THE
VINTAGE
GUIDE
TO
CLASSICAL
MUSIC

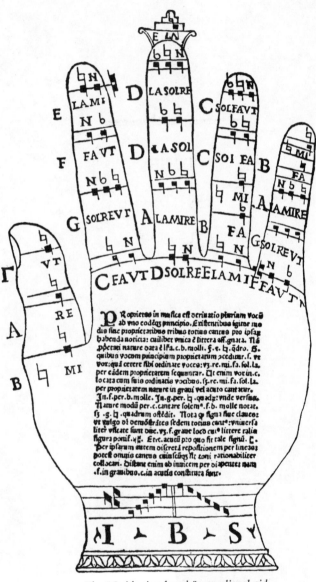

The "Guidonian hand," a medieval aid
for teaching music, attributed to Guido D'Arezzo.

THE VINTAGE GUIDE TO CLASSICAL MUSIC

JAN SWAFFORD

VINTAGE BOOKS

A DIVISION OF RANDOM HOUSE, INC.

NEW YORK

A VINTAGE ORIGINAL, FIRST EDITION
NOVEMBER 1992

Staff for this book:

Project supervision and design: IRWIN GLUSKER
Project coordination and layout: CHRISTIAN VON ROSENVINGE
Copy editing: ANNA M. JARDINE, PATRICK VANCE
Picture research: BARBARA HATCHER / WORDS AND PICTURES

Library of Congress Cataloging-in-Publication Data
Swafford, Jan.
        The Vintage guide to classical music / Jan Swafford. — 1st ed.
            p.   cm.
        "A Vintage original"
        Includes bibliographical references and index.
        ISBN 0-679-72805-8 (pbk.)
        1. Music appreciation.   2. Music—History and criticism.
    I. Title.   II. Title: Guide to classical music.
    MT6.S94V5   1992
    780'.9—dc20   91-50217
                                          CIP
                                          MN

This copyright page continues on pages 596–597.

Manufactured in the United States of America
10   9   8   7   6   5   4   3   2   1

For my mother, Lucille Swafford Johnson,
who started me in music and, against her better judgment,
did more than anyone else to keep me in it,
simply because it's what I wanted to do
and because I might turn out to be good at it.

ACKNOWLEDGMENTS

This book originated with Irwin Glusker, who encouraged me throughout the writing—sharing ideas and inspiration as well as some admirable meals—and then designed the book with his customary elegant touch. Joseph Spieler brought his talents as an agent to the business end and his background as an editor to the giving of good advice. (It was entertaining to steer a course between, respectively, the Mahlerphobe and the Mahlerphile.) My first studies for the book went to friends in the Northampton Writers' Group—Norman and Zane Kotker, Joanne Kobin, Carol Edelstein, Mordecai Gerstein, Betsy Hartmann; their enthusiasm helped convince me that this project might be workable after all. Old friend Steven Gerber contributed some useful caveats.

Early drafts were expertly tidied by editor and writer Mary Frakes. Once Mary had cleared out the underbrush, musicologist Raphael Atlas of Smith College not only took a critical look at the factual and interpretive side of things, but also added much good counsel on the writing—including the occasional sentence that went right into the copy. (Final responsibility for the facts, of course, is mine.) Then Robin Desser, my editor at Vintage, had her first crack at the book; every page is touched by her skill and sensitivity. Before Robin saw the final draft, my brother, writer and translator Charles Johnson, did some fine-tuning with his fastidious eye for grammar and usage. Thanks to Sybil Pincus, who detected my three different spellings of Nadezhda von Meck and similar crimes. Composer Randall Woolf computer-set the musical examples.

These people have made the book considerably better than I could have done alone. Writing is a social act, and I'm happy to acknowledge my debt and to call these helpmates not just associates but friends.

At left, a Cycladic harpist
of the third millennium B.C.

Medieval trio with vielle and flute.

CONTENTS

Haarlem's Saint Bavo Kerk organ,
played by Handel and Haydn
as well as the ten-year-old Mozart.

At left, "Still Life—Violin and Music," 1888,
by American painter William M. Harnett.

INTRODUCTION

Enduring works of music not only reflect their composers and their times, but have the capacity to reflect many peoples and many times. While every kind of music is intended to be heard, some is meant to be reheard and re-created in new performances, to grow in meaning, to become part of our lives and our culture, to represent the best we've done. In societies both Western and Eastern, these qualities define a body of music that is called "classical."

This book is a guide to Western classical music for present or potential music lovers. Like most such books, it is built on the notion that in understanding this music, knowledge is second in importance only to listening. Here I pursue that goal by combining two approaches that have traditionally been distinct. There are guides made up of unconnected essays on composers; and there are ones in which music drifts through history in the form of abstractions—polyphony, sonata form—that are taken up, in due course, by shadowy creative figures.

In contrast to the latter approach, my assumption is that while music contains abstractions, its primary meaning and purpose and fascination are not abstract but humanistic: music is something people do for people. So this book is a chronological history of music done largely in the form of essays on individual composers and their works. Here the string quartet does not "come to greater prominence in the later eighteenth century"; it comes to prominence mainly because Joseph Haydn wrote extraordinary quartets that have influenced musicians ever since. At the same time, the life, personality, and work of each composer are tied into historical developments and processes—the context of his time and his influence on others (until recently, alas, usually "his").

In the closing section of each composer essay I suggest a series of pieces that will give you a pathway into his work. Taken together,

---

At left, one of three Japanese prints making up "Concert of European music," late nineteenth century, continued on pages xvi and xviii.

the suggested pieces for all the composers add up to a basic library of classical music; this library is collected in the back of the book. There you will also find a glossary of musical terms and a list of further readings.

The composer essays are arranged in chronological order and grouped into historical period—Baroque, Classical, Romantic, and so on—each period prefaced by an introductory essay and concluded with briefer mention of additional composers. Each period also features essays dealing with broader issues: melody, polyphony, tonality, and the like. The reader should feel free to dip into the book anywhere she or he wants; each essay is complete in itself. When the book is read in order, though, the other dimension is revealed: an ongoing history of music.

Inevitably there are omissions, beginning with a number of less prominent but still worthy composers. I wish there had been room for Pachelbel, Boccherini, Takemitsu, et al.; but we have to stop someplace, and I didn't want to make long lists of "Others." By and large I don't go into "light-classical" music (i.e., the repertoire of "Pops" programs) or the details of operatic history because it seems to me these are separate, specialized subjects. However, some opera composers—mainly Wagner and Verdi—are included because their importance and influence went beyond opera. With regret, I also leave for other writers examination of jazz and non-Western music (I am a fervent dilettante of both). Duke Ellington is in the book because he is a distinguished composer by any measure; I couldn't imagine leaving him out.

I don't claim that the life of a composer tells you everything about his music. There are technical factors, too, that I touch on to the extent appropriate in a nontechnical book. I do claim, however, that a composer's life, personality, and milieu tell you as much about his music as anything else does. Haydn wrote over a hundred symphonies as compared to Beethoven's nine, because for various reasons a symphony for Haydn was a less weighty matter than it was for Beethoven. What symphonies were to Beethoven, operas were to Mozart; in both cases, they were the most ambitious of their works and what they preferred to be writing most of the time. As we move through the years we'll find that each new generation tends to raise the ante of its forebears: the achievements of Beethoven prepared

the way for Wagner's exalted notion of the artist, which led in turn to the still-more-exalted ideas of Mahler and Schoenberg. Meanwhile, that train of thought—involving the near deification of the artist—contributed to Stravinsky's disgust with the whole Romantic apparatus. While these historical developments did involve technical concerns, they were social, political, economic, and personal as well, so they fall within the scope of this book.

I am myself a composer, and like all musicians have strong opinions about my trade, which I am in the habit of venting. Listen to two musicians talking about a long-dead composer and it will often resemble siblings swapping tales about a fascinating if sometimes annoying uncle. There is some of that in this book, I hope—something of a musician's way of seeing and hearing things, and a manifest love of the subject.

All the same, this is not a critical book on what I think about music. It is about some remarkable composers and pieces that you might want to know. (Certainly you can't expect to like them all. I don't like them all myself. *What I like* is another book.) So I've kept my opinions on a tight rein; much of the wisdom here is common wisdom. Inevitably, since I have opinions, some of them lurk between the lines and a few creep into the lines. It's usually clear when that's happening—mainly in the section on twentieth-century music, which is my specialty, and regarding which there has been less time to accumulate common wisdom. The Afterword, called "Music: An Approach to Defining the Indefinable," contains my own, highly provisional, thoughts on the matter.

As per common wisdom, we'll find that even the greatest work is not perfect. Many of the faults in Bach and Beethoven are obvious to a child: Bach neglected to allow singers room to breathe, for example, and some of his arias are notoriously dull. In fact, all first-rate composers wrote more uninspired work than otherwise, and even their finest efforts are not necessarily less flawed than others. Great works, I believe, simply have the capacity to make their flaws irrelevant. When you are soaring amidst Beethoven's *Ode to Joy,* who cares if the form rambles and the soprano parts are too high? Nor do the stumbles of great creators make them less admirable. I say that it makes them more admirable; it reminds us that they are not gods but human beings who occasionally and miraculously spoke *as if* they were gods.

In recent years the very concept of greatness in the arts and in ideas has come under fire, often in the form of an attack on canons of Great Works. I have no quarrel with the idea of a canon if it is understood to be constantly evolving and somewhat arbitrary. But I submit that it is not *entirely* arbitrary. Quality exists and must be recognized; for all the difficulties in defining it, quality is real and important.

To a large extent, current attacks on the canon are mounted in the name of fairness to one excluded group or another. Nobody objects to the idea of fairness. Going beyond that, some have defined an attachment to quality itself as a form of elitism; for some reason, it's acceptable to call a basketball player or war hero great, but calling a thinker or an artist the same is branded elitist. These seem to me ultimately self-defeating habits of thought. While fairness is essential, so is quality. If we fail to recognize and appreciate the highest level of achievement, we fail to encourage any achievement, and we condemn ourselves to mediocrity. And in the long run that's not fair to anybody. The challenge is not to drag down quality in the name of fairness—or vice versa—but to encourage and honor both. This book is about quality, to better understand and honor its highest achievements in Western music. Fairness is another book, too—an equally important one.

Defining quality is, of course, the dilemma. If greatness in art were simply a matter of adding up pluses and minuses, judgment would be relatively easy. Certainly some critics throughout history have tried to do just that. But it has never really worked. All significant artists master the technique relevant to what they are trying to say, but somehow a masterpiece is more than the sum of its technical excellences. And clearly, "quality" is one more changeable and somewhat arbitrary concept. So where does this leave us? Are Greatness and Genius illusory, just a matter of public relations, cultural hegemony, a vast conspiracy of dead white males?

I don't think so. It's that greatness and genius—like love and compassion and joy and God, and most of the supremely important things in life—are vague and indefinable, more complex than we will ever be able to fathom, acting in mysterious ways spread tenuously across history and measureless numbers of people. We will never know what Bach has contributed to the human race: maybe not much, or maybe we could not have survived without him. Since such things finally come down to faith and speculation, here's a speculation of mine: greatness and genius *do* exist; but as with love, God, etc., we have to respect their mystery, believe without tangible confirmation.

For the sake of argument, I'll propose a practical definition of greatness in the arts. For some reason, time turns up certain names, certain works and bodies of work, that seem to have fixed themselves to the wall of history. "Great" works are that way because they have made themselves indispensable, even though the sources of their power remain elusive. Greatness is there because we seek it and need it. We may need it in different ways at different times, and as a result gravitate to different works, but the need remains.

No less do we need the mystery of art, which partakes of the great mysteries of life. Jorge Luis Borges wrote: "Music, states of happiness, mythology, faces molded by time, certain twilights and certain places—all these are trying to tell us something, or have told us something we should not have missed, or are about to tell us something; that imminence of a revelation that is not yet produced, is, perhaps, the aesthetic reality."

THE
VINTAGE
GUIDE
TO
CLASSICAL
MUSIC

WESTERN MUSIC
THROUGH
THE MIDDLE AGES

The heavenly choir gathered around Christ in Glory plays harps, psalteries, and bowed and plucked instruments. Romanesque portal in Galicia, Spain.

WESTERN MUSIC THROUGH THE MIDDLE AGES

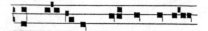

We no more know when and how music developed than when and how humanity did. Possibly they developed together: music may be as integral to us as our brains and hands and language. At least, no human society has been found without an indigenous music of untraceable antiquity.

We do know that music at the beginning was not a separate art, not separate from dance, poetry, worship. Art and religion were one, serving the eternal needs of societies—binding the community, sweetening labor, soothing the bereaved, expressing emotion, placating and entreating the mysterious powers of the world. It was only around the Middle Ages that music emerged as a distinct art and discipline. Or rather, partly emerged, and in some places: when a Western visitor to the East once complimented his host country's arts, a priest replied, "We don't have any arts. We just do everything the best we can."

Ancient and recent, "tribal" and "civilized," music has been perceived as an influence on life and feeling, something that resonates with the highest mysteries of life. To the Hindu god Krishna is attributed the saying, "People search for me in the things they love best. And it is in those things that I reveal myself to them." Music has long been a means of that search.

Now we'll begin to examine what we know of the story of one of the richest voices in the great global chorus of human musics: the Western classical tradition.

At the beginning of recorded history, music was already thriving. Until the advent of musical notation, however, which has fully developed only in the West during the last millennium, we know about music mainly from surviving treatises, paintings, traditions, tales: David playing the lyre for King Saul, Greek bards singing

Homeric epics, little bands of Egyptian girls serenading their queen with flute, harp, and lute.

As the foundation of Western culture and philosophy comes from the Greeks, so does the foundation of our musical ideas, even though the only tangible remains of Greek music are a few melodies in a notation hard to interpret. From written accounts we learn that the cult of Apollo favored the lyrelike instrument called the cithara and a music of restraint and purity, while followers of Dionysus performed their ecstatic dances to the keening of the double-piped aulos, a music of ecstasy and sensuality. The nineteenth-century philosopher Nietzsche would declare those two archetypes the eternal poles of art: the objective/Apollonian/classical, the subjective/Dionysian/romantic.

Greek musical theory dominated the West into the Middle Ages. Around 500 B.C., Pythagoras first described musical *intervals* (see Glossary) in terms of simple divisions of a sounding string: stopping the string in the middle (the ratio 2:1) produces an octave above the open string; stopping at the ratio 3:2 makes the interval of a fifth, 4:3 a fourth, and so on. Fully developed Greek theory established a number of scale patterns called *modes,* and the philosophical doctrine of ethos assigned expressive and moral qualities to each mode: the mode called Mixolydian, said Aristotle, makes men grave and sad, while the Phrygian inspires enthusiasm.

Early Christians acquired their sacred song from a number of sources, among them Jewish music. Medieval Christian song is known as *plainchant,* or simply *chant.* Like all the music in the world up to that time, chant is *monophonic,* that is, a single melodic line without harmonic accompaniment. The melodies fall into one of eight modes derived from the Greeks; the rhythm wanders freely, following the rhythm of the words. Latin-language plainchant was and often still is used for the Mass and other sacred services of the Catholic church. According to legend, sixth-century pope Gregory the Great collected and codified chant into its final form for use in the liturgy. In his honor, the main body of Catholic music has long been called Gregorian chant.

Unaccompanied Gregorian melody remains one of the glories of Christendom, among the most spiritually profound of all sacred music, and some of the most moving outpourings of pure melody in history. The haunting, floating world of chant is perhaps best approached in the more elaborate melodies for holidays, such as *Alleluia* and *Victimae paschali laudes* for Easter Sunday, and *Veni Sancte Spiritus* for Pentecost.

Naturally, popular music existed during the medieval Christian era, some for the sophisticated and some for the naïve, as always. But the secular side did not possess the tradition-preserving framework of the Church, nor its notation that began to develop around the ninth century. So until the later Middle Ages whole territories of secular music were born and died outside the notice of history.

We begin to find secular music written down and described after the tenth century, when loosely organized groups of musicians flourished across Europe—the highborn *troubadours* and *trouvères* in France, the *Minnesingers* and *Meistersingers* in Germany, the *scops* and *gleemen* in England. Hundreds of monophonic melodies by these minstrels have been preserved, mostly in the manuscripts of monkish scribes. In the twentieth century, early music specialists have liberated these songs and dances from the scholar's library and re-created them in all their worldly delights (see The Early Music Movement, p. 450). As with most secular music the rhythm is lively, the favorite subject love. The composer of most of these tunes is the ubiquitous Anonymous; but those of the greatest of the trouvères, Adam de la Halle, are identified and many have been recorded. His musical play *Jeu de Robin et Marion* is a prime example of this period's lilting and infectious song.

There is more to the period than good tunes, though. These minstrels virtually invented the modern Western concept of romantic

MELODY

Given that many people consider melody the main thing in music, the focus of their attention and interest, it is surprising how slippery the subject remains, and how many works of all kinds have found popularity without a strong melodic line. Rock 'n' roll, for example, is not a particularly melodic genre; the classic sixties tunes "Purple Haze" by Jimi Hendrix and the Beatles' "Come Together" are mostly a minimal chanting of two or three notes, and the recent rap style has no tune at all but only a text spoken rhythmically.

If melody were the main criterion of quality in classical music, Schubert might be considered the greatest of composers, with only a few people such as Verdi and Mozart holding a candle to him. Though Beethoven could write a dandy tune now and then, some of his finest movements are based on rather simple and featureless melodic material. Even the effect of the famous first movement of his *Moonlight Sonata* depends more on the harmony, rhythm, and dreamlike atmosphere than on the laconic melody. Similarly, much of Haydn's material is quite plain. A number of twentieth-century avant-garde and electronic pieces have made their point with nothing even approaching a tune.

So is melody overrated as the most important aspect of music? Yes and no. Many other things can make a piece work—the ex-

love, supplying it with its full litany of yearning, desire, frustration, and loss. Especially in the French songs of the later Middle Ages we see the kind of ritualized adultery (mostly, but not entirely, imaginary) that characterized courtly love in the age of chivalry. In this music and poetry all the shadings of love and desire have been captured with a youthful ardor that has rarely been matched (not even by all the convulsions of Richard Wagner in his version of the medieval masterpiece of courtly love, *Tristan und Isolde*).

Into the Middle Ages, Western music remained monophonic, as much non-Western music still does. Music was rhythm and melody and usually words, and nothing more. With an epochal evolution that began around the ninth century, Western music created some-

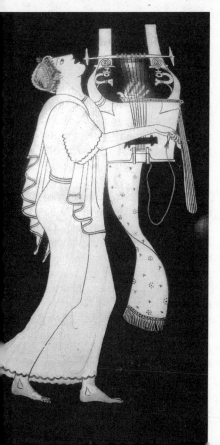

pressive unfolding, the handling of intensities, the harmonies, the instrumental colors, the rhythm. Usually, it's the marshaling of many such elements into an effective whole that makes a classical piece work. So as to tunes, let's put it this way: if the melody *is* the main point, the composer had better make sure it's a good one.

When the magic happens and one discovers a good melody, it is indeed one of the most marvelous things in music, for the composer

A Greek poet-singer accompanies himself on the kithara, a lyre played both with fingers and plectrum. From a red-figured vase of the early fifth century B.C.

thing that had never existed before: the art of *polyphony*.

This new kind of music took shape over several centuries. The first hints of it appear when theorists of the ninth century described a way of church singing in which two vocal parts moved in parallel intervals, usually hollow-sounding fourths or fifths. This way of singing was called *organum*. It was the first intimation of the musical revolution that the West has continued to expand and explore to this day.

Over years and centuries, by piecemeal creative experiment all over Europe and England, the idea of polyphony matured. The number of parts increased to three and four; the melodies began to grow independent of one another, each going its own way in the musical fabric. Since music had always been simply a matter of melody, the

as much as for the listener. A melody can't be forced; like a character in a novel, it must step up to the creator and reveal its shape and personality. An artist can refine that kind of inspiration but can't summon or predict it. A good melody is an ineffable gift of the Muse.

It is in those terms that we think of some of the great melodies of the world: folk songs such as "Greensleeves," "Barbara Allen," "Wildwood Flower"; popular standards such as "All the Things You Are," "Summertime," "Yesterday"; and classical melodies—Machaut's "Douce dame jolie," Bach's "Air on the G String," Mozart's "Là ci darem la mano," the finale of Beethoven's Ninth, Schubert's "Das Wandern," the opening of Stravinsky's

Le Sacre du printemps, and hundreds of others. A piece can be great without a great tune or without any tune at all, but melody remains a unique miracle of music. It's also the aspect that's most available, closest to us: you can't sing a chord progression or guitar part or tone color, but you can sing or hum or whistle a tune anytime.

The *Harvard Dictionary of Music* defines melody simply as "a coherent succession of pitches." Coherence is the deciding factor, then. But coherent *to whom* is the heart of the matter.

To most Westerners, Balinese gamelan pieces tend to sound like wandering streams of babbling notes; to the Balinese, they sound like variations on familiar tunes, and it is Western music that wan-

train of thought for centuries was concerned with *the combination of melodies,* which is finally what was called *polyphony* (see Monophony to Polyphony to Homophony, p. 88). For centuries the technique for composing polyphony was the same: you took an existing melody—usually from the Gregorian chant repertoire—and composed other melodies around it. Often the notes of the original chant were stretched out, making slow-changing drones amidst the added parts. Sometimes each of the melodies had its own text as well, and the texts might show a mixture of languages, such as French in one and Latin in another.

To keep pace with this new kind of music, notation also had to grow more sophisticated; polyphony was too complex to be remembered as music always had been. Primitive notation for chant dates

ders inexplicably. A frequent question among modern jazz novices is, Where's the tune? Ditto Schoenberg and Machaut novices. In their time, both Brahms and Puccini were accused of lacking melody.

In these and similar cases the melodies are there, but some listeners find them incoherent. In a way, a melody is like a sentence. If one understands the verbal language, the sentences make sense; if one understands the musical language, the melodies add up to something more than the sum of their pitches.

So where does all this leave us? With the following, I'm afraid: you recognize a melody when you hear something that sounds to you like one. A bit of a tautology, perhaps, but that's how it goes.

Whether we are hearing it or composing it, melody is largely a mysterious dialogue between ear and intuition. Still, as with all intuitive matters, our sense of melody can be sharpened by practice and experience. Some melodies are easy to follow ("Greensleeves," "Yesterday"), usually because their melodic line conforms to familiar patterns. Melodic patterns new to us (say, Indian or atonal) may take time, attention, and patience before we can discern their coherence.

Even if the essential nature of melody remains elusive, we can identify a number of organizing principles. Universally, a melodic line tends to be related unconsciously to the voice, whether or not voices are actually perform-

from around the ninth century. Modern musical notation would not be fully evolved until some seven hundred years later.

Among the first church polyphonists known to us by name is the French composer Pérotin, who worked in Paris in the early thirteenth century. Pérotin's *Sederunt Principes,* in four parts, is a marvelous example of early polyphony. This is sacred music with a dancelike vitality and a startlingly fresh sound to modern ears. Polyphony in those days had not been fully rationalized as to harmonic relationships among the parts, i.e., the handling of consonance and dissonance (see Consonance and Dissonance, p. 28). The result—again, to modern ears—is an intriguingly archaic harmonic language, with dissonant clashes sparkling among the voices.

Pérotin is the exultant, youthful song of the new millennium, the polyphonic revolution that would set Western music apart from all

Example 1

Shape:

ing it. For that reason we tend to interpret a rise in pitch as an increase in intensity, because higher pitches require more tension in the vocal cords; conversely, descending pitch tends to produce a sense of relaxation. Even in a rising and falling police siren one feels a rise and fall of tension. Leaps—large intervals—in a line increase tension because we sense that they are more difficult to sing. So a "good" melody, among other things, involves a satisfying and

coherent arrangement of rise and fall, leaps and smoothness, tension and release. This feature of a melodic line, like a line in a drawing, is called its *shape.*

Some melodies have smooth, relatively restful linear shapes, such as the famous one from Beethoven's Ninth: Example 1.

Others, like the theme that begins Mozart's G minor Symphony, have more jagged and dynamic shapes: Example 2.

(Of course, the shape of a mus-

Example 2

other traditions. We must also remember, though, that while a new world of possibilities commenced from this revolution, much would be lost as well. For one thing, the subtlety and nuances of the aural monophonic tradition withered when musicians stopped singing and playing by ear and began reading notes. Today one hears in non-Western traditions such as Indian music and the aural playing tradition of jazz what marvels can be accomplished with a single melodic line.

Some sixty years after the death of Pérotin was born the man who stands at the beginning of the long line of towering Western composers: Guillaume de Machaut. As Pérotin epitomized the archaic polyphonic style that came to be called *ars antiqua,* Machaut would bring to maturity the more sophisticated fourteenth-century polyphonic style that proudly called itself *ars nova,* "the new art."

ical line is not the only element producing tension. Beethoven, during the finale of the Ninth Symphony, intensifies his melody in several places by making it louder and surrounding it with busy accompaniments. Rhythm also plays an important role; the melody in Beethoven's Ninth is largely a smooth rhythmic flow, while the Mozart G minor theme has quick, nervous rhythms. Rhythm determines the character of a melody as much as does the shape of its line.)

In Western music, melodies are usually articulated by various subunits. Just as sentences have clauses and phrases, melodies have *phrases* and *periods.* The end of a musical phrase might be described as a breathing place, real or imagined. For example, here are two phrases making up the first period of a familiar tune:

1) Mary had a little lamb, little lamb, little lamb;

2) Mary had a little lamb, its fleece was white as snow.

As often happens, this song's first phrase sounds sort of like a "question" because it ends on an open-feeling, inconclusive pitch. Then the "answer" phrase ends on a note that sounds closed, conclusive, *cadential* (see *cadence* in Glossary). (What makes a note sound conclusive has to do with tonal organization, the built-in tensions within scales. To learn about that, see Tonality and Atonality, p. 268). In the West, the invention of harmony added a further dimension. We usually per-

The fourteenth century saw the literary work of Dante, Boccaccio, and Chaucer, and the revolutionary realism of the painter Giotto. As the power of the Catholic Church was sapped by the violent clashes of two rival papacies, artists turned their attention to the secular world. Their delicious vision of the pleasures of life, with its banquets and dances amongst the fountains of the gardens of love, persisted through the horrors of the Black Plague and the Hundred Years' War. That is the setting of the life and music of poet and composer Guillaume de Machaut.

He was born around 1300 in the Champagne region of France, had a clerical education, and took holy orders. For years he served as secretary in the retinue of King John of Bohemia; he also worked

ceive a melody as related to a harmonic underpinning—and the harmony creates its own tensions, relaxations, and articulations.

Few melodies have the childlike simplicity of "Mary Had a Little Lamb." Most are more subtle and complex, and include a measure of surprise. The various technical features (rhythm, shape, cadences, harmony, etc.) all work together to determine how tense or relaxed a melody is, how satisfyingly it progresses to its end, what moods it evokes. The possibilities of combination and interaction among these features are infinite—which is to say, there is an infinity of possible melodies. One can see why only the intui-

tion, which perceives wholes rather than parts, is able to find its way through the complexities involved in composing or understanding a good melody.

A couple of final ideas. The term *melody* is roughly synonymous with *tune*, but the latter often implies a self-contained unit such as a folk tune, with a beginning, middle, and end. *Melody* is a broader term that includes such subtypes as a folk tune or a symphonic *theme*. The latter is rarely designed to stand alone: a classical theme tends to be open-ended, less self-contained than a tune, more dependent for its effect on its context and function in a larger

for other noble houses including that of the future Charles V of France. These nobles, cultured men as well as warriors, probably kept him on more as a composer and poet than as courtier and secretary. After Machaut had accompanied King John on several military campaigns, the king died in the disastrous battle of Crécy in 1346, fulfilling his chivalric destiny by charging into the fray even though he was blind. Machaut settled from his travels in Rheims, where he remained as canon until his death in 1377. In his maturity all Europe recognized him as the premier composer of the age; he supplied music and poetry to the great courts of the time.

In our century his most famous work is *La Messe de Notre Dame,* one of the first polyphonic settings of the complete Ordinary of the Catholic Mass. (The Ordinary is that part of the Mass that is the same in every service, the sections called Kyrie, Gloria, Credo, Sanctus, and Agnus Dei.) In recent recordings of *La Messe de Notre Dame* one hears the sonority of the *ars nova,* less archaic to our ears than Pérotin, but still lean, open, with unexpected kinks in harmony and

work. Moreover, classical themes are often made up of *motives,* short melodic building blocks that can be detached and used as a basis for development or to construct other themes. The motives and phrases in the opening theme of Mozart's G minor Symphony are shown below: Example 3. As simple as the opening three-note motive is, it nonetheless dominates the entire first movement.

In symphonies, sonatas, and the like, themes tend to be preferred to tunes precisely because themes are less complete, easier to break up and rearrange and develop. They *need* to continue. That's the reason why symphonic themes can be effective even when they're not particularly "tuneful." In a large classical work, we are involved in a stretch of time that is like a little life, with peaks and valleys of interest but always an absorbing sense of unfolding. That's a dimension beyond the effect of a good tune. ◻

Example 3

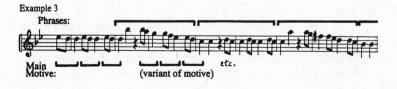

A fourteenth-century manuscript illumination depicts Guillaume de Machaut. His own era's "noblest bard," Machaut is now considered the first in the line of great Western composers.

melody that later polyphonists would smooth out, for well and ill. Yet there is something familiar about this sound too; in its strange harmonies and hazy tonality (based on the old church modes) it resembles nothing so much as the freedom and unpredictability of twentieth-century music. In both cases, the very old and the very new, one can turn to this music with a sense of adventure and refreshment after the familiar sonorities of the standard repertoire.

Though the *Mass* is his most famous work, the heart of Machaut is really in his secular music, in which he brought the world of the trouvères into the polyphonic age. There is a charming picture in one of the richly illuminated medieval manuscripts of Machaut's work: the composer in his study is visited by the angel Amour, who introduces to him three lovely ladies named Sweet Thoughts, Pleasure, and Hope. In his life and his music, Machaut embodied the world of chivalry and courtly love.

History records that when he was in his sixties, near the end of his life, the composer fell in love with a fair maiden of nineteen, and courted her in letters and poems and chansons, and she loved him in return. He rhapsodized in one of his letters to her, "I send you my book, *Morpheus,* which they call *La Fontaine amoureuse,* in which I have made a song to your order . . . & by God it is long since I have made so good a thing to my satisfaction; & the tenors are as sweet as unsalted pap . . . I am also sending you a ballade, which I made before receiving your sweet likeness: for I was a little hurt because of some words which had been said to me; but as soon as I saw your sweet likeness I was healed & free of melancholy." Cuisine may have changed from his day to ours, but love hasn't.

Machaut not only epitomized the soon-to-pass chivalric world, he also captured for all time the yearnings and pleasures of romance. His dozens of love songs, in all the poetic/musical forms of the day, are flowery and formulaic in language but delightful in their musical settings. "Douce dame jolie" runs, "Fair sweet lady, for God's sake do not think that any woman has mastery over me, save you alone. For always without deceit I have cherished you, and humbly served you all the days of my life without any base thought. Alas! I am bereft of hope and help; and so my joy is ended, unless you pity me." And so on and so on. Often Machaut followed the polyphonic technique of the time in which each voice has its own poem; in these polytextual works he creates subtle interrelationships of theme and sound among the words. He mastered the newly developed technical games of polyphony, such as canonic writing (see Fugue and Canon). At the same time, he produced some of the finest monophonic melodies of the age.

In the 1980s a group of musicologists, tabulating some obscure index of excellences, declared Machaut to be the Greatest Composer of All Time. (Beethoven came in second, by the way.) We don't have to go that far to declare that the rediscovery of Machaut, still in progress, is one of the most satisfying musical developments of recent decades. To date, there are only a few recordings featuring his work, but most are lovingly done. Absorbing this strange and bewitching music, one begins to understand his world and his stature. A farewell that one of his contemporaries composed on Machaut's passing shows the regard of his own time: "Men of arms, lovers, ladies and their knights, clerks, musicians, and those who write in French, all thinkers, poets, and all you who sing harmoniously with tuneful voice and hold dear the sweet art of music, give full feeling to your rightful grief, and lament the death of Machaut, the noblest bard."

A sixteenth-century
musicale with recorder, lute
cello and virginal.

THE
RENAISSANCE

THE RENAISSANCE
(CA. 1430–1600)

M usic lives in the world amidst the zeitgeist, the spirit of the times. The Renaissance, a flowering of learning, science, and the arts that transformed Europe after the mid-fifteenth century, was the first intimation of the modern spirit, and of music and art that seem familiar to us today. In music as in everything else, however, historical periods don't exist as sharp boundaries in the chaotic flux of events. Between Machaut, who embodied the medieval world, and the High Renaissance figure of Josquin Desprez, came a transitional period that included the composers of the Burgundian School who worked for the art-loving dukes of Burgundy in and around Brussels in the fifteenth century.

The leading Burgundian composer was **Guillaume Dufay**, born around 1400 in the area of Cambrai. His career as both composer and expert in canon law took him to church and court positions all over Europe, including several years at the papal chapel in Rome. Dufay wrote a good deal of both sacred music—mainly Masses and the shorter sacred form called *motet* (see Glossary)—and secular music, mainly French polyphonic chansons. What marks the music of Dufay and his Burgundian contemporaries, in contrast to their predecessors, is a limpid sweetness of sound: Dufay's music seems to hang in the air like billowing diaphanous fabric. His style is much the same whether sacred or secular: simpler than that of the past, often in three rather than four parts, with the emphasis on a lyrical top line that has a more concise profile than the wandering lines of Machaut. Dufay's harmony still has an archaic tinge to modern ears; he uses the old church modes, with their hazy tonality, but his sonorities seem fuller and richer than those of medieval music. The Burgundian School of the early 1400s and the Flemish School later in the century—collectively called the Netherlands School—also established the sacred vocal style that prevailed through the Renaissance: flowing polyphony most often in four equal parts.

An example of Dufay's sacred music at its most lovely is the Mass called *L'homme armé*. The title comes from a technique of the time in which an entire Mass was composed around a borrowed melody called the *cantus firmus* (literally, "fixed song," see Glossary), which lies buried in the polyphonic fabric. This was not a new idea; but where medieval composers normally used Gregorian chant cantus firmi, Netherlands School composers of Dufay's day and after liked to use popular tunes. Besides its function of unifying the whole piece, a popular cantus amidst a sacred work was an in joke for the attentive, especially enjoyable when the joke was a little racy—say, enlivening a motet to the Virgin with a cantus from an amorous tune like "My Mistress." Eventually the Church clamped down on that sort of thing, but not until the sixteenth-century Counter-Reformation. Though little is known about the song "L'homme armé" or the Armed Man that it tells us is "to be feared," it seems to have been one of the enduring hits of the era; there are dozens of "L'homme armé" Masses by composers from Dufay to Palestrina.

Along with his sacred music, Dufay's secular songs have been much recorded in recent decades, often alongside those of his colleague Gilles Binchois. In this music one hears reflected the quality of *jeunesse*, "youth," that was prized in the courtly life of the age, a blend of joyfulness, candor, elegant flirtatiousness, and precocious wisdom. Some recent recordings by early music specialists whose singing is as sophisticated as their scholarship are among the most beautiful of our time. (See Appendix for suggested recordings.)

Certainly the spirit of the fifteenth century was more worldly than that of previous ages. The milieu of artists in Dufay's era can be seen in a legendary party that he and Binchois attended in February 1454. Their patron, Burgundian duke Philip the Good, created this "Feast of the Pheasant" to drum up enthusiasm for a military campaign to retake Constantinople from the Turks. Notable in a day of eccentric amusements was a pie containing twenty-eight musicians wielding various instruments; two trumpeters playing astride a horse walking backward; a girl who sang a chanson of Binchois while mounted on a stag; an elephant ridden by a woman in white, symbolizing the Church astride the Infidel; a naked maiden draped around a pillar and guarded by a lion, symbolizing something or other; and finally a grand performance of a motet Dufay had written for the occasion.

Yet for all the worldly extravagance of the age there is a serene purity to its sacred music. In 1436 Dufay wrote his motet *Nuper rosarum flores* for the consecration ceremony of the Duomo in Florence. Of this work, whose structure is made to correspond in various ways to the proportions of Brunelleschi's stupendous dome, an eyewitness wrote an account that could describe much Netherlandish sacred music of both the fifteenth and sixteenth centuries:

> At the elevation of the Most Sacred Host the whole space of the temple was filled with such choruses of harmony, and such a concert of divers instruments, that it seemed . . . as though the symphonies and songs of the angels and of divine paradise had been sent forth from Heaven to whisper in our ears an unbelievable celestial sweetness. Wherefore in that moment I was so possessed by ecstasy that I seemed to enjoy the life of the blessed here on earth.

The High Renaissance was a nexus of intellectual, scientific, and artistic developments that began to gain momentum after 1450, all of which contributed to a snowballing spirit of discovery that became more than the sum of its parts. Among the developments were the invention of the printing press, which disseminated knowledge at an unprecedented rate; the invention of gunpowder, which spelled the end of armor-clad knights and walled towns, and with them the feudal age; the rediscovery of realism in the visual arts; and the development of the compass, which made possible new voyages of discovery. Above all, the rediscovery of the writers and philosophers of classical Greece and Rome—Aristotle, Plato, Homer, and Virgil—fueled a revival of learning, curiosity, and investigation.

Of course, the word *renaissance* means "rebirth," and what was reborn in that age was humanism: the sense that not the afterlife but life here and now is the proper concern of humanity, and that through reason and investigation we can discover things previously known only to the gods. Describing the true structure of the universe, Copernicus removed the earth from the center of the cosmos and set humanity sailing in the vastness of space. The new understanding of the classical nude and the science of perspective in painting made it possible to place convincing figures in a convincing illusion of space. In his 1477 work, *Book on the Art of Counterpoint,* Johannes Tinctoris declared that only music of the previous forty years was worth hearing. Historian and painter Giorgio Vasari felt similarly about the visual arts. Michelangelo, Vasari's favorite, imagined the human body as a tangible incarnation of divine spirit. Leonardo da Vinci applied his insatiable curiosity to every aspect of painting, mind, body, nature, mechanics. Martin Luther broke the spiritual monopoly of the Catholic Church and began the Protestant Reformation with a vision of individual responsibility to God. Shakespeare examined the passions of humanity with timeless wisdom and incomparable poetry. Everywhere there was an exhilarating feeling that marvels were being discovered and unimaginable marvels were to come.

From Renaissance humanism flowed the modern world, the modern consciousness: science, learning, philosophy, medicine, and the revitalized kaleidoscope and mirror of the arts. From the comparatively static and church-dominated society of the Middle Ages arose a searching, dynamic secular culture that has prevailed in the West to this day, a culture full of new marvels indeed (and horrors new and old, inextricably mixed).

In music, the High Renaissance saw the golden age of polyphony. At the summit of that art and of the Netherlands School stands Flemish composer Josquin Desprez, who was called *princeps musicorum,* the Prince of Music.

JOSQUIN DESPREZ

Though he was the most admired musician of his time, comparatively little is known about the life of Josquin Desprez. Born around 1440 in Burgundy, he probably sang in and conducted church choirs in his youth, among them the collegiate church of St. Quentin and, in a forecast of his cosmopolitan career, the Milan Cathedral in Italy. He may have studied with Flemish composer Johannes Ockeghem, whose intensely spiritual style and mastery of polyphonic devices Josquin absorbed.

We learn of Josquin's career through references to his presence in ducal courts at Milan and Ferrara, the Sistine Chapel in Rome, the court of Louis XII in France. He ended his years as canon of the collegiate church of Condé and died in 1521; surviving works include eighteen Masses, one hundred motets, and seventy secular vocal pieces. When Ottaviano dei Petrucci, inventor of music printing, published his pioneering editions in the early 1500s, he issued three times more works by Josquin than by any other composer.

Unlike Dufay's, Josquin's styles separate strongly along the sacred/secular line. His sacred polyphony has the otherworldly sound of the Netherlands tradition; it is largely in four parts, all similar in sound and equal in melodic interest. It was Josquin above all who established the principle of continuous imitation, the voices regularly picking up melodic motives from one another. He had a particular fondness for canon (see Fugue and Canon, p. 72); in all his music, there is a canon going on somewhere as often as not. He also continued two other traditions: borrowing popular songs and other melodies as cantus firmi for his sacred works, and using symbolic devices in which verbal or mathematical conceits are woven into the composition. For example, in his Mass *Hercules Dux Ferrarae,* dedicated to Duke Hercules of Ferrara, Josquin used as cantus a melody based on the vowels of the duke's name, which when associated with old names for notes translate to D C D C D F E D. One clearly hears this cantus moving in slower notes (as a cantus usually does) in the two-voice beginning of the Mass.

Of Josquin's Masses, perhaps the best known are the two using "L'homme armé," some of the many based on that secular tune, and *Pange lingua,* this one with a chant melody as cantus. Josquin was unusual in writing more motets than Masses, perhaps because these shorter religious works gave him more room for experimentation. For a taste of his motets, try *Veni sancte spiritus,* with its soaring depictions of spiritual light, and the somber *Absalon, fili mi,* with its conclusion that seems to descend into the grave.

His secular music is another matter, worldly-wise and irresistible. The texts range from tender love songs to nonsensical trifles to bawdy lyrics. His songs are more tuneful than his sacred music, with more of an emphasis on the top line. Nonetheless, he lavishes on them all the brilliance of his contrapuntal art; often a lilting melody will have a canonic shadow following after it. There is a lively rhythmic sense as well, almost jazzy in its dancing syncopations. (Instrumentation in the Renaissance was largely ad hoc; many parts were designed to be either played or sung, and instruments often doubled the voices in both sacred and secular music).

"Scaramella" is a prime example of his secular songs. Here the words are simply a pretext for music: "Scaramouche goes to war / With his lance and his shield," then lots of rum-tum-tums. In "Une mousse de Bisquaye," the singer meets a Basque girl who keeps repeating some incomprehensible phrase in her language, but is obliging all the same: "Long did we dally that morning, the Basque girl and I, and as I kissed her farewell, my hand on her breast, she replied, 'Soaz, soaz, ordonarequin.'" The tender "Mille regretz" is a farewell with perennial sentiments: "A thousand regrets to leave you and your fair face." Among the most charming is "El Grillo" (The Cricket), with its shameless imitation of crickets chirping.

While his secular songs are infectious, Josquin's sacred music is perhaps more of an acquired taste to modern listeners used to greater contrasts of color. For the patient, though, the serene sound of his church music—and that of later composers like Lasso and Palestrina—can reveal riches all the more precious for their subtlety. The Netherlandish church tradition that Josquin epitomized is one of the purest and most spiritual of sacred musics. If you went to heaven and the choirs sounded like that, it would seem just right.

ORLANDO DI LASSO

Among the sixteenth-century heirs of the Netherlandish polyphonic tradition is Orlando di Lasso (or Orlandus Lassus, ca. 1532–94), a prolific composer of immense vitality. He spent most of his career at the Bavarian ducal chapel in Munich, but his fame covered the continent. His relaxed and affectionate relationship with his noble employers is shown in letters like this one of 1572, a series of doggerel rhymes in a mixture of French, German, Italian, and Latin: "Most High, Most Mighty, Flighty, lord my Master Forever-

Orlando di Lasso conducts his musicians in the Bavarian Ducal chapel.

more: I have arrived at Munich . . . hale, hearty, and lazy . . . My wife, my little Rudolf, and my own person do kiss / in all humility the hands of your Excellency and of madam the princess, / while her rump feels no distress. / God preserve our cheerfulness."

Lasso wrote a good deal of magnificent sacred music, notably the *Prophetae Sibyllarum,* the *Penitential Psalms,* and a number of vivid motets. But he is better known today for his secular music, a polyglot variety of tongues and styles that reflect the impulsive, lusty, and cosmopolitan personality of the man. He was a master of the most convivial of Renaissance genres, the *madrigal,* which originated in Italy and spread around Europe and to England. Usually in four or five parts, madrigals are settings of short poems variously gay, lovelorn, pastoral, erotic; often they were sung among friends at home and on festive occasions. Lasso and later madrigalists chased after every image of the text, while at the same time maintaining an unbroken fabric. As with much other music of the time, it was common for an instrument to fill in on a part or two; all the lines were tuneful enough to work either way.

Among Lasso's more engaging outings are the archly cynical "Ich weiss mir ein Meidlein": "I know a young maiden wondrous fair—O take care, of her kind words beware . . . She fooleth, fooleth, fooleth thee!" The well-known "Matona mia cara" is deceptively pretty, given the roguishness of its lyrics: a German mercenary in Italy tries in broken Italian to woo a young lady ("Matona" is his attempt at "Madonna") out of her window to his bed in order to "Mi ficcar tutta notte." In contrast, the madrigal "Bonjour, mon coeur" can be numbered among the tenderest love songs of the era.

The epitaph on Lasso's tomb in Munich shows the esteem he enjoyed: "Here lies that Lassus who refreshes the weariness of the world, and whose harmony resolves its discord."

GIOVANNI DA PALESTRINA

In contrast to the broad stylistic range and richly expressive harmony of Josquin and Lasso—which might represent the romantic spirit in the Renaissance—is the classical restraint of Giovanni da Palestrina. He was born around 1525 in his namesake town near

Rome and came of age during the Catholic Counter-Reformation, when in response to the challenge of Protestantism the Church tried to cleanse itself of worldly excesses. Among the requirements of reforms made during the Council of Trent (1545–1563) were to restore church music to a pure vocal style, to banish instruments other than organ from services, to discard sacred works based on popular songs, and to see that the sacred texts not be obscured by too-elaborate polyphony. Though the old legend that Palestrina "saved" polyphony by satisfying all these requirements in his *Pope Marcellus Mass* is fanciful, he did manifest the restrained musical aims of the early Counter-Reformation, in the process creating one

CONSONANCE
AND DISSONANCE

The musical terms *consonance* and *dissonance* have long led two diverging lives. On one hand, they are technical descriptions of complementary states in music: consonance = relaxation, rest, resolution; dissonance = tension, suspension, instability. To some extent, these states are related to acoustic phenomena: consonant intervals and harmonies sound relatively smooth, dissonant ones relatively rough. (The operative word here is *relatively;* we'll return to it below.) The first thing to understand is that nearly all music requires an ebb and flow of tension and relaxation, and thus an alternation of dissonance and consonance.

The other, and more sordid, life of our terms has been as aesthetic and ideological weapons. Here the words leave behind their technical meanings and acquire subjective ones: consonant = beautiful and good; dissonant = ugly and bad. Conservative theorist Giovanni Artusi called Monteverdi dissonant and ugly, as many critics called Beethoven. Mendelssohn complained that you couldn't tell Chopin's wrong notes from his right ones. And so on, generation after generation leveling similar charges at Berlioz, Wagner, Stravinsky, Schoenberg, Stockhausen.

Berlioz conducts pandemonium in a caricature of 1846. Mendelssohn wrote: "One ought to wash one's hands after handling . . . his scores."

of the most lucid, consistent, and spiritual of sacred styles. Later ages would remember Palestrina as the ideal model of polyphonic music and the most representative of Catholic composers.

He spent most of his career in Rome, among his posts as organist and choirmaster of the Sistine Chapel and of St. Peter's. After his first wife died, he married into the family of a furrier, and ran the business despite his immense musical productivity. Because of the fur trade, Palestrina may have been the richest composer in history. At the same time, by his death in 1594 he had accounted for 104 Masses, 250 motets, and much other service music, plus 100 early secular madrigals for which he later "blushed and grieved."

His most famous piece today is the six-voice *Pope Marcellus Mass*, its fame mainly due to the legend of its saving polyphony. Nonetheless, this Mass epitomizes the Palestrina style: unaccompanied, the sound and sense of the text preserved, the emotion understated. What other composers would do with extravagant gestures to express the text, Palestrina might suggest with a subtlety of voice leading or chord spacing. This style represents the utmost refinement of Netherlandish polyphony; all voices are similar and equal, each has its own rhythmically supple and highly singable profile, and each voice resembles a plainchant melody. Yet everything works as a unity that unfolds like a gentle, crystalline stream—

While most of these complaints have not stood the test of time, they do reflect one historical reality: some styles have a generally higher level of dissonance (acoustically speaking) than others, and the overall level of dissonance in Western music indeed went up gradually from about the time of Mozart to about the time of John Cage, as composers steadily added more harmonic color to their palettes. By the middle of the twentieth century, acoustic dissonance in music had reached its furthest possible extreme with the incorporation of "white noise," which is all frequencies sounding at once (that's the sound you hear in empty TV channels).

And yet, from the time of Mozart to about the time of Schoenberg, one thing remained constant in music: the ebb and flow of tension and relaxation, relative consonance and relative dissonance. In other words, consonance is the stable and passive principle in

Example 4

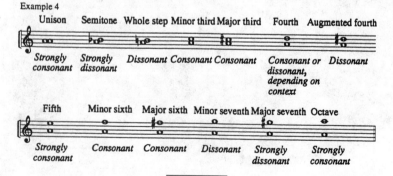

Unison	Semitone	Whole step	Minor third	Major third	Fourth	Augmented fourth
Strongly consonant	Strongly dissonant	Dissonant	Consonant	Consonant	Consonant or dissonant, depending on context	Dissonant

Fifth	Minor sixth	Major sixth	Minor seventh	Major seventh	Octave
Strongly consonant	Consonant	Consonant	Dissonant	Strongly dissonant	Strongly consonant

the musical equivalent of an ethereal Madonna by Raphael.

So consistent was Palestrina in his technique, his treatment of consonance and dissonance, his attention to the total effect of the parts, that composers and theorists ever since have studied his work and to some extent modeled their own exercises on his treatment of counterpoint. Haydn, Mozart, Beethoven, Mendelssohn, Brahms, and countless others spent their formative years studying counterpoint in Palestrina style (as abstracted in J. J. Fux's 1725 textbook *Steps to Parnassus*), and this study persists to the present. Perhaps more than to anyone else, music owes to Palestrina the preservation of the polyphonic idea: that in all kinds of music, whether overtly

music, dissonance the unstable and active. Both principles are necessary, but have been defined and treated differently over the years.

For example, Renaissance counterpoint had fairly strict definitions of consonant and dissonant intervals: Example 4.

As to chords, consonant harmonies for Mozart were the familiar major or minor *triads* (see Glossary). Other chords, dissonant for Mozart, often function as consonant for Debussy. A "consonant" chord for Bartók may be an ad hoc construction sounding smooth in comparison to more dissonant surrounding harmonies. One's impression of consonance and dissonance, then, is relative to context and to style.

In tonal theory of the eighteenth and nineteenth centuries, dissonant chords were required to re-solve to consonant (but things must not resolve too firmly or too often, or the piece stops in its tracks). There were standard procedures for harmonic resolution: this dissonant chord must resolve like so to this consonant one, a piece must end in the same key it began with, and so on through the rulebook. Then in the early years of the twentieth century, Arnold Schoenberg declared a "liberation of the dissonance" in his music, meaning that he would no longer resolve dissonance as tradition demanded. Nonetheless, Schoenberg and his fellow Modernists explored other means of creating peaks and valleys of intensity in their work despite a generally high level of dissonance. (This is possible because there can be rhythmic and melodic tension, as well as other kinds.)

Let's look at the terms in the

contrapuntal or not, the relationship of all the parts must be respected and shaped. Thus, in a way, maybe Palestrina did "save" polyphony after all.

Our tour of the Renaissance has had to skip some worthy figures, but I can't omit the **English madrigalists** of the Elizabethan Age, who produced some of the most beguiling secular music of any period. To be honest, the English language is a nuisance to set to music. It lacks the singable open vowels of Italian and Latin, the robust rhythm of German, the lyrical rhythm of French. In a rare collaboration of poets and musicians (some of whom were one and

---

broadest sense—consonance as producing rest, and dissonance as producing tension. Traditional tonal pieces begin from a point of rest, move through shades of tension mild and strong, and finally return to rest. The smaller curves of intensity in a piece are a microcosm of the piece as a whole: as a Classical-period melodic phrase usually involves a curve of relative rest-tension-rest, likewise does the entire work. In harmonic terms, a Classical symphony is a large genre in which true rest, complete consonance, only occurs at the beginning and end; the remainder of the piece is a journey through the large and small tensions of dissonant harmonies, modulations to other keys, and middle movements usually not in the home key. (These processes mirror physical and psychological effects of tension and release.)

Mozart especially had an incomparable gift for maintaining the flow in a piece by never quite letting the tension down. Even when his harmonies reach a point of rest, he uses rhythm or other devices to keep things going, keep up the tension until the end.

To summarize: consonance and dissonance are complex phenomena, partly acoustic and partly contextual, that apply to both small and large spaces of music. A dissonant chord creates small-scale tension; a modulation to another key creates large-scale tension. Each style of music defines its own values of tension and rest. But both consonance and dissonance are necessary. Without some degree of dissonance, music would tend to be flat and bland. Without relative consonance, it would tend to be flat and nerve-racking. □

the same), a group of Elizabethans produced a good part of the comparatively few first-rank settings of the language.

The main figures of this school, all of them living around 1600, include Thomas Campion, John Dowland, Thomas Morley, Francis Pilkington, Thomas Weelkes, Orlando Gibbons, and William Byrd. Poet, composer, and lutenist Dowland concentrated less on madrigals than on solo "ayres" accompanied by lute. His "Flow my teares" virtually defines the Elizabethan Age in music; that and other tunes such as "If my complaints" and "Can shee excuse my wrongs" count among the finest of the entire song repertoire, with a melancholy coloration unmistakably Dowland's. William Byrd, a Catholic in an Anglican country, is the only one of the group whose sacred music outstrips his secular; though he could turn out a sprightly dance tune like "John come kisse me now," he is at his best in sacred settings, among them his masses and the motet *Ave verum corpus*.

The English madrigalists were quite adequate to texts of sweet sadness, as demonstrated by Gibbons's sighing "Silver Swan," but perhaps they are most memorable in their moods of nimble gaiety. Thomas Vautor's "Mother I will have a husband" begins with that declaration and adds, "John a Dun should have had mee long ere this / He said I had good lips to kisse . . . / To the town, therefore, will I gad, / To get me a husband, good or bad." A madrigal of Morley's voices a perennial complaint: "April is in my Mistress' face, / And July in her eyes hath place, / Within her bosom is September, / But in her heart, a cold December." And there is Morley's "I goe before my darling," in which the lovers retire to a bower where, "Ther wee will together / Sweetly kisse each other, / And like two wantons, / Dally, dally, dally, dally." In these works and so many other madrigals, the music is as tart and spirited as the words.

For convenience, historians decree the year 1600 as the boundary between the Renaissance and the Baroque period, but the tradition of Renaissance polyphony flowed into the next century. It was in 1605, though, that Claudio Monteverdi, who bridged the two eras, felt it useful to distinguish between the *prima prattica* of the polyphonic style and what he called the *seconda prattica*. The latter was characterized by a new element in music: homophony. Its avatar was a strange, pseudo-Grecian concoction called opera.

THE
BAROQUE

Working drawing by
*Giuseppe Valeriani for
a setting of the opera*
Il Generoso di Tito.

THE BAROQUE
(1600–1750)

In 1601, Italian singer and composer Giulio Caccini signed onto a revolution with the preface to his collection of solo songs called *Nuove musiche* (New Music):

> In the days when the most excellent Camerata . . . was thriving in Florence, where not only much of the nobility but also the city's first musicians, intellects, poets, and philosophers met . . . I learned more from their savant speeches than I had in over thirty years' study of counterpoint. For those most knowledgeable gentlemen were always urging me . . . not to prize the sort of music which, by not letting the words be properly understood, spoiled both the sense and the verse . . . to suit the counterpoint (that mangler of poetry); but rather to adhere to the manner so much praised by Plato and other philosophers, according to whom music consists of speech, rhythm, and, last, sound—not the contrary. . . . Wherefore, having made a beginning [composing] songs for one voice alone . . . it seemed to me they had more power to delight and move than songs for several voices together.

This was one of the opening salvos that began the musical period we call the Baroque. As all revolutionaries must, Caccini mounted an assault on the edifices of the past, in this case on the very idea of polyphony. In the polyphonic style words were merely a pretext for music, said Caccini and his compatriots; counterpoint was the "mangler of poetry." Now, however, music was going to be cut down to size as the servant of words, as it was in ancient Greece. To that end, after various experiments, Caccini and other artists and dilettantes of the Florentine Camerata (all minor composers, as it turned out) created the new form called *opera*, modeled on their conception of ancient Greek drama. (See Seventeenth- and Eighteenth-Century Opera, p. 58.)

Beyond establishing a new musical genre, this creation would lead the way to a New Music indeed. The Florentine Camerata pioneered what became the norm for later generations, the idea that the most succinct and directly expressive kind of music is a single melody supported by harmonic accompaniment. Today we call that texture *homophony;* it is the offspring and complement of polyphony. An aria by Handel, a melodic section in a Mozart symphony, a Schubert lied, a Beatles tune, an Irish folk song—whether the accompaniment is a full orchestra or a single guitar, all are examples of homophony. In other words, with Baroque homophony the modern musical age began, and with it, what is today considered the standard classical repertoire.

Central among the styles of vocal declamation developed for opera was what came to be called *recitative:* singing that moves freely in a speechlike way, following the natural rhythms of its prose text, while the changing moods are reflected mainly in the harmony. Beyond that, Florentine composers pursued the art of solo song with relatively plain accompaniment. Among the corollaries of this new style was the *figured bass,* a musical shorthand in which numerical figures over a bass line indicate the chords to an accompanist, who uses them to improvise a background to the soloist. The instruments—low strings, harpsichord, etc.—playing the bass line and the chords are called the *basso continuo,* or just *continuo.* Baroque composers notated many works simply as a melody line for singer or player and a figured-bass line for the continuo accompaniment, which was so subordinate that the composer often did not bother to write it out in full.

The coming of the homophonic age thus represented a victory of the harmonic principle over the polyphonic. Before the Baroque, chords were considered the byproduct of counterpoint; though counterpoint survived the assaults of the seventeenth century, from then on it had to submit to the rules of chord movement that were first laid out by Baroque theorists. In other words, Baroque counterpoint is controlled by the harmony and put together over a strong bass line, usually with a featured top voice (including ornaments improvised by the players). The goal of the new harmonic art was to maintain clarity of tonality, to arrange the entire work according to a hierarchy of chords and keys gravitating around the main chord and key (see Tonality and Atonality, p. 268). The old tonally vague modal scales were swept from the field by the modern, stronger sense of tonality based on only two scales, the bright major and the dark minor.

Baroque is an odd and not particularly apt name for the period 1600 to 1750. The term actually refers to an irregular pearl; it seems to have been used in the mid 1700s to reproach the highly ornamented architectural style of the day and similar extravagances in other arts. So the term that came to represent the entire period in music is one that was originally used to deplore flamboyant bad taste. While much Counter-Reformation architecture and its offshoots, such as the florid French style in the time of Louis XIV, perhaps fit the term, it hardly encompasses the wide stylistic variety of the period. The Baroque was the era of Vermeer, whose painting is the opposite of ornate; it was also the time of Rembrandt, Rubens, Van Dyck, El Greco, and Velázquez. In literature the age saw Milton, Pope, Racine, Molière, Cervantes; in science, Newton, Galileo, Bacon, and Leibnitz. The modern scientific method was born in the seventeenth century. In music the period breaks roughly into three fifty-year stylistic units encompassing the very different styles of the pathbreaking Monteverdi, middle-Baroque masters such as Corelli, and the two giants of the late Baroque—Handel and Bach.

The designation *Baroque,* then, serves only as a handy traditional label for a rich panoply of arts and ideas. Still, some generalizations can be made about the period. Politically it was an age of absolute monarchy, exemplified by the glittering court of Louis XIV at Versailles. The courts hired artists more than did churches, so for the first time secular art outstripped sacred. The seventeenth century also saw the devastating Thirty Years' War, a struggle both religious and political that ended in 1648 with France and England ascendant, Germany in ruins, and the Holy Roman Empire a shell. In all the arts it was a period of magnificence and high drama: Rubens's dynamic diagonals and corkscrew figures; Rembrandt's unflinching documentation of his own decline in the self-portraits and the tragic drama of his historical paintings; the gigantic scope of Milton's *Paradise Lost;* the towering choruses of Handel; the dramatic sweep of Bach's *St. Matthew Passion.* All this romantic extravagance and

Baroque style epitomized: Gianlorenzo Bernini's Cathedra Petri, a flamboyant altar at St. Peter's in Rome.

emotionalism is nonetheless distinct from the *self*-expression of nineteenth-century Romanticism; the Baroque tended toward objective expressiveness.

The Baroque began in Italy with the second phase of the Catholic Counter-Reformation, which turned to architecture, painting, and sculpture to dazzle the masses with the splendor of the Church. The musical Baroque, part of the same spirit, began in Italy as well.

Central among its precursors was **Giovanni Gabrieli** (ca. 1553–1612), one of a series of extraordinary composers who worked as organists and choirmasters amidst the gold and filigree of the Basilica of St. Mark in Venice. (Others included the late-Renaissance contrapuntalist Adrian Willaert, Giovanni's uncle Andrea Gabrieli, and, later, Claudio Monteverdi.)

A grandiose place, St. Mark's demands grandiose music. Facing the great Piazza San Marco are five gold-mosaic arches on the cathedral's front and soaring golden towers above them. Thus Venice, a city devoted to putting on a glorious façade. The sumptuous religious and civic processions on the piazza and the marine regattas are further examples.

Like all the composers of St. Mark's, Giovanni Gabrieli wanted to fill the lustrous interior of the basilica with overwhelming music. To that end he made use of a group of galleries overlooking the ground level. He divided his singers and players among the galleries; the separate choirs answered one another from front, back, and sides, echoing phrases, joining for gigantic climaxes of sound coming from all directions. Thereby was perfected the *polychoral* style that would characterize much Baroque music—contrasting groups answering one another. Concentrating on effects of mass and texture, Gabrieli simplified his music, downplaying polyphony in favor of a more chordal approach (another foreshadowing of the Baroque). The simple lines were usually ornamented by players; a written long note, for example, might be turned into a rocketing scale passage.

Best known among Gabrieli's works today are the instrumental *canzone* (plural of *canzona,* "song") for divided groups of winds. They are most often played by brass choirs, making a marvelous effect as the dancelike rhythms chase back and forth among the groups. Among those pieces is the *Sonata pian' e forte* (Soft and Loud Sonata), famous for being one of the first pieces in which volume effects were expressly indicated. Effects of loudness and softness would become as much a feature of the Baroque as contrasting instrumental colors. Today's early music performances of Gabrieli's instrumental works make use of instruments of his time including organ, the wood-and-leather cornett (which sounds like a trumpet with a head cold), and the sackbut, an early trombone. Most grandiose of all are Gabrieli's polychoral motets for voices and instruments, among them *In ecclesiis* and *Nunc dimittis*. Stunning as these and the instrumental works can be in recordings, they sound still more so live. This is not the serene, heavenly choir of Palestrina, but rather a glory-blazing heaven flashing with gold and jewels—the new, improved paradise of the late Counter-Reformation.

From St. Mark's in Venice the polychoral style—and the color and dynamic contrasts it brought—spread across Europe. Among Gabrieli's students was Heinrich Schütz, a major predecessor of Bach and the finest German composer of the seventeenth century. The first towering figure of the Baroque, however, worked at St. Mark's as well: Claudio Monteverdi.

CLAUDIO MONTEVERDI

There is no single pattern for genius. Some are revolutionaries, some conservatives, some thoroughly of their own time. Italian composer Claudio Monteverdi was all three at once: a master of the old Renaissance style, he absorbed the new currents of the seventeenth century and, more than the petit revolutionaries around him, pointed the way toward the future of opera. He is the protean figure who unites the apparently contradictory musical worlds of Renaissance and Baroque.

Born to a doctor's family in Cremona on May 15, 1567, Monteverdi studied music at the town cathedral. At twenty-four he left Cremona for a position as composer, string player, and singer for the magnificent court of Duke Vincenzo Gonzaga of Mantua. Monteverdi would remain in Mantua for over twenty years, during which his publications would make him known all over Europe. The duke clearly valued this employee, taking him on vacations and military campaigns across the Continent. At the same time, Monteverdi resented his servant's position in the court; often he had to beg for his salary from contemptuous officials. In 1599 Monteverdi married singer Claudia de Cattaneis. He seems to have loved her wholeheartedly, a telling clue to which is the series of erotic madrigal texts that he set around the time of their marriage.

The heart of Monteverdi's work, and his musical laboratory, was his forty-year stream of madrigals. His first four books of madrigals

The spirited title page of the 1644 edition of
Fiori Poetici, *madrigals "... by the most illustrious and
most reverend Signor Claudio Monteverde."*

were in Renaissance polyphonic style, but he refreshed the old style
with a new intensity in portraying the images and emotions of the
text. Beyond having an adventurous harmonic sense in general, he
explored the expressive effects of dissonances, including ones not
classified by theorists of the time. This cavalier treatment of the
rules aroused the wrath of pedants, especially one G. M. Artusi,

who made it his mission to attack Monteverdi in a series of broad-sides. In these Artusi used the perennial language of conservative critics:

> Such composers, in my opinion, have nothing but smoke in their heads if they are so impressed with themselves as to think they can corrupt, abolish, and ruin at will the good old rules handed down from days of old. . . . We have reached the point of absurdity, but it is altogether possible that these modern composers will . . . find a way to turn dissonances into consonances and vice versa. . . . For such composers it is enough to set up a great roar of sound, an absurd confusion, an array of defects.

In the end these screeds did Monteverdi more good than harm; Artusi inadvertently drummed up curiosity and customers for the music he condemned. Still, the composer felt the need to defend himself, and began to do so in 1605 with the preface to his path-breaking fifth book of madrigals. In that and later writings Monteverdi outlined his ideas and aesthetics. First, he drew a line between the Netherlandish polyphony of the past, represented by masters like Josquin and Palestrina, and the new style of the Florentine Camerata and related composers (which theorists named *monody*). The old style Monteverdi denoted *prima prattica*, "first practice," and the new monodic style *seconda prattica*. In first practice the music tended to rule the text; in second, the text ruled the music. (Today we simply call the old style Renaissance and the new style Baroque. Note that while *homophony* is a general technical term, *monody* here indicates the kind of homophony heard in early-seventeenth-century Italian music composed for solo voice and accompaniment.)

Unlike Caccini and the other pioneering monodists, Monteverdi did not reject polyphony entirely. Rather he turned the old style toward the aims of the new style: his polyphony would express the text, too. Concerning expression, he wrote:

> It has seemed to me that the chief passions or affections of our mind are three in number, namely anger, equanimity, and humility. . . . The art of music clearly points to these three in its terms "agitated," "soft," and "moderate." . . . In the works of

past composers I have been able to find examples of the soft and the moderate, but I have never found an example of the agitated style [*stile concitato*], although Plato describes it as "the harmony which would fittingly imitate the speech and inflections of the brave man going to war." In view of this I have exerted myself with no little diligence and effort to recover this style.

In pursuit of a *stile concitato* Monteverdi invented the string tremolo, in which the bow rapidly repeats the same note; composers have made use of the device ever since. An allied effect is the string pizzicato—plucking the string.

The year 1600 saw the premiere of the world's second opera— Jacopo Peri's *Euridice,* mounted with great splendor in Florence. Among the audience for that premiere was Monteverdi. His madrigals had already been moving toward greater drama and portrayal of the affections; this new medium could give him the additional advantages of scenery, characters, and plot. His fifth book of madrigals, appearing in 1605, was dominated by the new monodic style. Rather than the old polyphony of equal voices, these madrigals are often for solo voices over a simple basso continuo accompaniment, resembling an aria or scene from an opera more than a traditional madrigal. This approach gave him freedom to pursue every nuance of the text while keeping the words intelligible. Monteverdi thereby became the first composer of genius to realize the full power of homophonic music.

After these experiments in monody he turned to opera. His first, *L'Orfeo,* was produced at Mantua in 1607. Though it is not the world's first opera, it is the first masterpiece of the genre. From that point Monteverdi began to set opera on a path toward more musical variety and, above all, stronger characters and drama. He enlarged the orchestra from that of previous operatic productions. This was by no means the modern orchestra, but rather a broad selection of instruments of the time: strings of both the violin and the older viol family, recorders, cornetts, sackbuts, timpani, organ, harpsichord, harp, and a collection of plucked instruments—guitars, lutes, theorbos, chittarones. Besides eleven soloists, their parts often demanding considerable virtuosity, *L'Orfeo* calls for a six-part chorus. While the characters do not entirely escape the mythical abstractions of early opera (most of whose stories were drawn from Greco-Roman sources), Monteverdi did make a beginning in expressing tangible characters with real emotions. When Orpheus sings, "I lived in dolorous grief," he sounds as if he means it.

Soon after the premiere of *L'Orfeo*, Monteverdi's wife died, leaving him with their two sons. He entered a depression from which he did not emerge for years. Putting aside new projects, he went to mourn at his father's home in Cremona. There, however, a summons reached him from Mantua, entreating a new opera with this grand peroration: "This is the time to acquire the greatest fame which a man may have on earth, and all the gratitude of the Most Serene Prince." Succumbing to this vision of glory, Monteverdi returned to Mantua to compose *L'Arianna*, which was premiered before thousands in 1608, to enormous acclaim.

With that work (now lost, except for its exquisite *Lament*) he did indeed acquire the greatest fame an artist could have. Nevertheless he retreated again to Cremona, complaining of constant headaches and "strong and rabid" itching. Besides his general melancholy, however, what he really itched for was a better job, preferably in Rome or Venice.

In 1610 he journeyed to Rome in search of a church position and a place in the papal seminary for one of his sons. As stock-in-trade he brought a collection of sacred works including his masterpiece, the *Vespers of the Blessed Virgin*, dedicated, with hope of good return, to Pope Paul V. (This sublime work thus joins Bach's B minor Mass in first seeing light as a job application.) At least Bach got the job; Monteverdi and son were both disappointed in Rome. His desire to leave the service of the Gonzagas, however, was backhandedly satisfied in 1612, when after the death of Duke Vincenzo the new duke unceremoniously sacked Monteverdi.

He languished in Cremona for a year until, out of the blue, he was summoned to take over one of the most coveted positions in Italy: *maestro di cappella* of the Basilica of St. Mark in Venice. He would remain there for the rest of his life.

Both Monteverdi and his music were assertive, mercurial, colorful—qualities that suited St. Mark's and Venice. His writings reveal a temperament self-confident and intellectually probing, but also much given to lamentation. Letters to his noble employers commence with the mandatory obsequious groveling but soon reveal his more pertinent demands: "I have indeed made [the dances], my Most Serene Lord, with the usual affection and ready willingness to serve you which I have always had and always will have, but not with the consent of my usual powers . . . for they are still in a weakened state from past labors, and so feeble that not medicine, nor diet, nor the interrupting of studies have restored them to their first vigor. . . . I shall then entreat Your Serene Highness for the love of God not to burden me ever again with so much business at once, or with such shortness of time."

Musing on Monteverdi in our century, Igor Stravinsky observed, "I feel very close to him. But isn't he the first musician to whom we *can* feel very close? The scope of his music, both as emotion and architecture . . . is a new dimension compared to which the grandest conceptions . . . of his predecessors shrink to the status of miniatures. The man himself . . . in his own letters, with their moodiness, anxieties about shortness of time, complaints of migraines, sounds not only strikingly contemporary to me but even, if I may say so, rather *like* me."

In a famous letter Monteverdi reveals his concern with expressiveness and realism by way of a testy response to a request to write music for a dialogue of winds: "The winds are to sing. How, dear Sir, shall I be able to move the affections by their means? [Now referring to his own operas:] Arianna moved the audience because she was a woman; and Orfeo moved them, being a man and not a wind. . . . [Now with patently false humility:] I feel, in my rather deep ignorance, that the whole fable does not move me a whit; and I hardly understand it either, nor do I feel that it will inspire me."

Despite his complaining, Monteverdi was generally content during his thirty years in Venice. He was admired extravagantly and paid accordingly, and had the finest musicians in the country at his command. Naturally, his production of sacred music increased in Venice, much of it in *prima prattica,* Renaissance polyphonic style. But he kept up a steady stream of *seconda prattica* secular works as well—madrigals, dance music for courtly celebrations, and dramatic works.

Among the major works of this period is the dramatic scene *The Battle of Tancredi and Clorinda,* showing the power of his flexible, expressive recitative style. It was the first to make use of "agitated" tremolos in strings, which must have been excitingly novel at the time. One also hears suggested in the string parts the trotting of horses, the clashing of swords (violin pizzicato, another novelty), and the sighs of the dying indicated by sudden changes from loud to soft. In his preface to the work's publication, Monteverdi boasts that the Venetian premiere in 1624 took place "in the presence of all the nobility, who were moved to tears."

In his later years Monteverdi's productivity declined. After a plague killed thousands in Venice during 1630 and 1631, he gave thanks for his survival by taking holy orders and writing a mass of thanksgiving. By that time the fashionable young composers of Venice were mostly his former pupils, and they seemed to be taking all the laurels available.

Yet in his seventies Monteverdi somehow roused himself again to his greatest powers, writing several stage works that picked up the innovations of the younger generation and carried them beyond the capacity of any other Italian of the day. The immediate stimulus for these pieces was the opening in 1637 of the first public opera theater in Venice (previously, operas had been performed in houses of the nobility). That hardly explains, though, the vitality of the two works that survive: *The Return of Ulysses* and *The Coronation of Poppea.*

Last of these is *Poppea,* from 1642, an opera of remarkable musical inspiration and psychological insight. With virtually his last creative gasp, the seventy-four-year-old composer produced something as fresh as any work of his youth. It was *Poppea* above all that set the new medium of opera on the right track: away from the decorous pseudoclassicism of the Florentine Camerata and toward real drama in music.

A year after the premiere of *Poppea,* and after a final visit to his homeland of Cremona, Monteverdi died in Venice in 1643. He was buried with splendid ceremony in Cremona. Fifty years after he died the most famous musician of his time, he was virtually forgotten. Perhaps his integration of polyphony and homophony was too personal to be useful to the new generation; and in any case, Baroque audiences were interested mainly in the newest music. The massive volumes of Monteverdi's works gathered dust in obscure libraries and much was lost. Only with the arrival of scholarly musicology in the nineteenth century did his music begin to emerge from limbo. In the twentieth century, especially with increasing performances of the *Vespers,* it has finally become clear that he stands among the greatest masters.

Not all Monteverdi's surviving output has aged well. Though this is true of all composers, especially prolific ones, it is perhaps especially true of Monteverdi. The long recitatives and agitated tremolos of his stage works like *Tancredi and Clorinda* were electrifying when the ideas were new; today one is apt to want more variety. Here, then, we'll concentrate on two characteristic madrigals and on the towering masterpieces of the *Vespers* and *Poppea.*

The madrigal *Se vittorie si belle,* for two tenors and continuo, begins "If love's wars bring such fair victories, become a warrior, my heart." The music is ebullient, vibrant, with a tender pause for the phrase "do not fear" before marching on to fanfares of victory. As with all his vocal work, this is not music to put on the stereo and half-listen to; its twists and turns need to be enjoyed with libretto in hand to see how he expresses the sense of every phrase.

The well-known *Zefiro torna* (West Wind), from the ninth book of madrigals, is for voices over a ground bass, a technique of the time that spins out melodies over a repeated pattern. Monteverdi often used such ground-bass forms. In this case, it's a short and sprightly bass pattern, the two voices above it vying with one another in accelerating feats of virtuosity that end with appropriately sighing, then soaring music for "now I weep, now I sing." In recent years these gems, and dozens of other Monteverdi madrigals, have been recorded by early music groups.

All that survives of his last opera, *L'Incoronazione di Poppea* (The Coronation of Poppea), is two hand-copied scores, neither by the composer, that show only the vocal parts, a simple basso continuo line, and occasional instrumental interludes. These scores have also been adapted in various ways for performances of the time; a few sections even seem to be by other composers. Nonetheless, what remains is enough to prove this the greatest opera of the seventeenth century and among the most brilliant of all time. Not until Mozart would another opera appear that seems less dated, less restricted by artificial conventions, more psychologically penetrating.

First onstage come the spirits of Fortune, Virtue, and Love. Fortune declares imperiously, "Hide thyself, Virtue! Poverty has struck thee!" Over Virtue's helpless protests, victorious Love declares the moral of the opera: "My mere changes of mood shall change the world." The theme of *Poppea* is the irresistible power of love to corrupt individuals and society. Yet the raptures of love and eroticism have never been more deliciously captured in music.

Emperor Nero, a depraved playboy, intends to replace his wife as empress with his favorite tart, the conniving Poppea. Despite the protestations of his mentor, the philosopher Seneca, and an attempt on Poppea's life by the empress, Nero does succeed in eliminating Seneca (celebrating his death with a drunken orgy), banishing the old empress, and crowning his shameful beloved amidst the sardonic laughter of the court. The beautiful final duet of Nero and Poppea seals the triumph of infamy.

Why did the aged Monteverdi take up such a perverse tale? It's hard to say, except that the story is full of rich characters to paint in music: the sultry, insinuating voice of Poppea; the brash and impulsive voice of Nero; the displaced empress now grieving, now murderous. Though all the characters are corrupt in some degree, all except Poppea reveal flashes of goodness, sympathy, and courage that are the more striking in a world where greed, violence, and caprice rule, a world perhaps resembling Monteverdi's Venice.

Given the sketchy sources, in our time the success of this opera depends on imaginative orchestration and staging by scholars and directors. Even then, the results will not please everyone, especially when heard only in recordings. Much of the work is pure recitative with simple accompaniment; there are few big dramatic scenes or full-scale arias. This is not the agile and ironic style of Mozart, with strongly marked divisions between aria and recitative, or the highly charged melodrama of Verdi. Instead, *Poppea* is a slow, stately dramatic unfolding rich in emotional—and moral—subtleties.

For those sensitive to it, however, the work is utterly absorbing. Monteverdi's voice in dramatic music is among the most elastic of all time; the music constantly changes to follow the emotions, shifting fluidly among recitative, arioso (short arialike sections), instrumental interludes, choruses, and full-blown arias with memorable lyric melodies. Of all operatic styles, one could argue that it is Monteverdi's that best reflects ever-changing reality, at least until the continuous orchestral fabric of Verdi's last two operas. It was Monteverdi above all who established the Italian operatic tradition, with its passionate emotionalism, that climaxed with Verdi two hundred years later.

Monteverdi's other masterpiece is variously called the *Vespers of 1610* or *Vespers of the Blessed Virgin*. Its music somewhat resembles that of *Poppea;* though laid out in more distinct sections, the *Vespers* is still a flowing, kaleidoscopic tapestry. Here the coloristic effects are heightened by Monteverdi's instrumental and choral mastery as well as his solo writing. Some choruses verge on Renaissance style, with imitative counterpoint, but most are closer to *seconda prattica,* and often of stunning beauty.

Part of the value of the *Vespers* is the freshness, to modern ears, of Monteverdi's musical language and his approach to sacred music. We do not find the heartfelt Protestant piety of Bach, but rather the religion of a worldly Venetian and Counter-Reformation Catholic. In Monteverdi's monodic music there was little difference between his sacred and secular styles. For the *Vespers* he creates a supple form whose primary tones are joyfulness and celebration that start right from the opening, which alternates brilliant fanfares with a lively dance tune. Now and then in history a work appears that captures all the currents of the time in a great synthesis. Among such works are Bach's B minor Mass, Beethoven's *Eroica* Symphony, and Monteverdi's *Vespers.*

The rediscovery of Monteverdi continues, revealing in loving performances more and more of the immense vitality of his imagination.

AFTER MONTEVERDI: HEINRICH SCHÜTZ TO JEAN-PHILIPPE RAMEAU

Among other masters of the early Baroque I have already mentioned German composer **Heinrich Schütz** (1585–1672), who studied Venetian polychoral style at its source, with Gabrieli and later Monteverdi at St. Mark's. Throughout his long career, most of it as music director of the electoral chapel in Dresden, Schütz adapted Italian Catholic style and techniques to the more austere requirements of German Lutheranism. In his early *Psalmen Davids* (Psalms of David), splendid polychoral works close to Venetian style, Schütz shows he had picked up the guiding principle of Italian monody: the primacy of the words. Schütz made the German language dance and sing as no other composer has.

These qualities are demonstrated in his famous work for soloists, strings, and two choruses, *Saul, was verfolgst du mich?*, from his collection called *Sacred Symphonies*. The music pictures the moment when Saul, the harrier of Christians, is stopped on the road to Damascus by the voice of Christ, crying the words of the title, "Saul, why do you persecute me?" This short piece builds to a hair-raising climax, the inexorable shouts of "Saul! Saul! Saul!" leaping among the choirs as they ring accusingly in his ears and his soul. Here as in so much Schütz the words seem to become music of their own power, and together they become meaning and emotion.

Major works of Schütz's maturity include the *Musikalische Exequien* (also called *German Requiem*) of 1636, for soloists, chorus, and instruments, one of the high points of seventeenth-century German music. The 1664 *Christmas Story* is wonderfully youthful for the product of an old man who had seen the horrors of the Thirty Years' War. Notable in this work is the vivid characterization of all the figures in the story.

For many years Schütz was mentioned in histories simply as one of the German predecessors of J. S. Bach. That he was, but Schütz is much more; the richness and individuality of his voice has just begun in recent years to receive the attention it deserves in recordings and performances.

After opera had established itself in the early seventeenth century, its monodic style percolated into all kinds of music. Besides the indirect influences, there were also direct spin-offs from opera—the genres called *oratorio, cantata,* and *Passion*. An oratorio is more or less an unstaged opera, a large-scale dramatic piece done in concert, the subject usually biblical. Like opera, oratorio makes use of soloists, chorus, and orchestra, and the operatic genres of overture, aria, recitative, and chorus. The most famous oratorio today is Handel's *Messiah,* though in contrast to most oratorios it does not have a story line. Cantatas resemble oratorios but are smaller in scale, secular as often as sacred, and sometimes for solo voice with instruments. During the Baroque, cantatas became one of the standard adornments of Lutheran church services (thus Bach's hundreds of cantatas), weddings, and secular ceremonies. Finally, a Passion in the Baroque is essentially an oratorio dramatizing the death of Christ; an example is Bach's *St. Matthew Passion*.

Central to the early development of oratorio and cantata was Roman composer **Giacomo Carissimi** (1605–1674). Probably the finest of his oratorios is *Jephte,* from the biblical story of the king who finds he must sacrifice his daughter to fulfill a promise to Jehovah. The recitatives in *Jephte* are among some of the most powerful ever written. Most memorable of all, however, is the celebrated final chorus of lamentation, in which Carissimi uses chains of dissonant harmonies to extraordinary effect; the music seems torn from a sorrowing heart.

The first important composer to pursue opera in France was Italian-born **Jean-Baptiste Lully** (1632–1687). Prolific, brilliant, ambitious, and cunning, Lully gained the favor of Louis XIV and finessed his influence into a virtual monopoly on opera in France. Though his stage works are a bit bloodless, they are also unfailingly elegant and engaging, and thus suited the times. In adapting Italian opera to French language and taste, Lully influenced French musical style for decades. A type of two-part overture he invented—the first section stately and slow, the second lively and fugal—spread across Europe as the "French overture." Both Bach and Handel would make extensive use of this form (an example being the overture to the *Messiah*). Lully's death is legendary among musicians: while beating time on the floor with a staff during a performance, he struck his toe and died of the resulting infection.

The Baroque was the first period in history in which instrumental music rivaled vocal; perhaps never before had the power of music in the abstract, unsupported by words, been so manifest. With this new emphasis on instruments came a flowering of purely instrumental forms and of virtuoso players. In the vanguard of this development was Italian violin virtuoso and composer **Arcangelo Corelli** (1653–1713). He specialized in the chamber music genre called *trio sonata* and the orchestral *concerto grosso*. Two things mislead about the term trio sonata: it usually involves *four* players in three parts—two treble instruments (violins, recorders, etc.), and continuo (harpsichord plus a low stringed instrument doubling the bass); and it is not the later sonata of the Classical period but usually a slow-fast-slow-fast arrangement of movements. (Terms like *sonata* and *symphony* were used loosely in the Baroque and have little to do with the Classical forms of the same names.) Movements of trio sonatas tend to resemble dances of the time, though Corelli's sonatas are more contrapuntal than dance music would be.

His concerti grossi vitally influenced the development of that Baroque orchestral genre. The main idea in a concerto grosso is the principle of contrast, seen in back-and-forth alternations of a large group called the *tutti* or *ripieno* (usually a string section) and a smaller group of two to four soloists called the *concertino*. As in all Corelli, one finds in his concertos a quiet dignity in slow movements and elegant liveliness in the fast ones. Later composers, especially Vivaldi and Bach, would bring more excitement and virtuosity to the genre, and both would also explore the solo concerto; but this idea of a single instrument featured against orchestra would come into its own later, in the Classical concerto.

Henry Purcell (ca. 1659–1695) stands as the only significant native English composer of the Baroque. During his brief life, Purcell rose to the forefront of British composers and served as organist of Westminster Abbey. Like most of his country's composers, he assimilated Continental styles: though he has a distinct voice, Purcell is a repository of the full range of the European Baroque.

He mastered both polyphony in the old style and the new Italian monody. We see his stylistic and expressive breadth in his incidental music for dozens of plays, his massive contrapuntal anthems for Anglican services, and especially in his cantatas and odes. Best known among the latter is the *Ode for St. Cecilia's Day,* a prime ancestor of Handel's English oratorios. Among his incidental music for plays, that for Dryden's *The Fairy Queen, King Arthur,* and some others is so extensive as to approach opera.

Purcell's most famous work is *Dido and Aeneas* of 1689, his only true opera and the only masterpiece of English stage music until the operas of Benjamin Britten in our century. Written for performance in a girls' school, it tells the classical story of Dido's love for Aeneas, which is fatally frustrated by sorcery. Purcell made the old tale into a moving and surprisingly intense one-hour drama. Dido's culminating song as she faces death, "When I am laid in earth," an anguished melody over a descending ground bass, is one of the finest moments in the operatic literature. With Purcell's death in his mid thirties, native British composition entered a period of somnolence that lasted more than two centuries.

Another important instrumental genre was the *suite*, usually composed for solo instruments such as harpsichord or lute but also written for larger ensembles. This was a collection of stylized (i.e., nonfunctional) dances of the time such as the sarabande, gigue, and so on, each with its own characteristic tempo, meter, and rhythm. German composers favored a suite based around the allemande, courante, sarabande, and gigue; the French tended toward a loose assemblage of a dozen or more short dances. Chief among French Baroque harpsichord masters was **François Couperin** (1668–1733), called *Le Grand* to distinguish him from other musical notables of his family.

Couperin's suites (*ordres* in French) epitomize both Frenchness and harpsichordness: they are buoyant, precious, ornamented to a dazzling laciness, overflowing with charm, and at times with a delicate pathos. Though most of his suite movements use dance rhythms, he gave them evocative or wry titles, making them into character pieces: "The Roving Shadows," "The Mysterious One," "The Dreamer." Hymns to worldly delights, these works are musical equivalents of the pastel world of love and intrigue seen in French painters of the time like Fragonard and Boucher.

Another outstanding French composer of harpsichord music was **Jean-Philippe Rameau** (1683–1764), who also wrote important chamber music and operas. His little *Pièces de clavecin en concerts* provide a delicious sampling of his chamber music. In his theoretical treatises, Rameau founded the modern approach to harmony; to this day, musicians study chords and chord relationships as Rameau first rationalized them.

Though national styles began to define themselves more strongly in the Baroque, notably in France, Italy still remained the homeland of the whole artistic period. Not surprisingly, then, the first musical giant of the late Baroque was Italian: Antonio Vivaldi.

ANTONIO VIVALDI

I t's hard to imagine now, but not so long ago one could have dinner in a nice restaurant without hearing Vivaldi's *The Four Seasons*. Though he was one of the most important composers of the Baroque, he was rediscovered in his full stature only in the middle of this century. From being—in America, anyway—the obsession of a few classical disk jockeys in the 1950s, he has ascended to ubiquity. He did likewise in his own time, until Venice got tired of it all and gave him the boot. Given Vivaldi's prodigious output it is not surprising that he did much of his composing on automatic pilot. The best of it, however, is dependably delightful, and something that J. S. Bach, among others, was eager to study and sometimes steal.

Antonio Vivaldi was born in Venice on March 4, 1678, and presumably studied violin with his father, who played at St. Mark's. A virtuoso violinist clearly planning a musical career, the young Vivaldi nonetheless spent ten years studying for the priesthood and took holy orders in 1703. That same year he also acquired a secular musical job in Venice that would occupy him for much of his life. Soon he begged off saying Mass and other priestly duties, claiming debilitating shortness of breath, perhaps asthma. The authorities noticed, however, that his energy in everything else seemed to be phenomenal.

Vivaldi's primary job might seem inconsequential but in fact was prestigious: music director, composer, and violin teacher of the Ospedale della Pietà, called La Pietà, a girls' orphanage and musical conservatory. As Venice seemed to be teeming with unclaimed children, there were four such orphanages in the city and all provided serious musical training. Audiences flocked to the regular Sunday and holiday concerts to see ensembles made up of teen-age girls expertly playing and singing.

For thirty-five years, Vivaldi churned out concertos and similar pieces by the basketful for La Pietà concerts, the total finally amounting to some four hundred works of that kind alone. To Stravinsky is attributed the quip that Vivaldi actually wrote the same concerto four hundred times. Certainly there is much that is prefabricated and predictable in these pieces, but one also finds a wealth

della Sanità   Magazzeni Publicò de Grano   Ponte dell' rio della Zecca   La Zecca   Procurat

of charm and beauty, as well as more variety than Stravinsky gave Vivaldi credit for.

For the Italian public of the time, which had an insatiable thirst for the latest music, Vivaldi was the ideal composer. Venice in particular was a music-mad city from the streets to the salons to the theaters and courts. A British visitor declared that street-corner musicians in Venice played as well as those onstage elsewhere. During Vivaldi's life six hundred operas were performed in the city's theaters. (Public concerts of instrumental music first appeared in the Baroque period. Though England and France were the pioneers in such concerts, Italian opera was performed for the public from the opening of the first theaters in the 1630s.)

By no means were concertos the only major works of the "Red Priest," as the Italian public dubbed Vivaldi for his flaming red hair and nominal vocation. He also produced forty-nine or so operas (twenty-one survive, but are rarely heard), ninety solo and trio sonatas, and reams of cantatas, motets, oratorios, and lesser works.

The Grand Canal of Venice in 1686, with San Marco in the distance.

Vivaldi claimed he could compose a concerto faster than a copyist could copy it, and he probably wasn't kidding. When a German visitor of 1715 asked him for some concertos, Vivaldi returned three days later with ten, several of them written in the interim.

Those were his halcyon days, when his music was heard constantly in Venice and his influence blanketed Europe. He spent much of his time on the road, performing and overseeing productions of his music. In Germany, Bach studied Vivaldi's scores, copied them for performance and arranged some for other instruments. From Vivaldi's crisp, propulsive style Bach absorbed a new conciseness of melody and form, and profitable lessons in rhythm.

The Four Seasons, a set of four solo concertos written in 1725, was enormously successful in Vivaldi's time and is again in ours. These concertos show off his personality at its most engaging—no great profundity of feeling or contrapuntal mastery, but rather a rhythmic drive that runs indefatigably through the fast movements, fine lyric melodies in the slow movements, great clarity of formal organization throughout, and notable imagination in writing for the strings.

Vivaldi was prized for his violin virtuosity as much as for his pieces. A visiting musical amateur of the time described his first hearing: "Towards the end [of the opera] Vivaldi played an admirable solo to accompany an aria, at the end of which he added an improvisation that really frightened me, for I doubt anything like it was ever done before, or ever will be again . . . [it was done] on all four strings, with imitations and at an incredible speed."

As seen in *The Four Seasons,* his writing for strings is also like nothing heard before. One finds flying scales, chattering chordal figures across the strings, imitations of birds, atmospheric murmurings. After centuries of compositions in which all parts, vocal and instrumental, tended to be interchangeable, the Baroque and above

SEVENTEENTH-
AND EIGHTEENTH-CENTURY
OPERA

Opera, the musical/dramatic genre that initiated the triumph of the homophonic style over the polyphonic, was born in the last decades of the seventeenth century amidst the creative ferment of a group of Florentine artists and intellectuals called the *Camerata.* The aesthetic theories and aims of the Camerata pushed a number of artists in the direction of a new kind of theatrical genre. Among the elements that would come together for that purpose were the madrigal tradition, with its emphasis on vivid picturing of the text; an aesthetic inclination away from polyphony and toward homophony (see Monophony to Polyphony to Homophony, p. 88); and the classical tradition of ancient Greece and Rome, which in that era represented the height of learning and the arts.

After a number of experiments and theoretical speculations, members of the Camerata pro-

The Brobdingnagian style of Baroque opera: Bernardino Galliari's proscenium curtain, painted in 1756 for Turin's Teatro Regio.

all Vivaldi created music that seemed to be the voice of the instrument speaking out of its inborn nature. Vivaldi's advances in this kind of idiomatic writing, following the lead of Corelli, were of incalculable importance to the development of instrumental music into the Classical period and beyond.

Vivaldi also set the standard formal outline for concerti grossi, which Bach and others would follow: generally there are three movements, fast-slow-fast; the quicker movements have a dramatic alternation of tutti and solo sections moving through various keys, and a spotlighted return to the home key near the end (the latter idea became a prime feature of Classical sonata form). In contrast, the middle movements are lyrical, with long-breathed melodies often resembling opera arias; soloists were expected to ornament these to taste. In his lucidity of form as well as his tendency to minimalize

counterpoint in favor of a homophonic sound, Vivaldi was more progressive, more a harbinger of the coming Classical style, than was Bach.

After 1730 the Italian public seemed to tire of Vivaldi. Church authorities harassed him for ignoring priestly duties and because of his long-standing affair with a well-known soprano. In 1738, after his thirty-five years of monumental labors for them, the directors of La Pietà turned him out. Two years later Vivaldi made a desperate journey to Vienna in hopes of support from his old patron, Emperor Charles VI, but he found the emperor had died. After several destitute months in Vienna so did Vivaldi, in July 1741. He was buried in a pauper's grave.

duced history's first opera, premiered in Florence in 1598: *Dafne,* with music largely by Jacopo Peri and libretto by Ottavio Rinuccini, after the ancient myth of Apollo and Dafne. In 1600, Peri and Giulio Caccini set Rinuccini's *Euridice* to music and mounted it as part of the wedding of Henry IV to Maria de' Medici in Florence; two years later Caccini premiered his own *Euridice* on the same text. The nominal idea of opera (its name being the plural of *opus,* "work") was to recreate ancient Greek drama as the Camerata imagined it. In reality, opera was hardly Greek but rather something quite novel in history—a drama sung in homophonic style accompanied by instruments, and sometimes involving instrumental inter-ludes, dancing, and choruses. Adding music to drama created new possibilities of expression, music amplifying the meaning and emotion of the words and the story.

The first operas were mostly sung in the new speechlike style called *recitative* (see Baroque section, p. 36, and Glossary). Although more musically appealing forms such as aria and chorus soon took over the main interest, during the next two centuries plots continued to be drawn from classical mythology and history. What touches of realism were achieved would be up to the composers' skill in giving recognizable humanity to figures from myth and legend. The first to do that, and thus the first modern

I will not detail many works here because one is not so likely to look for specific pieces as simply to "listen to Vivaldi," as one would "watch the ball game": it's always there, always different but always the same, unfailingly pleasant and not intrusive. In that he resembles some sort of Baroque Muzak—which is, alas, one of the reasons for his current popularity.

The omnipresent *Four Seasons* is a set of programmatic concertos, one per season, that follows with shameless literalism the texts of four sonnets. In the music as in the poems, birds chirp, breezes waft, thunder rolls, flies buzz, peasants dance, dogs bark, and Vivaldi has a high old time writing some of his most engaging and energetic music. One sees here why his contemporaries admired his *bizzarria*, his whimsicality. The marvel of these pieces is not only how he suggests the flavor of each season, but also how he keeps

opera composer, was Claudio Monteverdi, beginning with his first operas *L'Orfeo* of 1607 and *L'Arianna* of 1608. As seen in the essay on Monteverdi, in these and his later operas he brought homophony and recitative to a peak of beauty and expressiveness that would hardly be equalled until Gluck in the later 1700s.

The idea of opera spread around Europe throughout the seventeenth century, each locale evolving its own style. Roman opera downplayed recitative and concentrated on the more commercially attractive aspects—arias, choruses, instrumental preludes, and spectacular scenic effects: grand palaces, gods flying through the clouds, storms, naval battles.

Rome also introduced comic interludes between the acts of tragedies; these scenes, called *intermezzi*, developed into Italian comic opera—*opera buffa*. After decades of works produced largely in courts, Venice opened the first public opera house in 1637. This hastened commercialization; now catchy tunes and flashy stage-craft—seventeenth-century special effects—were required to bring in the crowds. Neapolitan opera, developing late in the century, established the primacy of the *da capo* (ABA) aria (see Glossary), of florid vocal virtuosity, the importance of *castrato* singers, and the fast-slow-fast "Italian overture." (The latter, called *sinfonia*, was a prime ancestor of the later Classical symphony.) Most

such detailed picturing of the text from falling into fragments. Magically, the music flows along as concise and unified as anything he wrote.

Among the most sheerly beautiful of his concertos is the one for violin called *L'Amoroso,* for its amorous tone. The first movement in particular has a breezy and exhilarating lilt like a fine day in May. Standing out among his other flocks of concertos is the set of twelve called *L'Estro armonico* (The Harmonic Whim) op. 3, published in 1712. Already showing the full-blown Vivaldi style, these works cemented his reputation alongside Corelli in the forefront of Italian instrumental composers. No. 11 in D minor, a concerto grosso with a concertino (solo) group of two violins and cello, opens the first and last movements with vigorous imitative sections before the tutti makes a dramatic entrance. The second movement spins out a beautiful melody for solo violin in the style of the lilting slow dance

celebrated of Neapolitan composers was Alessandro Scarlatti (1660–1725). Besides fathering his great son Domenico and about 115 operas, Alessandro also churned out the unstaged genres that were spin-offs of opera—some 600 cantatas and 150 oratorios.

French opera was its own world, integrating native and Italian elements. From the beginning, ballet was central to French stage music. So was sycophantic praise of the king, who was the main sponsor of opera. As we see in the section on the wily and prolific Jean-Baptiste Lully, in the process of maintaining his near stranglehold on the musical stage, Lully standardized the national style and the "French overture." Besides the operas of Monteverdi, Lully's and those of his rival Jean-Philippe Rameau are virtually the only Continental ones of the century to be heard nowadays (usually in excerpts). In England, Henry Purcell's superb *Dido and Aeneas* (1689) was a flash in the pan; the next important British operas did not appear until the twentieth century.

By the eighteenth century, opera had a wide public following, especially in its homeland of Italy but also in major cities across Europe. England preferred to import its opera and composers from the Continent. Around the end of the seventeenth century a group of Roman dilettantes had proclaimed

called *siciliano*. (As always in Baroque ensemble music, in the D minor Concerto the harpsichord plays throughout, improvising the continuo part from the figured-bass line, fleshing out the texture and providing rhythmic impetus.)

Bach arranged six of Vivaldi's *L'Estro armonico* concertos for organ or harpsichord. Most intriguing of Bach's reworkings, however, is the Concerto in A minor for Four Harpsichords and Orchestra, from a B minor solo concerto of Vivaldi. In full cry, Bach's version has an aviary twitter lacking in the rather heavy-footed original; but both have the inimitable Vivaldi rhythmic drive.

Vivaldi was not only one of the most prolific and infectious of Baroque composers, he was also responsible for some of the most productive musical ideas of his own time and was a vital influence on the next generation. Rarely has such an important artist managed to be so much fun.

the first of the periodic reform movements in opera, creating *opera seria*, with standardized three-act libretti based on classical history or legend. The most important seria libretti were written by the poet Pietro Metastasio, whose texts dominated the century. Most notable among those setting them was Handel; the death throes of his Metastasian opera seria in the mid 1600s are examined in his section. Seria and buffa remained standard operatic genres into the nineteenth century, however.

As detailed in their sections, the immortal names of opera in the later eighteenth century are Gluck the reformer and Mozart the dramatic genius. Gluck attacked the perennial problem of opera seria—that the musical elements tend to push aside the dramatic elements of story and character (not to mention acting, a chronic infirmity in opera production). In Mozart we see the joining of dramatic depth with opera buffa traditions—contemporary subjects and characters, sometimes spoken dialogue rather than recitative, more tuneful arias with more variety of form. After Mozart, who still largely stuck to the old traditions of separate "numbers" and a strong division between aria and recitative, composers of the next century would move toward continuous opera in two converging traditions: the German culminating in Wagner, and the Italian in Verdi. ☐

J.S. Bach amidst scenes of his labors: The St. Thomas Church, Observatory, and School with the later Bach monument.

JOHANN SEBASTIAN
BACH

In one of the gods' occasional literary touches, the name *Bach* is German for "brook"; and the music of J. S. Bach is one of the inexhaustible wellsprings of Western music. Even during the century after his death, when he was rarely performed, his influence inspired everyone it touched, among them Mozart, Haydn, Beethoven, and Mendelssohn. Today Bach is a major part of the great stream of Western music, his work absorbed into the hearts and minds of musicians and listeners everywhere.

We know far less about Bach's life than about later masters. Rather than playing the traveling virtuoso, he stayed home and did his job, and he found most of his jobs within a fifty-mile radius. To those who knew him he was simply the organist and composer at court or church, a skilled craftsman like a carver, not the kind of person one bothered to describe or memorialize. Of his life he left behind a couple of portraits of a fleshy, nondescript figure, some business letters (mostly recommendations of pupils and obsequious entreaties to the nobility), a few anecdotes, some successful children who remembered him fondly and patronizingly, and his music. Perhaps if we knew, as we do with Beethoven, more of his ideals, his hopes, his loves, his rages, his tastes in food and wine, we would be less in awe of him. But Bach the man lies hidden behind that stupendous body of work, and so it is hard to imagine him as anything but superhuman: many music lovers are apt to get Bach mixed up with God.

Johann Sebastian Bach was born into one of the most extraordinary musical families in history, in the German town of Eisenach, on March 21, 1685. Father Johann Ambrosius Bach, a violinist, expected his sons to follow the family trade. Bachs had been German Lutheran musicians for six generations; at one time in the early 1700s, thirty men named Bach held organist positions in Germany. In Thuringia, their region of the country, the word *Bach* was commonly used as a synonym for "musician."

Six generations of Bachs, musicians of Thuringia. This family tree begins with Veit Bach, a baker and amateur musician who died in 1619. Beside it are signatures of J.S. Bach's father Johann Ambrosius, then J.S. and his four famous sons.

From his father Sebastian received his first musical training on violin, but that did not last long; his mother died when he was nine and his father the next year. Sebastian was sent to live with his older brother Johann Christoph Bach, an organist in Ohrdruf. This brother saw to the orphan's musical and academic education—apparently grudgingly. One of the few stories that survive from Sebastian's youth is that Christoph forbade the child to use his best collection of organ music. Showing the curiosity and enterprise that would mark his life, Sebastian found he could extract the book from its latticed

43
~~Bernhard~~
geb. 160
gest. 1743

42
Tobias
Friedrich
geb. 1695
gest.

41
geb. 1703
gest.

40
Joh. Lorenz
geb. 1695
gest.

39
Wilhelm
Hieronymus
geb. 17
gest.

38
Joh. August
geb. 17
gest.

37
Joh. Friedrich
geb. 1703
gest.

36
Joh. Ernst
geb. 1722
gest. 1781

35
Joh. Günther
geb.

34
Joh. Christian
geb. 1696
gest.

33
Joh. Samuel
geb. 1694

22
Joh. Christian
geb. 1672
gest. 1707.

21
Joh. Valentin
geb. 1669
gest. 1720.

20
Joh. Nicolaus
geb. 1682
gest.

19
Joh. Christoph
geb. 1685
gest.

18
Joh. Bernhard
geb. 1676
gest. 1749

17
Joh. Christoph
geb. 1673
gest. 1727

16
Joh. Jacob
geb. 1668
gest. 1692

9
Joh. Nicolaus
geb. 1653
gest. 1682

8
Joh. Aegidius
geb. 1645
gest. 1717.

7
Joh. Christian
geb. 1640
gest. 1682.

4
Johann
geb. 1604
gest. 1673.

2
~~Bach~~
1626.

Johann Ambrosius Bach

Johann Sebastian Bach

J. C. Bach

W. F. Bach

C. P. E. Bach.

G. C. F. Bach

cabinet and spent six months copying the collection in the middle of the night (possibly contributing to a lifetime of weak eyesight). When his brother caught him at this, he callously took the copy from the boy.

After five years under his brother's harsh supervision, Sebastian was sent to Lüneburg to complete his studies while singing in the church choir (soprano and alto parts in church were handled by boys in that era). When his voice changed, he stayed on as a church harpsichordist and violinist; his skills in all aspects of music developed apace. In composition he apparently taught himself. A story from those years demonstrates Bach's tireless determination to improve his craft: thirty miles away in Hamburg worked the legendary organist Reinken; time and again, Bach made the journey on foot to Hamburg to hear the old master play.

In 1703 he took his first substantial position, as organist of the new St. Boniface Church in Arnstadt. Soon after began the wrangles with his superiors that would characterize his career—evidence of a creative ambition that outstripped his circumstances, a stubborn resistance to compromise, a tendency to ride roughshod over obstacles. He was chastised for "confusing" the congregation by "accompanying the hymns with curious variations and irrelevant ornaments"; he seemed too busy to rehearse the choir; his improvised hymn preludes went on too long (on hearing this, he obstinately made them too short); he got into a street fight with a bassoonist whose playing he had compared to a nanny goat. Most interesting of all, he had invited a "strange maiden" into the choir loft to sing. The maiden in question turned out to be his cousin Maria Barbara Bach, whom he married in 1706.

The authorities were still less amused by another episode. They had given Bach a month's leave to go hear the celebrated organist and composer Buxtehude in Lübeck, two hundred miles away. Bach made the journey, on foot, and stayed listening and studying for five months. Perhaps St. Boniface was happy to see Bach move on to an organist position at Mülhausen in 1706. By then he had a number of compositions to his credit—primarily cantatas (see Glossary) and works for harpsichord and organ. He stayed at Mülhausen for a year before taking a better-paying post as court organist, and later concertmaster, for the music-loving Duke Wilhelm Ernst of Weimar.

Bach labored in Weimar for nine years, during which he wrote some of his greatest organ works and fugues. Having absorbed the work of his German predecessors like Buxtehude and Reinken, he now studied the works of Italian composers, especially Vivaldi, copying and arranging their scores for performance. He picked up some of Vivaldi's melodic conciseness and rhythmic energy, tempering his dark German voice with a touch of Italian sunniness. Later he would study French style, with similar benefit.

For some time Bach was happy in Weimar. But in 1717 the duke's music master (*Kappellmeister* in German) died and Bach was not named as his replacement. This apparently rankled, and he brusquely asked the duke for his release. Wilhelm's response to this impertinence from a servant was to clap Bach in jail for three weeks. Finally, Bach received permission to leave for a new position he had already arranged, as Kapellmeister to Prince Leopold in Cöthen.

Young Leopold sang and played several instruments well. Bach led an orchestra of eighteen from the first violinist's desk, and the prince often sat in. During his nearly six years in Cöthen, Bach concentrated on writing secular music appropriate to a noble's court—concertos of various kinds, chamber music, and much keyboard music, including the first book of *The Well-Tempered Clavier* and the exquisite little *Inventions*.

The latter were mainly training pieces for his growing family. Bach would father twenty children, a fact musicians have snickered about ever since. But in those days tradesmen tended to have large families, partly in order to obtain free labor: wife Maria Barbara and the children were not only trained in music by Sebastian, they also served as copyists and assistants. Third son C.P.E. Bach would recall his family home as always "humming like a beehive"—the house full of children and visitors, father giving lessons, regular family concerts, and day and night the scratch of Bach's pen on music paper.

Life in those days was never without the darkest shadows. The average life expectancy was around forty; nearly half of all children died before adulthood, as happened with Bach's offspring. Childbirth strained the bodies of women; a rule of thumb was, "A tooth lost for each child." In the summer of 1720, Bach returned from a vacation with his prince to find Maria Barbara dead. She had borne seven children. We don't know the extent of his grief, but a year later he married Anna Magdalena Wülken, twenty, the daughter of a town trumpeter. She would be a magnificent helpmate; evidence of his affection for her is the notebook of little keyboard pieces he assembled for her instruction, and many of his performance parts are written in her hand.

Around the time of Bach's second marriage, Prince Leopold married a frivolous cousin who was indifferent to music, and the Kapellmeister's position accordingly diminished. Once again Bach began to look for something better, and his hopes settled on the church of St. Thomas in Leipzig.

The cantor of St. Thomas, Johann Kuhnau, had died and the position was open. Since it was one of the most important posts in Germany, the church naturally made an offer to the most famous composer available—not Bach, but rather Georg Philipp Telemann, a friend of Bach's and godfather to son C.P.E. At first Telemann accepted, then reneged when his old church raised his salary. Second choice Christoph Graupner could not get released from his current job. In 1723 the church finally settled for candidate number three, Bach. He would work at the church of St. Thomas for the rest of his life.

Compared to his previous positions, this one was prestigious and well paid. Leipzig was a cosmopolitan cultural and commercial center of some thirty thousand, with a university. Being cantor of St. Thomas was, in short, about as good a position as someone like Bach could aspire to, and it gave him unlimited opportunity for composing and performing. His duties included responsibility for all the choral and instrumental music at two churches—St. Thomas and nearby St. Nicholas—and a steady stream of compositions large and small. (In those days, remember, most of the music played was new music.)

By today's standards, however, Bach lived virtually like a slave. His family occupied rooms in St. Thomas's School next to the church, separated only by a thin partition from the dormitory of some fifty rowdy boys who sang in the choir in exchange for scholarships to the school. He could not go out of town without permission. Living conditions in his building were so unhealthy that of his first eight children born in Leipzig, six died.

Bach immediately fell into battles with the rector and town council over discipline in the school and substandard musical conditions, with the result that he was branded "incorrigible" and nearly lost his job. Eventually a new rector appeared who admired Bach, and things settled down. Always, though, there were wrangles with the authorities as Bach pushed doggedly to gain a free hand over his musicians.

Never could he be criticized for lack of productivity; he was expected to compose steadily and did so phenomenally. His output in the first decades at Leipzig included around 265 of his total of 295 cantatas (each some twenty minutes long), five Masses, six motets, four Passions, three oratorios, dozens of organ works, keyboard music including the second part of *The Well-Tempered Clavier*, scores of other instrumental works, hundreds of chorale harmonizations; all that on top of daily rehearsing and performing duties and teaching his family and private students.

Such productivity was not unprecedented for that age, in which craftsmen were required to work at a killing pace. Composing technique was rule-bound partly because it was geared to speed. Vivaldi and Telemann, among others, outdid Bach in sheer production. But what other composers lacked compared to Bach was not only the ineffable quality called genius; it was also his tireless determination to explore and grow. Telemann's music survives to this day as evidence of a talented craftsman doing his job, often with admirable grace and charm. But Bach rarely seems simply to be doing his job; he seems to be pushing always to extract the ultimate expression of the words, the deepest revelation of the musical material.

This miraculous creative energy is seen at every level of his work. It is seen in his constant struggle to improve the musical life of his church. It is seen in the way he often wrote out the ornaments (the rapid decorative notes in Baroque melody) rather than using the usual shorthand symbols; that way he got exactly the ornaments he wanted from the players, at the price of taking much longer to copy the piece. He used many of the standard chord sequences and melodic formulas of the day; but where other composers were content to play them out mechanically, Bach usually found ways to turn them into fresh gestures. Though in his gigantic output there is the inevitable percentage of less inspired work, his batting average was arguably higher than that of any other composer. (Perhaps only 15 percent of Haydn's and less of Handel's work survives in the standard repertoire. An educated guess is that half of Bach's output is regularly played and recorded.)

Rather than traveling, spreading his fame, playing the virtuoso as did the more celebrated Handel, Bach usually stayed home, so his renown was confined to his region and largely concerned his organ playing. Most who heard Bach considered him the greatest organist who ever lived; some said that he could play more on the organ pedals with his feet than most men could on the keyboard with their fingers. He published only about ten pieces and collections in his lifetime, notably the teaching pieces called *Clavierübung*, ''keyboard practice," *clavier* being the catchall term for any keyboard instrument. Manuscript copies of his music circulated, but many, especially the organ works, strained the capacity of the average musician.

All his work is marked, in one way or another, by a religious spirit. The foundation of his music was the Lutheran hymn, called *chorale,* which underlies much of his melodic writing as Gregorian chant underlies the work of Catholic composers. At the end of Bach's religious works appears the phrase *Soli Deo Gloria*—to God alone the glory. Even in his secular music he often wrote at the head the letters I.N.J., meaning *In Nomine Jesu.* As far as he was con-

FUGUE AND CANON

Fugue and canon are imitative contrapuntal procedures that have intrigued composers for centuries. First we'll examine fugue, the more flexible of the two and the richer in possibilities. Our model will be the "school fugue," as codified by nineteenth-century theorists, which has about as much to do with actual practice as the "average family" does with real families. Both are simply handy abstractions.

A fugue can be written for any medium, instrumental and/or vocal. It begins with a short tune done alone in one voice; this tune is called the *subject* and will recur throughout as the main theme. (In counterpoint we speak of individual parts as "voices" whether they are sung or played.) As the first voice finishes the subject, the second voice picks it up starting on a different pitch (that is, transposed); this second entry of the subject is called the *answer.* While the second voice is going through the answer (subject transposed), the first voice continues with other melodic material. If the latter material tends to accompany the subject throughout, we call it the *countersubject.* If there is a third voice, it usually enters with the subject starting on the original note; meanwhile the second voice might continue with the countersubject and the first voice do more or less what it wants (as long as it makes good counterpoint with the others). Bach and later composers

The circling voices of a Renaissance canon, "Salve Radix Varios," suggest the petals of a rose.

cerned, every note he wrote celebrated the glory of God. This spirit is the source of the joyousness that breaks out so often in his work, like the ecstatic voices of the *Et Resurrexit* in the B minor Mass. Through the centuries, his music has brought great joy to peoples of all faiths—and to people who profess no religion, or who believe only in the revelation of creators like Bach.

Like most composers of his time, he believed that music directly evoked feelings and symbolized ideas. With the "Doctrine of the Affections," Baroque theorists proposed a concise musical language, each gesture tied to specific emotions—excitement, grandeur, rage, mystic exaltation, etc. It was felt that one movement or

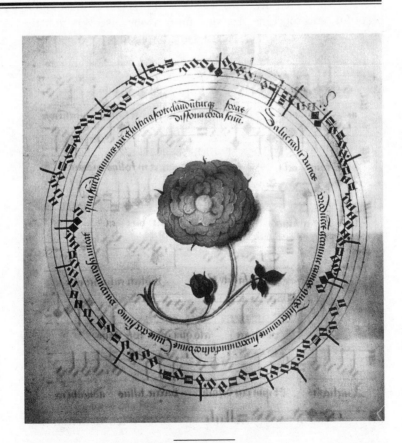

aria should have only one basic affection (in other words, mood). Also like other composers, Bach used symbols in his work: he regularly has voices crossing when Christ is mentioned, halo-like effects in strings when Christ speaks; sometimes he uses the divine number three and systematic numerological references based on the principles of the Jewish cabala. (The latter mathematical mysticism had spread among the intelligentsia of the Renaissance, and Bach picked it up.)

The aria "Wie zittern un wanken" from the cantata *Herr, Gehe nicht ins Gericht* (Lord, go not in judgment) shows how Bach can picture a text. The words speak gloatingly of sinners terrified before the judgment seat of God; they tremble, repeat themselves, accuse one another of their own sins. Bach's setting seems at first simple, beautiful, and touching. Looking further, one discovers that the oboe accompaniment repeats the same phrase over and over, like

---

often insert a brief episode, or "bridge," after the first subject and answer, to make the third entry more dramatic. So the three voices make a pattern something like this:

```
Voice 1: SUBJECT---COUNTERSUBJECT---                  FREE COUNTERPOINT---
Voice 2:              ANSWER--------------  EPISODE   COUNTERSUBJECT------
                    [subject transposed]     [free]
Voice 3:                                               SUBJECT------------------
                                                      [in original key]
```

We see this pattern in the beginning of this fugue from Bach's *Well-Tempered Clavier:* Example 5.

Entries can be adjusted at will in regard to range; often, as in the above, the first voice is in the middle/alto range, the second in the soprano, the third in the bass. There can be any number of voices; three to five are most common.

In a three-voiced fugue, the above pattern would constitute what theorists call an *exposition:* a series of entries on the subject. Usually an exposition is followed by a longer section of free counterpoint also called an *episode* (see Example 5). The rest of the fugue then proceeds in a series of subject entries (and/or complete expositions) and episodes (free counterpoint). This process moves through various keys, ending up in the home key with some sort of climax. Often that climax is

the sinners; that the accompaniment trembles, as they do; that the bass is missing, and therefore they have no foundation. With such subtleties, which never seem forced (as Handel's effects sometimes do), Bach paints the scene for the listener. Yet in the tone of the music Bach adds something that is missing from the fire-and-brim- stone text—a heartrending sense of pity for these sinners.

Bach was the last great master of the old polyphonic tradition. The art of polyphony is the hardest discipline in music because every- thing must serve two contradictory purposes: the melodic lines must be supple and free, but at the same time they must work with one another harmonically. At its highest level, writing counterpoint is an endeavor of Einsteinian complexity.

He not only mastered the grueling demands of counterpoint but reveled in them; he seemed happiest when posing himself the hard-

Example 5 – J. S. Bach, Fugue in C minor from *The Well-Tempered Clavier, Book I*

est problems. In the disciplined polyphonic arts of fugue and canon (see essay, p. 72), he is supreme; yet his fugues have been loved for generations not because they are abstruse but because the tunes are so good, the total effect so beautiful. Compared to his, the fugues of Mozart and Beethoven, which were partly inspired by Bach's, sound labored and self-conscious. Even in an unassuming little piece like "Jesu, Joy of Man's Desiring," Bach tosses off contrapuntal feats that few other composers achieve in their most ambitious works.

The trouble with his propensity for counterpoint is that it reduced him in the eyes of his more progressive contemporaries. His polyphonic style and his favorite musical forms—fugue, chorale fantasia, Passion, cantata—were obsolescent in his lifetime. Four of his own sons (Carl Philipp Emanuel, Johann Christian, Wilhelm Friedemann, and Johann Christoph) would lead the way toward the new Classical style, which was based on grace and lightness and

---

achieved by having entries of the subject overlap. This exciting effect, in which the subject seems to step on its own toes in its eagerness to be heard, is called *stretto* (from the Italian *stringere*, "to tighten"):

<pre>
              SUBJECT------(then free)
STRETTO: SUBJECT---(then free counterpoint)
              SUBJECT---(then free)
</pre>

A stretto has to be planned from the outset because the subject must be composed so as to make good counterpoint when combined with itself. In some pieces the climactic effect of the stretto is further enhanced by a sustained drone note, usually in the bass, called a *pedal point* (because organists play it by holding down one of the bass pedals).

Fugue appeals to composers largely because of its joining of discipline and freedom. To make such coldly logical patterns work fluently and interestingly in both melodic and harmonic dimensions takes a virtuoso command of counterpoint. Yet there can be considerable flexibility in the handling, and the episodes leave room for free invention.

Fuguelike procedures first appeared around the fifteenth century; German composers led in making freestanding fugues. (Germany always had the reputation of being the home of counter-

scorned old-style counterpoint. C.P.E., though he did much to preserve his father's music, also referred to him patronizingly as "the old wig."

In other words, J. S. Bach was a conservative who spent his life perfecting the dying polyphonic tradition. More than anything else, that is why the next two generations were largely deaf to his genius. Though he was the acknowledged leader of music in Leipzig, his last years were probably saddened by neglect; in any case, his productivity declined precipitously.

Two events stand out toward the end of his life. In 1747 he went to Potsdam to visit C.P.E., who worked at the court of Prussian king/conqueror/flutist Frederick the Great. The king was practicing flute when Bach's arrival was announced; he put down his instrument and cried, "Gentlemen, old Bach is here!" For hours Frederick

point, as Italy was the home of lyric melody.) The summit of the German fugal tradition is, of course, J. S. Bach. Recalled one of his pupils, "Bach considered his parts as if they were persons who conversed together like a select company." In *his* conversations, though, the company all speak at the same time, yet move together in harmony.

In Bach's fugues one finds myriad variants of the generalized pattern I have described. Some of his fugues have no stretto, some are nearly all stretto. He sometimes wrote *double* or *triple fugues,* with two or three subjects first presented in separate sections and finally combined in counterpoint; or there may be "double subjects" that always appear together in two voices. These are bogglingly difficult stunts, musical higher mathematics, but Bach brings them off as if they were simple as a folk song.

Bach's fugues have long been admired and studied by composers, but they have been loved by listeners simply because they can be such powerful music—for example, the monumental ten-minute fugue that begins his B minor Mass. Many climactic movements in Bach and Handel choral works are fugues. After Bach, and largely *because* of Bach, the fugue persisted. Besides writing freestanding fugues, Haydn and Mozart often used *fugato,* a short fuguelike section, in their works.

led Bach through the palace, showing off his collection of piano-fortes (the instrument was still in its early stages of development). Bach tried each, on one piano improvising a six-voice fugue and on another a fugue on a theme of the king's. It was a rare and satisfying day of acclaim for the aging composer. On his return home, Bach used Frederick's theme as the basis of a collection of contrapuntal tours de force that he sent to the king under the title *Musical Offering*.

The other story is more intriguing, with a touch of mystery. In 1733 Bach wrote two sections of a liturgical Mass, a Kyrie and Gloria, in an attempt to be named honorary Kapellmeister to the Catholic king of Poland and elector of Saxony. (He got the title, only to find it was without pay.) He probably used this music at St. Thomas, for the shortened Lutheran Mass. Then, from 1747 to

Beethoven became obsessed by fugue in his later years. Though fugues were written in the later nineteenth century mostly as a didactic exercise, truly creative ones were still being written into the twentieth, an example being the first movement of Bartók's *Music for Strings, Percussion, and Celesta.*

A canon might be described as a grown-up round. You all know rounds: "Row, Row, Row Your Boat" and so on. Likewise, a canon is a melody that is sung or played by two or more voices that begin at different times: the melody has to be written to overlap and make counterpoint with itself. Unlike rounds, which go round and round, most canons have a real ending. (A round is always a canon, but a canon is not always a round.) Most canons are

in two parts; following voices may enter on the same pitch as the first or on a different pitch. Compared to our fugue diagrams, the one for canon is simple:

MELODY--------------------
    MELODY--------------------

[plus an accompaniment if desired, and possibly more canonic voices]

Here's an example from Bach's *Musical Offering:* Example 6A.

The oldest known canon is the famous thirteenth-century English round "Sumer is icumen in." Josquin Desprez and his Renaissance contemporaries used the procedure regularly. As with fugue, there are myriad variations on the basic idea, and again a main exponent is Bach. His Goldberg Variations include, among other things, tours de force of canonic

1749, Bach filled out a complete Mass in B minor, adapting music from earlier works and adding some newly composed sections.

Therein lies the mystery. He could not use this Mass in his own church: it was the full Catholic form rather than the Lutheran one. Why would a practical Protestant composer in those days, who usually wrote for an immediate purpose, do something so useless?

We will never know for sure, but it is possible that he intended the B minor Mass as the crown of his work, his testament to God and man, in the highest musical form of the time. Certainly Bach could have had no inkling of his stature in the future, but the Mass implies that at least he had not given up on posterity. This masterpiece, which began as a job application and was assembled mainly from bits and pieces of other works, exists today as one of the greatest

Example 6A – J. S. Bach, canon
from *Musical Offering*

Sign indicates second voice starts here,
from beginning of theme

Canon a 2

THEME

ACCOMPANIMENT

writing throughout. He also wrote many freestanding canons, notably in the *Musical Offering*.

Following the lead of his polyphonic predecessors, Bach played all kinds of games with canonic voices: the second voice might be the tune upside down (inversion canon), backward (crab canon), twice as fast or twice as slow (diminution and augmentation canons). These tricks are often indicated on a single line by strangely located clefs and/or time signatures—a right-side-up clef followed by one upside down indicates that the second voice plays the tune upside down. An example from the *Musical Offering:* Example 6B.

monuments of the human spirit and imagination.

At the end of 1749, after decades of incredible labors, Bach's always weak eyesight failed completely. In January an English surgeon performed an operation on his eyes. The results were disastrous; Bach remained blind and his robust health was broken by the operation and medications. Bedridden, surrounded by his family, he prepared for the end. Legend says that in his final days he dictated to a pupil, note by note, his last work, an organ prelude he called *Before Thy Throne I Stand*. The main theme refers numerologically to his own name. It was his calling card to St. Peter.

He died after a stroke on July 28, 1750, and was buried in Leipzig at St. John's Church, in an unmarked grave: another anonymous servant of God.

Example 6B – J. S. Bach, puzzle canon from *Musical Offering*

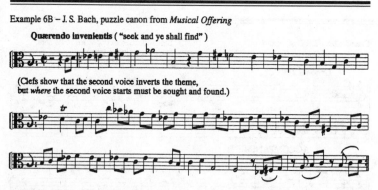

Quærendo invenientis ("seek and ye shall find")

(Clefs show that the second voice inverts the theme, but *where* the second voice starts must be sought and found.)

Bach and other composers also amused themselves and their players with what have been called "puzzle canons," in which the performers have to figure out how the other voices enter, and on what pitch, from arcane clues such as riddling texts. One puzzle canon is headed "Cry without ceasing," which turns out to mean that the second voice must ignore all the rests. Bach wrote one in the form of two contrapuntal melodies with the inscription "Christus Coronabit Crucigeros"; the solution is that two other voices are derived, crossing the first two in mirror form around the note C. With later composers, canons are likelier to appear in sections of a longer work. Brahms was fond of sneaking them in.

Fugue and canon have persisted to this day as a way of organizing counterpoint and a way for composers—and listeners, if they feel like following the game—to exercise their musical muscles. ❑

Of course, the story of his music did not end there. C.P.E. worked to keep his father's memory alive. In the hands of a few enthusiasts Bach's music found a haven. One of them was Beethoven's teacher Neefe, who had his pupil learn the entire *Well-Tempered Clavier* by heart. For the rest of his life, Beethoven kept a picture of Bach on his desk. Mozart well knew the work of Bach's four famous sons, who helped form his own style; but his late discovery of J. S. Bach affected Mozart profoundly, turning him toward a rediscovery of counterpoint. Haydn owned a copy of the B minor Mass, which may have influenced his late religious works.

So, contrary to later myth, Bach was never really forgotten. He had only gone underground, his work expanding every musical mind it touched. When Felix Mendelssohn revived the *St. Matthew Passion* in Berlin in 1829, the world began to awake to Bach's greatness. Then the early Classical composers, whose work had overshadowed him, seemed the dated ones, and Bach was revealed as the composer for all time.

In 1850 the Bach Gesellschaft (Bach Society) was founded to collect and publish what survived of his work. In the modern complete edition, that amounts to sixty volumes. It can be argued that those volumes constitute the most profound and magnificent body of work by a single mind, in any field, in the long human chronicle.

No one has come up with any sure measure for good and bad music or for genius in composers. Certainly, though, among the qualifications for a timeless genius like Bach are the matters of technique and expressive range. As to expression, he seems able to do anything at all: from artless little tunes like those in the *Notebook for Anna Magdalena Bach,* to folksy outings like the *Peasant Cantata,* to charming stylized dance music in the harpsichord suites, to moving melodic writing time and time again, to a tone of monumental nobility like the Sanctus from the B minor Mass, and even to despair—like the anguished opening of the *St. John Passion,* which depicts humanity in a world torn from God.

A master of emotional expression, Bach was also a supreme master of all the technical requirements of music—contrapuntalist, melodist, harmonist, and master of large and small forms. Nearly every musical genre that existed in his day, with the exception of opera, he explored and perfected. Certainly other composers have found potentialities of expression and technique that were unknown to Bach—for example, the intense subjectivity that Beethoven brought to music. But in Bach one sees the entire range of what the music of his age could do.

Beyond that, of all composers his notes seem the most indestructible. They have survived being arranged for modern orchestra, being electronicized, scat-sung, played by rock bands and the Japanese koto. (A record store of my acquaintance has a bin for these albums labeled "Schlock Bach.") If you enjoy such things, by all means indulge; the notes are still the same and some of the gold shines through the gilt. Likewise the recorded collections of lighter Bach pieces like "Jesu, Joy of Man's Desiring," "Sheep May Safely Graze," and so on. Below, however, I'll concentrate on the larger works, one medium at a time.

Long most popular of Bach's orchestral works are the six Brandenburg Concertos of 1721, which show off the composer at his most lighthearted. All follow the principle of the Baroque concerto grosso as Vivaldi perfected it, in which a larger group of instruments alternates with a solo group rather than a single soloist. The first concerto, for example, has a solo group of two French horns, three oboes, and a violin; the larger group is the normal string body of two violin parts, viola, cello, and bass, plus bassoon and continuo. The whole piece is marked by brilliant high-horn writing and the cheery patter of the oboes, as well as solos for the violin that are nimble here, soulful there. The second concerto has a solo group of four— trumpet, flute, oboe, and violin—and is in the usual fast-slow-fast movement pattern of the concerto grosso. The chugging music of the beginning sets a tone of dancelike good humor, the allegros being typically Bachian perpetual-motion machines. Notable here is the stratospheric writing for trumpet, a playing technique that was lost between Bach's time and the mid-twentieth century.

In some ways the most substantial of the Brandenburgs are the third and fifth. The third, for three groups of three strings plus bass, features stereophonic effects of material passing back and forth among ever-changing patterns of players and groups. Nowhere is Bach's gift for getting maximum mileage out of a small collection of ideas better seen than here: each movement produces constant variety from one or two themes. In the fifth the soloists are flute, violin, and harpsichord. Near the end of the first movement there is an astonishing cadenza for the harpsichord, in which an instrument that has hardly any range of volume seems to crescendo over several minutes to a climax of almost symphonic power.

Keep in mind that orchestras in Bach's time were not so standardized as they later became. As in the Brandenburg Concertos, the instrumental makeup tended to change from work to work, depending on what effects the composer wanted and which players were available that week. For a festive, outdoorsy piece, trumpets and drums and horns might be used; for a more modest piece, flutes or recorders with strings were appropriate. The four suites for orchestra show off Bach at his most festively secular, with lots of trumpets and drums. Try the Suite no. 3 in D; the long, songlike violin melody of the second movement has been popular for decades under the title "Air on the G String."

Bach was one of the first composers to write solo concertos of the type that became the norm in the Classical era and after. The best known of those are for harpsichord—no. 1 in D minor, no. 4 in A major, no. 5 in F minor. The athletic octaves that begin no. 1 show his rollicking side. This piece also exists in a version for solo violin; like all composers of the day who had to produce constantly, he regularly reused and rescored pieces for new purposes.

No less absorbing are the pieces for single instruments. Bach wrote the lighter of the collections for solo harpsichord, the French and English Suites, for the edification of young wife Anna Magdalena. Both these suites and the six partitas for solo harpsichord are mainly collections of stylized dances; Bach called the partitas "galanteries composed for the mental recreation of art lovers."

A step up in scope and seriousness brings us to one of the peaks of the keyboard repertoire—the Aria with Thirty Variations, generally known as the Goldberg Variations. Legend says they were written for a friend of Bach's named Goldberg and intended to be played nightly to alleviate the insomnia of Goldberg's employer, Count von Kayserling. If true, it was a strange assignment, composing a soporific, but Bach responded with an astounding expansion of the aria. On the bass line of that tune he erects a little universe of expression, everything from explosive gaiety to delicate wistfulness.

Crowning Bach's keyboard works are the forty-eight preludes and fugues, in two books of twenty-four each, that make up *The Well-Tempered Clavier*. The title comes from his conviction that keyboard tuning should be changed to an equal distance between all notes. Previous systems of tuning had used unequal intervals, which left some keys well in tune but others sour. With equal temperament, all major and minor keys are equally in (and slightly out of) tune, and therefore all are usable; and so in the collection Bach wrote two preludes and fugues in each major and minor key to show off the advantages.

The Well-Tempered Clavier is another astonishing outpouring of material, no two pieces alike, together covering an enormous span of expressive and stylistic territory. It took the composition of fugues higher than it had ever gone, but Bach took it still higher in another collection called *The Art of Fugue,* on which he was working when he died. Never has an almost scientific approach to the technique of composition been brought off with such musicality and expressiveness.

Among other major works for solo instruments are the three sonatas and three partitas for solo violin, and a corresponding set of six suites for solo cello. (Bach liked tidy numbering in his collections.) All were written, along with much other chamber music, during Bach's years at Cöthen. Of the violin pieces, try the Partita no. 2 in D minor; the concluding chaconne is justly famous, reaching a peak of grandeur that would not seem possible for a solo violin. Of the cello suites, I'll suggest the first two, the bright and cheerful G major and the dark D minor.

The organ music is a world to itself, where Bach stands alone at the zenith of the art. Start by exploring some of the popular favorites, like the expansive Passacaglia and Fugue in C minor, the Fantasia and Fugue in G minor, and the Toccata and Fugue in D minor.

The largest, broadest, deepest category of all Bach's work is the sacred music for voices and orchestra. The surviving cantatas number around two hundred. Most were written at top speed, because Sunday services of the Lutheran church required one a week, plus others for special occasions. In all, Bach probably composed some five cycles of fifty-eight cantatas for services.

Of course, not all this music stands at his highest level. There are plenty of torpid da capo arias (see Handel section p. 96) and whole cantatas with little inspiration. It has been said that though Vivaldi is the lesser composer, at least he generally knew when to shut up; the same can't always be said of Bach. But nowhere in all music run such rich veins of gold as in the cantatas. For a start at a lifetime's listening, we'll recommend three. The early *Christ lag in Todesbanden* (Christ lay in the bonds of death) is dark and tragic in tone. In contrast, *Ein' feste Burg ist unser Gott* (A mighty fortress is our God), from the same period, is one of Bach's most joyous, with a duet of surpassing loveliness on the text, "How blessed are they who call on God." *Wachet auf, ruft uns die Stimme* (Sleepers Wake) is another joyous one; the fourth section, in which Bach weaves a lilting melody around the chorale tune, found popularity in recent times in a scat-sung version.

Among the larger vocal works, the *Magnificat* in D major of 1723 is among his most engaging. Once again I have to use the word joyous for the brilliant opening of this sacred piece, with its dancing voices and pealing trumpets. Bach is the great master of spiritual joy, at times of a sustained intensity (as in the *Magnificat*) that seems to overflow the heart.

At the summit of Bach's music, and maybe of all music, lie two gigantic sacred works of contrasting import—the *St. Matthew Passion* and the B minor Mass.

The *St. Matthew Passion* is the more intimate of the two. It tells the story of Christ's death in alternations of narration and heartfelt reflection, interspersed with chorales and choruses. The great choruses set the scene and the emotional tone; sometimes the choir plays the role of the crowd, alternately reacting in horror to the story and at other times taking part: "Let him be crucified!" The Evangelist tells the story in solemn recitatives. In the arias, individuals speak of their anguish and their loss; "Come my heart and make thee clean," says the sublime final aria, "that my Jesus I may bury." The end is a stately dance to the grave. Pervading all is a sense of tragedy that transcends the particulars of any one religion. The universality of the Christ story is that we all suffer, all lose our beloved, all seek solace, all are crucified. The *St. Matthew Passion* expresses that sorrow and hope for all time and all humanity.

The B minor Mass is the more formal side of the religious experience—the drama, prayer, entreaty, celebration, and affirmation of the Catholic Mass. Here the tone is elevated and objective, starting with the enormous fugue on *Kyrie eleison* that forms the first chorus. There is no aspect of spirituality that is not touched in this work, from the lighthearted joyousness of the *Gloria in excelsis* to the stern proclamations of the Credo to the delicately lovely bass aria on *Et in Spiritum Sanctum*. Perhaps most unforgettable is the central *Crucifixus*, a depiction of the crucifixion in inexorable steps that seem to lead down into the silent blackness of the grave; then the *Et Resurrexit* erupts with cries of triumph and exaltation. In this Mass—at once one of the towering monuments of Western music, the human creative imagination, and the religious spirit—lie riches beyond measure.

The same words could stand for all Bach's output: riches beyond measure. He exhausted the possibilities of music in his time with a brilliance that exhausts superlatives. In him as with a few other artists of awesome fertility—Rembrandt, Picasso, Mozart, Shakespeare—one sees the closest humanity can come to the boundless fecundity of nature, which generates forms and glories and tragedies beyond measure.

DOMENICO SCARLATTI

Domenico Scarlatti is the great enigma of the Baroque. Of his life and character the record reveals more questions than answers. Most of what we know of him is his music: a number of stolid works in the conventional forms of the day and, from his later years, an audacious and brilliant collection of little harpsichord pieces that seem to have come out of nowhere, and on which his immortality rests.

He was born to an illustrious musical family in Naples on October 26, 1685, and christened Giuseppe Domenico. History remembers his father, Alessandro Scarlatti (1660–1725), not only for his fifty-plus operas and more than six hundred cantatas (some still performed today), but for their seminal influence on a generation of composers, above all Handel. For better or worse, it was Alessandro who established the *da capo* form as the standard for late-Baroque arias. His other musical children and relatives worked across Europe and England. Domenico would prove to be the best composer of the family, but he would hardly have the impact on his time that Alessandro did.

The child studied harpsichord and composition with his father and undoubtedly with others, but we do not know when and with whom. We know that at sixteen Domenico was appointed organist and composer of the royal chapel in Naples—evidence of both talent and nepotism, since Alessandro was music director there. Two years later came the premiere of two of Domenico's operas in Naples. The son seemed to be taking up his father's career path.

A possible reason for Domenico's later elusiveness and peregrinations, however, may have been his attempts to escape Alessandro's efforts to force him into the family mold as purveyor of fashionable entertainments to the nobility. In 1705, while working in Rome, Alessandro wrote to his patron, Prince Ferdinando de' Medici, "I have forcibly removed [Domenico] from Naples where, though there was scope for his talent, it was not the kind of talent for such a place. I am removing him from Rome as well, because Rome has no shelter for music, which lives here as a beggar. This son of mine is an eagle whose wings are grown; he must not remain idle in the nest, and I must not hinder his flight." Domenico apparently submitted for the moment to these forcible removals. He ended up in Venice for several years, doing we know not what.

We find him again in Rome in 1709, in the entourage of exiled Queen Maria Casimira of Poland. For her he wrote seven operas plus an oratorio and cantata or so. Some of these works survive, revealing Domenico at that time as no more than a competent dispenser of his father's kind of music. He was much in demand as a harpsichord virtuoso. In Handel's section I will tell of the legendary keyboard duel between him and the young Handel. Their contest, roughly a draw, left the two men mutual admirers.

The sketchy record continues with Domenico's 1713 appointment as music director of St. Peter's basilica in Rome. This was a prestigious post. All we know about this period of his life, however, is some surviving music—again, competent but uninspired. More intriguingly, at age thirty-two he took the trouble to obtain a legal document of independence from his father. Was Alessandro still trying to run his son's life? In 1719 we find Domenico, then thirty-four, taking a job the better part of a continent away from his father, as music director of the royal chapel in Lisbon, Portugal. This would prove to be the end of his wanderings and the beginning of finding himself as a composer.

It sometimes happens that artists fail to discover their forte until circumstance or luck spells it out for them: a painter of small canvases discovers her real metier is large paintings; an academic poet transforms himself with a style based on everyday speech. Away from the major European musical centers and away from his father, Scarlatti the composer of operas and cantatas was reborn as one of

MONOPHONY
TO POLYPHONY
TO HOMOPHONY

For most of human history, as far as we know, music was entirely a matter of melody and rhythm. Harmony in the Western sense was neither imagined nor needed, and in most non-Western music it still isn't: the music of India is a magnificent example of what can be done using only melody and rhythm. The term for such music, made from a single melodic line, is *monophony*.

The West's primary technical contributions to music have been the arts of polyphony and harmony. Our ideas of them took hundreds of years to evolve fully,

from around the ninth century to the seventeenth. Here is a brief summary of that long and digressive process.

When medieval church composers began to explore the epochal idea of multiple parts around the ninth century, they didn't simply put some chords under a tune; chords were a long way from being invented. All they knew was melody, especially the

Example 7 — MONOPHONY (a thirteenth-century illuminated chant manuscript). Detail from Beaupré's Antiphony, around 1290.

the most original geniuses of the keyboard miniature. That rebirth was a direct result of his job in Lisbon, which was primarily as teacher and composer for Princess Maria Barbara, the infanta of Portugal. The princess was strikingly homely yet destined to marry well, intended for a life of elegant uselessness yet determined to become a virtuoso harpsichordist. We know she was skilled because the music Scarlatti would write for her over some four decades is more challenging than any other of the time except for Bach's.

So in Lisbon he began writing little harpsichord pieces, one after another, for the amusement and edification of the princess. He called them *sonatas*—not the later Classical sonata but rather one-movement pieces some three to seven minutes long and displaying an unprecedented novelty of invention for such works. They may

have been intended to be played in same-key pairs, and they are often done that way today; but as with so much about Scarlatti, the evidence for such pairing remains inconclusive.

In 1729 Maria Barbara married the heir to the Spanish throne, the future Fernando VI, also a lover of music. The couple took Scarlatti with them to their court in Madrid. There he stayed for the rest of his life, one of the treasured private servants of a court as rich and extravagant as any in the world. In contrast to nearly all other artists, he appears not to have made a single complaint about his

time-honored repertoire of Gregorian chant. So naturally, when church composers began experimenting with multiple parts, they took an existing chant and added more melody to it. At first, the added melody was essentially the same as the original, moving in parallel intervals underneath, like a shadow. This style was called

Example 8 – POLYPHONY (Palestrina, Sanctus for *Missa Æterna Christi Munera*)

employers. During his early years with Maria Barbara he traveled occasionally, the journeys including one—only one—to Naples, to visit his dying father. He went to Rome in 1728 and there married Maria Caterina Gentili, sixteen, who bore him five children before her death ten years later. In 1742 he remarried in Madrid and had four more children. Four of his nine children survived infancy, about normal for the time; oddly for the time, none of the four took up the family trade of music.

The rest is hearsay, supposition, tantalizing fragments of fact.

---

organum. Then, over centuries, that second voice began to acquire more and more melodic independence; meanwhile, other voices were added. Finally, by around the twelfth century the texture of the most advanced church music consisted of two or more independent melodies sung or played together.

Thus was born *polyphony:* the art of combining two or more lines of smooth, effective melody, all working together. (Another common term for polyphony is *counterpoint.* Though the two words have slightly different connotations, they are usually used interchangeably.) For a time, the procedure in writing counterpoint was as follows: for a basis you took a Gregorian chant melody or another existing tune (which when used this way was called the *cantus firmus,* "fixed song") and composed other lines above and below it, one at a time. Later, composers tended to write all the

added parts at once, as they went along; still later, composers discarded the cantus firmus and wrote all the voices from scratch. (In counterpoint, each line is traditionally called a *voice* whether it is sung or played on instruments, and regardless of how many people are singing or playing.) As we learn in the section on the Middle Ages, musical notation developed along with polyphony, to preserve this unprecedentedly complex new music.

Of course, when melodies are combined harmoniously rather than randomly, the combination produces what we now call *chords,* or *harmony.* From the way melody and harmony look in notation, we say melody is the *horizontal* aspect of music and harmony the *vertical* aspect. Medieval polyphonists soon figured out that if melodies were going to sound good together, the "vertical" combinations had to fall mainly into consonant intervals such as thirds

The celebrated castrato Farinelli, also long employed by the royal family in Madrid, reported that Scarlatti was addicted to gambling and often ruined as a result, but that the queen invariably bailed him out. We know that in 1738 he became a Knight of the Order of Santiago, which among other things gave him the right to "wear clothes of velvet and silk in any color, rings, jewels, chains and clothing of gold." Sure enough, there is a portrait of the knighted Scarlatti sporting clothes of velvet and silk. He maintained a handsome house in Madrid. In her will Maria Barbara left Scarlatti two

or fifths (see Consonance and Dissonance, p. 28). During the Renaissance, sophisticated rules were developed to reconcile the horizontal and vertical dimensions. But the interaction of melodic lines remained the primary idea in polyphony; the harmony was considered merely the byproduct of the counterpoint. As I note in the pages on Bach, making counterpoint sound harmonious, reconciling the conflicting demands of supple melody and effective harmony, is one of the hardest disciplines in music. Nonetheless, the composer must make the result sound effortless and beautiful for the listener.

As we see in the Baroque section, in the seventeenth century, under the impetus of the new operatic style, music began to turn away from polyphony. Now for the first time, composers paid more attention to chords than to

Example 9 – HOMOPHONY (Mozart, *Piano Sonata in D major*)

thousand gold doubloons, a fortune, citing his "diligence and loyalty." But Scarlatti died before his queen, on July 23, 1757.

During his life the only publication of his work was an edition of thirty sonatas printed in London in 1738, under the modest title *Esercizi per gravicembalo* (Exercises for the Harpsichord). Admirers pirated these and others in further editions. As he had no predecessors for his extraordinary style, he had few heirs either. The publications and a few enthusiasts touched off a virtual Scarlatti craze in England; only there and in Spain did he influence other composers.

counterpoint. The new style of music was based on a single melodic line supported by harmonies: melody and accompaniment. This texture was eventually dubbed *homophony*. We are still in the homophonic age; an opera aria by Mozart, a folk song, a Gershwin tune, usually consist of one melody and some kind of chordal accompaniment. In the last four hundred years, composers have explored and expanded the idea of homophony in successive spurts of rule making and rule breaking. The *types* of harmonies have accordingly changed, from the familiar tonal chords of the past to the freer, often more dissonant harmony of the twentieth century; but the principle of homophony is still the same.

Here's a caveat: polyphony has never really died in the homophonic age. For one thing, composers have continued to write fugues, canons, and free counterpoint. And even in pieces that seem homophonic—a Bach chorale harmonization, a Mozart aria, a folk song arrangement, or brass parts for a pop tune—each part should move smoothly and melodically through the harmony. In the long run, there is no sharp distinction between polyphony and homophony. The best homophony still contains a lot of the old contrapuntal virtue of smooth melodic progress in each part. □

Example 10 – HOMOPHONY (American hymn, "Amazing Grace")

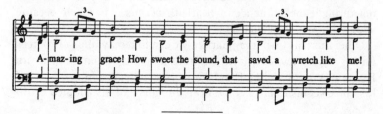

The artistic centers of the Continent—in Italy, Germany, France—hardly knew of his music during his life. His only recorded student of note was the Spanish minor master Antonio Soler.

The modern edition of Scarlatti's work comes to eighteen volumes, including over five hundred sonatas. As many as half of them may have been composed in the last six years of his life. The major existing source is the fifteen volumes, exquisitely hand-drafted and bound in red morocco, gold-embossed with the royal arms, that were the personal copies of Queen Maria Barbara. Not one manuscript in Scarlatti's own hand has been found. His singular legacy was a collection of fantasies composed by a phantom.

In one of his few surviving writings Scarlatti himself provided the perfect thumbnail description of his work: "an ingenious jesting with art." One is immediately struck by the wildness of his voice—the capricious melodic turns, the whirling extravaganzas-in-a-teacup, the mysterious fanfares, the startling shifts of chord and key. So much has been packed into these small spaces of time. Some have described his sonatas as tone poems in miniature, with whole dramas and characters and changes of scene.

While his approach is unique, it also prophesies the coming Classical style. Discarding the contrapuntal texture of the era's keyboard music, in which the lines tended to resemble vocal writing, he developed a new idiomatic treatment of the harpsichord. In that respect he was to the harpsichord what Vivaldi was to the violin, Chopin to the piano—a discoverer of new musical possibilities that grew directly from the nature of the instrument. He reveled in soaring arpeggios, wide melodic skips, chattering repetitions of one note. Where most Baroque composers still looked at a keyboard piece in terms of a consistent number of contrapuntal parts, Scarlatti didn't care if one chord had two notes and the next four; idiomatic figuration took precedence over counterpoint for him. All these usages would become characteristic of the Classical period (though not through the influence of Scarlatti, because his music became widely known only later).

Other than his own imagination, we can find only hints of sources for his style. Inevitably, one can trace influences from mainstream Baroque composers like Handel and especially Vivaldi. But part of his voice seems to have come from the music of his adopted country, Spain, and its national instrument, the guitar. Many of his pounding left-hand accompaniments resemble guitar strumming, their peculiar harmonic movements and startling dissonances suggesting similar effects in Iberian folk music. His rhythms sometimes resemble those of castanets.

Though there is a tremendous variety of idea and effect in Scarlatti's output, there is also considerable consistency in that nearly every sonata outlines some variation of *binary form*. This involves two large sections, both repeated; the first modulates from the home key to a closely related one, the second begins with some harmonic adventuring, then returns to the home key. Sometimes the whole piece gravitates around one thematic idea, something like: A A1// A2 A1 (each half repeated). Sometimes the second half of the first section, in its new key, has its own theme. He reliably returns at the end to the material that ended the first half, but transposed into the home key—a prophecy of later Classical sonata form.

One of his many variations on basic binary form is seen in the famous Sonata in E major K. 380. (The K. stands for Ralph Kirkpatrick, the best known of the scholars who have tried, with imperfect success, to arrange Scarlatti's output in some rational order.) The swinging-along main theme of the E major is proclaimed alone at first and then repeated in various registers, leading to a typically Scarlattian routine some have dubbed a "vamp" section, from a jazz term for marking time musically: a little motive is repeated over and over in the right hand while underneath, in the left hand, the chords progress in unpredictable ways. Next comes a contrasting part, in a new key, in this case a sort of ghostly horn call that is developed to the end of the section. This is all repeated. The second big section then treats only the horn-call idea, working back to the home key. The overall form here might be summarized A B//B1 B2. As usual, there is an exhilarating sweep into the final cadence.

Scarlatti's output is a torrent of tiny gems, so I won't detail many specific pieces here. There is a growing catalogue of good recordings by harpsichordists, pianists (Horowitz was a pioneer), and guitarists playing transcriptions. The pieces demand to be heard in performance or on the stereo with nothing else pending—lying down with headphones on is especially pleasant, I've found. Then you begin to discover his quirks of imagination: say, the startling two-fisted chords breaking into the F major K. 525; the almost Gershwinesque chromatic fillips that emerge in the G major K. 549; the way the D major K. 96 begins gaily with fanfares and builds steadily through the whole first half to a breathtaking climax—and that with an instrument unable to make a crescendo.

It was his idiosyncrasies that appealed to adventurous musicians of the eighteenth century lucky enough to know his music. An English historian of the time wrote, "Scarlatti's were not only the pieces with which every young [British] performer distinguished his powers of execution, but were the wonder and delight of every hearer who . . . could feel new and bold effects intrepidly produced by the breach of almost all the old and established rules of composition." It is a tribute to his imagination that in our century, which has sabotaged every conceivable old and established rule of composition, Scarlatti still manages to dazzle us with the audacity of his voice.

GEORGE
FRIDERIC
HANDEL

George Frideric Handel, whose art defines the grand and magisterial in music, was in his person fat and slovenly, gluttonous, bowlegged, bovine of expression, often to be seen lurching about the streets of London muttering to himself in German like some rummy ship-jumper. He was generally perceived to be mad in some degree; modern observers note evidence of manic depression, one symptom of which was his bizarre creative frenzies. All the same, by the end of a career of extravagant ups and precipitous downs, he had come to represent to his own time just about what he represents to ours:

one of those angel-smitten geniuses who are the glories of our species.

Then as now, that reputation was founded primarily on a single work of unprecedented popularity, *Messiah*. So magnificent and nearly ubiquitous is this oratorio that it has long threatened to crowd the rest of his work out of the public ear. That masterpiece was no fluke, however, but simply the most consistently inspired work of an artist who depended more than most on the inspiration of his muse. His contemporary, Bach, was the period's great architect in sound; Handel was its great improviser.

He was born Georg Friedrich Händel in Halle, Germany, on February 23, 1685, the son of a barber-surgeon with no love for music. Despite his son's early signs of prodigious talent, the father was determined that Georg would study law. The boy resorted to practicing on a muted spinet in the attic. Finally, on a visit to a relative at the ducal court of Saxe-Weissenfels, the duke heard Georg play organ and pressed the father to let him take lessons. Since the duke filled Georg's pockets with gold for the purpose, the father grudgingly agreed. Georg began to study at the Halle Lutheran church with F. W. Zachow, a prominent organist and composer.

By age twelve, Handel had progressed remarkably in studies of oboe, violin, and especially clavier (a blanket term for keyboard instruments). That year he became Zachow's assistant organist at the church. The teacher confessed he had nothing more to show this pupil; already Handel was composing service music, becoming known as a prodigy, attracting aristocratic patrons. In 1697 Handel's father died, but Georg nevertheless attempted to honor his father's wishes by enrolling in law school at the University of Halle. He lasted about a year before dropping out to become a church organist in Moritzburg. After another year, Handel left that job and took a place in the second violin section of the Hamburg opera house. This would seem a step down, but it is likely that he had already formed an ambition to write for the stage, and he headed for the primary source of German opera.

The director of the Hamburg opera house was Reinhard Keiser, the country's first important opera composer. As usual, Handel quickly made his presence felt, stepping in for an indisposed harpsichordist (who in that era also conducted the performance). Handel also got to know composer, singer, and keyboardist Johann Mattheson, another resident genius at the theater, and they became lifelong friends—except for one short but nearly fatal tiff. When Handel refused to relinquish his place at the harpsichord to Mattheson during a performance of the latter's opera, their argument developed into an extended fistfight, the two men rolling around the theater (to cheers from both audience and singers) and out into the street, where Mattheson pulled his sword and tried to stab Handel. A metal button on Handel's coat shattered the blade. That ended the duel and the quarrel; before long the two were great friends again. Mattheson would later write the first German biography of Handel.

The duel resulted as much from jealousy as anything else, and Mattheson was not the only jealous one. In 1704, director Keiser generously gave the libretto of *Almira* to the nineteen-year-old Handel to try his hand at opera. The result was a resounding success, which made Keiser very nervous. From then on, the director did not rest until he had hounded this young rival out of town. By 1706 Handel had had enough; he took his earnings and headed for Italy, to see what he could gain toward his art and his fortune. It proved to be much in both respects.

In Florence he mounted his opera *Rodrigo* to no particular acclaim, but in 1708 his Italian oratorio *La Resurrezione,* conducted in Rome by Arcangelo Corelli, made him instantly famous. The admiring Italians dubbed him *Il Sassone,* "the Saxon." He absorbed Italian style from its greatest masters, who became friends and patrons—among them Corelli, opera and oratorio composer Alessandro Scarlatti and his son Domenico, the latter on the verge of his own historic career. A feature of concert life in those days was public contests between virtuosos. Roman admirers of Handel and Domenico Scarlatti arranged a contest on organ and harpsichord in early 1709, at a concert in the home of Corelli's employer, Cardinal Ottoboni. It must have been an extraordinary evening, with two of the greatest keyboard players of all time unleashing their full powers in mounting feats of improvisation. At the end, the harpsichord laurels seemed to rest on Scarlatti, the organ crown on Handel, and the two men had become mutual admirers. It was said that when Scarlatti was complimented for his playing after that night, he would cross himself and speak of Handel. (Handel had only one peer as an organist—Bach—and they never met. It is not known if Handel ever heard of Bach at all.)

His triumphs in Italy made Handel one of the most celebrated young composers on the Continent. In 1710 he returned to Germany to take on the position of Kapellmeister—music director—to Elector Georg of Hanover, with a salary twenty times what Bach was then making at Weimar. But Handel was restless. He got leave to visit London and there produced his Italian opera *Rinaldo;* though this was largely an assemblage of previous material that Handel threw together in two weeks, it caused a sensation with the London public. The production was decked out with typical stage gimmicks of the time: the promised chariot drawn by white horses failed to appear, but there were two fire-breathing dragons, real fireworks, tenors dressed in royal robes sailing through pasteboard storms, and flocks of birds released onto the stage. (Addison and Steele, tireless satirists of operatic excesses, noted of the birds that "instead of perching on Trees and performing their Parts, these young Actors either got into the Galleries or put out the Candles.")

Handel returned to his job in Hanover for a while, then in 1712 got leave from the elector to return to London for a "reasonable" time and produce more operas. These found less success than *Rinaldo,* but works he wrote for the crown fared better, among them his *Birthday Ode for Queen Anne.* The queen gave Handel an annual stipend in hopes of keeping him around as a court composer.

Despite his job in Hanover, he did tarry in London. When Queen Anne died in 1714, things finally became a little embarrassing. Due to international royal relations, the new King George I of England was none other than the former Elector Georg of Hanover, Handel's neglected employer. Handel probably made himself scarce around court for a while. There is no truth, however, to the old story that he won the king's forgiveness with his *Water Music.* He and the king were reconciled long before that delightful work was written. It *may* have, as the story says, been the music that was played for the legendary party in 1717, when king and court floated down the Thames in barges accompanied by a bargeful of musicians playing Handel. That year he became music director for the duke of Chandos, for whom he wrote the *Chandos Anthems* and other works including *Esther,* his first English oratorio. He had established himself once and for all in England: Georg Friedrich Händel was now

George Frideric Handel. He would become a naturalized British citizen in 1726.

Such works as the *Water Music* were really only sidelines. Handel came to England to make his fortune writing opera for fashionable London audiences, who in those years craved stage spectacles in the Italian style and language. In 1719 a group of noblemen formed the Royal Academy of Music and named Handel one of the directors. The main intention of the organization was to produce Italian opera. Handel made scouting trips to Germany and Holland to round up the best singers. In the ten years after 1720 he would write fifteen new operas for the Royal Academy, several of them major hits.

Writing opera in those days was a market-oriented show-business operation and had to conform to the tastes of the time. Handel would compose most of the music for a given opera during the two or three weeks of rehearsals, all his work subject to the whims of producers and prima donnas. The whole thing was further dependent on a fickle, trendy London public that demanded as little plot and as much vocal and scenic pyrotechnics as possible. And anyway, these *opere serie* were in Italian, which hardly anyone understood. Between arias, the plot was advanced briskly by *recitative secco,* "dry recitative," the nadir of a once vital form of vocal recitation. Leading roles were often sung by *castrati,* named for the operation that made males permanent sopranos or altos. Despite the stupendous vocal skills of the best castrati, this grotesquerie was obsolescent even in Handel's day. In modern performances of Handel's operas, the castrato parts are usually transposed down and sung by tenors or basses, sparing us a mezzo-soprano Julius Caesar.

In contrast to the psychological subtleties we have come to expect from Mozart and later masters, a Handel opera aria is emotionally and formally static: according to the Doctrine of the Affections (see the Bach section, p. 73), each aria reveals only one affect of the character—tenderness, rage, melancholy, etc. It is usually written in *da capo* ("from the beginning") form, the ABA outline that was almost universal for arias of the time. The trouble is, unless the A section has uncommon appeal, its return after the B section can be deadly dull. This problem afflicts more da capo arias than not—including many by Handel and Bach.

By our standards, in other words, Handelian *opera seria* (see Seventeenth- and Eighteenth-Century Opera, p. 58) is dramatically absurd and musically dicey. There were and are rewards in them, however. Besides their musical gems, at which London audiences would stop talking and playing cards and actually listen, there were also on- and offstage feuds to keep things interesting. Opera was a kind of prize-ring sport, with heavily partisan fans. Handel's leading sopranos, Cuzzoni and Faustina, were bitter rivals; a 1727 performance was enlivened by an onstage hair-pulling, scenery-destroying catfight between the two ladies while their respective factions slugged it out in the hall. During a disagreement at their very first rehearsal, Handel somehow picked up Cuzzoni—who besides being foul-tempered and ugly was also quite hefty—and dangled her out a window. When she finally saw the logic of his argument, Handel pulled her back inside and warned, ''I know that you are a witch, but don't forget that I am the devil himself.''

For some time there was another rivalry between Handel and his Royal Academy codirector, composer Giovanni Bononcini. The fierceness of public sentiment in rooting for one or the other contributed two memorable new words to the English language. They occur at the end of a satirical jingle of the time concerning the feud:

> Some say that Signor Bononcini
> Compared to Handel is a ninny;
> Whilst others say that to him Handel
> Is hardly fit to hold a candle.
> Strange that such difference should be
> 'Twixt Tweedledum and Tweedledee.

Bononcini was finally caught with his hand in some other people's music and left the country in disgrace. Handel, who in a copyrightless age was an equally shameless plagiarist, managed to stonewall the matter. In fact, he was once caught lifting a tune of his rival's: ''It was much too good for Bononcini,'' he explained. Musicologists have detected him plundering at least a dozen other composers.

What remains familiar in Handel's operas today, besides the occasional revival of *Julius Caesar* and a few others, is some great individual pieces, best known of them the number from *Serse* long known as ''Handel's Largo.'' Perhaps his stage works will find a surge of interest someday; they contain, after all, some of his finest music. So far, though, the relative realism of Mozart and those who followed him seems to have undermined our ability to enjoy the more artificial pleasures of Handelian opera.

That artificiality finally became manifest to the London public—unfortunately, long before it did to Handel. The fatal blow came in 1728 with the appearance of John Gay's *The Beggar's Opera,* a work that went as far as possible in the opposite direction from Handel's opera seria style. While Italian seria appealed to aristocratic patrons with refined and virtuosic music, fantastic stage effects, and plots lifted from ancient history and myth, *The Beggar's Opera* aimed for

Hogarth turns his jaundiced pen on
an oratorio performance of Handel's day.

the middle class with a compendium of popular tunes sung in English, was staged relatively simply, and concerned London low-lifes gravitating around the villain Macheath. At the same time, Gay satirized the conventions and pretensions of Italian opera. His pot-pourri lasted a century onstage, one of the greatest theatrical hits of all time. (In our century, Brecht and Weill updated it into *The Three-Penny Opera*.) Within six months, the combination of Gay's competition and internal mismanagement had sunk Handel's Royal Opera.

A big-time impresario, Handel had his own money on the line. When the company went broke, so did he. But he would not give up; in 1729 he was back with a new company and a new series of operas. This venture struggled on in the face of growing public indifference. In 1737, with bankruptcy and beggar's prison waiting in the wings, Handel heroically turned out four operas—to no avail. That year his company, his personal finances, and his health all crashed at once. After suffering a paralytic stroke and mental collapse, Handel dragged himself to the baths at Aix-la-Chapelle raging at "this infernal flesh." He was fifty-two and apparently finished.

Yet at the end of 1737, Handel reappeared in London to put together another company for whom he wrote roughly an opera a year from 1738 to 1741. Finally, though, he got the message: Italian opera, the genre on which he had staked his career, was finished in England. The 1741 *Deidamia* was the last of his forty-six operas.

What could he do to pay the bills now? All along there had been a steady stream of smaller works—concertos, chamber music, choral pieces such as the 1727 *Coronation Anthems,* and orchestral works including the *Water Music.* But he wanted a grander canvas than such workaday stuff, however superlative the results.

The clue to his salvation had actually come as early as 1732, when he revived his English oratorio *Esther;* this was received encouragingly and he followed it with two more, *Deborah* and *Atalia.* Biblical oratorio could give him the epic scope and opera-style drama that he required at far less cost to produce than staged works. It would also prove to appeal powerfully to middle-class concertgoers. From 1738 to 1740, while he was still involved in his last opera company, Handel wrote four magnificent oratorios—*Saul, Israel in Egypt, Ode to Saint Cecilia,* and *L'Allegro, il Pensieroso ed il Moderato,* the latter after poems by Milton.

With these and later works Handel created a new kind of oratorio very different from the traditional Italian model. For one thing the texts were in English, which Handel set effectively despite his own erratic command of the language. Most of the stories were familiar ones from the Bible. The music reflected British influences, especially Purcell's church anthems. Though the subjects are usually religious, Handel's oratorios are not overburdened with piety. They are works for the concert hall, with all the musical color and dramatic flair of opera. In a change from opera, however, he made choruses rather than arias the main focus of his oratorios. The mighty Handelian choral style would become a model for composers of generations to come, though no one, not even Beethoven, quite came up to the level of his best.

In 1741 arrived a historic turn both in Handel's fortunes and in the history of choral music. The viceroy of Ireland invited him to Dublin to produce a charity concert. For that purpose Handel brought with him a new oratorio simply called *Messiah*. Unlike his usual oratorios with characters and plot, this was a loosely connected series of biblical prophecies and meditations concerning the coming of Christ. Handel had written the whole gigantic work in twenty-four days starting on August 22, 1741. Though later times would consider this speed a sign of divine inspiration, we have noted that Handel always wrote preternaturally fast, depending on improvisatory inspiration—and on liberal borrowings both from his own music and from others. A substantial part of the *Messiah* is recycled material. He took the chorus "For unto us a Child is born," for example, from one of his Italian duets (later the same music would do further service in an oboe concerto). The familiar *Hallelujah* was reworked from a chorus in one of his operas, where it was a paean to the reign not of the Lord God but of the Lord Bacchus—i.e., a drinking song.

Yet there *was* something special about *Messiah*, to Handel as to later ages. A servant reported that he worked at it like a man possessed, hardly sleeping or eating; at times he was so frenzied that he seemed to be going mad, writing until his fingers could no longer hold the pen. When he finished the *Hallelujah* chorus he sobbed, "I did think I did see all Heaven before me, and the great God Himself."

In April 1742 *Messiah* had its premiere in Dublin amidst delirious excitement. The hall was packed (women had been asked to wear hoopless skirts and men to forgo swords, to make more room), and hundreds more listened at windows and doors. It seems to have been one of those rare times in history when a transcendently great work is immediately perceived at its full value. The *Dublin Journal* was nearly at a loss: "Words are wanting to express the exquisite Delight it afforded to the admiring crowded Audience. The Sublime, the Grand, and the Tender, adapted to the most elevated, majestick and moving Words, conspired to transport and charm the ravished Heart and Ear."

Compared to the premiere, the first London performance the following year was a flop, though King George II was so moved during the *Hallelujah* that he rose to his feet, followed by the rest of the audience—and audiences ever since. Only some years later did *Messiah* catch on in London, after Handel initiated a series of annual charity concerts featuring the work and his own spectacular organ performances during intermissions. These concerts not only cinched the reputation of *Messiah* in England but his personal triumph as well: by the 1750s Handel reigned supreme in British music, beyond all rivalry. The English public, and the rest of the world, regarded him with awe. For generations after, until the mature Beethoven, Handel would represent music at its most majestic and sublime. Said Beethoven: "To him I bend the knee. For Handel is the greatest, ablest composer that ever lived."

As *Messiah* demonstrates, Handel had a smaller bag of tricks than Bach, but he used those tricks with unfailing brilliance and effectiveness. The basis of his attitude to musical expression came from the baroque Doctrine of the Affections, the quasi-scientific theory that proposed real connections between musical gestures (even particular keys) and specific physical and emotional states. In practice, this meant that composers consistently tried to paint words and ideas in their music, with widely varying results. When in *Messiah* the text chides that "all we like sheep have gone *astray*," the last word is set to a wildly drifting vocal line; we then "have *turned* [twisting line in fast notes] every one to *his own way*" [a note obstinately held]. While this obsessive text mirroring works well in that case, Handel at other times could slide into comedy—notably in *Israel in Egypt*, where the music representing the plagues of lice,

A period vocal part for the Messiah — *the aria*
"Who Shall Abide the Day of His Coming?"

flies, frogs, and such, is unintentionally hilarious. As we saw, Bach pursued the Doctrine of the Affections with more subtlety.

"For unto us a Child is born" from *Messiah* shows some of the most familiar and stirring Handelian effects. It begins with a jaunty tune on the title words, heard first in the sopranos alone, then in the tenors while the sopranos break into joyful roulades around them. Tenors and basses then do likewise. The line "and the government shall be upon his shoulders" is set to a striding and mounting line that builds voice by voice in imitation, to four parts arriving at, "and his name shall be called"; then come the climactic hammerblows of "Wonderful! Councillor! The mighty God!" while violins race ecstatically above. This gathering of imitative threads into a grand full-chorus proclamation is one of Handel's favorite devices, repeated dozens of times; yet he makes it work again and again—for example, three more times in "For unto us" alone, every one a harvest of goose bumps. Looking soberly and from a distance at Handel's tricks, it is easy to be cynical at his manipulations. When hearing them, however, few people with hearts connected to their ears can fail to be moved. Handel knew exactly where the heartstrings were and pulled them as well as anyone ever has.

Though *Messiah* brought him wealth and unrivaled fame, Handel's phenomenal productivity did not slack. The next years saw an unbroken stream of occasional pieces and big oratorios, some nearly equal to *Messiah;* among them is the fine *Jephte* of 1752.

It was while composing the latter that Handel began to have trouble with his eyes. For a while this caused him to break off; a note in the score of *Jephte* says, "Got as far as this on Wednesday, February 13, 1751, because of weakening of the left eye." After further deterioration he underwent three grueling operations on his eyes by the surgeon who had also operated on Bach. The results were the same for both men: total blindness.

Still, through the next eight years of his life Handel kept giving organ recitals, leading performances of his oratorios, revising older pieces with the help of an assistant. In the spring of 1759, seventy-four years old and sightless, he directed and played organ at ten oratorio performances in just over a month. At a production of *Messiah* on April 6, he fainted at the end and was helped home to bed. Sensing he would never rise again, he observed, "I should like to die on Good Friday." He missed it by a few hours, dying early on April 14, Good Saturday. Of his interment in Westminster Abbey a newspaper reported, "There was almost the greatest Concourse of People of all Ranks ever seen upon such, or indeed upon any other Occasion." It was a Handelian event.

As we have seen, Handel was a commercial composer start to finish, which is to say that his fortunes depended on the approval of a large public. He found this approval first in opera; when it faded he regained it with oratorio. This kind of career had ramifications in his style. In comparison to Bach the parochial church composer, Handel's melodies tend to be simpler and more concise (i.e., more popular), his harmony more conventional, and he usually downplayed counterpoint in favor of a homophonic texture. (Among musicians Handel is notorious for often writing phony fugues—pieces that start off like a fugue but soon lapse into simpler melody and accompaniment.) He also used much conventional melodic material, especially standardized cadence figures. But whatever his shortcuts and appeals to popularity, he made things *work*—his tunes are irresistible, his effects finely calculated, his rhythms infectious. When he is off his form he is stodgy and predictable; at his best he is still predictable, but exciting all the same.

Because of his popular appeal, Handel more than any previous composer reached the new middle-class concertgoing public that was forming during the Baroque, a change from the aristocratic elite that had once patronized opera and oratorio. Over the years his oratorios played a major part in developing that middle-class audience into the mainstay of classical music it has remained to this day. *Messiah* may be the most perennially beloved work of the entire standard repertoire (which itself is mostly based on middle-class tastes).

More directly, Handel made oratorio the most important form of English music and a prime embodiment of the nation's imperial ambitions. His victorious Israelites in *Judas Maccabaeus* and other works mirrored the British view of themselves as a chosen people. In a way, the British Empire was conquered to the strains of Handelian oratorio—both his and more overtly jingoistic imitators all the way to Elgar in the twentieth century.

Since the arrival in recent decades of the early music revolution, with its insistence on original instruments and authentic performance practice (see The Early Music Movement p. 450), the norms for playing Handel have changed radically. These days one rarely encounters *Messiah* done with Brobdingnagian choruses of four hundred or more, and the old grand reorchestrations of the *Water Music* seem overstuffed. Things have gone so far, in fact, that mainstream orchestras have been increasingly reluctant to touch the Baroque at all, leaving the period to early music specialists. Certainly this is overreaction. Except for extremes of romanticizing the Baroque, the music works in all versions. The stunning performances of harpsichord music by pianists such as Glenn Gould and Vladimir Horowitz prove that point. The real advantage for the modern listener is the many perspectives on Handel and the others available to us, from performances on modern instruments to the lean, clean early music versions with small choruses.

For recommendations I'll begin with the obvious—the *Water Music,* a loose suite of instrumental airs, dances, fanfarish pieces, and other bonbons that may have been played at that royal party on the Thames in 1717. Most familiar is the shortened version, six of the original twenty-one numbers, straightforwardly arranged for modern orchestra by Sir Hamilton Harty. These days, though, we also can find versions of the complete suite played on original instruments. In all avatars, this is Handel at his most high-spirited—no great seriousness, but lyrical and rhythmical pleasures at every turn.

The same could be said of the *Royal Fireworks Music,* which began life in 1749 with a splendid fiasco: amidst a crowded outdoor celebration of the British-French peace of Aix-la-Chapelle, the fireworks Handel's music was accompanying got out of control and set fire to a wooden pavilion, scattering the crowd—including King George—in panic. The original scoring was for whole choirs of oboes, bassoons, and brass, plus tympani and the bizarre twisting serpent horn. Harty's modern orchestration uses strings and the usual orchestral winds.

Less popular in style are the Concerti Grossi op. 6, all twelve of them written during three weeks of 1739. Handel's works in this Italian-born medium are closer to the sober Corelli than the more colorful Vivaldi; Handel does not indulge in as much fancy solo work as the latter. Still, these are impressive pieces, with some deliciously folksy movements. Try the Concerto Grosso no. 3 in E minor, with its charming polonaise that sounds like café music, and no. 7 in B-flat major, which ends with a rousing hornpipe.

Of his solo concertos, an old favorite is the Organ Concerto in F major, called "The Cuckoo and the Nightingale" because those birds are imitated in the second movement. As is typical of Handel this piece uses recycled material, in this case from one of the concerti grossi and two trio sonatas.

Following the tendency of named pieces to get the most attention, the most famous of Handel's harpsichord suites is no. 5 in E major, because the fourth movement has an infectious series of variations that a publisher named "The Harmonious Blacksmith"—apparently because a local smith was fond of belting out the tune as he hammered.

Despite the archaic conventions of his operas, they contain too much good music to be ignored totally. Perhaps one should take in a Handel opera the way his audiences did, as one might a contemporary jazz performance in a club—one chats, drinks, half-listens until something good comes along, and then one pays attention. In the occasionally revived *Julius Caesar* there is much that is extremely good, for which it is well worth wading through the languors of its nearly four hours (when we're lucky, the production has been trimmed of some of the music).

Finally we come to the choral works. Perhaps begin with smaller ones such as the *Coronation Anthems,* written for the ascension of George II in 1727. Including the well-known "Zadock the Priest," these are magisterial hosannas to the ruling class. *Acis and Galatea* of 1720 is a masque, a British stage form that was part ballet, part opera. Dryden and Pope contributed to Handel's text. That and the 1740 oratorio *L'Allegro, il Pensieroso ed il Moderato* have some superb music, Handel at his best. The same could be said of oratorios like *Israel in Egypt, Saul,* and *Jephte,* the latter his final large work.

That brings us to *Messiah,* the crown of Handel's music, the prime model for all later oratorio and perhaps the most popular classical work of all time. One could argue that no piece should be heard as much as this one is; there is a danger of its becoming a ceremonial relic rather than a living masterpiece. But at least the popularity of *Messiah* is earned. Has any other work in history, by any composer, been so consistently inspired? From touching recitatives to heartfelt arias to overpowering choruses, it is incomparable in its musical scope and variety, moving in nearly every minute of its two and a half hours. When one considers that despite herculean labors Beethoven possibly never wrote a full symphony at the top of his form, considers the lesser movements in Bach's large choral works, considers Wagner's "great moments and very dull quarters of an hour" (as Oscar Wilde put it), one is struck with awe at what Handel achieved in those twenty-four days of superhuman creative fire.

With Handel we end our survey of the Baroque, the period when modern ideas of music arose, today's concert life and standard repertoire of pieces began, and the modern political and scientific age commenced as well. The traditional ending date for the Baroque is 1750, the year Bach died and Handel was near the end of his creative life. While national schools had developed, by 1750 the general musical approach across Europe was an international style with Italian roots, which prepared the way for the international styles of Haydn and Mozart. The long tradition of improvisation in classical performance began to decline after the Baroque and has never recovered.

As to the overall impact of this period on Western culture, Alfred North Whitehead wrote in *Science and the Modern World:* "A brief, and sufficiently accurate, description of the intellectual life of the European races during the succeeding two centuries and a quarter up to our own times is that they have been living upon the accumulated capital of ideas provided for them by the genius of the seventeenth century."

Musical celebrities — Menuhin, Fischer-Dieskau, Rostropovitch, Horowitz, Bernstein, and Stern — sing an impromptu "Hallelujah Chorus" to celebrate the salvation of Carnegie Hall in 1976.

Eighteenth-century
French aristocrats
at a chamber concert.

THE CLASSICAL
PERIOD

THE CLASSICAL PERIOD
(1750–CA. 1825)

Some epochs are marked by fragmentation, parochialism, and competition, others by relative integrity, cosmopolitanism, and co-operation. In contrast to the periods on both sides of it, the musical era of around 1750–1825, which we call the Classical, was a time of consolidation and lucidity. All Europe shared a similar style and aesthetic. The techniques and forms and attitudes that coalesced in the first fifty years of this era, the time of Haydn and Mozart, were so powerful that they have been the dominant influence on Western music ever since. That, in fact, is a handy definition of what "classical" is: something that endures as a model because its elements are so poised as to represent, for all time, the miraculous illusion of perfection.

The Classical period in music tends to be associated with the movement called the Age of Reason or the Enlightenment, which began earlier in the eighteenth century. Following the scientific and intellectual advances of the previous century, thinkers such as Voltaire, Diderot, Montesquieu, Locke, Jefferson, and Franklin laid groundwork for a new human agenda—a willed progress toward humanitarian and democratic societies, based on the belief that through reason and science humanity is capable of understanding the world and controlling its own destiny, without relying on authoritarian decree or on whatever gods there may be.

Reason was the byword of the era: human deductive power was the means to discover the true order of the natural world and a just ordering of human affairs. As in the seventeenth century Descartes rejected all assumptions and systems of thought and built a new rational philosophy from the essential "I think, therefore I am," so the Age of Reason looked at received truth skeptically: truth was not revealed by the gods but had to be reasoned out. While reason was invoked by conservatives to justify the old aristocratic order, reason was also the instrument wielded by men like Voltaire to help overthrow that order.

The corollaries and repercussions of these ideas have thundered through history into our own time. They helped touch off the American and French revolutions in the later eighteenth century; they also refined the scientific method, leading to such epochal technological developments as the steam engine, power loom, cotton gin, and the harnessing of electricity. In turn, such technologies created the Industrial Revolution; as part of that upheaval, the industrially based middle class gained ascendancy over the old land-based aristocratic regimes, eventually using the new economic order called capitalism to sustain and control the new democratic societies.

What did this Enlightenment ferment mean to artists, who on the whole are far from philosophers? That is hard to pin down; yet there are unmistakable points of consistency among the arts and politics and philosophy of the period. To artists the spirit of the time said: pursue simplicity, directness, consistency; get rid of every unnecessary mark on the canvas, every unnecessary note in music; make images of objective truth, not subjective emotion; create democratically for the popular mind and ear and eye, avoiding what only the elite can understand; make forms that are solid, built to last, rational and natural and therefore universal; seek novelty from a firm foundation in norms and conventions; be ruled by the cool and ethereal image of Apollo, not the wild, self-indulgent, form-destroying Dionysus. Though in music the later eighteenth century was no more rule-bound than the past (in fact, Classical artists rejected any rule that seemed artificial), composers deliberately chose to restrain themselves, to cut down and strip away, to speak simply and plainly.

These ideals seem abstract on the page, and they have no direct and predictable application to music and the other arts of the Classical period. Yet it is with such abstractions that we can best grasp the startling difference in sound and effect of, say, Bach and Handel in 1750 and of Haydn and Mozart twenty-five years later. And it would be Haydn and Mozart above all who laid out the agenda for future music, who perfected the most significant traditions of form and procedure in Western classical music: symphony, sonata, concerto, string quartet, and the extraordinary principle of musical organiza-

The frontispiece to Diderot's Encyclopédie, *1751–80, celebrates
the Enlightenment, which shaped the aesthetics of the Classical style.*

tion later ages would call *sonata form* (see Sonata Form, p. 160).

Foreshadowings of the Classical style appear well back in the Baroque (just as the beginnings of Romanticism stirred within the Classical period). As early as the 1730s, German critic J. A. Scheibe wrote:

> Art must imitate nature. As soon as this imitation is exceeded, however, art is to be condemned. It is not art that endows nature with beauty but nature that endows art. . . . The more extravagant art becomes . . . the more it alienates itself from nature. It is therefore a fact that too much art obscures true beauty.

Though Scheibe was hazy about what he meant by "nature," it is clear that he was condemning aspects of Baroque style—heavy ornamentation, elaborate counterpoint, outlandish operatic conventions. J. S. Bach in his later years had to listen to a great many complaints of "too much art" from the younger and more fashionable composers around him in cosmopolitan Leipzig—among whom were some of his children.

We have met the figure of François Couperin, Bach's contemporary, a French master of grace, lightness, and charm. These would be stocks-in-trade to most of the artistic generation of the in-between period sometimes called *Rococo*, around the middle of the eighteenth century. In the visual arts the Rococo was a time of decorativeness even beyond Baroque tastes, a hyperbolic extravagance of ornament, a devotion to sheer pleasure: aesthetic meals of nothing but dessert. Rococo composers virtually abolished counterpoint; the main quality pursued was *galanterie*—simple, tuneful, and rather breathlessly precious (in the end, usually superficial as well). Among the composers associated with the Rococo are G. B. Sammartini and G. B. Pergolesi in Italy, and scattered around Europe, four sons of J. S. Bach, all of them more up to date and famous than their father had been—Wilhelm Friedemann, Johann Christoph, Carl Philipp Emanuel, and Johann Christian. Though none of the four was nearly the artist J. S. was, it took the world a long time to realize it. In any case, Johann Christian and Carl Philipp Emanuel stand among the most important and influential composers of the mid eighteenth century.

(In addition to his other gifts, J. S. Bach has history's best track record as a composition teacher. It is significant, though, that even he could not teach his talented sons the secrets of his own genius. From this we can draw two possible conclusions: 1) he didn't know how he did it; or, less likely but more intriguingly, 2) he *did* know and *did* tell his sons—and they didn't know what he was talking about.)

Johann Christian Bach (1735–82), youngest son of Johann Sebastian, worked largely in London and was usually called the "London Bach" to distinguish him from others of his clan. Trained first by his father and by older brother C.P.E., J.C. worked in Italy for some years before settling in London. As seen in pieces like the Concerto for Harpsichord (or piano) and Strings in E-flat major op. 7 no. 5, he epitomizes the Rococo. His lightness of touch influenced a whole generation of composers, notable among them the eight-year-old Mozart, whom J.C. befriended in London in 1764. The significance of J. C. Bach to Mozart's stylistic development is easy to hear: listened to casually, J.C. rather resembles Mozart on an off day. (Some of this effect is simply that both pursued the general galant style of the time, found everywhere in Europe.)

Element by element, form by form, the Classical style began to take shape during the Rococo. As the keyboard concertos of J. C. Bach guided Mozart, the piano music of his brother **Carl Philipp Emanuel** (1714–88) influenced composers from Haydn to Beethoven. Where J.C. contributed lightness, grace, and formal clarity to the international musical dialogue, C.P.E. (the "Hamburg Bach") added a darker element that the time called the *empfindsamer Stil*, "expressive style."

Though trained in the magisterial high-Baroque manner by his father, C.P.E. had a restless spirit, always on the lookout for new materials and new expressiveness. As Beethoven would be after him, he was famous for his fiery keyboard improvisations (on clavichord, harpsichord, and in later years on the piano—this was a transitional period for keyboard instruments). His clavier sonatas sometimes resemble improvisations, roaming nearly out of control from poetic galanterie to the near demonic. He seemed to be after something that the musical language of his period denied him—perhaps a kind of Beethovenian expressiveness. Only the formal control of Mozart and Haydn would make a Beethoven possible, however, and C.P.E. Bach had no such models. He remains a strange, elusive, fascinating figure in history. The rediscovery of his art is still in progress; the beginning point, in any case, is his keyboard sonatas.

As the invention of opera changed the face of music and initiated the Baroque, opera remained in the eighteenth century a touchstone of what was going on in music. As we saw with Handel, Italian Baroque opera seria finally began to sink under the weight of its exaggerated conventions. The times demanded a return to relative simplicity and realism on the operatic stage. The first composer to answer that need was **Christoph Willibald von Gluck** (1714–87).

Gluck knew how stale the conventions of Italian opera were; he composed some two dozen of them himself. German-born and Italian-trained, he had successes in England and Germany and ended up composing opera seria for the imperial court in Vienna. In his forties, Gluck came to know some people who were interested in reforming opera, getting rid of its castrato singers and their whirligig virtuosity, the absurd plots, the static da capo arias, the jarring contrast between dry recitative and florid aria. These reformers urged Gluck to follow the aims of the original creators of opera and make the music serve the words and the drama.

Being both an able composer and a canny professional who could tell which way the wind was blowing, Gluck picked up these ideas and carried them brilliantly, starting with *Orfeo ed Euridice,* produced at Vienna's Burgtheater in 1762. Later came *Alceste,* in the preface to which Gluck proclaimed his—and very nearly the age's—artistic credo: "I sought to confine music to its true function of serving the poetry by expressing the feelings and situations of the story without interrupting and cooling off the action through useless and superfluous ornaments. . . . I further believed that the greater part of my task was to seek a beautiful simplicity, and I have avoided a display of difficulty at the expense of clarity. I assigned no value to the discovery of some novelty, unless it was naturally suggested by the situation and the expression. And there is no rule that I did not willingly consider sacrificing for the sake of an effect."

All the same, these two pioneering operas did not appeal to the faddish Viennese public. Gluck's most resounding successes came hand in hand with his bitterest struggles, in Paris during the 1770s. Brought to the Paris Opéra by his onetime singing pupil Marie Antoinette, he produced two French operas based on Homeric legends: *Iphigénie en Aulide* and *Iphigénie en Tauride*. These works caused a sensation. French journalists and the public lined up in ranks pro and con, the favorite of the cons being Italian opera composer Niccolò Piccinni. Finally the whole musical world rocked with this trumped-up feud of Gluckists and Piccinnists and its attendant manifestos, conspiracies, and sabotage. For their part, the two composers stayed relatively aloof from the fray; in fact, Piccinni was not too proud to steal some of his rival's reforms.

In 1779, his conception of music drama in the ascendant but his person aged and ailing, Gluck retired to Vienna, where he was imperial court composer for Emperor Joseph II, one of the "enlightened despots" of the time who decreed some important social and economic reforms, including abolishing serfdom. (Also a patron of the arts, Joseph was generous with Gluck but later proved to be stingy with Mozart.) Crippled by strokes, Gluck spent his last years as an honored and benevolent figurehead. We find him applauding Mozart's *The Abduction from the Seraglio* in 1782; but he preferred Mozart's rival, Salieri. Gluck died in Vienna in 1778.

History remembers Gluck as the most important composer of opera between Monteverdi and Mozart. His direct influence, though, was mainly felt in France; decades later, Hector Berlioz would model his own operas not on Mozart but on Gluck. Still, the realism Gluck restored to opera has benefited every dramatic composer since—from Mozart to Wagner and beyond. Gluck avoided the da capo form and smoothed out the contrast between recitative and aria, making both music and drama more continuous, and enfolded all in a supple orchestral fabric. Wagner would carry those ideas still further.

To modern audiences Gluck tends, like J. C. Bach, to sound like Mozart Lite. He speaks the clean Classical language with all the grace but less of the expressive intensity and formal sophistication of Haydn and Mozart. Yet there are great beauties and tremendous stagecraft in his best works, most notably in *Orfeo* and *Iphigénie en Tauride*. I recommend experiencing these live or on film; seeing, for example, the scene of Orpheus in the underworld as it was intended, with the hero amidst the fires and caverns of hell, one can understand the impact on his time of an artist who, in contrast to most reformers, made his revolutionary statements with a voice modest and austere.

Now the minor characters have set the scene for the major players—Haydn and Mozart, who created the Classical ideal, and Beethoven, who in taking up and retooling the forms of his predecessors made them both more personal and more universal. The setting for the story will revolve entirely around one place: grand, corrupt, inconstant, and music-loving Vienna.

Overleaf, engraving: "Scenographic or Geometric Perspective View of Vienna, the Imperial and Royal Residence and Capital," commissioned by Holy Roman Emperor Joseph II in 1769. Numbered on the view are various Mozartean sites:

1. *The Royal Court Theater, where* The Abduction, Figaro, *and* Così *were first performed and* Don Giovanni *had its Vienna premiere.*

2. *Kärntnertor Theater.* The Impresario *was first performed here.*

3. *St. Stephen's Cathedral, where Mozart was married and his body lay before burial.*

4. *Site of the Freihaus Theater.* The Magic Flute *had its premiere here.*

5. *The lively Graben area, where Mozart lived in several apartments.*

6. *Kohlmarkt, location of Mozart's main publisher Artaria.*

7. *Schulerstrasse, where Mozart wrote* Figaro *during his salad days of 1784–87.*

8. *St. Peter's Church. Mozart lived nearby with the Webers in 1781.*

9. *House of the Teutonic Order, where Mozart was booted out the door by the archbishop's servant.*

In that era and later, Vienna was home to Haydn, Beethoven, Schubert, Brahms, Bruckner, Mahler, Schoenberg, Webern, and Berg.

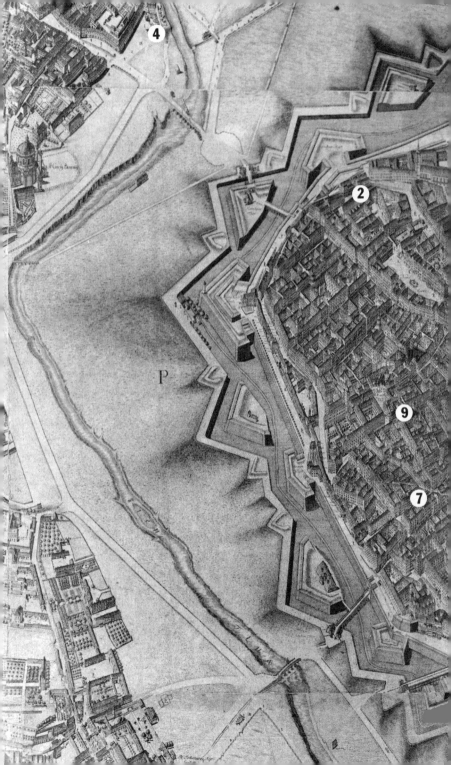

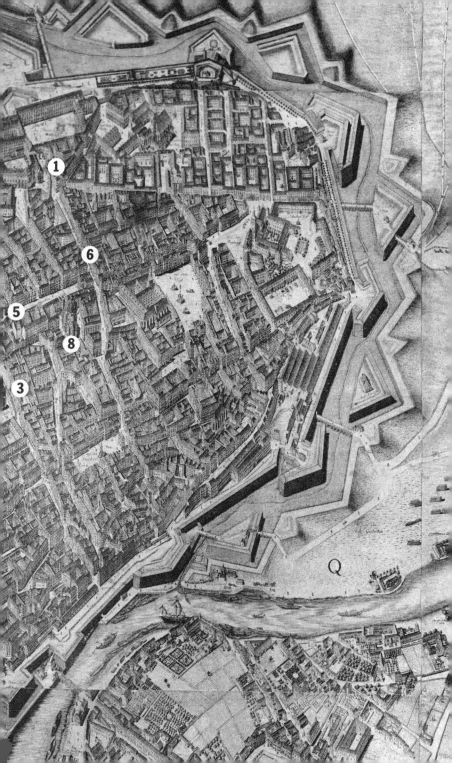

FRANZ JOSEPH HAYDN

History has tended to remember Joseph Haydn in a fatherly way, as "Father of the Symphony" and "Father of the String Quartet," and under his nickname of "Papa." Actually, he fathered neither the classical symphony nor quartet, nor any children, for that matter. The sobriquet comes from his personality, which was serene and generous and fatherly, and from his seminal effect on the whole of Western music. Every composer since has been in his debt; we are all in some degree his children.

Though his music is marvelously original and sophisticated, it does not wear those qualities on its sleeve. On the surface it sounds like the unassuming work of an unassuming man. Moreover, the bulk of his prodigious output remains in obscurity; dozens of operas, concertos, symphonies, and pieces for archaic instruments have not transcended their time and their context. But what survives in the modern repertoire is substantial enough for any composer. The joys of Haydn at his best are the surprising turns, the delight of someone we thought predictable suddenly kicking up his heels, breaking from reserve into something winning or passionate. With Haydn you must *listen:* listen for the humble little theme to flower into luxuriant variations, listen for the false recaps and phony endings and other pranks, listen through the expected for the pleasure of the unexpected.

He was born Franz Joseph Haydn in Rohrau, lower Austria, on March 31, 1732, second of twelve children of Matthias Haydn, a wheelwright and amateur musician. As a toddler Joseph showed tremendous love and aptitude for music, echoing his father's songs and pretending to play violin. Finally one J. M. Franck, a schoolmaster cousin a step above Joseph's peasant parents, took in the five-year-old boy, promising to teach him music. That Franck did over the next three years, though hardly in a kindly fashion; Joseph would recall that he got "more flogging than food" in his cousin's house. But his singing attracted notice, and when Joseph was eight

An unpretentious Haydn in a straightforward portrait.

Kapellmeister Reutter of the Cathedral of St. Stephen in Vienna accepted him as a choirboy.

There Joseph gained practical experience in music as a leading soloist of the choir, and endured more harsh discipline. His younger brother Michael, also destined to be a composer of stature, joined him as soloist. It seems to have been a wretched, near-starving life for the choirboys; Joseph had to sing on the street to earn pennies for extra food. Still, he received general schooling as well as training in voice, violin, and harpsichord.

In 1749, after his voice changed, Haydn was simply turned out onto the street with little more than the clothes on his back. Finding lodging with a sympathetic ex-chorister, he began giving music lessons, playing in street serenades, anything to earn his bread while he practiced and studied intensely on his own. He had become determined to make a career as a composer. His main tutors were the music of C.P.E. Bach and the contrapuntal exercises of Fux (which would train generations of composers). Finally he had enough pupils and playing jobs to rent a dingy attic room, buy a worm-eaten harpsichord, and begin to make his way in earnest.

It didn't take long. As early as 1751, two years after leaving St. Stephen's virtually a beggar, he had attracted enough attention to receive a commission for a comic opera, which was produced in Vienna and later around Europe (it is now lost). Otherwise he turned out small, practical pieces such as string quartets and the divertimenti that were the Muzak of the day—tunes to accompany the wealthy in their dining and amusements.

Perhaps the decisive year of Haydn's life was 1754, when he became a vocal accompanist, pupil, and manservant of Italian composer and singing teacher Nicola Porpora. Though this employer was stingy and abusive, he gave Haydn invaluable lessons in Italian language and music, and introduced him to the nobility. As Haydn would do all his life, he played his role of servant, kept his ambitions in view, and endured what he had to endure. And as it would all his life, his patience and industry paid off: in 1759 he got a job as music director for a Count Morzin, for whom he wrote his first symphony at age twenty-seven. More than one hundred symphonies would follow during the next three decades.

Around that time Haydn became enamored of one of his pupils and, as a working man now, felt able to ask for her hand. But the lady decided to enter a convent instead. When her father suggested Haydn marry the lady's older sister Maria Anna, he quickly and unfortunately agreed. As a wife, Maria Anna revealed herself to be an unalloyed shrew—bilious, spendthrift, and indifferent to her husband's career. "It was all the same to her," Haydn later said, "whether her husband was a shoemaker or an artist." She sometimes cut up his manuscripts to roll her hair. After a blusterous few years they were separated, but he continued to support her for the rest of her life. As things turned out, he would be able to afford it.

When Count Morzin went broke and had to let his musicians go in 1761, Haydn was snapped up by Hungarian Prince Paul Anton

*The conductor of an eighteenth-century concert
wields rolled-up music and stamps the beat.*

Esterházy to become Vice-Kapellmeister of his extraordinary private musical establishment. This was considered a plum job, though its status was that of a servant. Twice a day Haydn was to appear in uniform before the prince to receive orders. Among its provisions his contract stipulated, ''The said Haydn . . . must be temperate, not showing himself overbearing toward his musicians. . . . The said Joseph Haydn shall take care that he . . . appear in white stockings and white linen, powdered, and with either a pigtail or a tiewig. . . . He should conduct himself in an exemplary manner, abstaining from undue familiarity, and from vulgarity in eating, drinking, and conversation.'' Haydn obeyed; he presented himself properly powdered, he was exemplary, he abstained. In return, he received the chance to pull himself up by his own bootstraps as an artist. He entered the employ of the Esterházys a conventional minor composer; thirty years later, he emerged a world-famous genius who had changed the face of music. This servant had also secured for the illustrious house of Esterházy its only significance in history: as Joseph Haydn's employer.

Prince Paul died in 1762 and was succeeded by Prince Nicolaus Esterházy, dubbed "The Magnificent" for extravagances such as a diamond-studded uniform and the gigantic country palace called Esterház that he built on the model of Versailles. There Haydn lived in three rooms of the servants' quarters, following a rarely varying daily routine that included up to eight hours of composing. He created as a cook does—fast, mindful of available supplies, for daily consumption. If he couldn't come up with an idea he prayed until one appeared; then he labored away at the harpsichord.

His duties outside the study were enough to drain the energy of most men. Becoming Kapellmeister in 1766, he was in charge of all musical activities, musicians, and instruments at the palace. The palace of Esterház had an opera theater, marionette theater, two concert halls, an orchestra of about twenty-five and an opera company of about twelve. Haydn had to prepare and conduct two instrumental concerts and two opera evenings per week. A great deal of the music for all this performance was expected to be new work by himself; over the years he also mounted seventy-five operas by other composers. Esterház was, in fact, one of the main centers for opera in Europe. For much of his life Haydn considered himself primarily an opera composer.

An advantage of this boggling set of responsibilities was that Haydn had players at hand to read things over as soon as the ink was dry. Sometimes he would emerge from his study, assemble the orchestra to try out an idea, then return to work. In a famous paragraph he wrote of this experience:

My Prince was always satisfied with my works. I not only had the encouragement of constant approval, but as conductor of an orchestra I could make experiments, observe what produced an effect and what weakened it, and was thus in a position to improve, alter, make additions or omissions, and be as bold as

I pleased. I was cut off from the world, there was no one to confuse or torment me, and I was forced to become *original*.

By 1765, only four years after Haydn began working for the Esterházys, his work was so widely published and performed that a Viennese newspaper called him "the darling of our nation." He would remain that for the rest of his life. In the end his output would add up to some 108 symphonies, 68 string quartets, 47 piano sonatas, 26 operas (11 now lost), 4 oratorios, and hundreds of smaller pieces including around two hundred items for an unwieldy stringed instrument called the baryton, which Prince Nicolaus played. The bulk of this astounding production was written, to order, at Esterház.

The years passed calmly, industriously, and with much satisfaction. Haydn was a virtual slave in a gilded palace, but he was doing what he wanted to do and receiving appropriate acclaim for it. His breadth and originality expanded in Haydn fashion—carefully and deliberately. Whether he knew it or not (at Esterház he heard only distant echoes of his impact on the world), he was the main figure in forming the tastes and techniques of his day and, to a remarkable extent, of the future. And his popularity became such that an extensive cottage industry developed among composers faking Haydn; musicologists are still trying to straighten out the confusion.

Rococo composers such as Sammartini and Stamitz had derived the genre called *symphony* mainly from a Baroque Italian opera overture of the same name, along with elements of the dance suite. Haydn inherited this lightweight three-movement form, scored for strings, occasionally with two or three winds, and during his career made it into the most flexible, expansive, and significant orchestral form in Western music. In his Symphony no. 3 he began regularly using a minuet as the third (usually) of four movements. This was based on a dance that had been around for a century or so, which earlier composers had made into a nonfunctional instrumental piece. Haydn approached the minuet with immense variety over the years; a few times he sped up the tempo and called it *scherzo,* "joke," an approach that Beethoven would later make the symphonic norm.

Meanwhile, Haydn filled symphonic movements with a coloristic and expressive variety never before known to instrumental music. He phased out the Baroque continuo and expanded his forces to what, in some of his last symphonies, was virtually the modern orchestra—two each of flutes, oboes, clarinets, bassoons, French horns, trumpets (Beethoven would add trombones), timpani, and a string section (first and second violins, violas, cellos, basses). The number of strings varied from the dozen or so at Esterház to more than sixty in the group for which he wrote the Paris Symphonies.

In the matter of expression Haydn moved away from the Baroque Doctrine of the Affections, which limited each movement or aria to only one mood and one set of musical ideas. Instead, he looked for maximum variety and contrast in both expression and material; one movement can have a wide variety of contrasting melodic themes, rhythms, textures, instrumental colors, emotions. (Mozart and Beethoven would take this contrast still further.) Haydn also insisted on restoring to instrumental music some of the contrapuntal elements that the Rococo had eliminated; Haydn symphonies and quartets are rich in canons, fuguelike sections called *fugato,* imitative sections in general. A Haydn symphonic movement, and those by his musical descendants, has become a microcosm with myriad shadings of light and dark, potentially everything from tragic to playful, learned to naïve.

To hold together these new contrasts, Haydn had to create new kinds of musical continuity. Here is where Haydn for all his apparent artlessness was one of the most ingenious of all composers, perhaps surpassed only by Mozart: in the supremely difficult matter of achieving unity and continuity when the material is constantly changing direction. The chief solution to this problem was the principle called *sonata form,* detailed in a separate essay in this section. Other solutions included imposing on the musical fabric the regular phrasing of dance music; rather than the unpredictable phrase lengths of the Baroque, Haydn and other Classical composers established a norm of even phrases in multiples of two: two four-bar phrases make up an eight-bar phrase, two of those a sixteen-bar period, and so on. But that is only the *expected* norm; having established that expectation in the listener, a composer can play with tricks and subtleties of phrasing, as Haydn does constantly. When we tend to expect regular four-bar phrases, one of five or three bars make a striking effect. Similarly, Haydn simplified his harmony so that touches of chromatic color become all the more expressive in the generally plain landscape.

The early Baroque opera composers had created homophony; Classical composers developed more efficient approaches to homophony. Accompaniment figures often fall into the simple pattern called *Alberti bass*—a regular diddle-diddle that outlines the harmony while maintaining a rhythmic flow. In contrast to the flowery and complex melodic style of the Baroque, Classical themes tend to be unassuming; a good tune is always welcome, but in the main a theme must provide raw material for development. In fact, many great Classical works, such as Beethoven's *Eroica* Symphony, have no particularly striking melodies. Haydn was noted for using folklike tunes in his symphonic music; this makes for a robust, peasanty effect, for which he was called vulgar in his own time and is much prized today.

So it was with all the norms of phrasing, harmony, form, and the like: since the conventions are nominally set, Haydn can entertain, amuse, and astonish us by breaking them. He does this in ways both subtle and unsubtle, an example of the latter being the startling eruption that gave the *Surprise* Symphony its name. It has been observed that C.P.E. Bach is far more eccentric than Haydn, but Haydn tends to sound quirkier because he first convinces us that he's predictable. When everything is surprising, nothing surprises; but when most things are conventional, every deviation counts. Dressed in his decorous periwig and with his normally impeccable musical manners, Haydn is apt to kick us in the pants when we least expect it.

As with the symphony, so with the string quartet. Again, Haydn did not invent the medium; he modernized it. His first quartets, like his Rococo models, are essentially solos for the first violin, with the second violin, viola, and cello along for the ride. In the *Sun* Quartets op. 20, he invented a new approach in which all four instruments are treated nearly equally in the musical fabric. The *Russian* Quartets op. 33 took this approach further, adding a more thoroughgoing melodic development. Inheriting the string quartet as a slight genre akin to the Baroque suite, Haydn made it into the supreme chamber music medium and the most intimate of instrumental genres. From his day to the present, listeners have tended to hear a composer's quartets as the pieces most directly from the heart (as indeed they often are).

All the stripping down and simplifying in the Classical era by no means made for music simpler than that of the Baroque. Music needs both simplicity for comprehensibility, and complexity for depth, endurance, and effective organization. It makes less difference *where* the simplicity and complexity lie than that they are there. Bach is often dazzlingly complex on his polyphonic surface, but under the surface all is lucid design. Haydn and Mozart seem simple because their surface sounds that way, but under that surface lie tremendous complexity of form and sophistication of organization, harnessing an unprecedented variety of material. The difference is aesthetic: the Baroque aimed for the grand, magnificent impression; the Classical, for the artlessness that hides art, the unpretentious irony that masks deep feeling. The glories of the Classical aesthetic were the symphony, string quartet, solo concerto, and sonata—the richest, most malleable, most subtle instrumental genres ever invented—and the sonata form on which they are all founded.

Having thrived in isolation for two decades, Haydn in 1781 met his only peer at that time—Mozart. The forty-nine-year-old master and the young genius of twenty-five became close friends. Thereafter each influenced the other, and together they shaped and refined the musical forms that would dominate the future. The example of Haydn's *Russian* Quartets gave rise to the six quartets that Mozart dedicated to Haydn, and the example of Mozart's symphonies helped lift Haydn to his last and greatest works in that genre, the twelve *London* Symphonies. On the other hand, Mozart's operas revealed to Haydn that he was not the stage composer he had fancied he was. When asked for a comic opera in 1787, he declined with, "I should be risking a great deal, for scarcely any man can brook comparison with the great Mozart." Haydn was the only equal Mozart ever acknowledged: "He alone has the secret of making me smile, and touching me to the bottom of my soul." Few relationships in music have been as warm and fruitful as that of Haydn—sober, fastidious, self-effacing, plodding, and respectful of his superiors—and Mozart—childlike, mercurial, arrogant, effortlessly brilliant, and unable to knuckle under to the indignities of being a court composer.

Haydn's generosity to Mozart was characteristic of the man. He was ambitious but not competitive, stolid in his life but open to new ideas. A painter friend left this description:

Haydn was something under middle height. The lower half of his figure was too short for the upper. . . . His features were rather regular, his glance fiery yet temperate, kindly and inviting. When he was in a serious mood his features, along with his glance, expressed dignity. . . . His hawk nose (he suffered much from a nasal polyp which doubtless actually enlarged this organ) as well as the rest of his face was deeply marked with smallpox. . . . Haydn considered himself ugly and mentioned to me a prince and his wife who could not stand his appearance because, he said, "I was too ugly for them."

Ugly or not, Haydn was sensitive to feminine charm and often had his attractions reciprocated. In the 1780s he had a long affair with a young singer at Esterház, apparently passionate on his part, though the lady's interest seems mainly to have been in his money.

Haydn's hermetic life at the palace came to an end in 1790, when Nicolaus the Magnificent died and his successor dissolved the family musical establishment. Now without duties, Haydn could have rested on his substantial pension, his income from publishing and pupils, and his laurels. Certainly he was not sad to leave his familiar life: "The knowledge that I am no longer a hired servant," he wrote after three decades of uncomplaining service, "repays me for all my troubles." Rather than slowing down, however, he moved to Vienna and labored with his old diligence.

He was then nearing sixty, but some of his greatest achievements lay ahead. His last period of symphonic composition began soon after his retirement, when British musical entrepreneur J. P. Salomon persuaded him to come to London for a series of concerts. At a farewell party, Mozart said tearfully to his friend and mentor, "This is good-bye. We shall never meet again." He was right; in England the following year, Haydn was stricken to learn of Mozart's death.

He arrived in London on New Year's Day 1791 and soon found, to his astonishment, that he was treated with the wild acclaim once reserved for Handel. Newspapers carried rapturous doggerel about his music, visitors streamed through his door, he was invited to enough parties and banquets to fill every day. Haydn fled to the country and resumed his accustomed composing schedule (though remaining strenuous in partygoing). During the year and a half of his first visit and in a second visit in 1794–95, he composed the twelve *London* (or *Salomon*) Symphonies. He also carried on a romance with one Widow Schroeter, who he reported to friends in Vienna was "still handsome, though over sixty." Between visits to England he busied himself in Vienna with composing and pupils—among them an intractable young genius named Beethoven.

Many composers have concentrated on religious music late in life, no doubt hoping to induce the Lord to overlook a few sins. Haydn spent 1797 and 1798 on the enormous oratorio *The Creation,* a work that in the next century would rival Handel's *Messiah* in popularity. In the same years he began a series of Masses commissioned by Nicolaus II, the new Esterházy prince. His 1797 song "Gott erhalte Franz den Kaiser" became, to Haydn's intense pride, the Austrian national anthem. (He recycled it for a set of variations in a string quartet, which was therefore dubbed *The Emperor.*) His wife, Maria Anna—unchanged, unrepentant, and unmourned—had died when he was in London. He settled in a house near Vienna that Maria Anna had originally bought, she told him hopefully, for her widowhood.

From 1799 to 1801 Haydn labored mightily on another large oratorio, *The Seasons.* Though it found and still finds success, Haydn felt it had taken too much out of him for a secular piece with a rather lame libretto. In fact, he believed the strain of writing *The Seasons* exhausted him physically and creatively. Whether that was true or not, it was nearly his swan song. After sporadic composing over the next few years, he gave up. "I would never have believed," he lamented to a friend in 1807, "that a man could collapse so completely as I feel I have now. My memory is gone; I sometimes still have good ideas at the clavier, but I could weep at my inability even to repeat and write them down."

His last years were saddened by that decline, but he took unaffected delight in the flood of honors that came his way. The whole world seemed affectionately to know him as "Papa." He distributed his wealth among friends and benefactors going back to his childhood. Each day he sat down at the clavier to play his Austrian anthem, exclaiming with childlike pleasure when he played well. When he felt able he would receive guests and reminisce garrulously about old times, giving visitors a merry farewell: "Remember me to all the pretty girls!" In the spring of 1809 French forces began shelling Vienna and Haydn could not stand the shock; he died on May 31. Napoleon sent a detachment of French troops to see to the funeral. Two weeks later Mozart's Requiem was sung at a memorial service. Haydn would have been pleased.

In tracing a path through Haydn's work we will find constant change, experiment, development. To Haydn as to other professionals in his day, composing was several things at once: an art, a craft, a job, a means of making a name in the world in competition with hundreds of others. The art aspect was the unsearchable but all-important matter of inspiration, which can neither be taught nor learned (that part is up to the Muse, and she favors you or not, as she wills). The dimension of craft is something to which Haydn paid indefatigable attention, steadily refining his skills and, not incidentally, keeping a step ahead of his imitators.

The results of a career as successful and a music so fertile as Haydn's could be spectacular in more than financial ways. He was celebrated during his life as no classical musician is today, when such adulation tends to be reserved for stars of screen and pop music. Unlike his Viennese compatriots Mozart and Schubert, Haydn lived into his own legend and reaped the benefit of his labors.

There is nothing in music finer than the best Haydn string quartets. Certainly Bach and Beethoven have more depth, Mozart more magical perfection. Yet Haydn, the workhorse in this group of thoroughbreds, can reach their level at times because he was good at everything; he has more variety per movement and more originality than Bach or Mozart, was as good a melodist as Beethoven, and was the equal of anyone as an architect of musical forms.

He took over the string quartet as a vestige of the old Baroque dance suite and developed it into an ambitious genre similar to the symphony and sonata. The modern string quartet literature begins with Haydn's 1772 set of six, op. 20, called the *Sun* Quartets because the first edition had a sun on the cover. (Haydn rarely named his works, but they tended to pick up nicknames.) It was in the *Sun* Quartets that, for the first time, he began treating all four instruments nearly equally, rather than as an accompanied solo for the first violin. It was here also that he reclaimed a high level of counter-point for the Classical style; beyond the contrapuntal writing here and there throughout, three of the six quartets have fugal finales.

Another element of these quartets, and of much of Haydn's music in this period, has to do with expression. Like many German artists of that time, he was affected by the movement known as *Sturm und Drang,* "storm and stress." Led by the towering dramatist and poet Goethe, this was an assertion of human emotional life in all its ambiguity and complexity, as opposed to the cool rationalism of the Enlightenment. In practice, the movement produced a heightened expressiveness and subjectivity in the arts; in other words, the Sturm und Drang movement signaled the Romantic sensibility blooming in the middle of the Classical period.

While remaining at heart a classicist, the mature Haydn would also embody some of the expressiveness of Sturm und Drang while never letting go of the contrapuntal foundation called in those days the "learned style." These three elements, held in balance despite their apparent contradictions, helped him move beyond the pre-ciousness of the Rococo.

Of the *Sun* Quartets, I recommend op. 20 no. 4, with its unusually serious and introverted first movement and the Gypsy tunes in the minuet and finale. As often in his quartets, the minuet here is the second movement rather than the third. In this and all the first movements of the *Sun* Quartets, Haydn was near the fully developed sonata form (see Sonata Form, p. 160) with one important excep-tion: most of his sonata-form movements are really monothematic, the "second theme" a variation of the opening theme in a new key. Only later, perhaps under the influence of Mozart, did he start using more defined second themes. It is astonishing, though, how much variety he can create even in a monothematic movement.

The 1781 op. 33 quartets, sometimes called *Russian,* had an even greater impact than op. 20. Within months of their composition they were published and played around Europe, becoming primary models for the Classical string quartet and a particularly important influence on Mozart. Haydn described this set as "written in a new and special way." He probably meant a more developed equalizing of the four instruments and a heightened thematic logic, the melo-dies made up of contrasting motivic (see Glossary) elements that are fragmented in the development section and then reassembled in the recapitulation. (Unlike Mozart, who usually has fairly literal recaps, Haydn tends to change and develop his themes throughout a movement. While his themes may be less distinctive than Mozart's, he gets more out of them.)

Of the *Russian* Quartets, start with op. 33 no. 2 in E-flat, dubbed *The Joke*. He based the first movement on a set of ideas heard in the first four measures, and made the development highly contrapuntal. As in all these quartets the minuet movement comes second and is marked "Scherzo"; thus another common name for the set is *Gli scherzi* (The Jokes). This description can be confusing; though Haydn actually did invent the fast-tempo scherzo that Beethoven picked up, it was in later quartets. Here the "scherzo" movements are still minuets, maybe a little faster than usual, but earning their name with their lighthearted mood. The second quartet *(The Joke)* actually got its title from the last movement, which has no fewer than five false endings separated by pauses (perhaps to catch people chatting in the audience) before the rather sneaky real ending. Also wry in effect are some swooping violin glissandos in the scherzo, one of Haydn's myriad ironic touches.

Perhaps the peak of Haydn's achievements in the string quartet is the set of six, op. 76, called "Erdödy" after their dedicatee. No. 2 in D minor stands among the greatest quartets of all time, as both a model of compact construction and a marvel of expressive variety. It is called the *Quinten* (Fifths) from the opening theme based on that interval. The first movement is somber and intense in tone, the fifths theme omnipresent, the development brilliantly polyphonic. After a contrasting slow movement of relative lightness and grace, Haydn produces one of his boldest minuets—a two-part canon in bare octaves, so demonic in tone that it is known as the "Witches' Minuet." The last movement is typically racing and lightfooted, but begins unusually in minor before the final whisking-away of gloom with a turn to major.

Op. 76 no. 5, in D major, is called the *Largo* Quartet because of the slow movement that makes up nearly half the piece; this has some of Haydn's finest sustained melodic writing, approaching late Beethoven in its meditative profundity. In contrast is a warm and ingratiating first movement with lilting *siciliano* rhythm, a mellow minuet, and a whirling, whimsical last movement that starts with a series of final cadences, as if beginning with its ending.

Haydn was a competent performer but, as he put it, "no wizard" on clavier and violin. Perhaps for that reason he did not place the importance on his concertos that composer/soloists did; concertos were a vital part of the livelihood of virtuosos like Mozart and Beethoven, and the prospect of being paid tends to inspire an artist. Only two of Haydn's dozens of concertos have become familiar, and the main one is an oddity—the lovely Trumpet Concerto in E-flat. The standard trumpet of that time did not have valves; it was essentially a bugle with a limited range of notes. (The trumpet style of Bach's day, which achieved more notes by playing very high, had died out.) Haydn's Trumpet Concerto was written for an instrument with keys something like the later saxophone, giving it a full range of notes. For some reason this ephemeral contraption inspired Haydn to write some of the finest melodies of his career. The other well-known concerto is the D major for Cello and Orchestra op. 101; it has two movements of delicate charm and an earthy finale, with Haydn in his folksy vein.

The development of Haydn's symphonies paralleled that of his quartets, beginning with galant grace and ending with incomparable craftsmanship and a style on the brink of Beethovenian depth. Part of the explanation of why Haydn wrote around 108 symphonies (104 numbered) compared to Mozart's forty-one and Beethoven's nine, is that for most of Haydn's career a symphony was still a relatively light form, a cut above a divertimento but far from the earth-shaking affair that Beethoven made it (and Mozart approached only in his last three). The genre was simply less ambitious for Haydn than for later composers. Still, that does not make his best symphonies slighter works, only lighter ones.

Best known among the early symphonies are nos. 6, 7, and 8, from 1761, respectively called *Morning, Noon,* and *Evening.* These apparently were named by Prince Paul Esterházy, though the music certainly earns the titles; no. 6, for example, begins with a lovely evocation of sunrise. All three are full of Rococo charm and jolliness and are written in a soloistic way reminiscent of the Baroque concerto grosso.

A longtime favorite is the 1772 *Farewell* Symphony—no. 45 in F-sharp minor, for the early-Classical orchestra of two oboes, two horns, and strings. The material here is straightforward, though in the striding first movement Haydn takes the unusual step of introducing a new theme in the development. After a lightfooted adagio and playful minuet, Haydn produced one of his most famous jokes, which gave the symphony its name: toward the end the musicians pack up one by one and exit, leaving only two violins to play the final passage. Legend says this was a reminder to the prince that it was time for the musicians' vacation, and that he took the hint.

Two of the middle symphonies stand out. The bright and festive no. 48 in C major, from 1769, picked up the title *Maria Theresa* because it was erroneously thought to have been written for a visit by that empress to Esterház. It may have been played during her visit, which included a Haydn opera and a concert with Haydn and his orchestra dressed in Chinese costume playing in the palace's Chinese pavilion. In contrast, from the same year comes no. 49, called *La Passione* for its dark and expressive tone, an early harbinger of Sturm und Drang in Haydn. Every movement is in the same F minor, the moods ranging from penitential to urgent and nervous— not sunny Papa Haydn, but effective all the same.

As we saw, the finale of his symphonic career came with the twelve *London* Symphonies of 1791–94, nos. 93–104, also known as the *Salomon* Symphonies. Several of these have acquired nicknames, usually based on some feature in the piece. The most famous is called the *Surprise*, from the crashing chord that trips up a guileless little tune in the second movement, a sort of musical pratfall. Though Haydn may have joked that this effect was to "wake up the ladies," it was really designed to wake up London to his presence by an attention-grabbing effect, and it did the trick. The entirely delightful *Military* Symphony (no. 100) is aglitter and aboom with cymbals and triangle and drums, presumably military in import. The *Clock* Symphony (no. 101) got its moniker from the comical tick-tock bassoon accompaniment in the slow movement.

Haydn summed up what he had learned about the symphony with his last, no. 104, the *London*, a magisterial work with a touch of the peasant in the last movement—as Béla Bartók discovered many years later, it is based on a Hungarian folk song. That ready communicativeness, easily accessible yet immensely sophisticated, is Haydn's trademark.

Of the sacred works from the end of Haydn's career I will suggest two. As with his operas, which have never been successfully revived, the times posed barriers to sacred music. The spirit of the age was perhaps too secular and unpretentious to foster either first-rate serious opera or profound sacred music. The tone and pace of the Classical style as a whole are those of comic opera—light, bustling, often ironic, full of contrasts.

Yet Haydn overcame much of this limitation in his sacred music. Handel it isn't, but in the best of it one still finds some fairly fine Haydn. The *Paukenmesse* (Drum-Roll Mass, also called Mass in Time of War) of 1796–97, one of six Masses commissioned by Prince Nicolaus II, typifies Classical sacred music in its operatic style. This is especially noticeable in the solos and small vocal ensembles, which are consistently moving and effective, starting with the soaring, joyous soprano solo of the Kyrie. Notable throughout is the use of orchestral color to picture and interpret the words, as with the ominous timpani rolls that punctuate the Agnus Dei and its prayer for peace. Austria and France were warring at the time, and the meaning of those drum rolls was clear to his listeners.

The Creation of 1798 is still more operatic in approach. It is a gigantic work of manifold glories and manifest sins. Haydn could write superb arias, recitatives, and orchestral music; he was not always at his best in choruses, and like Handel he occasionally fell into naïve text painting (including some roaring lions in *The Creation*). The glories of this work begin at the outset, with the celebrated depiction of Chaos. Any composer will pull out all the stops for such an assignment, using every instrumental trick at his command and the most turbulent harmonies the style will bear. What strikes modern ears in Haydn's version of Chaos is not wildness, however, but rather a tremendous freshness of sound, avoiding most of the familiar harmonic and melodic grooves. It is as if Haydn were aiming for Wagner and getting surprisingly close. The climax, a mighty C major chord as the choir proclaims "And there was Light," is a soul-stirring moment that Wagner never had the craft (or the soul) to achieve.

The Creation has worn a little thin here and there since the success of its first decades, but it remains a much-loved masterpiece of the choral repertoire. The last public appearance of Haydn's life was at an 1808 performance, when during the piece the old man became so emotional that he had to be carried out of the hall in a chair. As he left, his onetime pupil Beethoven rose to kiss his hands and

forehead; at the door Haydn paused to raise his hand in final bene-
diction to the crowd and to his life in music.

Thus Papa Haydn, the most familiarly human of the great composers, the most unassuming, the one who seems to grasp our hand
as one of us. His achievement was no less impressive for its modesty of voice, nor his style any the less revolutionary for its aplomb.
In a letter near the end of his long, industrious, lucky life, Haydn
wrote an admirable artistic credo:

Often, as I struggled with obstacles of every kind opposed to my
works—often, as my physical and mental powers sank and I
had difficulty in keeping to my chosen course—an inner voice
whispered to me: "There are so few happy and contented men
here below—on every hand care and sorrow pursue them—
perhaps your work may someday be a source from which men
laden with anxieties and burdened with affairs may derive a
few moments of rest and refreshment." This, then, was a powerful motive to persevere, this the reason why I can even now
look back with profound satisfaction on what I have accomplished.

*Title page
of the first
edition
of Haydn's
"The Seasons."*

WOLFGANG
AMADEUS
MOZART

For nearly two centuries the story has been told and retold: Mozart the divine mystery, the incomparable freak of nature embodied in an impish and vulgar child, who wrote masterpieces before he was ten but was perpetually misunderstood, who was hounded by neglect to a pauper's grave. It is one of the most tragic and moving stories in the history of music.

But almost none of it is true. Certainly, Mozart was a prodigy equal to any, writing his first symphonies at eight, his first opera at twelve. Yet Schubert and Mendelssohn produced more original and important work in their teens than Mozart did. In contrast to Schubert, Mozart matured slowly and worked painstakingly (however quickly); most of his greatest work comes from his last ten years. Moreover, during that decade he was as respected as any composer alive and paid accordingly, earning more than Haydn did for most of his career. Often he received twice the going rate for writing an

opera. He ran out of money sometimes, as many successful people do, from a combination of bad management and bad luck. The begging letters he wrote to friends in later years are certainly pathetic; but by the time he died he had gone far toward paying back his debts and was on the verge, in his mid thirties, of real prosperity.

In the last year of his life, when legend has Mozart virtually starving to death, he may have had his best year, probably making well over the equivalent of $100,000. And though like anyone else he had relative hits and misses, he was far from being misunderstood. A contemporary German reviewer, who denounced *Don Giovanni* as something that "offends reason, insults morality, and treads wickedly upon virtue and feeling," felt obliged to add, "If ever a nation could take pride in one of her sons, so Germany must be proud of Mozart. . . . Never, indeed never before, was the greatness of the human spirit so tangible, and never has the art of composition been raised to such heights." Haydn, his only living peer, called Mozart the greatest composer he had ever known or heard of.

Thus in his own time Mozart commanded the same reputation, for more or less the same reasons, that he does now—as an incomparable genius and a model for the future. It was really the nineteenth century that misunderstood him, both his music and his life, and insisted on making his story into a grand Romantic tragedy.

As to his personality, while it is true that Mozart wrote some spectacularly pornographic letters to friends and family, and that he had a propensity for childlike romping in adulthood, other letters and contemporary descriptions reveal a man of immense acumen and intellectual vitality, fluent in several languages, a sharp observer of people and ideas, and a thoughtful artist capable of sober analysis of his own and others' work. And for a final blow at the Mozart legend, he was buried just like most Viennese of his day, rich or poor. The "pauper's grave" is another myth.

Accordingly, let's pose two new questions. First: Granted that the gods now and then confer phenomenal gifts on a child, why is it that only one person with such gifts ever grew up to be a Mozart?

That question is, of course, unanswerable. But the moral is that we can't attribute Mozart entirely to the gods. He had a good deal to do with it himself, some understanding the other prodigies lacked, some rankling dissatisfaction. He possessed a remarkable teacher in his father, who trained the child and then exposed him to the best influences of the age. Mozart studied the music of others all his life, gaining lessons that guided his own work. Whatever the confluence of forces that molded Mozart, they enabled him to mount higher and higher on a ladder that in his time only he possessed.

And the second question: Why the myths? Of course, there are inevitable gaps in the historical record and deficiencies in interpreting the evidence. But more significantly, both the Romantic nineteenth century and the Modernist twentieth shaped his life into something they wanted to believe: that all artists are neglected in their own time, tragic figures whose work can be understood only in the future. In reality, as I demonstrate throughout this book, most historically important composers were towering figures in their own time and sooner or later quite well understood, sometimes better understood in their lifetime than they have been since. For one example, it is only recently that we have rediscovered the shocking and demonic aspect of *Don Giovanni,* which the contemporary German reviewer saw quite clearly (even if he did deplore it). The perspective an artist's contemporaries always lack is that of history; we see Mozart and Beethoven in terms of their influence on the future, a dimension closed to their own era. In any case, the neglected genius is the exception. In these pages, only J. S. Bach, Charles Ives, and a few others come close to that model.

There is another Romantic and Modernist myth to which Mozart does not conform: that all geniuses are originals and pathbreakers. Of the three arguably supreme masters of Western music—Bach, Beethoven, and Mozart—that myth applies only to Beethoven, who was indeed a revolutionary. Original Bach certainly was; but the polyphonic basis of his music was outdated in his lifetime, with adverse consequences for his reputation. In his music as in his life, Mozart didn't much concern himself with the future. He was happy to be a man of his time writing for his time.

He lived in that brief period—around 1770 to 1800—when Western musical style had an unprecedented integrity, when similar aesthetic attitudes prevailed all over Europe. The language of Mozart's music resembles that of his Classical predecessors such as Haydn and J. C. Bach. Everything he wrote was within a genre—symphony, opera, quartet—that had a tradition and a set of norms and procedures to which he largely adhered. He functioned best within the Classical conventions, not opposed to them. And it may be that the kind of poise he achieved is possible only within the boundaries of such a tight tradition.

His relationship to his great peers, then, is one of quality rather than style or personality. If Beethoven teaches us the power of revolutionary vitality and individuality under disciplined control, and Bach reveals the full scope of human creative potential, then Mozart stands as the embodiment of the possibility of perfection.

Wolfgang Amadeus Mozart was born in the medieval storybook town of Salzburg, Austria, to Leopold Mozart and his wife, Maria Anna, on January 27, 1756. Leopold was a minor composer attached to the local court, and writer of an important book on the teaching of violin. After Leopold realized the scope of Wolfgang's talent, his major endeavor became the career of his son.

The miracle began when the three-year-old Wolfgang responded to his sister Nannerl's music lessons by picking out tunes on the harpsichord. Leopold began to give the toddler some lessons as well. We can only imagine his joy and wonder at what happened: the tiny child seemed to grasp everything he was shown, as if he had already known it. One day he picked up a violin for the first time and started playing. At five he began to compose little pieces.

Wolfgang's public debut—along with Nannerl, a comparable keyboard prodigy—came at the court of Munich in January 1762, when he was six. Then in Vienna he played for Empress Maria Theresa, after which he sat on the empress's lap and proposed to the young Marie Antoinette. Word of his performances flashed across Europe; he was regarded as a scientific phenomenon, like a talking monkey. Leopold was quick to grasp the potential for making his and his children's fortune.

Thus began Wolfgang's strange and marvelous childhood wanderings. In the summer of 1763, Leopold and the children set out on a tour that lasted over three years and took them to glittering courts and cheering concert halls across Europe and in London. From then until he was fifteen Wolfgang spent half his time on tour. It has been calculated that, by the end of his life, he had spent four of his thirty-five years in a stagecoach.

In other words he was a showbiz kid, his family life that of a traveling circus act. Leopold's advertisements for his shows were not subtle in hawking the product, though they did not exaggerate: "He will play a concerto for the violin, and will accompany symphonies on the harpsichord, the keyboard being covered with a cloth . . . he will instantly name all notes played at a distance. . . . He will finally improvise as long as may be desired, and in any key." Under these circumstances Wolfgang grew up like showbiz kids of all eras, with a shaky grasp of practicality and common sense. (All qualities Leopold possessed in oppressive abundance. In adulthood Nannerl ended up as pedantic and self-righteous as her father. They usually lectured with one voice against Wolfgang's schemes and rationalizations; they were, however, often right.)

Starting in 1769, Leopold took Wolfgang on three visits to Italy, during which the teen-ager absorbed Italian style, studied counterpoint, and picked up a row of honors including the papal Order of the Golden Spur. The latter resulted from one of his legendary tricks: writing down from memory, after two hearings, Allegri's famous

Miserere, which the Vatican had never let out of the house. Instead of censuring Wolfgang, the pope bestowed the knighthood on him. Thereafter he would occasionally sign himself "Chevalier Mozart."

The phenomenal memory this feat demonstrated was to become one of his most powerful tools. He was able to compose a work entirely in his mind—often during a stagecoach journey or while playing billiards—and remember every detail. Thus his music has the freedom and spontaneity of a mental improvisation. The score was copied out when he got around to it, which was usually at the last minute. (If things got complex, however, he had to sketch and revise like everyone else.) An example from his maturity is the overture to *Don Giovanni,* which he had worked out in his head but, what with parties and such, put off writing down until two days before the premiere. He then stayed up all night scribbling away, his wife feeding him punch and delicacies and telling stories to keep him awake, each page handed to copyists as it was done. The extraordinary result was sightread at the performance. "A few notes fell under the table," Mozart admitted.

The most productive aspect of his youthful travels was that everywhere Wolfgang soaked up the ideas and influences his father sought out for him; in the process he created a style that synthesized the musical features of several countries. The pervasive influence would be Italian lyricism and good humor. During a stay in London in 1764, he became close to Johann Christian Bach, Sebastian's son, whose galant and Italianate music epitomizes the early Classical style. Christian's music influenced Wolfgang as much as anybody's, until the more important model of Haydn arrived.

The end of every childhood journey was inevitably Salzburg, which early on began to frustrate him. There Leopold continued his post as music director to the prince-archbishop. In 1771 the old archbishop, who had always been agreeable to the travels of his renowned employees, died. His replacement was one Hieronymus von Colloredo; this new archbishop had stricter ideas about the place and duties of his servants. He began agreeably enough, raising Wolfgang's salary in his position as court concertmaster. But the archbishop chafed when the fifteen-year-old genius was called out of town to write operas in Munich and Milan.

By 1777 Mozart was itching to get a job anywhere but Salzburg.

Mozart, age 10, presides at the harpsichord in a Parisian salon during his second trip to France, summer of 1766.

He was kept in minor posts, mostly writing church music, which barely interested him. That year he went on a job-hunting trip, accompanied by his ailing mother, and ended up in Paris. Mozart was then nearing the first major challenge of his life: growing up. It is one thing for a ten-year-old to play brilliantly and compose symphonies, another thing for a young man of eighteen. In Paris, Mozart became for the first time a free-lance professional, competing with other professionals for the slim pickings available. He made the rounds of the salons and got some commissions, but essentially nothing happened. His mother died in July 1778, and early in 1779 he headed home feeling depressed and defeated. On the way, however, he stopped over at Mannheim, and there something of major import did happen.

In Mannheim he stayed with a family named Weber, whom he had met on the way to Paris. The household included four daughters, two of them excellent singers. The inevitable happened: Mozart began courting Aloysia Weber, prettiest and most talented of the four. He

wrote some of his finest concert arias for her and her sister Josefa.
(Years later, Josefa would create the role of Queen of the Night in *The
Magic Flute.*) But despite Mozart's passion for Aloysia Weber, the
return trip ended with another failure; she was interested in his
music, not his love. Meanwhile, Leopold, learning of his son's
intentions, furiously called Wolfgang home. Father Mozart considered the Webers beneath them; besides, he did not want his son
picking out a wife by himself. But as he slunk back to Salzburg,
Mozart wasn't through with the Webers, nor they with him.

Back home, he held a dreary job as court and cathedral organist.
By then he was a master of the pleasant galant style of the day, not
yet the profound and immortal Mozart, only the lucid and delightful
one, with a steadily growing list of symphonies, operas, chamber
and choral music in his portfolio.

In 1780 the elector of Munich, where Mozart had scored some
major successes, called him back to write an opera. The result was
Idomeneo, his first mature stage work and, in the end, the best of his

opera seria. He composed much of it during rehearsals, matching the music to the singers, observing stage effects, adjusting the timing of the action by cutting here and adding there. (One of his singers was a male alto named dal Prato, whom Mozart affectionately called "mio molto amato castrato dal Prato.") In the process he learned practical lessons in drama and stagecraft that would bear fruit in the later comedies.

Idomeneo made an immense impression at the time and remains worth hearing. But the genius of Mozart would finally prove to be in opera buffa—comic opera—rather than opera seria. As I've noted before, some scholars suggest that the Classical style doesn't work so well for tragedy. Its grace and dancelike lightness better fit the tone and rhythm of comedy, the breathless patter and fast-moving action. On the other hand, Mozart would find ways to inject seriousness, even tragedy, into the conventions of opera buffa.

After his triumph in Munich, Mozart ran head-on into the decisive event of his life—a liberating fiasco. Archbishop Hieronymus decided to rein in this wandering employee, to make him settle down and follow orders. In early 1781 he imperiously summoned Mozart from Salzburg to Vienna, where the archbishop was visiting. When his composer stood before him the archbishop unleashed a torrent of abuse at this servant who served him so ill. When Mozart tried to defend himself, he was physically booted out of the house.

At any rate, that's how Mozart wrote of the scene to Leopold. In the same letter he vowed to quit Salzburg and seek his fortune where the greatest musical fortunes of Europe and maybe the world were to be found: in Vienna.

He was then twenty-five and a free-lance composer in an age when that was a risky way to live. However brilliant as virtuoso and composer, he now inhabited a town crawling with the species, all of them ambitious and hungry. Once the Church had been the main consumer of art; now the aristocracy paid most artists' rent, if anyone did. Mozart hoped to attach himself to some court or other, which was the usual road to success. In the end, things would not work out that way.

At first he lived in Vienna with the Webers, who had moved there from Mannheim. Now that Aloysia had rejected him, the newly widowed mother began to push on Mozart the younger, less pretty, less talented (though she sang well) Constanze. He allowed himself to be persuaded, writing Leopold for his blessing on their union. Wolfgang and Constanze were married in August 1782, before Leopold's grudging and exasperated permission arrived. Because of the break with the archbishop and this impulsive marriage, relations between father and son cooled and stayed that way.

Constanze, then twenty, was no intellectual partner or soulmate, but that didn't seem to be what her husband was looking for. Mozart wanted an enthusiastic playmate and bedmate, and that the lively and flirtatious Constanze apparently was. Her new husband was a man-child who in one minute could be improvising sublimely in an elegant parlor, the next minute jumping over the furniture and howling like a cat. Long-nosed and rather bug-eyed, he was nothing much to look at except for a luxurious head of hair, his main vanity. In later years he seems to have resembled a fat little bird. He sometimes wrote letters full of wild scatological humor and lubricious endearments. ("Let me know your mind/Or I'll let off one behind." And worse. This peccadillo was common in that era; even his parents indulged in crude jokes.) At the same time, his letters reveal a droll and sharp-eyed observer of people and a certain generosity of spirit—except toward other musicians. The latter, accurately but tactlessly, he usually compared unfavorably to himself.

Whether in public or private he fidgeted nonstop, drummed his fingers on everything, paced nervously even while washing his hands. Constanze took to cutting his meat at table so he wouldn't slice up his fingers. He loved music and everything connected with it; otherwise he loved dancing, billiards, food, wine, parties, sex, and fun in general, with an insatiable animal enjoyment. Until his later years he was indifferent to literature, philosophy, politics— unless there was something in them he could use, and then he would seize them tenaciously. No more than anyone else could he explain the magical things that went on in his head. With Constanze, then, he needed no spiritual bond. But his letters show he was inordinately and lustily fond of her.

Just before his marriage Mozart caused a sensation in Vienna with an irresistible comedy, *The Abduction from the Seraglio*. This yarn of two noble ladies sold by pirates to a Turkish pasha was designed to take advantage of a then current Viennese rage for everything Turkish—coffee, candy, cigarettes, and pseudo-Turkish music (heavy on cymbals and drums). Enhancing the opera's salability was its form as a German *Singspiel*, a popular type of stage work rather like an American musical: songs linked with spoken dialogue. The Viennese ate up this concoction of Mozartean wit and exotic hokum.

Between *The Abduction* and his brilliant piano performances, Mozart became for a time the toast of the city. He and Constanze took a luxurious apartment and furnished it richly, including a fine billiard table. He indulged his taste for fancy clothes and a daily visit from his hairdresser.

Of course, they weren't really rich and never would be, even though he concertized often in the first few years and became one of the best-paid soloists in town. He could net the equivalent of over $6,000 for an evening's work, as much as some court officials earned in a year. All the same, Mozart had the unpredictable income of a free-lancer, vulnerable to threats from the state of the economy, the fickle tastes of the Viennese public, and the sabotage of his enemies. The success of *The Abduction* had been achieved, for example, despite machinations led by Antonio Salieri, head of the Vienna Opera and a favorite composer of Emperor Joseph II. Salieri did his best to slap down this brash young rival, planting men in the audience to boo and hiss. That's how the composer game was played. In that case it didn't work, but Salieri would be a formidable rival. He would enter history, in the end, not as a composer but as the nemesis of Mozart. (Though by no means the elegant monster portrayed in the film *Amadeus*. Salieri was simply more cunning at playing the games that all composers played. Moreover, Mozart later considered Salieri a friend, and apparently for good reason.)

For the rest of his life in Vienna, Mozart would work at full tilt and in his full maturity. The tide of his creation flowed serenely through all the disorder of his life, the periods of boom and bust and encroaching illness.

More than anything he wanted to write opera, but after *The Abduction from the Seraglio* he waded through dozens of librettos unable to find a subject that engaged him. He was bored with the classical gods and nymphs and shepherds that populated most opera seria, even Gluck's reformist ones. He would rather write opera buffa, with its amorous peasants and farcical schemes in contemporary settings. Those were real people, the kind of people he knew, and so were their problems. All the same, he also wanted comedy with meat on it, with an underlying seriousness of purpose. When he ran across Beaumarchais's notorious play *The Marriage of Figaro,* he knew he had found his subject.

By that time Mozart was a fixture at the court of Joseph II, emperor of the Holy Roman Empire. An "enlightened despot" and patron of the arts, Joseph had imposed wide-ranging reforms including abolishing serfdom, limiting the power of the nobility, and rationalizing burial practices. Joseph's reforms were so dictatorial, however, that in the end he would manage to alienate nearly everybody. Though he was chronically stingy in all matters, Joseph nonetheless kept a brilliant court. Another hanger-on there was poet, librettist, and adventurer Lorenzo da Ponte: half hack, half genius, phenomenally learned but also addicted to ladies and high living. Mozart approached da Ponte with the idea of *Figaro.* Da Ponte knew it well, and knew it could be trouble—Joseph had banned the play. But da Ponte promised to fix things with the emperor.

Though nominally a comedy, the play is a fierce indictment of the nobility in which barber Figaro and his betrothed, Susanna, battle the schemes of the philandering Count Almaviva—mainly his feudal right to sleep with new brides. Hearing of Mozart's plan to set this story, his rivals smelled blood; but da Ponte promised Emperor Joseph that they would clean up the objectionable parts, and Joseph agreed to lift his ban. Still, just under the jolly surface of the opera, the rage at social injustice remains. (Scholar Volkmar Braunbehrens—source of much of my myth-debunking information—suggests in his *Mozart in Vienna* that Joseph may deliberately have encouraged the production of *Figaro* as part of his own program against the feudal power of the nobility.)

Thus began the collaboration of Mozart and da Ponte that would produce three immortal operas. Perhaps the most perfectly realized of them all, *Figaro* was written in some six weeks of early 1786. Enemies in court (by no means limited to Salieri) tried to turn the performers against the music, but it soon won them over: a singer later recalled of rehearsals, "The players on the stage and in the orchestra were electrified. Intoxicated with pleasure they cried again and again . . . 'Bravo, maestro! Long live the great Mozart!' " At the premiere the length of the performance was nearly doubled because the audience demanded so many numbers be repeated. Emperor Joseph expressed his delight.

Then a sudden collapse. The public's attention was diverted by a catchy little opera called *Una Cosa Rara,* by the Spaniard Martín y Soler. Beyond that, the implications of a story about a barber humiliating a count were not lost on the nobility; they would not forgive Mozart—and perhaps Joseph—for that affront. *Figaro* went under in Vienna after only nine performances and for many years would rarely be heard there. A production in Prague soon after, however, was a stupendous success. Mozart proudly wrote his father, "Here they talk about nothing but *Figaro*. Nothing is played, sung, or whistled but *Figaro*. No opera is drawing like *Figaro*. Nothing, nothing but *Figaro*. Certainly a great honor for me!"

Inevitably, this triumph was temporary. In those days there were no royalties. One was paid to write the work and that was it; the piece could be sung everywhere and the composer made not a penny from it. The only way to survive as a free-lancer was to write and perform constantly, have constant successes, and hope the economy stayed strong. Around 1786, Mozart's creative activity flowered as never before. In six months from the end of 1785 to the spring of 1786, when he finished *Figaro,* he also completed three piano concertos, several pieces for Masonic services (he had become an active Freemason), a violin sonata, and many smaller works. Meanwhile, however, Emperor Joseph had gotten into a disastrous war with Turkey that was sapping the resources of the state and, inevitably, going hard on the arts. To make matters worse, Constanze Mozart was chronically ailing and spending a good deal of time at expensive spas. For his part, Mozart had always looked at money as something to spend and enjoy rather than put away for the future. Some sources suggest that he was making unwise loans and investments and/or indulging in gambling, though evidence in that direction is inconclusive.

For all these possible reasons, between 1788 and 1790 Mozart fell seriously behind and began abjectly begging loans from friends, especially his Masonic lodge brother Michael Puchberg. In 1789 he wrote Puchberg, "Great God! I would not wish my worst enemy to be in my present position. And if you, most beloved friend and brother, forsake me, we are altogether lost, *both my unfortunate and blameless self* and my poor sick wife and child. . . . Fate is so much against me . . . that even when I want to I cannot make any money.'' Such letters, and there are many, later helped create the myth of the neglected and impoverished Mozart. Yet the circumstances of his life at that time, difficult as they were, do not seem to have been quite as miserable as he painted them; one is apt to exaggerate when begging. In any case, within two years Mozart's finances would be stable again; historians have rarely noticed that by his death Mozart had begun to repay Puchberg, and Constanze took care of the remaining debts.

Among the rewards of the Vienna years was the warm friendship that developed with Joseph Haydn. The old master's worldwide acclaim had relieved him of the need to compete with anyone; besides, he was generous by nature. As we have seen, for all Mozart's harsh judgments of contemporaries, he was effusive in acknowledging his debt to Haydn.

Haydn's respect and generosity were rewarded by the dedication of six string quartets Mozart wrote from 1782 to 1785. Remarkable in their equal treatment of the instruments and their contrapuntal richness, these ''Haydn'' Quartets were perhaps the most laboriously worked over of all Mozart's music; the manuscripts show layers of revisions and rethinking. Three of them were first read through in Vienna on an evening in early 1785, with both composers playing and Mozart's father present. At the end a moved Haydn said to Leopold, ''Before God and as an honest man, your son is the greatest composer I know, either personally or by reputation.''

Prague responded to *Figaro*mania by summoning Mozart and da Ponte to write another opera in 1787. Looking for a sensational subject, they decided on the old Don Juan legend, eventually fleshing it out with technical advice from da Ponte's friend and fellow adventurer Casanova (who may even have contributed a scene or two). Da Ponte wrote the libretto ensconced in a room in a patron's house; in the next room was a table constantly supplied with food and wine; and a third room contained a young lady who appeared dutifully at the ring of a bell. Of the latter element of inspiration, da Ponte wrote, ''I would like to have loved her as a sister, but . . .'' Thus was put together one of the most powerful of all operas, the strange brew of comedy and tragedy and mythical resonances, *Don Giovanni*.

For all its refusal to fit any mold, the work had another resounding success in Prague—and another much-praised failure in Vienna. Emperor Joseph's response set the tone: "The opera is heavenly, perhaps even more beautiful than *Figaro*. But no food for the teeth of my Viennese." Some found the music too complicated, echoing the famous (and perhaps apocryphal) story of Joseph saying, "Too many notes, Mozart," and the composer replying, "Just as many as are needed, Your Majesty." More often, though, the music was praised while the story was condemned as immoral or foolish. Clearly, much of the lack of success in Vienna had to do with the opera's mixture of comic and tragic genres; the convention-bound Viennese wanted things to be one or the other. Yet by the time Mozart died, *Don Giovanni* was selling out all over Germany, Austria, and in Prague, the most popular of all his stage works (though the others were also widely produced).

Still, in those years money worries were pursuing Mozart like demons. When he did collect a good commission, it seemed to evaporate. In 1789, he was brought to Berlin by King William II of Prussia and paid extravagantly for a series of works, but he returned to Vienna with no money and no explanation. Constanze was pregnant more often than not—only two of their six children survived— and visiting her spas. To make miseries worse, Leopold died in May 1787, with too many issues unresolved between father and son, too many things left unsaid and undone.

Much of this was part of an artist's life in the eighteenth century. Da Ponte's memoirs detail a similar story of extravagant ups and downs, living in a palace one year and in squalor the next. Artists were beggars, really, parasites of the nobility, who themselves were known to go spectacularly broke. Mozart was already bouncing back financially by 1791, as da Ponte did time and again, but by the late 1780s Mozart was also intermittently but seriously ill. Perhaps kidney disease was slowly killing him; from the medical science of those days it is hard to tell. His physical decline, and Constanze's, spread its desperation into all corners of his life.

Yet his boyish spirits never entirely slacked, and neither did the inexorable flow of his inspiration. In one incredible span of six weeks in the summer of 1788, his fortunes at their lowest ebb, he wrote his final three symphonies, nos. 39–41. In these works he brought Classical symphonic form to the highest perfection it would ever reach, and pointed the way toward the scope and intensity that Beethoven would bring to symphonic music.

There were some transforming discoveries during his last decade. With his friend Baron van Swieten, a court librarian and musical amateur, Mozart began after 1782 to study J. S. Bach's *Well-Tempered Clavier* and *The Art of Fugue*. This study produced a revitalization of counterpoint that added musical and spiritual depth to Mozart's late masterpieces.

The other development was more surprising. Though nominally Catholic, Mozart joined a Freemason lodge in 1784. At that time the Catholic church—and Catholic Austria—tended to consider Masonry a diabolical conspiracy against divinely ordered authority. (Joseph, however, included Freemasons among his advisors. It was his predecessor and successor who drove the Masons underground.) For all his past indifference to politics, the democratic ideology of the Freemasons, who numbered among their members such Enlightenment figures as Voltaire, Goethe, and Benjamin Franklin, struck a deep chord in Mozart. The music he wrote for Masonic ceremonies had a tone of solemn grandeur new to his work. In the tenets of Masonry he embraced the ideals that later inspired Beethoven: liberty and the brotherhood of humanity. These two late discoveries, Bach and Masonry, would have much to do with his last masterpiece for the stage, *The Magic Flute*.

Before that, early 1790 saw the premiere of his and da Ponte's final collaboration, *Così fan tutte* (roughly, "They All Do It"). This story of betrayal generally follows the conventions of the period's sex comedies: two men callously subject their loves to a test of fidelity, and the ladies ingloriously fail the test. By the end, though, four lives are in a nasty mess and we are left wondering what's so funny. Mozart perhaps subverted the opera's popularity with his music, making the dilemmas too pointed, the supposedly comic sufferings too real. At any rate, for all its glories, *Così* has remained the least popular of the three great collaborations.

Mozart did not make the same mistake the next time: *The Magic Flute* is truly popular in style and story and had a huge success. Somehow he managed to make this preposterous bit of humbug the most profound of all his operas.

The impetus for *The Magic Flute* came from a colorful and somewhat sleazy figure named Emanuel Schikaneder. An actor, impresario, and Freemason, Schikaneder had played Shakespeare and other classics but had little artistic ambition beyond giving the public what it wanted. He established a theater where he produced and acted in comedies suitable to popular taste, with an emphasis on exotic subjects and flashy stage effects. Mozart and Schikaneder had become drinking companions; to keep his spirits up Mozart was now resorting to wine and song, and maybe women too. The actor was a fertile source of all.

In March 1791, Schikaneder proposed a project: a singspiel based on a fairy tale called *Lulu, or The Enchanted Flute.* Mozart agreed with no hesitation; he needed the money and couldn't be choosy. So Schikaneder started on the libretto, writing himself a slapstick role as the feather-clad bird-catcher Papageno. About a third of the way through, however, somebody else in town mounted a successful production of the same story. No problem: apparently Schikaneder simply switched everything around in the middle. The original heroine was the Queen of the Night, whose daughter Pamina is abducted by the evil Sarastro, head of a mysterious brotherhood; after the revision, Sarastro is revealed as a noble figure who kidnapped Pamina for her own good, and the Queen becomes a treacherous witch. In the process of revision the libretto picked up two undercurrents, one unfortunate and one fruitful.

The unfortunate element is a heavy dose of antifeminism: the Queen's major sin, it seems, is challenging the authority of men. Mozart probably paid little attention to this shabby attempt at dramatic motivation. What clearly moved him was that Schikaneder also made the play into a thinly disguised allegory of Freemasonry. Sarastro's brotherhood is much like a Masonic lodge, complete with pseudo-Egyptian ceremonials.

In the most dazzling feat of his career, Mozart turned the libretto's creaking assemblage of claptrap, platitudes, and misogyny into a sublime fairy tale for adults. It moves effortlessly from the artless and popular to the searching and profound. In Sarastro's arias and the choruses of the brotherhood speaks the solemn tone of his Masonic music. (George Bernard Shaw once said that Sarastro's arias are the only music ever written suitable for the voice of God.) As the choruses sing of a rebirth of wisdom, one hears the majestic opening chords of the new era of humanity, the dawn of Enlightenment and democracy. Even if in reality the new dawn would not prove so transcendent as it seemed in the anticipation, Mozart's music captured for all time the heart-filling grandeur of that dream.

By the middle of 1791 Mozart apparently knew he was dying. It had no effect on his output or even his travels. In the middle of that year he hastily composed an opera seria called *The Clemency of Titus* for a royal coronation in Prague, and went there to conduct the premiere. Far from his best, the work found no success. His letters of that period reveal an uncharacteristic brooding: "If people could see into my heart," he wrote Constanze, "I should have to feel almost ashamed—I find everything cold—ice cold." Yet a day or so later he would write with his old zest of eating a glorious meal.

The final horror arrived at his door in July 1791, in the person of a gray-clad stranger who refused to identify himself but commissioned Mozart to write a Requiem, a Mass for the dead. Accepting the commission and setting to work, he began to imagine that this stranger was Death himself and the Requiem his own. In a letter he raved, "I cannot remove from my eyes the image of the stranger. I see him continually. He begs me, exhorts me, and then commands me to work . . . I am on the point of death; I have finished before I could enjoy my talent . . . I thus must finish my funeral song, which I must not leave incomplete." (It's worth mentioning, however, that this letter may well be a nineteenth-century forgery.)

In the end he would leave the Requiem a magnificent fragment. Has there ever been more ominous music than the opening chorus? It is still firmly controlled Mozart, magisterial in tone and sensitive to every nuance of the text, but it is also the work of a man staring into his own grave. There speaks at times a depth of personal anguish that would not be heard in music again until the works of Beethoven's maturity. Throughout, the glow of Bachian counterpoint illuminates the Requiem; and it resonates with hope and rejoicing as much as with tragedy and death.

There is a simple explanation, by the way, for the mystery of the commission. The secretive messenger came from one Count Franz von Walsegg, a musical amateur who planned, as was his habit, to palm off the Requiem as his own work. After Mozart's death, the count confessed his scheme.

Two weeks before he died, Mozart conducted a newly written

Masonic cantata for the opening of a temple. It was his last completed piece. Two days later he took to his deathbed, still working on the Requiem. Word came that *The Magic Flute,* which had gotten off to a slow start, was shaping into a major hit. In bed Mozart began timing the nightly performances with his watch, saying, "Now is the Queen of the Night's aria. . . . Now comes Sarastro."

Further word arrived: some Hungarian noblemen had secured for him a generous yearly stipend that would mean the end of his financial worries. Such aristocratic endowment was the beginning of a new system for artists; Beethoven and later free-lance composers would make much of their living from such sources. Though the stipend capped a profitable year for Mozart and heralded a more secure future, it was all too late.

On the night of December 4, he struggled to sing parts of the

SONATA FORM, SYMPHONY, SONATA, AND RELATED FORMS

Our concepts of *sonata form,* the most important formal model of the Classical period and for a century after, descend partly from mid-nineteenth-century theorists who cooked up the idea as an abstraction of composers' procedures from about the time of Haydn on. As we found with the scholarly idea of fugue, only occasionally do pieces closely fit such definitions. Like other kinds of myth, standardized musical forms are not strictly "true" in the real world, but received in the right spirit they can be useful and even illuminating. In our discussions here, I'll move from the larger and more predictable aspects of sonata form (a.k.a. *sonata allegro* or *first movement* form) to the far more variable details.

What we call sonata form indicates a general way of organizing shorter pieces or individual movements of longer pieces. It developed in the Classical period out of

At right, a Beethoven sonata on one of his pianos. A virtuoso performer, Beethoven made demands on the piano that influenced its development.

Requiem with some friends gathered around his bed. Constanze, recently returned from another spa, was there with Mozart's pupil Franz Süssmayr, who had promised the dying man that he would complete the Requiem. (Süssmayr did as promised, and handsomely.) A doctor came and applied cold poultices to Mozart's feverish head; this precipitated a coma. When they checked him after midnight, December 5, 1791, he was dead.

The funeral was productive of many myths. Contrary to later legend, a number of people showed up. The services and burial were conducted according to the strict—and short-lived—decrees of Emperor Joseph, which were designed to eliminate extravagant funeral services and end unhealthy burial practices inside the city walls. So, as was done with most funerals in those years, the service was held in the city, at the Cathedral of St. Stephen, and later that evening the

body was carted outside the city walls for burial in a communal grave the next morning. Given that delay (partly required in case the corpse turned out not to be dead), few mourners in those days actually accompanied a body to the gravesite, which was always plain and unmarked. In fact, bodies were supposed to be interred in a linen sack and covered with lime; this may have been done with Mozart. The historical confusion entered in because these burial ordinances were detested and did not long outlive Joseph. Soon they had been virtually forgotten, and thus the myth of Mozart's receiving a pauper's burial was able to flourish in the Romantic era.

Mozart died anything but a poor or forgotten man. A memorial service in Prague on December 14 brought thousands of people to hear a Requiem Mass played by the finest musicians in the city; the newspaper account concluded, "countless tears flowed in painful

earlier procedures, mainly *binary form* (see Glossary). Sonata form has only indirectly to do with pieces called *sonata*. It can be found in numerous genres—symphony, string quartet, and sacred choral works, to name a few. Most commonly, first movements of instrumental pieces are organized according to sonata form.

This formal principle took shape as a way of realizing the far-ranging musical goals of the Classical period. Not only was the new musical rhetoric simplified; composers now wanted heightened emotional intensity but also stability, more contrast but also balance. These goals gave rise to new principles of organization founded on a sophisticated handling of key structure. Earlier, Baroque pieces changed keys during

their course and had concluding returns to the home key, but they largely stuck to one set of ideas and one mood throughout a movement. In the Classical instrumental works of Haydn, Mozart, and Beethoven, key changes became dramatic events, often signaled by thematic, rhythmic, and textural contrasts. To rationalize this new variety, composers of the period developed some habits of musical syntax and long-range organization which worked so well that they pervaded Western music for over a century. It was these habits that were later abstracted and dubbed "sonata form." (Haydn, Mozart, and Beethoven never heard of the term.)

Reliably in a sonata form movement, there will be three distinct

remembrance of that artist whose harmonies had so often moved our hearts to joy."

There was also a memorial service in Vienna, the music conducted by Antonio Salieri. For years a rumor would persist that he had poisoned Mozart. Though Salieri had possibly obstructed Mozart's career here and there, there was nothing to the rumor, nor did it damage Salieri's reputation. In fact, among other kindnesses, not long before Mozart died Salieri had sat through a performance of *The Magic Flute* alongside the composer and wildly applauded every number. Salieri went on to be an honored pedagogue who taught, among others, Beethoven, Schubert, Liszt—and Mozart's son Karl, who became a minor but respectable composer. Librettist Lorenzo da Ponte ended up in America, where he taught Italian at Columbia University and ran a grocery store, with a little bootlegging on the

---

sections. The first section presents the basic material of the piece; for that reason, it is called the *exposition*. In the next large section, material from the exposition is reexamined, "discussed," "argued," fragmented, reassembled, juxtaposed in new ways in a generally dramatic atmosphere; this second section is thus called the *development*. Finally the opening section returns, to some degree changed for the sake of variety and also to make it more stable and conclusive; this final section is called the *recapitulation*. These three sections—exposition, development, and recapitulation—are the basic constituents of sonata form movements. (Note that this organization resembles literary models, say, the form of an essay: exposition of ideas, development

of those ideas, final recap and summary. Metaphorically, one might call sonata form a logical discourse on stated themes, or a drama in the abstract.)

But I must immediately mention some variations on the above pattern. Sometimes there is an *introduction* before the exposition and/or a *coda* at the end of the movement. Since many sonata form movements are in faster tempos, the introduction is usually slow, a stately preface to the faster body of the piece. Usually the coda stays in the main tempo, but sounds more conclusive, more cadential. With these optional additions at beginning and end, we can have up to a five-section movement: *introduction, exposition, development, recapitulation, coda*.

A further variable: the exposi-

side. Constanze became a professional composer's widow, married a Danish diplomat, and survived him, too; his tombstone reads: "Here Rests Mozart's Widow's Second Spouse."

The cause of Mozart's death was laid at the time to "miliary fever," a diagnosis of vague import, later corrupted to the entirely meaningless "military fever." Current research suggests that rheumatic fever killed Mozart, probably helped along by his doctors, whose treatments included bleeding, a common and often lethal procedure of the time. In other words, neither poverty nor neglect nor poison killed Mozart, but rather the indifferent decree of the same gods who had so marvellously fashioned him.

tion section is usually repeated in order to reinforce the basic material. Until about the time of Mozart in the 1780s, the development and recapitulation were also repeated as a unit. (These two repeats reveal the ancestry of sonata form in the two repeated sections of the older binary form.) Thus we have this plan: exposition (twice)/ development-recapitulation (twice). Beethoven and later composers for the most part eliminated the repeat of the development and recapitulation. For that matter, modern performers sometimes omit both repeats, even that of the exposition. It's hard to defend these omissions on musical grounds (unless the music is so dull that nobody wants to hear anything twice).

Now let's examine the details of the "average" exposition, development, and recapitulation sections, keeping in mind that in practice there is tremendous variability from piece to piece.

The exposition is divided into two sections, which used to be called the "primary theme" and "secondary theme," with a "bridge" between them. The trouble is, sometimes there is only one real melodic theme in a movement (Haydn's "second theme" is often a variant of his first), and sometimes there are more than two (as we often find in Beethoven and later composers). Yet the idea of a two-section exposition is still valid in an important sense: the first section begins in the home key of the movement (also called the *tonic*), the bridge modulates to

The image of Mozart and his music has evolved steadily since his time. In his own day he was generally understood to be the equal of any composer who ever lived. When Beethoven arrived in Vienna shortly after Mozart died, the standard by which he was measured was, above all, Mozart.

Some composers of the nineteenth century claimed him as one of their own. Pointing to the expressiveness and the sometimes demonic intensity of his work, they declared Mozart to be the first Romantic in music. (His Classical restraint did not interest them so much.) But by the middle of the century the rage for Beethoven had pushed Mozart to the side; then he seemed little more than a laced and ruffled china doll, too decorous to encompass the heroic passions.

Always, though, his influence pervaded musicians. The art of

a related key, and the next section is in that key (the *dominant,* or the *relative major* if the tonic is a minor key).

In other words, the fundamental purpose of the exposition's two sections is not so much thematic as tonal, *a movement from the home key to a closely related key or keys.* Thus the sections of the exposition are better called: "first tonal group," then a transitional "bridge" to the "second tonal group." The opening of the first tonal group usually functions as the primary theme of the movement; it's the first melodic material we hear and may define the character of the whole piece. If the first tonal group is dramatic and assertive, the second tonal group will usually be contrastingly softer and more placid. At the end of the exposition there may be a brief concluding section, a *codetta* or "closing group" that helps to establish the new key. To summarize the "average" exposition: *first tonal group* (with the main thematic material), *bridge, second tonal group* (often with contrasting thematic material), and optional *codetta* (often with a closing theme).

Following the exposition, the *development* corresponds to the plot complications in the middle of a play or novel. Here the melodic themes, which are the "characters" in the piece, interact freely and dramatically, revealing new aspects of themselves, sometimes being dissolved into their constituent motives and recombined to form new thematic patterns. It is in the development that

Beethoven, Schubert, and Rossini was grounded in Mozart (and, of course, Haydn). Even Wagner and Tchaikovsky, despite their Romantic lushness, idolized him. In this century nostalgic evocations of the Mozartean world are found everywhere from Prokofiev's *Classical Symphony* to Strauss's high-Viennese *Der Rosenkavalier* to the works of Stravinsky's neoclassic period.

Only recently have we rediscovered his depths. It is true that emotions in Mozart tend to be veiled, like those behind the masks and ruffles of a costume ball. But hidden behind the masks are the timeless, universal passions. One sees this especially in the four great comic operas. Though all seem to be frivolous sex comedies, beneath their surfaces rages a world of murder, lust, seduction, betrayal, class struggle, and finally redeeming love. All that in lace, and with incomparable tunes to boot.

---

the composer most reveals his imagination and gift for variation (Beethoven was the great master of this process). Supporting the drama of themes is the drama of keys; the development tends to be highly unstable, with restless modulations from key to key, including ones far from the home key.

Then at the end of the development comes what is usually a central dramatic point of the movement: the retransition back to the tonic and the beginning of the *recapitulation*. Time and again, the best composers invest this familiar event with tension, suspense, and finally an almost revelatory sense of return and rediscovery (unless it suits their purpose to sneak into the recap). Once more, Beethoven is the supreme master of this game; whether it is the recap of the dramatic opening motto in the Fifth Symphony or the quieter main theme of the *Eroica,* the effect is invariably powerful. In a good recapitulation, the themes seem to bear the weight of what they went through in the development; they have a history now, they are characters we have seen in action, they have become richer and more meaningful. One thinks of the lines of T. S. Eliot: ". . . the end of all our exploring/ Will be to arrive where we started/ And know the place for the first time."

So the main point of the recapitulation is its sense of returning home to the opening themes and tonic key. This time things remain relatively stable: *the entire recapitulation stays mostly in the tonic,* with

This is not to ignore the technical brilliance. Most art exists within contradictions, centrifugal tensions that threaten to tear it apart. Such tensions can be dynamic and exciting. But in Mozart one finds a moment in history when all is poised in a radiant, Vermeer-like, apparently effortless balance. His music—even the less inspired—is a lucid world where nothing is wasted, everything is essential. For that reason, he is among the most challenging of composers to perform. The great pianist Arthur Schnabel said, "Mozart is too easy for children and too hard for artists."

The well-known smaller pieces are good places to start because they are entirely characteristic in style and quality. *Eine Kleine Nachtmusik* (A Little Night Music) presents four movements of distilled Mozartean charm, originally a serenade designed to accompany the

no major modulations to other keys. The themes may be more or less the same as in the exposition or may be varied somewhat. (Since the original second tonal group is now in the home key, the preceding second bridge often wanders a bit tonally, so that the tonic reenters with some sense of freshness.) By sticking largely to the home key, the recap functions as a resolution of the tonal tensions introduced with the first change of key in the exposition. Whether or not there is a coda, the end of the movement features a strong confirmation of the tonic key.

Here's a generalized summary of sonata form. For something fairly close to it in a familiar work, see if you can follow this pattern (with-

out introduction) in the first movement of Mozart's Symphony No. 40 in G minor.

—INTRODUCTION (optional).
—EXPOSITION.
 First tonal group (home key), bridge, second tonal group (related key), optional closing group. *Repeated.*
—DEVELOPMENT.
 (Variety of keys, thematic variation, sense of instability.)
—RECAPITULATION.
 First tonal group, second bridge, original second tonal group now in tonic. Everything relatively stable. (Up to about the time of Mozart, the development and recapitulation were repeated, though modern performances often

amusements of the aristocracy. The serene choral work *Ave Verum Corpus,* written near the end of his life, is among the most moving of his religious pieces. Equally fine is the Sinfonia Concertante in E-flat for violin, viola, and orchestra, a lyrical masterpiece from the Salzburg years.

The seventeen piano concertos written in Vienna as vehicles for himself stand at the peak of his instrumental music; at least a half dozen of them also mark the peak of the whole literature of solo concertos, with only Beethoven for company. From these I'll recommend two for starters, one bright and one dark. It used to be a commonplace that Mozart had a sunny C major approach to life and music. The Piano Concerto in C major K. 467 would seem to support that notion. (The K. numbers are taken from the definitive catalogue of Mozart's works, a chronological list compiled by Ludwig von

---

omit this repeat.) Big final cadence or—
—CODA (optional).
    Strong confirmation of the home key.

As we have seen, a movement in sonata form is as much a pattern of keys as of themes. The essential idea is a departure from the home key and, after a journey through closely related and then more distant keys, a final return to the home key in the recapitulation and a resolution of tonal tensions into the stable tonic key. (In many pieces, stable sections tend to be more homophonic, unstable sections more polyphonic.)

Now we can better see the underlying logic of sonata form as the Classical period shaped it, a sophisticated large-scale structure built up of interlocking units. Melodic phrases combine to form periods, periods build up into tonal groups, tonal groups build into large sections such as exposition and development, these large sections build up into the whole movement, and the individual movements build up to the whole piece. At every level, from the phrase to the whole piece, each building block tends to have a similar pattern of stability-instability-stability, rest-tension-rest (though never *complete* stability and rest until the end of the piece). As I note in the essay Consonance and Dissonance (p. 28), in this kind of structure the microcosm reflects the macrocosm.

This profound logic is the source of the power and preva-

Köchel in 1862.) This concerto indeed has the sunniest of outer movements. In the middle spreads one of the greatest of his slow movements, with a romantic languor that he never quite touched on again. Nowhere better than in this slow movement does Mozart show his unequalled gift for turning on a dime expressively, from pathos to pleasure, poignant question to richly satisfying answer. The movement was used to great effect in a romantic movie of the 1960s, and thus the whole piece is sometimes called the "Elvira Madigan" concerto.

Very different is the Concerto in D minor K. 466, which begins with a restless whisper that builds inexorably to shrill keening. This is the demonic side of Mozart, certainly more restrained than expressions of the demonic in later music, but electrifying for his time. The same applies to the maddened dance of the last movement. In

---

lence of what some scholars call the *sonata principle*. It is also the reason that this principle turned up again and again in all sorts of contexts beyond symphonies and sonatas. An aria or ensemble piece in a Mozart opera, for example, is often built in a sonatalike way, and so are many pieces called "overture."

The abstract logic and the flexibility of the sonata principle brought instrumental music to full maturity and independence in the Classical period, and insured its domination of the nineteenth century. Late in the century, the battle between "abstract music" and program music would be fought mainly between Brahmsian conservatives upholding the primacy of sonata form—and its tonal basis—and Wagnerian progress-

ives with looser, more literary concepts of form and more innovative ideas about harmony and tonality. By the twentieth century, the tonal system and its allied forms, especially sonata form, had been considerably bent and eroded (see essay Tonality and Atonality). Nonetheless, even Modernists such as Bartók and Stravinsky still found the old formal model stimulating; tone clusters and all, the first movement of Bartók's Fourth String Quartet still takes shape in sonata form.

If you're not quite sure what the genres called *symphony, sonata, string quartet,* and *concerto* amount to, refer to the Glossary (p. 539). From the time of Haydn well into the nineteenth century, most first movements of these genres were

between, the slow movement begins with deceptively gentle and bland gestures, but in the middle there is a startling surge of intensity. At the end of the concerto, like a curtain whisking aside, comes a sudden switch to D major, ending the piece with a burst of sunlight. This kind of turn to major, an old trick done a thousand times, Mozart makes seem like a revelation.

His voluminous output of chamber music shows the same mastery and variety as his piano concertos, building from the refined conventionality of the early work to the unique masterpieces of his last years. Of his string quartets I'll pick two of the six dedicated to Haydn—again, a light and a dark. D minor was one of his touchstone keys; time and again it brought out his most expressive side.

The D minor Quartet K. 421 is of almost Beethovenian pathos and

based on some variant of sonata form. What about the other movements?

Earlier in their careers, Haydn and Mozart tended to write three-movement symphonies in the general tempo plan fast-slow-fast. In their later symphonies they added the *minuet* as the third of four movements, making the rough pattern: fast, slow, medium fast, fast (sometimes the middle two are reversed, the minuet coming second). Their string quartets tended to have the same four movements. In sonatas for piano and for other instruments, Haydn and Mozart tended to write three movements: fast, slow, fast. Beethoven, who wrote four-movement symphonies, added a fourth movement to his sonatas as well, though he stuck to the three-

movement concerto plan. In his symphonies, quartets, and sonatas Beethoven also turned the courtly and elegant minuet into the lighter, faster *scherzo*.

Slow movements and finales are the most variable in form from piece to piece. One will find the occasional slow movement in sonata form, and often the finale as well. More common for the slow movement, however, are the models called *song form* and *theme and variations*.

The name song form reflects the often lyrical, songlike character of slow movements. It is also called *ternary*, from its simple ABA structure, the middle part contrasting in key and material. (Each letter—A, B, C etc.—in a formal diagram represents a theme or definable section of musical mate-

richness of texture in the first three movements; in contrast is the rather playful—though still minor-key—set of variations in the finale. From some startling harmonic effects in the beginning, the C major Quartet K. 465 is known as the "Dissonant"; after a serious first movement it builds to a dancelike finale, though none of it approaches the mythical Mozartean C major sunniness.

He is unusual among composers in that his string quintets are on the same level as his quartets. Part of the reason may be that Mozart liked to play viola in chamber music, so he was inspired by the richness of two violins, two violas, and cello. Best known of these are the genial and expansive C major Quintet K. 515 and the poignant G minor K. 516.

Though the assertion is getting redundant, I have to say again that Mozart's chamber music for winds marks the summit of another

rial.) The other common form for slow movements, theme and variations, might be diagrammed A A1 A2 A3, and so on; in all cases, a self-contained section called the *theme*—say, a small binary or ternary form—is followed by a series of variations on that theme. There is great variety as to what is being varied and how. Sometimes the composer preserves the harmony of the theme and writes new melodies around it; sometimes he decks out the original melody in new guises and ornaments; sometimes there are changes of meter or tempo, or changes from major to minor or the reverse. In all cases, there will be considerable variety of texture and effect from variation to variation. The game is to get maximum variety out of one piece of material. Haydn, a master

of the form, often starts with a plain and unpromising theme, then amazes us with the gold he extracts from it in the variations.

The *minuet* was originally a genteel dance and remained popular as such into the nineteenth century. Haydn and Mozart made it a regular feature of their four-movement symphonies and quartets, usually the third movement but sometimes the second. Minuets always have three beats to a measure, the tempo varies from stately to rather fast, and the tone is often courtly, though Haydn was noted for writing jokey and/or folksy minuets. The overall form is a large ABA, the middle part being the lighter *trio*. So sometimes the form is described as *minuet with trio*.

repertoire. Late in life he became enamored of the expressive sound of the clarinet, and the finest fruit of that is the Quintet in A K. 581, for clarinet and string quartet. His melodic eloquence is nowhere more penetrating than here; it has the grace of his earlier music, but the weight and depth of his last pieces. He was also one of the few composers before the twentieth century to write all-wind music at the top of his form. The best example of that is the Serenade in B-flat K. 361 for pairs of oboes, clarinets, basset horns (a sort of low clarinet), French horns, and bassoons. (A poetic slow movement from it was used in the film *Amadeus*.)

As a symphonist Mozart was often conventional; only six or so of his forty-one numbered symphonies are in the standard repertoire. (The same could be said of his piano sonatas.) But those six symphonies ascend to the heights of the genre. Of the earlier ones, try

---

Often the minuet section is also ABA, but in two parts—A / BA. Each of these sections is repeated; after the trio, these repeats are often omitted. The trio may have an A B A outline of its own. Are you sufficiently confused? A summary will help:

```
┌─ MINUET ─┐   ┌─ TRIO ─┐   ┌─ MINUET ─┐

     A            B            A
AA / BA BA // CC / DC DC // AA / BA BA//
```

When in the *Eroica* Beethoven replaced the minuet with the faster *scherzo*, he retained the three-beat meter (though it goes by much faster, making in effect one beat per measure triply divided) and the general formal plan of the minuet.

In the time of Haydn and Mozart the most common form for the last movement was the *rondo*, in which a recurring theme in the tonic key alternates with a series of contrasting episodes featuring other themes in other keys. A common rondo pattern is ABACADA, and so on—thus the name, because the main tune keeps coming around. Rondos are traditionally light and vivacious, with ironic or humorous effects. In finales one also finds a hybrid called *sonata-rondo*, which runs something like ABA/ C /ABA, with the first and last ABA resembling an exposition and recapitulation, respectively. In finales of nineteenth-century pieces the rondo was less common and there is considerable variety in approach; Beethoven's *Eroica* and Ninth Symphony, for example, have theme-and-variation finales,

two named works: the festive and nimble *Haffner* and the three-movement *Prague,* which seems to partake of the playfully wise tone of its near-contemporary *Figaro.*

That brings us to the sublime last three symphonies, nos. 39–41, written in those six weeks of 1788. No. 39 in E-flat has an almost Romantic richness of texture and expressiveness, the tone largely serious (though by no means solemn) until the spell is broken by the racing gaiety of the last movement. The Symphony no. 40 in G minor has perhaps never been bettered by any composer, including Mozart. It is another of his minor-key works that are soulful here, songlike there, at times demonic—especially the rocketing theme of the last movement. Throughout, one finds an astonishing economy of means and a seamless logic of unfolding. After the heaven-storming flights of Beethoven it has become harder to find the ex-

---

while others of his are in sonata form.

At this point, our abstractions of the structure of pieces break down and we are left with the particulars of each piece, which will have both elements of traditional formal models and unique aspects of its own. In any case, we must not confuse the form with the meaning. The point of Thoreau's sentence, "Most men lead lives of quiet desperation," is not that it has a subject and a verb; it is the succinct expression of a compelling idea. Similarly, the point of an exposition is not that it modulates from the tonic to the dominant; such a modulation is a commonplace of musical syntax. The meaning is in the particulars: the notes, the themes, the drama.

Here's a survey of the imaginary "typical" symphony, outlining the tempo, tone, and form of each movement. (String quartets, piano sonatas, etc., are similar in outline, but usually more intimate in effect.)

I. Medium to fast. Often "dramatic" or "heroic." *Sonata form.*

II. Slow. Often lyrical, songlike. *Song form* (ABA) or *theme and variations.*

III. Medium to fast minuet (18th century) or very fast scherzo (19th century). Dancelike. *Minuet-with-trio form.*

IV. Fast. Often light and vivacious (18th century) or epic-dramatic (19th century). *Rondo, sonata-rondo, sonata form, theme and variations, etc.*

pressive depth of a work like this. In a single movement Mozart can encompass a remarkable spectrum of contrast and variety; but unlike Beethoven, who always shows you how hard he's working, Mozart handles every turn of thought so effortlessly that one can easily miss how much is there.

The last symphony is not elegiac or valedictory but rather magisterial and somewhat impersonal; in reference to that tone, no. 41 has long been called the *Jupiter*. Its finale, a whirling tour de force of counterpoint, is perhaps the most striking of its four striking movements.

Finally we come to the operas. Once again, I believe, Mozart commands the summit of that repertoire too (though I would have to fight that out with partisans of Verdi and Wagner). *The Marriage of Figaro, Don Giovanni,* and *The Magic Flute* all show his unprecedented genius for physical and psychological characterization in music: in *Don Giovanni* we hear the comical gait of the manservant Leporello; in *Figaro* we find the slow burn of the Count's tantrums and the wise, resourceful, and erotic Susanna; and in all Mozart's stage works the orchestration—now limpid and sighing, now darting and dynamic—limns every nuance of the drama.

For all the variability in practice of these formal models, one should become conversant with their outlines for the simple reason that the composer expects you to follow the game. Haydn wants you to anticipate the recapitulation, for example, so he can play with your expectation (he loves false recaps). Beethoven wants you to be appropriately surprised when he adds an extra trio in the scherzo. Mozart wants you to enjoy how he coyly flirts with the final return of the rondo theme before he sneaks it up on you. Brahms wants you to understand how he's slipped into the recapitulation with a striking variation of the first theme. This shifting between expectation and surprise is part of the fun and fascination of classical music.

Though the above descriptions may sound formidably abstract and technical, remember that we already have a strong intuitive sense of musical form—just as we do the complexities of tonal harmony and of spoken language. Still, the more conscious we are of the various games composers are playing, the more we are drawn into the music. □

In *The Marriage of Figaro* servants fall in love, marry, and resist the depredations of the nobility, represented by the slimy Count Almaviva. Much of the work is very funny and very sexy, the music as brilliant as burnished silver. At the same time, the fun and games conceal a social drama of eternal relevance, a picture of those on the bottom of the totem pole fighting for dignity and freedom with the only weapons they possess, their wits.

If *Figaro* is burnished silver, *Don Giovanni* is old gold, its mixture of farce, brutality, and horror darker in tone. It is a comedy of eros, in which a murdering swine of irresistible charm seduces and corrupts everyone around him, including us, the beholders. By the time the ground opens and Don Giovanni is dragged unrepentant to hell, he takes some of our sympathies with him. Lust compromises all, and moral balance can be restored only by divine intervention—which, as Mozart and the rest of us know, never seems to happen in reality.

In *The Magic Flute* Sarastro has abducted Pamina from her mother, the Queen of the Night. Pamina is finally freed by her destined lover, Tamino, with the dubious aid of the clownish birdcatcher, Papageno (who finds his destined Papagena). After passing through trials of fire, Tamino ascends to the brotherhood of illuminated ones led by the godlike Sarastro, and the dark Queen's revolt against the light is suppressed.

Despite the hokum, in this work Mozart and Schikaneder stumbled on something more profound than perhaps either of them realized: a timeless parable of Love. We see the randy love of Papageno and Papagena, the exalted love of Tamino and Pamina, Sarastro's enlightened and divine love for all humanity. Surrounding and enfolding this spectacle is an uncanny magic, the magic of the flute and the boyish spirits that guide Tamino, and the magic of the composer's most radiant score.

Like all consummate artists, Mozart does not reveal his riches at once. So often he seems merely delightful; whole generations have expected little more of him. For many people, fiery Beethoven is the composer of their youth, when fire is sufficient. Often then, Mozart is the composer for age and experience, when indirection and restraint are understood and the rarity of work supremely well done is appreciated. At that point will always stand the sublime, elusive, incomparable Mozart.

Beethoven liked this 1818 drawing because it didn't tame his hair.

LUDWIG
VAN BEETHOVEN

Above the proscenium in Boston's Symphony Hall, one name rests in a marble medallion, presiding over the music like a resident demigod: Beethoven. In many concert halls around the world that design is repeated in one form or another. The reason for this single-minded iconography is that most of these halls were built in the late nineteenth century, when Beethoven was the unquestioned sovereign of composers, seeming to epitomize all music. Common opinion in this century has inherited that attitude.

Yet, in surveying the vast territory of music worldwide, how can anyone imagine that one composer could encompass all music? Is Beethoven really, once and for all, The Greatest Composer Who Ever Lived? Put so bluntly in our skeptical and pluralistic age, the answer is likely to be no. Bach and Mozart, at very least, would have equal claim to the crown of Western music.

There is another problem with Beethoven's traditional domination of music: it makes him very hard to hear with fresh ears, to approach at all. The West seems to be wary of great men. Many of us would rather worship athletes and actors than world-shaking heroes; the latter tend to scare us a little and bore us a lot. And it's oppressive, trying to come to terms with music that emanates from a demigod emblazoned in marble medallions flying above orchestras.

To approach Beethoven, let's forget the demigod and attempt to see the man: working at his desk, roaming streets and forests muttering and singing to himself, raging at his physical torments, too battered and too eccentric to make normal human connections. He was very good at his trade because he was born with the gift and worked at it as hard as one can work. The worst thing that can happen to a composer happened to him—losing his hearing—yet he chose not to die but to endure and keep on writing, and his music grew steadily broader and deeper until the end.

Ludwig van Beethoven was born in Bonn, Germany, on December

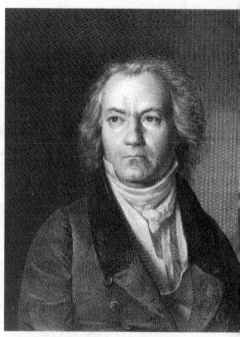

16 or 17, 1770. The town was a provincial center, with a prince and his court and a university. Ludwig's father, Johann, held a minor singing post at court; his mother, Maria, was the daughter of a court cook.

They were an unfortunate family. Johann drank and raged, filling Ludwig's childhood with humiliating scenes. Neighbors said of Maria Beethoven that no one ever saw her smile. She defended Ludwig against the abuses of his father, and the composer would honor her memory throughout his life, even as he tried to erase the memory of Johann. (For years he would encourage the rumor that he was the illegitimate son of a nobleman.)

When Ludwig revealed musical talent at an early age, Johann decided to exploit him, to create a child prodigy à la Mozart. In that spirit began Ludwig's brutal training in music, his father trying to

*As with his music, Beethoven's face inspired
a variety of responses. From left, the promising youth,
the strong-willed master, the Romantic demigod,
and finally the reality: a life mask at age forty-two.*

whip genius into him, locking him in rooms for hours to practice harpsichord and violin. Ludwig first appeared as a performer before the public at age six (Johann billed him as four), but made no great impression. Somehow, though, the child did not respond to this cruelty by hating music; instead, he seized on music as his salvation. And though he never would possess Mozart's miraculous facility, his teacher, court organist C. G. Neefe, realized that Ludwig was an enormous talent. Neefe kept the boy playing the preludes and fugues of J. S. Bach and supervised the first publication of his compositions in 1783.

By his mid teens Ludwig was Neefe's assistant and a professional in the musical life of Bonn. One could get good experience there, but to make a career as soloist and composer one had to conquer Vienna, the capital of Austria and the musical capital of Europe. In

1787 Ludwig made a trip to Vienna and played for an enthusiastic Mozart, but he was soon called home to find his mother dying. From then on, Ludwig would be the support of his father and two brothers, as Johann sank further into drink and despair.

Beethoven's talents, especially his extraordinary improvisations, became known around Bonn. The local aristocracy began to take him into their homes, hiring him to teach keyboard to their children. Beethoven formed lifelong friendships with some of these powerful and sophisticated figures, and they did much for him, gaining him entry into aristocratic circles and educating the barely schooled young man in literature and poetry. He became a fervent reader of Shakespeare and the Greek and Roman classics, as well as contemporaries such as Goethe and Schiller. At the same time, he absorbed the revolutionary democratic spirit that had spread across Europe from the French Revolution. His aristocratic friends never took the rough edges off Beethoven, but they encouraged him and fueled his spirit and intellect.

His great opportunity came in 1792: Joseph Haydn visited Bonn, was impressed with Beethoven's compositions, and invited the young man to study with him in Vienna. As Beethoven left home, his friend Count Waldstein gave him a letter with the grand peroration, "Receive the spirit of Mozart from the hands of Haydn." (Mozart had died in Vienna the year before.)

In the long run Beethoven did absorb the incomparable Viennese tradition, and then revolutionized it. But at first, things didn't work out that way. The Beethoven ego was already fully developed and he did not submit mildly to criticism. Haydn proved to be a desultory teacher and was exasperated by his brash pupil, whom the old master sardonically dubbed "The Great Mogul." For his part, Beethoven began seeing other teachers secretly; he studied Italian vocal composition with Mozart's supposed nemesis Salieri and counterpoint with the pedantic Albrechtsberger, who after a year gloomily prophesied, "He has learned nothing and will never do anything properly."

Friends from Bonn helped Beethoven bypass dozens of virtuoso competitors into the grand salons of Vienna; soon he was lionized by the cream of European nobility. From 1794 to 1796 he lived in the palace of Prince and Princess Lichnowsky, who treated him like a son. As at Bonn, aristocrats sent him their children for piano lessons. His radical sympathies did not deter him from accepting manna from the wealthy, nor did his politics—and sometimes boorish behavior—seem to bother his patrons.

At that point he was still most prized for his improvisations, in which he displayed a reckless emotionalism like nothing heard before. Wrote one witness, "His playing tore along like a wildly foaming cataract, and the conjurer constrained his instrument to an utterance so forceful that the stoutest structure was scarcely able to withstand it; and anon he sank down, exhausted, exhaling gentle plaints, dissolving into melancholy." Maturity as a composer would come when he began to contain that kind of expressive fire with a Classical sense of logic. The compositions of his first period most often reflect the decorous side of Haydn and Mozart, works such as the charming Septet op. 20, the first two piano concertos, and the First Symphony of 1800. Early on, though, there were flashes of the coming revolutionary in pieces like the C minor Piano Trio op. 1 no.3. The *Pathétique* Sonata, which appeared in 1799, is one of the first works in which he spoke with his full dramatic intensity.

Within a few years in Vienna, Beethoven had established himself as a keyboard virtuoso the equal of any in Europe, and a promising, if sometimes perplexing, composer. Yet around 1800 he declared that he was not satisfied with anything he had done: "I am now making a fresh start," he said. That start was marked in 1804 with one of the transforming works in musical history, his Symphony no. 3, titled *Eroica*, which began his second period of creativity.

The Third Symphony had a long background. For years Beethoven had embraced the democratic ideals of the French Revolution and was determined to attach his own work to that cause. This determination reverberates through his mature work in many ways, but the *Eroica* was specifically related during its composition to Napoleon Bonaparte. In the French conqueror Beethoven saw an enlightened liberator of the European masses, the kind of figure he himself wanted to be in music. So the original title of the Third Symphony was *Bonaparte*.

The story of the rejection of that title has been told many times: how Beethoven's pupil Ries arrived one day with the news that Napoleon had proclaimed himself emperor and Beethoven cried in fury, "Then he's nothing but an ordinary man! Now he'll trample on all the rights of men to serve his own ambition!" On the title page of the original manuscript one can still see Napoleon's name roughly struck out, replaced by *Sinfonia Eroica* (Heroic Symphony).

As was intended, the work had an impact on music like that of Napoleon on Europe—nothing was the same again. Beethoven took the Classical symphonic form of Haydn and Mozart and expanded its proportions, filling the larger space with more contrast, more themes, and a much expanded and dramatized development section. He built up the size and weight of the last movement; where the finales of Haydn and Mozart tend to be light and fleeting, the characteristic Beethoven finale is the counterpart in weight and intensity to the first movement, so that the symphony hangs between the two pillars of the outer movements. To compensate, he lightened the third movement, substituting for the traditional minuet the nimble scherzo. (As we saw, he was following Haydn's lead in the latter.)

Most of all, he now sought material more expressively charged than ever before. If the emotion in Mozart seems shrouded behind an elegant mask, and in Haydn behind his equanimity, the emotion in Beethoven is raw and face-to-face. In the myriad themes and towering climaxes of the *Eroica* one hears Beethoven the man, with all his elemental force and mercurial changes of mood. With him music became for the first time a revelation of individual personality—and therefore a revolution of musical democracy. Its main audience would prove to be the growing middle-class concertgoing public of the nineteenth century, an audience that had been nurtured by the Enlightenment spirit. Romantic composers like Schubert and Berlioz would seize this new expressiveness and take it to further lengths, to the brink of madness. Yet Beethoven *was* the true heir of Haydn and Mozart, the master of Classical form as they shaped it. Dionysus bridled by Apollo: no one before or since has accomplished such a merging of wildness and control.

Before he began to transform the musical world, Beethoven was already fated to a lifetime of suffering. He had always been robust of figure but weak in health. Around the turn of the century he realized with horror that he was losing his hearing. A deaf composer—it was impossible, absurd, unendurable.

On an 1802 vacation to the resort at Heiligenstadt he unburdened himself in a letter to his brothers that he never mailed but kept with him for the rest of his life. It has become known as the Heiligenstadt Testament. In it he writes that he wanted to die, but, "Only Art, only art held me back, ah it seemed impossible to me that I should leave the world before I had produced all that I felt I might, and so I spared this wretched life." He ends with almost incoherent sobs, "O Providence—grant me one pure day of *Joy*—the inner reverberation of true Joy has so long been a stranger to me—O when—O when O Deity—may I feel it once more in the Temple of Nature and Mankind—Never?—O it would be too hard."

He had to endure not only deafness but also a gauntlet of humiliating and debilitating diseases, painful intestinal troubles that led to chronic diarrhea, and eventually enlargement of the pancreas, cirrhosis of the liver, deterioration of bones in his skull, incessant lesser ailments. For years it was assumed that he had syphilis, as millions did in those days; recent science has speculated that he had a form of lupus.

Choosing life over death that summer at Heiligenstadt, he willed his own resurrection. At exactly that point he launched into the *Eroica* and the extraordinary music of the second period, which has been called his "heroic" period.

During that time he wrote, "I shall seize Fate by the throat; most assuredly it shall not get me wholly down." His art became the means of seizing fate. In his work he would rise above suffering and achieve triumph, and finally even joy. With that he made himself into the kind of figure that dominated the imagination of the nineteenth century, embodied in Nietzsche's superman and conquerors like Napoleon and Bismarck. The superhuman genius, the crown of the species, the revolutionary hero, the master of his own fate and transformer of the world: these are the qualities that made Beethoven the artistic hero of the century, the model for Berlioz and Wagner, the great icon in the mythology of Romanticism.

After the *Eroica*, Beethoven's progress over the next decade was one of steadily ascending expressive breadth and productivity, with a commensurate fame that spread around the world. Not that everyone approved of his innovations, and not that Vienna was particularly kind to him; the city had a way of giving the back of its hand to its great ones, as witness Mozart. In 1809 Beethoven even considered leaving Vienna for a proffered post at the Westphalian court of Jerome Bonaparte, but his wealthy friends established an annuity to keep him in town (it soon petered out, however). The climax of his public acclaim came at the Congress of Vienna in 1814, called to restore the power of the aristocracies after the Napoleonic Wars. There princes and kings paid court to Beethoven and he presented a concert with the premieres of two potboilers, *Wellington's Victory* and the cantata *Glorious Moment*, and also the wildly acclaimed Seventh Symphony (acclaimed for a change—most of his symphonies were initially received with bemusement).

Many observers sketched the Beethoven of those days in words and pictures. He was short (five feet four inches, the same as Napoleon), broad of chest and shoulder, dark hair thick and wild, his face unlovely, ruddy and scarred from childhood smallpox, his jaws blunt and powerful. To the Viennese his provincial accent sounded uncouth. First, though, one saw the eyes, glowing in repose, flashing in bursts of excitement. In those transports his whole face erupted into throbbing energy, and he could rave like Lear. He had a charming smile and was capable of grace and warmth in society, but that was marred by a grating horselaugh. He laughed like a man unaccustomed to it.

He lived in squalor, a terror to housekeepers. Often as he wandered the streets, humming and mumbling to himself, children would take him for a tramp and heckle him. With intimates he was often generous, emptying his pockets for them. At other times he could be cruel and arrogant; there are many letters in which he apologizes for his temper. When jovial in company—"unbuttoned," he called it—his humor was rough and boyish. Usually he looked sad; in his last years his face was so sickly yellow and lacerated with suffering that his friends could hardly bear to look at him. Time and again, though, when these things were observed by those who knew him, they would add that his nobility of mind and spirit shone through all the disorder of his life.

His sketches and manuscripts tell the same story. Nothing came easily to him, least of all composing. Where Mozart could dream up a whole piece in his head while playing billiards, Beethoven had to worry and whip every note into place in his sketches. The sketchbooks are amazing documents: gold being refined from raw ore, pedestrian ideas becoming revolutionary concepts, incoherence being forged into clarity and purposefulness. Even the final manuscripts are a morass of scrawls and blots and revisions on top of revisions. As he composed he sang and bellowed and cursed and pounded his fists as if he were tortured by all the demons of his own imperfections.

Often passionately in love, he was always disappointed. Among his lovers were daughters of princely houses and peasants. He proposed to several; but who would marry such an untamable man, so homely, so riddled with illness? Sometimes it was his own impossible standards that ended a romance. However much he longed for a soulmate, none appeared. There remains a letter to a mysterious "Immortal Beloved," residue from another perfervid and doomed passion.

His hearing did not vanish at once but came and went over many years. He last performed as a pianist in 1814, when it was sadly apparent that he could not always hear what he played. Over the years he accumulated a collection of ear trumpets in various designs; sometimes when composing he would hold a pencil in his teeth and touch it to the piano strings, to feel the vibration. After 1819 all conversation with him had to be written down. As his hearing worsened he became steadily more morose, suspicious, eccentric, drifting into a silent, solitary world.

That is the paradox of Beethoven, which astonished his contemporaries and those who have come to know him since: how a life so chaotic and torn could contain a spirit so magnificent and whole.

After 1814 everything seemed to go sour at once. His health further deteriorated and money worries harried him (apparently without reason, since his work sold well). Many of his wealthy friends and patrons left town, died, went broke, or were driven away by his tantrums. Weary of his profundities, the Viennese public turned to the sweeter pleasures of Rossini's operas. Beethoven also began to grope toward a new artistic direction, racking his imagination for fresh insights and possibilities in music. Perhaps most damaging of all was the relationship with his nephew that began in 1815, another great woe, this time self-inflicted.

His brother Karl had died that year, leaving a son of the same name. The aging, lonely composer conceived an obsession for the child and went to court to become his guardian, in the process grossly maligning the boy's mother. He took young Karl to his bosom with devastating consequences for both. Alternately he smothered Karl with affection and then forgot about him, sometimes leaving the boy for days without money for food. Karl, with no unusual intelligence or strength of character to begin with, drifted in a bewildering limbo, failed in his studies, took to drink and bad company. His famous uncle seemed to Karl a meddling old fool. In 1826, after a decade of constant friction, the desperate youth tried to commit suicide but failed even in that, managing with two shots only to wound himself. Beethoven responded with hysteria, but the attempt precipitated Karl's joining the army, to the relief of both.

Along with everything else, the struggles with Karl drained Beethoven's energy and creativity through much of the teens. His output was reduced to a trickle of works like the enigmatic *Hammerklavier* Sonata of 1819. The musical world concluded that the master had gone crazy or dried up. But for the second time, Beethoven turned his isolation and anguish into the means of his rebirth.

Imprisoned in the soundless world of his last decade, he found within himself the spiritual and technical resources to expand his work still further. As he transcended his own tragedies, his music seemed to transcend the limitations of music. In the 1820s new pieces poured from him in a rush. His last string quartets and piano sonatas are the purest expression of his third period, an apparently effortless freedom, the music seeming to float from idea to idea, beauty to beauty, but with the same inevitability as his earlier music. The tone is at times unearthly, at other times childlike, like the little march that breaks into the seriousness of the late A minor String Quartet op. 132. Also in the last works he pursued an obsession with counterpoint, perhaps sparked by his childhood study of Bach; he created the massive Handel-like fugues of the *Missa Solemnis* and the nearly berserk polyphony of the *Grosse Fuge* for string quartet. In the last pieces he seems more than ever to grip each listener person to person, saying something of tremendous import, however indefinable that import.

His third period was the final flowering of what he had learned in a lifetime of mastery in the Classical instrumental forms developed

Beethoven's cluttered study in a drawing made soon after he died in 1827.

by Haydn and Mozart. Beethoven had that most profound of musical abilities: he could make every note, every phrase, every period lead inevitably to the next and the next, ultimately forming a unified experience, a little world for the beholder to live in. A piece that may have taken years to write seems to give birth to itself as it goes, like an improvisation. This ability to shape large-scale musical forms is among the rarest gifts in the world. As evidence, consider that of the tens of thousands of Western composers in the last five centuries, only about a dozen have had such command of long stretches. Haydn and Mozart had the gift, Bach, a few others now and then. Many superb composers, among them Schubert and Schumann, never quite mastered large-scale musical architecture.

The piece that announces the third creative period also symbolizes Beethoven's personal and spiritual triumph. After a life of extravagant sorrow, the aged composer realized a long-held dream of writing a hymn to Joy, the joy that in the Heiligenstadt Testament of 1802 he felt was forever lost to him. The work is the Ninth Symphony, completed in 1823, its last movement a choral setting of Schiller's "Ode to Joy." For all its flaws (it is uncharacteristically rambling), the finale of the Ninth is a moving embodiment of the composer's final triumph, his reclaiming of joy. Perhaps the poem was on his mind when he wrote the ecstatic declaration, "I am the Bacchus who presses out the glorious wine for mankind. Whoever truly understands my music is freed thereby from the miseries that others carry about in them."

The end came amidst work and plans. Beethoven's friends had noticed in him a new lightness of spirit, perhaps a twilight sense of having got through it all and done his work well. A tenth symphony was in sketches. He had taken Karl on a visit to brother Johann in Gniexendorf, where he wrote the buoyant F major String Quartet op. 135. On the way home in December 1826 he hitched a ride in an open milkwagon in damp weather, and caught a chill. From there his strength declined as he lay in bed week after week talking hopefully of the future. Finally he fell into a coma, watched over by friends.

Nothing could be more aptly Beethovenian than his last moments, on March 26, 1827 (at least, as witnesses described them). It had been storming all day while he lay unconscious. Suddenly there was a flash of lightning and a tremendous peal of thunder. Beethoven sat upright, shook his fist angrily at the sky, and fell back dead.

Ten thousand people came from all over Europe to Vienna for the funeral. Among the torchbearers was Franz Schubert. There, symbolically, the torch of the unparalleled Viennese tradition was passed on.

People of Beethoven's stature remain alive in history and must remain; we need people like him to remind us of what, once in a while, humanity is capable. Most of all, of course, we need his music. But to stay alive, such figures and their works must be malleable, must serve different needs at different times. Those who can't transcend their times are not for all time.

It seems we have lost faith in what Beethoven represented to the Romantics—the world-shaking hero. Maybe that's just as well. Too many would-be world-shakers have failed, too many have betrayed us, for us to trust them. Perhaps the Beethoven we need now is the single, suffering and imperfect and triumphant man, the master of his particular fate, face to face with the single listener. The individual hero and no more, but immense all the same.

Where does one start to know Beethoven's music? Where does one start to know an ocean? From the cliffs of California? The beach at Rio? On a ship at sea? All equally possible, all inadequate. So we may as well plunge into the symphonies.

His Symphony no. 5 may be the most popular orchestral work ever written; for many concertgoers it is *the* classical symphony. It's not hard to see why. The Fifth is one of the most electrifying works in the repertoire: the first movement a rhythmic tour de force of white-hot intensity based on a single four-note figure; a second movement of exquisite lyrical grace; a third-movement scherzo that is grand rather than playful; and a glorious march of a finale, with a triumphant coda.

Unfortunately, familiarity has robbed the Fifth of its originality. Far from the archetype of the classical symphony, it is actually eccentric at every turn. The famous *dot-dot-dot-dash* motive of the first movement is strangely short for a symphonic subject, and many originally took it for a joke. The second movement contains one of the most sustained lyric melodies in the literature. The scherzo merges into the finale in an unprecedented way and pops up again in the middle of the finale. Moreover, the rhythmic intensity of the first movement has long been superseded in works such as Stravinsky's *Sacre du printemps*. The expressive and rhythmic ante has been upped considerably since the days when audiences were left gasping for breath by the opening movement.

In any case, the Fifth remains unique and indispensable. We don't have to swallow the old fable of the opening tattoo representing "Fate knocking at the door" to see the work as a symbolic struggle with fate, a struggle that Beethoven enacted in many works, in his music as a whole, and in his life: "I shall seize Fate by the throat."

The Sixth Symphony, called *Pastoral*, is a program piece in an old tradition of such pieces and prime inspiration for later Romantic program symphonies. It evokes the countryside to which Beethoven returned every summer for rest and inspiration. Within the music the fields lie sweet and calm, peasants dance, a thunderstorm breaks out, and so on.

The Seventh has variously been called another pastoral symphony and ''the apotheosis of the dance.'' Certainly the outer movements are dancelike, with an obsessive rhythmic momentum. These are not genteel French dances but heavy-footed, beer-drinking German dances, full of skirling strings and lusty horns. The grave slow dance of the second movement, with its mounting and sighing melodies, is one of the most beautiful in the repertoire.

The Ninth Symphony, called *Choral,* ends with the setting of Schiller's ''Ode to Joy'' for soloists and chorus, as mentioned above. The first three movements are strongly individual, each powerful, as

Beethoven's idea of a fair copy: the Kyrie *from the* Missa Solemnis.

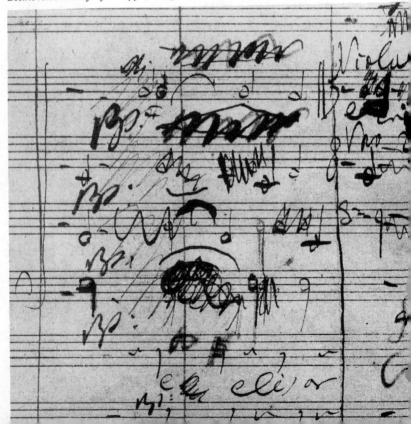

if all Beethoven's previous ideas were inflated to gigantic scale. Later composers would shamelessly steal, but none equal, the opening of this symphony, which seems to emerge from inchoate mist into colossal proclamations. The usual order of symphonic middle movements reversed, next comes the scherzo, this one whirling and pounding, with explosions from the timpani and an ingenuous peasant dance in the middle. The slow movement is third-period Beethoven at his most spiritual, a serene expanse in which almost nothing happens, except that two alternating melodies spin themselves into diaphanous variations of uncanny loveliness.

Then the finale, the first of its kind to use a chorus. A discordant eruption of sound and fury, a recollection of the earlier movements, and then a melody as simple as a drinking song, on which Beethoven builds a series of variations that range from the sublime—like

the soaring double fugue with ecstatic shouts of "Joy! Joy!"—to the near ridiculousness of a town-band military march. It may be that with the finale's simple tune, one that any child can hum and perhaps half the world knows, Beethoven was embodying his vision of democracy by reaching out to the whole of humanity: "Oh, ye millions," runs the telling line, "I embrace thee."

At the Vienna premiere of the Ninth Symphony in May 1824 (along with parts of the *Missa Solemnis*), stone-deaf Beethoven stood in front of the conductor setting the tempos for each movement. When the finale ended and a storm of applause broke out, the composer was still facing the players and marking time. One of the soloists had to turn him around to see the acclaim, which mounted louder and louder in a futile attempt to break through to him. It may have been the most glorious moment of Beethoven's career. Locked in his silence, he seemed hardly to understand or acknowledge it.

His Symphony no. 3, the *Eroica*, may be the greatest of the nine— at least its composer thought so. The first movement spins out multiple contrasting themes into an indefatigable outpouring of dramatic intensity. As second movement, a somber and striking funeral march. Third comes the first true Beethovenian scherzo, with chirping winds and a rustic trio of hunting horns. The finale's stately variations conclude with military fanfares in the brasses.

Beethoven's concertos—five for piano and one for violin—show a progression similar to that of his other series, beginning with decorous Classical outings and ending with prophetic masterpieces that would set the agenda for the Romantic period. Perhaps the finest of his works for soloist and orchestra is the Piano Concerto no. 4 in G major of 1809. Here he is at the furthest remove from showy virtuosity; instead, a searching and dramatic relationship unfolds between piano and orchestra. Rather than the usual extended orchestral introduction, this concerto begins with a few meditative measures for the piano that set the introverted tone of the work. The second movement seems to be a tentative and troubled dialogue between soloist and instruments. Finally in the last movement the tone shifts to bright and vivacious, building from one delight to the next. Though the following century would see many successful concertos, to find the equal of the Fourth Concerto one would have to look backward to Mozart.

Beethoven's sixteen string quartets span his creative life, a musical and spiritual journey of unprecedented magnitude. For a start, try the middle-period group of three, op. 59, called the Rasoumovsky Quartets after the dedicatee, one of the composer's princely benefactors. The first, in F, is known as the *Cello* Quartet because the opening features that instrument; the second, in E minor, has one of Beethoven's most affecting slow movements; the dramatic third quartet, in C, has been dubbed the *Hero.*

As noted above, it is in the five late string quartets, along with the last three piano sonatas, that we find the third period at its purest. One might start with the A minor Quartet op. 132. After an expansive first movement loaded with contrasts, the second-movement scherzo is an unassuming little tune that keeps getting stuck like a broken record, but which in its minimalistic course turns up delightful quirks. From there arises one of those exalted late slow movements, written as Beethoven emerged from another illness and headed, "A convalescent's holy song of thanks to the Divinity." From that point, except for a sprightly march, the quartet rarely leaves that tone of unearthly beauty, of a kind attained by no other composer.

Then one is perhaps ready for the similar mysteries and beauties and quirks of the other late quartets, opp. 127, 130, 131, 135. Along with these, take in the similar world of the last piano sonatas opp. 109–111. For a tour of the earlier and more bravura piano sonatas, try the named ones—the rhapsodic *Moonlight,* the *Pathétique,* and the stormy *Waldstein* and *Appassionata.*

There is so much more—an ocean. There is the *Missa Solemnis,* for example, which Beethoven regarded as the crown of his music. *Fidelio,* his flawed but still intensely moving opera, another hymn to freedom. The piano trios, such as the elegantly lyrical *Archduke.* The Fourth Symphony: among the lighter ones in tone, but maybe the most consistently inspired of the nine.

Don't be surprised if his works do not immediately reveal their depths. Beethoven unveils his elemental strength over time, the music growing with one's own spirit and understanding. He becomes part of one's joys and tragedies, attaches himself to them; because he was one of us, he was there, he knew and captured it all. One's journey through his work is the same as the journey of life, at its highest and wisest and most passionate.

THE
ROMANTIC
PERIOD

Richard Wagner,
in a fanciful rendering,
dreams up the Ring.

THE ROMANTIC PERIOD
(1825–1900)

Around 1844, French composer Hector Berlioz described his response to some works of music: "I feel a delicious pleasure in which the reasoning faculty has no share . . . emotion, increasing proportionately with the energy and loftiness of the composer's inspiration, soon produces a strange commotion in my circulation; my arteries throb violently; tears . . . often only indicate an advancing condition that is far from having reached its peak. In such cases, there are spasmodic muscular contractions, a trembling of all the limbs, a *total numbness of feet and hands,* a partial paralysis of the optical and auditory nerves; I cannot see, I barely hear; vertigo . . . a half swoon . . ."

In the same century philosopher Friedrich Nietzsche declared that the two eternal poles of art are the cool Apollonian and the ecstatic Dionysian. Clearly, Berlioz and his Romantic contemporaries were on the side of ecstasy. Whereas Mozart and Haydn wanted the listener to feel pleasure, wanted to inspire, uplift, even edify, now composers wanted to melt the heart, reduce to tears, astound, overwhelm, set hair on end.

The eighteenth century exalted ancient Greece and created placid neoclassic architecture and geometric gardens. The nineteenth exalted the medieval Gothic and preferred its castles in ruins overtaken by nature. The designation Romantic comes from the medieval *romance,* the kind of fanciful knights-and-ladies tale satirized in *Don Quixote.* Where the Enlightenment stressed reason and disinterested discourse, the Romantics loved legends, folk songs, the fantastic, irrational, and idiosyncratic. It was the time of Edgar Allan Poe, the eerie last songs of Schubert, the great collections of fairy tales and folk poetry, the exotic violence of Delacroix.

Previously I have described musical periods as being internally consistent; Gluck, Haydn, Mozart, and early Beethoven inhabit the same general aesthetic world. With the nineteenth century we enter an era that is all individual voices, each artist a law unto himself whether he is producing ingenuous little songs like Schubert's or operatic epics like Wagner's. Now begins the cult of the Genius. Romantic artists inflated their own image to that of demigods, half demons and half priests in a new religion of the subjective, the sublime, the magnificent and terrible. The presiding deity was Beethoven, dominating music as Napoleon and Bismarck dominated the battlefield. Music—elusive, boundless in suggestion, seeming to be pure emotion—was everywhere called the most Romantic of the arts. Walter Pater declared that all the arts aspire to the condition of music. And the essence of Romanticism, he wrote, is "the addition of strangeness to beauty."

The era saw the results of the previous century's democratic revolutions in the final triumph of the middle class in Europe and America, a culture based on capitalistic industry and commerce. Technology expanded into the full-blown Industrial Revolution; its fruits were railroads, steamboats, photography, steel, the telephone and telegraph, the practical uses of electricity. More sophisticated weaponry made the wars of the period—the Crimean, Franco-Prussian, and the American Civil War—more murderous than any before.

Increasingly through the century, the self-absorption and self-inflation of artists pulled them away from the mainstream of middle-class life; and just as well, said the artists, drawing around themselves a mantle of contempt for the commercial and popular. Words such as *philistine* and *bourgeois* on one side, *bohemian* and *decadent* on the other, became weapons in ideological battles. (They are still being fought, but both words and combatants seem increasingly battleworn.) Often disappointed in the present, artists for the first time believed that their day lay in the future: "My time is yet to come," prophesied Gustav Mahler, and it did.

Later in the century came the climax of its visual arts, with such figures as Manet, Degas, Renoir, and Whistler. Important philosophers included the Germans Schopenhauer, Nietzsche, and Hegel. Writing in German were the poet Heine with his heartbroken ironies, Hoffmann the fantasist, and Goethe, who seemed to embrace

A. COT. 1880

both Classic and Romantic in his gigantic reach. In his sculpture of the French novelist Balzac, Rodin created the definitive icon of the Romantic artist-hero: the writer looms erect as if at the edge of a precipice, wrapped in a robe that gives his whole form the blunt thrust of a phallus, his face at once magnificent, all-seeing, and racked with suffering.

In England, poets such as Wordsworth, Shelley, and Coleridge felt themselves part of a vanguard roaming in time, space, and the secret recesses of human consciousness. Awakening from an opium dream, Coleridge wrote his hallucinatory fragment of exotica, ''Kubla Khan'': ''In Xanadu did Kubla Khan/A stately pleasure-dome decree:/Where Alph, the sacred river, ran/Through caverns measureless to man/Down to a sunless sea.'' Sir Walter Scott spun fantasies of the age of chivalry and romance. Only later in the century did a strain of realism—elaborately furnished realism—turn up with writers such as Dickens and Hardy in England and Flaubert in France. In America, Emerson absorbed the German philosophers and their Eastern influences and turned them into a uniquely American philosophy called Transcendentalism, which exalted the visionary, self-reliant individual. Then came Thoreau, Hawthorne, Melville, and Whitman variously examining the exotic, mystical, and sublime with attitudes ranging from Whitman's self-described ''barbaric yawp'' to Hawthorne's haunted neo-Puritanism. Mark Twain served as skeptical jester for a time obsessed with the Ideal.

What held together all these visions, all this delirium and fragmentation? To some extent, tradition and history functioned as brakes. We see the effect of tradition clearly in music. Every composer must set himself off from the past, but he is still tempered and judged by the standards of the past. The standard by which young Beethoven was judged was that of Handel, Haydn, and Mozart. (Later, a composer is judged by his younger self; late Beethoven was reproached for not being early Beethoven.) Likewise, eras define themselves in contrast to the past while inevitably carrying on, in new dress, the traditions of the past.

At the same time as the Romantic era declared itself a revolution

In a seemingly ingenuous mix of Eros and Bathos, Pierre Auguste Cot distilled the Romantic impulse in The Storm, *painted in 1880.*

in expressiveness, it also saw an immense expansion of scholarly music history. It was the first period systematically to study and preserve the music of the past; thus Mendelssohn revived Bach's *St. Matthew Passion* and Brahms studied Scarlatti and Monteverdi. Whereas previous eras had wanted to hear the newest music and little else, now began the idea of "classical music" as, to a large extent, a museum. The effect on composers could be both enriching and debilitating. While the masterpieces of the past stood as monuments and exemplars, their steady accumulation weighed oppressively: "Who can do anything after Beethoven?" Schubert groaned; Brahms, writing his first symphony, spoke anxiously of the "tramp of giants" behind him. Never had composers been so aware of history and so self-conscious about their place in it. The Romantic period was the first artistic era to name itself.

The scholarly codification of forms, especially sonata form, added to the burden. The modern textbook definition of that form is an abstraction of Classical practice developed by nineteenth-century musicologists (see Sonata Form, p. 160). Often composers dutifully submitted to that abstraction at the same time as they struggled against its constraints. Among the results was that while the symphony reigned as the unquestioned king of musical forms, the Romantic period was, with some notable exceptions, not a great one for symphonies. New instrumental genres more congenial to the Romantic temperament were looser, more poetic and evocative, less burdened by tradition: dance-based pieces like the waltz, mazurka, polonaise; quasi-improvisatory piano works with names like fantasy, nocturne, impromptu, song without words; small, almost fragmentary pieces like Chopin's preludes (preludes to nothing) or the concert overture for orchestra (an overture to nothing). Orchestral music allied itself to literature, rationalizing its increasingly improvisatory forms with reference to ideas and stories, as did Liszt's tone poem *Les Préludes* and Berlioz's *Symphonie fantastique,* the latter based on a program of an artist's opium dreams. (The bizarre and sometimes terrifying visions produced by opium, the era's drug of choice, broadly influenced Romantic style and imagery.) The art song, formerly a minor genre, became one of the most important and characteristic embodiments of the Romantic spirit.

Many corollaries flowed from this situation. As the composer became a prophet and hero, his notes sacred text, improvisation and ornamentation declined, replaced by the performer's subjective interpretation of the score. Counterpoint and especially the old contrapuntal forms—fugue, canon, and so on—nearly disappeared except as academic exercises. More than ever before, the main focus of music was on melody. Romantic themes, both vocal and instrumental, tend to be lyrical and expressive, not with Classical-style dancelike rhythms and phrasing, but rather with the wandering rhythm of wandering feelings. An extended singing melody was its own justification; but because of that, sonata-form development sections often seem mechanical or perfunctory: the tunes resist development, sounding best in their original form.

In a way, much Romantic music is Beethovenian expressiveness and scope carried several notches further, but without the compensating discipline of his Classical foundation. Following Beethoven's lead, composers looked for still more color and emotion by means of heightened dissonance and chromaticism. From Schubert on, mainline Romantic music is characterized by a state of restless modulation from key to key, and sometimes stays suspended between keys, an analogy to the yearning, searching spirit of the age. The size of orchestral works expanded and the orchestra expanded along with them: from the typical Classical ensemble of thirty to forty musicians, the Romantic orchestra grew toward one hundred and beyond, and symphonies crept toward an hour in length. Berlioz dreamed of orchestras of thousands; Mahler approached that in his "Symphony of a Thousand." Technology contributed its part with key mechanisms that made woodwinds more efficient and valves that made brass instruments finally able to play all the notes. Many present-day major orchestras (such as the Vienna Philharmonic and the Boston Symphony) were founded during the nineteenth century. New conservatories trained musicians to the unprecedented level of skill that composers were now demanding.

The Classical period had evolved genres and forms—sonata, opera, etc.—and an attendant tonal system as concise, lucid, and objective structures. During the nineteenth century all these became increasingly fluid, subjective, and inflated. By the end of the century the old forms and tonality were beginning to unravel entirely.

While composers scorned the bourgeoisie around them, they nonetheless depended on the middle class for their audience and livelihood. In the Romantic era, no middle-class parlor was complete without a piano on which to play Beethoven or Chopin (or easier composers), and to provide background for songs by, say, Schubert and Schumann. There was a strong current of bourgeois sentimentality in much music, almost a straining toward sweetness and light even amidst "revolutionary" works. In the relatively new medium of the public concert, virtuosos such as Liszt and demon-violinist Paganini garnered rabid followings comparable to those of rock stars today. While the growing complexity and length of pieces made them harder for the average listener to grasp, at least the passion in the music was something nearly anyone could understand. That remains true: Romantic music is the most popular today, with the most works in the standard repertoire.

In the end, the split between composer and public, which opened and steadily widened through the nineteenth century, would have decisive consequences in our century, when Modernists made the break with the bourgeois public virtually into a credo. From that position an age of headlong exploration began: as we will see, Modernism to a large extent was Romanticism without brakes.

We'll begin our tour of the nineteenth century with two figures, one looking back and one forward: Rossini and Weber.

GIOACCHINO ROSSINI

Gioacchino Rossini was born to a musical family in Pesaro, Italy, on February 29, 1792, and at eighteen completed his studies at Bologna's Liceo Musicale. Three years later he found himself one of the most celebrated opera composers in that opera-mad country. After writing some one-acters for Venice, he had become instantly famous for the comedy *An Italian in Algiers,* which is still performed today. By then he had settled into the pace of two to four operas a year that he would maintain for his active career. His secret was a combination of prodigal genius (with a felicitous gift for melody), self-plagiarism (such as the overture that graced three different op-

At right, Rossini ca. 1860: elegantly fat, satisfied, and long retired.

eras), and a hack's attitude (he took every shortcut he could think of and never revised anything). Rossini once bragged, "Give me a laundry list and I will set it to music."

His masterpiece, written at age twenty-four, was *The Barber of Seville*, based on the first of two plays by Beaumarchais about the intrigues of the wily barber Figaro (the second play is *The Marriage of Figaro*, set by Mozart). Written in about two weeks, *Barber* had a fiasco of a premiere in Rome in 1816, but within a few performances it had become the audience favorite it has remained ever since. Where Mozart let Beaumarchais's underlying social criticism come through, Rossini plays it strictly for laughs. The result is perhaps the most effervescent and sheerly enjoyable opera buffa in history. Dur-

NINETEENTH-CENTURY OPERA

In the nineteenth century, opera settled into national traditions—most notably the French, Italian, and German. The Paris Opéra came to favor historical spectacles decked out with extravagant characters, big choruses, and ballets, as seen in the works of Giacomo Meyerbeer (1791–1864); his *Les Huguenots* of 1836 typifies what came to be called *grand opera*. (Now the term tends to be applied generally to all nine-

At right, a cross-section of the grandiose Paris Opera, completed in 1874.

ing the period Rossini spent in Vienna, the aged Beethoven gave this rival, who had turned the heads of the Viennese, a remarkably generous compliment about the *Barber:* "It will be played as long as Italian operas exist." So far, Beethoven has been right.

In 1829 Rossini was living in Paris, his primary home from then on, and there wrote what he considered his crowning achievement, the serious opera *William Tell*. Despite its considerable virtues, the Parisians hated it. (*William Tell* is sometimes produced these days, but is mainly known for its "Lone Ranger" overture.) Thereupon, after writing an incredible thirty-eight operas in nineteen years, Rossini went on vacation for the rest of his life. As for his reasons, he observed something to the effect that composing had become too

much like work. So over the next four decades he dusted his laurels, lived in the style of a wealthy bon vivant, ate well, exchanged one beautiful soprano wife for another, and entertained the great and talented of Europe in his home. The only creative efforts during his last years were a couple of religious works and the ironic little piano pieces he called *Sins of My Old Age*. He died in Paris on November 13, 1868, two weeks after throwing his last party.

While Rossini's style looked backward to Mozart, that of **Carl Maria von Weber** began the tradition leading forward to German Romantic opera and Wagner. Born in Oldenburg, Germany, in 1786, Weber first studied with Joseph Haydn's brother Michael and quickly gravitated to opera. After a number of wandering years as a conductor and pianist and a few stage successes, he was named conductor of the important Dresden theater. There he became fired

teenth-century opera in a grandiose mode.) Later came the smaller-scale French lyric style, represented by the most famous of the various versions of *Faust*, the 1859 setting by Charles Gounod (1818–1893).

Actually, the French grand opera tradition was established mainly by the last works of the Italian Rossini, whom I have profiled separately. After his successes in Italy, especially with *The Barber of Seville*, Rossini came to Paris and produced the pioneering grand operas *The Siege of Corinth* and *William Tell*. Meanwhile in France, Jacques Offenbach (1819–1880) created the lighter, more popular and sentimental genre called *operetta*, his best known being *Orpheus in the Underworld*

(1858). Offenbach also wrote a masterful full-scale opera, *Tales of Hoffmann* (premiered 1881). The most famous nineteenth-century operetta, however, is Austrian— the delightful *Die Fledermaus* (The Bat) by Viennese "Waltz King" Johann Strauss, which premiered in 1874.

In Italy, Rossini's successors were Vincenzo Bellini (1801–1835), whose sentimental lyricism is heard in *Norma;* Gaetano Donizetti (1797–1848), whose *Lucia di Lammermoor* and *La Fille du régiment* are still popular; and Giuseppe Verdi. As we see in the essay on Verdi, Italian opera had wide popular appeal, was the most lyrical and melodramatic of the national schools, and the least interested in fancy orchestration.

with the dream of creating a German national opera, divorced from Italian style. (He is thus also a precursor of the kind of musical nationalism that would flourish in the second half of the century.)

The first and finest result of that dream was the 1821 *Der Freischütz* (The Free-Shooter), reflecting German folk song, based on a German legend, and set in the depths of the German forest (the latter two elements to be characteristic of Wagner as well). Weber's story is a wild yarn crowded with ghosts and omens and magic bullets and hellhounds and pacts with the devil. Though *Der Freischütz* is only occasionally mounted these days, its handsome overture, along with those for *Oberon* and *Euryanthe,* is heard often at concerts.

Now we move into the full bloom of the nineteenth century with Franz Schubert, the first and possibly greatest genius of the Romantic period.

It would remain that way into the twentieth century, though Verdi would take everything in the Italian tradition to a higher level.

German opera remained closest to the Romantic mainstream; its prime ancestor was the Mozart of the exotic singspiels *The Abduction from the Seraglio* and *The Magic Flute.* The founder of German Romantic opera was Carl Maria von Weber; as we saw in his section, he established the folk-tale atmosphere and nationalistic approach. Finally came Wagner, who culminated German Romantic opera in his earlier works like *Tannhäuser* (1845) and, in creating the new ideal of music drama, influenced all opera from then on.

Elsewhere, composers in various countries turned their ambitions to creating nationalist operas, based on the stories and folk music of their own regions. Leading the way in Bohemia was Bedřich Smetana (1824–1884), composer of the folk opera *The Bartered Bride;* in Russia it was Michael Glinka (1804–1857), with works including *A Life for the Czar,* followed by the stage works of Rimsky-Korsakov, Tchaikovsky, and Musorgsky *(Boris Godunov).*

The streams of Wagnerism and nationalism would flow on into the twentieth century. In the essays on individual composers we will see how these streams variously mingled and diverged in the works of Richard Strauss, Debussy, Puccini, Gershwin, Berg, Schoenberg, Stravinsky, Janáček, and Britten. ◻

FRANZ SCHUBERT

Among the great naturals in music, Franz Schubert was in many ways the most remarkable. Compared to Mozart, Mendelssohn, and Rossini, he had the least training, matured at least as young as the others, was the most original, found the least public success, and died the youngest at age thirty-one. If Mozart had died at that age, we would have no *Don Giovanni,* no *Magic Flute,* no G minor Symphony.

Where Beethoven struggled with his material as if he were wres-

From the right, Schubert and Schubertians
Anselm Hüttenbrenner and Johann Baptist Jenger.

tling with the gods, and Mozart composed in his head, picking up the pen usually at the last minute, Schubert spent most of his time simply sitting and writing. "I work every morning," he said. "When I have finished one piece I begin another." Sometimes he finished several songs in a day. He seemed to live in and through music, to experience and feel things in his art that he may never have experienced and felt in his life. He never married, apparently never had a mature love. In his miserable last years he said that living was a burden and he would be glad to be rid of it. Instead of life there was music, bursting like a spring torrent from that squat, silly-looking figure. When he was not writing music he preferred to be playing or listening to it; failing that, to joke with his friends and drink himself into a stupor, like a boxer between bouts. His real life was on paper—a great deal of paper, fortunately, because his bodily existence was destined to be brief. From the beginning he wrote as if he knew how little time he had.

He was born Franz Peter Schubert in Lichtenthal, then a suburb of Vienna, on January 31, 1797, the only great Viennese composer actually to be born there. His father, Franz Theodor, was a school-teacher and amateur musician; he expected his three sons to become the same. At around eight, young Franz began to receive lessons in violin from his father and in piano from older brother Ignaz. Soon Franz had learned all Ignaz could teach him. That would become a regular pattern. After some lessons with a local choirmaster the old man said, "If ever I wished to teach him anything new, I found he knew it already." At the school of the Imperial chapel, where Schubert became a choirboy and student in 1808, his teacher finally threw up his hands as well: "I can't teach him anything else; he's learned it all from God himself."

Finally Schubert studied with someone who could teach him about writing for the voice—none other than Antonio Salieri, composer, teacher of Beethoven among many others, now enjoying an honored old age despite the continuing rumors that he had poisoned Mozart. Otherwise Schubert sang in the chapel choir, played violin in the orchestra, and, from about 1811 when he was fourteen, began to write little pieces. The boys were kept in a state of near starvation and poverty; he could not afford music paper and laboriously had to draw his own staff lines. Schoolmate Josef von Spaun, then and

A Schubertiad of 1826, the composer at the piano and guests including the poet Grillparzer, Spaun, von Schwind, and the Vogl sisters.

later one of his closest friends, heard some of Schubert's early efforts and began to supply him with printed music paper. That seemed to be all the boy needed to open the floodgates. Spaun could hardly provide the paper fast enough; Schubert filled it with incredible speed.

When he was sixteen he wrote a symphony, the next year a Mass. His pieces were played at school, in church, in family musicales at home. Though Franz's father initially resisted this obsession with composing, eventually he relented, though still pressuring his son to become a teacher. Franz obeyed in 1813, leaving the chapel school and training for a teaching career. From 1814 to 1817 he worked in his father's school, spending much of the time composing at his desk and whipping any boy who interrupted him. (Not knowing the reason, his superintendent commended him for his "method of handling the young.")

It was while teaching, at age seventeen, that Schubert wrote his first masterpiece, a song called "Gretchen am Spinnrade" (Gretchen at the Spinning Wheel.) Taken from Goethe's *Faust,* it is the soliloquy of an innocent girl who, as she sits spinning, proclaims her love for the worldly man who has seduced her; she is moved to her soul but hardly understands what she is feeling. The teen-aged Schubert's treatment of this passionate lyric is astonishing in every dimension, not least in his mature sense of the feeling behind the words. The melody is keening, with a mounting intensity as it wanders restlessly from key to key; equally remarkable is the piano accompaniment, a flowing pattern that is both the hum of the spinning wheel and the surging emotions of the girl. With this single small work—perfect, wise beyond his years, and epochal in importance—Schubert began his precocious maturity as a composer and also inaugurated the century-long tradition of the German Romantic art song, which we know by its German name: *Lied*.

Composers had written such lieder before, but those of Beethoven and Haydn and others are slight compared to what Schubert could do. He would take the lied for voice and piano to the highest artistic level, filling it with an unprecedented richness of melody, dramatic power, and psychological penetration. For lyrics he would turn to some of the best German poets—Goethe, Schiller, and Heine—and some of the worst; among the latter are Müller, whose saccharine poems Schubert made into his magnificent song cycles *Die schöne Müllerin* and *Winterreise*.

In 1815, still teaching, Schubert wrote a second symphony and 144 songs, sometimes a half dozen or more in a day. Among them was "Der Erlkönig," a Goethe ballad about a father riding through a storm with his child, who is seized and killed by the spectral king of the elves. Schubert made the verse into a little solo cantata, brilliantly shifting among the breathless narrator, the mounting terror of the child, the perplexed father, the seductive voice of the elf-king. Meanwhile the piano accompaniment is all pounding hooves and whirling wind. "Der Erlkönig" would earn Schubert his first public success and see print as his op. 1; it remains his most famous song and as remarkable as any of his career.

Such moments were still the exception in his output, however. In 1814, the same year as "Gretchen," he wrote his first stage work, *The Devil's Pleasure Palace*. More than a dozen operas and singspiels would follow over the next ten years, mounting to thousands of pages amidst his voluminous output of chamber music, symphonies, church music, and lieder. Only a couple of these operas would be performed in his lifetime, without success, and none has made it to the standard repertoire. Many were undermined from the beginning by a weak libretto, a lame imitation of *The Magic Flute* among them. Though he set words to music nearly every day, Schubert seems to have had an astounding lack of literary judgment. Convinced that opera was his best hope of attracting attention, he pursued it obsessively. The great irony of his career is that, having some of the most spectacular natural gifts in history, he spent much of his short life laboring in a genre for which he had no particular gift.

After three years of dutiful efforts to teach, as his father wished, Schubert resigned the only regular job he ever had and took up the life-style he would pursue for the rest of his years. Mostly he lived with friends and often was supported by them. He was lucky in his friends; though few had much money, they all had a little to spare to keep him going. In other words, he and his circle lived the classic bohemian life: on the edge of starvation, pursuing their various arts, looking for an audience, haunting the cafés and beer gardens of Vienna.

Schubert remained the center of this circle, the muse and pet of the group. Most of his friends were more sophisticated than he, some with talent and some not. They included his old friend Spaun and others from school days; the brooding writer and government censor Johann Mayrhofer, one of several who provided lyrics for Schubert; composer Anselm Hüttenbrenner and his brother Josef, a government minister; the wealthy and dissolute Franz von Schober, mediocre poet for some of Schubert's finest lieder, his primary supplier of living space and, perhaps, of women; painter Moritz von Schwind, who became a noted illustrator; and the singing Baron von Schönstein, eventually an important performer of Schubert's lieder. The group called themselves the "Schubertians," their evening rendezvous "Schubertiads." In these gatherings they listened to the composer's newest work, poets recited, and life and art and love were celebrated. Everyone contributed; Schubert was nicknamed "Kanevas" because of his usual question about a new face: *"Kann er was?"* ("What can he do?") (Another nickname was "Schwam-

merl''—''Tubby.'') Von Schwind and other artists of the circle left
drawings and paintings of these Schubertiads, with the bespectacled
figure of the composer presiding at the piano.

He was an unlikely centerpiece for this changing assemblage of
bohemians. Even his admirers admitted that Schubert looked preposterous: short, pudgy, pale, round-shouldered, often shabby of
dress, like the creature of close rooms and tallow candles that he
was. He stumbled about and dropped things and topped off his
undistinguished features with tiny egg-shaped spectacles. Shy and
inarticulate much of the time, he still managed childish pranks and
whimsies, such as his celebrated performance of ''Der Erlkönig'' on
a comb and tissue paper. After a day's composing he might, if he
had the money, take in an opera or a play with friends. Otherwise
he would pass the night in Viennese style: retire to a café for hours
of pipe smoking, a bit of coffee, and an appropriate amount of wine.
Sometimes he sat at the café piano playing dances hour after hour.
Recalled Anselm Hüttenbrenner, ''When the blood of the vine
glowed in him, he did not rant, but moved into a quiet corner to give
himself up to a comfortable frenzy. A smiling tyrant who, if possible, would destroy something—glasses, for instance, or a plate or a
cup. . . . He would sit there and grin and narrow his eyelids.''

Schubert composed anywhere, sometimes with a friend in the
same room writing poetry or music. He wrote quickly, but often
went through several drafts before he was satisfied with a piece.
Nothing stopped the incessant scratch of his pen. If spoken to he
might snap, ''Greetings. How's it going? Good,'' and keep on writing. Spaun, who was present during some of these creative trances,
recalled, ''Anyone who has seen him of a morning occupied with
composition, aglow, with his eyes shining and even his speech
changed, like a sleepwalker, will never forget the impression.''

Thus his devoted and marvelous friends kept him alive and working. In return he gave them the first glimpse of uncountable beauties, and gave them himself. After his funeral Schwind wrote to one
of the group, ''Schubert is dead, and with him all that was brightest
and most beautiful in our life.'' To the end of their days, many
Schubertians would say that their years in company with the pudgy
little man were the happiest they ever saw.

Such private adulation, however, did not attract big commissions.

Schubert was not without ambition, only without skill in realizing it—or the slightest competence with business or a budget. His main means of seeking success was to write opera after luckless opera. But his circle of friends and admirers steadily broadened and stories of the Schubertiads began to pique the curiosity of the Viennese.

His first foot in the door to a public reputation came in 1817, when his friend Schober convinced baritone Johann Michael Vogl to come and try out some songs. A large, imperious man nearing the end of a celebrated operatic career, Vogl came grudgingly, hummed through a few songs while Schubert played, and commented, "Not bad." As he left with some manuscripts in hand, he tapped Schubert on the shoulder and said patronizingly, "You do have talent, but you are too little the actor, too little the charlatan." But Vogl soon returned converted. He began to study the songs in earnest, realizing that he had discovered a genius and a new career as well: with Schubert as coach and the foundation of his repertoire, he would become the first lieder specialist. Vogl also became a friend and benefactor of the composer, who always had need of both; several times in the next decade they traveled together, performing for audiences wherever they went.

Things developed slowly. Vogl and others began to sing "Der Erlkönig" in public; at a Vogl concert in Vienna in 1821 the song was received with thunderous applause. That year, financed by some of Schubert's friends, it saw publication by the firm of Diabelli as op.1; following immediately came op. 2, "Gretchen am Spinn-rade." Diabelli must have been astonished to find these songs selling dozens of copies. The publisher began to buy, for outrageously low prices, songs from Schubert as fast as he could engrave them (which was none too fast). Schubert would later be portrayed by biographers as an unknown genius writing in a garret; in fact, by the end of his short life a substantial amount of his enormous output was in print from several publishers and selling briskly. It would have taken years in any case to catch up with his backlog; by the time op. 1 appeared, he had, at age twenty-four, written more than five hundred works of all kinds. The trouble was not that the world neglected Schubert but rather that he usually took any price publishers offered, and what they offered was shameful. Later, when his reputation was considerable, Schubert sold some of the great *Winterreise* songs for the equivalent of twenty cents apiece.

Why did his star not rise faster? As noted, he had no idea how to promote himself. Worse, he was not a virtuoso. Like most composers wanting to conquer Vienna, Mozart and Beethoven had first attracted attention as soloists; but being at best a fair accompanist for his own songs, Schubert could not follow that route to a career. (For similar reasons, there are no concertos in his output.) His shyness among strangers and his unimpressive looks did not help, either. Yet with every publication his audience grew, and musicians knew and respected him. Though Schubert may have met the town's resident demigod Beethoven only twice, the second time in a melancholy visit to the latter's deathbed, his name earlier appears in the deaf old man's conversation books. It was no accident that Schubert was chosen to carry a torch in Beethoven's funeral procession in 1827; by then many understood that Schubert was the likeliest man to carry on the torch of the Viennese tradition.

The year 1823 brought a mystery and a tragedy. Given an honorary membership in the Musikverein of Graz, Schubert promised to write a symphony in gratitude for that rather inconsequential honor. He began a work in B minor that was an extraordinary departure from his previous rather mild and Mozartean symphonies: it has a dark-hued first movement with mysterious whisperings, longing melodies, and impassioned outbursts, and a second movement of ineffable sweetness. Then came nothing, except a piano sketch of a scherzo with a few bars orchestrated. The two completed movements were never performed, never reached Graz, were hardly known; instead, his friend Anselm Hüttenbrenner allowed them to lie in a drawer for nearly forty years. Why the symphony remained unfinished is one mystery; why Anselm sat on it, knowing how good it was (he made a piano arrangement for himself) is another. It was finally premiered in Vienna in 1865, to spectacular acclaim, and soon known to the world as the *Unfinished* Symphony. In its yearning quality, its mingling of sweetness and suffering, it was the first true Romantic symphony and became one of the most popular orchestral works ever written. It also seems a confirmation of Schubert's most telling words about himself: ''Whenever I attempted to sing of love, it turned to pain. And again, when I tried to sing of pain, it turned to love.''

According to Schubert biographer George R. Marek, the answer to why the *Unfinished* Symphony remained that way might be simpler than it seems. Schubert may have been distracted by the news that he was fated to a long, brutal road to death.

Working on the B minor Symphony near the end of 1823, Schubert was stricken with headaches and back pains. He doggedly kept on working (but not on the symphony) as the symptoms grew worse, and finally consulted a doctor who probably made the diagnosis immediately: almost certainly it was syphilis, the scourge of the age. Schubert probably got it from the same source as did millions in the nineteenth century, among them Heine, Nietzsche, Smetana, and Schumann—from a prostitute. Vienna in the 1820s had some ten thousand prostitutes in residence, none of them examined by the health authorities.

Hardly anything is known about Schubert's relations with women. He spoke of an unrequited love in his youth, the like of which he never found again. This was Therese Grob, homely but a good singer, for whom Schubert wrote some of his early songs, and who finally married a baker. In 1818 and 1824 Schubert lived at the palace of a Hungarian count and taught his two daughters; there are hints of an infatuation with one of the daughters, or a romance with a chambermaid, but nothing conclusive. Some friends hinted that his benefactor Schober, something of a Mephistophelean character, might have introduced Schubert to the darker side of Viennese night life. Again, nothing conclusive. What is known is that prostitutes were the solace of most young Viennese men who lacked the means or desire to pursue marriage; there is no reason for Schubert to have been an exception.

Syphilis is a devious illness, toying with its victims. At times in those last years Schubert felt healthy, but then the symptoms— especially the violent headaches—would break out again. This process lasted through the final five years of his life. Soon after the first outbreak of the disease he wrote a friend: "I feel myself to be the most unhappy and wretched creature in the world. Imagine a man whose health will never be right again, and who in sheer despair over this ever makes things worse and worse, instead of better; imagine a man, I say, whose most brilliant hopes have perished, to whom the felicity of love and friendship has nothing to offer but pain, at best, whom enthusiasm . . . for all things beautiful threatens to forsake, and I ask you, is he not a miserable, unhappy being?

. . . Each night, on retiring to bed, I hope I may not wake again, and each morning but recalls yesterday's grief."

Yet during those despairing years Schubert composed without slacking, his work growing steadily in mastery and inspiration. From that period came the magnificent song cycles *Die schöne Müllerin* and *Winterreise,* dozens more lieder, string quartets, piano trios, and, in his last year, the C major Symphony, the three final piano sonatas, and the incomparable String Quintet in C major.

On March 26, 1828, a year after he had carried a torch to Beethoven's grave, supporters presented an all-Schubert concert at the Musikverein hall in Vienna. The overflowing house responded with tremendous enthusiasm to Vogl's rendition of songs, a string quartet and piano trio, a male chorus. There was encore after encore: a triumph at last, surely the first of many. Plans were initiated for another concert. But there would be no time for that.

In September 1828 Schubert moved to the suburban home of his brother Ferdinand, a teacher and composer, and kept to his usual composing schedule. Then in a restaurant one night he suddenly dropped his fork and cried that his food tasted like poison. Declining from that point, he finally took to bed, where he corrected publisher's proofs of *Winterreise.* On November 18 he became delirious, begging his brother "not to leave me here, in this corner under the earth; do I deserve no place above the earth?" When Ferdinand assured him he was in his bed, Schubert replied, "No, it is not true; Beethoven does not lie here." Next day he awoke from sleep, turned his head to the wall, whispered, "Here, here is my end," and died. He was buried a few feet from Beethoven's grave.

The epitaph on Schubert's tombstone, by the poet Grillparzer, reads, "The art of music here entombed a rich possession but far fairer hopes." It is a recognition that he died at thirty-one, very much in the middle of things, when he was just finding his voice as an instrumental composer and just attracting a public. Had he lived as long as Beethoven, he likely would have reaped all the honors the age could bestow. If the epitaph underestimates what Schubert had accomplished by the time of his death, that is understandable; rounding up and surveying that phenomenal body of work took most of the nineteenth century. The total finally amounted to over six hundred lieder, eight symphonies, twenty-two piano sonatas, thirty-five assorted chamber works, many short piano pieces, a wealth of piano works for four hands, six Masses, and fifteen operas. What he got to hear of his instrumental music had been spotty, some of the chamber music and symphonies (but not the major ones), played sometimes in public concerts, sometimes in private readings.

Discoveries large and small filled the decades after his death. Robert Schumann found the C major Symphony, Schubert's last and most ambitious, at the house of Schubert's brother Ferdinand in 1838. Around that time a London paper wondered sarcastically why the deceased Schubert seemed to be producing so many new songs; in fact, they were emerging piecemeal from cupboards and attics. In 1865 a conductor finally extracted the long-rumored *Unfinished* Symphony from old Anselm Hüttenbrenner by means of a promise to play Anselm's work. Soon after, young Englishmen George Grove (later of *Grove's Dictionary of Music and Musicians*) and Arthur Sullivan (later of Gilbert and Sullivan) went looking in Vienna for the lost incidental music to the play *Rosamunde*. They finally unearthed it—along with five symphonies, a trio, a Stabat Mater, and dozens of songs.

What has entered the standard repertoire from Schubert's output is a relatively small proportion, but still a good deal of music. As a teen-ager Schubert hit his stride as a song composer and never faltered. The flow of lieder masterpieces is consistent throughout, though there is the inevitable percentage of lesser work. From the beginning the songs are marked by his mastery of modulation, making for a characteristic shifting among keys, and most of all by an instinct for beautiful and expressive melody. No one has matched him in melodic genius, and that genius was to make a profound (though not entirely productive) impression on the whole of Romantic music. Increasingly, composers in the rest of the century would come to see melody, especially sighing lyric melody, as the main answer to everything. Schubert stamped both his strength and weakness on the period.

The weakness shows up most often in his instrumental music. His development in that area may be summarized as a growth from relying on tunes to carry a piece to a more mature understanding of large musical form, in which melody plays *a* part rather than the whole part. Robert Schumann spoke of the "heavenly length" of the gigantic C major Symphony (called "The Great" to distinguish it from an earlier symphony in the same key). As critics have pointed out, however, it is mainly the glory of the melodies that makes the symphony heavenly, rather than any Beethoven-like gift for creating an effective symphonic unfolding out of pregnant themes and a large rhythmic sweep. In his last instrumental works, however, Schubert began to find a rhetoric and syntax for himself in large forms, though death cut short that development.

The art of the German Romantic lied is unimaginable without Schubert, and in the songs of all its major figures one hears echoes of his voice—in Mendelssohn, Schumann, Brahms, Hugo Wolf, Richard Strauss, and Mahler (compare Mahler's *Songs of a Wayfarer* with Schubert's *Die schöne Müllerin*).

An introduction to Schubert might begin with his most beloved orchestral work, the *Unfinished* Symphony. The work has a unique coloration, beyond the Schubertian melodic and harmonic style. It begins, probably not for the first time in history, with a bass line in octaves, but the ominous and sorrowful effect is revolutionary: from the first notes the new Romantic expressiveness is heard, and that is carried on in the nervous rustling of the violins. When the main theme enters, a typically long-breathed lyric line, it is not heard in a single part but rather in a doubling of oboe and clarinet. Such a doubling would hardly have occurred to Mozart: Why not oboe *or* clarinet? Why both? Because the doubling gives a particular yearning coloration to the line—clarinet lending oboe smoothness, oboe lending clarinet poignancy. This kind of coloristic orchestration, which Berlioz would further develop in his music, would become a specialty of the Romantic era. The *Unfinished* is not only the first and one of the greatest of the period's symphonic works, it is also among the most personal and least derivative of Beethoven (though its style is still founded on the example of Beethoven).

The intense expressiveness of the *Unfinished* is a striking contrast to the lightness of the earlier Fifth Symphony in B-flat major, written when Schubert was about nineteen. Here the main inspirations are Mozart and Haydn, but beginning with the long singing theme of the first movement the voice is clearly Schubert's. Throughout, the work is engaging and nostalgic in its echoes of eighteenth-century galant style. Far different is his last, the C major Symphony, called "The Great," Schubert's closest orchestral approach to Beethovenian scope and seriousness. It begins with a grand horn proclamation, part of a huge introductory section that leads into a dancing allegro. The second movement alternates between a galant slow dance and lyrical sections, an example of Schubert's tendency to put a movement together by stringing one tune after another. Following a lusty scherzo, the finale is based on obsessive rhythms that rush nonstop to an ecstatic conclusion, the whole demonstrating Schubert's virtuoso command of modulation; things are always turning up in unexpected keys, phrases shooting off in surprising harmonic directions (a tendency going back to "Gretchen am Spinnrade").

The *Trout* Quintet may be the single most popular piece of chamber music in the classical repertoire. It has five movements, the added one being the fourth-movement variations on his lilting song "The Trout," which give the whole piece its name and much of its popularity. Those variations were a stipulation of the commission, which came from an amateur cellist friend who loved the song; another stipulation was that one variation should have a cello solo, but nothing too hard. Schubert obliged, meanwhile dispensing some of his most elegant melodic writing throughout.

Best known of the string quartets is the 1824 D minor, called *Death and the Maiden,* again because one of the movements has variations on a song of his by that name. It was written near the beginning of his illness; few of his pieces are so consistently tragic in tone. A dramatic proclamation in octaves begins a first movement of unrelenting intensity. The second movement starts off with the "Death and the Maiden" theme in a slow, implacable tread (the song concerns death stealing toward a young girl); except for a couple of brighter major episodes, the tone is somber. (Major and minor keys had for Schubert, maybe more than for any previous composer, the invariably happy-sad connotations that were becoming standard in Western music.) The scherzo of the quartet is still in minor, though with a wistful trio in major. For the finale Schubert uses the feverish rhythm of the old dance called *tarantella;* it is a swirling, breathless movement with a kind of demonic exhilaration.

His crowning achievement in chamber music, and the equal of

any by anyone, is the titanic String Quintet in C major, written in the last months of his life. Adding an extra cello to the usual quartet, Schubert reveled in the richness it added to the texture. Everything about this work is extraordinary—its breadth of expression from deepest tragedy to exultant joy to transcendent peace, its freshness of sound, its contrapuntal depth (the latter not usually one of Schubert's strong suits). The first movement is a gradual unfolding that often seems suspended between major and minor, hope and despair inextricably intertwined; it is a journey that takes the listener further and deeper in one movement than do many whole pieces. Delicate pathos introduces the second movement, dispelled by a violent and anguished middle section that seems to rise again and again before sinking to an exhausted finish. Then the scherzo, one of the most exciting ever written: the main theme a peasantlike dance of wild glee, scampering rhythmic drive, and marvelous lushness of texture; the middle a slow trio melancholy in tone. Rather than an anguished climax, the finale turns out to be one of the most exuberant of Schubert's life. By the end of this work as with few others, one feels one has traveled an immense distance—musically, emotionally, and spiritually.

Among the smaller piano works are two series of intimate pieces that influenced similar works throughout the century, the eight Impromptus and six *Moments Musicaux,* all with a considerable amount of Schubertian melody and brilliant piano writing (and with some of his liabilities as well—padding, rambling, sometimes cloying sweetness). Much loved by virtuosos is the monumental *Wanderer* Fantasy, its second section based on another of his songs.

At the zenith of his twenty-two piano sonatas are the last three, in C minor, A major, and B-flat major, the latter the finest of his piano works. This B-flat opus posthumous is at once the most Beethovenian of his sonatas and the most personal. It begins with one of his expansive and beautiful lyric themes; that mood of calm loveliness lasts throughout. The second movement falls into three broad sections, the middle another sustained melody, the outer sections a simple chord sequence turning constantly in new harmonic directions, which seems transfixed in a state of fatalistic despair. The mood begins to change with a wistful scherzo; then the final movement is light and lacy in mood, with intricate harmonic patterns. As with the C major Quintet, there is a valedictory air about the B-flat Sonata, as if Schubert knew (and probably he did know) that he was rousing his failing body to a final sprint.

Finally we come to the lieder, the heart and soul of Schubert. Almost any recorded collection will reveal his incomparable variety of ideas, accompaniments, and textures, clothing every nuance of emotion with his sublime melodic and harmonic gift. I have spoken of the dramatic canvas of "Der Erlkönig" and the passionate "Gretchen am Spinnrade." In contrast is the artless effect of the little "Heidenröslein" (Hedge-Rose) after Goethe, which like some other Schubert songs was absorbed so completely into the life of the people that most assumed it was a folk song. That lied, like many of Schubert's, uses the *strophic* form of the folk song, each verse set to the same tune (sometimes with changing accompaniment, sometimes with major-minor shifts). At other times he uses a *through-composed* approach, in which the song unfolds freely, following the words, the whole held together by thematic and harmonic relationships. Among songs of this type is "Der Erlkönig" and the hymn-like "Nachtstück" (Night Piece), sung by an old man welcoming death. Another stunning through-composed lied, one of the final set later grouped together under the title "Swan Song," is Heine's "Der Döppelganger" (The Double): among dreamlike, slow-striding harmonies, the singer tells of a spectral figure he sees standing before the home of an old lover; approaching closer, he discovers that the figure is himself, and cries out, "Pale brother, why do you mock the pains of love that tormented me so many nights, so long ago!" The music is equal to the scene in its nightmarish anguish.

As Schubert did not invent the lied but began its great tradition, so he did with the song cycle, a connected series of lieder outlining a story. With words by the minor poet Wilhelm Müller, *Die schöne Müllerin* tells of a young miller wandering in the forest who begins to work at a mill, but falls hopelessly in love with the miller's daughter who finally spurns him for a handsome hunter. In his despair he throws himself into the brook, which sings him to rest with a gentle lullaby. Not only does Schubert fill this sentimental tale with wonderful music, he makes its naïveté work for him by creating a kind of super-folk-style, the songs unfolding with apparent fresh-faced innocence while in fact everything is crafted with the highest sophistication. (One often strikes out humming a little Schubert tune only to get lost in the modulations.) As with a good deal of Haydn and other composers not interested in wearing their labors on their sleeves, this work is an example of art hiding art. When *Die schöne Müllerin* is done badly it sounds simpleminded; done well, it seems as ingenuous and profound as the hills are green.

Much the same could be said of the other great cycle of Müller poems, *Winterreise* (Winter's Journey). These songs were written in Schubert's last months, in the shadow of death, and they show it from beginning to end. The poet wanders aimlessly in a frozen landscape, seeking warmth and rest, finding only phantoms and emptiness. He is the eternal stranger, lost in the wilderness of the world. The end, in which he addresses a mysterious organ-grinder, is in its eerie singsong one of the most haunting moments in all music. As this was one of Schubert's several farewells to his own marvelous and tenuous life, it will be our farewell too.

FELIX
MENDELSSOHN

It is often noted that Felix Mendelssohn was aptly named: most of his life seems a collection of felicities. Born into a family who had the knowledge and means to shape his talent, coming to creative maturity earlier than any other major composer, he had by age thirty—after an almost unbroken series of triumphs—become the most beloved composer of his time. His story suggests, however, the weary conclusion that a perfect life is illusory, because in the end his inspiration proved unequal to his talent, and the first great sorrow he encountered was enough to kill him.

He was born Jakob Ludwig Felix on February 3, 1809, to Abraham and Leah Mendelssohn. His father was a prosperous banker, his mother an artist and musician. Abraham, son of the illustrious Jewish philosopher Moses Mendelssohn, would later modestly say of himself, "First I was the son of my father. Now I am the father of my son." When Felix was young the family moved to Berlin, where he and his comparably talented sister, Fanny, received their first piano lessons from their mother. Soon they were working with the best music teachers available and studying every day on a rigorous schedule, enforced by their father, that began at 5:00 A.M. Both also excelled in other interests and studies; Felix was particularly fine in drawing and painting. When it appeared that Felix's religion might be a barrier to his career in anti-Semitic Germany, Abraham converted the family to Protestantism; to distinguish his branch from the unconverted, Abraham changed their surname to Mendelssohn-Bartholdy. Felix would use that form.

We do not know how such dismal expediencies affected him. To all appearances Felix had a storybook childhood, making his public debut as a pianist at nine, as a composer at ten. During studies with Goethe's composer friend Karl Zelter, Felix became a favorite of the old poet and often played for him. Zelter kept his pupil on a steady diet of Bach, stressing the study of fugue. At age twelve Felix produced nine fugues, five symphonies for strings, two operas, and numerous smaller pieces. The next year his father arranged a series of Sunday musicales in which the finest musicians in Europe performed with Felix and played his works.

At age sixteen, with a substantial body of music already to his credit, he came to full maturity with his extraordinary Octet in E-flat for strings, which outdistances anything done at that age by Schubert or Mozart. Next came a work of equal imagination and skill, the overture to Shakespeare's *A Midsummer Night's Dream;* he conducted the first performance in 1826.

By no means were Mendelssohn's achievements limited to composition. As a teen-ager he was already one of the finest pianists of his time, but he would become still more celebrated as a conductor. In 1829, when he was twenty, he conducted the Berlin Singakademie in the epochal revival of Bach's *St. Matthew Passion,* performed for the first time since Bach's day. So profound was the impression it made that this one event kindled the great revival of Bach's music in the nineteenth century. Mendelssohn then set off on a three-year grand tour of Europe, everywhere exciting admiration. This included the first of his ten visits to England, where his star would always burn brightest; he became a special favorite of Queen Victoria (in a famous letter, Mendelssohn tells of accompanying the queen in his songs at Buckingham Palace). He also visited Scotland, a trip whose main fruit was the superb overture *Fingal's Cave* (or *The Hebrides*) and the *Scotch* Symphony. Throughout his travels he practiced his drawing and wrote delightful reports home to Fanny and his parents. With his sunny personality and striking good looks he made friends everywhere, especially among the leading musicians of Europe.

It would seem that things could hardly get better, but for a time they did. In 1836, at twenty-seven, Mendelssohn became conductor of the venerable Leipzig Gewandhaus Orchestra; true to form, during his tenure he made it into the greatest orchestra in the world, broadening its repertoire both into the moderns and deeper into the past. The following year he married clergyman's daughter Cécile Jeanrenaud, a beauty of eighteen; their exceedingly happy marriage produced five children. A few years later he led in the organization of the new Leipzig Conservatory, where he taught piano and composition. All the while he kept up a steady output of pieces large and small; important works completed in the decade after 1833 include the *Scotch* and *Italian* symphonies and the Violin Concerto in E minor. By 1845, however, his schedule was getting the best of him and his luck was running out.

Mendelssohn's obsessive labors had strained his delicate constitution. Though already ailing from the effects of overwork, he insisted on going to England in 1846 to conduct the premiere of his oratorio *Elijah.* It was, as usual, a triumph, but the trip further damaged his health. He kept to his killing pace in Leipzig and returned to England the following year. Finally admitting he needed a rest, he canceled his performing and teaching duties and fled to

Frankfurt for a vacation. Upon arrival he received the news that his beloved sister, Fanny, had died. The deaths of his father and mother had shaken him for a time, but in his weakened state this unexpected blow did worse; at the news he shrieked and fell unconscious to the floor with a ruptured blood vessel in his head.

He emerged from the attack a changed man, sapped of his vitality and cheerfulness. The next months were full of depression, bouts of pain, and steady decline. His main creative work was the String Quartet in F minor op. 80, clearly a work born in sorrow and suffering. He died at thirty-eight in Leipzig on November 4, 1847. The musical world was stunned; memorial services were held throughout Germany, in England, and in Paris.

Mendelssohn came to maturity at an extraordinarily early age and pursued the limpid and lovely style of his teens until his death. When he experienced the kind of shock and misfortune that can deepen a talent like his, he did not survive. The great musical question of his era, as posed by the young Schubert, was, "Who can do anything after Beethoven?" That dilemma, which obsessed the entire nineteenth century, Mendelssohn simply sidestepped. He was a Classicist who allowed himself a tincture of Romantic expressiveness. His virtues, in the double handful or so of really great works, are polished perfection, delicate touches of pathos and melancholy, and long stretches of sheer delightfulness. Schumann, a very different composer, was not too proud to admire and covet his friend's mastery of form: Schumann composed from fickle inspiration, Mendelssohn from solid craftsmanship.

His reputation for sweetness and light brought acclaim in his lifetime and partial eclipse thereafter. He was the favorite of Victorian England, but that only testifies to his domesticity. This term is not unfair, given such items as the *Songs Without Words,* his main contribution to the Romantic literature of sentimental parlor pieces for the piano. (Some of these were actually written by Fanny, who in allowing them to see print under her brother's name submitted to the time's shameful attitude that composing—or any creativity—was unseemly for women.)

To get acquainted with Mendelssohn we'll proceed roughly in

chronological order. There is no need to start with his more approachable pieces because everything is approachable.

The 1825 Octet in E-flat major for strings is one of the most miraculous works in history. That a large-scale piece this genial, original, and sure-handed could come from a youth of sixteen would be considered impossible if he hadn't done it. (His teacher Zelter could not have helped him much; Zelter never wrote anything nearly as good.) If Mendelssohn had been able to build from the Octet rather than rest on it . . . but he didn't. He may, in fact, have never equalled it. A gem of chamber music, it begins with a warm and spacious first movement, gently lyrical second movement, light and airy third (the first of Mendelssohn's trademark "fairy scherzos"), and a lively and charming finale with masterly fugal writing.

Next on the list is the following year's Overture to *A Midsummer Night's Dream,* one of the finest and most evocative character pieces of the century. Here the skittering, elfin Mendelssohn is in full steam, the music picturing every aspect of Shakespeare's comedy from the sighing of the lovers to the jackass bray of Bottom. All this tone painting is characteristically Romantic, as is the magical atmosphere of the whole; but in Mendelssohn everything is expressed in Classically derived form, in this case the usual sonata form of the overture. From this early masterpiece forward, in an age of thick orchestral palettes his scoring had a fine clarity.

Some fifteen years later, he added to the overture thirteen pieces of incidental music for Shakespeare's play. He was able to match the style of his youthful masterpiece because he had never really left it. Most familiar of these pieces are Puck's scherzo, a quiet nocturne for the lovers, and the Wedding March. (Along with Wagner's from *Lohengrin,* the latter has probably married a good percentage of the Western world.)

From Mendelssohn's 1829 trip to Scotland came the overture *Fingal's Cave,* also called *The Hebrides.* Beginning with a grand and hypnotic rocking of waves, it sweeps on to evoke birds, surf, and storm, in strict sonata form. Richard Wagner, not a fan of Mendelssohn, nonetheless admired the pictorial imagination of this work: "Mendelssohn was a landscape painter of the first order," he wrote, "and *The Hebrides* is his masterpiece."

Of the symphonies, the *Italian* (1832) is a good beginning. From the airy and exhilarating opening theme Mendelssohn is at the height of his powers, the music magisterial in its logic, restrained but compelling in its expressiveness. After a minuetlike scherzo, in the last movement appears the only definably Italian touch in the symphony—a driving saltarello, the traditional fieriness of that dance tempered with a touch of his *faerie* mode. On nearly the same plane of pleasantness and mastery is the *Scotch* Symphony, finished in 1842 after years of labor.

Prolific as he was, Mendelssohn could still be endlessly painstaking. An example is his Violin Concerto in E minor, perhaps the finest concerto of the century after Beethoven's (though fans of Brahms might disagree). Written for his violin virtuoso friend Ferdinand David, and with some of the solo part probably written *by* David, the concerto was six years in gestation before Mendelssohn let it go in 1844. Rather than the usual long orchestral introduction to the first movement, he plunges right in with a seductive solo for the violin, setting a tone of delicate pathos that is maintained throughout. In all three movements the soloist plays almost nonstop, yet the orchestra is a full partner in the musical dialogue. After a lyrical and beautiful slow movement, the finale is a typically light and sparkling allegro. On that note, we will leave one of the most sparkling, and also perhaps most tragic, of composers.

HECTOR BERLIOZ

Among the vanguard of French Romanticism in the nineteenth century were Eugène Delacroix, painter of harems and massacres; Victor Hugo, writer of the populous *Les Misérables* and *The Hunchback of Notre Dame;* and Hector Berlioz, who followed his first teacher's advice to pursue "Babylonian" effects in his music. All had great impact on their time. In Berlioz's case, the extravagance of his ideas and his unprecedented orchestral imagination would pervade the rest of the century.

In my introduction to the Romantic period I noted Berlioz's hyperbolic response to music. Such effusions would characterize his life and work, along with a steady self-absorption in contemplating and reporting them. Not surprisingly, Berlioz was the first signifi-

Berlioz broods in old age.

cant composer to write memoirs; every true Romantic is a poseur. Much of what has been written about his contemporary Hugo applies as well to Berlioz—his egocentrism, his delirious amours, his faith in progress, even the vulgarities and "heroic banality" of some of his pages. It was an age when artists were expected to be excessive, profligate, on the edge of sanity. (Jean Cocteau said: "Victor Hugo was a madman who believed himself to be Victor Hugo.")

In other words, Berlioz's personality and self-consciousness were symptomatic of his time. To keep himself and his work anchored, however, he dosed himself with a touch of Classicism. His music is sometimes outrageous, but never out of control; rich and sometimes bizarre in orchestration, but never sloppy. In his music, though not in his life, he realized his wildest fancies with a fine clarity of means.

Christened Louis-Hector Berlioz, he was born on December 11, 1803, in the town of Côte-Saint-André, near Grenoble. His father was a prosperous physician, his mother a pious Catholic who believed the stage and concert hall were gateways to hell. Intended from birth to follow his father into medicine, Hector gravitated instead to music, learning guitar and flute (he never played piano), teaching himself from books, and composing. At eighteen he was sent to Paris to study for his medical degree, but over the dogged protests of his father and the hysterical entreaties of his mother he ended up studying music at the Paris Conservatory.

Lesueur, his first teacher, had been Napoleon's court composer; it was he who suggested the gigantic, "Babylonian" effects that suited the temperament of his young protégé. Lesueur also informed Berlioz that he was a genius, and Berlioz never wavered in that faith. He idolized the favored geniuses of Romantics everywhere—Beethoven, Shakespeare, Goethe, Hugo.

Berlioz's first major work was a huge Solemn Mass, which he produced twice in the 1820s. Though it brought him some attention, the expenses of mounting it beggared him for years (a foretaste of much of his career). To make matters worse, after he repeatedly tried and failed to gain the Paris Conservatory's prestigious Prix de Rome, his father cut off his allowance.

The heroic, excessive, and notorious part of his life began when he attended a Paris performance of Shakespeare's *Hamlet* in 1827. The role of Ophelia was played by a shapely and earnest young Irish actress named Harriet Smithson. Though the production was in English and Berlioz hardly understood a word, by the end of the play he was desperately smitten with Harriet. The combination of Shakespeare and female beauty overloaded his circuits; he stalked the city all night in a paroxysm of frustration and desire. For the next five years—until their actual meeting—the image of Harriet Smithson ruled his life.

After deluging her with letters to no avail, he conceived the idea of conquering her with music, of writing a great symphony in which, he wrote, "the development of my infernal passion is to be portrayed." Thus the genesis of the most thoroughly Romantic masterpiece in the orchestral literature, the *Symphonie fantastique*. It is based on a clearly autobiographical program that Berlioz later disavowed, but which remains essential for understanding the music. A young musician of "morbid sensibility and ardent imagination," frustrated in love, tries to kill himself with opium. But instead of death, the drug gives him powerful hallucinations, and these constitute the five movements of the symphony: he recalls when he first saw his beloved and felt a transport of passion; he sees her dancing at a ball; he is calmed by a scene in the fields; he has murdered her and is executed at the guillotine; his corpse becomes the centerpiece of a witch's sabbath during which the beloved appears as a grotesque hag. As Berlioz could not escape the image of Harriet Smithson, so is the *Fantastique* haunted by a melody he described as an *idée fixe*. Representing the beloved, it turns up in a new guise in each movement, from the delicately lyrical first appearance to a shrieking parody in the witch's sabbath.

The originality of sound and concept in the *Symphonie fantastique*, and a sustained power of invention astonishing in a composer of twenty-six, made it into one of the seminal works of the century. Its unprecedentedly expressive treatment of the orchestra, the moods ranging from the ethereal beauty of the beginning through the elegant ballroom scene, the thunderous march to the scaffold, and ending in the demonic sabbath, helped fuel a revolution in the art of orchestration. Whereas earlier composers wanted instruments to sound like themselves and present the music clearly and efficiently, now the orchestra was free to murmur, to shout, to howl like devils if necessary. Berlioz's orchestration book of 1844 was among the first of its kind and remains among the finest. With a Classical approach to Romantic expression, his book carefully categorizes the emotional effects of tone colors and scoring techniques.

The *Fantastique* also initiated the great age of program music. As sonata form and other Classical models ossified or withered, an accompanying story could take over the function of organizing and justifying the music. Equally important, Berlioz's use of the idée fixe inspired cyclic symphonies like those of Schumann, in which themes reappear in more than one movement, and similar approaches in Liszt's work. (Liszt heard the 1830 premiere of the *Fantastique* in Paris; from then on he was a friend, partisan, and student of Berlioz.) For the young Richard Wagner, Berlioz and the *Fantastique* were an incitement toward the development of his own style, his orchestration, and his idea of leitmotif so much like the idée fixe.

Harriet Smithson, however, did not attend the premiere of the work she had so weirdly inspired. Berlioz claimed that he had exorcised her spell with the symphony, and, anyway, he had found solace with a coquettish young pianist named Camille Moke, to whom he became engaged. Moreover, on his fourth try he finally won the Prix de Rome by writing a cantata sufficiently orthodox to please the jury. The award involved three years' residence in Rome. Berlioz went there reluctantly and mostly chafed, though his long tramps in the countryside and mountains would later inspire works such as the *Roman Carnival* Overture and *Harold in Italy*. In Rome he also made the acquaintance of Mendelssohn; the amiable young German found Berlioz's person and music too intemperate for his taste, but he remained polite as always.

During his stay in Italy Berlioz learned that Camille Moke had thrown him over for a rich piano maker. Vowing to murder her and her complicitous mother together, he set out for Paris with two loaded pistols and a disguise as a chambermaid—a wig and dress. He made it just past Genoa before the absurdity of the plan became manifest to him; so he meekly went back to Rome—but only after writing the overtures *King Lear* and *The Corsair*.

Returning to Paris in 1832, he produced a concert featuring the *Symphonie fantastique* and its weaker sequel, written in Italy, called *Lélio*. The hall was full of young artistes with velvet coats and pale, fierce faces, demanding to be astonished. And by sheer coincidence, who should show up but Harriet Smithson, in Paris at that time trying to revive a faltering career. Poet Heinrich Heine, also present, recalled the performance: Berlioz with his "monstrous antediluvian hair'' played the timpani, glaring with haunted visage at the actress and pounding with greater fury when their eyes met.

It worked. Along with most of the audience, Harriet was transported, bewitched. Now in spite of herself she began to respond to his renewed entreaties. But not all at once, and meanwhile both their families violently opposed the idea of marriage. Berlioz begged, demanded, tried to poison himself before her eyes. Finally in October 1833 they were wed in Paris. And that, even more dramatically than usual, ended both obsession and romance. With her acting career in ruins, Harriet turned shrewish, jealous, and prematurely aged. After several tempestuous years and one child, they separated. Berlioz took up with singer Marie Recio, but supported Harriet until her death in 1854.

With the *Symphonie fantastique* Berlioz made a name but not a fortune. He never would secure a reliable living or achieve his greatest dreams. He wanted to teach at the Paris Conservatory and write operas; but his enemies forestalled a teaching post (though he did become the Conservatory librarian) and, after his *Benvenuto Cellini* failed at the Paris Opéra in 1838, he never got another chance at the stage until it was too late. Instead, he remained a free-lancer, having to make most of his living in a way he despised, though he was superb at it: writing about music for newspapers. In his articles and reviews he promoted the music of Liszt and Chopin and Beethoven, fought against the cavalier treatment of composers' scores in opera houses, and crusaded for progressive musical ideas in general. His writings are still in print and make entertaining reading.

Now and then his music found favor in Paris, but in between were long periods of struggle and neglect. Around Europe he became a hero to what a later age would call the avant-garde, but to the musical establishment of Paris he was the enemy. Music in France was carried on as power politics of the most vicious kind, a boiling cauldron of intrigue, alliance, and betrayal. A case in point is the premiere of Berlioz's monumental Requiem. He had long wanted to write a Mass for the dead and finally wangled a promise of a commission from the minister of fine arts. Immediately patrons of Cherubini, the conservative head of the Conservatory, pulled strings to block the commission. They failed, and Berlioz went to work in a fury of creativity, largely writing the enormous piece in three months. After he had finished the work and made the complex arrangements for the premiere, the ministry canceled the concert without explanation—and expected Berlioz to pay the expenses incurred. "I defy them to wear me down," he proclaimed, grimly pursuing his own machinations.

With help from friends in high places, the chance for the Requiem came in December 1837, with a memorial ceremony at the Invalides Chapel for a general killed in Algeria. At the premiere the chapel was lit with thousands of candles; the royal family, diplomatic corps, and all fashionable Paris were in attendance, and Berlioz had been given the Babylonian forces he asked for: 190 players, a chorus of 210, plus four brass choirs in the corners of the chapel and sixteen kettledrums, all primed to make enough noise to wake the dead. At the performance Berlioz sat next to the conductor, on alert for a final act of sabotage, and indeed it came: at a critical moment, just before the apocalyptic brass eruption of the *Tuba mirum,* the conductor deliberately laid down his baton and took a pinch of snuff. Berlioz leaped up and marked the beat, and the brass entered on time. For the moment his determination paid off; the Requiem gained him immense acclaim from critics and public alike.

In the end, though, this triumph changed little. His enemies continued their campaigns against him and were successful often as not. Meanwhile his reputation flourished elsewhere, especially in Germany where Liszt and Schumann crusaded on his behalf. Beginning in the 1840s, Berlioz toured Germany, Italy, Austria, Hungary, England, and Russia, conducting his music often to great applause. In his memoirs he writes of admirers kissing his coattails after a performance. (It was, as I have said, an extravagant era.) In an 1844 concert in Paris, he conducted the orchestra and chorus of his dreams, numbering over one thousand and requiring seven assistant conductors. Caricatures of the time depict the gaunt, hawknosed Berlioz hovering like a great bird above orchestras of uncounted thousands and including heavy artillery (see page 29); it was not far from the truth.

From 1856 to 1858 he labored on his most ambitious work, the operatic epic *Les Troyens* (The Trojans), weighing in at over six hours. But lacking the combination of energy, patronage, luck, and cunning that Wagner commanded to bring his giant music dramas to the stage, Berlioz fought for years to produce *Les Troyens,* to little avail. Finally the second half was modestly produced in 1863, to modest success. By then Berlioz was worn down by the fray—exhausted, bitter, and racked by an agonizing intestinal neuralgia. He responded to news of audiences showing up for the opera with, "They are coming, but I am going."

His swan song was the little comic opera *Beatrice and Benedict;* lovely, lyrical, full of hope, entirely delightful, it was everything Berlioz himself no longer was. He managed to conduct a brilliantly successful premiere in Baden-Baden, Germany, in 1862. That same year his wife, Marie Recio, died (he had married her after Harriet's death); five years later, the death of his son in Havana removed what little joy in life he had left. He lived as a recluse in Paris until he died at sixty-six on March 8, 1869. Within a few years, the Paris establishment that had thwarted Berlioz at every step had virtually deified him.

Berlioz wrote no significant chamber music or piano music; nearly everything he did was big. His work, said Heine, "causes me to dream of fabulous empires filled with fabulous sins." Partly because of that extravagance, Berlioz remains the most controversial of all major nineteenth-century composers. We find one modern writer saying, "his melodic materials were usually second-rate," another declaring him "the greatest melodist since Mozart." Only in the last decades has he been generally taken seriously by musicians and critics. Few deny that there are problems in his music—awkward harmonies, strange voice leadings, failed experiments of various kinds, and a degree of rant and rave in place of substance. His peccadilloes, however, are integral to Berlioz and to his sometimes crude but always authentic voice.

To begin getting to know him, I recommend the inevitable *Symphonie fantastique.* Like Stravinsky's *Sacre du printemps,* Berlioz's first masterpiece has never lost its capacity to shock. The quirky rhythms, surprising harmonies, and startling orchestral outbursts, alternating with a marvelous lyricism, have made it an audience favorite from the beginning.

Much the same could be said of his overtures, especially the familiar *Roman Carnival,* originally part of the opera *Benvenuto Cellini.* A combination of scintillating prestos and soulful melodies brilliantly orchestrated, it is among the finest concert overtures in the repertoire.

Harold in Italy is another program symphony, with an inspiration less crazed than that of the *Fantastique*. It was based on one of the Romantic classics of the time, Byron's *Childe Harold*. Not for the only time, Berlioz took prodigal liberties with his model; Byron's Harold never went to Italy, but Berlioz dispatched him there to disport in the landscape that the composer had loved in his Italian stay: Harold meditates on the mountains, joins a band of brigands, and so on. The commission for the piece came in 1832 from virtuoso performer and composer Niccolò Paganini, who wanted a viola concerto to show off his new Stradivarius instrument. Berlioz made the viola soloist, representing the figure of Harold, an obbligato part in an orchestral symphony. Seeing how little the viola got to play, Paganini refused to touch the piece; but when he first heard it, one of Berlioz's warmest and most handsome scores, Paganini ran to the podium and kissed the composer's hands, later sending a large check with the note, "Beethoven is dead and Berlioz alone can revive him."

Less familiar is the series of songs called *Les Nuits d'été* (The Nights of Summer), for soprano and orchestra. Accompanied by an untypically delicate handling of the orchestra, the voice spins out some of Berlioz's most beautiful melodies. He had the Romantic gift for memorable lyric tunes, and seldom more graciously than here.

Finally try the monumental Requiem, of which Berlioz wrote, "If I were threatened with the burning of all my works except one, it is for the Requiem that I would ask for mercy." This is no work of sincere piety but rather the Napoleonic-style outpouring of a composer who wanted to make a noise in the world and went about the task literally. When the four brass choirs cut loose in the *Tuba mirum* and later sections, the effect is fully as stupendous as he intended. Yet there is also a good deal of quiet and subtle music in the Requiem, alternating with its invigorating touches of the vulgar, the maudlin, and the anomalous. (As an example of the latter quality, I submit the orchestral hiccup that accompanies the *Lachrymosa*.) A live performance is a memorable experience; or listen to a compact disc, to get as close as possible to the full-voiced splendor of a composer who was sometimes egregious but rarely dull, determined to astonish and succeeding as well as anyone.

ROBERT SCHUMANN

Robert Schumann exists in history less as an integrated figure than as a series of fragmentary images: a man sitting in a corner whistling to himself, a slayer of philistines, a husband in the shadow of his wife, an irreplaceable composer for piano and voice, a failed symphonist, an enigma, a madman. This fragmentation was not unknown to him; to some of his avatars he even gave names: impulsive Florestan, dreamy Eusebius, wise Raro. He was all these and none of them. His best and most characteristic works are collections of miniatures—songs, little character pieces: fragments.

He was born Robert Alexander Schumann in Zwickau, Germany, on June 8, 1810. The father was bookish—author, publisher, editor—and likewise the son. Robert spent his youth reading the Romantic imaginings of Byron and the like, and hoped to be a poet. At the same time, he developed an early interest in playing the organ; with the encouragement of his father, he began at age seven to compose little pieces. By the time of his father's death in 1826, he had resolved his indecision between poetry and music by determining to create poetic music.

His widowed mother, however, wanted him in something more profitable and respectable. At her insistence he made gestures toward studying law in Leipzig and Heidelberg, but spent more time with music. Finally at the end of 1829 he wrote home an unequivocal declaration: "I have . . . arrived at the conviction that with work, patience, and a good master, I shall be able within six years to challenge any pianist. . . . Besides this, I also possess imagination, and perhaps aptitude, for individual creative work." Soon after, he returned to Leipzig to study piano intensively with his good master (and later worst enemy) Friedrich Wieck.

In Leipzig from 1830 to 1832 he practiced incessantly, composed a little, and spent hours improvising dreamy phantasmagorias with the pedal down. From these years come his remarkable early opus numbers, including *Papillons* and *Die Davidsbündlertänze*. The latter title, "Dances of the League of David," referred to the mythical characters—Florestan, Eusebius, et al.—that he presented half seriously as an aesthetic guerrilla band, little Davids battling the giant musical sins of the day: empty virtuosity, shallow conservatism, and philistinism in general. In April 1834 Schumann and a few colleagues started a periodical, the *Neue Zeitschrift für Musik* (New Journal for Music), which in its ten years under Schumann as editor and chief critic became the most important voice of progressive musical ideas in Germany. In the *Neue Zeitschrift* Eusebius proclaimed the arrival of Chopin with, "Hats, off, gentlemen, a genius!" The music of Berlioz found a champion there as well, and in Schumann's last years of writing he greeted Brahms as "the young eagle."

By the time his magazine was launched much had changed in Schumann's life. He had become entirely a composer because he could no longer be a pianist: his right hand was crippled. His explanation for this disaster was that he had invented a device to immobilize his recalcitrant fourth finger during practice, and the device had paralyzed that finger. Modern medical opinion suspects a different cause: a side effect of the mercury used in those days to treat syphilis. Whether Schumann was another victim of that disease we will never know for certain, but it would also explain the bouts of madness. His first serious breakdown came in October 1833, when after fits and fainting spells and lacerating depression, he tried to throw himself out a window.

By the mid 1830s Schumann seemed to be back on an even keel; he was writing important criticism in the *Neue Zeitschrift,* composing some of his finest piano works, and falling in love with the daughter of his piano teacher. He had known Clara Wieck since she was nine; she was her father's prize pupil and one of the first to perform

Schumann's work in public. He had played the uncle with her until he realized that she had become a high-spirited and handsome woman of sixteen, who silently idolized him. Slowly their old games and secrets became something more significant.

When Friedrich Wieck realized what was happening he was outraged; it was perhaps a combination of protectiveness toward his daughter and doubts about both Schumann's prospects and sanity. For four years Wieck attacked their romance with every weapon at his command, including threats to murder his onetime protégé. The lovers sustained their relationship with secret notes and meetings. Finally in 1840 they sued her father; after a sustained court battle humiliating for them all, Friedrich lost. Robert and Clara were married on September 12, 1840. That day, she wrote in their diary, was "the fairest and most momentous of my life."

He called Clara the guardian angel of his genius. Though one of the finest pianists of her generation, she would, in deference to him, suppress her considerable talents as a composer, as Fanny Mendelssohn had done before her and Alma Mahler would after. Clara and Robert published some songs jointly under his name; he sometimes borrowed her themes as an homage to her.

During the first year of their marriage Schumann wrote 140 lieder, most of them, naturally, love songs. They included all his greatest cycles: the *Liederkreis* on Eichendorff lyrics, *Frauenliebe und -Leben* (Woman's Love and Life), and *Dichterliebe* (A Poet's Love) on verses by Heine. In these works he brought to the tradition of the German lied his own singular voice, less melodious than Schubert, but more poetic.

That was his "song year." Unlike most composers, it was his pattern to concentrate obsessively on one medium at a time. His first twenty-three opus numbers were all for piano; in 1840 came the flood of songs. Meanwhile, Clara was prodding him to write a symphony. He stalled, neither the first nor last composer to tremble at the spirit of Beethoven looming over his attempts at the orchestra. Suddenly in early 1841, during four days of heated inspiration, Schumann drafted his first symphony, which he called *Spring*. It was premiered to great applause by his friend Mendelssohn and the Leipzig Gewandhaus Orchestra. He immediately wrote another in that "symphony year" of 1841, but after the premiere he decided to put it on the shelf. Later revised, the work would be heard in 1853 as Symphony no. 4. The "chamber music year" of 1842 produced three string quartets, a piano quartet, and a piano quintet.

Then the strain of his compulsive working habits brought on another breakdown. Like most Romantic artists, and in contrast to Classical craftsmen, Schumann wrote mainly from inspiration, constantly feeding on his emotions. He composed all three of his string quartets, for example, in one month. With such a creative method one is always on the verge of sliding into confusion, excesses, or worse. Insanity seemed almost an occupational hazard for Romantic artists.

Mendelssohn brought Schumann to the new Leipzig Conservatory in 1843, but Schumann proved too brooding and vague to be a good teacher, and his conducting had similar problems. Energetic and obstinate Clara pushed him to conduct when he had no gift for it; she wanted him to have a glittering performing career like hers. They had two children now and the responsibility of a family weighed on him as well. Once again the ominous symptoms gained on him. Already depressed and unable to concentrate, he developed a maddening itch.

In 1844 he resigned from the Leipzig Conservatory and from the *Neue Zeitschrift* editorship (though he kept contributing) and accompanied Clara on a concert tour of Russia. Then came another breakdown, the worst yet. Searching for rest and change, he and Clara moved to Dresden; they lived there quietly for five years as he tried to recover his health. In that period he completed his Piano Concerto in A minor, his Symphony no. 2, and the opera *Genoveva;* the latter floundered at its Leipzig premiere and has remained in limbo.

In 1850 they moved to Düsseldorf, where he had secured a conducting position. Again, it did not work. He was irascible and forgetful on the podium; sometimes in performance he became so absorbed in the music that he forgot to beat time. By 1853 an assistant had to take over his duties. Meanwhile his work found a public only slowly; it lacked the ingratiating charm that made nearly everything of Mendelssohn's instantly popular. After one of Clara's performances, someone asked him, "Are you musical too, Herr Schumann?"

By then illness and domesticity had changed him from his impulsive and crusading youth. Eusebius had taken over; he had withdrawn into himself. A visitor dispatched to get some musical

Young Clara Schumann, eager and expectant; old Clara, having done and seen more than enough.

information could rouse Schumann to say only, "Do you smoke?" After being asked this three times, with long pauses, the visitor finally gave up. Evenings Schumann tended to spend alone in a café, at a table to the side, his lips pursed in silent whistling; finally the whistling seemed to be going on all the time. A friend wrote, "His eyes . . . looked as if he had something he must fathom and listen to intently deep in his own soul." Even in company he seemed to be alone. Where once he had been in the vanguard of the newest musical ideas, he finally embraced the conservative Brahms and nearly ignored the progressive Wagner.

And madness stalked him. On a tour of Holland with Clara, a considerable public success for them both, he began to hear voices and terrifying music in his head. To his friend the violinist Joachim he wrote in early 1854, "The night is beginning to fall." On February 6 of that year he fled his family and threw himself into the

Rhine. Pulled from the water, he asked to be committed. The last two years of his life he spent at an asylum near Bonn, sometimes lucid, sometimes lost in voices and horror. Brahms visited him from time to time; fearing his reaction, the doctors did not allow Clara contact with her husband. She would sit out of sight and watch him through a window. Of his visits to Schumann, the normally reticent Brahms wrote moving letters to Clara, with whom the young composer had fallen irrevocably in love. Death released Schumann at age forty-six, on July 29, 1856.

Like Schubert and Mendelssohn, Schumann bloomed early; though he lived a little longer than they did, his significant work was done by his mid thirties. He began as a piano composer and is usually at his best when there is a piano involved, whether the medium is song, chamber music, or concerto. With the orchestra he was ambitious but somewhat at sea; though his symphonies contain much fine material, the scoring can be opaque and heavy-footed when the musical ideas call for transparency and lightness. Nor was the large-scale development of ideas his (or his time's) forte. He was aware—painfully aware—of the gnawing question of what to do after Beethoven, but he did not survive long enough to propose any solid answers.

We find his strongest work, then, in songs and character pieces for the piano. The main virtues of these small masterpieces are the marvelous writing for the keyboard and his genius for harmony. With new chord colors, poignant use of dissonances, and long-delayed harmonic resolutions, Schumann contributed to the development of coloristic harmony that would absorb Wagner and, later, Debussy. In Schumann for the first time a single chord can be an event, and the movement from chord to chord, often free from conventional expectations, makes for a continually fresh harmonic flow.

Despite his deficiencies in longer forms, there are innovations as well. In the last three of his four symphonies Schumann picked up, mainly from Berlioz, the idée fixe, the notion of repeating a theme in various movements of a work. This way of unifying multimovement orchestral works came to be called the *cyclic symphony;* it would be around for the rest of the century and into the next, showing up in composers as diverse as Brahms and Charles Ives.

Among Schumann, Chopin, and Liszt, the piano was remade into a different instrument from what it had been for previous masters—more brilliant, with flitting, glittering, even roaring figuration that now seems inevitable for the keyboard, but which had to be discovered. Of Schumann's piano music, the finest may be the 1835 set of pieces called *Carnaval* op. 9, teasingly subtitled "Little scenes on four notes." Those four notes are among the personal references that mark the twenty-one "scenes": they are A-S-C-H, the name of the town where Schumann's then sweetheart lived, and which in the traditional German note names become A-E♭-C-B. He uses various permutations of these pitches for melodic material throughout the piece, an attempt at unifying what is actually a rhapsodic form. (Schumann composed at the piano and usually followed his nose more than traditional patterns.) What really unifies *Carnaval* is the personal and programmatic element—the in joke of the cabalistic themes and the titles of the movements, among them the commedia dell'arte figures of Harlequin and Pierrot, fellow artists Chopin and Paganini, Chiarina/Clara, and his own avatars Eusebius and Florestan. The work concludes with an impetuous "March of the 'Davidsbündler' Against the Philistines." *Carnaval* was the real beginning of Schumann's early and short-lived maturity. Few geniuses have announced themselves with such élan and such charm.

As a song composer Schumann followed his idol Schubert in many respects, but added a great deal to the lieder tradition as well. Besides his gift for poetic evocation, he exercised his pianistic imagination to make the accompaniment equal to the voice. With Schubert one remembers the tune; with Schumann one is just as apt to remember a piano phrase. For example, in his setting of Eichendorff's classic Romantic poem "Mondnacht" (Moonlit Night), part of the *Liederkreis* group, the piano creates an atmosphere enfolding a simple but engrossing vocal line; together, voice and piano capture the dreamlike suspension of the poem.

"Im wunderschönen Monat Mai" ("In the lovely month of May") begins Schumann's greatest song cycle, *Dichterliebe* (A Poet's Love), with words by Heinrich Heine. From the achingly sweet-sad lyricism of the first song it moves through the shades of love and loss, embodied by a remarkable variety of piano textures and colors, before fading into a wistful cloud of reverie at the end. These songs stand with Schubert's finest cycles at the pinnacle of the German lieder tradition.

For an introduction to Schumann's instrumental music, one might start with the Quintet in E-flat for Piano and Strings, written in three weeks of September 1842. It is the first masterpiece in history for this marriage of piano and string quartet and helped inspire quartets by Brahms and Dvořák. Schumann's first movement is dramatic and propulsive, the development section mostly a piano solo. Second comes a funeral march à la Beethoven's *Eroica*, but in rondo form; the somber march alternates with lighter material. The scherzo is typically driving, leaping, full of fascinating rhythmic notions, and has two contrasting trios. In the finale there is a pounding, folklike theme; near the end, melodies from first and last movements combine into a double fugue (more interesting in conception than execution—traditional counterpoint was not Schumann's forte either). Though entirely Schumannesque, the quintet often sounds proto-Brahmsian as well.

That is even more true of the Piano Concerto in A minor of 1841–45, Schumann's finest work involving orchestra. It stands as one of the most perennially popular of Romantic concertos and the direct ancestor of Brahms's works in the genre. With the inspiration the piano always brought him, and with the necessity of scoring delicately behind the soloist, Schumann avoids overscoring and finds some of his most attractive ideas. The first movement fantasia sustains a tone of restless yearning, with ravishing thematic material. A light and charming second movement Intermezzo flows directly into the allegro vivace finale, a rhythmic tour de force with some of the most sparkling piano writing of the era.

The Symphony in D minor, written second but numbered fourth, is the most integrated of his four symphonies, all the movements sharing melodic material. An aggressively leaping theme and persistent march rhythms makes for a dramatic opening movement. In contrast, the following *Romanze* begins with a wistful theme in cellos and oboe, leading to some beautiful lyric episodes. The scherzo is one of Schumann's most memorable, minor and darktoned, with an intense rhythmic drive. After a slowly swelling introduction in D minor, the finale breaks out joyfully in major, marchlike material alternating with lyrical. In this symphony, the

Piano Concerto in A minor, and the late Cello Concerto in A minor, we realize what music may have lost as a result of Schumann's illness and early death: one of the century's most individual and gifted miniaturists making himself into the symphonist he dreamed of being.

FRÉDÉRIC CHOPIN

From his own time forward, Frédéric Chopin has seemed the most aristocratic of composers, the creature of elegant salons, the composer for dandies and fainting ladies. As a matter of fact, he *is* all those things. He is a significant composer, however, because he accomplishes so much more. Like his personality and his fashionable milieu, his music conceals more than it reveals. If he is sometimes precious and redolent of the drawing room, he also intimates the passions that lie under the brocades and trivialities; if he is sometimes limp and sentimental, he is more often virile and commanding. What the finest musical minds of his time admired so much in Chopin was that he expressed so many miniature worlds; nothing you can say to characterize him, even in a specific genre like the waltz or polonaise, will do justice to the myriad caprices of his imagination. And with his chosen vehicle, the piano, he was and remains what Beethoven was to the orchestra: pervasive and inescapable. In discovering what seems the piano's natural voice, he remade the world's conception of it once and for all.

Frédéric François Chopin was born on March 1, 1810, in Zelazowa Wola, near Warsaw, to a French father and Polish mother. His father ran a boarding school for aristocratic children, with whom Frédéric grew up. Showing musical talent virtually from the cradle, he was provided with the best piano teachers and made a sensational debut on his eighth birthday. He soon became a pet of the aristocracy, playing in their musicales. His repertoire included his own little pieces, among them the Polish dances called polonaise and mazurka that he would compose for the rest of his life. By the age of twenty Chopin was a mature artist whose singular style was already formed; the great G minor Ballade dates from that year. After visits to Berlin and Vienna, where he was dazzled with the musical life, he decided in 1830 to go on the road to make his fortune. He left Warsaw carrying a silver urn full of Polish earth. That symbol of his native land would accompany him everywhere—everywhere but Poland, which he never saw again.

After several frustrating months in Vienna, Chopin tried Paris. Though for a while he was neglected there, so desperate he even considered setting out for America, he finally caught the ears of fashionable Paris and became its favorite. As performer and composer he inspired not only devotion in his public but profound respect among his peers. Friends and admirers included Liszt, Berlioz, Mendelssohn, and the writers Heine and Balzac. Schumann called him "the boldest and proudest poetic spirit of the time."

Schumann would not have said the same about Chopin's personality. Effeminate and dandyish, a salon-hopper and name-dropper, impressed with anyone famous, he was extravagantly neurotic, delicate in health, an egregious snob, and fashionably anti-Semitic (excepting his converted friends Mendelssohn and Heine and the rich Rothschilds). He was, in other words, exactly what the French aristocratic world expected their artists to be. He flowered in that elegantly vicious, style-obsessed, pleasure-hungry world. (His letters reveal another side—charming, ironic, observant, loyal to old friends, a wholehearted Polish nationalist, and, finally, courageous in facing death.)

In public Chopin largely played his own music, shaping its rhapsodic surface with a delicate and sensuous touch. In contrast to the thunderous playing of Liszt, Chopin never used fortissimo but rather shaded his dynamics downward toward the intimate and nearly inaudible. He was celebrated for his unprecedented rubato, in which his right hand played with a flexible, wandering rhythm over the left hand's strict tempo, a union of freedom and control that would hardly be equalled again until the advent of jazz in the twentieth century.

But his approach did not please the bourgeois public who were ravished by Liszt. Chopin's harmonic colors were so original, his dissonances so startling, that even as sensitive a listener as Mendelssohn complained, "one does not know at times whether [the notes he plays] are right or wrong." In view of the nervous, over-heated tone of much of his music, rival pianist John Field (from whom Chopin took the idea of the nocturne) called him a "sickroom

*Chopin, looking as spectral as a nocturne, here sits
for one of the earliest photographs of any composer.*

talent." Shrinking from such criticism, Chopin bitterly told Liszt in 1835 that he was retiring from public recitals: "I am not fitted to give concerts. The crowd intimidates me; I feel asphyxiated by its breath . . . but you, you are destined for the crowd, because when you do not captivate your public, you have the wherewithal to overpower it." Though lack of money would sometimes drive him back to the concert stage, from then on Chopin largely retreated to the salons of the beau monde that idolized him.

Chopin and Liszt would finally come to a parting of the ways, due as much as anything to mutual jealousy. But in 1836 they were still friends, and Liszt introduced Chopin to George Sand, the notorious cigar-puffing novelist who called herself by a man's name and wore men's clothes—though her taste in lovers ran to men and lots of them. Fastidious Chopin was scandalized at first by this outlandish figure, but she set her sights on him and, being by far the more aggressive, finally conquered him. Chopin had experienced infatuations before, had consummated an affair or two (and maybe had a homosexual attachment in Poland), but the long romance with George Sand would dominate, exalt, frustrate, and finally consume him.

The two of them spent the winter of 1838–39 on the island of Majorca. It was a disastrous time; already in poor health, Chopin developed chronic bronchitis and had nightmares and hallucinations. One night Sand found him sitting at the piano paralyzed with terror. Nonetheless, he composed steadily during that winter, mainly completing the magnificent twenty-four preludes. Chopin's favorite composers were Bach and Mozart (he never liked Beethoven); the preludes were his testament to Bach.

George Sand left a portrait of Chopin's creative style: "[Inspiration] came on his piano suddenly, complete, sublime, or it sang in his head during a walk. . . . But then began the most heartrending labor I ever saw. It was a series of efforts, of irresolutions, and of frettings to seize again certain details of the theme he had heard . . . his regret at not finding it again . . . threw him into a kind of despair. He shut himself up for whole days, weeping, walking, breaking his pens, repeating and altering a bar a hundred times, writing and erasing it as many times, and recommencing the next day with a minute and desperate perseverance. He spent six weeks over a single page to write it at last as he had noted it down at the very first." In this consuming quest for perfection we see Chopin the immortal artist as opposed to Chopin the hothouse flower and drawing-room pet. He loved the sophisticated and superficial life, but the artist in him was stronger. The airy flights of his music, which seem as free as improvisations, were the products of furious labor and the highest level of craft, like a rococo hall that appears to be all clouds and confections but is held up by solid architecture.

Chopin left Majorca barely alive, but his health soon improved and the relationship with Sand became relatively stable, though never less than stormy. In winter they lived in Paris, in summer at her château in Nohant. His career and his creative powers were at their zenith in 1841 and 1842; his craft and expressiveness dug deeper and deeper while his innovations in harmony and piano style pervaded the musical world.

But his health declined again after 1842 and his relations with Sand along with it. For years she had devotedly nursed him through his illnesses and put up with his neurotic ways; but finally she tired of her increasingly troublesome and spectral lover, whom she began to call "my dear corpse." The inevitable break came in late 1846, which also marked the end of his creative life. He felt Sand had killed him. Certainly, he was now dying in earnest from tuberculosis. (That and syphilis were the twin scourges of the century.)

During his miserable last years Chopin kept performing; he needed the money. An 1848 concert tour of England and Scotland further damaged his health and gained him nothing. He returned to Paris to die, breathing his last on October 17, 1849. At his request, Mozart's Requiem was sung at his funeral. Buried with him was the Polish earth that he had carried since he left Warsaw.

Except for two early piano concertos (strong in piano, weak in concerto), a late cello sonata, and assorted minor pieces, Chopin wrote entirely for the piano, the only major composer to limit himself so consistently to one instrument. On the whole, he avoided the traditional large forms; only a few works are called sonatas, and they tend to be loosely connected series of movements. Most of his works bear names typical of Romantic free genres—nocturne, scherzo, ballade, prelude, impromptu, étude. And there are many dance pieces, some of them based on the Polish genres that he knew and composed from childhood: mazurka, polonaise, and waltz. Though these pieces are small in scale, he made them large in effect. What some composers require a symphony or a sonata to say, Chopin could put into the ten minutes of a ballade or nocturne.

As noted before, his piano style seems to be the innate voice of the instrument, liberated for the first time. Every work he wrote is identifiably his in every measure, yet there is an immense variety of ideas and colors from work to work. His novelties in both texture and harmony were not studied or formulated so much as they were discovered at the piano by constant experiment, part of the reason why his pieces seem improvisatory even when they were painstakingly worked out. Some generalizations can be made about his piano writing: the left hand often plays widely spaced chordal figures that give an airy openness to the texture while keeping the rhythm going; meanwhile, the right hand can spin lacy flights of fantasy, or play a simple tune and then immediately turn it into a flowery variation. Usually there are implied counterpoints in the figuration, making a shadowy background melody supporting the foreground.

A good place to start with Chopin is his 24 preludes, designed to echo Bach's in the *Well-Tempered Clavier,* and having a similar tour through the keys. They are a remarkable collection of little pieces, each based on a single texture and idea, some fully fleshed out and others truncated like a fragment of a longer work: "sketches, beginnings of Études . . . ruins, eagle wings, a wild motley of pieces," wrote Robert Schumann. They largely proceed in contrasts, no. 1 breathless and impulsive, no. 2 bleak and somber, no. 3 a whirlwind, and the celebrated no. 4 a slowly sinking lyrical suspension. And thus these preludes continue, some grand, some slight and sentimental, some joyous, some morbid unto despair.

Chopin largely forswore the extremes of virtuosity that Liszt and others of the time wallowed in, but his études are among the first such finger exercises and technical studies to attain musical significance. Starting with the roaring cascades of the first étude, these are exhilarating examples of Romantic virtuosity. Similar pieces are the impromptus, midway between the virtuosic and lyrical. An example is the Impromptu in A-flat op. 29, an ABA form in which the outer sections are a dizzying whirligig with nearly berserk harmony, the middle simple and lyrical with typical vary-as-you-go melodic lines in the right hand.

His waltzes are relatively light pieces, but show his usual variety. Here one senses the emotions surging beneath the gallant surface of this genre. (Schumann: "If he were to play [his waltzes] for dancing, half the ladies among the dancers would have to be at least countesses.") Very different are the polonaises, maybe the most nationalistic of Chopin's works. Though their material ranges from the heroic to the elegiac, they tend to be massive and magisterial. Some of them, especially the famous Military Polonaise, no. 3 in A major, reflect his feelings about the doomed Polish uprising against the czar in 1831. It is primarily these works, and the more adventurous and idiosyncratic mazurkas, that made Chopin Poland's native composer and a prototype of musical nationalism in the nineteenth century. (Just before Poland surrendered to the Nazis in World War II, the first notes of the Military Polonaise were played defiantly over Radio Warsaw.)

Among the most sustained and developed genres are the nocturnes and ballades. The Nocturne in D-flat of 1835 is a finely controlled study in sustained lyricism; its languid opening melody sounds operatic, reminding us that among Chopin's friends was bel canto opera composer Bellini. In this poetic night piece his rhapsodic right-hand figuration is in fine form. The ballades are one of his most personal genres; there is nothing else quite like them. Though they tend to resemble rondos in form, with the main theme turning up in alternation with other material, their overall effect is improvisatory. The Ballade no. 1 in G minor, written when he was twenty, has a ruminative introduction in octaves, then a darkly passionate theme of a Slavic type that would persist in piano music all the way to Rachmaninov; this alternates with faster material and brilliant figuration. The Ballade no. 2 in F major begins with a lovely and almost childlike little folk tune that is shattered by an eruption of fury; after further similar contrasts, the little tune seems to lie broken at the end.

William Faulkner observed that one can present the truth plainly or put it in a chalice. Chopin presented his work in the richest and most filigreed of chalices, but filled it with a full measure of human experience and truth.

251

FRANZ LISZT

The life of composer and virtuoso pianist Franz Liszt could be seen as an ongoing illustration of the old maxim, "The road of excess leads to the palace of wisdom." Except that Liszt never really left the road and never quite made it to the palace. His journey was marked by approximately equal parts genius, charlatanism, generosity, self-serving, skirt-chasing, monkish withdrawal, and shameless grandstanding. Some of the same descriptions apply to his music, which even at its innovative best can still slide into tub-thumping vulgarity. In any event, his public, especially the legions of women, worshipped him from beginning to end. It is said that some countess or other wore to the day of her death, in a gold locket at her breast, one of Liszt's cigar butts.

He was born on October 22, 1811, in Raiding, Hungary. From his earliest years he was trained on piano by his father. When it became obvious that the boy was a prodigy of Mozartean dimensions, in 1821 a group of Hungarian noblemen paid for his family to go to Vienna, where Franz studied piano with the famed technician Czerny and composition with the ubiquitous Antonio Salieri. Liszt always said that in Vienna he played for Beethoven, who delightedly rewarded him with a kiss, but the story may be hype: Beethoven was stone deaf by then. At thirteen Liszt's one-act opera *Don Sanche* was performed to some acclaim, but he withdrew the score and never tried the stage again. By the time he moved to Paris in 1824, he was becoming one of the most renowned pianists on the Continent. When his father died in 1827, he knew his son's career was secure if only he didn't let the glitter get to him. (The father's prophetic last words: "I fear for you and the women.") Soon after that Liszt had the first of his numberless affairs, this time with a girl of sixteen; when her father broke it up, he went into a two-year funk marked by the kind of compulsive piety that would periodically mark his life.

In 1830 Liszt met three artists who revitalized him: Berlioz, his model for form and orchestration in the grand style; Chopin, who revealed new ways of writing for the piano; and the violinist Paganini, who dazzled him with his unparalleled virtuosity. For two years Liszt sequestered himself, practicing technique with fierce determination, and returned to concert life styling himself "the Paganini of the piano." Hype notwithstanding, he may have been the greatest keyboard master who ever lived. His compositions at that point were largely designed to show off his wares; ranging from the splendid to the dreadful, the works have been foundations of the virtuoso repertoire ever since.

His audience was the vast new bourgeois concert-going public. Unlike his friend and rival, Chopin, Liszt knew what this audience wanted and was happy to provide it. Since he happened to be blazingly handsome and a born showman, success was assured. His concerts, for the first time called "recitals," were an extraordinary blend of seriousness and circus, spiritual communion and erotic feeding frenzy (which applies to much of the Romantic period as well). Wrote one observer, "Constantly tossing back his long hair, with lips quivering, he swept the auditorium with the glance of a smiling master." Another recounted: "As the closing strains began I saw Liszt's countenance assume that agony of expression, mingled with radiant smiles of joy, which I never saw in any other human face except in the paintings of our Saviour . . . he fainted in the arms of a friend who was turning the pages for him, and he bore him out in a strong fit of hysterics."

Liszt's first sustained liaison began in 1835 with the married Countess d'Agoult, who, like George Sand, wrote novels under a man's name. They traveled around Europe and had three children, among them Cosima, who would inspire musicians herself. Meanwhile he pursued some passing fancies, including George Sand, the legendary Lola Montez, and the model for Dumas's "Lady of the Camellias." By 1844 the countess was weary of Liszt's extracurricular dalliances and left him. He took up with the Russian-Polish princess Carolyne Sayn-Wittgenstein, beautiful, eccentric, cigarsmoking authoress of the outlandish twenty-four-volume *The Inner Causes of the Outer Weakness of the Church*. Well versed in inner and outer weaknesses, the princess tolerated her lover's and stayed with him the rest of his days, serving as, among other things, his ghostwriter for several books (mainly extensive and inaccurate ones on Chopin and on Hungarian music, of which he was an enthusiast but hardly an expert).

She also managed to turn Liszt to religion again, convincingly enough so that the pope made him an abbé in 1865. Liszt retired to

*Liszt in his later years, displaying
the famous profile, somewhat worse for wear.*

Rome for two years, spending his days in penitence and prayer and his evenings with the ladies. Later he took on minor orders but never became a full priest; the Church was too wary of his peccadilloes to allow that. Once Liszt insisted on confessing to the pope in person; exhausted by the endless enumeration, the pontiff finally exclaimed, *"Basta,* Liszt; go tell your sins to your piano."

After 1848 he virtually retired from concertizing and became court Kapellmeister of Weimar. During eleven years in that post he composed voluminously and also conducted and promoted the music of others. The chief beneficiary of his efforts was Wagner; among other works, Liszt conducted the premiere of *Lohengrin.* Together the two men led the radical musical faction in Europe under the banner of Wagner's "Music of the Future." Liszt's dozens of piano transcriptions, arrangements, and variations of other composers' work also helped popularize Beethoven and Schubert symphonies, Schubert songs, and a great deal else.

His last decades were spent in Weimar, Rome, and Budapest—composing, teaching, proselytizing for new music, seeking holiness, and getting in trouble with young women. Among several notable piano pupils was conductor Hans von Bülow, who married Liszt's daughter Cosima and was a leading Wagnerian until Wagner stole Cosima for himself. Liszt and Wagner suspended relations for some time. Even before they were reconciled, though, Liszt still promoted Wagner's work.

In his last years a fat and warty Abbé Liszt, as he liked to be called, was virtually a one-man shrine to whom young composers came to be blessed; Borodin, Fauré, and Debussy were among the pilgrims. At age seventy-five Liszt made a "Jubilee Tour" of Budapest, Liège, Paris, and London; his works received all the old enthusiasm from the public. He then made his own pilgrimage to Wagner's Bayreuth, where despite illness he insisted on hearing *Parsifal* and *Tristan und Isolde.* During the latter performance, pneumonia set in; he died of it on July 31, 1886.

All but his most charitable admirers admit that Liszt is erratic, only occasionally at his best. All the same, his music has survived, and not only the virtuosic side of it. No one could deny his incalculable importance to later nineteenth-century music: without Liszt's prose-lytizing and his musical ideas, Wagner and other artists might have been stillborn.

After the undisciplined excesses of his virtuoso period, Liszt labored for years to corral the wild horses of his imagination into effective large concert works. He matured not by imitating the past but by developing techniques appropriate to his own novel ideas of musical construction. These ideas and techniques constitute his most important legacy.

A primary ingredient of the Music of the Future agenda that he and Wagner promulgated was the concept of a synthesis of arts. In Liszt's case, this led to the *symphonic poem* (or tone poem): an orchestral work, usually in one movement, based on a literary or philosophical idea. The main inspiration for this new genre was Berlioz's *Symphonie fantastique;* Liszt simply took the programmatic concept of that work several degrees further (as he did with Berlioz's orchestration, his idée fixe, and his extravagances generally).

An old audience favorite among Liszt's thirteen symphonic poems is *Les Préludes* (1856). There is no specific program here but rather a general idea from the poet Lamartine: "What is our life but a series of Preludes to that unknown song of which death strikes the first solemn note?" It is a characteristic Lisztian amalgam of innovative harmony, rambling formal organization based on recurring themes, and episodes ranging from the grand to the garish to the soggy-sentimental. Still, in a performance with a modicum of restraint, *Les Préludes* can add up to a powerful experience.

Among the best and best known of his virtuoso piano outings is the program piece *Mephisto Waltz* no. 1 of 1860, one of several works in a self-styled demonic vein. The program is based on Goethe's play *Faust,* a Romantic favorite: Faust seduces a girl at a dance while Mephistopheles provides the devilish fiddle accompaniment. Liszt makes the piano into a kind of superviolin, building brilliant figuration to a frenzied climax. Together, Liszt and Chopin would bequeath to the future an idiomatic understanding of the piano and a compendium of ideas in writing for it that composers would mine for the better part of a century.

Though he was an enthusiastic Hungarian nationalist, Liszt barely spoke the language and only occasionally lived in his native country. His pieces in a "Hungarian" vein were mainly based on the tunes of Gypsy street bands rather than true Hungarian folk music, which Bartók and Kodály would be the first to document. Still, Liszt's attempts at nationalism would contribute much to the nationalistic movement of the nineteenth century and beyond. His Hungarian Rhapsodies, especially no. 2, are well-loved bonbons of the light classical repertoire.

Several of his most important works appeared in the 1850s, when he had deepened his control of form and thematic relationships. Increasingly in his mature music, the melodies of a whole piece are derived from a small collection of basic themes; this technique would influence composers starting with Wagner (his leitmotif idea) and as far into the future as Bartók and Schoenberg. The massive Sonata in B minor for piano, the culmination of Liszt's piano music, is less a traditional sonata than (as one critic put it) "a great rhetorical rhapsody on a few motifs." In its single movement it contains some of his finest and most visionary pages. There is a similar motivic treatment in the Piano Concerto no. 1 in E-flat, whose main theme is a typically plaintive, chromatic lyric line that undergoes transformation in each of the four movements. This bravura concerto is one of the essential works of the Romantic grand style.

Similar pieces by his friends Berlioz and Wagner inspired Liszt's *Faust* Symphony of 1853–57. The first three movements are portraits respectively of Faust, Gretchen, and Mephistopheles (a mocking scherzo); the finale is a choral setting of the "Chorus Mysticus" that ends Goethe's play. Besides containing some of Liszt's most effective orchestration and musical ideas, the *Faust* Symphony shows the radical harmonic style that so much affected later composers; the opening is so chromatic that it approaches atonality. Wagner promptly stole it for *Die Walküre*.

Near the end of his life Liszt wrote several enigmatic, meditative little piano pieces that were music of the future indeed; they suggest the harmonic style of Debussy and anticipate Schoenberg. Among these is the extraordinary *Nuages gris* (Gray Clouds), which features highly chromatic melodic lines over chords of unprecedented dissonance and ambiguity, and ends with an unresolved dissonant chord. With these final works—spiritual, searching, and perhaps with a touch of despair—Liszt wound up the singular odyssey of his searching life.

RICHARD WAGNER

The first half of the Romantic period in music was dominated by Beethoven, the second half by Richard Wagner. Other composers were intimidated by the looming presence of their great predecessor; Wagner deliberately assumed the mantle of Beethoven and attempted to go still further. The earlier nineteenth century established the religion of art; Wagner declared himself high priest of that religion. Others wrote large, ambitious works; Wagner wrote epic music dramas with world-transforming intentions. One simply attended other composers' operas; Wagner established a shrine for his seventeen-hour, four-night cycle, *Der Ring des Nibelungen,* (The Ring of the Nibelung), presented as a quasi-religious festival to a convocation of pilgrims. By the late nineteenth century he would haunt the Western cultural tradition as pervasive myth and sacred monster.

His stupendous ambition and the ruthlessness with which he realized it would have been only another episode in the crowded history of Romantic egomania were it not for one inescapable fact: even if Wagner failed to be the universal genius he considered himself, he was still an artist of a very high order who forever changed opera, the orchestra, and the tonal language of Western music. Beyond that there was the widespread influence of his intellectual framework, the Music of the Future agenda that was in some respects logical and provocative, in other respects atrocious and proto-Nazi. Other composers had influence; Wagner had a way of thinking named after him. As we shall see, a significant biographical feature of most composers into the next century was how they lined up in regard to Wagnerism.

Richard Wagner was born in Leipzig, Germany, on May 22, 1813, to the family of a police official who died six months after his birth. A year later his mother married actor and family friend Ludwig Geyer, who may in fact have been Richard's father (the jury is still out on that, but Wagner himself apparently suspected it). In any

*Wagner in silks and satins. "By nature," he wrote, "I am luxurious,
prodigal, and extravagant, much more than Sardanap and all
the other old emperors." He might have said the same of his own music.*

case, Geyer's artistic interests permeated the family. Richard's three sisters and brother all became actors, and from childhood he was fascinated by the dramas of Goethe and Shakespeare. Under the spell of Beethoven, Richard also became interested in music and had desultory lessons in piano, violin, and theory, but he would remain largely self-taught. By his mid teens he was composing in earnest; 1832 saw his first published work, a piano sonata, and a symphony that had a couple of well-received performances. He then spent a few months at the University of Leipzig, majoring primarily in wine and women.

In 1833 Wagner's brother brought him into the theater of Würzburg as chorusmaster. This was the beginning of sixteen years' work, off and on, as an opera conductor. At age twenty-one Wagner finished his first opera, *Die Feen* (The Fairies); very much in the spirit of Rossini and Donizetti, it was never performed in his lifetime. His second effort, *Das Liebesverbot* (based on Shakespeare's *Measure for Measure*) was premiered in March 1836 at a theater at Magdeburg where Wagner had been working. It was a fiasco sufficient to bankrupt the company. Meanwhile in Magdeburg Wagner fell in love with actress Minna Planner, whom he married in 1836. Pretty and conventional, Minna would never understand his ideas or his colossal aspirations. Already at age twenty-two Wagner had begun making notes for his autobiography. He said later that he knew from the beginning that he was great, but it took a while to figure out what he was going to be great at.

After several frustrating jobs in opera houses, Wagner went to Paris, where he finished *Rienzi* and *Der Fliegende Holländer* (The Flying Dutchman). Despite his history of failure he expected fame and fortune on the opera stage; instead, after much struggle and near starvation he ended up in debtor's prison. His disastrous first sojourn in Paris ended in 1842 when *Rienzi,* an old-fashioned grand opera à la Meyerbeer, was produced with great success in Dresden. Meyerbeer, a Jewish opera composer then at the height of his fame, had given Wagner advice and practical help. Wagner repaid him eight years later by attacking Meyerbeer in a contemptible anti-Semitic screed called *Judaism in Music.*

The 1843 premiere of *Der Fliegende Holländer,* which was nearing Wagner's mature musical style, found less success in Dresden but at least earned him further respect. That led to a prestigious appointment as Kapellmeister to the Saxon court, which included directing the Dresden Opera. Wagner spent six years in that post, conducting a wide spectrum of the operatic literature and producing his *Tannhäuser*. Though still in the Weber tradition of German Romantic opera, this work marks the beginning of Wagner's maturity. Not well received at first, it gradually found a wide audience despite the steady sniping of conservative critics. It was quickly followed by *Lohengrin;* this opera would have a more complicated performance history, because Wagner's life was about to become highly complicated.

In 1848 he wrote a libretto called *Siegfrieds Tod* (The Death of Siegfried), based on ancient German and Scandinavian myths. It was the first step toward the stupendous undertaking that would remain his primary concern, despite competing projects, for over twenty-five years. Around the same time he made the acquaintance of Franz Liszt, who became an important champion of Wagner's music. (Liszt and Berlioz, both of whom contributed much to his style, were the only living musicians Wagner recognized as colleagues. Others he divided into disciples or enemies.) Also in 1848, Wagner joined a revolutionary movement called *Vaterlandsverein*. Though he was in the employ of the Saxon court, his politics were socialist—or maybe more generally anticonservative, since conservatives were his main opponents. Wagner supported the movement's May revolution of 1849, but when it was crushed he did not wait around for the dust to settle. With an arrest warrant pursuing him, Wagner fled, ending up in Zurich, Switzerland. His twelve-year exile had begun.

Though Liszt would conduct the premiere of *Lohengrin* in Weimar in 1850, Wagner now had little hope that other new works would be performed. (He did not even hear *Lohengrin* until 1861.) Before going to Zurich, he made a trip to Paris looking for opportunities. The main fruit of this visit was an affair with a young married woman named Jessie Laussot. To his disgust, she finally refused Wagner's offer of eternal bliss with himself. So he went to Switzerland with the carping Minna, who wanted him to make a steady living writing what people wanted to hear.

Instead, for several years he composed words rather than music. First came a series of polemics—*Art and Revolution, The Artwork of the*

Future, Opera and Drama. In these Wagner laid out a revolutionary agenda for his future stage works. Like several others in the history of opera (among them Gluck), he called for a return to the Greek ideal of drama. In Wagner's interpretation, that meant overthrowing the last centuries' accumulation of operatic conventions and pursuing a unified conception: away from the artificial division of recitative and aria, away from the traditional dominance of music on the operatic stage, and toward an equalizing of music, text, drama, movement, and design. Thereby, he said, the ancient unanimity of the arts would be reinstated. Wagner named such an integrated form the *Gesamtkunstwerk,* "total work of art," and he proposed to call the result *music drama* rather than opera. In music drama no element was to exist for itself; everything would serve the story and the meaning.

Like ancient Greek theater, music drama would be a kind of religious ritual based on indigenous myths and legends. Also in keeping with Greek ideals, Wagner anointed the artist as the embodiment of the voice and spirit of the people, a manifestation of national and racial blood brotherhood. In turn, the artist served and exalted the people from whom he derived his inspiration and stories and language. (From then on, nationalistic movements in music would tend to present themselves in similar terms.)

In later writings Wagner would attribute the corruption of society to materialism, militarism, industrialization, a mercenary church, meat-eating, and racial mixture. Germans, being the least racially contaminated, were to lead in the redemption of humankind. The means of this redemption would be art, "the living representation of religion." And at the forefront of German artist-redeemers would be . . . Guess Who. (With similar mythical/spiritual/authoritarian doctrines, the Nazis would anoint themselves avatars of the German racial spirit.)

At the same time that he was formulating this sweeping aesthetic philosophy, with its inextricable blend of authentic vision, racist lies, and self-serving humbug, Wagner was also writing the text of its intended vehicle. Working backward in the story from *Siegfrieds Tod,* he dramatized the old German epic that begins with the theft of gold by the gnomish Nibelungs and leads inexorably to the fall of the gods. This tale would be embodied in the four-opera cycle *Der Ring des Nibelungen: Das Rheingold, Die Walküre* (The Valkyrie), *Sieg-*

fried, and *Die Götterdämmerung* (The Twilight of the Gods). The latter two were based on the original *Siegfrieds Tod;* but where the hero Siegfried had originally been the focus of the drama, now the Valkyrie Brünnhilde and the king of the gods, Wotan, became more important figures. The immense canvas of the *Ring* was held together by a few overriding themes: the spiritual weakness of gold's power, the failure of masculine force, the regeneration of humanity by feminine love. In the end, the redeemer of humankind would be not the sword-wielding Siegfried but rather the self-sacrificing Brünnhilde.

In 1853 Wagner published the librettos of the four operas, beginning the struggle to try to raise interest and wherewithal for their realization on the stage. Given that the *Ring* was perhaps the most ambitious single project ever conceived by one creative mind, and that its creator was living in poverty and exile at the time, it was some kind of audacious proposition. In fact, for many years Wagner did not expect to see it produced in his lifetime. Nonetheless, in 1854 he began composing *Das Rheingold.* (Though Wagner was generally strapped for money he always lived in luxury. His main financial procedure was simply to borrow large sums and never pay them back. The world in general, he felt, owed him whatever he required. Eventually, he more or less got it.)

As he composed the *Ring,* his theories found their practice. The most noticeable of his departures from previous opera (already suggested in *Holländer*) was to erase the traditional boundaries between recitative and aria; along with such divisions he also discarded the old strongly marked short phrases in melodic writing. In the *Ring* the music is continuous, the orchestra plays nonstop, and the vocal lines take the form of rhapsodic semirecitative over the orchestra—what would later be called *unendliche Melodie,* "endless melody." This new long-breathed melodic style would demand a new kind of singer, one male version of which is the *Heldentenor,* "heroic tenor." Where in the past the instrumental ensemble had been an accompaniment with occasional pictorial touches, Wagner made his orchestra into a full participant in the music drama, functioning as commentary, explanation, reflection. The orchestra fulfills, in other words, the function of the chorus in classical Greek drama. The characters live and love and die amidst the voluptuous instrumental web, which unfolds like a gigantic symphony.

To further integrate music and drama, the music is saturated with short melodic/harmonic ideas called *leitmotifs*, literally, "leading motives." Each motive is associated with a person, a situation, or an idea. For example, each character—Siegfried, Brünnhilde, Wotan, etc.—has a basic leitmotif; other motives (there are dozens) include Siegfried's Sword, the Magic Fire, Valhalla, The Rhine, and so on. Leitmotifs are the melodic material of the operas in a way similar to themes in symphonies, but while they are carrying the music they are also contributing to the story. When Siegfried sings of Brünnhilde, we hear her theme in the orchestra; a leitmotif can subtly suggest a character or idea not mentioned in the text at the time; it can prefigure events, even contradict what a character is saying or tell us he is lying (if, of course, we've done our homework and know the leitmotifs). Having thus unified, to his own satisfaction, the words, drama, and music, Wagner would eventually try to incorporate the stagecraft into the overall concept.

In the end, though, his music drama does not work out quite as planned. Wagner considered himself a genius as playwright, poet, stage director, and philosopher as well as composer—himself a unanimity of all the arts to be united in the *Gesamtkunstwerk*. In reality, he was simply a musical genius. And so in the *Ring* and his other operas the drama is sometimes static, the story silly, the poetry only serviceable. But never mind—the music can be glorious. And the drama has some unforgettable episodes: the giant Fafner, cobuilder of Valhalla, watching as his original payment for the job (namely, Wotan's sister-in-law) is slowly covered by the stolen Rhinegold that Wotan offers him instead, until the king of the gods is forced to throw in the all-powerful ring to cover the dazzling glint of the maiden's eye; Wotan and the gods ascending the rainbow bridge to Valhalla accompanied by a grandiloquent march that is in fact bitterly ironic—Wotan knows that his shiny new palace has been paid for by a crime that will eventually bring them all down, palace and gods alike; the guileless Siegfried, in search of this interesting new sensation called *fear*, bantering with the hungry dragon; Siegfried listening to the magical bird, in which Wagner's luminous orchestration creates an extraordinary suspension of time.

At its best, the *Ring* has the unmistakable feel of true myth, and a musical subtlety and grandeur fully equal to the subject. It is also filled with memorable characters—the brooding, guilt-ridden, and henpecked Wotan, the powerful but callow Siegfried, the flirtatious Rhine Maidens, and Brünnhilde, at once warrior and passionate woman, avatar of the new age of love that replaces the old, inadequate age of masculine heroism. (The Nazis had to stand the meaning of the *Ring* on its head to co-opt it as their own myth.) Perhaps no composer or poet or philosopher in history could have fully realized the pretensions of these dramas, but Wagner came amazingly close. Even if, in the end, music once more wins out over the other elements on the stage, the Wagnerian ideal of music drama would continue to inspire generations of composers including Richard Strauss, Debussy, and Berg.

In a letter to Liszt written as he worked on the *Ring,* Wagner was remarkably candid (if full of false modesty) about himself: ". . . my talents, taken separately and individually, are not great at all; I am something and achieve something only when I bring all of them together in an effect and when they and I are recklessly consumed therein. Whatsoever my passions demand of me, I become for the time being—musician, poet, director, author, lecturer, or anything else." By nature he required something intoxicating to move him, some stage entirely his own, a form that he had invented for himself. He created music drama in his own image, as a shrine to his genius. Once that was done, the main problem would become money; that required other talents, to which once again he would prove adequate. But as if things were not already complicated enough when he set out toward the *Ring,* his extramusical passions made them worse.

Wagner attracted disciples in Zurich, among them wealthy silk merchant Otto Wesendonck and his handsome wife, Mathilde. As Otto was helping support Wagner, Wagner fell in love with Otto's wife. Finally, while Minna was visiting Germany in 1854, Wagner and Mathilde Wesendonck became lovers. In the image of their passion (which must have been sensational), he conceived the sustained erotic delirium of *Tristan und Isolde.* So it happened that in 1857—he and Minna now living on the Wesendonck estate, the affair with Mathilde openly acknowledged, with Minna hysterical and Otto accommodating—Wagner put aside the *Ring* and began writing *Tristan.* Originally planned as a practical little number to produce some cash, it grew into a gargantuan production of phenomenal orchestral imagination and musical audacity. (The first attempt to produce *Tristan* would be abandoned after fifty-seven rehearsals.) One memorable evening the relevant parties assembled to hear Wagner read the completed libretto; Hans and Cosima von Bülow were also in attendance. Thus, as Victor Borge nicely puts it, "He read it aloud to his wife, his mistress, his mistress's husband, his future mistress, and his future mistress's husband. They all said they liked it."

Wagner finished composing *Tristan* in Venice and Lucerne in 1859. Then he went to Paris—where Minna left him for good—and spent over two years trying to get *Tannhäuser* on the stage of the Paris Opéra. When he had added the Venusberg ballet to the beginning to satisfy French tastes, the opera was mounted in March 1861, only to be booed off the stage by a cabal organized by the fashionable Jockey Club. Paris having frustrated him again, Wagner left for Germany. After a dozen years of exile, he had been granted amnesty.

The next years saw some conducting, much controversy, much high living, and the libretto for his only comedy, *Die Meistersinger von Nürnberg*. Like *Tristan*, *Die Meistersinger* would use the music-drama apparatus developed for the *Ring*. Still, each opera has a definable sound of its own, *Die Meistersinger* relatively light and cheery, *Tristan* dense and chromatic. *Die Meistersinger* also satirized Wagner's critics, especially Eduard Hanslick, conservative leader of a faction that identified itself with Brahms: the opera's pedantic Beckmesser was originally called Hans Lick.

Meanwhile, the affair with Mathilde Wesendonck having run out of steam, Wagner took solace in some less frenzied amours. But things were in a generally disastrous state and the *Ring* still in limbo. In 1864, then living in Vienna, he had to flee his creditors. At that point, now fifty-one years old and apparently at the end of his rope, Wagner found a redeemer of sorts.

His redeemer for the moment was nineteen-year-old King Ludwig II of Bavaria, builder of useless fantastical castles, homosexual, and well on his way to full-fledged madness. Ludwig had conceived an obsession for Wagner and his operas. (By then *Tannhäuser* and *Lohengrin* were enormously popular in Germany.) The king summoned Wagner to Munich, paid off his mountain of debts, installed him in regal surroundings, and promised him whatever he wanted. Wagner played the king like a fisherman with a prize catch on the hook, reeling him in with a string of letters, telegrams, and poems. The immediate result was the 1865 premiere of *Tristan* in Munich.

By then Wagner had secured a new mistress. One can only wonder how he did it. He was a small man with a large unhandsome head and a variety of nasty chronic ailments. He had the emotional maturity of a spoiled child, complete with tantrums if he did not get his way. His sole topic of conversation was himself, his ideas, his needs. He treated benefactors with fawning obsequiousness and employees with contempt. But his personal magnetism and determination must have been irresistible. With incredible callousness he had again appropriated the wife of one of his admirers—Cosima von Bülow this time, whose husband, Hans, was one of the leading conductors of the age and a fervent Wagnerian. Cosima also happened to be the daughter of Wagner's friend and supporter Franz Liszt; though Liszt was hardly puritanical, the affair incensed him enough to break with Wagner for years. Yet such was the force of Wagner's spell that neither von Bülow nor Liszt slacked in his efforts on the composer's behalf. "If it had been anyone else but Wagner," explained von Bülow, "I would have shot him." The first of Wagner and Cosima's three children was born in 1865; with incomparable cheek, they named her Isolde. Hans von Bülow dutifully pretended the child was his own.

Wagner's enemies used this scandalous situation as leverage to hound him out of Munich in 1865. Wagner and Cosima settled in Triebschen, Switzerland, near Lake Lucerne. In 1870, following her divorce, they were married. After years of incessant turmoil, exile, money troubles, and bitter musical and political struggles, Wagner was astonished to find a measure of peace and contentment, the first of his life, with the adoring Cosima. Also enhancing his contentment were a growing number of disciples and the continuing supply of manna from King Ludwig. Among the new disciples was young philosopher Friedrich Nietzsche; after years of hero-worship, however, Nietzsche would become a formidable adversary whose anti-Wagner polemics would become part of his philosophical writings.

In a hopeful frame of mind Wagner finished composing *Die Meistersinger* and, in 1869, picked up composition of the *Ring* where he had left off a dozen years before, in the middle of *Siegfried*. As always, he worked day after day in a trance, dressed in silks and stroking satin as he composed. (His taste in clothes had to do with both extravagance and a skin condition.) In 1874, some twenty-five years after the initial conception, the unprecedented project was finished: *Der Ring des Nibelungen* was complete.

By the time it was finished he knew where it would be staged, in the form he had imagined from the beginning: a quasi-religious festival for pilgrims from around the world. In 1872 the little town of Bayreuth had donated to Wagner a site for a theater. Two years later, Wagner and Cosima moved into Villa Wahnfried near the site. With money raised from private subscriptions, from Wagner Societies that had sprung up worldwide, from benefit performances conducted by Wagner, and contributions from King Ludwig, his theater

---

TONALITY AND ATONALITY

A mong musical terms bandied about with little notion of their real meanings, *tonal* and *atonal* may top the list. Let's detach these concepts from ideological banners and see what they actually are.

Tonal music earns its label because it has a main tone, on which is built a main chord, either/both making up a kind of audible home plate called a *tonal center*. Now go to the Glossary and read what a *scale* is. Now, remember the syllables used for the notes of the scale from the song in *The Sound of* Music? *Do* (a female deer) *Re Mi Fa Sol La Ti,* which brings us back to *Do*. Well, *Do* is the tonal center of the scale and of the key. Here are some scales from among the twelve major and twelve minor scales available. Note the *key signature* at the beginning of the line,

---

At right, Composition 8, *by Wassily Kandinsky, a pioneer abstractionist, who like Paul Klee and other painters of the early twentieth century saw painting as analogous to music.*

was completed in 1876. It was called the Festspielhaus, the "festival house." In August of that year the first complete performances of *Der Ring des Nibelungen* were heard at the first Bayreuth Festival. His operas are still heard there every summer, the productions supervised by his descendants.

Wagner's troubles were not over when his great work finally saw light. Though the first performances brought enthusiasts and reporters from all over the world, there were bitter attacks in the press (in his career Wagner probably received more critical bile than any other composer), which led to reduced attendance, huge debts, and suspension of the festival. Meanwhile, Wagner's age and struggles were reflected in his health. By 1880 he was hard at work composing *Parsifal* despite a series of heart attacks and debilitating outbreaks of his old skin ailment. With great satisfaction he supervised the premiere of *Parsifal* at the renewed Bayreuth Festival in 1882. In

September of that year he went to Venice in search of a cure. On February 11, 1883, he began an essay called "On the Feminine in Human Nature." In the middle of the second page, after writing the words "love-tragedy," he was seized by a fatal heart attack. Cosima sat alone by his body until the next day. He was buried in the garden of Villa Wahnfried at Bayreuth.

Today few people worship Wagner and his ideas so fanatically as thousands did in the nineteenth century. Now we tend to see him as a composer like others, with his strengths and weaknesses. His harmonic innovations remained controversial into the twentieth century, but history has certified them. His operas, for all their failings, their "great moments and very dull quarters of an hour" (to

which shows which notes are flat and which sharp: Example 11.

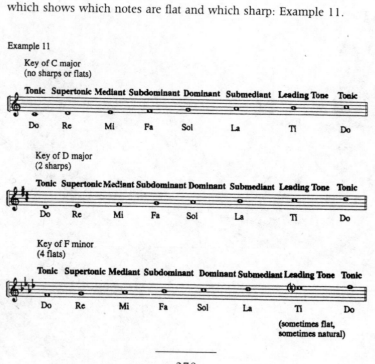

Example 11

quote Oscar Wilde once again), are still on the stage and still power-ful. The *Ring* has shown surprising flexibility: often departing from the traditional gloomy Teutonic approaches with their horned hel-mets and brass brassieres, contemporary productions have devised modernist *Rings,* postmodernist *Rings, Rings* interpreted as psycho-sexual theater and as allegories of the decline of capitalism. These interpretations have found resonances in the music and the drama, a reliable sign of work destined to endure. So much of the *Ring* remains immensely vital, from the moments of true mythical magic to the consistent passion of its love stories and even to its moments of comedy.

If Wagner is no longer a demigod, if in light of later history some of his racial ideas stand out in their full malevolence, he nonethe-less remains a great composer and an abiding influence. As we shall see, Verdi reflected Wagner's ideas in his old age. Debussy went

---

The tonal center is also known as the *tonic* note. *Tonic, Do, tonal center, key note*—all mean the same. And the three-note chord built on that note, the *tonic triad* (see Glossary for *triad*), is the main chord in the key. When a piece is in the key of C major, then, the notes used are from the C major scale and the tonic triad is a C major triad. In C minor, the tonic triad is minor: Example 12.

All the notes in the scale have their own importance and func-tion relative to the tonic and to one another. The tonal system is as hierarchical as the court at Ver-sailles: you've got your key note/main chord—the *tonic;* your second most important—the *domi-nant* (which is *Sol*); third on the totem pole—the *subdominant (Fa);* the *leading tone (Ti)* to get you back to the *tonic (Do),* and so on. In the hands of a skilled composer, these relationships are manipulated to create an ebb and flow of tension and release, expectation and sur-

Example 12 – Triads in C major

	Tonic triad	Supertonic triad	Mediant triad	Subdominant triad	Dominant triad	Submediant triad	Leading Tone triad	Tonic triad
Kind of triad:	Major	Minor	Minor	Major	Major	Minor	Diminished	Major

from enthusiasm to hostility, but the presence of Wagner is manifest in every page he wrote. The Second Viennese School of Schoenberg, Berg, and Webern picked up where Wagner left off; the operas of Schoenberg and Berg are extrapolations of Wagnerian ideas. Even John Cage's essays, "How to Improve the World (You Will Only Make Matters Worse)," are in part, perhaps, a distant riposte to the Wagnerian vision of the artist as high priest and world-transforming hero.

Wagner's influence begins, as I said, with his reform of opera, turning it into a continuous symphonic fabric. Moreover, his orchestration is opulent and inventive, with myriad gradations of color and texture. He physically expanded the orchestra, using triple woodwinds or more, including sometimes a dozen or more French horns, adding his middle-sized Wagner tubas to fill in between horns and trombones. Wagner was the first composer to grasp the

---

prise. That is the beauty of the tonal system, whose myriad possibilities have allowed it to work so nicely for so long.

So we have *keys*, which are named after their *tonic* note, and which use the major or minor *scale* of the same name; and on each note of the scale a *triad* (or other chord) can be built. Music having this kind of organization, which is most of the Western music we're familiar with from Bach to rock, is *tonal music*. Our system of tonality had evolved by around 1600; the ensuing "common practice" period lasted through most of the nineteenth century and in some styles, like pop and folk music, continues to the present.

This explanation may sound dauntingly abstract, but so do the rules of everyday grammar. Simply by growing up in Western culture, we assimilate the Western tonal language and respond to it intuitively, as we do our native speech. When we're in the key of, say, F minor, we hear quite clearly (if unconsciously) when the music *cadences* (see Glossary) "home" on the note F or the F minor triad. People growing up in other musical cultures don't hear tonal functions as we do. Though our system sounds natural and inevitable to us, it is still a learned language—and each tradition has its own language: Example 13.

A given tonal piece is often dubbed by its home key, as in "Symphony in B-flat major."

full potential of the new valved brass instruments; the sonorities of pealing trumpets and heroic horns and trombones in sumptuous harmony are the most characteristic aspect of his orchestral sound. He also explored unprecedented effects of strings in multiple parts, producing everything from voluptuous low textures to hanging clouds.

To a large extent the Wagnerian style united the chromatic harmony of Liszt and the orchestration and general giganticism of Berlioz. But Wagner took everything far beyond his models: what Berlioz, for example, could not quite bring off in his epic opera *Les Troyens*, Wagner accomplished in the *Ring*. In the end, perhaps the most fertile part of his legacy was his harmony. As noted in the essay Tonality and Atonality (p. 268), he carried chromaticism further than any other composer of the century, exploring new kinds of dissonance, new chord colors, and fluid key relationships that

Example 13 – Mozart, *Piano Sonata in D major*

Chords on
scale degrees: I   vi   ii   V   I   ii   I   V

Does that mean the whole thing stays resolutely in that key? Not at all. In many long pieces only the first and last movements are based in that key, and those movements also *modulate* (move to other keys) during their course. Part of the point is to provide harmonic variety with a tour through assorted keys. As much as anything, the classical symphony and sonata are *about* patterns of key change

and key relationships. (See Sonata Form, p. 160.)

But in most tonal pieces, whether by Bach or Mozart or Brahms, there will be a return to the home key—both within each movement and in the piece as a whole. For example, the triumphant effect of the eruption of the last movement in Beethoven's Fifth Symphony has less to do with the tune, which is rather

finally, in *Tristan*, stepped over the line into atonality. After 1900, probably no Western composer was untouched by Wagnerian harmony and orchestration.

For an introduction to Wagner, one should certainly start with recorded collections of excerpts from his works. Though his music dramas did not have the traditional separate numbers, they still contain preludes, overtures, and set pieces. Wagner himself established the tradition of performing these in concert.

As a group, the familiar excerpts are a compendium of imaginative specimens of orchestral writing. Where Schubert and Berlioz had doubled instruments as an expressive special effect, say, a clarinet and oboe together on a melodic line, Wagner mixed colors as a

---

plain, than with the dramatic return to the home key of C after a long stretch of harmonic ambiguity. Just as the notes and harmonies within a key gravitate around the tonic and finally cadence on it, likewise the series of keys in a long piece gravitate around the original key and finally return home to it. A first movement beginning in G minor ends in G minor; the second and third movements usually begin and end in other keys; and the final movement will begin and end in G again (often pieces that begin in minor end in what is called the *parallel major*—G minor becomes G major).

To summarize: classical tonal music involves a hierarchy of notes and harmonies organized in major and minor keys and gravitating around a tonal center called the tonic.

So where did atonality come from, and why?

It's characteristic of artists never to be satisfied, always to be looking for something fresh. They do this not out of perversity but because they get tired of the same stuff: if you're only redoing what's been done before, why bother? By finding new colors, by pushing at barriers, artists refresh themselves and their art.

Thus it was with composers and the tonal system. Through the nineteenth century they began to bend and expand the traditional rules in various ways. Beethoven was a leading culprit, having a

rule. The result is a new richness of sound, a prime example being the *Prelude* and *Love-Death* from *Tristan und Isolde,* a traditional concert grouping from the beginning and end of the opera. This spiritualization of sexual energy climaxes with Isolde's ecstatic death; the instruments seem to throb and sigh with an eroticism both literal and metaphysical: the universe as created and sustained by desire.

There are also remarkable coloristic effects in the prelude to *Lohengrin,* which depicts the descent to earth of the Holy Grail. This begins with high hanging chords for divided strings, an ethereal sound unknown in orchestral writing before Wagner. The familiar *Ride of the Valkyries* from *Die Walküre* is a wild scherzo that uses the full resources of the orchestra to paint the Valkyries soaring across the sky, riding to Valhalla with the souls of heroes; their music is full of pounding steeds, joyful cries, and flashes of lightning. *Siegfried's Rhine Journey* from *Die Götterdämmerung* is a guided tour of the

thirst for fresh key relationships and tending more and more to postpone resolving to the tonic. Richard Wagner took that process several degrees further; his melodies and harmonies often move chromatically, that is, slide around between the normal notes of the major or minor scale, and that sometimes keeps the sense of key ambiguous for long stretches. Moreover, in his search for voluptuous colors, Wagner often used dissonant chords, including some that weren't in the book. Finally, in the opera *Tristan und Isolde,* finished in 1859, he decided to express the continual yearning of the lovers by unrelenting harmonic tension, which only occasionally resolves: the music is often in a state both keyless and

keyed-up (if you've been in love, you know the feeling). In this way Wagner invented atonal music.

However, nobody called it that yet, though musical conservatives did apply a number of unsavory adjectives to *Tristan*. The adjective we're after came to be used in the twentieth century, and it was applied to the mature music of Arnold Schoenberg. In his early work Schoenberg had stretched Wagnerian chromaticism until he realized that he may as well forswear tonal scales and keys; he had burst their boundaries. By the time of his *Pierrot lunaire* (1914), Schoenberg's music was floating free in chromatic space. His harmonies, often unprecedentedly dissonant, were no longer tied down to the old chord formations and

legendary German river by means of leitmotifs—the Rhine motif, the Rhine Maidens, Siegfried's horn call, and so on. *Siegfried's Funeral March,* a magnificent tone painting from the same opera, conjures up a somber processional through misty forests. *Forest Murmurs* from the middle of *Siegfried* contains some of Wagner's most extraordinary pages; here the music evokes breezes and birdsong in a magical shimmering quietness. A good example of lighthearted Wagner (hardly the Mozartean variety, of course) is the *Dance of the Apprentices and Entry of the Masters* from *Die Meistersinger.*

In recommending a complete opera with which to get to know Wagner, one faces a dilemma: there is no easy introduction to such works. One could begin with *Die Meistersinger,* perhaps the most approachable of the lot, unless *Tannhäuser* is. With the *Ring* there have been some beautifully done productions for television and

functions but were free to take any shape and sound he needed—and he rarely seemed to need a triad: Example 14.

It was a disgruntled critic who dubbed the style of *Pierrot* and Schoenberg's later music—along with that of his pupils Webern and Berg—*atonal,* meaning without tonality. Schoenberg hated the term, but nobody listens to composers in these matters.

Like Wagner, Schoenberg and his disciples arrived at their approach less from iconoclasm than from historical and artistic necessity, (though there were certainly some iconoclastic proclivities involved). As Webern explained, it was generations of composers, not they alone, who had bent tonality out of shape. Besides, they wanted to explore an expressionist emotional world, plunging into

Example 14 – Schoenberg, atonal Minuet from *Suite for Piano*

Numbers indicate order in basic 12-tone row (see Schoenberg section)

video; the late-1980s neo-traditional television version from the Metropolitan Opera was justly applauded.

But besides the barrier of its length, the *Ring* comes loaded with imposing philosophical and political baggage. Some of the other operas inflict heavy doses of religion. (For all its musical virtues, the Christianity of *Tannhäuser* is certainly the most hypocritical. Wagner writing a paean to piety and contrition? Who's he kidding?) So I will go out on a limb and recommend as a start the most extravagant music drama of all and arguably the greatest: *Tristan und Isolde.*

Fueled by Wagner's obsession with Mathilde Wesendonck, *Tristan* is the world's greatest exploration of fatal passion, a gigantic hymn to crazy love that proposes to spiritualize the rapturously physical. Based on an ancient Celtic romance popular in the Middle Ages, the story relates an unintended love: Tristan is conveying Isolde, new bride of his master, King Mark of Cornwall, across the

---

the human unconscious to a depth the relatively tranquil and predictable old keys could hardly attain. Eventually, Schoenberg rationalized atonality into the *twelve-tone* system (see essay on Schoenberg, p. 388).

To summarize: atonal music avoids a sense of key or tonal center in favor of making all notes and harmonies relatively equal in importance. It is a kind of musical democracy in place of the old tonal hierarchy. Atonality characterizes some, though by no means all, of this century's classical music. (By the way, while much atonal music uses quite dissonant harmonies, that is not inevitable: "atonal" and "dissonant" are not synonymous, as is often assumed.

Nor is atonal synonymous with "ugly" any more than tonal is with "pretty." (See Consonance and Dissonance, p. 28.)

Two parting thoughts. First, like most things in art and reality, the distinction between tonal and atonal is not absolute. Much of Bartók, for example, is highly chromatic and harmonically innovative, with no major or minor scales, but still has a sense of a note that functions as a tonal center. This is sometimes called *chromatic tonality*—still a center, but defined in nontraditional ways. Charles Ives, Igor Stravinsky, and other composers explored *polytonality*, the simultaneous juxtaposition of more than one key. Many

sea from Ireland, when they are slipped a love potion that is really only a symbol of their unconscious attraction. Their forbidden love proceeds inexorably to the climax of Isolde's love-death on the body of her lover. Just before embarking on the work, Wagner had embraced philosopher Arthur Schopenhauer's Romantic (and Buddhist) longing for the night-bliss of death; thus the deaths of Tristan and Isolde represent not tragedy but rather fulfillment. In this opera the Romantic obsession with the transcendent and unattainable finds its most intoxicating expression.

Moreover, the musical language that Wagner invented to express this longing and ecstasy is one of the most brilliant imaginative creations in Western music. As detailed in the essay Tonality and Atonality (p. 268), it is a texture of almost continual chromatic yearning, the ultimate in nineteenth-century harmonic ambiguity. The very first chord in the piece, a poignant throb of indecipherable

---

composers have used the archaic scales called *modes*, which have a weaker sense of tonal center than do major and minor scales; this approach is called *modality*. Some kinds of Western music from folk to the blues gravitate around the immemorial, worldwide, five-tone scale called *pentatonic*. (If you've ever played around with the black keys of the piano, you've played pentatonic music.)

And second, both tonal and atonal music have their place and their expressive value. Tonality gives us the reassurance of knowing where we are, of being able to predict more or less where things will come out. Atonality cuts us off from our moorings, and by obscuring the future forces us more deeply into the ebb and flow of the moment. Atonality can be unsettling or frightening, as in some of Schoenberg, Webern, and Berg; but it also can be mystical and otherworldly, as in György Ligeti's music in the film *2001* and some of Charles Ives's transcendent moments.

Shakespeare had his joking *Midsummer Night's Dream* and his despairing *King Lear* and everything in between. Music deserves the same range of expression, even if its specific emotions are harder to pin down. All human feelings are part of all of us; it takes the full range of musical possibilities—from consonant to dissonant, tonal to atonal—to encompass that universe of feelings. □

tonality, may be the most famous single sonority in all music, known to musicians as the ''Tristan chord.''

The effect of *Tristan* in every respect—harmonic, melodic, coloristic, and emotional—is almost unimaginably rich. Among other things, listening to it becomes something of a tour through the succeeding history of music, because its riches were mined by generations of composers. En route, one hears prime inspirations of Franck and Bruckner and Mahler, hears where Tchaikovsky got this and Debussy got that, where Verdi was intrigued, where Schoenberg began, where even Charles Ives found something to use.

Thus Wagner, a man hard to forgive but an artist impossible to ignore. He made sure of that. Now for the aftershocks.

Kirsten Flagstad, celebrated Wagnerian soprano,
decked out as Brunnhilde for a Hollywood publicity photo.

Verdi in his seventies composed two operatic masterpieces.

GIUSEPPE VERDI

Given that history's two greatest composers specializing in opera were contemporaries, it is striking how little they resembled each other—at least until Giuseppe Verdi arrived at some of the same conclusions as Richard Wagner. The German Wagner rationalized the concept of music drama in a culture that worshipped theories. The Italian Verdi had no theories, only powerful instincts and a tradition going back to Monteverdi, founded on strong feelings expressed by soulful melody. Wagner conceived opera in instrumental terms and his characters as abstractions. Verdi thought in vocal terms and his characters are individuals overflowing with life. While Wagner preached socialism and was authoritarian in practice, Verdi began by simply writing what the common people expected and, as he grew in depth and sophistication, brought his audience along with him. For many years after both had died, Verdi's work seemed like a hayseed in the path of the Wagnerian juggernaut. But by the middle of the twentieth century, when the vast edifice of Wagner's *Gesamtkunstwerk* was showing its age, Verdi's melodies and his fine-honed sense of drama remained fresh and vital. In the end, though, each in his own fashion had moved toward the goal of music drama, in which every element is marshaled in service of the story.

Giuseppe Verdi was born on October 10, 1813, to the family of an illiterate innkeeper in the village of Le Roncole, near the small town of Busseto. In childhood he was given music lessons by the village organist; soon he took over his teacher's job. As a teen-ager, already composing music for local functions, he became an assistant to a brewer in Busseto named Barezzi, who admired his talent. Verdi, meanwhile, admired the brewer's daughter Margherita. Finally, in 1828, Barezzi raised money to send the boy to Milan to make his fortune. Verdi began inauspiciously by getting rejected for entrance to the Milan Conservatory. In a historic blunder, the professors declared him "lacking in musical talent."

Verdi began to study composition privately and found conducting jobs. In 1836 he married Margherita Barezzi, his patron's daughter. Three years later he convinced La Scala in Milan, Italy's leading opera house, to stage his first opera, *Oberto*. It was well received and Verdi was immediately signed by a publisher and commissioned for more operas. Next was to be a comedy called *Un Giorno di regno* (King for a Day). But between 1838 and 1840 Verdi's life turned nightmarish: he fell ill and his two young children died, followed by his wife. Somehow he managed to finish his comedy; it was an embarrassing failure. Prostrate with grief, Verdi vowed never to compose again.

Some months later, the manager of La Scala pressed a libretto on a resistant Verdi. The composer took the book home, slammed it down on a table, and discovered that it had fallen open to a striking text for a chorus. He began to take peeks at the libretto; all night the words rang in his ears, forming into melodies. Finally there was nothing for it but to break his vow and start composing. The result came to be known as *Nabucco*, a.k.a. Nebuchadnezzar, a riot of Hebrews, Babylonians, massacres, falling idols, and other Cecil B. DeMille-ish hullabaloo, all set to a whang-bang score short on subtlety but long on clout. At the 1842 La Scala premiere, the public went mad over it. In the first year more tickets were sold than there were people in Milan. Suddenly Verdi was famous all over Italy; hats and ties bore his name, restaurants christened sauces after him. Two operas later, *Ernani* was received with even greater acclaim in Venice; productions followed in Paris, London, and New York. Now he was famous around the world.

Then followed what he called his "years in the galleys." During those six years he wrote nine competent but undistinguished operas (except for *Macbeth*, of 1847), his first crack at Shakespeare and the strongest of his early works). Some were hits, some not. What they did accomplish was to make him rich enough to do what he really wanted to do. What that turned out to be was to go back home and buy a farm. From then on, his country estate called Sant' Agata, near Busseto, claimed his energies and enthusiasms nearly as much as did music. Living there with him was soprano Giuseppina Strepponi, who had sung the lead in *Nabucco*. After many years of living together unwed (despite scandalized neighbors), they were married in 1859.

From the beginning, Verdi's popularity had to do with more than his music. It also reflected his connection to the Risorgimento movement, Italy's struggle for a united country free of Austrian domination. Throughout his early career, Verdi had to pick his way through a minefield of Austrian censors who snooped through his work looking for revolutionary overtones and constantly demanded changes. Certain subjects were held to be suspiciously political; for a time *Joan of Arc* was changed to *Oriette of Lesbos*, *Ernani* to *The Pirates of Venice*, even *Moses* to *Pietro*. It did no good. When the exiled Jews in *Nabucco* sang of their grief, audiences understood it as a protest against the Austrians. And so on through the other operas. Finally a new slogan began to be shouted in the streets, scrawled on walls: *Viva Verdi!* As everyone knew, this formed the acronym for the nationalist cry, "Viva Vittorio Emanuele Re d'Italia" (Long live Victor Emmanuel, King of Italy). When the censors protested, it was easy to respond that the slogan simply acclaimed everybody's favorite composer. For all these reasons, Verdi became *the* Italian composer of his time. But though a fervent nationalist, he was no rabble-rouser; he let his music express his convictions indirectly.

The admiration and rewards Verdi found in his lifetime were almost unprecedented in music history, but no amount of success satisfied him as an artist. His five-decade career was marked by steady growth from the conventional blood-and-thunder melodramas and rumbustious orchestration of his early works to the Shakespearean depth and masterful scoring of his last two operas. Clearly, Verdi viewed his work not simply as entertainment: "I do not wish to find in art what [Rossini] does, simple pleasure," he wrote. "To have been amused! That is a way of speaking that even when I was a young man always made me blush and still arouses my ire." He also struggled against the dismal performance standards of the time. His letters are full of complaints: "The artists were singing as badly as they knew how . . ."; "I ask you whether this Opera could be staged worse, in spite of a good cast? . . . I cannot and will not allow any performances of this *Macbeth* at La Scala, at least not until things have taken a turn for the better." The soprano who sang the first Lady Macbeth—in Florence—recalled that Verdi put her and the tenor through 150 rehearsals for one duet, and for good measure one more during the intermission of the premiere. (The duet brought the house down, she added.)

His real maturity began with the three great operas of the early

1850s—*Rigoletto, Il Trovatore,* and *La Traviata.* The soul of the Italian musical spirit had always been vocal melody, but in these works Verdi directed his melodic sense to the service of the drama as never before in Italian music. "La donna è mobile" from *Rigoletto,* the world's favorite aria to sing in the shower, was not only a hit from the outset (Verdi printed hundreds of copies to sell at the premiere), but also defines the personality of the philandering duke. Later in the opera the same tune, heard sung by the duke in the distance, tells Rigoletto that his hired assassin has not killed the person he was supposed to. Something of a throwback, *Il Trovatore* has an incomprehensible plot, but its melodies have insured its popularity; after its premiere, it was running in three theaters in Venice simultaneously.

La Traviata got off to a slow start. Its 1853 premiere in Venice was a debacle, largely because the soprano playing Violetta, supposed to be dying of tuberculosis, was so conspicuously fat and healthy. At one point when she collapsed, ostensibly near death, she raised a cloud of dust that obscured the stage. Meanwhile the leading tenor lost his voice and the baritone could hardly be heard. The audience was in stitches, though Verdi was hardly amused. After a revision and a new production, *La Traviata* caught on and stayed on to become one of the most beloved of all operas.

Among the works of his full maturity were two written for Paris, *I Vespri siciliani* and *Don Carlos,* for which Verdi adapted the Meyerbeerian grand-opera style that he knew would go well there. *La Forza del destino* was written for St. Petersburg; its striking overture is one of Verdi's best known. In his operas for home consumption, Verdi still had to contend with Austrian authorities: *Un Ballo in maschera* originally concerned the assassination of Swedish King Gustave III, but since an Italian had just tried to assassinate Napoleon III, the plot seemed provocative to the ever-alert censors. So for a while the locale was changed to make it as exotic as possible—Boston, Massachusetts. Meanwhile the characters retained very Bostonian names like Riccardo, Renato, and Silvano. These farcical games ended when Italy was unified in 1861. Such was the respect accorded Verdi that he was elected to the first national parliament; he dutifully stuck it out for five years before returning with relief to music and farming.

In 1869 came what appeared to be his last hurrah, and a splashy one it was. The khedive of Egypt commissioned an opera from Verdi on an Egyptian subject, to be premiered in Cairo as part of the ceremonies for the opening of the Suez Canal. Delays with the libretto (Verdi kept his writers on a short leash, questioning everything down to the last word) and the French-made costumes and scenery put off the premiere until 1871. As the khedive had planned, the premiere in the lavish new opera house was a royally vulgar show. The cast numbered three hundred, all with lavish costumes, and hero Radames's helmet and shield were of solid silver. The cream of European and Egyptian society were there including the khedive's entire harem, which took up three loges. Not in attendance was Verdi, who wrote of the occasion, "the sentiment produced in me is one of disgust and humiliation . . . [this *Aïda*] was no longer art, but a trade, a pleasure party, a hunt." All the same, with his usual habit of giving his audience what it wanted while at the same time serving his own artistic conscience, Verdi had seen to it that *Aïda* was appropriately grandiose and pseudo-Egyptian, especially in its celebrated Triumphal March. Nonetheless, it is one of his most original, ambitious, and magnificent scores, with a new dramatic intensity and richness of orchestration.

In 1874 Verdi wrote a Requiem as a commemoration of the death of novelist and patriot Alessandro Manzoni. His style in this his only sacred work is forthrightly operatic. The agnostic Verdi concerned himself not with the afterlife but with a humanistic—and characteristically Italian—memorial for the living. Meanwhile, after *Aïda* Verdi had apparently retired from opera to concern himself mainly with horses, chickens, and fertilizer.

But it only seemed so. Verdi devoted fifteen years to developing his farm into a modern operation of which he was inordinately proud. But in fact during those years he never entirely gave up on plans for the stage. Having spent a lifetime making himself a dramatist, he was looking for a new direction and the right story. For some time he toyed with an opera on Shakespeare's *King Lear,* but he could not get the libretto he wanted. Besides, he was convinced that the grand tunes and shameless melodramas of his past works would not get far in an operatic world now under the spell of Wagner. He felt obsolescent.

Finally in 1879, having been alerted that Verdi might countenance something Shakespearean, the brilliant librettist (and composer) Arrigo Boïto presented him with a libretto based on *Othello*. Despite protestations that he was too old, Verdi allowed himself to be convinced. Over several years a score accumulated, at once unlike anything he had written and a summation of everything he had written. As we will see below, in his *Otello* he took on Wagner on his own turf, music drama, but did it in his own way. The 1887 La Scala premiere of *Otello*, which drew audiences from around the world, received the most tumultuous reception of Verdi's life. The seventy-three-year-old composer took twenty curtain calls, ending only when he appeared onstage in hat and overcoat. His carriage was dragged to his hotel by throngs of admirers, who milled about all night shouting his praises.

Surely now Verdi was ready to retire. But a few years later Boïto showed up with another Shakespearean libretto, this time a comedy: *Falstaff*. Verdi's only previous comedy had been the old, calamitous *Un Giorno di regno*; but as with *Nabucco* and *Otello* the words seduced him. And incredibly, in his eighties he once again produced a masterpiece. Premiered at La Scala in 1893, *Falstaff* is as fresh and youthful a work as ever hit the stage, one that stands with Mozart's *Figaro* and Rossini's *Barber* at the peak of the comic opera literature.

The main labor of Verdi's last years, one in which he took great pride, was to build and endow a Home for Aged Musicians in Milan. It was in part a memorial to his beloved wife, who died in 1897. After she was gone he sank into depression. Not able to bear living alone on his estate, he moved to Milan, where he dragged through the days. After a stroke, he died at the Grand Hotel on January 27, 1901. As his body was conveyed to his grave at the musicians' home, a quarter-million people lined the streets in homage.

Verdi worked in an Italian operatic tradition that was largely its own world, and in that world Romanticism was only a distant echo. His musical forebears are not Schubert and Berlioz and Liszt but rather Rossini and Bellini and Donizetti. And whereas the classical tradition elsewhere in Europe was a middle-class and aristocratic affair,

Italian opera was a people's art, the most significant popular music of the country. Its public expected tear-jerking melodramas, preferably with a bracing amount of bloodshed, everything expressed in terms of bel canto vocal style (see Glossary). Verdi never really challenged these assumptions until his last works, but he took them further than anyone else both musically and dramatically.

For over a century there has been a spirited debate concerning to what extent Wagner influenced late Verdi. One extreme says not in the least, the other that Verdi's last operas were essentially Wagnerian. I will not take sides here, except to point out that Verdi knew and admired Wagner's operas; in a letter of 1883 he wrote, "Sad! Sad! Sad! Wagner is dead! When I read the dispatch yesterday, I was simply aghast. . . . A great personality has passed away!" His last two operas, *Otello* and *Falstaff,* have a considerably extended role for the orchestra, verging on a Wagner-like participation in the drama, as well as a more progressive harmonic language and a vocal approach moving away from bel canto toward something more declamatory. And as I noted, he was concerned that his earlier style would be dated in comparison to Wagner.

However one interprets the above, it is also clear that his style not only fit the Italian tradition but carried it into the next century, toward Puccini and Leoncavallo. Opera everywhere in the nineteenth century was moving away from the separation of aria and recitative in distinct "numbers" and toward a continuous flow of music. Verdi wrote more or less continuous opera from *Rigoletto* on. The astonishing innovations of his last years may partly have been inspired by the presence of Wagner, but as always he did things his own way. A stubborn, determined man of tremendous integrity, Verdi imitated no one, especially Germans. He believed that each country had to follow its own traditions. When German conductor Hans von Bülow, the champion of Wagner and Brahms who at first had dismissed Verdi's Requiem, wrote a contrite letter to the old maestro declaring, "Now I admire and adore you!" Verdi responded graciously and added a credo at once nationalistic and universal: "I see that truly superior artists judge without preconceptions as to school, nationality, period. If the artists of the North and the South have different tendencies, it is well that they should be *different!* Everyone ought to keep the *characteristics inherent in their nation,* as Wagner said so very aptly. Well for you, who are still sons of Bach! And we? We too, sons of Palestrina."

For an introduction to Verdi one could start with *Rigoletto*, the highest achievement of mainstream nineteenth-century Italian opera, or with *Otello*, the most forward-looking of his works. Based on a Victor Hugo play, *Rigoletto* is the story of its eponymous hero, humpbacked court jester to the duke of Mantua. Responding to his employer's abduction of his daughter, Rigoletto hires someone to assassinate the duke. Daughter Gilda, meanwhile, has responded to her more-or-less rape by falling in love with her abductor. After a series of those dubious coincidences to which opera is addicted, the assassin's victim given to Rigoletto wrapped in a gunny sack turns out to be Gilda. In another operatic tradition, father and daughter sing an extended duet as she expires. With tunes as good as these, however, one should be willing to suspend any amount of disbelief: "La donna è mobile," "Caro nome," "Questa o quella," and other arias are what Italian opera is all about. And the character of Rigoletto is one of the most fascinating in the literature—twisted, bitter, and murderous, he is still ultimately consumed by love of his daughter and his drive to protect her.

A beloved masterpiece from that period is *La Traviata* (The Wayward One). Based on a play by Dumas called *La Dame aux camélias*, which in turn was based on a true story, the opera tells of consumptive courtesan Violetta and her doomed love for Alfredo. One of the great weepers of the operatic stage, it is overflowing with some of Verdi's loveliest inspirations.

That Verdi, after a fifteen-year hiatus, could return to opera with the freshness, vitality, and originality of his last two works is one of the miracles of music. Of the dozens of Shakespeare adaptations by dozens of composers, these are the only ones worthy of their models. In *Otello*, Verdi and Boïto transformed the tale of the jealous Moor, driven to murder his wife by the machinations of Iago, into a true operatic story, not just a play set to music. For example, whereas the original play never really accounts for Iago's malevolence, here in a dramatic masterstroke he proclaims his nihilism in the chilling "Credo in un Dio crudel" ("I believe in a cruel God"). No longer is melody the focus of the opera; now Verdi integrates all the elements into his Italianate version of music drama. The voices range from declamatory style to arioso to full-blown arias; but even the latter blend into the smooth flow of the music. In counterbalance to Iago's snarling and sly tone is the love music between Otello and Desdemona; the theme of "the kiss," repeated, tragically, as Otello dies, is an outpouring of unforgettable beauty and youthful warmth—and that from a composer in his seventies. Beautiful as it is, even this music is absolutely in the service of the drama.

Having done the incredible with *Otello,* Verdi went on to the still more incredible with *Falstaff,* based on Shakespeare's beloved figure of the rotund schemer and tosspot. With the same general approach as its predecessor, this opera is even more sophisticated in its means. Now one finds no big arias or spectacular climaxes. The declamatory style is in the ascendant, the patter singing a vital element of the comedy, everything small-scale and intimate, the pace breathless, the orchestration light and supple as quicksilver. The work ends with Verdi's final testament, a burst of ironic wisdom in the form of a rowdy fugue on "The whole world is a jest . . . Every mortal being/laughs at every other one,/but the best laugh of all/is the last one." A great man and a marvelous instinctive artist, Verdi left us pondering that last laugh.

His last two operas have never quite found the popularity of the great earlier ones. Many opera buffs are inclined to think them not lyrical enough; they have few of the melodic transports that are the lifeblood of Italian opera. Others, though, see his last two works as the equal of Mozart at his best—which is to say, among the greatest of all operas. With them, Verdi climaxed the Italian operatic tradition that Claudio Monteverdi had begun nearly three hundred years before, and brought that tradition into the twentieth century.

A playbill for the premiere of Rigoletto
at La Fenice in Venice.

JOHANNES BRAHMS

The First Symphony of Brahms begins with a grand sweeping gesture, sounding like an apotheosis of symphonic music at its most magisterial. Few composers have spoken that language with such assurance, and Brahms was very nearly the last who would. Steeped in tradition, he saw himself as its vessel, a weaker vessel than the giants of the past. In that he undervalued himself, but he under-

stood rightly enough that parts of his tradition—Romanticism, tonality, classical forms—had nearly run their course.

Brahms expressed his feelings about this decline, as about most things, with ironic resignation rather than despair. His response was to gather the scattered elements of Western musical tradition into a great twilight synthesis. Elsewhere, the music of the future was being shaped by Wagner and his heirs. By the time Brahms died, Debussy had written his revolutionary *Prelude to the Afternoon of a Faun* (1894). The next fifteen years would see Stravinsky's raging *Sacre du printemps* (1913) and the first atonal works of Schoenberg. Brahms wrote in the knowledge that he was near the end of a line.

Brahms in his bearlike maturity.

Johannes Brahms was born in the slums of Hamburg, Germany, on May 7, 1833. His father, Johann Jakob, was a musician, mediocre and itinerant for much of his career but finally a double bass player in the Hamburg Opera. Seeing that Johannes was interested in music, the father arranged for piano lessons early on, and his son made admirable progress. At age fourteen, in one of his first public appearances as a pianist, Johannes included on the program a piece of his own.

But no prince appeared to become his patron, and his family was both fractious and poor. Then as later, he had to make his living the hard way. In his youth that meant playing in waterfront brothels, where the women and sailors treated him as a plaything. As a result, his relationships with women were permanently soured—at least that would be his own explanation for his chronic aversion to matrimony. Otherwise he earned his keep churning out hackwork, mostly arrangements of light pieces published under pseudonyms. At the same time he was making himself into an imposing composer and pianist.

In 1853 Brahms went on a concert tour with Hungarian violinist Eduard Reményi that set in motion his early success. Reményi introduced Brahms to the celebrated violinist Joseph Joachim, who was impressed with the young man; it was the beginning of a lifelong friendship. Joachim in turn introduced Brahms to Liszt and Schumann. The meeting with the former did not go well; no lover of Liszt's music, Brahms managed to fall asleep as Liszt played.

How Brahms's music struck Robert Schumann in Düsseldorf can be gauged from Schumann's diary entry of September 30, 1853: "Brahms to see me (a genius)." Schumann went on to amplify that conviction in the *Neue Zeitschrift für Musik;* in the article "New Paths" he declared the twenty-year-old Brahms to be one "vouchsafed to give the highest and most ideal expression to the tendencies of the times, one who would not show us his mastery in a gradual development, but like Minerva spring full-armed from the head of Zeus." In fact, Schumann was only partly prophetic. The early works Brahms had shown the older composer, including his three sprawling piano sonatas, were about as far as he would go in the direction of progressive Romanticism, the tendency of the times. Instead, Brahms had a long and backward-looking development ahead of him.

All the same, Brahms took Schumann's prophecy with solemn seriousness. He determined indeed to carry his tradition to its "highest and most ideal expression," even if that expression was in a more conservative direction than what Schumann expected. Schumann, for his part, did not have much longer to be concerned about his young protégé. He wrote his article, found Brahms a publisher, and virtually adopted him into the family, but soon after landed in the asylum that would be his final residence. Concerned for Schumann's wife, Clara, Brahms took an apartment over hers and shored her up through the terrible last two years of her husband's life. Clara Schumann was one of the finest pianists of her time, brilliant and creative herself, and dependent for emotional support on the young Brahms. Almost inevitably, he fell in love with his mentor's wife, fourteen years his senior.

It must have been an extraordinarily wrenching time for him and Clara. Both deeply loved and grieved for the mad, dying Schumann. Neither knew what to do with Brahms's growing passion. "Would to God," he wrote Clara in that period, "that I were allowed this day . . . to repeat to you with my own lips that I am dying for love of you." Though Brahms would have other loves, he would never again write such unconstrained and heartfelt words to anyone else. When Robert Schumann died in 1856, Clara had to decide what to say to her would-be lover. We will never know what she said or when things were resolved. Perhaps they never were resolved. Clara and Brahms remained friends but went their separate ways. Often over the next forty years there would be tensions between them, but always they would respect their strange, indefinable, but inescapable connection. Many times she was the first to hear a new work of his and to give advice, which he often took; she was among his favorite interpreters of his music. Well into his bachelor middle age, he would write Clara, "I love you more than myself and more than anybody and anything on earth."

Within a few years after Robert Schumann's ringing prophecy, the young Brahms began to fulfill it. He acquired a public, admirers in high places; the talismanic comparison to Beethoven was evoked. Back in Hamburg, people took to calling his musician brother Fritz "the wrong Brahms." For some time Johannes led a peripatetic existence, conducting in Vienna and elsewhere, performing on piano, and composing with growing strength and maturity. In 1863 he hoped to be named conductor of the Hamburg Philharmonic; he thought he would be happy to spend his life conducting his home-town orchestra. But he did not get the job. For years he was bitter about the snub, feeling that it condemned him to a wandering and uncertain career.

The first important work completed in this period was the Piano Concerto no. 1 in D minor. Brahms played the solo part at the 1859 first performances in Hanover and Leipzig. In his early Romantic style, the concerto was associated in his mind with Schumann's breakdown and the ensuing web of sorrows. The strange, swirling beginning may even depict Schumann's suicidal plunge into the Rhine. He told Clara the second movement was a portrait of her. Typically, Brahms buried his anguish under dry humor when he described to Joachim the concerto's Leipzig reception:

> I will force this hard and pointed steel pen . . . to relate to you how it came about that here my concerto has been a brilliant and decisive—failure. . . . The first and 2nd movements were listened to without the slightest display of feeling. At the con-clusion three pairs of hands were brought together very slowly, whereupon a perfectly distinct hissing from all sides forbade any such demonstration. . . . I believe this is the best thing that could happen to one; it forces one to concentrate one's thoughts properly and increases one's courage. After all, I am only ex-perimenting and feeling my way as yet. But the hissing was too much of a good thing, wasn't it?

The concerto soon caught on, but another chorus of hisses greeted the 1866 premiere of the first three movements of the *German Requiem*. Undaunted, he kept adding to and performing it. By the 1870s this Requiem, dedicated to the memory of his late mother and containing some of the most exquisite choral music of the century, was admired all over Europe.

The Requiem's connection to his mother was typical. Though supporters held Brahms's work to be the ideal of "abstract" music, with no program attached, most of his pieces related directly to his life. Said one scholar, "There is a story at the back of all Brahms's great works, but it is a personal story, not a dramatic one like the stories of Berlioz and Liszt, and it is told only in music." Some examples will illustrate.

During the two years he waited at Clara Schumann's side for her husband to die, he worked on a piano quartet in C-sharp minor. He, Joachim, and Clara all were unsatisfied with the results, so he changed its key and tinkered with it off and on for nearly twenty years before it was premiered in its final form as the Piano Quartet in C minor. Of it he wrote his publisher, "You may place a picture on the title page, namely a head—with a pistol pointed at it. This will give you some idea of the music. I shall send you a photograph of myself for the purpose. Blue coat, yellow breeches, and top boots would do well." The whole suggestion is nominally a joke, but the costume he cites is that of Goethe's novelistic hero Werther, who kills himself over a hopeless love for a friend's wife. The somber quartet is sometimes called the "Werther."

Soon after his hopes for Clara were dashed, Brahms fell in love with a young singer named Agathe von Siebold. He wrote songs for her and they played together—both music and children's games—during country vacations. Clara Schumann, seeing them walking arm in arm at one point, left town in a jealous rage. Everyone assumed Agathe and Brahms would be married, and they apparently exchanged rings secretly. But then at the last moment Brahms pulled back in horror of the altar. "I love you!" he wrote to her. "I must see you again! But I cannot wear fetters." She understood the message and broke off the engagement. When friends deplored his behavior he admitted, "I have played the scoundrel toward Agathe." Some years later he produced his farewell to her: the String Sextet in G major, among the most meltingly beautiful of all chamber works. The climax of the first movement proclaims a theme built on letters from her name: A-G-A-H-E (in German notation, B-natural is called H). "Here," he told a friend, "I have freed myself from my last love."

In fact there would be other loves, several of them young singers. But he would not lead them on as he had done with Agathe. How far these amours went is hard to say. Brahms also had a lifelong weakness for prostitutes, no doubt the result of his teen-age years playing in brothels. Determined to be unfettered but not lonely, he fashioned the motto *Frei aber Froh*, "free but glad." Its musical symbol, the notes F-A-F, appears here and there in his music. But if he was a confirmed bachelor, he still never lost his delight in sweet young things.

By the 1870s Brahms was the most conspicuous of his generation's composers; during the first half of the decade he also conducted the eminent Gesellschaft der Musikfreunde orchestra. Already he had begun to acquire the academic and other honors that would mark the rest of his career. His first major orchestral work, *Variations on a Theme by Haydn* (there is also a two-piano version), was received with great acclaim on its 1873 premiere by the Vienna Philharmonic. But the question on everyone's mind was, When is he going to write a symphony?

The same question very much troubled Brahms's mind. In his youth he had left after a performance of Beethoven's Ninth declaring, "I must write music like that!" As with most composers of the century, this youthful ambition turned into a burden. He would come to say, "You will never know how the likes of us feel when we hear the tramp of a giant like [Beethoven] behind us." He first tried to write a symphony in his twenties, but that effort turned into the First Piano Concerto. As early as 1862 he had completed a symphonic first movement, sketches for which went back half a decade, but that draft languished for years.

All this was characteristic of him. He refused to let anything second-rate out of the house. If composers can be divided into sprinters (like Mozart) and plodders, Brahms was the model plodder, refining his ideas over weeks and years at desk and piano and during long walks. We will never know how many works he destroyed; probably more than he kept. Not wanting history snooping in his workshop, he also destroyed most of his sketches. Promising ideas he would tenaciously rework and recast until he was satisfied. Several pieces changed media in their course, sometimes several times. As an example, he began the great F minor Piano Quintet as a string quintet with two cellos, revised it somewhat in that form, then entirely redid it as a sonata for two pianos, and finally in 1864 put it into final form for string quartet and piano. That process took two years. As we saw with the C minor Piano Quartet, these kinds of revisions could go on for decades—possible because Brahms's style hardly changed after his late twenties.

So in his tortoiselike fashion he kept picking away at a symphony. In 1876, when he was forty-three and after some twenty years' gestation, the First Symphony finally saw light at Carlsruhe. Response was respectful but mixed. Not for the last time, some made the astonishing accusation that he was unmelodious. Conservative critic Eduard Hanslick, champion of Brahms and flayer of Wagner, was guardedly enthusiastic. Clara Schumann found parts of the First a bit academic. All realized that it was very much in the spirit of Beethoven, though certainly in Brahms's voice. Conductor Hans von Bülow went so far as to call the First Symphony "Beethoven's Tenth"; the comparison probably both pleased and exasperated Brahms. (Von Bülow also invented the idea of "The Three Great B's"—Bach, Beethoven, and Brahms.) A comment that the choralelike theme of the last movement sounded like the analogous one in Beethoven's Ninth brought from Brahms the curt response, "Any jackass can see that!"—implying that anyone with brains could also see that he had added something of his own. Performances of the First quickly followed around Europe, with similar results. Few listeners realized that this symphony was destined to be one of the most popular ever written. For Brahms, now that he had gotten through the dreaded initiation, the symphonic floodgates seemed to open; the Second Symphony followed within a year, and by 1885 the Third and Fourth.

After years of wandering, with intermittent Viennese sojourns, Brahms finally settled there in 1878. The city was still the musical center of Germany and Austria and the home of his artistic ancestors going back to Haydn. In a cluttered three-room apartment on the Karlsgasse that grew shabby with the years, Brahms lived the winters of his bachelor life. Mornings began with the ritual of brewing the strongest possible coffee. Alone in his living room he liked to play with tin soldiers. He took long walks around the city, greeted by admirers, saying hello to his favorite streetwalkers, giving candy to children from the bulging pockets of his grizzled waistcoat. Brahms bought everything cheap and traveled third class; with regard to his beloved beer and cigars, he was concerned more with quantity than quality. It is said that over his writing desk he kept the famous (and inaccurate) etching depicting the cart carrying Mozart's body to a pauper's grave. Probably it was there to remind Brahms of what he planned to avoid; he would leave a comfortable estate and not go alone to his grave. Parsimonious as he generally was, he could be generous. Once he gave his father a copy of Handel's *Saul,* saying that if the old man were depressed he would find solace in it. When his father finally tried the suggestion, he found banknotes inside each of the uncut pages.

Which brings up his wit. Brahms was brusque and sardonic much of the time, his barbs pointed enough to be remembered. When the violist in a string quartet asked if he liked their tempos, Brahms replied, "Yes—especially yours." To ladies rehearsing Haydn's *Creation:* "Why do you drag it so? Surely you took this faster under Haydn." After an evening of sarcasms at the expense of friends in a café, he left and then returned to add, "If there is anyone here I've failed to insult, I apologize." In 1881 he grew whiskers, only then becoming the bearded bear familiar in photographs. (In his youth he had been slender, blond, blue-eyed, smooth-faced and handsome. He never lost the warmth and occasional roguish twinkle in his eyes.) Bear or not, he had many loyal friends of both sexes and all ages, to whom he was loyal in return. He was happiest in the summers, which he usually spent at resort towns in the mountains; in those pleasant surroundings he did most of his composing. Winters he largely spent performing in Vienna or on the road.

He studied the music of the past incessantly, especially Bach and Beethoven but going as far back as Josquin; he also edited editions of composers from Couperin to Dvořák. He believed that music was in decline. Once when playing a Bach sonata in C with Joachim, he threw to the floor his own sonata in the same key, crying, "After that, how could anyone play this stuff?" And another time: "The fact that people don't understand and respect the very best things, such as Mozart's concertos, is what permits men like us to become famous." Never had a composer of his stature felt so much under the onus of history and so humble about his ability to measure up. Perhaps he believed that music needed a shot in the arm of some kind, and knew he was not the man to administer it.

Instead, he spent his career restating, in his own way, the gestures of the past, in the genres of the past, in the language more or less of his time. He succeeded in that nearly impossible endeavor by sheer genius and stubborn toil. Among other efforts he spent years teaching himself Palestrina-style counterpoint, a labor that bears fruit on every page of his mature music. One way and another, he made himself a musical craftsman the equal of any who ever lived (except, perhaps, for Bach).

As his music and attitudes were conservative, Brahms inevitably became the hero of those who despised the radical Wagner. As would happen later with Schoenberg and Stravinsky, Wagner and Brahms would represent the musical poles of their time. How did they view each other?

Though he would not be the one to sustain the feud, Brahms inadvertently began it. In 1860 he, Joachim, and a few others drew up a manifesto critical of the progressive school. Mainly aimed at Liszt, it was intended to draw numerous signatures before being made public. Instead, it got into the papers with only four signatures, including Brahms and Joachim, and was viewed as a personal vendetta against Wagner.

That did not keep Brahms from making a courtesy call on Wagner in 1864. It would be their only meeting. Typically, Wagner was charming and complimentary in person, but later attacked Brahms in print. The more celebrated Brahms became, the more savage his enemies. Wagnerians regularly organized goon squads to disrupt Brahms performances. Wagner's bitterest printed epithet for Brahms, again displaying his anti-Semitism, was "a Jewish czardas player." (Brahms was not Jewish, but he did admire Hungarian folk genres such as the czardas and tried his hand at Hungarian style.)

The real leader of the anti-Wagner faction was not Brahms but the critic Eduard Hanslick. His virulent attacks on Wagner were based not so much on musical quality as on a set of abstractions centered around the idea of "absolute" or "pure" music. By this Hanslick meant a philosophy of music as separate from poetic or literary ideas, moving listeners purely by relationships of tones. Music can only express itself, said Hanslick, not anything else. His bêtes noires were the writers of music drama and program music—mainly Wagner and Liszt. Wagner got even by creating in *Die Meistersinger* a caricature of the critic, the fatuous and pedantic Beckmesser.

Though Brahms certainly deplored program music, he probably was not convinced by Hanslick's ideal purity either; music for Brahms had always been a way to help put his feelings to rest. And up to a point, Brahms respected Wagner and said so. In his treasured manuscript collection was a section of *Tannhäuser*. When in

1875 Wagner wrote an icy demand for Brahms to return that score ("it can be of no value to you except as a curiosity"). Brahms testily complied ("I do not collect 'curiosities' "), but demanded a replacement. Taken aback, Wagner sent, with a slightly less chilly note, a deluxe score of *Das Rheingold*. Brahms replied with remarkable warmth: "What you have sent me gives me so much pleasure that I cannot abstain from telling you . . . my deep gratitude for the splendid present I owe to your kindness." Later Brahms went to see the first two operas of the *Ring*. A strange sideshow to his relations with Wagner was his friendship with Mathilde Wesendonck, Wagner's old mistress and the inspiration for *Tristan und Isolde*. With cavalier disregard for her onetime lover that would have made Wagner apoplectic, Mathilde invited Brahms for a visit and proposed to house him in the very cottage that was the scene of the affair. Though sleeping in the famous bedchamber would surely have tickled Brahms, he never took her up on the offer.

Though it is hard to imagine Brahms attempting an opera, he did contemplate the idea off and on. In the end he stayed away from the stage much as he stayed away from marriage: "It would be as difficult for me to marry as to write an opera. But after the first experience I should probably undertake a second."

In May 1896 came the long-dreaded news that Clara Schumann had died. She had been ill for some time. In anticipation of the end he had written his deeply felt *Four Serious Songs*, which he could never bear to hear performed. However expected, her death still shattered him. For four decades their love had been interwoven with frustration and uncertainty, but nevertheless it had sustained him. He rushed to her burial and at the graveside caught a cold that seemed to linger. Finally he went to a doctor, who discovered that Brahms had advanced liver cancer, the same disease that had killed his father. He was not told, but surely he knew how to interpret his growing fatigue and pain.

In March 1897 Brahms attended a performance of the Fourth Symphony in Vienna. A member of the audience recalled that night:

A storm of applause broke out at the end of the first movement, not to be quieted until the composer, coming to the front of the artists' box . . . showed himself to the audience. The demonstration was renewed after the second and third movements, and an extraordinary scene followed the conclusion of the work. The applauding, shouting house, its gaze riveted on the figure standing in the balcony . . . seemed unable to let him go. Tears ran down his cheeks as he stood there, shrunken in form, with lined countenance, strained expression, white hair hanging lank; and throughout the audience there was a feeling of a stifled sob, for each knew that they were saying farewell.

At the end of that month he wrote to his stepmother one of his ironic notes: "I've gone to bed awhile, for the sake of variety . . . But don't be afraid, nothing has changed, and all I need is patience as usual." He died five days later, at sixty-three, on April 3, 1897.

In his art Brahms was a union of opposites, a Romantic in expression but a Classicist in form and technique. The manifest emotionalism of his music—the source of its popularity—is held in check by traditional formal and tonal logic. Though his harmony is more colorful than Beethoven's, it is less adventurous than that of Wagner and Liszt. Sometimes the strains of his paradoxical approach show in sonata-form developments that make musical sense but don't quite pay off emotionally; the subjective feelings seem to struggle against the objective constraints of their form. A good deal of the time, though, Brahms subdued this conflict of loyalties and forged a kind of resolution. In any case, it was the only approach that suited his personality—stolid, bourgeois, at once painfully sensitive and stubbornly reticent. The exquisitely longing, twilight tone of much of his music has to do with both his tastes and his nostalgia for a world that was irrevocably past. In other words, if his backward-looking is to some extent a weakness, it is also part of his strength and scope: in Brahms the whole of the Western musical tradition from Palestrina to Schumann speaks in an individual and eloquent summation. After him, the tradition had to find new paths.

His craftsmanship is displayed even in parlor pieces for the piano like the Intermezzo in A major op. 118. In the course of it an apparently simple harmonic underlining of a melody verges on canon, a charming harmonic turn is created by putting an earlier melody in the bass, and throughout there is a masterful rhythmic and thematic development. (Brahms's thematic techniques much influenced Schoenberg, for all the latter's Wagnerism.) Similarly, in the atmospheric Intermezzo in B minor op. 119, Brahms plays ingenious games with the harmony, keeping the key sense suspended and sometimes implying different keys in each hand.

Despite his sophistication, Brahms also enjoyed dabbling in lighter music. The best-known example is the artless little "Cradle Song," the most beloved of its kind ever written. He admired the waltzes of Johann Strauss, Jr., once signing an autograph album with the melody of Strauss's "Blue Danube" and adding, "Unfortunately not by yours truly, Johannes Brahms." He tried his hand at Strauss's game in two sets of *Liebeslieder* (Love Song) Waltzes for two pianos and voices. His love of Hungarian folk music is reflected in four books of Hungarian dances, in Gypsy songs, and in chamber works such as the last movement of the G major Quintet op. 111.

Though the most familiar of Brahms's works are his symphonies, a good way to make his acquaintance is through the chamber music. There are only around twenty opus numbers of chamber works, far fewer than by Beethoven and others, but they include pieces as strong as any in the literature.

I suggest starting with something atypical in its sweetness and directness, however complicated the feelings that went into it: the String Sextet no. 2 in G major of 1865, the one he wrote to put to rest his love for Agathe von Siebold. It begins with a throbbing figure in the viola and builds through one felicity after another to an achingly beautiful climax on the notes representing Agathe's name. Of near-Mendelssohnian grace is the second-movement scherzo, in which, shortly after the beginning, he sneaks in an inversion of the theme against counterpoint above; a lusty folklike trio provides contrast. In the third movement theme and variations there is a touch of sadness in the form of a starkly descending chromatic line, but that is dispelled by a vigorous animato. The finale begins with a whirlwind which quickly dies down to a warm lyrical melody.

Three years later came perhaps the greatest of his chamber works, the Piano Quintet in F minor. The first movement is of almost symphonic scope, impassioned and tragic in tone, with a fierce rhythmic urgency. After a calm and lovely slow movement comes one of his most exhilarating scherzos, contrasted by a faux-naïf trio.

The final movement stays largely in minor but still manages, after a solemn introduction, a tone of ironic playfulness. Throughout, there is a typically painstaking evolution of thematic ideas that unifies all the movements.

In 1890 Brahms felt written out and declared to his friends that he was hanging up his pen. That resolve lasted until 1891, when he first heard the clarinetist Richard Mühlfeld and could not resist composing for him. The works for Mühlfeld began with a clarinet trio; then came what Brahms described as "a far greater piece of foolishness," the Quintet in B minor for Clarinet and Strings. There is a sweet-sad autumnal glow to this work, coming from a man not that old but feeling old, and in supreme command of his craft. The heroic posturings and melancholy outbursts of his earlier works no longer interested him; here, most of the material is "unobtrusive" (his word) but quietly beautiful all the same. Meanwhile, he took care to show off every nuance of the clarinet. His last chamber works were two sonatas for that admired player and instrument.

Of the larger works, I'll begin with the *German Requiem*, completed in final form in 1868. As we have seen, it was partly a memorial to his mother. Not being a religious man in the usual sense, Brahms bypassed the traditional text of the Requiem Mass and set verses from the German Bible that expressed his own feelings about death. So many moments in the seven sections attain a luminous beauty, especially the opening "Blessed are they that mourn" and the familiar "How lovely is thy dwelling place." Perhaps most memorable of all, with a kind of transcendent sentimentality, is the final "Happy are they who die in the Lord." Brahms demonstrates as well as anyone that some of the greatest work borders on sentimentality—but stays on the right side of that border. (Unless you are of the opinion of George Bernard Shaw, who wrote that Brahms's Requiem can be borne patiently only by the corpse.)

Among the concertos—two massive ones for piano, one for violin, and a double concerto for violin and cello—I'll recommend starting with the Piano Concerto No. 2 in B-flat, premiered in 1881 with Brahms at the piano. This work is at once monumental and straightforward, with little of the pomp and portentousness of his other concertos. In keeping with its length—over forty-five minutes—its four movements cover a great deal of expressive territory:

the first movement solemn and imposing, the second faster, darker, and more passionate, the third gently songful, and the last movement surprisingly carefree and light.

Finally I come to the symphonies, which are invariably ranked next to Beethoven's as among the finest ever written. Here we see Brahms at his most ambitious and his most self-conscious. The gravity with which he approached his symphonies is reflected in their orchestration; they have a weighty sound to match their intended effect. In the end, Brahms was able to surmount his own awe in the face of history and fashion works of timeless breadth and power.

Most agree that the Symphony no. 1 in C minor, though not necessarily the most sophisticated, is his finest, partly because the material is so compelling. It begins with a searing, pounding slow introduction that leads to a craggy and dramatic allegro. The two inner movements are calmer, the third not the usual scherzo but a charming allegretto. The final movement returns to a weighty tone in an extended slow introduction that mounts to a pealing horn solo said to be inspired by a horn Brahms heard in the Swiss Alps. The last movement proper begins with the famous chorale melody, introduced sumptuously in low strings. (This is the tune always compared to Beethoven's "Ode to Joy," but Brahms's theme sounds majestic with a touch of melancholy rather than joyful.) The regal assurance of this melody is challenged by much tumultuous and even anguished music in the finale, but the symphony ends in a burst of triumph.

From there go on to the Symphony no. 3, sometimes called Brahms's *Eroica*. It certainly begins heroically, with two ringing chords followed by a towering pronouncement from the full orchestra. But like all Brahms symphonies, it covers a large territory; the heroic tone is balanced by the wistful lyricism of the third movement and much use of intimate, chamberlike sonorities. In some ways most striking of all is the finale, which contains everything from quiet whisperings to soaring melodies to heroic proclamations, but whose last third is largely soft and elegiac, an unlikely ending for a big symphony, but beautifully realized. Then try the other two symphonies: the lighthearted and pastoral no. 2 and the valedictory no. 4.

In the symphonies as in all Brahms's major works, his constant looking backward may be the source of his twilight yearning, his sweetness, even his rage and heaven-storming transports. For Brahms the past contained the only true giants, contained the hope of Clara and of love. Perhaps the tragic sense in his music is the tragedy of time's passing. For that loss and yearning in all our lives, Brahms speaks truly and indispensably.

ANTONÍN DVOŘÁK

Most of the familiar works of Antonín Dvořák are "absolute" pieces like those of his mentor Brahms—symphonies, chamber music, and so on. Yet while Dvořák uses the conventional genres and harmonic means of the late nineteenth century, everything comes out with an ethnic coloration that is unmistakable even if one knows nothing of his roots in Bohemian folk music. That vivid and engaging coloration, a complex of characteristic melodic turns, rhythms, and harmonic usages, is as hard to pin down as a national cast of features or personality type, but it's there all the same. One hears it most clearly in pieces like the rustic dances of the *Dumky* Trio or the rambunctious bagpipe whirls in the last movement of the Eighth Symphony. But even in the *New World* Symphony, an attempt to write in the spirit of another country, the Bohemian tone is manifest. It is as if Dvořák had attempted to whip up a gumbo but unconsciously blended the spices to his old-world taste.

Though he was not the first musical nationalist of the nineteenth century, he remains the model of the type. Everywhere, artists of the era were caught up in a new ethnic awareness and desire for political and cultural independence from foreign domination. All the same, there is a good deal more to Dvořák than patriotism and folksiness. Though his musical education was slow and painstaking, at bottom he was an instinctive genius who virtually breathed music. That facility infused all his best work with a youthfulness that may be his most endearing quality. Fifty years ago some critics were predicting that his scores would eventually gather dust in libraries: he was too affable to be really good. Instead, the years have failed to tarnish his freshness and have only made his music steadily more beloved.

Antonín Dvořák (pronounced *dvor'zhok*) was born on September 8, 1841, in Nelahozeves, a town in the Bohemian region of what is now Czechoslovakia, then under Austrian rule. Antonín's father was an innkeeper and, like most of his countrymen, an amateur musician. He reared his son to follow the same life. Instead, the boy neglected innkeeping and spent most of his time playing and listening to the folk music of the region. After years of the father protesting and the son doggedly studying violin, piano, and theory, Antonín was allowed to go to the Organ School in Prague. Upon graduating he began playing violin in cafés and orchestras. As he made himself into a composer, he scratched out a living on the violin for over ten years, a time, he wrote, of "hard study, occasional composing, much revision, a great deal of thinking, and very little eating." He produced stacks of pieces, most of which he kept back or destroyed. In those years he studied only "with God, with the birds, and the trees—and myself." Though his idol was Beethoven, another primary influence was Bedřich Smetana; with works such as the serenely lovely tone poem *The Moldau* and the opera *The Bartered Bride,* Smetana had fathered Bohemian national music.

In 1873 Dvořák left behind his miserable playing jobs; soon he would begin a long teaching career at the Prague Conservatory. That same year he married Anna Cermak and had his first major success with the cantata *Hymnus*. In 1874 he won the Austrian State Prize for the Symphony in E-flat; he would win three more years in a row. In 1876 Brahms sat on the panel that awarded him the prize for the nationalistic *Airs from Moravia*. That time he was also given a yearly pension and Brahms placed the work with a publisher. On Brahms's suggestion, Dvořák composed the *Slavonic Dances* that soon made him world famous.

Once Brahms gave him a leg up in his career, Dvořák needed little further assistance. Like Mendelssohn, he was a composer of manifestly delightful music, with touches of boldness but nothing too unconventional, so audiences everywhere received his work with open arms. Though Dvořák wrote within the German stylistic orbit, his personality owes (or convinces us it does) more to the fields and woods of Bohemia than to German theories and formal traditions.

Brahms, so burdened by history in everything he wrote, admired in his protégé exactly that ingenuous freshness and facility.

Also like Mendelssohn, Dvořák was adopted by the British. In 1884 the first of his nine visits there saw the premiere of his *Stabat Mater;* he conducted the second performance of the piece for an audience of twelve thousand. These English tours and related commissions allowed him to buy a country estate in southern Bohemia, where he summered happily with his growing family and a cacaphonous houseful of birds. The Symphony no. 8 in G major op. 88, one of his most engaging, was premiered in June 1891 at ceremonies in which he received an honorary doctorate from Cambridge University.

His report of that day to a friend shows a great deal about the man, who was by then one of the most famous and honored composers alive: "I do not like the celebrations, and when I have to be in one of them, I am on pins and needles. . . . Nothing but ceremony, and nothing but doctors. All faces were serious, and it seemed to me as if no one knew any other language than Latin. I looked to the right and to the left, and did not know to whom I was to listen. And when I realized they were talking to me, I had quite a shock, and was ashamed at not knowing Latin. But . . . I think that to compose the *Stabat Mater* is, after all, more than to know Latin." He seems like a wide-eyed rube in the presence of the great and sophisticated.

How much of that attitude was genuine is the question. When somebody complained that Dvořák seemed incapable of talking about anything but music, an acquaintance suggested, "Did you try talking to him about pigs?" Yet while as composer he lacked the formal mastery of Brahms or Beethoven, he was anything but unsophisticated. Often the form of Dvořák's large-scale works holds up better than that of Schubert and Schumann. He seemed to grasp the intricate demands of symphonic writing with the same instinctive understanding with which he produced little Slavonic dances. Perhaps the best guess is that Dvořák was not as guileless as he seemed, but cultivated a naïve streak that he knew was the source of his voice and his authenticity.

So he resembled a humble Bohemian peasant who felt lost in cities and at home only among his fields and his birds. One of the few recorded exceptions to his generally sweet temper is that he was a bad loser at cards. He had a childlike obsession with railroads and would sometimes travel for miles to watch a favorite train go by. It is said that he visited stations so regularly and knew the schedules so well that people assumed he was a train conductor. Eventually he would be induced to travel to America as much as anything by the prospect of beholding the glories of Grand Central Station.

Oddly enough, the most productive part of Dvořák's life was spent in a foreign country ostensibly imitating its music. In 1891 the persistence and admirable bank account of an American lady named Jeanette Thurber convinced Dvořák to come to New York and head the National Conservatory, which she had founded. He arrived in the United States in 1892; during his nearly three years of residence he would write some of his finest works and set off a seismic shock among American composers.

The story of his American works and attendant controversy is complicated, but simple enough in outline. Despite a heavy teaching and performing schedule, Dvořák maintained his usual steady output. He wanted to do something to honor his host country, in the process perhaps stimulating the creative life of native composers. He had become entranced by spirituals sung to him by a black student of his named H. T. Burleigh; meanwhile, he had also been introduced to American Indian melodies. For Dvořák all this heady new experience touched off a ferment of ideas and creativity that would virtually explode across the American musical scene.

In a newspaper interview, Dvořák declared with more enthusiasm than accuracy: "I found that the music of the Negroes and of the Indians was practically identical. [In fact they are not remotely similar, unless in the sketchy notation of scholars.] I therefore carefully studied a certain number of Indian melodies . . . and became thoroughly imbued with their characteristics. [He would never be imbued with anything but Bohemia.] It is this spirit which I have tried to reproduce in my new symphony. I have not actually used any of the melodies. I have simply written original themes embodying the peculiarities of the Indian music."

The symphony in question is the one he titled *From the New World,* which had a sensational reception at its 1893 premiere by the New York Philharmonic. The idea that a certified Great European Composer had written something based on indigenous material enraptured an American public chronically insecure about the country's artistic credentials. Actually the symphony is about as American as Puccini's high-Italian *Girl of the Golden West.* Like Puccini's opera, Dvořák's *New World* owed its inception and some measure of inspiration to America, but in the end stands as one of the greatest manifestations of the Czech/Bohemian spirit. The same can be said of his *American* String Quartet, though that may actually quote an Indian tune or two.

Dvořák wrote this quartet during a vacation in the little Czech-speaking town of Spillville, Iowa, where he went in an attempt to assuage his growing homesickness. But the sojourn among his countrymen only sharpened his yearning to return home; he sailed back to Prague in 1895, leaving in his wake a highly productive turbulence. Though by that time the concert life of America was booming, its classical composers were mostly pale imitators of European models. To the inspiration of some and the irritation of others, Dvořák had the audacity to propose as a foundation for native symphonists the folk music of African-American people and Indians: "I suggested that inspiration for truly national music might be derived from the Negro melodies or Indian chants. . . . The most potent as well as the most beautiful among them . . . are certain of the so-called plantation melodies and slave songs. . . . The music of the people is like a rare and lovely flower growing amidst encroaching weeds. . . . The fact that no one has as yet arisen to make the most of it does not prove that nothing is there." He was proposing, in other words, that American composers do what had worked so well for himself and other European nationalists. The *New World* was a kind of object lesson in how to go about it.

The results of Dvořák's modest proposals included, on one hand, racist carpings about the very idea of using black and Indian material, scholarly altercations over how "American" Dvořák's American-written pieces really were, and protests from German-trained composers like the popular Edward MacDowell: "Masquerading in the so-called nationalism of Negro clothes cut in Bohemia will not help us." On the other hand, a new generation of artists took to heart Dvořák's suggestions and began writing pseudo-Negro and pseudo-Indian symphonic works that proved to be, in the end, not much more than earnest and quaint. The trouble in the United States, unlike more homogeneous European countries, had always been, *Which* people are *the* people? *Which* music is *the* national music? It would be Charles Ives who would finally find a way around these dilemmas to realize Dvořák's call for a vital music national in means but universal in scope.

So Dvořák returned home to his teaching, his beloved countryside, his honors and love from the Bohemian people. For some reason, though, his work declined after the American years. The main productions were several operas and tone poems, none among his best works. Dvořák's last years were saddened by Bright's disease and the failure of his opera *Armida*. On May 1, 1904, he suddenly died of a stroke amidst his family at the dinner table. He was buried in a state funeral on a day of national mourning.

For an introduction to Dvořák's music one may as well start with the most popular of his works, since it also happens to be one of his best—the Symphony no. 9 in E minor op. 95, *From the New World*. It is three movements of infectious folklike melody, luminously scored, and a finale of rousing trombonic banality. The last movement also includes an engaging development of what seems to be "Three Blind Mice." The famous tune of the second movement (later decked out with words to make the ersatz spiritual "Goin' Home") is one of which the composer, and the world, were particularly fond. This entire work, like so many of his, captures the lyricism and lilt of folk music in a way few classical composers have ever managed to do—and does it in a mainstream European symphonic style that also attains moments of grandeur on a Brahmsian scale.

The Symphony no. 8 in G major may actually be the most winsome of the lot. The last movement, for example, begins with one of the sweetest of broad Brahmsian tunes for the cello section, then transforms the same melody into a boisterous folk dance. The relatively somber Symphony no. 7 in D minor, neglected for many years, may be the most substantial of his symphonies. There Dvořák consciously evokes the heights of the symphonic tradition as represented by Brahms and Beethoven, and nearly reaches those heights.

His Cello Concerto op. 104, mostly written in America, is one of the most familiar of Romantic concertos, with an especially moving slow movement. The *Slavonic Dances*, two sets of them in versions

ANTONÍN DVOŘÁK

both for piano duet and orchestra, have long been "Pops" favorites.

To sample Dvořák's chamber music, begin with the piano trio called *Dumky*, op. 90. It is named for a Slavic peasant dance characterized by soulful slow interludes alternating with hearty rhythmical music. The trio is a somewhat loose assemblage of six *dumky*, contrasting in moods; the first three are joined so that the whole work still approximates the standard four movements. Dvořák loved the *Dumky* and often played piano in performances. (Brahms edited it for publication and in his enthusiasm may have added a few touches of his own.) The Piano Quintet op. 81, one of the great Romantic works for that medium, is unceasingly songful. Like the *Dumky*, it is full of ear-grabbing Dvořákian "hooks."

Most admired of Dvořák's chamber music is the String Quartet in F major op. 96, which he called the *American* for its supposed Indian melodies. It seemed to burst out of him during three idyllic weeks in Spillville, amidst walks in the countryside and organ-playing for local church services. Indian tunes or no, from the beginning this is old-country Dvořák at his most brilliant: the opening seems to break out like a gabby and delightful old peasant talking about life and love and the weather. In a way that's what Dvořák was, and why he's such an agreeable companion.

MODEST MUSORGSKY

In the celebrated Clock Scene of Musorgsky's *Boris Godunov*, Czar Boris has just heard an account of the murder of the young czarevitch, which Boris had arranged himself in order to gain the throne. Learning that the youth's body had remained miraculously uncorrupted for days, the czar cries "Enough!" Then, step by step, he loses his senses. His voice moves from song to groans to shouts. Finally he has a hallucination of the bloody child, the orchestra growing like an accusing thunder to overwhelm his cries of terror and anguish. At the end, in a wasted, empty voice, he begs God for mercy.

The scene is a depiction of searing emotion that few other composers ever managed on the operatic stage—and there are other comparable scenes in *Boris*. "The artistic presentment of beauty alone is sheer childishness," Musorgsky wrote; "I am a realist in the *higher sense*—i.e., my business is to portray *the soul of man in all its profundity*." Through the fiasco of his life, the patronizing attitudes of his friends, the poverty and alcoholism, Musorgsky understood with fine clarity what he was doing and why, and he found his own means of accomplishing it. That may not be the definition of a polished artist, which he was not, but it is a workable definition of a great one, and that Musorgsky was, in the handful of works he managed to finish before the bottle finished him.

Modest Petrovich Musorgsky was born on March 21, 1839, in the village of Karevo, in the province of Pskov. His father was a prosperous landowner and music lover. Modest first studied piano with his mother; he later had lessons in the city where he would spend his life, St. Petersburg. Following a family tradition, he attended a cadet school there and graduated into the military, by which time he had become an accomplished pianist and amateur composer. His first published piece, a polka, appeared as early as 1852. Piano playing, good looks, and an amiable disposition made him popular with fellow soldiers and with women. The main things he would learn in the service, however, were the traditional soldierly arts of drinking and carousing.

In 1857 this young dandy and musical dabbler was transformed into a driven artist. That year he met several composers including César Cui and Mily Balakirev. Fired by their vision of a new Russian music, he began to study with Balakirev and to compose in earnest, though at first with no striking results. In 1858, at nineteen, he left the military to devote his life to music. For a time his family helped support him.

Two years later Musorgsky enjoyed his first success when Anton Rubinstein conducted the Scherzo in B-flat major at St. Petersburg. Soon after, Musorgsky had a nervous breakdown, an early sign of what would prove to be a fragile temperament. Then in 1861 came the historic freeing of the serfs by the czar; the effect on Musorgsky's landowning family was disastrous, however, and in 1863 he had to take on a job as a government clerk. He would remain in lowly desk jobs, subsisting on starvation wages, until nearly the end of his life. After his mother's death in 1865, his depressive episodes and his drinking worsened, initiating a long slide to disaster.

Much of the time he roomed with composer friends, among them Nicolai Rimsky-Korsakov. He took up operas one after another, worked on them for a while, then wandered into something else. Yet his talent began to be noticed; an 1867 article first spoke of the "mighty handful" of St. Petersburg composers—Musorgsky, Rimsky-Korsakov, Cui, Balakirev, and Alexander Borodin—who were committed to forging a new national art from Russian sources. They would come to call themselves "The Five," and history has done likewise. Friends recalled Musorgsky as the most literary member of the group and the most trenchant thinker about the relations between music and society. Those concerns are all embodied in the great work of his life.

In 1868, putting aside a work based on Gogol's comedy *The Marriage,* Musorgsky took up *Boris Godunov,* a historical drama by Pushkin about a czar who seizes power by murder but cannot escape his own conscience. The story was made for Musorgsky's gifts and dramatic ideas, a full-blooded Russian tragedy that he could treat in a style based on folk song and on the rhythms and inflections of the Russian language. He would call *Boris* a "musical folk-drama."

His technique had to be discovered as he went along, because his studies in traditional theory had been desultory and his aims were different from—and often opposed to—traditional ideas of musicality and the Italianate style that dominated Russian opera. Music was not mere entertainment or an abstract discipline for him; it spoke to the people as much as possible in their own voice and temperament: "I foresee a new kind of melody which will be the melody of life. With great pains I have achieved a type of melody imitating that of speech." Elsewhere he described his approach as "melody justified by sense." His work often is beautifully lyrical but in a novel way, following the sound and sense of the text.

Musorgsky painstakingly worked out his ideas at the piano, guided not by rules but by his finely tuned ear and a consciousness steeped in folk music. His startling harmonic colors, unprecedented dissonances, and inventive atmospheric effects are not geared for prettiness but for dramatic truth. Often he departed from the standard major and minor scales to use the ancient modal scales of folk music. (All these features were to have tremendous influence on composers of the next century—Debussy, Ravel, Stravinsky, Proko-

fiev, Bartók.) While Musorgsky lies firmly in the Russian tradition of full-bodied sound and extravagant expressiveness, he has neither the self-indulgent purple patches of Tchaikovsky nor the pseudoexotic voluptuousness of Rimsky-Korsakov. Musorgsky is really the least Romantic of the Russians. Romantics are dreamers; he was a realist. Like all the best nationalist art, his tragedies, his violence, his visionary transports are universal, not personal: "the soul of man," he wrote, "in all its profundity."

Nicolai Ghiaurov in the role operatic basses dream of: Boris Godunov, in a production by the San Francisco Opera.

After revisions that added more conventional elements (including some love interest), *Boris Godunov* was accepted by the Imperial Theater in St. Petersburg and premiered there in February 1874. As intended, it spoke to the people. It was taken up especially by progressive youths, among them revolutionaries who saw it as a call to action against long-standing corruption and injustice. Songs from *Boris* were sung in the streets. But the more educated musicians, including Musorgsky's friends, condemned its stylistic innovations as signs, in Rimsky-Korsakov's words, of "clumsiness and illiteracy." Meanwhile the authorities were not slow to notice the political implications of a story involving a popular revolt against a murderous czar. On orders that may have originated with the royal family, the opera was first cut by censors, then dropped. It would go into eclipse for years before emerging in the twentieth century as the epitome of Russian nationalism in music, a revelation of the country's people and soul (and its guilty conscience).

The period he spent on *Boris* was the only time in his life that Musorgsky marshaled his energies and kept the vodka at bay long enough to complete an operatic project. Most of his other mature output—except for the finished and marvelous songs—is a patchwork of sketches, some finished by other and lesser composers. Toward the end he became fat, red-nosed, and buffoonish; reduced virtually to rags and begging, he was often found in drunken oblivion or brawling in the streets. A friend called him a "perfect idiot." Through his last years he attempted without success to finish two new operas, the tragic *Khovanshtchina* and the comic *Fair at Sorochinsk.* He died following a bout of delirium tremens on March 28, 1881, just after his forty-second birthday.

Some years after his death began a rebirth of his music, sparked primarily by Rimsky-Korsakov, who orchestrated *A Night on Bald Mountain* and made two "improved" versions of *Boris,* taming the wildness of Musorgsky's voice and decking it out in sumptuous orchestral garb. It is a measure of the strength of the original that all this retooling did not manage to kill the explosive power of the work. Only in the later twentieth century did Musorgsky's rawer but more compelling original version challenge Rimsky-Korsakov's on the stage. Meanwhile several composers, most notably Maurice Ravel, took a crack at orchestrating the 1874 piano suite *Pictures at an Exhibition,* the only other major work Musorgsky managed to finish. In Ravel's version, it is one of the most colorful and popular pieces in the orchestral repertoire.

A succinct introduction to Musorgsky is his little orchestral tone poem *A Night on Bald Mountain,* a picture of a witches' sabbath. As orchestrated by Rimsky-Korsakov, it is a delightful outing of mock diabolism, with whizzing violin effects for spirits, orgiastic writh-ings, and lots of demonically braying trombones. What carries it, finally, is not the orchestral tricks but rather Musorgsky's harmonic and melodic and descriptive imagination.

That imagination is in full strength in his programmatic piano suite *Pictures at an Exhibition*. It is based on drawings by Mu-sorgsky's artist friend Victor Hartmann, whose death had terribly depressed the composer. Long obscured by versions orchestrated by others, the original piano suite has emerged to take its deserved place in the virtuoso literature as a tour de force of musical and pianistic brilliance. The broad striding of the opening "Prome-nade," representing the composer walking through the gallery, recurs periodically throughout. Otherwise we find an evocative set of little descriptive pieces: among the pictures in the gallery, here is a grotesque gnome, there children playing in the Tuileries of Paris, across the way two Polish Jews debating, one shrill and one solemn. At the conclusion, based on a drawing of an architectural project, comes the lofty music for "The Great Gate of Kiev." Ravel's famous orchestration of *Pictures* is both creative and self-effacing: masterful in handling the orchestra, yet in every way serving the music.

Before plunging into his opera, perhaps sample Musorgsky's songs, which approach operatic drama and intensity. He wrote fewer than Schubert or Schumann, but enough to make him one of the great songwriters of the century. Given his general lack of disci-pline, the short form of the song allowed Musorgsky to concentrate his energy, and the effect can be spectacular in song cycles such as the *Songs and Dances of Death* and *Sunless*.

Like all operas, *Boris Godunov* is best heard in live performance. Rather than a continuous story, it is a series of scenes, each with its own shape. The magnificent Coronation Scene, for example, seems to gather bit by bit as the crowd swells in the great square; then arise the joyful shouts of the people and the singing of an old Russian hymn, everything seemingly enfolded in the gigantic pealing of bells. Yet after the frenzied shouts of "Glory!" the first words of Boris in his moment of triumph are: "My soul is sad! Strange, dark forebodings and evil presentiments oppress my spirit." And so the tale unfolds, power and misery and treachery and madness; in scene after scene Musorgsky finds ways of conveying overwhelming emo-tion that are as original as they are effective. There are many operas more perfect than *Boris,* but few more realistic in expression and richer in human understanding.

Musorgsky was probably the most talented composer Russia ever saw before Stravinsky. It is sad to contemplate what he might have become if his circumstances had been better, if his friends had understood him better, if the opera had been an unequivocal success, if he had mastered his thirst—and if and if.

On the other hand, maybe there should be no sadness at all. Maybe he was born to write *Boris Godunov* and, having accomplished that, could only die, like a salmon that has spawned.

PETER
ILYICH
TCHAIKOVSKY

Perhaps no composer of renown has had so many complaints registered against him, while still staying in business, as Tchaikovsky. Among his own severest critics ("I have suffered all my life from my incapacity to grasp form"), he himself began generations of carping, from both enemies and friends, about his tendency to be prolix, bombastic, glib, and vulgar. Yet from his own time to ours, he has been one of the most popular of all composers, especially important as a gateway for listeners into the world of classical music. (I am among those who at age fourteen thought the *1812 Overture* was the swellest thing ever written.)

I will not be so cynical as to suggest that Tchaikovsky is popular *because* he is prolix, bombastic, etc. Plenty of other composers are even more so, without commanding his following. He prospers partly because in the long run he transcends his faults; he recognized and struggled tenaciously against them, with some success. His musical hero, surprisingly enough, was Mozart; perhaps this enabled him to keep a bit of Classical rein on his rampaging passions. But clearly, heart-on-sleeve emotion is his main stock-in-trade. In his music and his life, Tchaikovsky was the archetypical Russian artist: a hectic blend of spiritual aspiration and extravagant self-indulgence, a saint and a charlatan, self-inflated and self-loathing, fatalistic and more than a little mad.

Peter Ilyich Tchaikovsky was born on May 7, 1840, to the comfortable family of a mining engineer in provincial Votkinsk. He soon revealed a fragile and hysterical temperament; his nurse called him "a child of glass." When Peter was ten he was placed, to his horror, in a boarding school in St. Petersburg; the family moved to the city soon after. Always passionately attached to music, he studied it off and on through his childhood but attended law school and graduated to become a government clerk. Finding the work intolerable, he began paying more attention to music. Finally, over the protests of his family, he left his job in 1863 and went to a music school just founded in St. Petersburg by pianist and composer Anton Rubinstein. There his compositions brought him much attention. A friend, later a powerful critic, wrote him, "In you I see the greatest, or rather the only, hope of our musical future." He graduated in 1865 and soon found a position teaching at the new Moscow Conservatory, run by Anton Rubinstein's brother Nicholas.

For some ten years he led a stable life filled with composing, teaching, and newspaper criticism. Soon after moving to Moscow he wrote his sister, "My nervousness has completely vanished, and I am gradually acquiring the proper professional demeanor. My hypochondria is also disappearing." Work on his First Symphony interrupted this relative contentment; amidst frenzied labors and lacerating uncertainties he had a nervous breakdown in the middle of the piece. After a summer's recuperation he finished the symphony, only to have Anton Rubinstein reject it for performance. But Nicholas Rubinstein conducted the symphony, called "Winter Dreams," in Moscow and it found tremendous success. (It is still heard occasionally and has its charms, though there is little of the familiar Tchaikovsky personality.)

Many of his works had at first to contend not only with his own self-doubts but with crushing responses from musicians including his friends. Tchaikovsky introduced the First Piano Concerto to Nicholas Rubinstein in 1874, and later wrote of the reaction: "Then burst forth from Rubinstein's mouth a mighty torrent of words. . . . It appeared that my concerto was utterly worthless, absolutely unplayable; passages were so commonplace and awkward that they could not be improved; the piece as a whole was bad, trivial, vulgar." When his Violin Concerto was played in Berlin in 1881, conservative critic Eduard Hanslick wrote: "The violin is no longer played: it is yanked about, it is torn asunder, it is beaten black and blue. . . . We see wild and vulgar faces, we hear curses, we smell bad brandy. . . . Tchaikovsky's violin concerto brings to us for the first time the horrid idea that there may be music that stinks in the ear." This review oppressed Tchaikovsky to the end of his life; he could recite it word for word. Yet both concertos triumphed in his lifetime, and he had the satisfaction of hearing Nicholas Rubinstein play the piano concerto.

The relative stability of Tchaikovsky's life began to disintegrate, in ways both productive and tragic, in late 1876. At that point he got some minor commissions from a fabulously wealthy widow named Nadezhda Filaretovna von Meck, who had become enthralled by his music. Next summer she sent him a gift of three thousand rubles, beginning a relationship that would go on for thirteen years, with one notable peculiarity: during the entire time, they never once met. Their friendship was carried on entirely in affectionate and almost daily letters. Sometimes they stayed near each other during vacations; on her request he would walk past her window so she could see him. A few times they came face to face, and turned and fled. After years of this bizarre relationship, she finally asked to meet him. He turned her down.

The first important fruit of her beneficence was the Symphony no. 4, which with the words ". . . to my best friend" he dedicated to his patroness. But despite her paving the way, the work would be born in tumult and suffering.

In Russia in those days, concert life had a hyperbolic, almost crazed quality. It is said that after piano recitals young ladies were known to shoot themselves because they felt the rest of their lives would be an anticlimax. Music student Antonina Milyukova seems to have been something of that type. Having conceived an obsession for Tchaikovsky's music and transferred it to the man, Antonina courted him in 1877 with a combination of adulation, begging, tantrums, and threats of suicide. Then in the middle of composing the Fourth Symphony, he allowed himself to be persuaded to marry her, partly because he had already decided that marriage was the only way out of the great dilemma of his life.

The dilemma was his homosexuality. Being generally conventional—in fact reactionary—in his life and opinions, and living in a country where homosexuality was a capital crime, this was a constant source of anguish and fear. Even before meeting Antonina he had written his brother Modeste, who was also homosexual, "I will seriously consider entering matrimony with any woman. I am convinced that my *inclinations* are the greatest and insuperable barrier to my well-being, and I must by all means struggle against my nature [Tchaikovsky's emphasis]." So an unstable and hypersensitive artist struggling vainly against his sexual orientation married a young woman who was neurotic, unintelligent, and apparently sexually insatiable. It was a formula for nightmare, and the nightmare began virtually the day they were married. For him over the next three months followed despair, mental breakdown, and finally an attempt at suicide.

His family stepped in to extract Tchaikovsky from Antonina, and a sympathetic Madame von Meck bestowed on him an annuity of six thousand rubles. Slowly he recovered and completed the Fourth Symphony. The next year, he would leave the Moscow Conservatory and with his patroness's help become a full-time composer. Antonina did not survive the disaster; after years of deluging Tchaikovsky with pleas and blackmail threats, she was committed to an insane asylum, where she spent the last two decades of her life.

The rest of Tchaikovsky's years were a patchwork of glowing successes and humiliating failures, exaltation and despair. His ballets, starting with *Swan Lake* and going on to *The Sleeping Beauty* and *The Nutcracker,* made him a staple of the dance stage worldwide. Some of his operas, especially *Eugen Onegin,* were well received. Though during an early attempt at conducting he had developed the hallucination that his head was falling off (through the piece he held on to it with one hand), he finally returned to the podium to conduct his own work regularly. One of his most triumphant periods was an 1891 concert tour of America; he began it as the centerpiece of the opening of Carnegie Hall in New York. He was astonished at the love and respect given him in America: "I am a much more important person here than in Russia," he wrote home. "Isn't that curious?"

By then he had endured the final great blow of his life: in 1890 Madame von Meck suddenly cut off her support with a fabricated explanation of financial difficulty. Tchaikovsky no longer needed the money, but his pride was stricken. She never replied to his queries, and her real reasons have never become known.

Only fifty but looking aged beyond his years, he seemed to get steadily more world-weary and fatalistic, and all those feelings were poured into his last and most personal symphony, no. 6, which brother Modeste christened the *Pathétique*. Tchaikovsky conducted the first performance in St. Petersburg in October 1893. Though the symphony was received coolly, he felt uncharacteristically pleased with it: "I give you my word of honor," he wrote his publisher, "that never in my life have I been so contented, so proud, so happy, in the knowledge that I have written a good piece." It was in that spirit, perhaps feeling too elated to be cautious, that he hastened his death nine days after the premiere.

On November 2, having lunch with Modeste in St. Petersburg, he took the dangerous step of drinking a glass of unboiled water in cholera season, saying to his brother's protest, "One can't go tiptoeing about in fear of death forever." The ravaging disease, which had killed his mother, set in soon after. He died on November 6, 1893, murmuring the name Nadezhda Filaretovna.

A good deal of Tchaikovsky verges on light-classical, and those pieces are as good a place as any to begin. The *1812 Overture*, written in 1880 to commemorate the Russian defeat of Napoleon, is a spacious and stately work featuring the gentle accompaniment of live artillery. Though he dabbled in nationalism in works such as *1812* and *Marche slave* (1876), Tchaikovsky was really an internationalist with strong German affinities. (Rimsky-Korsakov and the other unforgiving nationalists of the Russian Five deplored his eclecticism.

For his part Tchaikovsky was usually cordial to the Five; despite his fears and neuroses, he could be generous and fair even to his critics.)

Of the ballet scores, long most popular is *The Nutcracker*, which has become as much a part of Christmas as *Messiah*. This story of a Russian nutcracker come to life in a girl's dream is set to music as fairylike as anything written for the stage, with a lightness of touch that reminds us (for once) that Tchaikovsky's hero was Mozart.

Somewhere between light- and heavy-classical lies the orchestral fantasy *Romeo and Juliet*, first written in 1870 and extensively revised over the next decade. It features a good deal of broad songlike melody interspersed with long stretches of blood-stirring Tchaikovskian agitation.

The First Piano Concerto is a mainstay of the bravura concerto repertoire. It commences with a grand melodramatic gesture and soon arrives at a definitive illustration of what might be called the late-Romantic doctrine of the Big Tune: a sobbing, throbbing melody that goes right for the jugular. (Tin Pan Alley later turned it into the song "Tonight We Love.") After a lyrical slow movement the finale is Russian in tone, with a Cossack flavor.

Tchaikovsky's first three symphonies are occasionally revived, but his reputation as a symphonist rests on the last three. In the Fourth he found his voice—gloomy, fatalistic, tending to minor keys, but with gay and marchlike episodes that can be brilliant and exciting at times, at other times thunderously inane. To its dedicatee, Madame von Meck, he wrote a long program for this symphony; its tone is defined by a recurring horn call, which he said represents "that fateful force which prevents the impulse to happiness from attaining its goal."

The Fifth Symphony is hardly less fatalistic, though perhaps more lyrical. It opens with a darkly brooding theme that appears, in differing guises, in each movement. As usual with Tchaikovsky, there is an unrelenting rhythmic drive in the fast movements. The slow movement features another of his songlike themes. A delicate and lilting third-movement waltz reminds one of his ballet scores (in fact, all the symphonies frequently sound balletic). The finale is a vigorous and intense minor-key march.

From the beginning the Sixth Symphony, the *Pathétique*, strikes a tone of anguish: the opening is a low bassoon solo extraordinarily foreboding in effect. While the symphony is a tour of Tchaikovskian trademarks, here they are more intense and heartfelt than ever. The means, on the other hand, are often novel: a strange but charming "waltz" in five-beat time, an airy scherzo, the main theme of the adagio lamentoso finale both tragic and hymnlike. Whether Tchaikovsky intended it to be or not, in its unprecedented depiction of naked suffering the *Pathétique* was the valedictory song of his anguished and pathetic life.

RICHARD STRAUSS

Richard Strauss was a wunderkind, born into a musical family and given the best training available. He found early fame with a series of brash and audacious symphonic poems, went on to a couple of still brasher and more audacious operas, and then drew the line on both audacity and evolution. Thereafter Strauss lived on

Strauss projected nineteenth-century program music well into the twentieth.

through half the Modernist century, gradually running out of inspiration, in his comfortable late-Romantic mode. His best works have survived because he was a brilliant musical mind, a fine craftsman, and a man who knew how to draw a crowd. His personality of a petit bourgeois salesman insured that there was a good measure, and sometimes more than a good measure, of commercial appeal in everything he did. He wrote with one eye on the music and one on the box office.

He was born in Munich on June 11, 1864. His father, Franz Strauss, was principal horn of the Munich Opera and a Wagner hater, his mother heiress to the mighty Pschorr brewing company. Frau Strauss began teaching Richard piano when he was four; Franz took over to supervise a thorough musical education for his son, sending him to various teachers in town. Richard began composing at age six, was soon writing orchestral works, and had his first piece published at twelve. Before he reached twenty he had heard a symphony, string quartet, and violin concerto publicly performed. Writing at the time in a conservative style influenced by Brahms, he was already a master of orchestration in the grand Romantic manner.

Strauss came to the attention of conductor and pianist Hans von Bülow, the mover and shaker we have encountered as an associate of Liszt, Wagner, and Brahms. In 1884 von Bülow brought the young man to his Meiningen orchestra as assistant conductor. Strauss there began a conducting career paralleling his composing, which would finally take him to the Berlin and Vienna operas as music director. It was in Meiningen that Strauss converted to the Wagnerian creed. Thus the son of a famed musician who had ridiculed Wagner in person would become the new generation's avatar of the Wagner/Liszt/Berlioz tradition of "music as expression."

To Strauss, that meant expressing tangible dramatic and emotional ideas through music. He wrote two symphonic poems that would, as they were intended to, make him world famous—*Don Juan* (1888) and *Death and Transfiguration* (1889). With these and later programmatic works Strauss extended into instrumental music the Wagnerian leitmotif technique, in which musical ideas represent characters and images. Where previous symphonic poems had been based on hazy stories or allegories, Strauss's are implied dramas: Don Juan's tale is told with musical gestures related to specific aspects of the story, Don Juan, for example, having his own themes. Strauss was reluctant to spell out his programs; instead, his followers wrote elaborate explanations that he more or less approved (one for the later *Ein Heldenleben* [A Hero's Life] runs to seventy thematic illustrations). Whether or not the familiar programs exactly match what Strauss had in mind, his music *sounds* illustrative; one seems to hear horses and love songs and comic interludes and executions and sheep and philistines and windmills. (This is a prime reason why the Straussian style would later be epidemic among movie composers).

With his early, but nevertheless masterful, symphonic poems, Strauss became the darling of the progressive Wagnerian faction and the bane of the conservative Brahmsians. Von Bülow christened him "Richard the Second," an extraordinary endorsement for a composer in his mid twenties. (No one could then imagine that within two decades Wagnerians would be the old guard.) In the 1890s Strauss extended his string of important symphonic poems with *Till Eulenspiegel's Merry Pranks, Thus Spake Zarathustra, Don Quixote,* and *A Hero's Life* (the hero in question being Strauss himself, represented in quotes from his music). Later, when the quality of his orchestral music fell off, he would keep himself profitably controversial with his stage works.

Having already written a fine body of lieder, to which he would add for the rest of his life, Strauss completed his first opera in 1894, the frankly Wagnerian *Guntram*. It had an unsuccessful premiere in Weimar and a disastrous one in Munich. From the experience Strauss did claim one prize, however—he married the production's lead singer, Pauline de Ahna. Imperious and clever, Pauline would virtually run Strauss's life from then on, managing his business affairs, even telling him when to compose. Strauss, arrogant with everyone else, meekly submitted to Pauline's discipline.

A second opera, *Feursnot* of 1901, also failed. For his next libretto he chose something guaranteed to attract attention, Oscar Wilde's scandalous play *Salomé*. With music as gloriously lurid and decadent as the drama—the most notorious episode being Salomé's ecdysial "Dance of the Seven Veils"—the opera caused the intended sensation. Among other flaps, the Metropolitan Opera in New York withdrew it after one performance generated rabid moralistic outrage. Strauss recalled playing some of *Salomé* for his aged father, who groaned, "Dear Lord, all this nervous music! It's like having your pants full of June bugs." Strauss also liked to quote Kaiser Wilhelm II: "I'm quite fond of [Strauss] otherwise, but he is going to *do himself a lot of harm* with this [Wilhelm's emphasis]." With satisfaction, the dollar-conscious composer would add "Thanks to this harm, I was able to afford my villa at Garmisch!" (The storybook Bavarian village was his home most of his later life.)

Salomé was followed by the even more sensational opera *Electra*. Though time and a higher ante of dissonance and decadence have eroded some of its impact, this ancient tale of murder and revenge still manifests its near-psychotic ferocity as well as its musical and dramatic brilliance. *Electra* was the first of six collaborations between Strauss and Hugo von Hofmannsthal. The latter, already a famous poet and dramatist, would prove to be one of the finest librettists opera has seen, in the splendid company of Mozart's Da Ponte and Verdi's Boïto. Their second and greatest project was as far as possible from the crazed world of *Electra*: the delicately ironic, neo-Mozartean *Der Rosenkavalier* of 1910.

That work also represents the summit of Strauss's career. For twenty years he had bedazzled the musical world and represented the last word in modernism. But in 1910 the real Modernists, Schoenberg and Stravinsky, were about to step onto the scene, and Strauss would never be able to keep up with them. Instead, for the rest of his life he issued work after work in the same style, with the same skill, but never again with quite the same inspiration. Not that the later works are devoid of interest, as witness the pleasures of Hofmannsthal operas like *Die Frau ohne Schatten* and *Arabella*. But somehow the air had gone out of Strauss. He was satisfied to be a wealthy and honored anachronism.

His nadir was from 1933 to 1935, when he declared allegiance to Hitler and served as head of the Nazi Reichsmusikkammer. He dutifully went about purging German music of Jewish, modernist, and other "unwholesome" elements, until it came to condemning his own Jewish librettist, Stefan Zweig. Happy to ruin the lives of people he didn't need, he refused to condemn someone he did, so his honeymoon with the Nazis ended. Strauss spent most of the war living in Switzerland. He was enough of a collaborator to be tried by the Allies after the war, but was let off.

This cozying up to the Nazis shows his self-serving side. Strauss was vain, petty, rivalrous, and avaricious. Since his wife kept him on a short allowance, he insisted his orchestral musicians play cards with him and he regularly fleeced them. Perhaps the most succinct description of his personality came from conductor Hans Knapperts-busch: "I knew him very well. We played cards every week for forty years and he was a pig."

Strauss left his last regular conducting job, at the Vienna Opera, in 1924. Thereafter he composed, guest-conducted, and collected his money and honors, with only the war years and their aftermath to trouble him. In 1946 he produced the finest work of his last years, the elegiac *Metamorphosen* for twenty-three strings. He died at Garmisch on September 8, 1949.

After Strauss conducted the Munich premiere of the symphonic poem *Don Juan* in 1889, Hans von Bülow wrote home, "Strauss is enormously beloved here. His *Don Juan* . . . had a wholly unheard-of success." From its first torrential eruption, *Don Juan* seizes listeners by the throat and never lets go. Critic Olin Downes wrote of the "fierce onslaught of the opening measures . . . in which Strauss unmistakably revealed his genius." As in much Strauss, there is a kind of breathless chromatic excitement in the work, the orchestra bustling from one striking color to another. Sometimes his pieces can sound like a long introduction to something that never quite happens; but here, in representing the legendary lover's endless searching and frustration, the restlessness is appropriate to the story. After much fuss and fury, the music arrives at brief stability with a noble proclamation by six horns in unison, sweeping upward like mighty portals opening. When at the end, in Strauss's words, "at last disgust seizes hold of [Don Juan] and this disgust is the devil that fetches him," the music falls suddenly into an unforgettable gray bleakness, with a dissonant stab from the trumpets.

One sees another side of him in the comic *Till Eulenspiegel's Merry Pranks* of 1895, with its Viennese lightness and charm. The program is based on the old legend of an incorrigible rogue and prankster: Till makes his appearance in an absurd leaping and hiccuping horn line that trips up anyone trying to find the beat; then, represented by horn or piping clarinet, he plays tricks on ladies in the marketplace, dresses up as a priest, falls in love, mocks the philistines, and so on. Finally he is caught and executed, but his laughing spirit seems to fly up from the gallows. As with most of Strauss's symphonic poems, the vagaries of the story are reined in to some extent by Classical forms. Strauss called *Till* a rondo, which it approximates, Till's tune being the rondo theme; other of his symphonic poems tend to be laid out roughly in sonata form.

From there go on to the other major tone poems—the sumptuous *Death and Transfiguration, Thus Spake Zarathustra* (which for all its virtues never quite fulfills the promise of its magnificent opening, familiar from the movie *2001*), *Don Quixote* (with its prophetic section of dissonance representing the voices of sheep), and the self-promoting *Ein Heldenleben*.

For an introduction to Strauss's operas begin, of course, with *Der Rosenkavalier* (The Cavalier of the Rose). In this sublime comedy of an aging princess giving up her young lover to his destined bride, the story is decked out with Mozartean sexual confusions, many laughs, many waltzes à la Johann Strauss, and an operettalike story set in a bygone, make-believe Vienna. There is no reason why this opera should be more than a frivolous and nostalgic confection, but it manages to be a great deal more. Librettist Hofmannsthal supplied the memorable figure of the worldly-wise princess renouncing her last love, the headstrong youth dazzled by his first love, and a vivacious cast of supporting characters. In the "Presentation of the Rose" scene and throughout, culminating in the glorious soprano trio at the finale, Strauss's music makes *Der Rosenkavalier* into an unreal but compelling world, floating outside time like a magical bubble in the imagination.

Musicians and critics have often deplored programs for imposing irrelevant and limiting elements on music. And many have deplored Strauss's sins, his frequent facility, banality, and commercialism. But as in *Der Rosenkavalier*, Strauss for all his faults could take up ideas that should not work and bring them off by sheer skill and cleverness. Certainly disgust never seized him as it did his Don Juan; Strauss's *Four Last Songs*, his haunting final work, is an eloquent meditation on the coming of death. Perhaps without his grandstanding he would have been little more than a technician. Like Don Juan, Strauss is a bit of the cynical seducer; but however wary of him we may be, he still knows how to get to us.

GUSTAV MAHLER

With the symphonies of Mahler—sprawling assemblages of the sophisticated and folksy, beautiful and grotesque, grandiloquent and naïve—so much comes to rest and so much begins. The incomparable Viennese tradition that dominated Western music from Haydn to Brahms ended in convulsion and exhaustion with the haunted figure of Mahler. He also culminated nineteenth-century symphonic giganticism: his Third Symphony takes almost two hours to play; his Eighth requires nearly the performing forces of its title, "Symphony of a Thousand." After Mahler, there was little choice for composers but to cut back in scope and size. Yet he pointed the way toward that, too; despite the size of Mahler's orchestra, his genius for transparent and coloristic scoring led to the chamber-sized ensembles of the Modernist century.

So Mahler was no less a culminator of the past than a harbinger of the future. Among his disciples was Arnold Schoenberg, founder of what has been called the Second Viennese School, whose ideas transformed twentieth-century music. But even more was Mahler a spiritual barometer, in both his aspirations and his malaise. His fairy-tale fanfares, his sentimental tunes juxtaposed with grand perorations, his monumental climaxes that seem to strive for transcendence only to end in defeat—all are at once a cry of hope and a sounding alarm. In the fragmentariness of his consciousness and the violence of his stylistic incongruities, he announced the violent incongruities of a new era: "Ours is a century of death," wrote Leonard Bernstein, "and Mahler is its spiritual prophet."

Gustav Mahler was born in Kalischt, Bohemia, on July 7, 1860, the second of fourteen children of a Jewish distiller. Shortly after Gustav's birth the family moved to the provincial town of Iglau. His childhood there was an inextricable mingling of artistic stimulation and tragedy. The family early recognized and encouraged his musical talent. He spent much of his youthful years happily hanging around the local military barracks, learning dozens of soldiers' songs and playing them on the accordion. Revealing an almost religious sensitivity to nature, the boy gloried in the hills and forests of the region. Meanwhile, his parents' marriage was miserable and

Mahler, implacable as conductor and composer.

the father abusive, seven of his siblings died in childhood, one brother was mentally handicapped and another a suicide; when Gustav was eleven he witnessed a brutal rape. The hypersensitive child kept his spirit alive by living in music and dreams and ambitions. Later he would say that all the horrors of his childhood, and some of the joys as well, were connected in his mind to everyday music, to folk song and the cheap tunes of cafés and organ-grinders.

At age fifteen he was accepted into the Vienna Conservatory. There his talent and ambition revealed themselves in academic honors and a friendship with older composer Anton Bruckner, then lecturing at the university. Mahler's first published work was a piano arrangement, made at eighteen, of Bruckner's Third Symphony. His mind grew amidst the café debates of the students. He embraced Wagnerian ideas, including vegetarianism; for some time he would live on water and fruit and spinach.

Encouraged by his teachers to compose, for several years Mahler experimented with operatic projects that never quite took shape. Creatively frustrated for the moment, in 1880 he found a summer job as an apprentice theater conductor at Bad Hall. It was the beginning of a conducting career that took him quickly to fame. By age twenty-eight he was conducting at the Royal Opera House in Budapest. From there he went to the Hamburg Opera as protégé of the ubiquitous Hans von Bülow, making a tremendous impression on Brahms and the critic Hanslick. Mainly because of their support, in 1897 he became director of the Vienna Opera, then in decline. In his ten years there Mahler rebuilt the company into one of the strongest and most innovative musical organizations in the world, nearly every production setting new standards of quality and imagination.

Yet there as everywhere else, Mahler also made himself a hated man. A relentless taskmaster willing to sacrifice himself and everyone else in pursuit of his vision, with every successful production he further eroded his support and his own physical and mental wellbeing. Anti-Semitic Vienna also resented him because he was born a Jew, even though he had converted to Catholicism virtually as a prerequisite for conducting at the Opera. Mahler had never practiced Judaism and was hardly interested in the Catholic church; his own beliefs approached some kind of pantheism. But the forced conversion was one more division in an already neurotic and divided nature. "I am thrice homeless," he would say. "As a Bohemian born in Austria. As an Austrian among Germans. And as a Jew throughout the world.''

Much of his frustration arose because at heart he wanted nothing more than to leave conducting and simply be a composer. Given his theater schedule it is incredible that Mahler composed at all in those years; yet his output was voluminous. Driving himself as he drove everyone else, he formed the pattern of sketching works during brief summer vacations in the country and then orchestrating them in the mornings before going to work. Three unsuccessful romances in the 1880s produced three of his early pieces: the cantata *Das Klagende Lied,* the song cycle *Lieder eines fahrenden Gesellen,* and the Symphony no. 1. Even in these early works his style is almost fully formed. By the time he resigned his Vienna position in 1907, he had completed eight large symphonies and four collections of songs.

He had also, in his forties, married the beautiful Alma Schindler, handling the courtship in typical Mahler fashion: he took her walking shortly after they met, announced they were to be married, and consummated their bond virtually on the spot. Though Alma had shown considerable talent as a composer, he ordered her to stop composing; she must devote herself to taking care of him and their children. Strong-minded Alma was not long in chafing at his endless demands; in his last years he backtracked desperately in fear of losing her, and begged forgiveness for stifling her composing. After Mahler's death she would go on to marry two more prominent artists, architect Walter Gropius and writer Franz Werfel.

Mahler found few champions for his early work and was not widely taken seriously either during his lifetime or for decades after. He echoes, often in stream-of-consciousness form, both popular music and voices of the grand tradition—especially Beethoven, Schubert, Wagner, and Bruckner—though every page also has his unmistakable voice. Mahler's music began to appear at a time when Brahms and Wagner were defining, in contrasting ways, each with a style of strong consistency, what the Western tradition was. To the musical world of his time, Mahler's symphonies seemed a paradoxical babel of styles wrapped up in random forms. The First Symphony, for example, begins with a portentous introduction à la Beethoven's Ninth, but its main theme is a charming little folk tune from one of his earlier songs; the second movement is a robust

Austrian dance called a ländler; the third is based on the nursery tune "Frère Jacques," put into minor and strangely foreboding in effect; and while the finale is mostly intense and sometimes nearly delirious, the end becomes an explosion of transcendent joy (or at least an attempt in that direction).

Mahler's image as a pretentious failure and poseur did not change for many years after his death. There is certainly a measure of clumsiness, sentimentality, and bad judgment in his work; too often he attempts to whip up an overwhelming effect with slight or shop-worn material. But as I have said before, simple perfection does not add up to greatness. The overall vision of Mahler is his strength, not the debatable details. Not seeing that vision, critic after critic complained that Mahler was careless and never found a real style. In the 1930s, Boston Symphony commentator Philip Hale sounded the usual damning litany: "It was his ambition to continue the work of men he revered, Beethoven and Wagner. In spite of his indisputable talent he was not the man to do this. In the nearer approaches to the ideal that was in his mind he was simply an imitator; not a convincing, not even a plausible one. One has found through his symphonies restlessness that at times becomes hysterical . . . [ideas] often naïve, at times beautiful, but introduced as at random and quickly thrown aside."

Mahler endured such complaints constantly. Even as Hans von Bülow promoted Mahler the conductor, he impeded Mahler the composer. "If this is still music," von Bülow said of the Second Symphony, "I know nothing of music." Thus for many years, Mahler's work had to be kept alive by a small group of supporters. The first was Richard Strauss, who premiered the Second Symphony in 1895. Mahler later said of Strauss, "If his success had not opened a path for me, I should now be looked on as a sort of monster." The line of zealots that began with Strauss continued with conductors including Bruno Walter, Willem Mengelberg, Otto Klemperer, and Leonard Bernstein. Only the Eighth Symphony, premiered in Munich under Mahler's baton in 1910, before an audience that included some of the most important artists of the day, had a significant initial success. Even when audiences responded with enthusiasm, as they did to the Second, critics tended to be savage.

An International Mahler Society was formed in 1955; on its shield appears Mahler's prophecy: *"Meine Zeit wird noch kommen"*

("My time will come"). It seems that his time could not come until the century had seen a full measure of disintegration and desperate attempts to rebuild. As Bernstein said, the time of Mahler is after the Holocaust and the Bomb, after the fragmentations of modern culture and art, after attempts to maintain some kind of stability and spiritual idealism in a threatening and unbalanced world. The kind of wholeness the music of the past symbolized no longer seems attainable; however admirable and moving wholeness is, we cannot quite believe in it, cannot live it. Himself fragmented, uprooted, and death-haunted, Mahler speaks to our time with supreme orchestral craft and supreme spiritual uncertainty. In him Romanticism culminated and disintegrated. He is the first voice of the post-Romantic era, the herald of Modernism.

In 1907 Mahler came to New York, drawn by a munificent salary as the new head of the Metropolitan Opera and by a hope of making enough in a few years to retire to full-time composing. He immediately established his usual dictatorial style and began making the usual enemies. The next year he also became conductor of the New York Philharmonic. As with past positions, the quality of the music making shot up abruptly in the organizations and he kept to his grueling composing schedule. But Mahler no longer commanded his old physical and mental energy. The illness and death of one of his two daughters in 1906 had prostrated him; the next year a doctor had diagnosed a heart condition that was virtually a death warrant. Once again Mahler responded to disaster by keeping his head down and continuing to work. But he was shaken to the core. "With one blow," he wrote his young protégé Bruno Walter, "I have simply lost everything I ever achieved in clarity and comfort. I stood face to face with nothingness, and now at life's end I must again learn to stand and walk, like a beginner."

Superstitious about the fact that Beethoven, Schubert, and Bruckner died after nine symphonies, he named the collection of Chinese songs that constitute his actual ninth symphony *Das Lied von der Erde* (Song of the Earth). Then, proclaiming that he had cheated the curse, he went on to his Ninth and Tenth symphonies. But he did not complete the Tenth; in the end, he would still join the ranks of composers with nine finished symphonies (a good example of the gods' sense of humor). All his late works are leave-takings.

On the manuscript of the Tenth one sees his tortured exclamation, "My God, why hast thou forsaken me!"

His end was nearing in any case, but events in New York hastened it. Accustomed to getting his way whatever the obstacles, Mahler found himself for the first time fighting enemies who had more weapons and strength than he had—mainly the society ladies of the Philharmonic board of directors, who were unwilling to give up any of their power to a mere conductor. Wrangles with the board and tensions with Alma further strained Mahler's health. In early 1911 he came down with a throat infection in New York and returned to Europe, where his condition worsened. On May 18, 1911, he lay on his deathbed in Vienna, barely conscious, conducting with his finger on the quilt. Finally he whispered, "Mozart . . ." and died.

Mahler wrote little other than symphonies and songs, and his symphonies are never far from song, especially the kind of childlike folk song seen in *Des Knaben Wunderhorn* (The Boy's Magic Horn), based on a famous collection of German folk poetry. The twelve *Wunderhorn* songs that Mahler set for voice and orchestra between 1892 and 1901 are a good introduction to his art. His settings seem like fairy tales in sound. The subjects range widely—war, love, hunger, humor. The naïveté of the text is mirrored in Mahler's simple, direct, strophic settings reminiscent of Schubert (who also knew how to appear artless). But the sophistication of the treatment is seen in the crystalline orchestration, illustrative of every image in the text and enchanting to hear.

After three increasingly ambitious symphonies that climaxed with the Brobdingnagian Third, in the Fourth Symphony (1900) Mahler deliberately produced something relatively cheerful and compact. It begins with a touch of jingling Orientalism, and throughout there is an intimate, exquisite charm to the music. The second movement is one of Mahler's several dances of death, but this one has a kind of puppet-show tone. The finale involves a setting of a folk poem called "The Heavenly Life," in which paradise is imagined as a place full of wonderful things to eat: "Good apples, good pears and good grapes! / The gardeners permit everything! / If you want roebucks or hares you'll find them / Running about in the open streets!'' In the Fourth, Mahler is typically masterful with the orchestra. Every instrument seems remade and at the same time more itself than ever before. An oboe, a French horn, a violin sound like characters in a kaleidoscopic drama, each color and personality individual yet each contributing to the whole. And the sound of the ensemble, whether silky and caressing or jangling or marchlike, has an interior glow that no other composer achieved—except perhaps Debussy and Stravinsky, arguably Mahler's only peers as orchestrators. Another Mahler thumbprint: while his harmonic world is not particularly radical, he does take the unusual step of ending a symphony in a different key than that of the beginning: the Fourth starts in G major and ends in the relatively distant key of E major.

In the 1894 Second Symphony, after the Fourth the most popular of the lot, one finds Mahler in his colossal mode, with all his prodigal inconsistencies on display. Naming the Second the *Resurrection,* he wrote, ''I have called the first movement 'Celebration of the Dead' . . . it is the Hero of my First Symphony whom I bear to the grave.'' The Hero, needless to say, is the composer himself. After the sustained and sometimes alarming tumult of the first movement, there follows a graceful andante moderato in the style of an Austrian folk dance. Most immediately compelling of the five movements is the whirlwind scherzo of the third, an instrumental reworking of his satirical *Wunderhorn* song ''St. Anthony Preaches to the Fishes'', alternately beautiful and lusty and grotesque. The halolike fourth movement, called *Urlicht* (Primal Light), introduces a contralto singing a folk poem about salvation: ''[may] the dear Lord vouchsafe him a little light to show the way into the blessed life beyond.'' Then in the choral finale, which Mahler called ''a colossal musical fresco of the Day of Judgment,'' he attempts to resurrect his hero-self by sheer decibels. After much music of indubitable excitement, the soaring choral perorations of the conclusion are, depending on taste, either monumentally inspired or monumentally cheesy. (Even Mahler's excesses are worth hearing in a good performance, though. From his years of conducting he absorbed an extraordinary understanding of the immediacy of performance and how to make notes leap off the page into sound. When conductor and players are up to the job, he is reliably thrilling when heard live.)

Also among the most popular large Mahler works, and perhaps the culmination of his art, is the song-symphony *Das Lied von der Erde* (The Song of the Earth), which he completed in 1908 and never heard performed. Though it did not get the layers of revisions to which he subjected all his works after hearing them, it is hard to imagine that he could have significantly improved this heartrending farewell to life. After the twin disasters of his daughter's death and the discovery of his heart condition, Mahler found a collection of translations from Chinese poetry that echoed his feelings. He set six of them for solo voices in *Das Lied*, alternating between tenor and contralto. Never was Mahler's orchestration more diaphanous and expressive, never closer to capturing word and emotion in the sheer color of sound. First comes a vibrant but haunted drinking song with the refrain, "Dark is life, is death." Second is a slow movement called "Autumn Loneliness": "My heart is weary, My little lamp has gone out with a sputter, it urges me to go to sleep." Then follow three irresistible little scherzos, all radiant images of the joys of life and love and the beauty of the earth. Finally comes the "Farewell," every word and note filled with Mahler's vision of his approaching end: "Where am I going? I shall wander in the mountains; I am seeking rest for my lonely heart. I shall wander to my native land, to my home . . . Still is my heart; it is awaiting its hour. Everywhere the lovely earth blossoms forth in spring and grows green anew! Everywhere, forever, horizons are blue and bright!" With the words "Forever . . . forever . . ." the symphony seems to fade into the distance.

Then go on to the other and more problematic symphonies, for example the gigantic, rambling, but powerful Fifth, or the Seventh with its two nocturnes and brilliant finale. Among his song cycles for voice and orchestra, the *Rückert Lieder* are perhaps the most subtle. In expressing these troubled lyrics, his orchestra sounds almost desiccated, all bone and sinew in unprecedented instrumental combinations.

Mahler said a symphony must be "a world," and his symphonies, like their composer, contained much—too much to have the control and integrity of past composers. As I have noted, earlier composers knew so little music compared to us and to Mahler; for the most part Mozart knew living or recently dead composers, from a few countries, most of them writing in similar styles. Consistency

Mahler conducting: silhouettes from a contemporary postcard.

came naturally to artists in the Classical era. Mahler, even more than Brahms, felt the burden of the centuries' music weighing on him, in addition to the burdens of his own tragic life. It is not surprising that he was diffuse. Rather it is admirable that he managed to get so much of it down on paper, everything from the highest spiritual aspiration to the deepest horror. Now, at last, we understand him. Now, at last, Mahler's time has come.

OTHER NINETEENTH-CENTURY
COMPOSERS

French composer **Georges Bizet** (1838–75) spent his early career writing theater and instrumental works with scant to modest acclaim. Then, on the verge of middle age, he composed one of the finest and eventually most popular operas ever written, and died of a heart attack three months after its premiere. The opera was *Carmen,* the story of the fiery Gypsy who seduces soldier Don José and then gets bored with him, with results fatal to both. Contrary to later legend, it was not a failure at its 1875 Paris premiere but rather a middling success—surprising, given its daring subject and echoes of Wagner, whom the French despised virtually out of patriotic duty.

Within a decade after Bizet's death, *Carmen* was acclaimed

Scene from Carmen Jones, a 1940's black version of Bizet's opera.

around the world. The main reasons were the tunes, which are infallibly vivacious and memorable, and the sexy story. Though it lacks the psychological penetration of Verdi or the grand sweep of Wagner, *Carmen* is commendably less sentimental than the former and less pretentious than the latter. Among its other virtues are splendid orchestration and fascinating main character. In a way, Carmen is the female counterpart to Mozart's Don Giovanni. Both stand as mythical images of the power of sex, but the difference is that while Don Giovanni has a heart and soul of ice, Carmen really does, however briefly, love Don José. Bizet was no Mozart, but he had a warmer subject and he was equal to her.

Carmen did not quite receive the acclaim it deserved partly because its style, German-influenced with a Spanish veneer, was more international than French. **César Franck** (1822–90) had similar problems, but even more so. Born in Belgium but spending most of his life as a pious and hard-working teacher and church organist in Paris, Franck was late to develop, a slow worker, and often ridiculed as a composer. Yet in his generation he represents the best of the cosmopolitan tradition in France and wrote a handful of finely crafted pieces that have become staples of the standard repertoire. Among his chamber works, best known is the handsome and expansive Violin Sonata, written when he was sixty-three. It typifies his style, Romantically lyrical and expressive while maintaining a certain Classical detachment. It also shows his tendency to use thoroughgoing cyclic form, thematic ideas being developed through all four movements. His harmonic approach might be described as Lisztian chromaticism turned up a notch. Best known of all Franck's works is the D minor Symphony of 1889, which begins with a dynamic burst of energy and rarely flags in inspiration. It has long been one of the most popular nineteenth-century symphonies.

Anton Bruckner (1824–96) was a little, timid, silly-looking organist with gargantuan ideas. He idolized Wagner, at whose feet he once fell crying, "Master, I worship you!" But for all his prolixity and his obsequiousness to Wagner, Bruckner had a singular and powerful musical personality, and a contrapuntal mastery that makes his nine symphonies into densely woven polyphonic designs.

Bruckner had a hard time getting his immense works into the

concert hall. For one thing, he generally acted like a nincompoop, such as the time he attempted to tip one of his conductors during their bows. For another, he was a convenient target of anti-Wagnerians and not much good at fighting back. At the premiere of his Third Symphony in Vienna, he began conducting with a large house and at the end turned to find that all but twenty-five of the audience had skipped out; he stood paralyzed, with tears pouring down his face. But the 1881 premiere of his Fourth Symphony was a major victory. After that people got nicer to him in Vienna, and by his death his name was becoming known outside Austria.

All nine Bruckner symphonies are rather similar in style, approach, and material, though the last three are probably the strongest. Except for the last, on whose finale he was working when he died, all are in four movements, typically beginning sort of like Beethoven's Ninth—nebulous stirrings in the strings from which themes gradually emerge. All are large, brassy in the manner of Wagner, but with a uniquely Brucknerian lyricism, notably in the expansive slow movements. (Big adagios were among the propensities his pupil Mahler picked up.) All Bruckner's proportions are large; where other symphonists have themes, he has "theme-groups." His scherzos tend to have an inexorable rolling momentum and a rustic Austrian cast.

The Fourth Symphony is a good place to get to know Bruckner. He dubbed it "Romantic" and it is relatively light (for him). The Seventh is a heftier and quite handsome piece. The Eighth is his mightiest; after the typical Beethoven-like opening, rustic scherzo, and singing slow movement, it ends with a finale that unleashes the brass as if a dozen cavalries were coming. No doubt it's too long and too loud and just generally *too,* but if you're susceptible, it's worth the trouble.

Like Mozart, **Camille Saint-Saëns** (1835–1921) was a phenomenon from childhood. Unlike Mozart, his career loped comfortably from triumph to triumph: acclaimed first symphony produced at age eighteen, most revered musician in France by his twenties, admiration from such compatriots as Berlioz and Liszt. In addition to composing and being a virtuoso pianist, Saint-Saëns wrote books on philosophy, literature, and the arts. Still more unlike Mozart, he was finally never really a great composer, being unwilling to sully his facility with depth or originality. But at his best Saint-Saëns is certainly a charming composer, and never more so than in his lighthearted set of bestiary caricatures called *Carnival of the Animals* (1886), a favorite with generations of children. From the same year comes the grand and spacious Symphony no. 3, called the *Organ* Symphony because that instrument is featured. This work shows him at his most engaging: eclectic, hedonistic, suave, and slick. Also much admired is his short, sweet Cello Concerto in A minor, from 1873.

Among the most popular nationalist composers of the late nineteenth century is the Norwegian **Edvard Grieg** (1843–1907). His work, most of it in shorter genres, is marked by graciousness of effect, dewy lyricism, and wistful harmonies. Thinking mainly of his piano music, Hans von Bülow called Grieg "the Chopin of the North." He is best remembered these days for his two orchestral suites of pieces originally written to accompany Ibsen's strange fairy-tale play, *Peer Gynt*. (While these are reliable crowd-pleasers, Grieg himself was hardly enthusiastic about them all. Of the now-famous "Hall of the Mountain King" he admitted to Ibsen, "I have written something for the hall of the Troll king which smacks of so much cow manure, ultra-Norwegianism and self-satisfaction that I literally cannot bear to listen to it.") Best known of his large pieces is the Piano Concerto in A minor, whose dramatic opening flourish seems the distilled essence of the Romantic concerto.

Leader of the nationalistic Russian Five toward the end of the century, **Nicolai Rimsky-Korsakov** (1844–1908) started off in a naval career but gravitated to music. His conservative style is enlivened by his gift for fairy-tale atmosphere and his phenomenal orchestral skill, which he passed on to his student Igor Stravinsky. (For who knows what reason, there seems to be an innate Russian genius for orchestration, as there seems to be a propensity for painters in Holland and symphonists in Vienna.) Rimsky-Korsakov's *Capriccio Espagnol* is one of the all-time tours de force of instrumental imagination; the whole orchestra seems like a tambourine pouring out its soul. The "Pops" favorite *Scheherazade* unfolds as a lush and exotic musical representation of *The Thousand and One Nights*.

Alexander Scriabin (1872–1915) represents the darker and more outlandish side of the Russian artistic psyche. Beginning as a virtuoso pianist and writer of Chopinesque salon pieces, Scriabin turned increasingly to his private brand of mysticism. Where Wagner had wanted to transform the world gradually with myths, ideas, and sumptuous music, Scriabin wanted to transform it in one blow with a sort of hyper-*Tristan* orgasmic rapture. To that end he spent his last years planning a stupendous synthesis of arts called the *Mystery,* decked out with elaborate color symbolism and pervaded by his "mystic chord." It was supposed to be staged at a lakeside temple in India for "worshippers" in whom it would induce the "supreme final ecstasy." Before his *Mystery* got off the ground, however, Scriabin died in an embarrassingly mundane manner from a carbuncle on his lip.

In his mature work Scriabin was one of the first to take post-Wagnerian harmony to the brink of atonality, exploiting the voluptuous haziness of that language for his own cabalistic ends. The last three piano sonatas, nos. 8–10, are a good place to begin with his music; no. 10, full of delirious trills, attains a genuinely visionary effect. His 1908 orchestral work called *The Poem of Ecstasy* is often played; despite its title, it is a pleasant essay in orchestral post-Wagnerism.

As Scriabin was Russian to the core without overt nationalistic apparatus, likewise was **Sir Edward Elgar** (1857–1934) English. The musical voice of the Edwardian Age, Elgar was the first significant English composer since Purcell, some two centuries before. Though he did not use folk tunes or the like, he is unmistakably British the way dark wainscoting or a certain cut of clothes is British. It is a tone, an attitude: dignified, expansive, high-toned, and inspiring. Thus the appropriateness of generations of school graduates marching bravely into the future to the strains of his *Pomp and Circumstance* no. 1. His plush, expressive-but-not-excessively-so orchestral style is best heard in the 1899 *Enigma Variations,* a quite lovely series of portraits of friends based on an unstated theme, and the Second Symphony of 1911, into which one can sink as into a comfy chair. Elgar wrote a good deal of now dated choral music, but his 1900 *Dream of Gerontius* has endured as one of the finest of British oratorios.

With transitional figures such as Strauss, Mahler, and Scriabin, we have seen the final flowering and decay of Romanticism. The nineteenth-century artistic movement that had begun with bound-

The first important English composer in two centuries: Elgar in 1919.

less idealism and exaltation of the human imagination had become (except for a few first-rate artists in their best work) variously over-blown, conventional, decadent, egomaniacal, fin-de-siècle—in short, exhausted, as all ideas and movements must be, sooner or later. By the beginning of the twentieth century, music, like other arts in the West, needed new directions, new blood, new infusions of ideas. Inevitably, in a still thriving and vital tradition, the new infusions would come, mostly picking up where Romanticism left off. Today the Romantic century is the most popular period among listeners. As we will see, for all its reputation for controversy and revolution, the twentieth century would come closer than any other period to rivaling that popularity.

Swing Landscape, *1938, by*
American painter Stuart Davis.

THE TWENTIETH CENTURY

THE TWENTIETH
CENTURY

T he zeitgeist, the spirit of an age, is hard to define, especially when one is living in the middle of it, before distance has revealed its broad outlines and scholars have affixed their tidy labels to the picture. For most of this century we have called our arts modern and our music New Music (the latter term echoing the fourteenth-century *ars nova*, the seventeenth-century *Nuove musiche*). In the last decade or so before this writing, the main stylistic label bandied about for the arts has been postmodernism. Last month in my newspaper I read about the decline of postmodernism. Any day now, a newspaper will arrive at my door announcing some brave new -ism.

For all the problems in defining cultural labels, however, they are at least a recognition that during a given period something is in the air—in short, that the zeitgeist is real, however intangible. So what has characterized the Modernist century?

Socially and politically it has been characterized by turmoil and violence on an unprecedented scale, including two world wars. At the same time, it has seen the concept of democracy rise to enjoy near-universal lip service; even totalitarian societies such as Stalin's Soviet Union felt it prudent to call themselves "democratic." The last Western rejection of democratic ideals came from Stalin's fellow demagogue Hitler, in Germany. Both men initiated incredible programs of terror and genocide, Hitler mainly against Jews, Stalin against his countrymen in general. Meanwhile the United States, which after the world wars emerged with the Soviet Union as one of the twin world superpowers, preached democratic ideals and the international helping hand while pursuing overtly or covertly imperialistic adventures from the Philippines to Vietnam.

In science and technology this century has seen more epochal breakthroughs every decade or so than used to be seen in a century.

After millennia of humanity relying on transportation by foot, horse, ox, etc., in little more than a generation much of the world changed to motorized transportation. It was sixty-six years from the first heavier-than-air flight to the first landing on the moon. In general, the developed countries have become completely reliant on sophisticated technologies, from the electrical devices invented earlier in the century to the computers that have become commonplace in the recent past. As technology has broadened its control over our lives, our primeval relationship to nature has receded further and further from our awareness. All together, these changes have made life more efficient and in many ways more comfortable, and at the same time more complex and stressful.

Among the most pervasive technological developments have been broadcasting and recording. From about the 1920s on, these new media have disseminated music of all kinds at a rate phenomenally faster than in previous centuries, when all music was live. We are accustomed to riding subways, shopping, eating, and making love accompanied by music, whether we want it or not. Music has changed from being a person-to-person communication, performer to listener, to an inescapable background noise. The modern world is filled with a stupendous babel of machines and media, drowning out silence and the sounds of nature.

In the arts as in technology, the rate of change became dizzying and then more dizzying. In the visual arts it has been the time of revolutions and manifestos, from the great Modernist founders such as Cézanne and Picasso, through the painters of the early century dubbed the Fauves (wild beasts), through Surrealists such as Dalí and Max Ernst, to the major and minor masters of such schools as Abstract Expressionism and pop art. Nearly to a man and woman modern artists have shared the dream of discovering new languages, new sounds, new ideas, new orders of art and society. Yet for all their schools and common quests, modern artists can also be described as lonely individualists, islands, with troubled and ambiguous relationships to the public and the world around them.

Technically, Modernism can be explained as a steady expansion and exploration of artistic materials and means and ends. Sociologically, it can be charted as a series of explosions and scandals, such as the riot that greeted the premiere of Stravinsky's *Le Sacre du printemps*. Artistic schools, movements, scandals, and rebellions

349

have galloped past seemingly year by year. We have named previous musical eras of fifty or more years Classical here, Romantic there. So far in the ninety-plus years of this century we have seen, roughly in order, these subdivisions of the Modern spirit in music: nationalism, post-Romanticism, impressionism, expressionism, neoclassicism, futurism, Gebrauchsmusik, experimentalism, serialism, post-Webernism, electronic music, aleatoric music, minimalism, neoromanticism, postminimalism, postmodernism—and (no kidding) post-postmodernism.

This century also saw the emergence of the African-American styles called ragtime, blues, and jazz, whose influence spread across the world, and then the onset of the Age of Rock 'n' Roll. In recent decades the juggernaut of Western popular culture has invaded societies everywhere. In Singapore, in Thailand, in Bali, Vietnam, and Rio de Janeiro today, one mainly hears Western-style rock blaring from radios, television, bars, and stereos. There has been a concomitant decline of indigenous folk and classical traditions worldwide. In the West, a generation of conservatory-trained composers have claimed elements of rock in their music. At the same time, non-Western music has had a growing influence on Western composers. A multicultural eclecticism has been a Modernist fixture since Picasso began to study African masks, Debussy heard a Javanese gamelan, Ravel heard New Orleans jazz.

It is not surprising that listeners, performers, and creators in this century have often found themselves confused and uncertain. Perhaps an eternal law of art is that, for everything discovered, something of value is forgotten. When the West invented polyphony, for example, it forgot many of the nuances and subtleties of monophony, which survive in aural traditions such as Indian music. In response to the century's artistic glut and flux, many people in the West have held determinedly onto the musical past—the older, more reassuring -isms—as a kind of talisman against the unending shock of the new.

Yet, paradoxically, in many ways this has been a healthy century for music, about as good as the West has ever seen. The steady dissemination of music by the media has expanded audiences in every direction. The sheer playing skills of classical musicians, professional and amateur, have improved dramatically. The early music movement has reclaimed the sounds of the past while refreshing our sense of the familiar repertoire.

For all the revolution and counterrevolution and shocking of the bourgeoisie, the century has produced a respectable collection of composers who have found a major audience. A look at the following pages will reveal more prominent composers in the twentieth

Influenced by African art and jazz, Picasso painted
his familiar masterpiece Three Musicians *in 1921.*

century than in any other period (though there are more *pieces* in the repertoire from the nineteenth century). Undoubtedly, time will weed out some, as it has thousands of older composers, and will discover a few who have been overlooked. But in any case, our time has seen its share of music that is likely to last as long as humanity lasts.

Our tour of this century will gravitate around two figures who have seemed to be the poles between whom the battles of New Music have been fought: Igor Stravinsky and Arnold Schoenberg, the former leading the triumphantly popular faction, the latter the father of generations of serialists who have only occasionally been embraced by the larger public. For most of this century these two men have been hailed and damned as the great icons of Modernism, New Music, avant-gardism to the brink of anarchy. Yet both rejected these labels and insisted on their continuity with Western tradition. "I am a conservative who was forced to become a radical," said Schoenberg. "Be a revolutionary if you must," Stravinsky told a group of students, "but never be an anarchist. Not even the *nicest* anarchist."

These and related matters (such as the epochal decline of traditional tonality and forms) will be examined as we tour this vertiginous century. I will avoid, however, the tendency in histories to ascribe change in music mainly to the expansion of technical means. That plays a great part in change, but so do social, economic, and psychological factors. For example, a good deal of what generated the Modernist revolution—a revolution both creative and destructive, exhilarating and demoralizing—was the earlier triumph of the individual artistic vision during the nineteenth century. Innovators such as Schumann and Wagner enthroned artists as virtual demigods, demanding that the public come to them, never they to the public. Many composers and other artists of this century inherited that mind-set. Yet in the long run the Romantics depended on the public for their livelihood and for that reason, at least, had a built-in brake; they could not afford to forget that they were in the business of communication. Many twentieth-century composers, making their living as teachers or conductors, were free to follow their ideas wherever they led—whether to profound and fruitful work or to myriad dead ends. To a great extent, Modernism has been Romanticism without brakes.

CLAUDE DEBUSSY

One tends to think of musical revolutionaries in terms of noise or provocation: the pounding dissonances in Beethoven's *Eroica*, Stravinsky's raging *Sacre du printemps*, the overripe decadence of Schoenberg's *Pierrot lunaire*. Yet among the most radical of all musical voices was the languid and understated one of Claude Debussy. All revolutionaries have bent this and expanded that and overthrown the other; Debussy threw nearly everything out, all at once: traditional harmonic syntax, foursquare rhythm, Romantic melody, Classical forms, lush orchestration. Though in his work one can discern influences from Couperin through Wagner to Musorgsky and the Javanese gamelan, he still is remarkably unlike anybody who preceded him. At the same time, to our ears he seems entirely familiar; the extraordinary synthesis of his style sounds so natural that it is hard to believe no one had thought of it before. His influence on all subsequent Western music—classical, jazz, and popular—has been pervasive.

In his own time, Debussy's voice was like the intrusion of a dream world into sound. The language of tones had been made suddenly rich and strange; the heavy Romantic orchestra is now light and subtle, illuminated from within like the Art Nouveau glass of the era. Even individual instruments seem remade into visions and suggestions: a flute becomes the memory of a caress, a cymbal becomes a chill ocean spray. Compared to Debussy's luminescent orchestra, that of Wagner and Brahms seems turgid and opaque; compared to the intoxicating perfumes of his harmonies, later innovators of the twentieth century seem almost puritan.

Debussy was born into a family of small-time farm workers, artisans, and merchants in the Paris suburb of St. Germain-en-Laye on August 22, 1862, and christened Achille-Claude Debussy. When he was three, father Manuel Debussy's china shop failed and the family moved to Paris. The Debussys were poor and family life was scattered. Two of the four children lived with a better-to-do aunt, Mme. Roustan; for Claude there is no record of any formal schooling. Manuel was determined that this son be a sailor. Instead, Claude became fascinated with music. After he had some beginning piano lessons, Mme. Roustan paid for more serious studies with a Mme. Mauté de Fleurville, who had studied with Chopin. (She was also mother-in-law of the poet Verlaine, who would become a prime inspiration of the mature composer.) Claude made remarkable progress; at the age of eleven he was accepted into the venerable, rigorous, tradition-bound Paris Conservatory.

He would spend over a decade there as a student, variously desultory, dutiful, brilliant, and rebellious. While winning prizes and medals, he also befuddled teachers with his ideas. Stories about Debussy became legendary at the Conservatory. During a classroom piano improvisation César Franck shouted at him, "Modulate! Modulate!" and Debussy calmly replied, "Why? I'm perfectly happy where I am." When his composition teacher Guiraud told him, "I'm not saying that what you do isn't beautiful, but it's theoretically absurd," Debussy responded, "There is no theory. You merely have to listen. Pleasure is the law." Nonetheless, he spent a good many years intermittently submitting to traditional studies in harmony and counterpoint, aiming for the most prestigious of Conservatory honors, the Prix de Rome.

During his teens, meanwhile, Debussy found a job as pianist for wealthy Russian widow Nadezhda von Meck, the patroness of Tchaikovsky. For three summers, this child of near slums and near squalor traveled with her elegant household, playing four-hands with madame and teaching piano to her daughters during tours of European capitals and at her estate in Russia. Von Meck found her young employee witty, a good mimic, overflowing with talent. In Russia Debussy absorbed the country's music—a good deal of Borodin and especially Musorgsky, though not so much Tchaikovsky.

Then for nearly five years, as he closed in on the Prix de Rome, Debussy was consumed by love for a student of his, a married woman named Mme. Vasnier. Just how far this romance went is not recorded, but from 1880 to 1882 he wrote some lovely songs for her.

Finally Debussy won the Grand Prix de Rome in 1884, with a conscientious academic cantata called *L'Enfant prodigue* (The Prodigal Son). Next year he began the traditional three-year stay at the Villa Medici in Rome. There, having achieved his long-sought goal, he discovered that he hated Rome, hated the food, hated the other students, hated writing the *envoi* pieces he was obliged to send to Paris, and could hardly bear being away from Mme. Vasnier. His

Debussy: fastidious Bohemian and refined voluptuary.

main solace was the scores of Wagner operas; he immersed himself in them as did so many other devotees in those days. His first *envoi* piece, *Zulëima,* the Conservatory judges declared "bizarre, incomprehensible, and impossible to play."

In the spring of 1887, well before the expected three years were up, Debussy returned to Paris for good, there writing his third *envoi* piece, *La Demoiselle élue* (The Blessed Maiden). Its restless modulations, wandering rhythms, and "decadent" air show that he was groping toward a new style. The next few years would be the most critical of his career.

Debussy settled into the bohemian life of Montmartre, composing and scraping by in artistic poverty. Unable to rekindle whatever it was between him and Mme. Vasnier, he acquired a mistress, Gabrielle Dupont, whom he called "Gaby of the green eyes." She would stay with him for ten years. Debussy, with his flowing cape, broad-brimmed hat, and languid, feline grace, was a familiar figure in the streets and nighttime cafés of Montmartre. To hide an abnormality—low bony knobs protruding from his forehead—he brushed his dark hair forward in bangs. As his style matured, his swarthy faunlike face came to seem the embodiment of his music.

Around 1887 Debussy began to frequent the Tuesday meetings of the Symbolist poets, among them Baudelaire, Verlaine, Rimbaud, and Mallarmé, who declared that art must appeal to the senses and intuition before the intellect. The method of Symbolism, wrote Mallarmé, was "to evoke in a deliberate shadow the unmentioned object by allusive words." Debussy would become the tone poet of that art of mist and suggestion. Like the Symbolists as well, he was addicted to the nameless mysteries and obscure horrors of Edgar Allan Poe, as translated by Baudelaire.

One by one, the inspirations he needed appeared. He was well aware of the revolutionary French painters of the time, who had been condemned by critics as "impressionists"; the name had stuck to them as it later would to Debussy, to his unending disgust. Monet, Renoir, and fellow painters took their canvases outdoors and with vaporous brushstrokes tried to paint light itself, in its evanescent subtleties flitting across stone and water and landscape. Their atmosphere drifted into Debussy's work. Equally important to Debussy's growth was the Paris Exposition of 1889, where he was entranced by the playing of a Javanese gamelan. This exotic, mesmerizing music, enfolded in the bronze resonances of gongs, revealed to the onetime Paris Conservatory denizen that wholly new territories of sound existed outside Western tradition. The music of Java showed him further paths away from both German-dominated Romantic rhetoric and the dogmas of the Conservatory. It confirmed his intuition that fugue and counterpoint, symphonic development, and preordained form were not inevitable; that sheer intoxicating harmony and melody could be sufficient—if he could make them intoxicating enough.

In 1891 came another momentous connection when Debussy met Eric Satie (1866–1925), whose anti-Romanticism was expressed in little piano pieces with outlandish titles ("Three Flabby Preludes for a Dog," "Pieces to Make You Run Away") that enclosed novel harmonic experiments. Debussy would later orchestrate two of Satie's demurely lyrical piano pieces called *Gymnopédies*.

Another influence Debussy first embraced and then rejected, but never entirely escaped: Wagner. His Wagnerian years climaxed with two visits to Wagner's theater at Bayreuth in 1888 and 1889, where he heard *Die Meistersinger, Tristan und Isolde,* and, most significantly, two performances of *Parsifal.* Shortly after the second visit came a violent reaction: "Don't you see that Wagner with all his formidable power—yes, in spite of his power—has led music astray into sterile and pernicious paths?" he proclaimed to the Wagner-loving Symbolists. He called Wagner "the old poisoner." Yet behind every page of Debussy's mature orchestral music lie the innovations of the German master, especially in Debussy's opera *Pelléas et Mélisande.* At times Debussy was even willing to admit it; in his opera, he said, he sought to create "an orchestral color illuminated as from behind, of which there are such wonderful effects in *Parsifal.*" His rebellion against Wagner was like that of a son against a domineering but inescapable father.

From all those influences musical, visual, and literary, and guided by his extraordinarily acute ear, Debussy slowly fashioned his revolutionary musical language. Between 1887 and 1889 he wrote two collections of songs on Symbolist texts, in which his mature style is discernable: *Cinq poèmes de Baudelaire* and *Ariettes oubliées* on poems of Verlaine. From 1890 came his first major hit, the *Suite bergamasque* for piano, containing the soon-to-be-ubiquitous "Claire de lune." Then in 1894 he completed the first work showing the full force of his genius: the delicate little orchestral tone poem *Prélude à l'après-midi d'un faune,* which would transform the face of Western music just as decisively as did far longer and louder works by Beethoven and Wagner.

Stéphane Mallarmé's poem "L'Après-midi d'un faune" (The Afternoon of a Faun) epitomized the Symbolist aesthetic of elliptical allusion. One admirer called it "this famous miracle of unintelligibility." In the poem, a faun seems to be dreaming over his panpipes about a dalliance, perhaps imaginary, with two nymphs. To suggest the images and atmosphere of the text, Debussy created harmonies and orchestral sonorities of refined sensuousness. From the first sighing notes in the lowest range of the flute (whose silky eroticism had awaited discovery by Debussy) we are in another world. Where composers of the past shaped progressive harmonic patterns, Debussy shapes each chord as an event in itself, the harmony drifting apparently free as air, above which the melodies spin out in fluid arabesques that drift across the boundaries of the meter. While there is still a general sense of key, tonality has become flexible, sometimes disappearing in a haze of ambiguity. "I love music passionately," Debussy said, "and because I love it I try to free it from barren traditions that stifle it. It is a free art, gushing forth—an open-air art, an art boundless as the elements, the wind, the sky, the sea!"

The piece was first played, badly, in Paris in December 1894, receiving its expected share of critical venom, but it still made an indelible impression on progressive artistic circles. Mallarmé wrote nebulously to Debussy, "Your illustration . . . presents no dissonance with my text; rather does it go further into the nostalgia and light with subtlety, malaise, and richness." Debussy's first and only string quartet, premiered in 1893, provoked further enthusiasms and controversies.

From around 1892 date the first sketches of the opera *Pelléas et Mélisande,* whose libretto is a play by Symbolist poet Maurice Maeterlinck. Debussy set this otherworldly drama with few changes. He had always been a slow worker, apparently due both to painstaking care and to bohemian laziness; *Pelléas* was in gestation for nearly ten years before he was ready to look for a performance. Meanwhile his reputation had grown to the point that he was able to secure a prestigious premiere at the Paris Opéra-Comique. Aiding in that reputation had been the premiere of the three orchestral *Nocturnes* around the turn of the century. It was these works, with their descriptive titles ("Clouds," "Festivals," "Sirens") that got Debussy tagged once and for all as an impressionist.

As plans for producing *Pelléas* began to take shape during 1901, so did the makings of disaster. At first Debussy received the blessing of playwright Maeterlinck, partly on the assumption that Maeterlinck's mistress would sing the role of Mélisande in the premiere. Then the Opéra-Comique announced that it was giving the leading role to the young and winsome Scottish-American soprano Mary Garden. An enraged Maeterlinck nearly challenged Debussy to a duel, and tried to sabotage the production; "I am compelled," he wrote in *Le Figaro,* "to wish that its failure should be resounding and prompt."

Meanwhile, the copying of the orchestral parts was botched, so that in rehearsals the orchestra could hardly tell sharps from flats. Moreover, at the last minute it was discovered that the opera's thirteen changes of scene were impossible to manage in the time allowed in the score. Having chewed over the work note by note for a decade, Debussy had to sit down and, in a few days, compose substantial orchestral interludes to buy time for the scene changes. The dress rehearsal was made still more nerve-racking by a scurrilous pamphlet (probably by Maeterlinck) that appeared outside the theater, and by the shouts and laughter of the playwright's partisans in the preview audience. If that were not enough, the censor suddenly demanded the excision of an entire scene, calling it indecent.

Somehow, the premiere on April 30, 1902, was a success—astounding not only because of the controversy that attended the performance, but also because of the opera's style, which understates everything and largely avoids lyrical melody in favor of a speechlike approach. Despite the carping of some critics (one called *Pelléas* "musical hashish") the opera began to sell out. Many of its partisans were Parisian students and young artists hungry for revolution, the type who had been the natural audience of progressive composers at least since Berlioz, and who now made Debussy into their cause and their champion: among those pale artistes the cult of *debussysme* arose (and promptly got on its namesake's nerves). As the composer reached forty, *Pelléas* helped secure for him an international audience. Within a decade the opera had been heard in New York, London, and around Europe. Mary Garden would remain the definitive Mélisande. Today the work seems to epitomize that legendary era, the age of Art Nouveau, of Aubrey Beardsley, of cryptic and elegant decadence.

By 1905 Debussy was world famous and twice married. In 1898 he had left Gaby of the Green Eyes for Rosalie Texier, whom he married the next year. (He had to give a lesson on their wedding morning to pay for the reception.) It was a passionate match with the woman he called "Lily-Lilo"; he had threatened suicide if she wouldn't marry him, and dedicated the *Nocturnes* to her as "proof of the deep and passionate joy I find in being her husband." The trouble was, there was little more to it than passion. Rosalie was a dressmaker of no unusual intelligence or sensitivity to music, though she was charming and devoted to Debussy.

Within a few years Rosalie's charms had worn thin. In 1904 Debussy suddenly ditched her and eloped with Emma Bardac, then the wife of a wealthy banker, formerly the mistress of composer Gabriel Fauré. Paris buzzed with the scandal, and buzzed louder after the despairing Rosalie shot herself (she recovered). Debussy and Emma both secured divorces and were married at the end of 1904. Most of the opinion, including that of close friends, ran against Debussy; many said he had abandoned Rosalie for Emma's money. In the long run, however, they proved to be a happy and not particularly wealthy couple. Her income was tied up in litigation and they lived mostly on his earnings as composer and critic. In the first decade of the century he resorted to newspaper writing to pay the bills. (Like Berlioz, Debussy wrote some marvelous prose that is still in print.) The couple had one child, Claude-Emma, whom he called "Chouchou"; to her he dedicated the lighthearted piano suite *Children's Corner* of 1906–08.

Debussy's output increased after the premiere of *Pelléas*, partly because the demand for his music had increased. Notable among his works during the century's first decade is the sea-symphony *La Mer* (1903–05), the masterpiece of musical impressionism and one of the great orchestral tours de force of all time; it completed the remaking of the orchestra that Debussy had begun with *Prélude à l'après-midi d'un faune.* At the same time, he was writing a good deal for the piano; in works such as the *Estampes* (Etchings) of 1903, he combined his kaleidoscopic harmonic palette with innovations in pedaling and texture to create the first genuinely original piano sound since that of Chopin. He planned several more operas, notably one on Poe's "The Fall of the House of Usher," but none got further than sketches. His output of songs, among the finest bodies of vocal work in the century, would continue nearly to the end of his life. From 1908 he began conducting his work on tours that took him around Europe and to Russia. Among the friendships of his later years was one with the young Igor Stravinsky; it began as a fatherly relationship and became one of mutually admiring colleagues.

Around 1910 Debussy began to have nagging ailments that developed into a protracted decline from cancer. As his condition worsened he had to rely on morphine to control the pain; there were operations and radium treatments. Finally, describing himself as "a walking corpse," Debussy retired into near seclusion, where he kept composing with fierce determination. Much of the music of his last years is paler, perhaps, than his best work, but all is worthy of his genius. The most impressive piece of that time is the ballet *Jeux,* written for Nijinsky and the Ballets Russes (of whom you will read in the Stravinsky section). *Jeux* is Debussy's most enigmatic and forward-looking score, but it was a failure at the time. On top of that failure and his illness, the coming of World War I oppressed Debussy even as it awoke his patriotism: he proudly began to sign himself "musicien français." His last completed work, and one of the finest of his last years, is the Sonata for Violin and Piano.

Before beginning that last masterpiece, he had written in a sad letter of 1916, "As Claude Debussy is no longer making music, he no longer has any reason to exist. I haven't any hobbies; the only thing they taught me was music." He died during a German bombardment of Paris, on March 25, 1918. Amidst the tumult of the war, one more death was hardly noticed. As the sparse funeral procession wound through the torn streets, a shopkeeper was heard to explain, "It seems that it was some musician."

Pierre Boulez, who has conducted some of the most lucid Debussy performances of our time, wrote, "He retains a power of seduction that is mysterious and spellbinding; his situation at the beginning of the contemporary movement is that of a spearhead, but solitary. . . . We cannot forget that the time of Debussy is also that of Cézanne and Mallarmé: a triple conjunction, at the root, perhaps, of all modernity . . . [Debussy] had to dream his revolution no less than build it." I would add: he is one of the few Modernists inviting to approach, who may often be mysterious but rarely is intentionally mystifying. He learned the traditions of the past thoroughly and then taught himself to forget them, remaking music as his ear and intuition guided him; and therefore his music was written to be heard, to lie well in the ear. The goal was not to attain the profundity of Beethoven but rather to ravish the mind and senses with the perfumes of mystery and dream.

I have mentioned his revolutionary harmony, the foundation of his art: he revitalized traditional chords, putting them together in new ways whether in streams of parallel harmonies or in virtually keyless successions; and he invented chords never heard before. He was the father of generations of modern composers who consistently avoided the expected resolution of dissonant chords to consonant. For him as for later composers, shades of dissonance were simply colors in his palette. He let his rhythms float free from the traditional strong and weak beats of meter; at times different parts of the orchestra seem to be going at different speeds at once. He explored a polyglot collection of scales, from the ancient church modes to the whole-tone and pentatonic—five-tone—scales of the Orient (in using modes he followed the lead of composers like Musorgsky and Liszt, but took it much further). So many influences, from so many sources from the musical to the visual, combined with Debussy's own far-reaching imagination to produce the sophisticated yet apparently effortless synthesis of his style.

Like most major composers, Debussy wrote some small works that have become light-classical favorites. These include, above all, the lyrical piano confection "Clair de lune" (Moonlight) from *Suite bergamasque,* and *Children's Corner,* a suite for piano. Most familiar from the latter is "Golliwogg's Cakewalk," with its touches of American ragtime and sarcastic allusion to Wagner's *Tristan.*

Of the longer works, the natural starting place for making Debussy's acquaintance is the one marking the beginning of both his mature orchestral work and of musical impressionism—*Prélude à l'après-midi d'un faune,* described above. Then go on to the *Nocturnes* for orchestra, completed in 1899. The first, "Nuages" (Clouds), uses static, wandering streams of harmonies to represent its subject; it seems to be composed of intangible mists. Next is the contrasting "Fêtes" (Festivals), with breathless rhythms; in the middle, with a more stately pace, comes what Debussy called "a procession . . . passing through the festival and blended with it." For the final movement, "Sirènes," Debussy uses wordless women's voices to represent the song of the Sirens; appropriately, their music is mesmerizing, timeless, enticing.

The peak of his orchestral output is *La Mer* (The Sea), in which Debussy caught in tone the rhythms and masses and fluid energy of the ocean, which he never saw except from shore; his only voyages on water were two trips across the English Channel. The three movements—which he called "sketches"—are named "From Dawn to Noon at Sea," "Play of the Waves," and "Dialogue of the Wind and the Sea." *La Mer* is the closest Debussy came to a symphony, its breathtaking finish his closest approach to a traditional climax. There are marvels for the ear in every measure of this score; the orchestra groans, roars, sighs, babbles, erupts in sprays of light and color. In this work we see the essence of what (for lack of a better word) we call musical impressionism: rather than telling a story complete with emotions, it evokes a scene complete with its atmosphere and moment-to-moment unfolding.

Another kind of scene is heard in *Iberia,* completed in 1910 as part of three orchestral *Images.* This is perhaps the greatest orchestral portrait of Spain, coming from a composer who had spent exactly one day in that country, where he saw one bullfight. Besides conjuring up the rhythms, sounds, and images of Spain, toward the end Debussy creates one of his most original orchestral effects, turning the whole string section into a kind of superguitar.

Of the piano works, I recommend beginning with the first book of preludes, written in 1910. Here Debussy, without giving up any of his unique personality, finds multiple resonances with history: with the preludes of Bach, the suites of character pieces by Bach's French contemporary François Couperin, and above all with the preludes of Chopin, who revolutionized the piano in his time as Debussy did in his. (It is significant that in writing pieces called preludes, Debussy picked the most amorphous of old genres, avoiding more predictable Classical ones like sonata or rondo.) All these preludes have titles, most of them given after the music was written; Debussy preferred to speak of "colors and rhythmicized time"—i.e., abstractions. Evocative abstractions they are. Among the most famous is "La Cathédrale engloutie" (The Sunken Cathedral), named for the tale of the drowned cathedral of Ys, which for the eyes of the faithful rises from the waves each dawn with bells tolling and priests chanting. Here Debussy relies on the rarely used middle pedal of the piano to sustain bass notes through changing harmonies; the result is a remarkable richness and blending of sonorities that build to a towering climax of pealing lines that are melodies and harmonies at the same time. Immediately follows the nimble "Danse de Puck," seemingly danced on breezes and boughs. The set ends with "Minstrel," one of Debussy's American-tinged outings, this one with droll rhythms and imitations of drums.

Finally, try *Pelléas et Mélisande,* but with this caveat: if you require from opera what Verdi gives you, it won't be found in these tableaus from myth and dream—no big tunes, no big emotions, no teary melodramas. Boulez called *Pelléas* "a world endeavoring to be beyond time." Lost in a forest, King Golaud finds Mélisande, a princess who seems to have come from nowhere; he takes her back to his castle and marries her; then, slowly and with "a great innocence," Golaud's young half brother Pelléas falls in love with Mélisande; at last, finding them together, the maddened Golaud kills Pelléas. Soon Mélisande dies after giving birth to a daughter.

For the opera Debussy invented a new vocal style, a declamation following the natural rhythms of French and enfolded in an orchestral fabric of extraordinary subtlety. Occasionally, at moments of emotion, the voices fall almost unnoticeably into lyric phrases. In the same way, the characters seem to drift between being symbolic representations and real people; this inconsistency has dated the play, but Debussy turned it to his purposes. Erik Satie, who longed to set the story himself but knew it was beyond his powers, gave Debussy the key to his anti-Wagnerian, though secretly Wagnerian, approach with the orchestra: "There is no need for the orchestra to grimace when a character comes on the stage. Do the trees in the scenery grimace? What we have to do is create a musical scenery, a musical atmosphere in which characters move and talk." That atmosphere and the half-real, half-intangible characters and passions and tragedies that inhabit it, are the most marvelous things about *Pelléas,* the highest achievement of the singular art of Claude Debussy.

JEAN SIBELIUS

The reputation of Jean Sibelius has swung precipitously up and down since his own time, when he was treated with a veneration rare in this century. Since his strange mid-life retirement, he has been called everything from the greatest symphonist after Beethoven and Brahms, to a "vulgar, self-indulgent provincial." It is generally admitted that dozens of his bill-paying items like *Valse triste* are lightweight at best. But in his symphonies and some of his tone poems Sibelius was a worthy inheritor of the Romantic tradition, and he added to that tradition a coloration somber and sometimes savage, as dark-toned as the winters of his native Finland, yet also capable of grandeur and old-world grace. As Dylan Thomas in poetry is Sibelius in music: not quite as great as he sounds, but still there is that *voice* whose ringing and rhetoric are compelling and inimitable.

Sibelius was born to the family of an army surgeon in the Finnish town of Tavastehus on December 8, 1865. In his youth he studied piano and violin; the first compositions date from around age ten. His father dispatched him to Helsinki University in 1885 to study law. Within a year, though, Sibelius had changed to the Helsinki Conservatory, where his mentors were the nationalist composer Martin Wegelius and the progressive composer/pianist Ferruccio Busoni. With the help of a government grant, the young man completed his studies in Berlin and Vienna. A friend's description of Sibelius as a student suggests much of his music as well: "His nature was delicate and impressionable; his sensitive imagination found outlet in music at the slightest provocation. His thoughts always strayed, his head was always in the clouds, and he continually expressed such original and bizarre ideas that [a friend] said

Sibelius during his long retirement.

that in his normal mood he was like the rest of us drunk." (In younger years Sibelius was often literally drunk as well.)

On his return home in 1891, Sibelius joined the "Young Finns" group, who were militating for independence from Russia. Determined to use his art to rouse national consciousness, he turned for ideas to the Finnish national epic, the *Kalevala*. The first of his pieces derived from those ancient stories was the symphonic poem *Kullervo*, from 1892. Next year came *En Saga*, a failure at first but soon to contribute to his skyrocketing fame. By then he had married Aino Järnefelt; their rustic country home at Järvenpää, to which they moved in 1904, was named "Ainola" after her. To the end of his life they would never leave for long that cabin in the pines.

His style was already formed, his musical thumbprints in place: the growling brass crescendos, the predilection for unmixed instrumental colors and low registers, the ineffable harmonies in whispering strings, the driving folklike melodies (though he never used an actual folk tune), the pervasive intimation of nature. "I love the mysterious sounds of the fields and forests, water and mountains," he said. "It pleases me greatly to be called an artist of nature, for nature has truly been the book of books for me."

In 1893 Sibelius began to teach at the Helsinki Conservatory. Four years later he was given a government stipend, which he would receive annually for the rest of his long life. Soon followed the tone poem that would most identify him with the spirit of his people, and also the beginning of his career as a symphonist.

As part of a patriotic program in Helsinki in December 1899, Sibelius unveiled his tone poem *Finlandia,* an impassioned portrait of his country. It immediately became identified with the nationalistic struggles of Finland, in the way certain choruses of Verdi had taken on patriotic overtones. Legend says that the Russian authorities were so concerned about the inflammatory effect of *Finlandia* that they forbade performances, so that it had to be played under other names. Later evidence suggests that Sibelius himself helped spread this tale, but there is no doubt that the work stamped itself on the national consciousness as part of its identity. From then on, Sibelius was *the* Finnish composer. Meanwhile, the First Symphony of 1899 began his series of seven, in which he forged a personal reconciliation of the past and future of symphonic music.

His reputation began to spread through Europe in the early years of the century, at the same time as his health declined alarmingly; he developed a cancer of the throat that afflicted him for some time. The haunted Fourth Symphony is partly a reflection of that mental and physical anguish. In 1908 the cancer was successfully removed. For years after, Sibelius fearfully shied away from his beloved alcohol and cigars.

An indication of his international reputation came in 1914, when Sibelius visited America under the sponsorship of wealthy music lover Carl Stoeckel. He conducted his work, including the first performance of the tone poem *The Oceanides,* to immense acclaim and received an honorary doctorate from Yale. After his return to Finland, however, the war forced Sibelius into seclusion. Royalties from his German publishers ceased and inflation devalued his government stipend; he sank into poverty, turning out hackwork for money. Meanwhile, a murderous civil strife in Finland claimed the life of his brother. Twice the "Red Guard" ransacked Ainola. Somehow during this period Sibelius managed to write his triumphant Fifth Symphony, which was premiered in December 1915. Despite its public success, he would do two major revisions of the Fifth in the next few years.

In the 1920s, Sibelius enjoyed a worldwide reputation maybe greater than any of his contemporaries—certainly he was more beloved than thorny Modernists like Schoenberg and Stravinsky. The trouble was that Sibelius knew music was turning to paths he could not follow, even though he by no means deplored the radicals (he admired Stravinsky, for one). Perhaps Sibelius felt that his post-Romantic style was anachronistic, or perhaps he ran out of ideas that excited him. For whatever reason, after 1924 he no longer conducted in public and his work trickled to a halt: the 1926 incidental music for *The Tempest* was his orchestral swan song, and a few minor piano pieces from 1929 were the last works he gave the world. For the rest of his life there were rumors of a new symphony. Sibelius played cat and mouse with those rumors for years, but after his death not a note of an eighth symphony was found.

He lived in retirement through World War II and into the fifties, receiving visits from musicians, enjoying the spread of his music but staying well out of public life, and died at home on September 20, 1957. Thousands of his countrymen came to pay their respects as he lay in state in Helsinki. He was buried in his garden at Ainola.

Sibelius wrote some hundred songs, 130 piano pieces, fifty works for solo violin and piano, many choruses, two string quartets, and an opera. Nearly all these works are minor and some are regrettable (he suppressed the opera himself). His reputation mainly rests on four or five symphonies, a handful of tone poems, and the Violin Concerto.

Over the years he has been both over- and underrated. Even at his best there are problems: miscalculations in orchestral balance, elaborate transitions to nowhere in particular, allegros that stumble and fall, pages of brassy banality. But besides the soulfulness and authority of his voice and the novelty of his Finnish musical accent, he also added forward-looking ideas to symphonic thinking. In traditional sonata form, themes are presented, recast and boiled down in the development, and then recapitulated. Sibelius reversed that procedure, using seminal motives that are combined and recombined to create themes. In other words, where traditional symphonies feature the deconstruction and then reconstruction of stated themes, a Sibelius symphony sprouts themes from seedlike motives. This new logic produces fresh and organic forms: a piece seems to grow melodies as it goes, like a flower blooming.

Finlandia, its importance as a nationalistic icon aside, is to Sibelius's work what the *1812 Overture* is to Tchaikovsky's: a perennial hit that makes its point not with subtlety but rather with heroic brass and throbbing tunes. Far more delicate, and nearly as popular over the years, is the tone poem *Swan of Tuonela* (1893), whose program is taken from the *Kalevala:* "Tuonela, . . . the Hades of Finnish mythology, is surrounded by a broad river of black water and rapid current, in which the Swan of Tuonela glides majestically and sings." The song of the swan is represented by a floating melody in English horn, supported by uncanny harmonies in muted strings. It is a good example of Sibelius's gift for achieving striking intensity and atmosphere with the simplest of means. Another audience favorite for many years is the Violin Concerto of 1903–05, which features some of his most passionate themes.

Sibelius's best symphonies may be approached more or less in order. The Second Symphony of 1901 begins in a novel way, for all its simplicity: a gently gliding string accompaniment leads to a piping rustic theme in woodwinds, the kind of tune one finds oneself whistling on a fine day in harvest time. The second movement takes a turn to the tragic; the final two are a whirling vivacissimo of a scherzo and a majestic finale with striking, slowly mounting climaxes. (A teacher of mine used to find the finale graphically erotic. There's something to that.)

The 1911 Fourth Symphony is quite another matter: from the groaning strings of its opening to the bleak, wandering gestures of its conclusion it is a world of shadows and uncertainties. Critics have always had trouble with this work; some have written of its "baffling simplicity," its "complete absence of sensuous appeal." Some say it is Sibelius's least characteristic piece, others that it is his distilled essence. Certainly the Fourth came from an agonized time of his life and reflects that in its mournful themes, its moments of oddly grave exuberance. Frustrating sometimes in its peregrinations and non sequiturs, the Fourth is still arguably one of the most absorbing and original symphonies of this century, its enigmatic apprehensions and incompletenesses—and its attenuation of tonality—representing the composer's closest approach to Modernism. It is also as good an example as any of his gift for extracting the last drop of feeling from every gesture. (And he does it without Tchaikovskian bathos: if Sibelius "extracts" emotions, Tchaikovsky wrings them ragged.)

The Fifth Symphony, premiered in 1915 but not finalized until 1919, begins with a rising horn line as sweet as a summer sunrise, which is also the seed-motive that generates most of the themes in the work. The first movement is really two, a dreamlike section that meanders like clouds in a breeze, and a vivacious scherzo. Next comes a movement made from variations on a gently lilting rhythmic pattern; it has some of the most elegantly beautiful pages in Sibelius's work. The finale again joins two ideas, a hearty scherzo and an expanse of Brahmsian loftiness.

Finally, try the Seventh Symphony, Sibelius's last, completed in 1924. It is relatively short and in one movement, and the orchestra is fairly small, but still it manages to attain great breadth and a kind of twilight grandeur. The Seventh has often been compared to the ineffable spirituality of the late Beethoven quartets; for both composers these late works represent their furthest expansion of traditional forms, the usual boundaries and procedures submerged into an unbroken organic unfolding. Melodies seem to grow before our ears, to melt into other melodies or into floating mists. Throughout, the Seventh harks back to the nineteenth century; chorales, scherzos, graceful dances appear and disappear like an echo. In this last symphony of this often unsatisfactory but irreplaceable genius, we seem to be eavesdropping on waves of feeling and memory in Sibelius's own fading creative consciousness. Like Brahms, Sibelius is a poet of what used to be, his melancholy the melancholy of things past.

MAURICE RAVEL

From the time of Couperin in the eighteenth century well into our own, the mainstream of French music has been consistent: a spirit more Classical than Romantic, more subtle than splashy, more lyrical than dramatic, more restrained than passionate. (Even Berlioz, the great exception, is touched by these qualities.)

Ravel, his dress as impeccable as his music.

In the crystalline pastels of Maurice Ravel one finds a distillation of musical Frenchness. Always paired in history with Debussy as the twin pillars of musical impressionism, Ravel is perhaps better described as a postimpressionist; he brought his own lucid and classical vision to bear on the innovations of Debussy and crafted a distinctive personality. Debussy, intoxicated by his sounds, aimed to intoxicate the listener. The enigmatic Ravel, in his quiet study shut off from the world, pursued a fastidious perfection he knew would always elude him.

Maurice Ravel was born on March 7, 1875, in the town of Ciboure in the Basque region of southwestern France, near the Spanish border. His father was a Swiss engineer, his mother Basque. The composer would retain through life a fascination with things Spanish, as much a part of him as his chiseled Basque features. Soon after his birth the Ravels moved to Paris, where Maurice began to study piano at seven and harmony at twelve. In 1889, like generations of French musicians before him, he entered the Paris Conservatory; he would inhabit its classrooms for sixteen years.

Around 1894 Ravel began to compose, his work already showing signs of his mature style. Among those who influenced him at that time was the eccentric Erik Satie, whose harmonic experiments had previously made an impression on Debussy. Composer Gabriel Fauré, with whom Ravel began to study in 1897, gave his pupil an indelible dose of classicism while helping Ravel refine his style. Among the first demonstrations of Fauré's influence is the wistful piano piece *Pavane pour une infante défunte* (Pavane for a Dead Princess) of 1899, which was an immediate hit and remains one of Ravel's most-loved works (often heard in his orchestrated version). With the *Pavane* and the *Jeux d'eau* (Play of Water, 1901) for piano, Ravel made a name for himself in France. His String Quartet, completed in 1904 and dedicated to Fauré, was greeted as a masterpiece and remains in the repertoire as one of the most ravishing chamber works of the century.

During his student years Ravel joined a group of young avant-gardists who called themselves the "Apaches," after the French term for a street thug. He gained friends and collaborators during late-night debates about new work and new ideas; among others, the young Stravinsky frequented the Apache meetings. One of the group later wrote, "Ravel shared our preference, weakness, or mania respectively for Chinese art, Mallarmé and Verlaine, Rimbaud, Cézanne and Van Gogh, Rameau and Chopin, Whistler and Valéry, the Russians and Debussy."

Traditionally, the official ticket to success for a French composer was the Conservatory's Prix de Rome. Berlioz, Bizet, and Debussy had all gone to great trouble to secure the prize with the required proper cantatas. Ravel made his first try in 1901 and won second place. Three more attempts followed, the last in 1905, when he didn't even make the finals. That a composer of Ravel's stature was brushed aside, however, begat a scandal that had cafés and school-rooms humming all over Paris. In the wake of the scandal the head of the Conservatory resigned, to be replaced by Fauré. Disgusted by the devious machinations of official awards, Ravel never again competed for the prize and in later years twice refused the Legion of Honor, France's highest distinction.

Like Debussy, Ravel avoided academe. He did have the occasional private pupil, notably British composer Ralph Vaughan Williams (whose work hardly shows the imprint of his teacher). In his social life, Ravel was a riddle: little seemed to reach him, little escaped. He never married and lived with his mother until her death, had many friends but kept them at arm's length, and largely preferred his family, other peoples' children, his cats, his collection of curios, his solitude. Still, among friends he was a marvelous wit and practical joker; he was known to turn his head in the middle of a conversation and emit birdlike shrieks. His sexuality, or lack of it, has been the subject of much inconclusive speculation. He seemed to live in and for his music.

After the Prix de Rome imbroglio, the only serious controversy in Ravel's uneventful life had to do with Debussy. Legend says that Debussy felt the younger man's String Quartet was too imitative and this estranged them. In fact, they maintained cool but cordial relations and Debussy advised Ravel, contra some critics, not to change a note of the quartet. In 1907 a public flap broke out when Ravel found himself accused of plagiarizing Debussy in the *Histoires naturelles* and other works. Certainly Ravel had mined Debussy for sounds and ideas (perhaps one reason he bloomed early). However, while Ravel did pick up some of his predecessor's modal scales, rich dissonances, and harmonic perfume, he used them in different ways. Where Debussy often lets his harmonies drift freely, Ravel uses novel harmonies in traditional progressions. It's often hard to figure out what Debussy was up to and why, but to some extent one can analyze a Ravel work in terms of traditional harmonic practice. Certainly, Ravel is no second-string impressionist. His songs, some of the finest of the century, reveal a lyric gift at least equal to Debussy's, and if Ravel began by absorbing the other's epochal innovations in piano writing, the older composer in later years showed he had learned from the younger. Ravel's virtuosic *Gaspard de la nuit,* one of the most original piano works of its time and a masterpiece of impressionistic evocation, may have influenced Debussy.

"I did my work slowly, drop by drop," Ravel once said. "I tore it out of me by pieces." And why did he take such pains? "My objective . . . is technical perfection. I can strive unceasingly to this end, since I am certain of never being able to attain it. The important thing is to get nearer to it all the time." His friend Stravinsky called Ravel "a Swiss clockmaker"—high praise from one who aspired to the same precision. Ravel's drive to perfection is most audible in his lapidary orchestration, in which both simple textures (as in the *Mother Goose* Suite) and kaleidoscopic instrumental masses (as in *Daphnis et Chloé*) are handled with unfailing effectiveness and brilliance. It is arguable that Debussy, Ravel, Mahler, and Stravinsky represent the summit of orchestral virtuosity in Western music.

All the same, Ravel's goals were far from academic notions of technique for its own sake. "Great music must always come from the heart," he said; "Music should always be first emotional and only after that intellectual." In the end, Ravel's precision does not add up to coldness but rather to a tightly reined warmth and charm. His art is lightweight compared to the great Germans and even compared to Debussy, but it is captivating all the same. "Ravel rules an enchanted world, made up of children, gods, fairies, tender animals, turbulent puppets," a biographer has written. "It is the kingdom of Ariel." The later Moderns tend to astonish and overwhelm. Ravel prefers to seduce.

Ravel's international reputation grew through the teens, based mainly on his piano pieces such as the *Pavane* and orchestral gems such as the *Rapsodie espagnole* (1908) and *Ma Mère l'Oye* (Mother Goose, 1912). When he received a commission from Sergei Diaghilev, impresario of the Ballets Russes, Ravel was determined to make *Daphnis et Chloé* his masterpiece, standing in for the symphonies he never attempted. He spent over two years working on this nymphs-and-shepherds ballet, which is at once his most voluptuous and most controlled score. Premiered in Paris in June 1912 to mixed reviews, it has become one of the enduring hits of the twentieth century. With *Daphnis* as the epitome of his grand style, Ravel thereafter simplified his means and ends, working toward a true neoclassicism (as did Stravinsky and other composers in that era). The gentle *Le Tombeau de Couperin* (The Tomb of Couperin), written as a piano suite in the years 1914 to 1917 and some of it orchestrated later, harks back to the charm of eighteenth-century French music.

Rejected for combat duty during World War I because of his short stature and delicate constitution, Ravel served as an ambulance driver at the front until a physical breakdown sent him home to Paris. Soon after his return, his beloved mother died in January 1917. From that point Ravel's health began to decline and along with it his creativity, though there were still masterpieces to come. In 1921 he moved to a villa he called "Le Belvédère" in Montfort-l'Amauray, thirty miles from Paris, which was his home from then on.

During the twenties he traveled around Europe conducting his work. In 1928, despite his deficiencies as a pianist and conductor, Ravel received tremendous acclaim on a concert tour of the United States. Like many Frenchmen he was fascinated by wild and woolly America, but most of all he took every opportunity to soak up jazz, calling it one of the most important musical developments of the century. He befriended George Gershwin, whose influence on his Violin Sonata's bluesy slow movement Ravel was happy to acknowledge. Jazz ideas would also be strong in the two piano concertos he wrote in the next few years. Ravel returned to France to compose *Bolero* for a Spanish ballet by Ida Rubenstein. This mesmerizing tour de force of orchestration swept through the musical world and overnight made Ravel the most celebrated living French composer. For his part, Ravel was dubious about the piece, which is made up of a simple verse and refrain melody repeated with inexorably mounting force. *Bolero,* he cautioned, was "orchestration without music—a long, very gradual crescendo." (One could see this work as a forerunner of present-day minimalism, though with far more instrumental virtuosity than any minimalist has managed.)

Thereafter Ravel's creative and physical decline accelerated. His two piano concertos of the early thirties (one for the left hand, written for a pianist who had lost an arm in the war) are fine works, but not quite up to his usual level. In 1932, minor injuries from a taxi accident seemed to linger, finally resolving into a mysterious brain disease that caused him great pain and periodic paralysis. Perhaps worst of all, Ravel was tormented by musical ideas that he could not manage to write down. Finally, in desperation, he agreed to a risky brain operation. He never awakened from it, dying at age sixty-two on December 28, 1937.

Even though Ravel was a master of fine line and delicate tracery, his most famous works are in his extravagant mode. *Bolero* (1928) is one of his most brilliant, unfolding along an unchanging theme and relentless drum rhythm, the orchestra slowly expanding to an over-whelming climax. Also in a Spanish mode is the *Rapsodie espagnole,* much of which is like castanet-haunted dreams. Ravel seemed to remember Spain in his genes, and to write of it from that uncon-scious depth.

Where Debussy's favorite Russian was Musorgsky, Ravel's was the more sumptuous and exotic Rimsky-Korsakov. One sees that connec-tion in the grandest of all Ravel's scores, *Daphnis et Chloé,* most often heard in the second of two suites Ravel arranged from the ballet. The beginning "Daybreak" section seems to rise from a far horizon into full blaze, with the cries of birds and whirling clouds of sunstruck colors (here Ravel is a mainstream impressionist). Pan plays his pipes in the "Pantomime," in a twining flute solo almost as famous as Debussy's at the beginning of his *Prélude à l'après-midi d'un faune* (while the latter uses the sultry low tones of the flute, Ravel sets his panpipes in the silvery high register). The "General Dance" of the finale builds in chains of brilliant effects to a concluding Ravelian delirium: both dreamlike and exact, wild but always under control. (*Daphnis* owes much to Debussy, most noticeably in the wordless women's voices at the end, much like those that end Debussy's *Nocturnes.* In comparing the two, however, it is the differences that are striking, with Ravel by far the more calorie-loaded.)

One also finds an atmosphere of dream and delirium in *La Valse,* an homage to nineteenth-century Viennese Waltz King Johann

Strauss. Here Ravel uses all his orchestral sorcery to conjure up phantoms dancing in a cloud of reverie. The ending of *La Valse* verges on hysteria, as if the ballroom were exploding before our ears. Also in his expansive style is his resplendent orchestration of Musorgsky's *Pictures at an Exhibition,* discussed in the essay on Musorgsky.

The more restrained and Classical side of Ravel—always there, even when covered by cream—is seen in works like the delicate piano (and later orchestral) work *Pavane pour une infante defunte* and the String Quartet, the latter a revelation of how fresh the same old two violins, viola, and cello can be made to sound. His ingenuous side may be heard at its most engaging in the orchestral suite of fairy-tale pieces called *Ma Mère l'Oye* (Mother Goose), originally piano pieces for children.

Ravel is usually passed over lightly in histories because he added little to the art of music other than his own voice. Debussy, Stravinsky, Schoenberg et al. revolutionized musical technique, and Ravel learned from all of them. Yet Ravel is one of the most beloved of all twentieth-century composers because he turned his genius and his patient labors not toward technical novelty but toward what *worked:* what sounded best from the instruments, what entertained, charmed, dazzled the ear and the imagination. Such aesthetic pragmatism may not be the highest ambition in art, but it has its place, and it became increasingly rare as the century went on.

CHARLES IVES

From the lonely years of its creation to the present, the music of Charles Ives has refused to settle into any convenient slot in Western tradition. In one vertiginous page of the second movement of his Fourth Symphony we find stacked up, in various keys and at top volume, a brass-band march, "Turkey in the Straw," "Marching Through Georgia," and various other wildcat tunes in assorted keys and rhythms, including a four-hand piano in which the lower hands are ragtimey and upper hands nearly atonal. It makes, in short, the damnedest racket you ever heard, which is just what Ives intended it to do. Then the symphony's next movement is a lovely, more or less traditional fugue based on a hymn tune.

The effect and intention of all this still baffles many listeners today, who despite the artistic anarchies of our time still expect a composer to be one thing or another, naïve or sophisticated, popular or classical, modern or otherwise. Ives was all these things at one time or another—and sometimes simultaneously. When the Fourth Symphony was written, in the second decade of this century, its style and meaning were simply incomprehensible. Compared to the other great musical innovators, whatever their struggles with the public, Ives wrote in the most profound isolation of them all, and the furthest from any mainstream current.

Despite his stylistic elusiveness, though, one thing has been clear since the belated onset of Ives's public career: he was the first to thoroughly explore the Modernist musical vocabulary—polytonality, polyrhythm, dissonant counterpoint, atonality, tone clusters, quarter tones, chance music, spatial music, and on and on (see Glossary). Some of these techniques evolved in his work between a decade and a half century before anyone else thought of them. At the same time, in his use of national tunes, ragtime rhythms, hymns, marches, and other popular material, he created the first truly American idiom in music and the first systematic synthesis of "high" and "low" music. He was thus a prophet of both Modernism and postmodernism, without really belonging to either. In the end, he was a one-man milieu. The only label that really applies to Charles Ives is *Ivesian*.

That is because none of the above mattered much to him. Experiment, pluralism, nationalism—these were all means to an end. The real point was how his music reflected and exalted the finest and most eternal things in life. The ultimate task of art, Ives wrote in his *Essays Before a Sonata,* was to transcend art, to attain "a conception unlimited by the narrow names of Christian, Pagan, Jew, or Angel! A vision higher and deeper than art itself!" If he was sometimes impatient with the more pedestrian demands of art, from the need for clear scores to the practicalities of writing for orchestra,

Ives dreamed of "A vision higher and deeper than art itself."

his exalted conception of music and its place in the human community still shines through his greatest work.

Charles Ives was born on October 20, 1874, in the small New England manufacturing town of Danbury, Connecticut. Though the Iveses had long been known in Danbury as businessmen, bankers, and such, father George Ives had gone into music, directing bands and teaching around the region. George groomed his son to be a concert pianist, and though that never interested Charlie (partly because he was painfully shy), he did become a prodigy as an organist, a professional church musician from his early teens. While training Charlie in musical fundamentals, George also bequeathed to his son an experimental attitude: as Charlie watched and listened, George tinkered with quarter tones, spread his musicians around the town square to hear effects of space, had his children sing in one key while he accompanied in another, tried to capture the sound of bells on piano. When Charlie, as a drummer in the band, practiced drum parts on piano by playing with his fists (thereby inventing tone clusters), George did not object as long as the boy knew the "rules," too. This background—constant participation in community musical events both highbrow and low, his father's mix of experiments and traditional training, plus the boy's inborn talent—led naturally to the precocious works Charlie wrote in his teens, among them the rollicking *Variations on America* for organ, with its polytonal interludes. These days the piece is a "Pops" favorite in orchestrated form.

At Yale from 1894 to 1898, Ives studied with Horatio Parker, a leading composer and teacher of the time. Conventional in his ideas, Parker laughed off Ives's musical experiments but still taught the young composer to think like a symphonist, to build large forms and relate themes to one another. Besides the conventional pieces Ives wrote for Parker (some of them, such as the Romantic-style First Symphony, works of striking maturity for his age) and the private experimental pieces, Ives also wrote light music for fraternity shows and local theater orchestras. Sometimes in the orchestra pit he would roughly stack up popular tunes and fraternity songs in different keys and, amidst the laughter of the crowd, absorb the results with his keen ears and steel-trap memory. The conflicting streams of music that he pursued at Yale, the experimental and conventional, classical and popular, would remain part of him for the rest of his life, sometimes separate and sometimes mingling. Meanwhile at Yale, he held down the most prestigious church organist job in New Haven and played on intramural football and baseball teams. Ives later admitted that his main interest in college was sports; outside music, his grade average was D-plus.

At some point during his college years, Ives decided that his career would not be in music. A discouraged George Ives, before his sudden death in 1894, had probably advised Charlie not to make a living that way; it couldn't support a family. In addition, at Yale Ives had begun to realize that people could little tolerate his experiments; they were all right for a joke, but not to be taken seriously. Ives insisted on exploring new musical materials, but also hoped for a family and a living; he did not intend, he later wrote, to "starve on dissonances." So after graduation in 1898, he moved to New York for a job as a five-dollar-a-week clerk with the Mutual Life Insurance Company. He would be an insurance man for the rest of his working years—a very fine insurance man, as it turned out.

The pattern of his life was already set. He had always done many things at once—work, sports, studies, socializing—and had crammed music around the edges, day by day. So he kept going that way, at an incredible pace. Living in apartments with collections of Yale friends, he worked at the office, pitched on company baseball teams, studied some law, for several years held church organist posts, hung out in nightspots with friends spelling the house pianist, and nights and weekends composed a great deal of music, everything from staid pieces for church choirs to the beautiful and relatively conservative Second and Third symphonies to experimental pieces of growing audacity and confidence.

In 1903 Ives wrote the *Country Band March,* a satire of small-town musicians that involved elaborate polyrhythms and quasi-accidental counterpoint. In 1906 came *The Unanswered Question,* a "Cosmic Landscape" in which the "Perennial Question of Existence" is posed by a trumpet against a quiet background of strings (the silent universe), and four woodwinds dubbed the "Fighting Answerers" run futilely in search of an answer. At last the trumpet intones the Question once again, and is answered by silence. Both musically and philosophically, *The Unanswered Question* was, for all its slightness, a seminal work for Ives. For the first time in music, it sets three independent groups against one another in loose juxtaposition, the details of alignment left to chance. Moreover, each group has its own style: while the string background is made of mysterious, slow-cycling tonal chords, the trumpet Question is of indefinite tonality and the Answerers become increasingly atonal and dissonant in their frustration. (Stravinsky, who admired some Ives works, said he'd rather this one be "The Unplayed Question.")

The Unanswered Question also reflects the Ivesian philosophy that a question is truer and more heroic than an answer in the sublime immensity of creation. With such ideas in mind, Ives could not be satisfied with what he called "nice easy-chair sounds"—even though he was still writing conservative pieces and always would.

While his traditional works found favor in church performances, nobody could countenance his wilder ideas, the ones he most cared about. Unhappy with his compromises, Ives resigned from his last church job in 1902 and went underground as a composer. That year marked the last public performance of his music for over two decades.

Ives was not entirely alone through this long artistic isolation. He hired musicians to play over things, sometimes inviting friends to listen. In 1908 he married Harmony Twichell, daughter of a noted Hartford minister. A settlement-house nurse and amateur poet, Harmony became the kind of supporter and approving audience Ives had lacked since his father died. Harmony believed with all her abundant heart and mind that her husband was a genius. If he had no real audience other than her, that, for a time, was enough.

After their marriage, his business career and his creative maturity bloomed together. With a partner he founded Ives & Myrick, which by the mid teens had grown into the largest insurance agency in the country. Ives is remembered to this day as a pioneer in the insurance business, the inventor of systematic estate planning and organizer of some of the first schools for agents.

At the same time, he gave himself completely to his most visionary musical ideas. Writing for his own ear and imagination, no longer held back by the practicalities of performance and the humiliations of audience rejection, he took his art to astonishing heights of daring and imagination. Between 1909 and 1916 he worked in a kind of fury. His output of those years included the

Second String Quartet, *Three Places in New England*, most of the *Holidays* Symphony, the Third and Fourth violin sonatas, the *Concord* Sonata, the Fourth Symphony, and dozens of songs including "General William Booth Enters into Heaven," most of the works that would later secure his reputation.

In these pieces, for all their wide-ranging explorations, Ives never abandoned the foundations of his experience, mainly his Danbury childhood. Much of his music is a texture of quotes of familiar marches, hymns, and national songs; nearly every piece is a picture of a remembered scene. In Danbury he had heard thousands of voices singing hymns at camp meetings, bands passing one another in parades, taps played over the graves of war heroes, his father's cornet soaring over church congregations, the bells and bands and fireworks of holidays, old men singing war songs and weeping, Bach and Beethoven played on parlor pianos and wheezy church organs. These cherished memories of the music of ordinary people became the substance of his art, not for their own sake, but for what they represented. Danbury was a community where people did what people do—gather to worship, to celebrate, to memorialize the dead, all accompanied by music. Danbury was anyplace and everyplace. For Ives, music was never an abstraction but rather an embodiment of universal human experience. "Music," he once wrote in a letter to Harmony, "does not represent life, it *is* life."

For twenty years he worked in the office, composed at home, was father to their adopted daughter and, when World War I came, did volunteer work on top of it all. But the irony was that while blessed with extraordinary talent and energy, Ives did not have the constitution to sustain them. In October 1918 he suffered a devastating heart attack. Recovering to some degree, he returned to business and to music. But though he wrote some important songs in the twenties and reworked a good deal of previous material, he never again conceived and completed a major piece. His last work, the elegiac song "Sunrise," dates from 1926. Physically and creatively, something had gone out of him that he never recovered.

His health declined steadily. By 1930, when he retired from business, Ives was spending long stretches helpless in bed. Through the ensuing invalid years his spirit and personality never dimmed; he remained vivacious, unpredictable, playful, sometimes cantankerous but unfailingly generous and kind. He and Harmony spent much of the year at their country house in West Redding, Connecticut, just over the hills from Danbury. The riches he had earned in business flowed into musical and charitable causes around the world; the number of musicians and friends and relatives and causes he helped will never be fully known.

Despite appearances, Ives was never a Sunday composer writing for his own amusement. He had every intention of getting his work before the public sooner or later, somehow or other. Immediately after the heart attack, with mortality suddenly weighing on him, he laid out enormous sums to engrave and print the *Concord* Sonata and a book of songs. He sent these printings to musicians by the hundreds. Meanwhile, in 1919 he wrote the *Essays Before a Sonata;* in the guise of essays on the literary subjects of the *Concord* Sonata (Emerson, Hawthorne, the Alcotts, Thoreau), they embody his ideals of art and its place in life.

The music he sent out in the 1920s garnered responses ranging mostly from polite dismissal to outrage. But here and there these strange works found receptive ears. Among those who pored over them were George Gershwin, pianist John Kirkpatrick, and self-proclaimed "ultramodern" composer Henry Cowell, who would become Ives's first major champion. Performances began to appear, often greeted (contrary to later legend) by critical response both enthusiastic and perceptive. By the early 1930s, Ives had become to a small group of enthusiasts a beacon for what American music, and all music, could be, a symbol of freedom and high courage.

But for the remainder of his life—which thanks to Harmony's care managed to be a good many years—Ives only slowly emerged into greater recognition. The 1930 and 1931 performances of *Three Places in New England,* by Nicolas Slonimsky and the Boston Chamber Orchestra, and especially John Kirkpatrick's triumphant premiere of the *Concord* Sonata in 1939, brought two major works before the public. In 1946 Ives won the Pulitzer Prize for the mild Third Symphony, premiered forty-two years after it was finished. He growled to the press, "Prizes are badges of mediocrity"—and then proudly hung the award in his study.

Ives died on May 19, 1954. *Time* magazine had a brief notice, saying that some people went so far as to call Ives the greatest American composer. In the next decades a good deal of the world came to the same conclusion. Beyond the American part of it, though, Ives has also come increasingly to be seen as one of the century's more important composers of any nationality. Today he is a significant influence in the Soviet Union; there is a Charles Ives Society in the Netherlands as well as in the United States.

The music of Ives has its problems, and they are as large as his imagination. Many of his pieces aren't really finished because there was simply no time. The pieces he cared most about, though, such as the *Concord,* were painstakingly revised in draft after draft. Like Schubert, Ives accomplished so much, his imagination and scope were so far-reaching, that it has taken generations for the world to begin to catch up with him.

Ives wrote every kind of piece there is, from artless children's songs to some of the most complex things ever put on paper. Sometimes he combines naïve and complex, consonant and dissonant, "old" and "new" ideas in one piece, as in the Fourth Symphony, where he follows the hullabaloo of the second movement with the ingenuous and traditional fugue. So it is not hard to find entries into Ives's world; many of his pieces are easily accessible, like the *Variations on America* and songs such as "Charlie Rutlage" (a hell-for-leather Western tune) and the lacy and lovely "Two Little Flowers" (written for daughter Edith).

A good place to start with the larger works is the Second Symphony (1900–02), which also turns up on "Pops" programs. For all its lightness of touch, its Yale songs and fiddle tunes and splashes of humor (Ives ironically throws in ideas from Bach, Brahms, Tchaikovsky, and Dvořák), this is a work of great importance, the first symphonic work in history with an unmistakably American voice. The long struggle for an American idiom, which Dvořák had nurtured during his stay in the country, here bore fruit; but nobody knew that until a half century later, when Leonard Bernstein premiered the Second Symphony (Bernstein's best-selling second recording of the piece was made just before his death in 1990). The Third Symphony is a transitional work, more complex in counterpoint than the Second, but still based on hymn melodies and highly ingratiating.

Ives was one of the most prolific songwriters of the century. The songs range from early ones such as the beautiful and rather Brahmsian "Feldeinsamkeit," to folksy outings ("Charlie Rutlage"), to meditations on hymns ("Watchman"), to a style of prophetic Modernism (as in the craggy tone clusters that accompany "The Majority"). Finest of all the songs is his setting of Vachel Lindsay's sardonic/serious poem on the founder of the Salvation Army, "General William Booth Enters into Heaven." Ives seems to play the poem for laughs, with drumbeats and banjos and shouts of "Are You Washed in the Blood of the Lamb?" from a chorus of drunks and floozies, all of it growing ever more raucous and funny. Then he transforms everything with a quiet, hymnlike ending. With that simple, eloquent gesture Ives says, Yes, after all, they *are* washed in the blood of the Lamb. It is a magical moment, and a paradigm of a good deal of what Ives is about: the mundane transmuted into the spiritual, the ordinary becoming the sublime, the paradoxes and contradictions of life reconciled before our ears.

Then one can go on to the grander, more challenging territories of the Ivesian world. The *Holidays* Symphony is really four separate movements that make up a kind of "Four Seasons." "Washington's Birthday" begins with an evocation of bleak winter and ends with a rambunctious barn dance; "Decoration Day" reflects both the tragic and festive aspects of that holiday honoring the war dead, with its second half a rousing march. "The Fourth of July" is a phantasmagoria of fireworks, crowds, and not-entirely-sober singing; and "Thanksgiving" is full of rich polytonal harmonies, climaxing with a soaring choral hymn.

Three Places in New England (ca. 1908–14) was the first of Ives's orchestral works to be circulated and remains the most familiar. The first piece is named for the Saint-Gaudens statue in Boston Common commemorating the Civil War's first black troops; Ives's work, a meditation on the heart of the American dilemma, resembles a dreamlike blues, with complex shimmering harmonies. In contrast, "Putnam's Camp" is an uproarious march full of wrong notes and players losing the beat (most of it taken from the satirical *Country Band March*). Finally comes "The Housatonic at Stockbridge," an unforgettable masterpiece of American impressionism. Based on a walk Ives and his wife took by a river in autumn soon after they were married, it sets a simple folk tune against a swirling orchestral texture that rises to a towering vision; its raging climax cuts off to reveal quiet harmonies suspended in strings, which drift unresolved into silence.

Near the end of his creative life and at the furthest reach of Ives's musical explorations lies the Fourth Symphony (1909–16). At once a musical autobiography, a summation of the Romantic symphony, a prophecy of the transcendent music of the future, and an apotheosis of American hymnody, it is one of the epic imaginative works of the twentieth century, comparable to Joyce's *Finnegans Wake,* Proust's *Remembrance of Things Past,* Schoenberg's *Moses und Aron.* Like those works, the Fourth is a deep, wide, sprawling, and sometimes bewildering evocation of the profoundest questions of life. In the first movement, the chorus sings of a Traveler searching for the "glory-beaming star" of the spirit. The next three movements are the Traveler's journey. The second movement, a massive Ivesian scherzo called the "Comedy," brings the Traveler to Vanity Fair, which turns out to be a clamorous modern city; in its climaxes the Comedy mounts to a teeming pandemonium that has to be heard to be believed. The third movement, the quiet fugue on a hymn tune, is set in a New England church.

These middle movements represent answers to the questions of life, but only provisional ones. In the final movement the Traveler, who is all of us, journeys into the world of the spirit, in music of extraordinary visionary intensity. At the end, a wordless chorus intones the main theme, musical and metaphorical, of the symphony, the hymn "Nearer, My God, to Thee." The music seems to fade into the stars, still in motion, still searching. Ives knew he wasn't complete yet and neither were we and maybe neither were the angels, but he believed with all his heart that we would get there, one of these days. A work of universal religion, the Fourth Symphony was his supreme effort to bring us a little Nearer.

Maybe the main reason Ives is not really a Modernist is his inexhaustible optimism. He represents a kind of alternative, an exploratory path without the usual Modernist baggage. More than anything Ives wanted his music to be a catalyst for the innate greatness and spiritual progress of the human community. Soberly considered, his faith in music and in humanity was misplaced. But who has believed more passionately in all of us? Who in our time has had a more magnificent delusion?

Schoenberg in an Expressionist self-portrait.

ARNOLD SCHOENBERG

No composer has had more baggage attached to his very name than Arnold Schoenberg. His name and achievement have been the subject of diatribes, dismissed with grudging respect, used as a litmus test, sabotaged by both enemies and disciples. Somewhere behind all the shouting is the real Arnold Schoenberg, the composer who first fully explored the territory that others named atonality, and who—more importantly—created a hyperbolic and sometimes violent expressive world perhaps closer to the raw unconscious than any other music. His jagged melodies, spiky harmonies, and screaming trumpets are symptomatic of his century's spiritual climate. Still, in his most heartfelt works he suggests the possibility of redemption, a redemption all the more profound for being hard-won.

Conservatives have accused Schoenberg of being a dispenser of musical mathematics. Radicals have pilloried him for being too attached to the past, for not going far enough. One could argue both accusations, and maybe they help explain his perennial failure to gain the public that Modernists like Stravinsky and Bartók have. But here I will avoid mathematics and polemics and concentrate on his life and the emotional impact of his music. Schoenberg lived in a time of artistic revolution, of the revolutionary psychology of Freud, of Expressionist artists such as his friend Oskar Kokoschka, who were trying to paint the abysses of the Freudian unconscious. Impressionism, born in France, is all outdoors, fields and ocean spray, the outside reflected from the inside. Expressionism, born in Germany, is the most inward-looking art. And sometimes that inner eye falls on terrors, hallucinations, monsters.

In his time, of course, the terrors were outside as well. Around Arnold Schoenberg, a lapsed Jew who was driven back to the faith, grew the chaos and anarchy that came to fruition in the Nazi era. He saw it all, felt it all, and resonated with it all. Eventually he would attack that chaos and anarchy with faith: faith in the God of the Old Testament and in a new way of composing music.

He was born Arnold Franz Walter Schönberg in Vienna on September 13, 1874 (later, in America, he would Anglicise the spelling to Schoenberg). His father, Samuel, ran a shoe store and raised his children as Orthodox Jews in a virulently anti-Semitic society. Arnold took up violin and cello in his youth, mainly teaching himself; also on his own, he began writing little pieces. Samuel died when Arnold was sixteen and the boy worked several years in a bank to support his family. Already he was determined to be a composer; he spent his free time studying music and playing chamber works with friends.

Among those friends was an up-and-coming composer named Alexander von Zemlinsky. For some time Schoenberg studied informally with Zemlinsky, who was two years older and the only teacher Schoenberg ever had. The student picked up Zemlinsky's passion for Wagner. (And picked up a wife, too; Schoenberg married Zemlinsky's sister Mathilde in 1901.) During this period Schoenberg turned to making a living orchestrating popular music and operettas; he later estimated he had done six thousand pages of hackwork.

In 1897 the first Schoenberg piece was heard in public, a string quartet played in Vienna. Two years later, when he was twenty-five, came his youthful masterpiece, the string sextet *Verklärte Nacht,* written in three weeks of heated inspiration and today the most popular of his works. Then in 1900, a performance of some new songs was greeted by protests. From then on, Schoenberg would say, "the scandal never stopped."

But he was not yet the particular kind of scandalous figure he later became. So far he was a post-Wagnerian Romantic when Wagner was still considered revolutionary. Schoenberg based his early music above all on the restless chromaticism of Wagner's *Tristan und Isolde*, carrying that restlessness a notch further. Among Schoenberg's mentors was the still scandalous post-Wagnerian Richard Strauss. When Schoenberg moved to Berlin in 1901, to conduct in a cabaret started by some friends, Strauss secured a scholarship for the young man and a job teaching composition at the Stern Conservatory. Around that time Schoenberg sketched the gigantic *Gurrelieder* for voices and orchestra, the grandest work of his post-Wagnerian period. It would not be heard until 1913, when it found an enormous success rare in Schoenberg premieres.

In 1902 Schoenberg moved back to Vienna, where he and Zemlinsky founded a short-lived organization to promote new music. The honorary president of this group was Gustav Mahler, who became a champion of the young composer. Mahler would not always agree with Schoenberg's music, but the older master never reneged in his support—in contrast to Strauss, who within a few years was declaring, "I think [Schoenberg would] do better to shovel snow than scribble on music paper."

Schoenberg continued teaching. In the autumn of 1904 he acquired two pupils who would follow his ideas in the process of becoming major composers themselves, Anton Webern and Alban Berg. The year 1905 saw the premiere of another big Romantic work, the orchestral *Pelleas und Melisande*, finished in 1902 and based on the same Maeterlinck play as Debussy's opera (which had been unknown to Schoenberg). By then, though he did not yet realize it, Schoenberg was preparing to leave behind the sumptuous post-Wagnerian style of his first period and to move into a kind of music that seemed to have come from another world.

The transformation began in works of 1905–07, among them the String Quartet in D minor (the first published, so-called no. 1) and the Chamber Symphony no. 1. In both works the continual chromaticism strains the boundaries of traditional tonality while the dense counterpoint challenges the ear's ability to keep up with it. At its premiere the D minor Quartet provoked an audience riot, which would become a regular feature of Schoenberg performances. The String Quartet no. 2, premiered in 1908, was the last major Schoenberg work to contain a key signature, a sign of connection to the old major-minor scales. In the last movement of that quartet, which includes a soprano voice, the music omits a key signature and launches into an unprecedented harmonic freedom, beginning the atonal epoch with the words, "I feel the breath of other planets."

Besides its position in the history of Modernism, the Quartet no. 2 reflected a tumultuous period in Schoenberg's life. He and his wife had been studying painting with the young Expressionist artist Richard Gerstl. In the summer of 1908, Mathilde Schoenberg ran off with the painter. She was persuaded to return, but the despairing Gerstl killed himself. Somehow Schoenberg and his wife were reconciled and the marriage survived until her death in 1923. The Quartet no. 2 is dedicated to Mathilde.

During this period of personal turmoil, Schoenberg was also struggling with the monumental decision to abandon the tonal system, which for centuries had been virtually the mother tongue of Western music. He knew what he would be up against, creatively and personally. In 1909 he wrote, "I already feel the opposition that I shall have to overcome. I suspect that even those who have believed in me until now will not be willing to see the necessity of this development. It is not lack of invention or of technical skill that has urged me in this direction. I am following an inner compulsion that is stronger than education." Thus wrote a man who considered himself the heir of Beethoven, Bach, Brahms, and Wagner, one on whom history weighed with even more authority than on most creators. I have earlier mentioned his confession, "I am a conservative who was forced to become a radical." He came to see himself as the reluctant avatar of the historical necessity of overthrowing tonality. When a stranger once asked him, "Are you *that* Arnold Schoenberg?" he replied with weary irony, "Well, no one else wanted to be, so I had to take the job."

With the Piano Pieces op. 11 and op. 19 (1907–11) the new language established itself. These begin the second period of Schoenberg's work, sometimes called free-atonal, sometimes atonal-expressionist. As noted in the essay Tonality and Atonality, the word *atonal* was slapped on Schoenberg's music by a disgruntled critic. Schoenberg declared the word absurd, saying that it implied "without tone," and proposed instead the term *pantonal*. Nonetheless, atonal became the standard term for music that avoids keys and tonal centers. To help erase a sense of key, Schoenberg largely banished traditional chord formations and melodic contours, decreeing what he called "the emancipation of the dissonance." No longer would dissonance be considered subordinate to consonance, nor would dissonant chords be required to resolve into consonant, as they had in the past. Debussy had taken similar steps, but had not gone as far; Schoenberg's free-atonal music is consistently more dissonant than anything before. By these means he endeavored to replace the hierarchies of tonality, and its seven-tone scales, with a more nearly democratic treatment of all twelve tones of the chromatic scale.

This period can be called *free*-atonal because Schoenberg was following his intuition rather than rationales and theories. The rationales would come later. Partly because he was feeling his way into a new world, the pieces of this period are mostly miniatures. He did not yet feel confident to create large forms; he was also reacting against the giganticism of his earlier late-Romantic style. The expressionist aspect has to do with the effect of this music, so close to paintings of that era, to Kokoschka's and Beckmann's tortured visions and violently clashing colors (also characteristic of Schoenberg's own paintings).

The first masterpiece of musical expressionism was Schoenberg's *Pierrot lunaire* of 1912, a collection of twenty-one miniatures for soprano and chamber ensemble, based on the old idea of a *melodrama*—poems recited with musical accompaniment. For the recitation Schoenberg notated every word of the text (poems by the Belgian Symbolist Albert Giraud) on a musical staff, controlling not only rhythm but speaking pitch. He thereby invented a technique he called *Sprechstimme*, literally, "speech-voice." Somewhere between normal speaking and singing, this technique in its very strangeness is an ideal vehicle for musical expressionism. *Sprechstimme* would become a staple technique of Schoenberg and his disciples.

At its Berlin premiere in October 1912, *Pierrot* was greeted by the usual donnybrook in the hall. But progressive and avant-garde circles responded with tremendous enthusiasm; some understood that this work was as epochal in its implications as Beethoven's *Eroica* had been in its day, and *Tristan und Isolde* after that. Among the audience for the early performances of *Pierrot* was Igor Stravinsky, then working on *Le Sacre du printemps*. Later, Stravinsky recalled *Pierrot* as "the great event in my life then." Those two works, *Pierrot lunaire* and *Le Sacre*, very different in sound and implications but both creations of tremendous originality and impact, launched Modernism in music on its triumphant and contentious career.

The opposition that Schoenberg had anticipated now dogged his steps—more virulent opposition, though, than he could have imagined. At the same time, he had a small but zealous following. Like his fellow Viennese Sigmund Freud, Schoenberg was a controversial and messianic leader surrounded by a group of apostles. Through the distractions of persecution and adulation Schoenberg forged on, composing and explaining himself. For the 1912 London premiere of the *Five Pieces for Orchestra*, he described the music in Freudian terms: "This music seeks to express all that swells in us subconsciously like a dream; which is a great fluctuant power, and is built upon none of the lines that are familiar to us; which has a rhythm, as blood has its pulsating rhythms, as all life in us has its rhythm; which has a tonality, but only as the sea or the storm has its tonality; which has harmonies, though we cannot grasp or analyze them nor can we trace its themes." Critics of the *Five Pieces* did not respond in kind: "If music at all, it is music of the future, and we hope, of a distant one." "We must be content with the composer's own assertion that he has depicted his own experience, for which he has our heartfelt sympathy." But critic Ernest Newman, after noting that a third of the audience was hissing, another third laughing, and the remaining third apparently stupefied, concluded, "I take leave to suggest that Schoenberg is not the mere fool or madman that he is generally supposed to be. May it not be that the new composer sees a logic in certain tonal relations that to the rest of us seem chaos at present, but the coherence of which may be clear enough to all of us some day?"

Questions of coherence and logic came to preoccupy Schoenberg as the teens wore on. By then he was teaching in Berlin, having been hounded out of Vienna by attacks both musical and, increasingly, anti-Semitic (even though he had converted to Christianity in his youth). Berlin turned up students and a wealthy patron, and he began to conduct his work. But his creative output had been slowing for some time; finally he bogged down in composing a biblical oratorio called *Die Jakobsleiter* (Jacob's Ladder). Part of the reason was World War I. Schoenberg underwent training for the German army but had to be released due to asthma and other health problems. More significantly, he was no longer willing to follow his instincts in composing. He felt the need to impose some discipline on anarchic free atonality, the Pandora's box he had opened. Between 1915 and 1921 Schoenberg completed nothing as he searched and pondered.

Meanwhile he stayed active as a performer and teacher. Settling after the war in Mödling, near Vienna, he founded the Society for Private Musical Performances with Webern, Berg, and other supporters. Through the four years of its existence and 117 concerts, the Society was a singular organization in the history of music: one expressly designed to keep the general public away from composers. The works on the programs (some radical, some not) were rehearsed as much as necessary, only Society members could come to concerts, and neither the press nor applause were allowed. On one hand, this arrangement deepened the isolation of the contemporary composer from the larger public; from then on, the milieu of atonal music tended to be isolated and ingrown. On the other hand, the Society made it possible for the first hearings of some the most important works of the century to be played in sympathetic surroundings.

One can hardly blame Schoenberg for his retreat from the public. Perhaps no composer, not even the much-vilified Wagner, has ever had such bile thrown his way. By no means an unsociable man or one who despised the world, Schoenberg was driven by the world's hostility toward suspicion and paranoia, rarely attending performances of his music outside the Society. Though he did not force his methods and ideas on students (his teaching was based on tradition) and was honest and forthright with them, he could also be brutally frank, wounding, and quick to imagine slights and betrayals. His life was punctuated by feuds, the most celebrated of them in the 1940s, when he bitterly attacked his friend Thomas Mann for creating a Schoenberg-like composer in the novel *Doktor Faustus*. Even with Webern and Berg there were periodic tensions. Schoenberg recognized his tendency to paranoia; in 1924 he wrote in a letter, "Unfortunately, the better sort of people become enemies faster than friends because everything is so serious and important to them that they are perpetually in a defensive position . . . I am speaking of my own defects." But as the saying goes, even paranoids have enemies. Schoenberg had more than his share, even before the Nazis.

By the 1920s, Schoenberg was world famous—or perhaps more accurately, world infamous. He did not entirely lack official acclaim, however. In 1924, on his fiftieth birthday, he was honored by the mayor at the Vienna Town Hall, a chorus from the Vienna Opera sang his magnificent early work *Friede auf Erden* (Peace on Earth), a magazine issue featured him, and his disciples produced a book of essays on his work and ideas. By then he had a new wife. Mathilde had died in 1923; the next year he married Gertrud Kolisch, sister of string quartet leader and Schoenberg champion Rudolf Kolisch. In 1925 he began a long teaching stint at the Prussian Academy of Arts in Berlin.

Those were his halcyon years. Contributing to his happiness was the fact that he was composing again at his old prolific rate. The problems he had come up against in the previous decade had been resolved into what he named the "method of composing with twelve tones" (sometimes called *dodecaphony*). With this systematic method he intended to bring atonality to heel within a musical language as well grounded and consistent as the previous centuries' tonal language.

Worked out in the heat of composition in pieces from 1921 to 1923, the twelve-tone system operates, in general, like this: all the notes in a work are derived from a single arrangement of the twelve notes of the chromatic scale; this arrangement, freely chosen by the composer, Schoenberg called the *row*. The twelve-tone row is the theme of the work, but its function goes far beyond the old melodic themes. Sometimes the notes of the row, or sections of it, are presented as a melodic line; and sometimes row segments are stacked up to form harmonies. This is possible because of the "emancipation of the dissonance," which made any kind of chord possible;

thus any succession of notes can be used either as a chord or a melodic line. A primary aim is the general equality of all chromatic notes, with no overall tonal implications (See Tonality and Atonality, p. 268).

Besides the original form of the row (also called the *prime*), other forms are available. The row may be presented backward (called the *retrograde* form), upside down (the *inversion*), or in retrograde inversion. Finally, the row can be transposed to begin on any of the twelve notes of the chromatic scale. The twelve possible transpositions, multiplied by the four forms of the row (prime, retrograde, inversion, retrograde inversion), generate forty-eight versions of the row, any or all of which may be used in a given piece.

That is the outline of Schoenberg's twelve-tone system. There are various corollaries. Rhythm was not part of the original scheme and for the moment could be handled freely. To avoid lines that resembled the old major-minor scales, Schoenberg and other twelve-tone composers tended to write jagged melodic lines full of large leaps. The harmony usually stays at a high level of dissonance, partly for expressive reasons, partly to avoid familiar chords with their tonal implications. (Nothing in the scheme requires steady dissonance, however. Some later composers used rows to write sweet-sounding pieces with clear tonal centers. Part of the reason for the system's later success, in fact, was that it does not dictate style but rather allows room for a composer's personality.)

Two important goals underlie the twelve-tone system. The aesthetic goal is to unify a composition more thoroughly than ever before by basing its melody, harmony, and counterpoint on a single unifying structure—the row. Secondly, Schoenberg aimed to replace the old tonal system with a new system of equal validity. "I have discovered something," he boasted to a student, "that will guarantee the supremacy of German music for the next hundred years."

What has happened to that prediction since the 1920s? For a long time, it seemed that the prophecy would indeed come to pass. Schoenberg's pupils Webern and Berg became extraordinary composers and both took up the twelve-tone system in their later music. Together, the three became founding fathers of what has been called the Second Viennese School, the heirs of Viennese composers from Haydn to Brahms. Many other composers embraced the twelve-tone method during Schoenberg's lifetime. After World War II, the method was extended into the idea of *serialism*, a more thorough-going treatment of his ideas. In serialism, rhythm, volume, texture, and other aspects of composition are controlled as pitch is in Schoenberg's rows. So rows and rowlike constructs were renamed *series;* now there also could be rhythmic series, and so on.

The primary model for serial theory, however, was the more systematic techniques of Webern, so the new style came to be called *post-Webern*. Serialists dismissed Schoenberg for being too attached to the rhythms and forms and emotionalism of the past, thus the young Pierre Boulez's proclamation, "SCHOENBERG IS DEAD." In Europe after World War II, young avant-garde composers such as Boulez and Karlheinz Stockhausen preached post-Webern serialism as a historical necessity and holy cause. In America, composer/theorist Milton Babbitt treated serialism as a branch of mathematics, working out his compositions in numbers, only at the end turning his calculations into notes.

Meanwhile, the counterforce to serialism was Stravinsky and his followers. From the twenties to the fifties, the Stravinsky and Schoenberg schools were the two warring, mutually exclusive camps of modern music, the relatively tonal, neoclassic Stravinsky side tending to find public success, the atonal Schoenberg side tending to find indifference if not hostility. Then in the mid fifties, after Schoenberg's death, Stravinsky suddenly converted to serialism. It was as if a commanding general had gone over to the enemy. Stravinsky's defection sealed the triumph of post-Webern serialism, and more generally the worldwide ascendancy of the musical avant-garde. By the sixties it seemed that serialism was indeed the future of music, an international language that had replaced the old mother tongue of major-minor tonality.

As has become clear in the last decade or so, that expectation did not pan out. The reasons were many. For one thing, Schoenberg's followers didn't help the cause in the way they expressed their enthusiasm. In an article on Schoenberg written for a popular reference work, we find this edifying tidbit: "Obviously, the identity of contour patterns which characterizes the close relationship between the first hexachords of the inversion of the concerto series and the inversion of the quartet series must then hold true for the first hexachords of the original of the concerto series and the inversion of the quartet series." *Obviously*. There is a great quantity of this sort of flapdoodle in writings about Schoenberg, despite the fact that he deplored meddling in his workshop. When Rudolf Kolisch wrote that he had ferreted out the row in a piece, Schoenberg fired back, "I can't utter too many warnings against overrating these analyses . . . my works are twelve-tone *compositions*, not *twelve-tone* compositions." Few followers of Schoenberg have taken that advice. Instead, they have treated the twelve-tone technique, which was a means to an end, as *the* end.

Moreover, many on both sides of the issue have used the public success of Schoenberg, Webern, and Berg as a litmus test of the success of all twentieth-century music: if audiences don't accept atonality and/or serialism, then they don't accept Modernism. By that test, twentieth-century music is a failure. But in fact, as I have noted before, a great deal of work from this century has found a major audience and is part of the standard repertoire. Why should atonal music be the litmus test?

In the long run, Schoenberg's prophecy failed mainly because audiences refused to attend the revolution. Even though individual twelve-tone and serial works found favor here and there, more often listeners stayed away from serialism and, increasingly, from anything they perceived to be avant-garde. Even after the lag always necessary for absorbing the new, the lag after which composers such as Bartók and Stravinsky were widely accepted, audiences continued resolutely to reject most serial music. The reasons for that rejection are in some ways mysterious and in any case beyond the scope of this book. Perhaps the logic of serialism is more mathematical than musical; perhaps serialism has insufficiently to do with what things *sound* like; and perhaps and perhaps. Certainly, some magnificent serial pieces—Stravinsky's *Agon* among them—have yet to find the public they deserve.

Despite composers' gestures of defiance (Babbitt's 1967 article "Who Cares if You Listen?" is a notorious example), in the long run too few people showed up, that's all. However well twelve-tone and serial methods acquit themselves in some pieces, Schoenberg was given his chance and was proven wrong about the system's universality. Composers are still in the aftershocks of that realization, still wondering what next. So far, no one has raised another such flag and asked the world to salute it.

These matters all lay in the future in the early 1930s, when Schoenberg had more immediate concerns. From 1930 to 1932 he wrote the first two acts of his projected three-act opera *Moses und Aron,* on his own libretto. It is at once his most ambitious work in the twelve-tone method, a turn to a more objective and less expressionist style, and a harbinger of his return to Judaism. During those years the Nazis were securing their stranglehold on Germany. In March 1933 his employer, the Prussian Academy, declared its intention of becoming *Judenfrei,* "free of Jews," in conformity to Nazi policy. Schoenberg did not wait around for the other shoe to drop. In May he emigrated to France, where he officially converted back to Judaism. Not only his spiritual yearnings but the very persecution he had experienced had driven him back to the faith. In October he sailed for the United States to take a teaching position at the Malkin Conservatory in Boston.

By the next year failing health had shown him that he could not endure the Massachusetts climate. He moved across the country to the benign airs of Hollywood, where he taught in 1935 and 1936 at USC and then established himself at UCLA. He would remain in Los Angeles until university rules made him retire at seventy. In 1941 he became an American citizen.

Schoenberg lived a peculiar life in Los Angeles. Pupils flocked to him and he taught several important American composers of the next generation, including John Cage. He had the company of a group of European artistic émigrés who were sitting out the war in Los Angeles, Thomas Mann among them. On the other hand, while Schoenberg and Stravinsky lived not far apart in the same city and had friends in common, they apparently never once met—which now and then may well have involved one of them spotting the other and running. Strangest of all, Hollywood luminaries courted Schoenberg. Fashionable pianist/actor/neurotic Oscar Levant took lessons and wrote twelve-tone pieces. Producer Irving Thalberg sounded out this famous émigré about doing a movie score; Schoenberg demanded $50,000 and total control of the music, and that ended that. He became a Ping-Pong buff and played tennis with movie people. More significantly, he struck up a warm and mutually admiring friendship with George Gershwin; when the still young American genius died, Schoenberg wrote a moving tribute.

Despite social and professional successes, however, Schoenberg was never really reconciled to America. It seemed to him a country populated mainly by yahoos, and in any case the prevailing musical power was Stravinsky. All the same, from the American years come some of his finest works, including the Violin Concerto, Piano Concerto, String Quartet no. 4, and *A Survivor from Warsaw*. Performances remained scarce. Leopold Stokowski was among the few major conductors willing to take a chance on Schoenberg, and his insistence on playing the Violin Concerto is said to be why Stokowski was fired as conductor of the Philadelphia Orchestra.

In 1944, with the war ending and after a forced retirement, Schoenberg hoped to return to Germany. He was prevented by health problems and by lack of money: his UCLA pension was small, and he and Gertrud had three young children. In 1944 he applied for a Guggenheim Fellowship to finish the third act of *Moses und Aron*. That organization, which had long given generous stipends mostly to mediocre composers, rejected his application; and thus *Moses und Aron* was never finished. In 1946 Schoenberg had a severe heart attack but was revived by an injection directly into his heart after it had stopped beating. From that experience came the anguished String Trio, which he described with grim humor as "the only piece ever written by a dead man."

His last years were spent as an invalid, though he kept at teaching and composing as best he could. There were some satisfactions: overflowing crowds at a series of Los Angeles concerts in his honor during 1949, his seventy-fifth year; the publication of *Style and Idea*, an important collection of his writings; and being named honorary president of the Israel Academy of Music. He died in Los Angeles on July 13, 1951.

Perhaps I have scared you away from Schoenberg's music. That wasn't my intention, but it would not be fair to claim that it is nice, straightforward stuff. The real problems with Schoenberg's mature music are probably not so much dissonance (gloriously dissonant pieces by Bartók have become popular) or lack of melody (much Beethoven is hardly more melodic than Schoenberg). The problem may be that Schoenberg is *unpredictable:* the music develops constantly, repeating almost nothing literally; the rhythm wanders, only occasionally having a steady pulse; the texture is often densely contrapuntal; and the atonal language erases the usual tonal expectations. The result is that his music, by denying us expectations about the future, forces us into the present. It resembles our psychological perception of time, which is constantly in flux. Most of the music we are familiar with has a clocklike pulse; that is the rhythm of the body. Schoenberg and his followers worked almost entirely in the volatile rhythm of the mind and emotions.

So some listeners feel lost in space with Schoenberg. Like many important artists of the century—among them Joyce, Eliot, Picasso, and Faulkner—Schoenberg does not come to us but demands that we come to him. That gauntlet flung down before the public has been characteristic of Modernism. There is nothing wrong with such a challenge if the rewards are equal to it. For many people the music of Schoenberg has been a transforming experience. For many others he has been at least someone to delve into, now and then. It is certain that he powerfully illuminates some aspects of the human psyche, and some corners of the potential musical universe, that no one else illuminates.

(There is one more thing I should mention about Schoenberg and a good deal of the music that followed him: you can't put it on the stereo as background music. Many listeners make Bach and Beethoven and Debussy into an accompaniment for other activities—little more than Muzak. Schoenberg and other Modernists demand to be heard with full attention. Many find that a fault; I call it a virtue.)

With Schoenberg one should probably start with *Verklärte Nacht* (Transfigured Night), originally for string sextet, later arranged for string orchestra. It is the only work of his to appear regularly on standard programs. The title and inspiration come from a poem by Richard Dehmel, about a woman who confesses to her lover that she bears a child not his; his forgiveness transforms the child and their love. The style is dense late-Romantic chromaticism. That some of *Verklärte Nacht* is featureless and sentimental must be expected from a composer of twenty-five, but there is also music of great beauty in it, and some really inspired moments. Among the latter is the dark surging of the introduction, which is later transformed into a radiant high texture symbolizing the transfiguration of the lovers.

Moving into his atonal-expressionist period, one finds the *Five Pieces for Orchestra* of 1909, among the most astonishing works in history: a Viennese who a decade before could have shaken Brahms's hand has created a new musical world, complete in all its parts, of an impact and strangeness that have hardly diminished to this day. The first movement explodes with a tone of feverish agitation, advancing to a kind of monstrous climax that sinks to an ominous clock-tick. The second movement sustains a quiet, lyrical melancholy amidst a birdlike background chatter. In some ways most revolutionary of all, the third movement is little but pulsating, slowly changing, cryptic chords, a tour de force of coloristic orchestration and near-impressionistic evocation (at one point it was called "Summer Morning by a Lake"). The brief fourth movement alternates frenetic music with lyrical interludes. Finally comes "The Obbligato Recitative," an endless, mysterious melody that progresses through the orchestra within a thick wash of atonal polyphony.

Then move on to *Pierrot lunaire* (Moonstruck Pierrot, 1912), for *Sprechstimme* voice and chamber ensemble, in its own way maybe the most shocking and fascinating piece Schoenberg ever wrote. The Pierrot of the poems is the white-faced clown of old French pantomime and puppet shows. Starting a twentieth-century tradition for voice and mixed chamber ensembles, Schoenberg selected a different palette of instrumental colors for each of the twenty-one settings, using all the players only in a few pieces. The music, always atonal, ranges from arcane canonic writing to unanalyzable stream of consciousness. Schoenberg wrote the pieces with heated inspiration, sometimes two or more in a day.

But for all the historical importance of its medium and technique, what makes *Pierrot* unforgettable is its tone of fantastic and sometimes stifling dream. It is life as a savagely ironic clown-play. The music is entirely equal to the weird imagery of Giraud's poems, which are like Aubrey Beardsley at his most decadent: "The Sick Moon" runs in part, "You somber, deathly stricken moon, / There on the heavens' darkest couch, / Your gaze, so feverishly swollen, / Charms me like a strange enchanted air. // Of insatiable love-pangs / You die, die, by yearning overwhelmed, / You somber, deathly stricken moon!" At the end Schoenberg leaves behind the decadence, achieving a marvelous mystery and yearning with the last whispered line: "O ancient perfume—from fairy-tale times!"

Contrary to many people's idea of Schoenberg, the hyperbolic atmosphere of his expressionist period is by no means his only style. In the twelve-tone works of the twenties and after he attained, in his own terms, a kind of neoclassic balance (though still spiky and challenging compared to the milder Moderns). But the expressionist works are arguably his most compelling. They speak from a malaise that was more than the composer's, a malaise that was spreading inexorably through Germany and Europe. Schoenberg was a prophet of spiritual crisis as much as of new musical paths. For both reasons, he lies at the heart of Modernism.

Of the twelve-tone works, I recommend starting with the most genteel of them, the Piano Concerto (1942). Originally planned as a practical item for Oscar Levant, it grew into one of the finest and most ambitious concertos of the century—and one that flirts with tonality despite its twelve-tone basis. (Schoenberg wrote some tonal pieces in his later years, observing that "there's still plenty of good music to be written in C major.") The Piano Concerto is four movements in one, the first section moderate in tempo with an unmistakable waltzlike lilt, then a frantic second section, tranquil slow movement, and a fast conclusion marked *giocoso,* "humorous." Perhaps because of its original intention, the concerto has some of his most lucid, least contrapuntally loaded music. The Violin Concerto of 1936 is darker, more complex, and richer. In its demonic energy it harks back to the expressionist period, but it also contains some of Schoenberg's most beautiful lyrical writing.

Among the memorable works of Schoenberg's last years is *A Survivor from Warsaw* (1946–47), for male *Sprechstimme* voice and orchestra. Based on stories from the Nazi concentration camps, this work packs an enormous impact into its six minutes of narration and musical illustration. The end, when Jewish prisoners on the way to the gas chamber suddenly break into the prayer *Shema Yisroel,* is one of the most moving passages in the music of our time.

Finally, there is Schoenberg's unfinished opera *Moses und Aron,* the work that was closest to his heart in its search for faith and in its metaphorical reflection of his own life. Schoenberg's libretto is an interpretation of the biblical story of Moses, filled with a transcendent vision of God but unable to articulate it to his people, and his brother, Aron, who glibly waters down Moses' inspiration to sell it to the crowd. Throughout, Moses speaks in guttural, groping *Sprechstimme* while Aron's honey-tongued tenor soars above. It is the primeval struggle between the visionary and the pragmatic, the idealistic and the commercial, the internal spiritual quest and the external institution. (Among the allegories of the work is that the musical symbol for God is the BACH motive: B♭-A-C-B.)

Clearly, Schoenberg identified with Moses, whose unbending devotion to truth makes it impossible for him to communicate with the multitudes, but who nonetheless is destined to lead his people to the promised land. But the opera goes far beyond the composer's situation in its examination of the dilemmas of the spiritual life. *Moses und Aron* is one of the great philosophical dialectics of the stage, musical or otherwise.

Often the work is static in action, as much oratorio as opera. The most musically striking parts are the choruses, beginning with the opening burning bush scene in which the voice of God is portrayed in an uncanny texture of floating, many-stranded vocal lines and simultaneous *Sprechstimme*. In deliberately shocking contrast to the rest is the Golden Calf scene, with its orgies and naked virgins and human sacrifices and deliciously lurid orchestral accompaniment. Some have argued that even though Schoenberg never composed music for the brief third act, the opera is better as it is, ending with Moses' despairing cry, "O Word! Thou Word that I cannot speak!"

Like much Schoenberg, *Moses und Aron* is not for everyone. But a few outstanding performances (notably the one recorded by George Solti and the Chicago Symphony) have shown that the work can achieve at least a measure of the kind of broad communication of which Schoenberg/Moses despaired in the opera itself.

Moses und Aron is perhaps the essential work in coming to terms with this troubling genius. Schoenberg was an artist accused of anarchy and destruction who longed for faith and wholeness. It has been observed that both *Die Jakobsleiter* and *Moses und Aron,* his main testaments of religious faith, break off before the point of fulfillment, of union with God. A similar destiny has befallen Schoenberg's other article of faith, his other attempt to meet the threat of chaos: the twelve-tone method, which has not fulfilled its promise of being a universal musical language for the twentieth century. There are profound questions, profound metaphors and allegories in these struggles for salvation. The dilemmas do not make Schoenberg any less important and fascinating, but rather more so. I say again: he is at the heart of Modernism.

IGOR STRAVINSKY

When Igor Stravinsky died in 1971, it was said that for the first time since the death of Guillaume de Machaut in 1377, the West was without a great composer. Perhaps that overstates the case, but there is no doubt that with Stravinsky's passing something significant came to an end: the generation of Modernists who came of age when the Romantic tradition was still alive, and who from that foundation revolutionized the art of music. The generations who followed Stravinsky founded their revolutions *on* revolution, and nearly broke the thread of Western musical tradition.

Stravinsky's creative path was winding and to many observers puzzling. Having begun with a series of audacious and Dionysian works, in mid-life he declared his allegiance to Apollo and became leader of the conservative camp of Modernism. Then in the last decades of his long career he threw the musical world into an uproar by taking up serialism, which had been the method and creed of his enemies.

Only later, after his death, could we begin to understand what lay under Stravinsky's changing masks. From the beginning, he was a classicist at heart. His works were created with superb precision and poise, whether he was shaping the wild stamping and howling of *Le Sacre du printemps,* the hard edges of his neoclassic music, or the severe polyphony of the late serial works. And one more thing unites all his music: like Debussy but even more so, Stravinsky was a man drunk on the colors and rhythms and architectures of sound. After his youth he forswore the literary emotions the Romantics attached to music because he no longer needed them; the music alone was fascination and exhilaration enough.

In each of his disguises, Stravinsky changed the history of his art. Many composers since have aspired to, and none have achieved, his rhythmic imagination, his genius with the orchestra, his gift for making history his own. He is the ubiquitous figure in the music of our century. Even the exotic swells and angles of his face, captured in photographs and in drawings by Picasso, became a Modernist icon.

He was born Igor Feodorovich Stravinsky on June 17, 1882, in the summer resort of Oranienbaum, near the Russian musical capital of St. Petersburg. Igor was the third of four sons of Feodor Stravinsky, a leading bass of the Imperial Opera. Receiving piano lessons in his childhood, the boy also soaked up opera and the other pleasures of a musical family. But his parents were against his taking up a musical career and sent him to law school in St. Petersburg. Then in 1902 he met Nicolai Rimsky-Korsakov, the dean of Russian composers and master of orchestration in the grand style. After looking over some of the youth's piano pieces, Rimsky-Korsakov advised him to study music privately, but not to give up law. Instead, Stravinsky left school to devote himself to composing. In 1906, as he prepared himself for a musical career, he married his cousin Catherine Nossenko; they would have four children.

Starting in 1903, Stravinsky studied intensively with Rimsky-Korsakov. In 1908 he composed the short, brilliant *Feu d'artifice* (Fireworks) both to celebrate the wedding of his teacher's daughter and to show off what he had learned about the orchestra. He mailed the piece to Rimsky-Korsakov and awaited a response; instead, the package came back unopened with the note, "Returned due to death of recipient." Heartbroken, Stravinsky composed a funeral dirge. He would never have another teacher. Besides, in two years he would be one of the most celebrated composers alive.

A St. Petersburg concert of 1909 featured his *Feu d'artifice* and *Scherzo fantastique*. Among the audience happened to be Sergei Diaghilev, celebrated promoter of everything new in the arts. Diaghilev was organizing a troupe with which he intended to revivify the dance in his country, the Ballets Russes. He hired Stravinsky to orchestrate a couple of Chopin pieces for a production. When that went well, Stravinsky received a commission for an extended work called *L'Oiseau de feu* (The Firebird).

He worked on the score for a year. During rehearsals for the premiere in Paris, Diaghilev pointed out the twenty-eight-year-old composer to one of his dancers and said, "Keep an eye on him—he's about to be famous." That production of the Ballets Russes turned out to be an assemblage of legends made or in the making: Stravinsky's brilliant music in the Rimsky-Korsakov tradition (but with

Two Modernist icons: Stravinsky as drawn by his friend Picasso.

a mixture of impressionist influence and his own burgeoning musical personality), the choreography of Fokine, the dancing of Madame Fokine and Karsavina, and the designs of Bakst. The premiere was a sensation; overnight, Stravinsky secured a place in the musical world.

Immediately Diaghilev pressed his composer to come up with something even more spectacular for the next year's Paris season of the Ballets Russes. Stravinsky was already thinking about it, as he later recalled: "One day, when I was finishing the last pages of *L'Oiseau de feu* in St. Petersburg, I had a fleeting vision . . . I saw in imagination a solemn pagan rite: sage elders, seated in a circle, watched a young girl dance herself to death. They were sacrificing her to propitiate the god of spring." Diaghilev shared Stravinsky's excitement about this story as an outline for a ballet. But instead of plunging right into it, Stravinsky decided to warm up with a programmatic piece for orchestra with piano: "In composing the music, I had in mind a distinct picture of a puppet, suddenly endowed with life, exasperating the patience of the orchestra with diabolical cascades of [arpeggios]. The orchestra in turn retaliates with menacing trumpet-blasts. . . . Having finished this bizarre piece, I struggled for hours to find a title which would express in a word the character of my music. . . . One day I leapt for joy. I had indeed found my title—*Petrushka,* the immortal and unhappy hero of every fair in all countries."

Finding Diaghilev agreeable to this idea as well, Stravinsky set to work turning it into a ballet. The score, with its surging fair scenes and childlike radiance and shadowing evil, was completed in May 1911. Less than three weeks later, *Petrushka,* one of the finest and most perfect ballets of all time, premiered in Paris, with choreography by Massine and the great Nijinsky in the title role. (All that survives of Nijinsky's performance are a few photographs of him in costume, but they are unforgettable.) Stravinsky had outdone himself; the success of *Petrushka* was even greater than that of *The Firebird.* Given the novelty of the music, there was more than a little scandal as well. Later, Stravinsky would say that the success of this work, whose unprecedented musical language had come entirely from his intuition, gave him a confidence in his ear that never left him. Now he was ready to return to his vision of the girl dancing herself to death in a circle of elders.

This ballet was called *Le Sacre du printemps* (The Rite of Spring). Stravinsky composed it knowing exactly how extraordinary were its barbaric colors and ferocious dynamism. In the door of the closet-sized room in Clarens, Switzerland, where he wrote much of it at an upright piano, he carved a proclamation: "Here I am composing *Le Sacre du printemps*. Igor Stravinsky." (The lady downstairs was not impressed; "Monsieur Stravinsky plays only wrong notes," she huffed.) The last section, the "Sacrificial Dance," he worked out at the piano but for some time could not figure out how to write down. No music had ever used this kind of constantly shifting accents and rhythmic patterns. He solved the problem by changing the time signatures in nearly every measure; this became a stylistic signature of his music.

During the time he worked on it, *Le Sacre* seemed to come out of his heart and soul in a way nothing had before. To a friend he wrote: "I have penetrated the secret of the rhythm of spring." And in an article written at the time of the premiere (an article he later disowned, perhaps because it revealed too much of himself), he described the work in visionary words: "I wished to express the sublime uprising of Nature renewing herself—the whole pantheistic uprising of the universal harvest . . . the obscure and immense sensation of which all things are conscious when Nature renews its forms; it is the vague and profound uneasiness of a universal puberty. Even in my orchestration and my melodic development I have sought to define it . . . I have tried to express in [the] Prelude the fear of nature before the arising of beauty, a sacred terror at the midday sun, a sort of pagan cry. The musical material itself swells, enlarges, expands. Each instrument is like a bud which grows on the bark of an aged tree." He ended by calling *Le Sacre* "this work of faith." One finds here a sort of religious ecstasy, the rarest and most profound kind of artistic creation.

Diaghilev had entrusted the choreography to Nijinsky, who only recently had begun directing ballets. The complex rhythms of the music, pounded out on piano by Stravinsky, bewildered the inexperienced choreographer, so Nijinsky largely ignored the rhythm in arranging the primitive tableaus he had imagined. Some steps involved the dancers' leaping high in the air and coming down on their heels with a bone-shaking crash. Pierre Monteux meticulously taught the score to the orchestra through some forty hours of rehearsal. A dress rehearsal, with a number of invited observers, went peacefully enough. Nothing prepared Stravinsky for what would happen at the Paris premiere in the Théâtre des Champs-Élysées on May 29, 1913.

The opening solo in the bassoon's highest register began, so high some musicians could not identify the instrument. Today, as one of the most familiar beginnings in all music, it still sounds uncanny, like some moaning of the earth. That first time, how indescribably strange it must have been. Writer Carl Van Vechten, who was present, described the next moments:

A certain part of the audience, thrilled by what it considered to be a blasphemous attempt to destroy music as an art, and swept away with wrath, began very soon after the rise of the curtain to whistle, to make catcalls, and to offer audible suggestions as to how the performance should proceed. Others of us bellowed defiance. The orchestra played on unheard, except occasionally when a slight lull occurred. The figures on the stage danced in time to music that they had to imagine they heard, and beautifully out of rhythm with the uproar in the auditorium . . . [A] young man occupied the place behind me. He stood up during the course of the ballet to enable himself to see more clearly. The intense excitement under which he was laboring, thanks to the potent force of the music, betrayed itself presently when he began to beat rhythmically on the top of my head with his fists. My emotion was so great that I did not feel the blows for some time.

Around the hall, fistfights broke out. The Princesse de Pourtalès stood grandly in her box and cried into the fray, "I am sixty years old, but this is the first time anyone has dared to make a fool of me!" Another well-dressed lady was seen to spit in the face of a demonstrator. Debussy, pale and shaken, begged the people around him to be quiet; nearby, Ravel was shouting, "Genius! Genius!" The musicians kept going despite the pandemonium in the hall and a blizzard of programs pelting into the orchestra pit. Conductor Monteux, Stravinsky would recall, "stood there apparently impervious and as nerveless as a crocodile."

The horrified composer left his seat soon after the shouting began. Slipping backstage, he found Diaghilev flicking the house lights in a futile attempt to calm things down, while Nijinsky stood on a chair shouting numerical cues to his dancers, who could not hear the orchestra. Stravinsky spent the rest of the performance holding on to Nijinsky's coattails and listening to him scream, "Sixteen! Seventeen! Eighteen!" and so on. That is what happened at the birth of Stravinsky's child of ecstasy, his work of faith.

Legend has Diaghilev after the performance sobbing in the Bois de Boulogne. What actually happened, according to Stravinsky, was that he, Diaghilev, and Nijinsky retired to a restaurant, where "we were excited, angry, disgusted, and happy . . . Diaghilev's only comment was: 'Exactly what I wanted.' . . . No one could have been quicker to understand the publicity value."

But despite the succès de scandale, something had gone out of Stravinsky. No doubt it is too dramatic to say that the change happened that night (the extraordinary *Les Noces* was to come), but it began to happen at that time. He would never again write anything like *Le Sacre du printemps,* neither in style nor in audacity. There would be no more testaments of faith so close to his heart; later testaments would be more orthodox religious works such as the *Symphony of Psalms.* For the rest of his long life, Stravinsky would assume a series of disguises, basing his music as much on historical models as his own imagination. These disguises would turn out to be marvelous indeed, some of the finest music of our own or any other time. But never again would he write something as unprecedented and overwhelming as *Le Sacre.* He had outdone himself for the last time.

That evening in the spring of 1913 was the symbolic beginning, with a bang, of twentieth-century music. In fact, Schoenberg's *Pierrot lunaire* had made an equally important beginning the year before in Berlin. But Schoenberg did not have the glamour of the Ballets Russes backing up his revolution, and Paris in those years was the epicenter of the new in the arts. So in history books if only partly in reality, *Le Sacre* begins musical Modernism. It shook the Western tradition to its foundations; it made Stravinsky the champion of the avant-garde and the bête noire of traditionalists. He was seen as the musical counterpart of his friend Picasso, the Cubist and Primitivist. Just under a year following its tumultuous premiere, after the first concert performance of *Le Sacre,* Stravinsky was paraded through the streets of Paris on the shoulders of a cheering crowd. Around the world, the same pattern was enacted: violent rejection at the early hearings, soon followed by enthusiasm. By the thirties, the work was famous—and safe—enough to accompany animated dinosaurs in Walt Disney's *Fantasia* (Stravinsky was outraged but helpless to stop it).

But even as he was being anointed leader of the revolution, Stravinsky was leaving it behind. In the works of the next years he searched for new directions, all involving some kind of retrenchment. The masterpiece of the mid teens is the choral work *Les Noces* (The Wedding, 1913–17), in its fierce concentration nearly on the level of *Le Sacre* in originality and impact. But for *Les Noces*, after experiments with various kinds of ensembles, he cut the accompaniment down to a sinewy and monochrome collection of four pianos and percussion. This reduction, concentration, and boiling down continued into World War I. The war made the splashy ballet productions of the past impossible in any case. Stravinsky responded by producing a practical little number: a fable of a soldier, his violin, and the devil, for dancers, reciter, and a few instruments—the oddly haunting *L'Histoire du soldat* (The Soldier's Tale, 1918).

Stravinsky spent the war in Switzerland, intending to return home to Russia when hostilities ended. When the Russian Revolution broke out in 1917, he was enthusiastic at first, hoping for a more liberal government. But things steadily deteriorated; finally the Communists confiscated his Russian property, plunging Stravinsky and his family into financial miseries that plagued them for years. Further insults would come from his homeland: Russia refused to honor international copyright laws and kept the royalties from Stravinsky's early ballets; yet the government also vilified him as a bourgeois Western artist and virtually banned performances in Russia. Meanwhile, the war drove Diaghilev's Ballets Russes into a decline from which it would never quite emerge, and the irreplaceable Nijinsky slipped into insanity. On top of it all, Diaghilev could never forgive Stravinsky for writing music for anyone else. The two men continued to work together, but under great strain, until the impresario's death in 1929.

Still, Stravinsky returned to the Ballets Russes immediately after the war, fulfilling Diaghilev's commission to arrange some pieces by the eighteenth-century composer Pergolesi. The result, *Pulcinella*, is far more than an arrangement; using Pergolesi's melodies virtually unchanged, Stravinsky nonetheless made them his own. He wrote that with *L'Histoire du soldat* he had made "the final break with the Russian orchestral school in which I had been fostered." Now with *Pulcinella* he began to construct a new orchestral sound, one recalling the eighteenth century but turning the old ensemble into something lean and glowing. With this score he rediscovered the genres and sounds of the past and found ways to turn them to his own purposes.

His new aesthetic of clarity, economy, restraint, and "pure" music, inflected by the sounds and techniques of both Modernism and earlier periods, came to be called *neoclassicism*. By no means was it unique to Stravinsky; many artists and composers of the time rejected the emotionalism and expansiveness of the Romantics. One of the earliest examples in music is Prokofiev's *Classical Symphony* of 1917. In the twenties even Schoenberg and his followers returned to the old forms, writing suites with minuets and such. Though Stravinsky's neoclassicism involved a more conservative approach than Schoenberg's, it parallels the Austrian master's development of the twelve-tone method. Both composers rationalized their music to a greater or lesser degree, pulling back from the threat of chaos that had shadowed their intuitive explorations of the previous decade.

By 1923, the year of the chilly but still beautiful, harmonically spicy but still tonal Octet for Winds, Stravinsky's neoclassicism was fully formed. With various permutations, it would remain his style into the 1950s. Along with that style came a categorical rejection of the Romantic aesthetic that had once been his. "I consider," he wrote in his 1936 *Chronicles of My Life*, "that music is, by its very nature, essentially powerless to *express* anything at all, whether a feeling, an attitude of mind, a psychological mood, a phenomenon of nature." Later, as part of an anti-Wagnerian tirade, he declared, "It is high time to put an end, once and for all, to this unseemly and sacrilegious conception of art as religion and the theatre as a temple." Stravinsky thus kicked the artist off his Romantic throne and abjured wild Dionysus in order to embrace the modest and serene Apollo—a symbol of which is his 1928 ballet *Apollon Musagète* (Apollo, Leader of the Muses).

For the rest of his life, Stravinsky would pursue a vision of purity and abstraction. "My music . . . is not free from dryness," he admitted. "But that is the price of precision." That crystalline precision shaped the masterpieces of his neoclassic years, among them the Concerto for Piano and Wind Instruments (1923–24), the opera-oratorio *Oedipus Rex* (1927), the *Symphony of Psalms* (1930), and the Symphony in Three Movements (1942–45). In that period he also began to appear as conductor and pianist in his own works.

Starting in the 1920s, his music was a prime inspiration for French composers such as Milhaud and Poulenc, and for pedagogue Nadia Boulanger, who inculcated the gospel of neoclassicism in young American composers including Aaron Copland. Yet in those years Stravinsky's neoclassic music was widely denounced by critics, who declared that he had lost the fire and inspiration of his early ballets. It is amazing now to read the contempt once vented on his middle-period masterpieces: of *L'Histoire du soldat* and *Pulcinella* a critic wrote in the forties, "Poor, half-starved things that they were, they have scarcely had the energy to last twenty years." Of *Les Noces:* "Its lack of color palls, its insistent rhythms numb rather than excite." Of *Apollo:* "an inane group of musical statuary." The young Pierre Boulez, while declaring Schoenberg dead, also booed Stravinsky's new works in concerts.

Much of the world, having forgiven Stravinsky for *Le Sacre du printemps,* refused to forgive him for not producing more of the same, for being so un-Modern as to write music of audience-pleasing charm and grace (for all the dryness). So even while his neoclassic style was an inspiration for a good deal of music by other composers, it was also accompanied by choruses of condemnation.

His personal life had changed dramatically since 1920, when he had taken up residence in Paris, eventually gaining French citizenship. A daughter had died of tuberculosis, followed in 1939 by his wife, Catherine. Meanwhile, the French had always treated him as an outsider and were among the most relentless in condemning his new works. In 1939, Stravinsky fled both the war and his critics for the pleasanter climes of Hollywood, California. With him came his mistress of over fifteen years, painter Vera de Bossett. He and Vera married in Bedford, Massachusetts, in 1940. They would have a marvelous partnership.

His relations with America had deepened since his first tour of

1925. Conductor Serge Koussevitzky, long a Stravinsky champion, had commissioned the *Symphony of Psalms* (1930) for the Boston Symphony. Visits of the following decade had revealed to Stravinsky that he had many admirers in America, some of them with handsome bank accounts with which to commission new works. After settling in Hollywood, he joined more or less the same colony of expatriate European artists that Schoenberg was part of (though, as mentioned previously, for over ten years they somehow managed to miss running into each other). In 1939 and 1940 Stravinsky gave the prestigious Norton lectures at Harvard; the result was collected into the book *Poetics of Music*. In 1945 he became an American citizen.

Stravinsky remained fruitful in his new country, turning out works beginning with the Symphony in C, written for the fiftieth anniversary of the Chicago Symphony. Like Schoenberg, he flirted with the idea of doing film music, but nothing quite came of it. Like many good Americans he was willing to prostitute his art a little, now and then, for an appropriate sum. Among the more notorious rent-paying items is the 1942 *Circus Polka*, written for the terpsichorean efforts of Barnum & Bailey elephants.

The climax of his neoclassic period was reached in 1951, with the completion of his only full-scale opera, *The Rake's Progress*, based on a tantalizingly weird Hogarthian libretto by W. H. Auden and Chester Kallman. (There had been several earlier short and/or sort-of operas—*The Nightingale, Renard, Mavra, Oedipus Rex*.) For this story of Tom Rakewell, who makes a pact with the devil and pursues a life of singularly unsatisfying debauchery, Stravinsky returned to the structure and some of the sound of Mozartean opera. It was as if Wagner and late Verdi had never existed; the *Rake* has separate arias, choruses, and the like, even recitatives accompanied by harpsichord. But it is the spirit of Mozart seen through a Stravinskian prism: less interest in emotion and psychology than in sonority, spectacle, and lyrical melody.

Then came the historic turn to serialism. As I detail in the Schoenberg section, Stravinsky's conversion scattered the warring camps of atonality and neoclassicism and helped pave the way for the triumph of the post-Webern style. For reasons technical, aesthetic, and personal, Stravinsky decided that the future of music lay in counting to twelve. By that time, his great rival was dead. With the *Rake,* perhaps Stravinsky felt his neoclassic vein was mined out, after thirty years of working it. In the late forties he had acquired an amanuensis, a young man named Robert Craft, who was an enthusiast of serial music. Craft introduced his employer to Webern's work, at that time enjoying an enormous vogue among European composers. Serial ideas began to show up in sections of Stravinsky pieces, the choral *Canticum Sacrum* of 1954 and the ballet *Agon,* written for his longtime collaborator choreographer George Balanchine. Finally came the largest of the late religious works for voices, *Threni* (1958), composed entirely in serial technique and, with its sparse instrumental textures and chains of vocal canons, among his most austere works.

His last years were full of honors and the satisfaction of having lived well into his legend. The celebrated in every field were his companions; Pope John XXIII greeted Stravinsky like an old friend and sat him down to gossip about what all the artists were up to. Stravinsky continued to perform and record his music. In 1962 he finally returned to Russia, where he was moved by the acclaim he received everywhere in the homeland that had denounced him for so long. Premier Khrushchev received him at the Kremlin.

In 1968, Stravinsky was shown the original score of *Le Sacre du printemps,* which he had not seen for nearly fifty years. Producing a pen, he wrote a bitter note at the end of the score about the riot at the premiere:

> May whoever listens to this music never experience the mockery to which it was subjected and of which I was the witness in the Théâtre des Champs-Élysées, Paris, Spring 1913.

It still hurt.

With Craft he sat for interviews, a very old master airing for history his ideas, his memories, his views of various music, his faltering creativity, his declining health and extravagant hypochondria, the dynamics of his creative life, his profound and lifelong love of strong drink.. That figure of the old master—puckish, observant, wise, charming, erudite, sometimes cantankerous, sometimes drunk, and always fascinating—is the Stravinsky the world will always know. He died in New York on April 6, 1971. As he had asked, he was buried in the Russian section of the island cemetery of San Michele in Venice, near the grave of Sergei Diaghilev.

A musician once recalled that the first piece by Stravinsky he ever heard was the *Symphony of Psalms,* and he realized with the first notes that the composer was a genius. The symphony begins with an E minor chord, laid out absolutely against the traditional rules, with a wide gap between low and high notes, and in an orchestra without violins or violas. As so often in Stravinsky, this single sonority has an impact more striking than whole melodies by some composers. One thinks also of the unforgettable bassoon solo that opens *Le Sacre,* the deliciously sour horn chords at the beginning of the Concerto for Piano and Winds, the weird, pealing clarinets in the *Symphonies of Wind Instruments.*

To understand Stravinsky's achievement with instrumentation, contemplate this fact: the orchestra of *Le Sacre du printemps* has about the same makeup as that of Wagner's *Ring,* and is mostly made up of the same collection of instruments as in a Mozart symphony. Individually and collectively, Stravinsky reshaped the personalities of orchestral instruments. Where the strings had always been the most lyrical and voicelike section, in *Le Sacre* and elsewhere he could make strings into percussion instruments of astonishing rhythmic force. Where French horns had been mostly background drones in the Classical orchestra and, equipped with valves, the noble stentorian voices of the Wagnerian and Brahmsian style, in *Le Sacre* the horns are set to howling like moose in heat. Even when Stravinsky imitated the Classical sound, as in *Pulcinella,* his orchestra has a resonance and a glow that almost make Mozart seem horse-and-buggy. (When we compare the *musical* ideas, mind you, it's a different horse and buggy.)

Yet perhaps the most striking thing of all about Stravinsky is his rhythmic style. Its basis is what has been called the *unit pulse*—a chugging pulsation (usually at the eighth- or sixteenth-note level) that is inflected by continually shifting accents and/or metric groupings. The most familiar example of the unit pulse is the ''Dance of the Adolescents'' section near the beginning of *Le Sacre,* built around the strings' pounding polytonal chords in eighth notes, their irregular accents reinforced by savage yawps in the horns. At times Stravinsky superimposes differing inflections of the unit pulse, a steady foundation pattern and a shifting pattern above it. At other times, as in the breathtaking cadenza of the Piano Concerto, short measures of three to eight sixteenths race by, each measure in a different meter, things further complicated by syncopated accents going against the metric pattern. It is not surprising that in his early neoclassic years, when he looked around for ideas in the past and present, Stravinsky became fascinated by ragtime and jazz. He produced some pieces he called ragtime, and ragging syncopations (see Glossary) are a prime feature of the Piano Concerto. Meanwhile, the Dixieland jazz combo was a model for the small ensemble of contrasting instruments in *L'Histoire du soldat*. He remained a jazz enthusiast to the end of his life.

Stravinsky's harmonic ideas underwent a steady evolution through his career, from the Debussy-influenced style of *The Firebird* to the atonal harmony of the last works. *Petrushka* pioneered in the systematic use of polytonality, with its characteristic juxtaposition of C major and F-sharp major; the famous "Petrushka chord" is a combination of those triads. In *Le Sacre,* Stravinsky explored *polychords*—superimposed triads. In the neoclassic works both polytonality and polychords are used in subtle ways to produce effects that often sound like familiar harmonies slightly skewed. For most of his career, Stravinsky was a tonal composer; his novelties were based on the old Western concepts of chord and key. Even in the late serial works he looked for patterns that would create tonal implications.

In his approach to form, Stravinsky moved from the episodic, ad hoc structures of the early ballets to a neoclassic interest in sonata form and other traditional models. Even then, he put pieces together in a personal way some have called *block form:* the formal units are arranged in discrete blocks that he sometimes shoves together without transition. In Mozart, such a sudden shift of direction is a special effect; in Stravinsky it is the norm, the music progressing in almost cubistic sections starkly juxtaposed.

His melodic style is as characteristic as the other elements, though it also changed over the years. Earlier he tended to use aphoristic, folklike themes; part of the success of *Le Sacre* has been the almost primitive directness and obsessiveness of its little tunes, which resemble those of Russian folk music. In his neoclassic period he wrote longer, more lyrical themes in deliberate imitation of

Baroque, Classical, and even Romantic models. As his interest in melody grew, so did his interest in counterpoint; his serialism resulted as much as anything from a desire to explore abstract polyphonic structures.

The fundamentals of Western music are melody, harmony, rhythm, counterpoint, timbre (that is, tone color), and form. In all those dimensions, Stravinsky opened up territory that others have been exploring ever since. No less than Schoenberg is Stravinsky at the heart of Modernism. But where Schoenberg's atonal revolution was rationalized, cabalistic, and controversial, Stravinsky's innovations (most of them intuitive rather than theoretical) were of broad practical value. In examining some of his pieces, we will find not only magnificent music, but some of the most significant contributions to the art of music since those of Haydn, 150 years before.

I suggest getting to know Stravinsky's work more or less in chronological order, tracing his path in all its turns. *The Firebird* is the first of the major ballets; a suite drawn from it may be the most popular Stravinsky piece in the repertoire. The story follows a Russian fairy tale decked out with a magic Firebird, a disappearing castle, golden fruit, an evil magician to imprison beautiful maidens, a hero to rescue the maidens and take one for his bride. The music is voluptuous in the Russian manner, clearly an offspring of Rimsky-Korsakov, but the personality of Stravinsky dominates from the first mysterious whisperings in the basses. Most spectacular of all, and most prophetic of the composer's future, is the "Dance of Kastchei," with its booming tuba and dazzling orchestral roulades.

Petrushka creates a very different world than the previous ballet. It is the story of the puppet Petrushka, a fixture of Russian fairs, who is always in love with the Ballerina, always rebuffed, always abused by the Moor. Here they come to life and Petrushka suffers in reality before the Moor kills him and he becomes a puppet again. The music represents the sounds of a Russian fair, painted with a brush as sure-handed as the Impressionists': the bustling throngs, the accordions (the whole orchestra becomes a superaccordion), the hurdy-gurdy with a broken note, the drunks, the dancing bears, and through it all the wretched Petrushka being chided in squalling outbursts of trumpets. Even the rhythms seem to reflect the jerky motions of puppets. But if this work were only a tour de force of exotic ideas and vibrant orchestral sounds, *Petrushka* would simply be another *Firebird*. I suspect that its enduring fascination lies in its tone: Stravinsky captures the strangeness of stories of dolls imbued with life; he sustains a tone of mingled ingenuousness and malevolence, a child's world suffused with adult evil.

Then came *Le Sacre du printemps,* one of the few revolutionary works in history that has never lost its capacity to shock. Here Stravinsky conjures up the inspiration of the work, his vision of pagan Russia and its rituals. We hear preparatory ceremonies called "The Adoration of the Earth"—"Games of Rival Tribes," "Ritual of the Ancestors," and so on—and then the climactic sacrifice, the virgin who dances herself to death. The piece ends with a crash, representing the great cracking of river ice that from time immemorial has announced to Russians the advent of spring.

In its stamping strings and screaming horns, its birdlike flute cries and rampaging percussion, *Le Sacre* sounds as implacable as thunder. There is a quality of nature and the old pitiless nature cults, the feel of the cave paintings. And as with all those things, there is a savage grandeur and beauty in *Le Sacre*. The secret of this work is that for all its willful primitiveness, it is among the most sophisticated of creations. There has never been a more original and ingenious display of orchestral virtuosity—page after page of unprecedented colors and overwhelming effects—yet all is consummate, nothing tentative or experimental. As with Picasso's response to African masks in the same years, this is supreme artistic mastery dedicated to an evocation of the primitive.

Then move on to *Les Noces* (The Wedding, 1914–17), for chorus, soloists, four pianos, and percussion. Here Stravinsky uses a Russian peasant wedding as a canvas for his most concentrated exploration of rhythm. The story is sketchy, the libretto mostly repetitive chants ("Combing her tresses,/her bright golden tresses,/combing her tresses . . ." and on and on), the accompaniment monochrome, the melodic material mostly small cells repeated with minuscule variations. Much of the time the voices are nearly percussion instruments, with hypnotic chanting and grunting and whooping. After the bridegroom's incantatory song of love to his new bride, the work ends with bell-like strokes on the four pianos. (*Les Noces* is often quite comical, by the way, especially when the drinking begins at the wedding feast.) Recordings, good as some are, inevitably mute the visceral impact of this work. To appreciate its power, one needs a good live performance; then it sounds like some fantastic tribal music of a land that never existed. *Les Noces* is the last of Stravinsky's transcendent feats of imagination. After it come gentler pleasures.

L'Histoire du soldat (The Soldier's Tale, 1918), besides being one of his best-known pieces, is also a transition toward neoclassicism. It was billed as "a narrative ballet in five scenes, to be read, played, and danced." The story, a Russian folk tale, concerns a soldier who returns from war with a violin, which is his soul; he gives it to the devil in return for a book that promises to answer any question. As usual in such transactions, the devil gets his due. The narrator recites the story and dancers pantomime it. The music, scored for a heterogeneous collection of seven instruments, includes Stravinskian versions of various familiar genres—chorales, a march, a ragtime, and the like. Above I describe *L'Histoire* as oddly haunting. Stravinsky is often haunting, but what is odd is how he manages to achieve that in a style so cool, desiccated, and sardonic. There is a kind of studied meanness in his little chorales and marches, that may be off-putting at first but in the long run contributes to the fascination of this miniature masterpiece: it could have been merely quaint, but he makes it unsettling and memorable.

The Octet for Wind Instruments of 1923 is Stravinsky's first full-fledged neoclassic work and one of his most genteel. Here everything is sparkling and good-humored from the coy trills of the opening, through the rocketing bassoons of the second movement theme and variations, to the wry march of the finale. From now on in his music we find few Russian themes or sounds; he and his music have become cosmopolitan Parisians.

A strangely neglected work in the Stravinsky canon is the Concerto for Piano and Wind Instruments of 1923–24. Despite its solemn introduction, the outer movements feature some of his jazziest inspirations, the piano sounding like a nimble offspring of harpsichord music and Scott Joplin. In contrast, the slow movement is a broad expanse of rich harmonies and soulful melodies.

Perhaps the greatest work of his neoclassic period, and the peak of his religious music as well, is the *Symphony of Psalms* for chorus and orchestra, written in 1930 for the fiftieth anniversary of the Boston Symphony. The text of the three movements is Psalms in

Latin. (Stravinsky liked Latin because it is a dead language, thus abstract and formal.) For the orchestra, Stravinsky omitted some of the warmer instruments—violins, violas, and clarinets. He wanted a music of severity and devotion, and he got it. The first movement builds slowly to a fine choral climax, the second has an extended orchestral fugue leading to a choral fugue. The last movement begins and ends slowly, with a muscular allegro in between. The long coda, one of the most unforgettable of Stravinsky's time-suspending expanses, slows finally to a stretch of sublime serenity, capping a work of faith that hardly seems possible in a century of anxiety, violence, irony, and despair.

While the *Symphony of Psalms* is an outpouring of religious sentiment, the *Symphony in Three Movements* is dominated by images of World War II that Stravinsky saw in films and newsreels. (He admitted this connection despite his enmity toward "expression" and program music.) This symphony begins with a dramatic upward sweep, introducing a first movement of relentless rhythmic energy and dark instrumental colors; the last movement is equally kinetic. In between comes music originally sketched for the film *The Song of Bernadette;* it is intriguing to imagine how this music of quiet dancing grace would have worked for the sequence showing the girl's vision of the Virgin Mary.

Finally, I suggest the masterpiece of Stravinsky's old age, *Agon,* written for George Balanchine's New York City Ballet and completed in 1957, near the composer's seventy-fifth birthday. It was a ballet for twelve dancers with no plot at all, entirely abstract, its title a Greek word for contest. *Agon* is a nexus between Stravinsky's past and future, beginning with elegant brass fanfares in his neoclassic mode, going on to some of his finest dances including an ethereal quasi-seventeenth-century galliard, with striking textures of flutes, bass harmonics, harp, and mandolin. The piece becomes steadily more chromatic until it reaches serialism, then returns to the opening tonal fanfares. One would have to go back to Verdi, and before him Monteverdi, to find a composer of such advanced age writing music so vital and forward-looking. Stravinsky never lost his searching spirit, his goading dissatisfaction, his youth. It is the youthfulness of *Agon* that is so astonishing and so moving. Some people (I am one of them) feel that after *Le Sacre du printemps, Agon* may be his greatest creation.

I could mention a good deal more, of roughly equal value—*The Rake's Progress*, the Violin Concerto, *Oedipus Rex* among them. By a long shot, Stravinsky produced more first-rate works than any other composer of this century. And as I said, his influence is as incalculable as that of Haydn.

To some extent, Brahms had been the last glorious gasp of both the Classical and Romantic traditions in their original shapes and genres. By the time Brahms died and Stravinsky was beginning his career, Western classical music was becoming old and tired. With his first ballets, Stravinsky gave his tradition a shot in the arm that helped revivify it for fifty years—in other words, as long as he lived. From him, composers of this century learned many of their best lessons. We have had no such teachers since.

BÉLA

BARTÓK

Almost inaudibly, a melody begins in violins, a haunting and lonely sound like the sighing of distant wind. The melody floats, turning on itself, drifting free as the wind and at the same time certain and purposeful. As it sinks back to its opening note, another group of strings picks up the melody, and now two voices move together in a strange, wandering counterpoint.

That is the beginning of *Music for Strings, Percussion, and Celesta*, an unbridled masterpiece by a repressed and tragic man, Béla Bartók.

The innocuous title hardly suggests the expressive breadth of this work for two antiphonal groups of strings. It is a score of strange beauties, wild joy, demonic fury, mystery, awe, and final affirmation. Throughout, one hears an unmistakable voice, passionately humanistic, at once Hungarian and universal. Though some who knew him considered him a saint, Bartók was not religious; his faith lay in nature and humanity. Inevitably, the torturous course of this century did not make his life or his work any easier.

He would die in America, like his peers Schoenberg and Stravinsky, but before them, and before the world had quite understood his stature. He had neither their notoriety nor their gift for trailblazing. He is a linking figure between Schoenberg's atonal and Stravinsky's neoclassic schools. While they invented, he listened and learned and composed in his Hungarian-inflected voice, which remains to this day an exotic strain amidst the pervading German, French, and Italian accents of Western classical music. His techniques and most of his ideas about music he kept to himself; he led no factions and left no disciples.

Yet for all his stretches of dissonance and deliberate barbarity, Bartók is the warmest of the Modernist giants, the widest in expressive range, even in his rages the closest to us in his humanity. In contrast to Stravinsky's rejection of the very idea of expressiveness, Bartók declared, "I cannot conceive of music that expresses absolutely nothing." And contra the theorizing of Schoenberg and his disciples, he told a professor, "It is no good asking why I wrote a passage as I did . . . I can only reply that I wrote down what I felt. Let the music speak for itself."

In a rare moment of personal revelation, Bartók once said that he was born twice. The first birth was on March 25, 1881, in the small Transylvanian town of Nagyszentmiklós. His father died when Béla was seven; his mother, Paula, a piano teacher, nursed him through a childhood full of illness—bronchitis, pneumonia, skin disease—and gave him his first music lessons. His fragile health erected a wall between Béla and the friends and pursuits of youth; music was his refuge, and he soon revealed a tremendous talent. At age ten he made his first public appearance as both pianist and composer.

From 1899 to 1902 Bartók attended the Royal Academy of Music in Budapest, though his work was still periodically interrupted by illness. He studied composition but concentrated on piano, becoming a keyboard virtuoso. Then in 1902 he heard a performance of Richard Strauss's *Thus Spake Zarathustra* that galvanized him. Leaving behind the Brahmsian approach of his earlier music, Bartók began writing in a Straussian late-Romantic style that culminated in the tone poem *Kossuth,* which had a well-received 1903 premiere in Budapest. A programmatic portrait of Louis Kossuth's doomed 1848 revolt against Austria, the work was intended as a contribution to the Hungarian nationalistic movement of Bartók's time, the continuing struggle against Austrian rule. At the premiere, Bartók took his bows in native costume. *Kossuth,* however, was only a temporary style for Bartók; it was not his rebirth.

That transforming moment came in the most unexpected way in 1904, in the resort of Gerlice Puszta. In the next room a young girl from the town of Kibéd sang to her child a melody that astonished Bartók with its chromatic, primeval sound and unconstrained rhythm. He asked the girl where she had learned it; from her grandmother, she said, just an old village tune like many others. During some probing in the countryside, Bartók realized with mounting excitement that among the peasants of Hungary and neighboring regions lay a repository of undiscovered music of a unique character, a folk legacy corrupted in the "Gypsy" and "Hungarian" melodies of Liszt and Brahms, who tamed the music by forcing it into conventional scales and foursquare rhythms.

Bartók and fellow composer Zoltán Kodály spent years tracking through the hinterlands of the region, collecting these Magyar songs. Further field researches would introduce Bartók to Rumanian, Transylvanian, Serbo-Croatian, and Bulgarian folk music; later travels into North Africa and Turkey added more exotic styles. The results of his and other collectors' labors were finally published in some twelve volumes, thousands of melodies, one of history's great works of ethnomusicology.

"Those days I spent in the villages among the peasants," Bartók later wrote, "were the happiest of my life." But there was far more to his studies than either the pleasures of the countryside or a scholarly interest in folk music. This music was the means of his own artistic awakening, the second birth that freed him from the domination of Strauss and Liszt and created his own voice as a composer, a voice growing from the musical soul of Hungary.

In 1907, Bartók began a faculty career of nearly thirty years at the Royal Academy of Music in Budapest, but only in the piano department. Believing that each composer must find his own way, he refused all his life to teach composition. Two years later he took a momentous step in his personal life. One morning he brought home a sixteen-year-old pupil named Marta for a lesson, introducing her to his mother. The lesson seemed to go on for a very long time, and he announced that Marta would be staying for lunch. Later that day he mentioned to a shocked Paula Bartók that the girl would be staying for dinner and then added, grudgingly, "We're married." When his friends at the conservatory discovered that fact and sent their congratulations, he heatedly accused them of meddling in his business. In 1923, with similar mysteriousness, he would divorce Marta and marry Ditta Pásztory, another young piano student. With each wife Bartók would have one child.

Though he by no means lacked humor—usually expressed as bitter irony—Bartók tended to be withdrawn, somber, often depressive. The experiences of his life rarely mitigated that temperament. A friend, trying to talk him out of a creative block around 1910, recalled, "I had never before observed in anyone the tight lips and unchanging deathly pallor with which Béla Bartók listened to me." Another musical friend remembered how a silent Bartók "stared at me with wide questioning eyes, quite often for fifteen minutes at a time." Said conductor Antal Dorati: "There was never such a pair of eyes! Large, burning, piercing—his looks had something of a branding iron—they seemed to mark everybody on whom they fixed."

To the end of his life Bartók remained introverted to the point of being a cipher, unable to function in ordinary social terms, with the intractable guardedness of the painfully sensitive. He viewed life with minute seriousness, ingrained fatalism, and unbending idealism. But mostly he held his feelings in check behind the tight lips and pale, sculptured features. Only in music did his emotions flow without constraint, the savage relentlessness, the rage sometimes approaching hysteria, but also the nobility of spirit and the extraordinary sensitivity to the magic and mystery of life.

As Bartók felt his way toward artistic maturity, his studies of folk music gradually pervaded his creative work. Rarely did he disturb the integrity of his wellspring by stealing material or by direct imitation; integrity in all things meant a great deal to him. Rather, the songs of his country came to inflect the shapes and modes and colorations of his music: "It is necessary," he wrote, "for the composer to command this [folk] language so completely that it becomes the natural expression of his own musical ideas." He became the Hungarian equivalent of other nationalist composers such as Musorgsky in Russia, Verdi in Italy, Smetana and Dvořák in Bohemia, Ives in the United States. At the same time, the chromaticism and rhythmic energy of folk music led Bartók in the direction of European Modernism, toward the primitivistic ferocity of Stravinsky's *Sacre du printemps*, the chromaticism of Schoenberg (though Bartók never took up the twelve-tone method or entirely abandoned tonality). Like Schoenberg and Stravinsky, he denied that he was revolutionary: "In art there are only fast or slow developments. Essentially it is a matter of evolution, not revolution."

So Bartók had an eclectic temperament, picking up what he heard and making it his own, whether it was a peasant song or the work of refined cosmopolitans like Debussy and Stravinsky. While not a mainstream neoclassicist, he was often closer to the old Classical patterns than his contemporaries, many of his works showing the influence of sonata form, and he wrote fugues and cantatas. The musical result of this wide eclecticism was his singular fusion of the primitive and sophisticated, violent and lyrical, atavistic and futuristic: in him spoke age-old peasant songs, the Classical traditions of Mozart and Beethoven, and the liberated harmonies and rhythms and timbres of the new century.

Though he wrote feverishly when the mood was on him, in the long run Bartók was unprolific and his development slow, and there were long unproductive periods. It took decades for him to arrive at his maturity. The String Quartet no. 1 of 1908 began a series of masterpieces that string players sometimes call the New Testament (Beethoven's quartets being the Old), but not until the Second Quartet (1917) did the folk influence flower. Finally, a decade later, in the Third Quartet, he was the mature Bartók.

By then success had come, however ambiguously. In the decade after the premiere of *Kossuth* he had made little headway with the public. When his 1911 opera *Bluebeard's Castle* could not find a performance, he virtually quit his public career and concentrated on folk music studies and on writing a ballet, *The Wooden Prince*. Then in 1917 this ballet was staged in Budapest to considerable acclaim; that led to a successful performance of the opera and a publishing contract for his music. The *Dance Suite* of 1923, a prestigious commission for the anniversary of the joining of Buda and Pest, was played in major cities worldwide. In the mid twenties Bartók began to perform again in public, making his first American tour in 1927. To the detriment of his career as a virtuoso, however, he programmed more of his own piano music than bread-and-butter items.

By the 1920s he was generally recognized as the leading Hungarian composer, but he remained controversial. His piano writing in particular did not endear him to recital audiences used to the singing lines and voluptuous sonorities of the Romantic literature; as in the deliberately provocative *Allegro Barbaro* (1910), Bartók treated the piano as the percussion instrument it actually is: hammers striking strings. His keyboard music, including much of the first two piano concertos, is often marked by lean sonorities, pounding figures, and harmonies dissonant sometimes to the point of tone clusters. A stiff manner onstage did not help; in his recitals he refused to ingratiate himself either musically or personally.

Another difficulty was that, as the old Hungarian nation broke up after World War I, his association with folk music seemed patriotic to some, to others a dangerous influence. He despised both the short-lived Communist government after the war and the following reactionary administration of Admiral Horthy, which abused the peasants and minority groups that Bartók saw as the lifeblood of the country (and of his music). His association with the music of "alien" ethnic groups was condemned; the head of the Academy of Music wrote in a newspaper attack on Bartók that he considered it "culpable for us to be in any way concerned with the culture of our minorities." All these tensions seemed to ride on Bartók's frail but unbending back. "I have never meddled in everyday politics," he wrote, "but . . . every bar of music, every folk tune I have recorded has been a political act." His internal strength and integrity allowed him to keep going, but at a cost no one could tell.

At the turn of the century he had been a defiant nationalist when that ran against the status quo. By the 1920s he had left nationalism behind as well: "My own idea—of which I have been fully conscious since I found myself as a composer—is the brotherhood of peoples, brotherhood in spite of wars and conflicts. I try—to the best of my ability—to serve this idea in my music; therefore I don't reject any influence, be it Slovakian, Rumanian, Arabic or from any other source. The source must only be clean, fresh and healthy! Owing to my . . . geographical position, it is the Hungarian source that is nearest to me, and therefore the Hungarian influence is the strongest." As did Charles Ives around the same time, Bartók here proclaimed his intentions as universal, however national his accent.

During the 1930s Bartók revealed the breadth of his full maturity. By then he had achieved the ambiguous success of most innovators: he was admired by progressive musicians around the world and by a small group of adventurous listeners; to the general public, though, he remained a distant and perplexing figure. Still, he began the decade with a work that quickly found wide popularity: the dancing, lyrical Piano Concerto no. 2. In the middle of the decade came the monumental *Music for Strings, Percussion, and Celesta,* and the *Sonata for Two Pianos and Percussion.* In the bleak year of 1939, when Nazi domination of Hungary was in the offing, Bartók in a period of some eighteen days wrote one of his most delightful scores (in the outer movements, at least), the *Divertimento* for strings. Also during the thirties he assembled, from the pieces he had written for his son's lessons, the graded piano series called *Mikrokosmos,* which begins with the simplest tunes for children and progresses though an education in the musical sounds and techniques of this century.

As many European artists did in those years (including Herbert von Karajan), Bartók could have stayed home during World War II, remained in his comfortable job in familiar surroundings, kept his opinions to himself, given occasional lip service to the Nazis, gone through the war with little bother and come out smelling like an "apolitical" rose. He never considered that option. Compromise in any matter large or small was unthinkable to him. In his late fifties he left his homeland for the United States and began the most heroic, the most miserable, and the final period of his life.

As he put it, Bartók Béla (the Hungarian form of his name) had achieved a measure of success; in America he would have to start over again as Béla Bartók, foreigner. Arriving in the United States in 1940, he was welcomed by a small group of admirers, but the general concertgoing public knew him, if at all, as another of those fearful Modernists. A Boston critic had once brushed him off with, "the composer was regarded . . . by the audience as, if not stark mad, certainly an eccentric person."

His friends did the best they could to help, but found that trying to help Bartók was a difficult proposition because of that magnificent, infuriating integrity. He categorically refused to accept gifts of money or anything else, refused several offers to teach composition in prestigious schools, refused all but a few piano students, refused to accept advances for work he might not be able to complete. Finally he did take a small job at Columbia University, cataloguing Serbo-Croatian folk music collected by somebody else. Occasionally there would be a concert engagement or a lecture, but not often. Overwhelmed by the demands of adapting to a new country and culture, tormented by the noise and confusion of New York City, he did no composing for the two years he worked at Columbia. Meanwhile, he began to be afflicted with mysterious aches and fevers.

When the Columbia job ended, Bartók, Ditta, and their son were on the verge of starvation. Desperate to find a way to help him despite his vigilance against any hint of charity, his friends finally resorted to giving him fictitious royalties for records of his music that had never actually been sold. Such measures barely kept the family alive. Those who knew Bartók in those days were at once exasperated and awed by him. As disease consumed his body, his spirit seemed to burn more and more powerfully through the great, piercing eyes.

His final surge of creativity began in 1943, as he lay despairing in a New York hospital, the mysterious illness seemingly coming to a head. By then his doctors had probably diagnosed leukemia; he was never told, but he saw clearly enough that he was dying. One day, into the hospital room swept the imposing figure of Boston Symphony conductor Serge Koussevitzky, who had a commission in hand for Bartók and refused to accept the composer's protests that he was too sick to work. The effect of this offer was electric. In short order Bartók was out of bed and heading for Asheville, North Carolina. Away from the city, close to the earth and woods again, he fell into one of his creative furies, writing day and night, scribbling even as he chatted with friends. "Here," he happily wrote his publisher, "time makes no difference." The main fruit of that period in Asheville was the *Concerto for Orchestra,* premiered by Koussevitzky and the Boston Symphony in December 1944. Bartók painfully made the journey to Boston for the premiere and could not conceal his delight in the performance and the enthusiastic audience reception. The concerto would soon become one of the most beloved works in the contemporary repertoire. It was the last piece of his he ever heard in public.

With that work finished, he was back in time again; he knew there was precious little of it left. At home in New York, he frantically worked on a Viola Concerto (finished from the sketches by a pupil), the Sonata for Unaccompanied Violin commissioned by Yehudi Menuhin, and the Piano Concerto no. 3. The latter had been sketched in Asheville; its second movement is full of the bird calls of the Carolina countryside. He intended the concerto as a final gift for Ditta, to help support her performing career after he was gone; he made sure it was one of his most lyrical and ingratiating pieces.

As he neared the end of the concerto, in pain and failing, his doctor arrived to take him from his desk. Knowing he would never leave the hospital alive, he begged the doctor to let him finish; there were only seventeen measures to go. The doctor refused. For the only time in his life, Bartók wrote the word *Finished* on the manuscript. At the hospital, he said near the last, "I am only sad that I have to leave with my trunk full." He died on September 26, 1945, just as the *Concerto for Orchestra* was waking up the American public to his genius. In the next months there were a torrent of performances worldwide. His pupil Tibor Serly finished the Third Concerto; a devastated Ditta Bartók could not bring herself to play it for nearly twenty years.

I have noted that Bartók picked up ideas from both sides of the Schoenberg-Stravinsky fence and made them his own. His work sometimes has the sophisticated primitivism of Stravinsky's *Sacre du printemps,* for example, but Bartók adds a distinctly Hungarian flavor. While his rhythmic style owes much to Stravinsky's unit pulse, Bartók tends to fall into the irregular meters of Balkan music, such as 5/8, 7/8, and other dance meters with some beats longer than others. Where Stravinsky tends to change meter lengths regularly, Bartók often writes whole pieces in these sprung rhythms.

His harmony to some extent bridges the gap between Schoenberg's chromatic atonality and Stravinsky's skewed tonality. Bartók's usual approach has been called *chromatic tonality*—the music roams in chromatic space with quite free harmonies, but in various ways it defines a tonal center. The first and final movements of the *Music for Strings, Percussion, and Celesta* gravitate around the note A; one might say they are "on" A, rather than "in" it (that is, not "in" a traditional key). He once said of a highly chromatic spot in the Violin Concerto no. 2, "I wanted to show Schoenberg that one can use all twelve tones and still remain tonal." Bartók also makes use of the modal scales of folk music, which are neither major nor minor; sometimes he stacks up different modes at once, creating *polymodality*—similar to polytonality, which tends to use major and minor scales. Bartók may often be as dissonant as Schoenberg, but his dissonances seem more expressive and coloristic than those of serial composers (in whom dissonance tends to be grayer and more relentless). In fact, few composers have used dissonance as expressively as Bartók; it helps to create the chromatic haze that enfolds his "night music," intensifies his savage moments, contributes to the folklike humor of other passages. Since (in contrast to Schoenberg) Bartók often used the traditional consonant chords as well, he commanded an extraordinary harmonic range, literally everything from triads to tone clusters.

It is in his melodic voice that he is most distinctive. As his pieces can cover a wide stylistic range in their course, his melodies range from simple folk tunes to a kind of wandering, sighing, chromatic line of which the beginning of *Music for Strings, Percussion, and Celesta* is the model. While his orchestration is not quite up to the brilliance and glow of Stravinsky, Bartók had a characteristically open, pure-colored instrumental sound. His percussive treatment of the piano I have already mentioned; only occasionally, as in the Third Piano Concerto, did he allow himself a more traditional lyrical piano style. He regularly experimented with novel instrumental effects; some of the sounds most associated with him are the percussive effect of snapping a string off the fingerboard (now called the "Bartók pizzicato"), the spooky pedal glissando on the usually rock-solid timpani, and other percussion effects such as cymbals being played with a fingernail or knife blade. (The next generation's obsessive timbral experimentation, in which sometimes fascinating, sometimes banal sounds are tortured from once familiar instruments, is an echo of Bartók's interest in new sounds.)

In the end, it is inadequate simply to call Bartók eclectic. We should better call him one of the great synthesists of the century, who drew on a variety of influences to produce a personal style. The breadth and universality of his music results in large part from the breadth of his sources.

Maybe the best entry into his musical world is the *Concerto for Orchestra* (1943), one of the milder works typical of his American years. It is not his deepest piece, but it has a compelling lyricism and evocative power. And it is a good introduction to his style, from the "night music" of the opening to the breakneck Gypsy fiddling of the finale. In the middle three movements come some of the most splendid musical wit and charm he ever produced, including a lampoon, complete with Bronx cheers in the brass, of an inane Shostakovich tune (from the Seventh Symphony) that had irked him.

Smaller in scale but equally enjoyable is the *Divertimento* for string orchestra (1939), whose dancelike outer movements are close to the folk tradition. The work was mostly written, along with the Sixth String Quartet, during four weeks of "vacation" in 1939. The middle movement of the *Divertimento* is entirely serious, featuring a relentlessly growing, spine-chilling, banshee music that may well be an evocation of the horror that was advancing across Europe in 1939.

Of the six string quartets, the most accessible may be the Fourth, a wild, Gypsyish work that is one of the most electrifying outings in the chamber music repertoire. The piece shows Bartók's concern with symmetrical structures: it is in five-movement "arch form," with the outer movements arranged symmetrically (in tempo, thematic relationships, and character) around the keystone of the slow, songful, "night music" middle movement; the middle movement itself has a symmetrical ABA form; and there are symmetries in the details of the pitch structure: melodies in mirror images, chords arranged in mirrored intervals around a central point, and so forth. (Though Bartók never used Schoenberg's twelve-tone method, he had his own cabalistic techniques; he just didn't give lectures about them, as Schoenberg and his disciples did.) After the Fourth String

Quartet, try the calmer Third and the richer but more austere Fifth Quartet.

The Second and Third piano concertos are in his milder vein, with a good deal of folklike melody. The Second in particular sports some of the most lighthearted pages he ever wrote, including most of the first movement. The Third Piano Concerto, though written in the shadow of death, has a gentle lyricism that makes it one of the more intimate of his larger works. Similarly, the Violin Concerto no. 2 has a first movement of surpassing grace and beauty reminiscent of Mendelssohn's concerto, and a final movement in the traditional form of a theme and variations.

At the peak of Bartók's achievements lie two more complex works, complex not only because of their thornier idiom but also because of their expressive range and contrasts. The *Sonata for Two Pianos and Percussion* is among his most brilliant efforts, full of striking timbral effects and innovative treatment of the percussion (such as his trademark timpani glissandos).

The crown of his work is the *Music for Strings, Percussion, and Celesta*. I have described the drifting melodies and dark colors of the first movement; it is actually a fugue as systematic as one by Bach, though its flowing lines are more like a dissonant version of Renaissance polyphony. The second movement is rhythmically explosive and at times demonic; the third features one of his intervals of "night music," with chirping percussion and soulful soliloquies; and the finale is an ebullient movement that culminates in a metamorphosis of the work's opening theme. During its course this work seems to touch on feelings from bleak despair through joy to triumphant affirmation.

There is a lesson that, in one way or another, all great artists demonstrate, Bartók as well as any: to be deeply personal, deeply of a time and place—and, let's not forget, to write well—is also to be universal. A countryman wrote of Bartók, "His pagan barbarity, his explosive and angrily defiant melancholy, his demoniacal instinct . . . these are all echoes . . . of the thousand-year-old Hungarian psyche." They are also echoes of the immemorial human psyche. Of all musical nationalists, Bartók achieved the broadest scope: he is one of the great humanists of our century's music.

A L B A N   B E R G

Like his teacher Arnold Schoenberg and his colleague Anton Webern, Alban Berg embraced the new world of atonal music with intentions as much expressive and spiritual as technical. It is often observed that of the founders of the Second Viennese School, Berg wrote the most passionate music, the closest to the Romantic past. At the same time, he was in some ways the most cabalistic of the three, the most obsessed with formalistic structures, numerology, arcane symbolism. Thus the madness and tragedy of his opera *Wozzeck* is contained by rigorous application of traditional musical forms; and in the most personal of his chamber works, the *Lyric Suite*, scholars have discovered the story of a love affair symbolized in numbers and letters and words. No matter what the rigor, however, in Berg the expression is the most conspicuous element. For that reason, though he was the least prolific and innovative of the great Viennese moderns, from the beginning he has been the most nearly popular. The day has not quite come, but surely will, when *Wozzeck* will stand in the repertoire alongside peers such as *Don Giovanni* and *Otello* as one of the most powerful operas ever written.

Alban Berg was born in Vienna on February 9, 1885, and only occasionally left the city during his life. His family were well-to-do merchants; he had a thorough education and developed wide-ranging literary interests. In his mid teens he was stricken by asthma, which would afflict him from then on. Having picked up an interest in music from his brother and sister, Berg began in 1900 to write songs and piano pieces under the influence of Brahms and Mahler.

At eighteen, depressed by the breakup of a love affair and failures at school, he had a nervous breakdown that led to a suicide attempt. His recovery was confirmed the next year by the most important event of his life: he began to study composition with Arnold Schoenberg, who would be Berg's only teacher and also his hero and protector.

Berg studied with the pioneer of atonality from 1904 to 1910, quickly developing from a dilettante into a master composer with an unmistakable voice. A small inheritance made it possible—barely—for Berg to devote his life to music. His growing skill may be traced through the early opus numbers, written under Schoenberg's guidance; from the pale but promising Piano Sonata op. 1 to the powerful String Quartet op. 3. Meanwhile he became close friends with Webern, another Schoenberg pupil. In 1911 Berg married Helene Nahowski; on the face of it, their match would be nearly ideal, but as we will see, Berg had a secret life.

His first masterpiece, the *Altenberg Lieder* op. 4, for soprano and orchestra, was completed in 1912. It would have an unfortunate history. At the 1913 first performance of two of these songs, done in Vienna under Schoenberg's baton, one of the worst audience riots of the century broke out, rivaling the one that same year at the Paris premiere of Stravinsky's *Sacre du printemps*. The police arrived to stop the concert. An outraged critic wrote of these songs, "We thought we knew all the discords which human ingenuity can devise, but . . . can they be the birth pangs of a new art, these zoological expressions that would make the real menagerie seek cover?" Berg's horror at the debacle was not lessened when the prickly Schoenberg also condemned the music. Shaken, Berg put the *Altenberg Lieder,* among the finest and most beautiful works of his career, on the shelf. They were not heard again until seventeen years after his death.

Somehow, Berg's creativity survived the hostility of the public and the censure of his mentor. In May 1914 he saw the Vienna premiere of *Woyzeck,* a play of expressionist sensibility written in the previous century by the prophetic George Büchner. Berg, composer of less than a handful of small, promising but spectacularly unpopular pieces, decided on the spot to make the play into the world's first atonal opera. This ambitious and unlikely scheme was the beginning of ten years of intermittent labor.

World War I put on hold most things artistic. Berg enlisted in the German army, but given his poor health, the training and his duties nearly killed him. After a year he was assigned to a desk job in Vienna, but his work allowed him little time for *Wozzeck*, as he would call his version. With what time he had, he carefully shaped the play (which had been a series of sketches discovered after Büchner's death) into an incisive drama. His own experience of the military, the gray life of the barracks, the drudgery and humiliation, gave Berg an intense identification with the hapless soldier whose sufferings he would portray so indelibly.

After the war he began composing the music for *Wozzeck*. Meanwhile, with Webern and Schoenberg he cofounded the Society for Private Musical Performances, which between 1918 and 1922 aired new works for invited audiences, with critics excluded and applause forbidden. Later, Berg would become an important figure in the International Society for Contemporary Music; his personal charm would make him an effective proselytizer for his own and others' work.

Having finished *Wozzeck* in 1920, he faced the problem of arranging a performance of what amounted to one of the most challenging works in history, for players and listeners alike. He had a reduction made for voices and piano and printed and sold it himself, often delivering the copies in person. The resulting interest led, in 1924, to a performance of three excerpts in a Frankfurt orchestral concert, which in turn caught the attention of Erich Kleiber, courageous new music director of the Berlin Opera. There Kleiber conducted the premiere of the complete *Wozzeck* on December 14, 1925, more than ten years after Berg had first seen the play. The results were sensational, for well and ill.

As was still de rigueur for important avant-garde premieres in those days, the performance went forward to the accompaniment of shouts, whistles, and brawls in the audience. The tall, pale figure of the composer took his bow at the end amidst a cacophony of bravos and boos. Next day appeared one of the most brutal newspaper reviews in history:

When I left the State Opera last night, I felt that I was not leaving a public place, dedicated to the arts, but a public insane asylum. On stage, in the orchestra, in the audience—only lunatics. The work of a Chinaman from Vienna. My name will be, from tomorrow on, Moses Sewersmell [note the anti-Semitic touch], if this is not a deliberate swindle. Fragments, rags, sobs, belches. Tormented, ugly-sounding cackle. A fountain-poisoner of German music. The man who committed the crime of this work relies confidently on the stupidity and baseness of his fellow men. . . . He is a musical mountebank, a composer dangerous to the public welfare . . . one has to ask, in all seriousness, whether and to what extent occupation with music can be criminal. This is, in the realm of music, a capital crime.

So excessive were the reviews, good and bad, that Berg's publisher had them all printed up in a booklet. The next year, a production in Prague touched off a riot that brought in the police; in the melee, the mayor of the city collapsed with a heart attack. The next production was heard, of all places, in Leningrad in 1927, which convinced some Viennese that Berg must be a Bolshevik in addition to a madman and a criminal. (That Russian production made a profound impact on the young Dmitri Shostakovich, among others.) A decade later, the Nazis would brand Berg and his ilk as "degenerate" artists, purveyors of cultural Bolshevism.

But these controversies were only the birth pangs of a masterpiece, which before many more years had been staged, triumphantly, around the world. In the first decade after the premiere, *Wozzeck* had seen some hundred and fifty performances across Europe and a critically acclaimed American premiere by Leopold Stokowski. So far, this timeless story of a little man and the society that torments and kills him has yet to become an audience favorite, but it has nonetheless stayed onstage as the closest thing to a popular opera the musical avant-garde ever produced.

In musical idiom *Wozzeck* is free-atonal (see the Schoenberg section, p. 388), held together by systematic deployment of traditional forms: the opera contains a fugue, a passacaglia, a rondo, and so on—even a symphony in five movements. It was only after this work that Berg took up, in parts of the *Lyric Suite* (1925–26) for string quartet, the twelve-tone method of his teacher Schoenberg. But there is more to the *Lyric Suite* than that. In 1977, a score annotated by Berg was discovered, which declared the work to be "a small monument to a great love." The great love turns out not to be Helene

Berg, but one Hanna Fuchs-Robettin; the score revealed Berg's ten-year affair with a married woman. Besides the fervor of the music, the symbolism of the two lovers is seen in every aspect of the score, from tempo indications such as andante amoroso and adagio appassionato to a theme based on their entwined initials (H-F and A-B, in German notation the notes B-F-A-B♭). There are also quotes from Wagner's *Tristan und Isolde* and typically Bergian numerological symbols. He considered 23 to be his fateful number—he had his first asthma attack on a July 23—and Hanna's to be 10.

By 1930, Berg was working on another opera that the musical world was now eagerly awaiting: *Lulu*, based on two plays by Frank Wedekind about a femme fatale who destroys everyone around her and then herself. In 1932, he bought a small villa he called "Waldhaus," on the Wörther-See in Carinthia, spending his summers composing there.

Of the three pioneer Viennese atonalists, Berg was the warmest in personality. His friend and publisher Hans Heinsheimer wrote of him, "He was unusually tall but always slightly stooped, as if bowing in grace and elegant humility to the world. . . . He had a beautiful face, a smiling, almost mocking mouth, great warming eyes that always looked straight at you. Most of the many photographs that survive do him small justice . . . they have neither the twinkle in the eye which we all remember nor the suffering that we also knew so well." Berg was one of those people everyone felt privileged to know. Despite his always fragile health, he loved walks in the country, long drives in his American automobile, and sports; Heinsheimer fondly recalls him at soccer matches leaping up to cheer his team waving his long arms and his big sombrero. Berg was rarely free from physical pain, but few people were more alive.

He had been working hard at *Lulu* month after month at his villa, whose walls were covered with diagrams of its twelve-tone rows. Finishing the condensed "short score," he had begun to orchestrate the enormous work. As he had done with *Wozzeck*, he extracted a suite of pieces from *Lulu* that Kleiber premiered, to great acclaim, in Berlin in 1934. In the spring of that year, Berg interrupted work on the opera to write the Violin Concerto, commissioned by the American violinist Louis Krasner. Composed in four months—remarkable for the methodical Berg—it was inspired by the death of nineteen-year-old Manon Gropius, daughter of his friend and patron Alma

Mahler Gropius (the remarried widow of Gustav Mahler). Dedicated "To an angel," the work is among the greatest concertos of the twentieth century. Berg would never hear it, nor finish orchestrating *Lulu*.

Shortly after completing the concerto, he was stung by a wasp; the sting developed into an abscess, and that into blood poisoning. Two weeks after attending the premiere of the *Lulu* Suite, he died in Vienna on December 24, 1935. For years *Lulu* would be heard in incomplete form, the third act done only in dialogue or pantomime, because Helene Berg refused to release the completed short score of the third act. Only in 1979, after her death, with the short score orchestrated according to Berg's indications, was the complete *Lulu* heard at last.

Berg wrote only thirteen mature compositions, of which a handful—the two operas, the *Altenberg Lieder*, the *Lyric Suite*, and the Violin Concerto—represent him at his best. No other composer has built such a momentous reputation on so few works (though in total duration, Webern's output is even smaller). Moreover, Berg's style was so personal that in contrast to Schoenberg's and especially Webern's, it has had little influence on later music. The fact that he remains unquestionably a giant of his time is testimony to the impact of those few pieces.

To start with Berg, I suggest the Violin Concerto and the opera suites—Three Orchestral Excerpts from *Wozzeck* and the *Lulu* Suite. The Violin Concerto proves, among other things, that the twelve-tone system presents no barrier to music of great beauty. In it Berg characteristically arranges his rows not to erase but rather to suggest tonal centers and traditional chords; in much of his music the old familiar sounds often seem to float, nostalgically and hauntingly, just out of reach. This work in memory of "angel" Manon Gropius contains moments of violence, but more music of ethereal spirituality. As usual in Berg, it is rife with symbols, some overt and some hidden. Most noticeable is a recurring quote from the Bach chorale setting, "Es ist genug" (It is enough), which suggests resignation in the face of death (the chorale melody is the last four notes of Berg's twelve-tone row, so it is part of the fundamental structure of the piece). But other clues reveal that the concerto is also autobiographical: it refers to the numbers Berg associated with himself and his secret mistress, Hanna, and quotes a folk song referring to a "Mizzi," the name of a servant girl who in his youth bore a child of his. In fact, the Violin concerto is a double requiem—for the "angel" and for himself.

I believe Berg's opera *Wozzeck* to be one of the most eloquent experiences the theater has to offer, riveting in every minute, the expressionistic music wedded seamlessly to the words and the drama. I might also argue that here the Wagnerian ideal of the *Gesamtkunstwerk,* the total work of art, finds at last its true realization.

The opera tells the story of poor soldier Franz Wozzeck, taunted and abused by his captain, victimized by a doctor whose experiments have weakened his body and addled his mind, his only life and hope residing in his mistress, Marie, and their child. But Marie is callously seduced by a drum major, who returns to the barracks after their tryst to humiliate and beat Wozzeck. In his rage and despair, Wozzeck murders Marie and then, slipping into insanity, drowns himself. At the end, their young boy is playing with a group of children when someone runs in to announce that his mother is dead. He does not understand. The other children run off to gape at the body, leaving the boy playing alone with his stick horse.

The story is unrelentingly bleak, but Berg said the keynote of his interpretation was pity: pity for the oppressed of all times and places, pity for suffering humanity. Of the "abstract" forms that he used throughout—the rondo, the symphony, and so on—Berg wrote, "No matter what knowledge one has of the multiplicity of musical forms contained in this opera . . . no one . . . should really concentrate on anything else but the idea of this opera, which transcends the individual destiny of Wozzeck." For the listener it is not a matter of forms, but of the way the music seems to *be* the story in all its details, until one cannot imagine either without the other.

So many moments of the score remain engraved on the memory: Wozzeck's repeated cry of "We poor folk!"; the scene in which Marie sings a gentle lullaby to her child, and the later one when she reads from the Bible, in anguished *Sprechstimme,* the story of Christ and the adulteress; the eerie moaning of the sleeping soldiers in the barracks; the berserk out-of-tune piano in the shabby barroom where Wozzeck appears, covered with blood, after he has stabbed

Marie; the macabre, slowing chords that writhe up through the orchestra as he drowns; and the blank babble of winds at the end as the child plays on uncomprehendingly, the music saying that this tragedy has not ended but will go on as long as there are cruelty and victims.

As noted in the Schoenberg section, keeping free atonality under control proved an almost impossible task; Schoenberg instituted his twelve-tone system to impose order on the chaotic chromatic scale. The traditional musical forms in *Wozzeck* were Berg's way of corralling his notes. Nonetheless, it has been said that in Berg chaos and incoherence, musical and spiritual madness, often seem to threaten and sometimes to boil over. In *Wozzeck,* that threat is part of the drama and its meaning, part of the monstrous world that it inhabits, which, as former soldier Berg knew, was part of his world and always had been.

Beyond *Wozzeck* lie more difficult works. The *Lyric Suite* has some of the thorniness one associates with twelve-tone music, but its six movements also contain music of powerful and transparent expression from its opening, marked "jovial," to its "desolate" close. And there is *Lulu,* which some have called the composer's masterpiece and one of the greatest of all operas. Critics of that mind tend to take inordinate interest in the work's ingenious twelve-tone technique. The *Lulu* Suite is the best introduction to this complex and paradoxical work. For many, though, the essential Berg remains *Wozzeck,* which alone is enough to make its creator one of the immortal voices of Western music.

ANTON WEBERN

Anton Webern loved the Austro-German tradition and considered himself part of it. Wagner and Mahler were his heroes no less than they were for his mentor, Arnold Schoenberg. But after picking up where the past left off, Webern retreated as far as possible from the lush giganticism of late-Romantic music—retreated, in fact, to the brink of silence. In a lifetime of intensive compositional labors, Webern produced thirty-one mature pieces, few lasting more than ten minutes. The whole body of his work amounts to some four hours. Often the pieces themselves seem to be made of enigmatic wisps of sound applied to the void.

In his own time he was far less known than Schoenberg and his friend Alban Berg, and to this day Webern is performed and recorded far less than his fellow Viennese atonalists. Relatively few people, in other words, have ever understood Webern's lapidary miniatures. Yet so far-reaching was his impact on serial composers after World War II that the whole era bears his name: the post-Webern period. While so many of his followers seem merely to be playing mah-jongg with notes, however, Webern is the real thing; his little pieces can speak volumes. And a good deal of his influence has been fruitful and lasting. He taught Western composers the beauty and terror of silence, and the value of making every note count.

Anton von Webern (he would drop the aristocratic *von*) was born in Vienna on December 3, 1883, the son of a mining engineer, and as a child studied piano with his mother. In 1906 he received a doctorate in musicology from the University of Vienna. By then he was studying with Arnold Schoenberg. Shy, awkward, naïve in many respects, Webern was among the most devoted of Schoenberg's pupils; he followed in his master's steps as Schoenberg developed the concepts of free atonality and, later, the twelve-tone method. As he was doing with Alban Berg, Schoenberg gave Webern strong technical equipment and a commitment to exploring new musical paths, and at the same time allowed Webern room to develop his own personality. Webern would always be the most classically minded of the three, the most careful, the most concentrated. His tastes and his gifts were for extremes of purity and economy.

His "graduation" piece when he finished studies with Schoenberg in 1908 was the orchestral *Passacaglia* op. 1, written in the post-Wagnerian style of his teacher—highly chromatic but still tonal. Then in two song cycles, op. 3 and op. 4 of 1909, Webern followed Schoenberg into the free-atonal idiom; these pieces show the aphoristic brevity characteristic of him. That same year he wrote his first masterpiece and one of the seminal works of the century: the Five Movements for String Quartet. No less significant are the Six Pieces for Orchestra (1910), with their extraordinary novelty of orchestral color.

The furthest point of Webern's boiling-down process came with the Six Bagatelles for String Quartet op. 9, which all together last three minutes, and whose shortest movements last eight measures. Even though he habitually thought his pieces were twice as long as they actually are, Webern was painfully aware of the obsessiveness of what he was doing: "I had the feeling here that when all twelve notes had gone by, the piece was over. . . . In my sketch-book I wrote out the chromatic scale and crossed off individual notes. Why? Because I had convinced myself: this note was there already. It sounds grotesque, incomprehensible, and it was unbelievably difficult."

The pieces of this period, though, have a strength and impact far beyond their minuscule proportions. Writing about the Bagatelles, Schoenberg put his finger on the promise of Webern's approach: "One has to realize what restraint it requires to express oneself with such brevity. You can stretch every glance into a poem, every sigh into a novel. But to express a novel in a single gesture, joy in a single breath . . ." One might compare Webern to the Japanese haiku, another tiny form of sometimes monumental import, which often seems to float on silence, breaking only briefly, cryptically, into sound.

Webern's free-atonal period lasted from 1908 to 1927; during the last twelve years of that period he wrote only lieder. Meanwhile he taught occasionally and for several years was an unhappy conductor of operettas. After World War I he settled with his wife and children in Mödling, just outside Vienna, and with Berg and Schoenberg founded the Society for Private Musical Performances. After those concerts ended in 1922, Webern began a dozen years as conductor of the Vienna Workers' Symphony and Chorus, a socialist organization of musical amateurs that he developed into a nearly professional group. He also served as music director of the Austrian Radio and went to London several times to conduct the BBC Orchestra. A friend recalled a triumphant performance Webern gave of Mahler's Eighth Symphony; at the end, when cheers broke out, he hoisted the heavy score over his head, so that it could receive the acclaim.

When Schoenberg developed the twelve-tone method in the mid twenties, it was inevitable that Webern would take it up as well, and that he would pursue this new musical logic with the utmost discipline. Beginning with the Three Sacred Folk Songs of 1924, he turned the twelve-tone technique into a language of almost scientific exactness. In the canonic second movement of the *Piano Variations* (1926), for example, each chromatic note appears in only one register, and all the notes lie symmetrically around a central note A. Time and again Webern explored elaborate canons, palindromes, and similar formal rigors; his Symphony begins with a double canon—two canons going on at the same time. Webern took Schoenberg's row techniques several degrees further, to the verge of controlling all aspects of the composition—pitch, timbre, rhythm, even loudness. As we saw in the Schoenberg section, the post-Webern generation would call this approach *serialism,* and take it still further.

Webern spent most of World War II in Vienna. By then Berg had died and Schoenberg, endangered by his Jewish background, had left for America. Performances of Webern and his "degenerate" colleagues were banned by the Nazis; the government had also stripped Webern of official positions. But Webern's dirty little secret, which after the war his admirers did not care to examine, was that in many respects he sympathized with the Nazis and craved their approval—even though he stayed close to Schoenberg and other Jewish friends. Two of Webern's daughters were married to party members and a son volunteered for the army. If we want to be generous, since Webern was by no means a heartless or militaristic man, we might call his politics a sign of extraordinary naïveté.

In any case, he paid with his life for staying in the country. In early 1945 he fled the Allied air raids to Mittersill, to stay with his daughters. There, after the collapse of German forces, his son-in-law was involved in the black market. On September 15, 1945, two American soldiers were sent to arrest the son-in-law. After dark, Webern stepped out of the house to have a cigar and on his return bumped into one of the American soldiers, who panicked and shot him. Webern died as he had lived, in near obscurity. Within a decade, for well and ill, his ideas would be one of the most potent forces in contemporary music around the world.

A major influence on the post-Webern generation of composers was simply the sound of his later chamber music: the wide melodic jumps, the refined dissonant harmony, the gestures leaping in and out of silence, the textures sometimes made up of one or two notes at a time from each instrument (the latter is sometimes called *pointillism,* after Seurat's painting technique of single dots). But these influences were perhaps superficial. For one thing, Webern did not intend his music to sound like a grid of isolated points. Instead, he wanted melodic lines made up of changing instrumental colors melting into one another, according to the principle Schoenberg had named *Klangfarbenmelodie,* "tone color melody." When Webern heard a performance of his highly pointillistic Symphony that failed (as most do) to make those connections, he could only echo his critics: "A high note, a low note, a note in the middle—like the music of a madman!" Then and later, too much of Webern's music and ideas have been imparted by bad performances.

More significantly, Webern bequeathed to later composers the idea that a row is a series of intervals. Serial music, then, is a matter of composing with patterns of musical intervals rather than with themes or motives. Beyond that, as noted above, he suggested the possibility of using series to control rhythm, texture, tone color, and loudness. American composer Milton Babbitt, for example, has written pieces in which there are twelve rhythmic values, twelve levels of loudness, and so on, each aspect controlled by a series. Pierre Boulez, Karlheinz Stockhausen, and others would exercise similar control; this approach is called *total serialism.* (Many composers gave that up after the 1950s. It turned out that total control tends to sound totally random, an interesting concept philosophically, but not so interesting musically.) Finally, many composers would follow Webern in refusing to repeat anything literally, whether a steady rhythmic pulse or a thematic pattern. "Once stated," said Webern, "the theme expresses all it has to say. It must be followed by something fresh."

In the end, Webern was after something more than refining serial technique. He was looking for a universal law, a system tight as mathematics, inevitable as nature. "With me," he said, "things never turn out as I wish, but only as is ordained for me—as I must." He spent his life searching for that *must,* which became a religion for him: "Adherence to the row is strict, often burdensome—but it is *salvation!* The dissolution of tonality wasn't our fault—and we did not create the new law ourselves; it forced itself overwhelmingly upon us." One can see why, after the horror and chaos of World War II—after all the vast irrational tragedy set in motion by the same dreamy Romantic culture that gave us Schumann and Wagner—composers embraced the serial salvation that Webern promised, something pure and rational and inevitable. The trouble was, in the end serialism didn't interest the public as much as it did composers. As seen in the Schoenberg section, serialism failed to live up to to its promise as the new international language of music, replacing the old tonal language.

The fact that I have devoted a good many words to music that will take less time to listen to than read about is a long-standing tradition in discussions of Webern and serialism. So without more ado, here are a few pieces that I believe to be masterworks of this century, ones many sensitive and open-eared listeners can understand.

The *Passacaglia* op. 1 (1908) might be called Webern's equivalent of Schoenberg's popular, post-Wagnerian *Verklärte Nacht*. It is a clearly Romantic work rich in texture and expressiveness. With that piece under one's belt, maybe it's not so hard to grasp the remarkable Five Movements for String Quartet of 1909 (many prefer Webern's later arrangement for full string orchestra). This is the concentrated world of his mature atonal music; the twelve minutes of these pieces, the distilled essence of expressionism, contain more emotional clout than many composers can manage in an hour. Webern said that the Five Movements, like most of his music at that time, was a response to the death of his mother in 1906. Certainly it has a tone of almost unbearable tragedy, a *King Lear* in miniature. The first movement is made of nervous dashes, throbs, twitterings rising out of silence, sudden shifts of direction that are at once inexplicable and inevitable. (Its effect has much to do with some of Webern's characteristic timbral devices: the glassy sound of strings playing *sul ponticello,* at the bridge; the clatter of *col legno,* in which the wood of the bow strikes the strings.) The second movement sustains a heartbroken melody over muffled harmonies, every note carrying an extraordinary expressive weight. The third is a jittery scherzo, erupting and climaxing in seconds, rushing past before you know it. The fourth movement consists of mysterious, distant textures with eerie scraps of melody. The finale begins with a broad theme, then sinks to sad, sour harmonies over a sighing repeated motive in the cello: it is a hymn to desolation.

The Six Bagatelles for String Quartet (1913) are even shorter—three minutes. Bagatelle literally means "trifle." The mood here is playful and coy: some of these pieces are like a girl who sneaks up to whisper something in your ear and then runs away laughing. Their absurd brevity almost seems part of the joke. Yet each piece has its own personality, shape, and rounding off—even if the end trails off into obscurity.

The Six Pieces for Orchestra op. 6 (1910) relates a very big story in a very short time. It begins with broad gestures (broad for Webern) with perhaps a background of uncertainty; then a second movement secretive, rustling, building to a crisis that ends with violent, almost palpable blows. The third is empty, amorphous, elusive. Then the cataclysmic fourth movement: low rumbles and thuds with distant anguished cries and shouts above, a middle section of pinched melodies and low groans, and finally the percussion and brass mount to a screaming climax that chokes into terrifying silence. The fifth movement is soft again, delicate, with a kind of wounded beauty. And in conclusion a movement made of serene melodies floating through the orchestra, barely accompanied, with soft echoes of earlier movements, settling finally to distant bells achingly resounding. The Six Pieces is a work of tragic poetry and supreme orchestral imagination. To my mind it is also, along with Schoenberg's *Five Pieces for Orchestra,* a prophecy of violence and madness, of the next forty years in Germany. Webern would never surpass the devastating impact of this piece. And what other composer could approach that impact with such economy of means?

The later, twelve-tone pieces are more subtle, less dramatic, less exciting in most respects. A good example is the Symphony op. 21 (1928), a symphony in two movements that lasts under ten minutes. In the rare good performance (such as the von Karajan recording), the first movement has a stately, slow lilt as its complex canons unfold; the second movement is spry, dancing, and jovial: Viennese.

Even at his most expressive, Webern can be hard to follow because he demands so much, demands that you listen profoundly and with your heart to every note. Webern even managed to warm Stravinsky's chilly old heart; Stravinsky became almost rhapsodic in this tribute from one master to another: "We must hail not only this great composer but also a real hero. Doomed to total failure in a deaf world of ignorance and indifference, he inexorably kept on cutting out his diamonds, his dazzling diamonds, of whose mines he had such a perfect knowledge.''

PAUL HINDEMITH

In histories of thirty years ago, what is now called the trio of twentieth-century giants—Stravinsky, Schoenberg, and Bartók—was a quartet, the fourth member being Paul Hindemith. He was the conservative of the group, the upholder of tonality and traditional values of craft, writer of fugues and passacaglias, inspiration of the "Back to Bach" faction. Well, *sic transit gloria mundi:* today Hindemith seems a bit of an also-ran and, despite mighty efforts as a pedagogue and theorist, largely irrelevant to the Modernist age. Certainly, though, among his hundreds of pieces large and small lie a number of works proven in communicative power and popularity.

Paul Hindemith was born in Hanau, near Frankfurt, on November 16, 1985. He played violin in his youth and at fourteen began serious study in Berlin. From 1915 to 1923 he served as first violin of the Frankfurt Opera. By the time he left that position he was already numbered among the most important young German composers. His first major success had come at the Donaueschingen Chamber Music Festival in 1921. As composer and as violist of the celebrated Amar String Quartet, Hindemith would be a star of those legendary festivals through the 1920s.

Then still finding his way as a composer, he allied himself with various groups in the vibrant German art scene of that decade. He was associated with the *Neue Sachlichkeit* (New Objectivity) movement, a branch of neoclassicism that called for a return to older forms and styles. At the same time, for a while Hindemith seemed to be a part of the *Zeitkunst* (Contemporary Art) group that exalted jazz, popular arts, and generally trendy ideas; the most famous fruit of this movement was Kurt Weill's *Three-Penny Opera*. Hindemith's main *Zeitkunst* works include the comic chamber operas *Neues vom Tage* (News of the Day), with its notorious soprano in the bathtub, its typewriter chorus, and "hate duet"; and the bizarre *Hin und Zurück* (Forward and Back), in which story and actors go to the middle and then proceed backward to the beginning, like a movie run in reverse (the music and words approximate the same effect). Hindemith soon got over such youthful follies, however. The *Sachlichkeit* would prevail, and the rest of his career would be notable for sobriety unto humorlessness.

There was a further ideological association that he proclaimed himself and then spent the rest of his life trying to escape: the idea of *Gebrauchsmusik*, "useful music." He introduced the term to indicate music intended for specific practical purposes and contexts, saying that a composer ought to know where and how a work was to be used before composing it. The idea was taken up by both

THE EARLY MUSIC
MOVEMENT

I happen to own one of the first recordings ever made of a Baroque work for large ensemble using the original instruments of the time. It is a 1961 record of Handel's *Royal Fireworks Music*, with various Boston and New York musicians doing their darnedest at their first try on Baroque trumpets and horns, keyless oboes, serpent horns, and so on. It's a great record for parties. With its medley of cracked notes from the brass, blatting oboes, groaning bassoons, and with everybody splendidly out of tune, the rendition sounds like a bad day in the junior high band room. Almost as much fun is the accompanying

scholarly treatise, which explains that in Handel's day brass instruments—simple curved tubes lacking valves and thus with a restricted range of notes—could not be played in tune. We are told that, believe it or not, this is what Handel really sounded like, and it apparently didn't at all bother those primitive folks back then.

Nowadays most of the recordings we hear of Baroque music, and increasingly of Classical music as well, are done on original instruments just like those de-

Surrounded by seventeenth-century musical instruments, this richly clad Dutch gentleman strums the lute.

friends and enemies. To friends it was an answer to the supposed abstruse and antipublic attitude of radicals such as Schoenberg; to enemies, it represented a philistine devotion to pragmatism and popularity. Hindemith later wished he'd kept his mouth shut; "It has been impossible to kill the silly term," he lamented. Still, through his career he wrote a good deal of attractive, practical music for young musicians, notably the *Plöner Musiktag*, a day's worth of pieces starting with the stately Morning Music for brass and ending with an Evening Concert.

In the 1930s, Hindemith reached his mature style, which would persist with little change nearly to the end of his life. Its most notable feature is a steady concern with fluid, lyrical counterpoint, often chromatic and sometimes dissonant, but never atonal and

usually resolving eventually into the old triadic harmonies. By then a teacher at the Berlin High School of Music, he published the first of his major educational works, *The Craft of Musical Composition*.

Craftsmanly and neo-Baroque as his career and music had become, however, he still managed to raise the hackles of the Nazis. Besides being modestly modernist in style, Hindemith had also married a woman of Jewish descent, associated with Jewish musicians, and had written an opera, *Mathis der Maler* (Mathis the Painter), about an artist who joins a popular uprising against German tyranny. Propaganda Minister Goebbels unleashed a broadside of condemnations: "cultural Bolshevism," "spiritual non-Aryanism," music "unbearable to the Third Reich." Accordingly, in 1935 Hindemith began to travel outside the country, among other things

scribed above. So smooth and familiar do they sound that many of us don't even notice that the Vivaldi piece we're hearing on the radio features the mellow sounds of authentic Baroque violins and oboes and trumpets. Of *course* brass could be played in tune in Handel's day. Musicians then knew as much about their trade as we do. Our 1961 original-instrument pioneers just hadn't figured out how to use the brass tuning holes and how to control the instruments. Since then, so expert have players become on original instruments that they have virtually taken over the pre-Classical literature. As the conductor of a mainstream group once known for Baroque performance said when asked why he no longer did Baroque music: "In that period, the early music people have won."

These "early music people" play music on the instruments of its time in performances as historically accurate in style as possible. In a way, the movement was an outgrowth of the rise of scholarly musicology in the nineteenth century, which led to the rediscovery of composers such as Bach and Monteverdi. In that time, performances of older music were done as a matter of course on current instruments and in current style. When Mendelssohn and Brahms played Bach, they brought to the performances the elaborate expressive apparatus of Romantic music and played it with the full nineteenth-century orchestra, often with enormous choruses as well.

In the twentieth century this approach slowly changed, as scholars began to dig deeper into the sources and find more about the

establishing a Western-style music education system in Turkey. In 1939 he settled in the United States, and the next year took a faculty position at Yale, where he would stay until 1953.

In America during the forties, Hindemith probably wielded more influence than his fellow refugees Stravinsky and Schoenberg (Bartók, also in the United States, was hardly noticed until just before he died). He composed at his usual relentless pace, taught composers, issued new pedagogical books, gave the Norton lectures at Harvard, and pursued a pioneering interest in early music played on original instruments. His principal ideas as teacher, theorist, and musical philosopher were consistent and forcefully expressed: music is a moral force, atonality is impossible in theory and deplorable in

how in addition to the *what*. Pioneers such as England's Arnold Dolmetsch led in the revival of long-silenced instruments such as lute, recorder, harpsichord, and viol. Starting in the 1920s, the great Wanda Landowska doggedly convinced the musical world to accept the reintroduction of the harpsichord in Baroque music. It is hard to imagine now, but for many years efforts to bring back "obsolete" instruments met with tremendous resistance, in part because they were a direct attack on the Western obsession with Progress in all things. As that attitude began to give way toward a respect for the past on its own terms, rather than as a way station on the road to the glorious present, attitudes toward performance also changed. Conductor Arturo Toscanini led a new generation of

performers in calling for utter fidelity to the score and an end to Romantic interpretive extravagances.

So the early music movement was part of a change in attitudes in the twentieth century, an evolution both philosophical and practical—away from thoughtless assumptions that newer is better, away from the irrelevant accretions that tradition had applied to history, and toward a pluralistic understanding of musical styles. Each generation of early music performers moved closer to authenticity. In the 1940s Paul Hindemith led pioneer American original-instrument performances with Yale students. In the fifties and sixties, the New York Pro Musica issued many popular recordings of medieval music, notably the twelfth-century liturgical

practice, an overinterest in tone color is mere sensuality, and so on. In short, he attempted to become a bastion against some of the primary tenets and techniques of Modernism.

The main works of his American years included the *Ludus Tonalis* (Play of Tonalities) for piano, his response to Bach's *Well-Tempered Clavier*, which embodied his ingenious theories of tonal relationships; the Requiem for President Roosevelt based on Walt Whitman's "When Lilacs Last in the Dooryard Bloom'd"; and the last of a series of twenty-six sonatas for single instruments and piano, one sonata for every orchestral instrument. The latter pieces, and a related set of concertos, came from Hindemith's desire to create systematic bodies of well-crafted works to expand the standard repertoire. Many of them also show his unfortunate propensity for

---

drama *The Play of Daniel*. Harpsichordists such as Gustav Leonhardt used instruments more faithful to Baroque models than Landowska's, and developed playing techniques at once more responsive to the historical evidence and full of imaginative innovations. When the early music movement had become at once scholarly and creative, neither arbitrary nor slavishly "authentic," it had reached maturity.

The unreachable goal of "authenticity" has two aspects. The easier aspect, though it's hard enough, is mastering the instruments for which the music was created. In medieval and Renaissance music, these include recorders, lutes, oboelike shawms, the violin ancestors fidel and rebec, the trombone ancestor the sackbut, and the like. In Baroque music, one finds the older string family called viols, the buglelike Baroque trumpet, the harpsichord, and the Baroque violin. The latter has gut strings (modern violins have a metal top string and metal-wound bottom strings), a shorter fingerboard, and a bow that is slightly convex—curved outward away from the hair, rather than concave as is the modern bow. The convex Baroque bow allows one to play up to four strings at once, and gives a characteristic swell to long notes; also, Baroque music is usually played without the vibrato that modern string players give to nearly every note by shaking the left hand. (From our perspective it is astonishing to realize that, in the nineteenth century, incomparable stringed instruments made by the Stradivaris and Amatis

stamping out reams of pages of consistent style and craft but little inspiration. There are exceptions to this tendency, though, such as the handsome Sonata in C for Violin and Piano of 1939.

In 1953 Hindemith moved to Switzerland, which became home base for wide-ranging travels as conductor. His composing pace never slacked. The major work of his last decade was *Die Harmonie der Welt,* an ambitious opera based on the life of the Renaissance astronomer Kepler, which occupied Hindemith for some dozen years and embodied his ideas about art, society, and the cosmos. Even admirers of Hindemith, however, tend to see this work as an intriguing failure, overintellectual in concept and sometimes arid in execution.

Hindemith died in Frankfurt on December 28, 1963. He had

were taken apart and refitted with longer fingerboards. On the other hand, art lovers in the same century cut three inches off the *Mona Lisa* so it would fit a new frame.)

Later Classical-period instruments are mostly modern in name, but still significantly different in details—still no metal strings, no valves on the brass, and none of the elaborate mechanical keys that the nineteenth century added to flutes, clarinets, and other woodwinds. The modern symphony orchestra is essentially that of the late nineteenth century, and so is primarily designed for lush Romantic music. Today's Baroque and Classical original-instrument orchestras have fewer players than the full nineteenth-century complement; the overall sound is quieter, less brilliant and colorful, but also

more mellow, homogeneous, and transparent.

The other, and more dicey, aspect of authenticity is performance practice: How does the notation work? How do you interpret those sometimes mysterious symbols for ornaments (trills, shakes, mordents, and so on)? What kind of sound should you aim for? From the beginning of the early music movement in this century, there have been two rival philosophies, roughly describable as the "objective" and "subjective" schools. The former studies every available clue about the performance practice of a given time and creates a style that resolutely conforms to the evidence. The "subjective" school usually studies the same sources and then makes an imaginative leap, admitting that in the absence of re-

erected his ideological and theoretical framework as a challenge to Schoenberg's, his own conservative contribution to a new language of music; dozens of composers around the world absorbed Hindemith's ideas, their music often sounding all too much like him. The younger generation of serialists and avant-gardists, the wave of the future, simply ignored him. Gruff and contentious in personality, early set in his creative ways, Hindemith had been willing to spend his career playing the nay-sayer and lonely individualist.

I'll recommend three works to get to know Hindemith, all longtime favorites and among the most attractive works of the century.

cordings from Bach's day there's no sure way to know what his performances really sounded like; it's the modern musician's task, they believe, to keep the music alive by keeping it creative.

In practice, the objective school tends to give more sober, clean, and cool performances, while the subjective interpreters are apt to have a more expressive sound. Both schools can produce marvelous results. The best live performance of Bach's B minor Mass I ever heard was by Christopher Hogwood and the early music chorus and orchestra of the Handel and Haydn Society; the next day a Boston critic, probably a follower of the subjective school, deplored the dryness of what was in fact a lucid, understated, and yet inspired performance. Another current early music superstar is

John Eliot Gardiner, of the subjective school, whose passionate interpretations of Baroque music on original instruments are some of the finest of our time.

In all cases, the music and the public are well served. When the Academy of Ancient Music's original-instrument performances of Mozart symphonies appeared in the 1970s, the effect was revelatory. Every note could be heard, down to the second bassoon; the violin octaves of the G minor Symphony opening, which in modern orchestras had always sounded overlush unto saxophonish, were more restrained and yet just as expressive, and the whole orchestra had a beautifully integrated sound. It was not long before mainstream orchestras began to adjust their playing style in response to original-instrument

The early *Kleine Kammermusik* of 1922, for five winds, is full of a piquant wit and charm surprising to those who know his later music. It starts out with a driving energy and engaging tunefulness that never flag through the five movements.

The *Symphonic Metamorphosis of Themes by Carl Maria von Weber* belies the sobriety of its title; it is among the liveliest of his orchestral works. Loosely based on Weber melodies, the four movements form more or less a symphony, complete with jazzy, percussive scherzo and a brassy and bracingly Hollywood-vulgar march.

Long most famous of Hindemith's orchestral works is the symphony *Mathis der Maler,* based on music from his opera of the same name about the sixteenth-century German painter Matthias Grünewald. Premiered in Berlin in 1934, the symphony caused much

performances, cutting down the numbers of strings to the levels Mozart was used to, paring away vestiges of Romantic style in the playing. These days, modern orchestras tend to sound more like an "original" orchestra than they once did in Baroque and Classical literature.

As we go further back in history, the evidence for playing and singing styles becomes skimpier, and it is never less than ambiguous. (Mozart, for example, apparently yearned for larger string sections than he usually got. So what should we do?) All that survives of Monteverdi's seventeenth-century opera *The Coronation of Poppea* is a skeletal score mostly on two lines, the voice part and the bass part. Occasionally there will be an instrumental interlude written on several lines,

but these do not always indicate which instruments are intended. So from knowing what kinds of instruments made up Venetian opera orchestras in those days, and from a few clues about performance practice, modern players and directors make a reconstruction that can never be anything but provisional. Nonetheless, in a good performance Monteverdi's masterpiece still comes through.

Still less do we know about earlier practice. The vocal notation of Josquin and other Renaissance polyphonists, among other omissions, did not precisely indicate how the words and music lined up. We're not sure if instruments ever doubled choral lines, or only sometimes, or most of the time. From period drawings of choruses that seem to show them straining,

trouble for Hindemith and celebrated conductor Wilhelm Furtwäng-
ler; the latter got himself banned by the Nazis for conducting and
defending the work (but later returned to their good graces). The
symphony is in three movements, each based on an episode in the
opera. "Angelic Concert" lives up to its title with the opening gossa-
mer harmonies, then has a bustling allegro developing several
themes contrapuntally; in a characteristic tour de force, these
themes are finally combined with a traditional German chorale melody, bringing the movement to a sonorous close. "Entombment" is
an expansive and somberly beautiful slow movement. Finally, "The
Temptation of St. Anthony" recalls the scene in the opera where
Matthias experiences the horrifying subject of one of his paintings,
St. Anthony beset by demonic visions. The music is hectic and

---

some have concluded that the authentic sound for Renaissance
choral music should be keening
and nasal. Others think that idea
is silly. There *is* a general agreement, anyway, that plush operatic
voices and big choruses are inap-
propriate for pre-Classical music.

Many secular monophonic
songs and dances survive from
medieval times, but all are written
down in a single line without instrumental indications and often
in ambiguous notation. The variability of interpretation can be seen
in comparing renditions of the
"Lamento di Tristan," a fourteenth-century tune that survives
in an Italian manuscript of the
time. Many early music groups
simply play the tune straight;
I have heard it done on harp,
recorder, rebec, and so on. A
Waverly Consort recording goes

through the main tune gently on
soft plucked instruments in parallel fifths, then adds the full
complement of vielle, recorder,
psaltery, drum, and the like for
the dancelike "Rota" that ends
the piece. The Early Music Consort uses rebec, viol, lute, organ
drone, and drum, and makes the
piece into a stately processional;
here the rota is faster, but not so
lusty as with the Waverly's. The
Studio der Frühen Musik, noted
for its improvisations and imaginative interpretations, makes the
same tune richly orchestral, with
elaborate ornamentations added
by the players and a generally
Middle Eastern sound (they sur-
mise that there was much Moor-
ish influence on European music
in those days—after all, the lute
came from the Arabic stringed instrument the oud).

quasi-grotesque, but ends in victorious alleluias from the brass.

In the relatively conservative, postmodern atmosphere of the present day, the time would seem to be ripe for a Hindemith revival. It hasn't happened yet, so we'll wait and see. History, for its part, has not yet figured out what to do with him.

SERGEI PROKOFIEV

Sergei Prokofiev grew up a prodigy with one of the most spectacular creative gifts of our time, left his native Russia after a youthful series of scandals and triumphs, and then, after sixteen years of

---

The effect of the early music movement has been both pervasive and salutary. It opened up a marvelous new literature from the medieval and Renaissance periods, reclaiming long-neglected masters such as Pérotin, Machaut, and Josquin. And the performances refreshed our ears with the sound of dozens of rediscovered instruments, among them the mellow lute, nasal cornett, buzzing krummhorn, and the now-familiar harpsichord. Moving on to Baroque and Classical works, scholars made mainstream musicians far more aware of the evidence relating to performance practice, and thus brought a new level of authenticity to the familiar repertoire.

Most early music specialists have let go of the illusion that we can really find out everything about how Machaut, or Bach, or even Haydn played their music. Going further, many have admitted that our way of doing any music cannot help but reflect our times. As Joel Cohen of the Boston Camerata puts it, "There is only one civilization we can ever hope to express completely and authentically—our own." Thus the term "authentic" performance has tended to give way to the more modest "historically informed." Scholarly research helps keep performers honest, but beyond that it's up to us to make the music live. In the end, early music is simply the name of a twentieth-century performance tradition that has its own past and will have a creative future. As such, it is one of the most exciting developments of contemporary musical life. □

unhappy labors in America and Europe, fled back to the arms of Mother Russia. There in the last decades of his life he would keep, for a while, one uneasy step ahead of the Stalinist thought police. That his risky decision to return home was nonetheless fruitful for his art is shown in the fact that most of his best work, which has made him one of the most popular composers of the century, was written in Russia.

Prokofiev was born into a well-to-do family on April 23, 1891, in the Ukrainian village of Sontzovka. He first studied piano with his mother and at five began to make up little pieces. By age nine he had completed his first opera. At thirteen he was accepted into the St. Petersburg Conservatory, where he studied with Rimsky-Korsakov among others, composed voluminously, and excelled as a pianist. Already he showed his experimental side; when he played his First Piano Concerto for a graduation competition in 1914, Conservatory head Alexander Glazunov fled the hall with hands over his ears. Such was the respect Prokofiev's talent commanded, however, that the jury still gave him first prize. Even finer would be his first symphonic work, finished three years later, the beautiful, irrepressible, not in the least radical Classical Symphony. Those two paradoxical sides of his personality, the classic and the experimental, would coexist surprisingly happily throughout his career.

By the time he graduated from the St. Petersburg Conservatory, Prokofiev was already notorious around Russia. Generally seen as some sort of futurist, he played that role in works of his postconservatory years, such as the piano pieces *Sarcasms* and *Visions fugitives*. In their touches of the mordant and grotesque mingled with compelling lyricism, these already show the composer's mature style. On a performing trip to London, the twenty-two-year-old composer impressed Sergei Diaghilev, impresario of the Ballets Russes, and received a commission for a ballet. That became the primitivistic *Scythian Suite,* clearly in the vein of Stravinsky's *Sacre du printemps* but with a unique personality as well. Diaghilev never produced that work, but the two would become collaborators through the twenties in Paris.

Before that, Prokofiev tried to make his way in the United States; he emigrated here in 1918 intending to stay. But the country did not live up to his hopes. His playing tended to find favor, but as composer he was treated as a barbarian, a Bolshevik, a madman: ''Russian chaos," the critics cried, "a carnival of cacophony," music evoking "visions of a charge of mammoths on some vast immemorial Asiatic plateau." One night, he wrote later, "I wandered through the enormous park in the center of New York and, looking up at the skyscrapers that bordered it, thought with cold fury of the marvelous American orchestras that cared nothing for my music, of the critics who balked so violently at anything new, of the managers who arranged long tours for artists playing the same old hackneyed programs."

So to Paris. There, at least, Modernism was understood. For ten years Prokofiev was associated with the Ballets Russes, part of its roster of legendary artists that had included Stravinsky, Ravel, Debussy, Picasso, and Nijinsky. Among Prokofiev's ballets for Diaghilev and the company were *Chout* (The Fool) and *The Prodigal Son*. Meanwhile he toured around the world. American champions, among them Serge Koussevitzky, kept him coming back to the States; in Chicago in 1921, Prokofiev conducted the premiere of his fantasy opera *The Love for Three Oranges* and played in the premiere of his Third Piano Concerto. Back in Paris, he married Spanish soprano Lina Llubera (whom he would later leave for the young poet Mira Mendelsohn).

All the same, despite the successes in Paris, Prokofiev felt he was living and composing in a vacuum. Finally there seemed to be only one alternative. "I've got to live myself back into the atmosphere of my native soil," he wrote a friend. "I've got to see real winters again, and spring that bursts into being from one moment to the next. I've got to hear the Russian language echoing in my ears. I've got to talk to people who are of my own flesh and blood, so that they can give me back something I lack here—their songs, my songs. Here I'm becoming enervated. I risk dying of academicism. Yes, my friend—I'm going back!"

Russian musicians and authorities welcomed Prokofiev back in 1934, and he launched into a busy schedule of composing. Among his efforts of the thirties were the classic film scores for *Lieutenant Kije* and *Alexander Nevsky*, both of which he turned into concert pieces; the ballet *Romeo and Juliet*; the Second Violin Concerto; and *Peter and the Wolf*, which will introduce children to the instruments of the orchestra as long as orchestras exist. Still, there were rumbles, and sometimes worse, from officialdom about his progressive tendencies, even though his style had become significantly simpler and more populist since his return.

To keep critics at bay, Prokofiev dutifully composed light pieces and toadying official works such as the *Toast to Stalin* of 1939. Meanwhile, he lived the comparatively luxurious life of the state-supported artist. During World War II Prokofiev contributed patriotic pieces and, in 1944, his somber orchestral masterpiece, the Fifth Symphony. Also during the war he finished the gigantic opera *War and Peace*. Then Stalin, after routing the Nazis, turned his attention once again to his people. The dictator was a sensitive fellow, for a politician; he really paid attention to what was going on in the arts. For that reason, those who directed the wrong play, wrote the wrong poem, composed the wrong notes, tended to disappear. In 1948 the roof fell in on composers.

One would think that Prokofiev, who along with Shostakovich was one of the stars of Soviet music, and who had returned to Russia partly because he wanted to draw closer to his people, would have escaped the lash. Instead, it fell heaviest on him. The buzzwords of the denunciation were "decadent formalism," which more or less meant Modernism, art for art's sake, which is "unable to reflect the greatness of our people." Moreover, Prokofiev had been an associate of Diaghilev, "the degenerate, blackguard, anti-Russian lackey of the Western bourgeoisie," and friends with Stravinsky, that "servile and corrupt musical businessman."

These were not polemical words or fighting words; they were potentially lethal words. Atonality could be a capital crime in Stalinist Russia. Like Shostakovich and others, Prokofiev made haste to grovel. "The Resolution of the Central Committee," he wrote in a famous apology, "has separated decayed tissue in our composers' creative production from the healthy part. No matter how painful it may be for many composers, myself included, I welcome the Resolution. . . . As far as I am concerned, elements of formalism were peculiar to my music as long as fifteen or twenty years ago. Apparently the infection was caught from contact with some Western ideas. . . . I must admit that I, too, have indulged in atonality, but I also must say that I have felt an attraction toward tonal music for a considerable time. . . . I should like to express my gratitude to our Party for the precise directives of the Resolution, which will help me in my search for a musical language accessible and natural to our people, worthy of our people and of our great country."

The work he offered in atonement, however, the 1948 opera *A Tale of a Real Man,* was condemned by the authorities. His wife, meanwhile, was imprisoned on political charges. Finally, Prokofiev simply retreated, played it safe, and thus ended his significant creative life. The Stalin Prize he received in 1951 certified that he was reprieved for the moment. Further problems were circumvented by Stalin's death on March 4, 1953, and Prokofiev's, in Moscow, the next day.

In his autobiography, Prokofiev listed, with his accustomed precision, the primary elements of his music:

> The first is classical, whose origin lies in my early infancy when I heard my mother play Beethoven sonatas. . . . The second is innovation. . . . The third is the element of the toccata, or motor element. . . . The fourth element is lyrical. . . . I should like to limit myself to these four elements, and to regard the fifth element, that of the grotesque . . . as merely a variation of the other characteristics. In application to my music, I should like to replace the word grotesque by "Scherzoness," or by the three words giving its gradations: "jest," "laughter," "mockery."

We see here the description of a composer whose art is founded in the forms and procedures of the past, with a strong element of rhythm and lyric melody, but who adds to these elements a taste for experiment and grotesquerie. In practice, that means traditional clarity of form and gesture, but with modernistic elements of various kinds: the craggy leaps in the melodic lines, the dissonant chords amidst traditional ones, the quirky juxtapositions of tonal harmonies, the sudden jumps from key to key. (Though he tinkered with atonality here and there, his music is usually tonal.) There is an unmistakable Prokofiev sound; in the orchestra, that often involves superimpositions of dark textures of low strings and brass, shot through with brilliant high timbres like sunlight breaking through lowering clouds. His rhythm is always muscular and powerful, whether it is lumbering bearlike or leaping along athletically.

Some critics have referred to the latter as his "football" quality. Not surprisingly, Prokofiev was very fond of the bass drum.

These might seem to be elements of a patchwork style, but the music doesn't sound like that. Prokofiev was a natural, a born composer; everything he did comes out with a compelling musicality that synthesizes the most heterogeneous elements into unity. That is one reason why he has attained such popularity despite the surface modernisms of his material. Another is his endless supply of memorable melodies. Once heard, it is hard to forget the whistling tune that represents Peter in *Peter and the Wolf*, the lusty "Troika" in *Lieutenant Kije*, the loping "Dance" from *Romeo and Juliet*.

Prokofiev's most famous orchestral piece is probably the Classical Symphony of 1917, a conscious effort to write something Mozartean in a modern idiom. This work anticipated the neoclassic movement of the next decades—though, oddly, it is Prokofiev's only real essay in neoclassicism. The music is light and charming throughout, with some of the most felicitous moments he ever achieved. The same could be said of *Lieutenant Kije* (1934), a suite Prokofiev drew from his score for a film satire about a fictitious soldier with a bureaucratic life of his own. The sections proceed from "The Birth of Kije" in the minds of aides to the czar, to a "Romance," "Kije's Wedding," "Troika," and finally "The Burial of Kije," when he is killed off. The main glory here is the merry tunes, most of them accompanied by his characteristic vigorous oompahs.

From the extensive ballet music he wrote for *Romeo and Juliet* in 1935, Prokofiev extracted three suites, the best known being the second. The sections are "Montagues and Capulets," "Juliet, the Maiden," "Friar Laurence," "Dance," "The Parting," "Dance of the West Indian Slave Girls," "The Grave of Romeo and Juliet." In grand and stately tones the music captures the unfolding of the drama, from the foreboding beginning to the irresistible dances and love music to the sorrowful music of the end.

The Third Piano Concerto (1921) has long been the most popular of his five. The first movement begins with one of his breezy tunes, then launches into a sprightly allegro with brilliant piano writing. Second is a series of variations on a gentle, sighing theme that is put through some highly contrasting metamorphoses, from slow to fast, meditative to fantastic. The finale is one of his athletic outings, full of irony and mockery, that builds inexorably to a glittering, goose-bump finish.

The Fifth Symphony is surely the most impressive of his seven. Written during World War II, the first movement begins gently but is overtaken by a tone dark and tragic, with anguished themes spreading above the groaning accompaniment. For the second movement there is a scherzo, but rather than the usual joking one this becomes relentless and frighteningly mechanistic. The slow movement is almost unrelievedly tragic in tone, and the finale builds to a savage conclusion. Prokofiev said the Fifth was a testament to "the spirit of man." One of the great works to come out of that war of mechanized extermination, it is a melancholy testament, but nonetheless grand and ultimately triumphant—and not lacking in his characteristic charm in many pages. The Fifth is one of the best demonstrations that, for all his sometime facility and superficial splashiness, Prokofiev understood high tragedy and could make it into music. He was not quite a first-rank composer, perhaps, but his best work has something approaching the skill and the emotional scope of one.

AARON COPLAND

For a man who has long seemed the quintessential American composer, Aaron Copland poses some surprising conundrums. The one most often noted is why someone of Russian-Jewish background, reared in Brooklyn, would end up writing highfalutin cowboy music with a French accent. Beyond that, how and why did he make the transition from being called a nearly murderous Modernist to the most genial and avuncular of composers? Or *was* there a transition? Among other things, these paradoxes add some depth and ambiguity to a body of work that can seem so plain and direct that it threatens to become simplistic. At his best, though, Copland's Modernist side adds bite to the folksiness, and the combination can produce considerable strength and subtlety, not to mention fun. In those pieces he is a one-man melting pot. As with film director John Ford, Copland's primary subject is the myth of the American frontier, of the vast spaces, the small sorrows, the hopes and joys of everyday people.

Aaron Copland was born in Brooklyn on November 14, 1900, the son of a Jewish store owner who had emigrated from Russia. Later Copland would recall, "I was born on a street in Brooklyn that can only be described as drab. . . . It fills me with mild wonder each time I realize that a musician was born on that street." Drawn irresistibly to music, he studied piano from age thirteen and at seventeen began lessons in harmony with the conservative composer Rubin Goldmark. His first published piece, *The Cat and the Mouse* of 1920, was already more modernistic than his teacher could countenance. In 1921 Copland went to Paris, looking for inspiration in the city that Stravinsky, Picasso, Joyce, and other revolutionaries were making the artistic hub of the world.

There Copland ended up as the first American pupil of the brilliant teacher Nadia Boulanger, who would go on to inculcate the doctrine of Stravinskian neoclassicism in a generation of composers from the States including Virgil Thomson, Walter Piston, and Roy Harris. From Boulanger, Copland gained a solid technical foundation and a superb understanding of the orchestra. Though his crystalline scoring would owe much to the model of Stravinsky, he would always have a distinctive sound.

In 1924 Copland returned to New York, where over the years he would work indefatigably as a composer, performer, and advocate of new music. His style at that time was heavily influenced by jazz; he had seized on that still new African-American music as the most direct path to his goal, which was "to make the music . . . come out of the life I had lived in America." He had left Paris fired with the determination to create a true American concert music (not yet knowing that Charles Ives, working in isolation, had already done that two decades before).

During the twenties Copland had a number of important performances, however ambiguous their reception. In January 1925 the New York Symphony under Walter Damrosch premiered his Organ Symphony, written for Nadia Boulanger, who played the organ in the first performance. After the piece, Damrosch turned to the audience and added a sardonic postscript that would be long remembered: "If a young man at the age of twenty-three can write a symphony like that, in five years he will be ready to commit murder!" (For years after, Damrosch apologized every time he saw the composer.) Over the next few years Boston Symphony conductor

*Copland promoted new music
and new composers in books and
on his radio program,
"Aaron Copland Comments."*

Serge Koussevitzky, an unequivocal admirer of Copland, conducted the Organ Symphony, the jazzy and ironic *Music for the Theatre,* and the Piano Concerto.

By 1930 Copland had abandoned overt jazz elements in his music, though it would remain part of his rhythmic style. For several years he pursued a severe avant-garde idiom, typified by the concentrated and somewhat serial Piano Variations of 1930. Meanwhile he became involved with various projects in behalf of his profession—the League of Composers, new music concerts with composer Roger Sessions, and lectures and articles that would make up a series of books beginning with the 1939 *What to Listen for in Music.* In 1932 Copland co-founded the Yaddo Festival in Saratoga Springs, New York, starting those concerts with his own historic performance of songs by Ives, which gained much attention for the old Yankee. Copland would always be a generous promoter, his generation's major statesman of new music. Among his other efforts, he helped found the Arrow Press, which published a broad spectrum of American Works, and the American Composers Alliance. From 1940 to 1965 he was a mainstay of the summer school at Tanglewood, teaching dozens of young composers. Among his protégés was Leonard Bernstein; the two men would have a close working relationship to the end of their lives (they died within a few weeks of each other).

By the 1930s Copland had established a solid reputation among the relatively few people who followed avant-garde music. But he began to be unhappy with his isolation from the mainstream. Stimulated by left-wing ideas that proliferated in America during the Depression, he began to look for a style that would be closer to the people. "During those years," he would write, "I began to feel an increasing dissatisfaction with the relations of the music-loving public and the living composer. . . . It seemed to me that we composers were in danger of working in a vacuum. . . . I felt that it was worth the effort to see if I couldn't say what I had to say in the simplest possible terms." For inspiration and material he looked to folk music of various kinds, from New England to Southwestern to Latin-American. *Simplicity* would be his talisman.

The first work of what came to be called his "Americana" or "populist" period was the orchestral *El Salón México* of 1936. Based on dances Copland had heard in Mexico, it was designed to communicate to the average concertgoer and did so. *El Salón* became an enormous success, of a kind few contemporary works were finding in that period. That and the following pieces in his populist style belong to what is usually considered Copland's third period (the first period including the youthful jazz-inspired works, the second the severe style represented by the Piano Variations). However, Copland never really left his second style; it would crop up now and then and return full force in his late serial pieces.

In a few years, from the late thirties into the forties, he produced all his most beloved works—notably the two cowboy ballets *Billy the Kid* (1938) and *Rodeo* (1942), and his masterpiece, the ballet *Appalachian Spring* of 1944. All use borrowed folk material, such as the Shaker tune "Simple Gifts" in *Appalachian Spring*. But Copland had absorbed folk style so completely that his own melodies now sounded like the voice of his country speaking its native musical tongue. To that he added his brilliant orchestration, in which the busiest textures are transparent and the familiar instruments seem expressive in their very sound: a clarinet playing a single sustained tone somehow becomes a Copland clarinet, and a viola section can touch your heart with a couple of notes arranged just so. His harmonies are expressive and elegant whether consonant or dissonant, and even when he is using familiar chords and chord progressions he makes them sound fresh and new. And finally, his work sustains a characteristic rhythmic energy, based mainly on the shifting accents of jazz but no longer sounding merely imitative. The "Americana" style was now fully formed. As far as the public was concerned, from the late thirties into the fifties that style—represented by Copland, Thomson, Harris, Piston, and several others— would be *the* American concert music.

Copland's most ambitious work for orchestra appeared in 1946, the Third Symphony, a massive work sometimes magnificent and sometimes frustrating. Its finale incorporates an earlier piece, the stately *Fanfare for the Common Man* of 1942, which over the years has served as everything from college-graduation music to a title tune for TV news coverage of the Olympics. Also in the forties, by way of a patriotic contribution to the war effort, Copland produced the *Lincoln Portrait*, in which spoken excerpts from Lincoln's writings are accompanied by orchestral music using folk tunes the president might have known. Between 1939 and 1961, Copland wrote music to accompany eight films. Of those, his score for *The Heiress* won an Oscar; the music for *Our Town* and *The Red Pony* he made into orchestral suites. His one opera, *The Tender Land,* appeared in 1954; periodically revived, it has yet to secure a place in the repertoire (though a 1990 recording was a classical best seller).

To nearly everyone's surprise, in 1950 Copland returned to his severe style with the Piano Quartet, which uses serial methods. Thus he anticipated Stravinsky in turning away from a popular style to a serialism that audiences found hard to absorb; this would be the general tendency among composers of the next twenty-five years or so. Despite the complaints of many of his devotees, including Leonard Bernstein, he used serial techniques in several more works of the next years, including the orchestral pieces *Connotations* (1962) and *Inscape* (1967). Critics have long tried to find the connections between the two streams of Copland's music, the experimental and the folksy. With typical matter-of-factness Copland explained it this way: "You [can't] just happily go on doing what you always had been doing and get away with it. Going into 12-tone seemed to me to be giving myself possibilities I wouldn't otherwise have had, and it never occurred to me that by adopting a method that so many other people were working with that I was somehow betraying myself."

In 1971 Copland returned one final time to his Americana style in the touching Duo for Flute and Piano. Then he put down his pen, saying he had done enough. Into the 1980s he would be active as a conductor, but would not attempt any new work. Among the dozens of honors of his later years was the Presidential Medal of Freedom. After years of declining health, Copland died in North Tarrytown, New York, on December 2, 1990.

For an introduction to Copland, I'll suggest one of his most characteristic and attractive works, *El Salón México*. Here one finds in a nutshell his lucid and sinewy orchestration, his imaginative reworkings of folk tunes, his sprightly dance rhythms. Then go on to the two cowboy ballets, *Billy the Kid* and *Rodeo*. The former is the more expansive, with evocations of the broad prairie, of dances and gun battles, in what seems to be their definitive musical representation. *Rodeo* is more of a boisterous hoedown, with buckaroos and gals and fiddlers all over the place.

Appalachian Spring has the same idiom, but more subtly and movingly presented. The scenario of the Martha Graham ballet was a simple story of a young couple getting married and beginning their life together. Copland made three versions of the music—the original for chamber ensemble, a somewhat shorter suite for full orchestra (the best known), and the complete ballet redone for full orchestra. The suite may be, and justly so, the most-loved orchestral work ever written in America. It is music of quiet grace here, dancing joyfulness there. The most famous section is the variations on the Shaker song "Simple Gifts," a tune Copland rescued from obscurity. His genius for evocation, his simplicity hiding great sophistication, and his understated emotion are never better seen than here. The original chamber version is equally fine, with an introspective and spiritual quality that is somewhat swamped in the suite for full orchestra.

The Piano Variations (1930) represent Copland's more austere and challenging side. A terse seven-note theme undergoes a series of metamorphoses, every note of the piece derived from the theme in ways reminiscent of Webern's serial technique. The total effect is at once forbidding and magisterial, curt and expressive.

In the Third Symphony Copland clearly intended to integrate all of his work, from the folksy to the forbidding. The result is a fascinating piece, often engaging, often disappointing, sometimes majestic and sometimes trying too hard to be. The first movement begins with one of his broad landscapes, building to heroic proclamations; though there are moments of peace, this movement has an ominous undercurrent. Second comes a characteristic lilting scherzo introduced by brassy fanfares. The slow movement may be the most intriguing and most unsatisfying; it feels odd, uneasy, wandering—and what does the intrusion of a cheery, dancelike section mean? The finale emerges from the third movement, with winds building to the majestic "Fanfare for the Common Man" section. The movement then turns into yet another cheery dance. But what do those chilling dissonant chords signify, breaking suddenly into the dance and leading to a mysterious babbling section?

The piece ends with grandiloquent proclamations, heavy on brass and gongs and bass drum.

The fascination of the Third Symphony, it seems to me, goes beyond the attractiveness of its material on one hand and its peculiarities on the other. Maybe it reveals some genuine deficiencies in Copland's formal control. Or, more interestingly, perhaps here Copland hinted at conflicts and passions that lay beneath a surface personality that never cracked, a surface affable, giggly, statesmanly, never controversial (he kept his homosexuality under wraps to the end). The symphony seems, in other words, to be following some unstated program that might account for its vagaries. Maybe here Copland for once explained himself—but only in music that he never explained in words. With this enigma he crowned his long, successful, generous, and to all appearances untroubled life in music.

DMITRI SHOSTAKOVICH

To be an artist in a totalitarian state and survive both physically and creatively, one must play a surreal game with mortal stakes, a game of submission and humiliation, of periodic betrayals of self and others, of tentative advances and desperate retreats. The main rules are: never be what you seem, never mean what you seem to say. Dmitri Shostakovich played cat and mouse with the Soviet authorities for his entire career, alternately provoking them and knuckling under, while dozens of friends and fellow artists fell into the abyss. He must have lived with almost unimaginable fear, waiting decade after decade for the final denunciation, the knock on the door. You could see it on his face in later life, in the eyes nervously darting behind the thick glasses, the endless cigarettes, the weary masklike features.

He survived three interlocking hells: the Russian Revolution, World War II, and the Stalinist holocaust. His sadly uneven output gains much of its power from our understanding of what he lived through and tried to embody in his work. It is no surprise that his most familiar tones are savage irony and tragedy. In many passages he seems to be straining to encompass something too big to be contained in notes, some anguish and horror beyond the possibility of expression. As with all serious art produced under a dictatorship, with Shostakovich one must read between the lines, behind the notes, to find the real meanings and the real voice. At his best, in guarded but no less profound tones he mourns for his friends, his country, and for all victims of all tyrannies.

Dmitri Dmitriyevich Shostakovich was born in St. Petersburg on September 25, 1906, to a family enjoying its last years of prosperity before the Russian Revolution. His father was a government engineer and musical amateur; his mother, a concert pianist, gave him his first lessons. He entered the Petrograd Conservatory in 1919, during the post-Revolutionary tumult and famine. The head of the Conservatory had to petition for more rations to keep this talented pupil from starving. Shostakovich's graduation piece was the First Symphony, written at eighteen, which within a few years had been played around the world. It remains one of his best-known works.

In 1930 he scored another major success with an opera called *The Nose,* based on a Gogol fantasy about a clerk's nose which, separated from his body, becomes a government official. Premiered in Leningrad during a period of relative lenience toward experimental art, the work put an aggressively modernistic musical style at the service of satire and fantasy. Some official rumbles about bourgeois decadence appeared, but nothing too serious.

Things were going well for Shostakovich in those days. He wrote the first of many film scores and two ballets, including the popular *Age of Gold* (its story of a Russian soccer team reflects the composer's lifelong obsession with sports). He had secured a solid career in his own country and a growing international reputation. In 1932 he married Nina Varzar. Of their two children, son Maxim would become a noted conductor and specialist in his father's works.

With the opera *Lady Macbeth of the Mzensk District,* completed in 1932 and premiered two years later, Shostakovich went still further in provocative subject matter and musical style. The story concerns a woman who murders her husband and father-in-law in order to marry her lover; she gets caught and finally kills herself. Shostakovich's music shows the influence of Berg's expressionist opera *Wozzeck,* but with graphic illustrative touches such as the trombone

*Shostakovich, with no time to court the Muse,
wrote fast, in ink, on the final score.*

slides that accompany an offstage tryst of the lovers. He saw her less
as a monster than a victim of society—not communist society, of
course, but the old czarist one. In the same period, perhaps in an
attempt to reassure the authorities, Shostakovich wrote a ballet
called *The Limpid Stream* about the pleasures of life on a collective
farm. The ballet was a hit, but *Lady Macbeth* was a sensation; a

production of the latter in Moscow packed in audiences for two years, and in Europe and America the opera was hailed as the best of its kind to come out of Soviet Russia.

All the acclaim ceased suddenly when, it is said, Stalin dropped into this famous production and was not amused. In January 1936 an unsigned *Pravda* article—the most feared, since they usually came from on high—appeared under the title "Muddle Instead of Music." It condemned *Lady Macbeth* as "the coarsest kind of naturalism. . . . The music quacks, grunts, growls, and suffocates itself in order to express the amatory scenes as naturalistically as possible." The article ended ominously by predicting that if he did not change his ways, the composer "could end very badly." Such an end, in the Soviet Union, did not mean merely lost prestige and commissions; it could well mean a bullet in the back of the head. Even worse, a second article denounced *The Limpid Stream* as vulgar and showing "contempt for our national songs." Unnerved, Shostakovich withdrew his Fourth Symphony, then in rehearsal. *Lady Macbeth* would not be heard again until 1963, revised and renamed *Katerina Ismailova;* it would find success comparable to its premiere production. The Fourth Symphony would finally be premiered in the same decade. In 1936, all Shostakovich could do was knuckle under and try to write something safe. Somehow he managed to redeem himself with one of his finest scores.

That return to official grace came with the Fifth Symphony of 1937. Its conservative idiom and heroic tone found favor both with audiences and with officials, who presumably did not notice its troubling undercurrents. The Fifth, at once direct and powerful yet shot through with ambiguities, became Shostakovich's most popular work and still is. The hundred-thousand-ruble Stalin Prize, awarded in 1940 for the Piano Quintet, showed that Shostakovich was again an approved composer.

As had happened with Prokofiev, World War II brought Shostakovich the opportunity to display his patriotism in music and deeds, and his patriotism seems to have been quite genuine. In the United States, the Soviet Union, and the Allied countries of Europe, he became a symbol of Soviet resistance; a picture of Shostakovich in his volunteer fireman's hat appeared on the cover of *Time* magazine. His most celebrated effort of the war was the 1941 Seventh

Symphony, called *Leningrad* from its dedication to that war-ravaged city. The work was performed hundreds of times during the war in most of the Allied countries, over sixty times in America alone in 1942 and 1943. However, though it is still heard now and then, the Seventh has not worn too well past its function as an Allied icon. The first movement especially, which depicts the coming of the Nazis with a banal tune repeated some dozen times steadily louder, can be a chore to sit through. (Bartók razzed the movement in his *Concerto for Orchestra*.)

One would have expected Shostakovich at that point to be an unassailable figure. Besides achieving heroic status during the war, he was a leader of several Communist party organizations and had written stacks of patriotic pieces and film scores. But in the Russia of those years, only Stalin was unassailable. In 1948 official condemnation descended on most of the leading composers (as detailed in the Prokofiev section). Shostakovich's Eighth and Ninth symphonies and Third String Quartet were denounced for their "formalist perversions and antidemocratic tendencies . . . alien to the Soviet people and its artistic tastes." Performances of his music ceased; he was released from teaching duties at the Moscow Conservatory; everywhere he was suddenly a pariah.

Like Prokofiev, a terrified Shostakovich publicly recited his mea culpas: he deplored bourgeois artists, saying music must cease to be a "toy in the hands of satiated gourmands and aesthetes and . . . again become a great social force." And for his part, "I am deeply grateful for all the criticism contained in the Resolution. I shall, with still more determination, work on the musical depiction of the images of the heroic Soviet people." He got out of danger this time with the oratorio *Song of the Forests* (1949), a paean to Stalin's glorious reforestation program, which won Shostakovich his third Stalin Prize.

Nicolas Slonimsky, Russian-born writer and musician, observed that Shostakovich had been "the barometer of political current in Soviet music. Whenever the line changes, Shostakovich is made the prime target of either praise or vehement denunciation." After Stalin's death in 1953, life became less risky for artists, and Shostakovich reigned as the dean of Soviet composers. While he kept hedging his bets with patriotic works, he also took bolder chances. The fifties saw toadying pieces like the cantata *The Sun Shines on Our*

Homeland and the Twelfth Symphony, dedicated to the memory of Lenin and gushing with noisy, stern-but-joyful heroic bombast of the approved sort. Other works of that period, though, show the serious Shostakovich—the Tenth Symphony of 1953, perhaps his finest, and some of the string quartets that all along were his private rebellion against his times. Meanwhile his reputation grew in the West, even though many saw him as tainted by his willingness to kowtow to the establishment in return for the cars, the money, the vacation cottages and private shops of the approved artist.

After the party-line Twelfth Symphony, Shostakovich felt safe enough to release one of his most powerful and courageous works, the Thirteenth Symphony (1962), subtitled *Babi Yar*. Written for vocal soloists, chorus, and orchestra, it is based on poems by Yevgeny Yevtushenko that speak of Russian tragedies of both past and, by implication, present. The titular first movement is a meditation on the Nazi massacre of thousands of Jews at Kiev, and a condemnation of continuing anti-Semitism in the Soviet Union: "Over Babi Yar there are no monuments . . . I am terrified. / I am as old today / As all Jewish people . . ."

For Shostakovich this symphony reflected years of concern with the Jewish plight, an earlier example being the Piano Trio op. 67, much of it based on Jewish melodies. Still, I suspect that, as usual, there are broader dimensions to his concern. Yevtushenko's "Babi Yar" says, "I imagine that I'm a Jew. / Here I wander through ancient Egypt." Poet and composer are talking directly about Jewish suffering under Hitler, but indirectly about that of Russians under Stalin. Meanwhile they knew that the Soviet government would be constrained by world opinion from coming down too hard on a work that condemned anti-Semitism; such a condemnation would itself be anti-Semitic. As it was, Premier Nikita Khrushchev insisted that Yevtushenko add a few lines to the text noting that others besides Jews were victims of Nazi atrocities. In that form, the Thirteenth found acclaim in the Soviet Union. Thus we see the tormented logic of artistic production in a totalitarian state, even in the relatively mild days of Khrushchev. In the end, perhaps the real theme of the Thirteenth Symphony is in the fourth movement, called "Fears": "I remember fears being in power and force / At the court of the triumphant lie."

There are triumphant lies and triumphant lies. Stalin was one kind, Shostakovich another: his art may be seen as a triumph over the words he was forced to speak. Near the end of his life he said to a friend: "I never lie in music." After years of illness, reflected in the bleak leave-takings of his Fifteenth Symphony and Fifteenth String Quartet, Shostakovich died in Moscow on August 9, 1975.

Four years later, a book was published in New York called *Testimony: The Memoirs of Dmitri Shostakovich,* "as told to and edited by Solomon Volkov." In the book, the composer paints himself as a victim of the Soviet system, his endorsements of that system as a ruse, his entire work as a secret rebellion and a series of tombstones for friends murdered by Stalin. However, that book itself may not be what it seems. Most evidence, including the opinion of Shostakovich's widow and son Maxim (the latter now living in America), suggests the book is a fraud, though in some degree it probably reflects Shostakovich's actual life and opinions. Volkov has refused to produce the manuscript. The smoke and mirrors continue even after the composer's death: one wonders if Volkov fabricated the book to convince the West that Shostakovich was not the loyal Communist drone he was long considered to be. If so, the book had the desired effect.

In any case, the music of Shostakovich stands as a flawed and compromised legacy, but one that at times was worthy of a vast and harrowing subject. The heroism and significance of art surviving amidst chaos is something the West needs to hear and understand. A Russian artist once observed, "In Russia, few things are possible and everything is important. In America, everything is possible— and nothing is important."

Shostakovich's Symphony no. 5 in D minor (1937) remains one of the relatively few symphonies of its time to have settled into the standard repertoire, probably because of its communicativeness and its conservative idiom, often reminiscent of Mahler. The first movement begins with solemn dramatic proclamations and goes on to a wide range of ideas from slow to marchlike. Next is a scherzo, with a typically sardonic undercurrent. These first two movements have contrapuntal stretches, but next comes a broad expanse of pure lyrical counterpoint, with not one note wasted or out of place; one of his finest slow movements, its tone is unremittingly somber (as in much Shostakovich, minor keys predominate throughout). The finale begins with a brassy and perhaps deliberately banal march tune; like the first movement, this is rich in contrasts. From the Fifth, one might go on to the lyrical Tenth Symphony (1953) and the dark and magnificent Thirteenth, discussed above.

A good introduction to his chamber music might be the Piano Trio no. 2 in E minor op. 67 (1944), written to commemorate the death of his friend Ivan Sollertinsky. Since much of it is based on folk tunes, this trio is among Shostakovich's most melodious instrumental works. Here one sees why the poet Anna Akhmatova said he could write "as though the flowers had suddenly begun to talk." A relatively calm and folksy first movement is followed by one of his motoric scherzos. The elegiac slow movement uses the old form of the chaconne, a series of variations over a repeated bass. Perhaps a response to the first reports arriving in Russia about the Nazi concentration camps, the last movement uses Yiddish folk tunes in a pounding, relentless dance of death. (Shostakovich often drew material from Jewish music, saying that even its dances can express despair, can mask tragedy with gaiety.)

Shostakovich's fifteen string quartets are one of the century's most notable bodies of chamber music. As I said above, he relegated to these personal, nearly private works many of the feelings and the technical adventurousness he could not afford to display in his more public pieces. Among the best known is the String Quartet no. 8 in C minor (1960), in five conjoined movements. It was written while Shostakovich was working on a film score in the ruined city of Dresden, site of an Allied fire-bomb attack during World War II that incinerated thousands of German civilians. The quartet is dedicated "to the victims of fascism and the war." But the notes tell us there is another dimension: dominating the entire work is the motto D-E♭-C-B, which in German notation is D-S-C-H, letters derived from the composer's name. The quartet also uses themes from several of his symphonies and other works including the E minor Piano Trio and *Lady Macbeth*. Moreover, it quotes a well-known Russian song with the line, "Exhausted by the hardships of prison." In other words, this quartet is a self-portrait of the composer, brooding once more on a scene of devastation. It begins in a tone of foreboding, each part entering with D-S-C-H. Then erupts a frenzied and some-times hysterical allegro, another of his dances of death, followed by a skittering scherzo based again on the D-S-C-H motto. A slow fourth movement features suggestions of the *Dies Irae* (Day of Judg-ment) melody, a Gregorian chant long associated with death and apocalypse. The final movement is a weary, bleak meditation on the D-S-C-H motive, which seems to drift into silence.

The String Quartet no. 11 is a more enigmatic work, laid out in seven short movements including a quiet scherzo with drones and folk tunes; a painful recitative, the violin sawing away crazily over rakingly dissonant chords; an étude with nimble figures playing around a Russian tune, and so on. It ends with a blank, fading high note in violin.

Like much Shostakovich, these two quartets are composed largely in shades of melancholy, rage, despair, devastation. A good deal of what makes them worth hearing and ultimately life-affirming is their very existence, their paradoxical vitality. They are an abiding testament that nothing, not even the worst things in the world, can make a true singer stop singing.

BENJAMIN BRITTEN

In England, Benjamin Britten is honored as the most significant native composer since Henry Purcell, and the man who woke En-glish opera from its three-hundred-year somnolence after Purcell's *Dido and Aeneas*. To the rest of the world, Britten is simply one of the most admired composers of the century, his works marked by ready communicativeness whether their technical means are traditional or modernistic. Clearly, communication was Britten's main intention. "I believe in the artist serving society," he said. "It is better to be a bad composer writing for society than to be a bad composer writ-ing against it. At least your work can be of *some* use." Toward that end of creating useful work, he brought high craftsmanship and an innate musicality that helps unify an eclectic range of influences.

He was born Edward Benjamin Britten on November 22, 1913, in Lowestoft, on the coast of Suffolk. He would recall, "My parents' house directly faced the sea, and my childhood was colored by the fierce storms that sometimes drove ships into our coast.'' A prodigy, he played piano from early childhood and by age fourteen had completed a symphony, six string quartets, and ten piano sonatas. In his teens he studied with a noted British composer whose influence would be memorialized in Britten's youthful masterpiece, Variations on a Theme of Frank Bridge (1937). Between 1930 and 1933, he pursued piano and composition, not very happily, at the Royal College of Music.

Britten had some major successes in his early twenties, among them his Simple Symphony, based on melodies from his childhood works. His main training ground as a dramatic composer, he would say, were the many scores for documentary films and radio dramas that he wrote in the early thirties, for which he had to turn out

Britten with his companion and greatest interpreter, tenor Peter Pears.

evocative music with a minimum of means. Among the films was the classic *Night Mail*, with narration written by W. H. Auden; the poet would become Britten's close friend and occasional librettist.

In 1939 Britten followed Auden in fleeing the war to America; with him was his companion, lover, and longtime collaborator, the tenor Peter Pears. For the rest of his life, most of Britten's music for tenor, including the title role of *Peter Grimes*, would be written for Pears's unique, clarion voice. In the United States, far from the war raging in Europe, Britten completed some of his finest works, including the song cycle *Les Illuminations* and the *Sinfonia da Requiem*. He also first tried his hand at an opera, *Paul Bunyan*, on an Auden libretto; at its premiere in New York, he reported, the opera was "politely spat at."

In 1942, an attack of homesickness took Britten back to England. On the journey over he wrote his choral work *A Ceremony of Carols*, which has since become a Christmas favorite. Meanwhile he had secured an opera commission from Boston Symphony conductor Serge Koussevitzky. A pacifist and conscientious objector, Britten spent the rest of the war concertizing around England and working on the commissioned opera, *Peter Grimes*. In 1945 he produced a series of orchestral variations on a Purcell piece, called *The Young Person's Guide to the Orchestra*. The work has been nearly as popular as Prokofiev's *Peter and the Wolf* in introducing children to orchestral instruments.

Peter Grimes was premiered in June 1945, the first performance in the reopened Sadler's Wells Opera House, whose doors had closed years before during the German blitz. The opera was thus both a symbolic and a musical event; the postwar reviving of the English operatic stage with an ambitious new work. All scheduled performances were sold out before a note had been heard. Many feared that *Peter Grimes* could not live up to the anticipation; in fact, it went beyond what anyone had hoped. Edmund Wilson wrote after the premiere, "The opera seizes on you, possesses you, keeps you riveted to your seat during the action and keyed up during the intermissions, and drops you, purged and exhausted, at the end." Soon it was having that effect in theaters around the world. Leonard Bernstein conducted the American premiere at Tanglewood, a legendary evening in the history of that summer festival. Everywhere, *Peter Grimes* solidified Britten's reputation as one of the leading composers of his generation. It also revivified British opera and stimulated dramatic composers around the world.

Britten settled into the Suffolk coastal village of Aldeburgh, near his birthplace. In 1948 he and Pears founded the Aldeburgh Festival, an annual event whose initial purpose was to produce chamber operas by English composers. There over the years many of Britten's works were first heard. The festival gradually expanded into a wide range of concerts, art exhibits, and the like, a major feature of which were song recitals by Britten and Pears. In addition to giving numerous piano performances that featured his own work, Britten became an authoritative conductor. He had always believed in the idea of the composer-performer, a tradition mostly fallen by the wayside in the twentieth century. To this day, many of the finest recordings of Britten are played or conducted by the composer. He and Pears also made some handsome recordings of Schubert, Britten playing that music as much "from the inside" as he did his own.

Britten's career from the fifties on lacked variety, perhaps, but it was notable for productivity. He lived a carefully controlled life made up of steady composing—an opera usually in the works, other pieces fit into the schedule here and there—plus performing and organizing the Aldeburgh Festival. He wrote through the morning in his studio and spent much of the rest of the day swimming in his pool or walking on the seashore plunged in thought.

The works of Britten's later years broke little new ground but confirmed the nature and vitality of his gift. He had one of the widest stylistic orbits of any modern composer, encompassing everything from the simplest consonant music to strong dissonance, and occasional forays into his own version of twelve-tone writing. Even at his most chromatic, though, Britten always remains tonal, or at least polytonal. His broad stylistic command enabled him to produce effective pieces for children's performance, such as *Let's Make an Opera* of 1949. Many of his most ambitious works are notable for their stylistic mixture; at times the diversity gets out of hand, but more often things cohere into an integrated style.

His vocal works are marked by strong lyricism and a characteristically free handling of the text. His settings can sometimes seem awkward; at other times he illuminates a line by breaking away from its expected accents. While his music is always expressive, there is a certain classical distance and formalism as well; in his chamber opera *The Turn of the Screw* (1954), for example, each scene has a variation on a twelve-note theme heard at the beginning.

As influences turned up, Britten integrated them into his work. Early ones included Mahler and Berg. A visit to Indonesia produced the glittering gamelanlike music of the ballet *Prince of the Pagodas* (1957). Later, exposure to Japanese Noh plays led to the three ritualistic chamber operas he called "Parables"—*Curlew River, The Burning Fiery Furnace,* and *The Prodigal Son* (they were designed for small-scale performances in church). In the sixties, a friendship with Russian cellist Mstislav Rostropovich inspired a cello sonata, two solo suites, and the Cello Symphony. An abiding influence in all his work was the British tradition of Purcell and the Elizabethan madrigalists. Without either the folk-based style of his contemporary Ralph Vaughan Williams or the plush old-school sound of Elgar, Britten is still British to the core, not least in his pragmatic, no-nonsense approach to his craft.

Britten was stricken by a heart ailment in the mid seventies and had to end his public career. He had just finished his final opera, and one of his finest—*Death in Venice,* based on the Thomas Mann story of an aging writer who falls fatally in love with a young boy. Clearly, this story had strong personal resonances for Britten. He had written much music for boys' voices, and a primary recurring theme of his dramatic works is wounded innocence. Near the end of *Death in Venice,* the doomed writer dreams of a struggle between Apollo and Dionysus. Here Britten seems to symbolize the tensions in his hero, in his music, in the music of his time, and in his own soul: Form or freedom? Obedience or license? Discipline or ecstasy?

Britten was knighted by Queen Elizabeth in 1976. As his health declined, he kept at composing until his death in Aldeburgh, on December 4, 1976.

Britten wrote first-rate work in many forms, but the heart of his output is vocal music: eleven operas, thirteen song cycles, ten cantatas, and many smaller pieces. A good introduction to his work might be the popular *A Ceremony of Carols* (1942), originally written for boys' voices and harp, sometimes heard in a full-chorus arrangement. With its integration of Gregorian chants and imaginative reworkings of medieval English carols, it has become a favorite item of Christmas choral performances. Especially memorable are the warm lyricism of "There is no rose of such virtue / As is the rose that bare Jesu," and the leaping close canons of "This Little Babe." Here one sees several Britten trademarks: material drawn from British tradition, a love of boys' voices, a ceremonial quality designed for church performance, and a gift for filling out rigorous formal ideas with ingratiating music.

Some of those qualities also mark his work for string orchestra, Variations on a Theme of Frank Bridge (1937), in which his childhood teacher's theme is taken through a variety of transformations including caricatures of Rossini and a Viennese waltz. There is a brash vitality to this work, as if the young composer were confidently announcing his presence to the world. Over the years the prolific Britten produced his share of stolid workaday stuff, but to the end of his life he never lost the ability to dazzle with bursts of youthful energy.

For an introduction to his operatic music, one could start with the Five Orchestral Interludes from *Peter Grimes,* often performed at orchestral concerts. These character pieces are done in the opera with curtains closed. They open memorably with the breezy high strings of "Dawn," then go on to the electrifying "Storm," ringing "Sunday Morning," "Passacaglia," and quiet "Moonlight."

While *Peter Grimes* is Britten's best-known opera, there are several of comparable strength, among them his chamber opera of 1954, *The Turn of the Screw.* It is based on Henry James's enigmatic story about ghosts haunting two children entrusted to the care of a fearful young governess. The motto of the opera, a line taken from Yeats, is, "The ceremony of innocence is drowned." We have, then, another of Britten's stories about lost innocence, children threatened by the adult world and adult evil, with lurking sexual undercurrents. The ghostly Peter Quint enthralls young Miles as the dead Miss Jessel threatens Miles's sister, Flora. At the end Miles repudiates Quint, only to fall dead. The music ranges from bright children's songs to unsettling episodes all the more powerful for being understated: Miles sings to his unsuspecting governess a strange, mesmerizing song, called "Malo," taught to him by Quint. And there is Quint's song to Miles: "I am all things strange and bold . . . I am the smooth world's double face . . . In me secrets and half-formed desires meet." However compact and restrained, *The Turn of the Screw* is a theatrical masterpiece.

That opera might prepare one for the larger canvas of *Peter Grimes,* the story of a sadistic fisherman responsible for the death of two boy apprentices. With unerring dramatic instinct, Britten paints Grimes as an antihero not without sympathy and humanity, struggling against spiteful townsfolk, the implacable sea, and his own growing madness.

In many ways Britten's most ambitious effort is the *War Requiem* of 1961, a flawed but still impressive work for chorus, soloists, and orchestra. It weaves together the traditional Latin Mass for the Dead with antiwar poems by Wilfrid Owen, a young officer killed in World War I. The point of the *War Requiem* is how the words of the liturgical text are reinterpreted and often rendered hollow by the realities of death in war: for example, the Latin text *Quam olim Abrahae* (Thou didst promise to Abraham and his seed) is undercut by Owen's bitter recasting of the Abraham story, in which the angel appears to tell the father not to sacrifice his son, "But the old man would not so, but slew his son—/ And half the seed of Europe, one by one." In this work we see Britten's prodigal inconsistencies on display, from the fusty brassiness of the *Tuba mirum* to several memorable solos and duets. For all its problems, the *War Requiem* will probably survive as one of our time's most impassioned indictments of war and its heroic myth, which Owen called "the old Lie." Britten seems to have been a religious man, but he was a clearsighted humanist as well, not least in his determination to contribute to the larger community rather than stay aloof from it.

OTHER TWENTIETH-CENTURY COMPOSERS

Our roundup of other twentieth-century composers will inevitably contain more names than the roundups of other periods. After any artistic era, it takes time for musicians, the public, and historians to sort out which figures and trends seem the more significant (not that such sorting is ever definitive). And as I noted at the outset, things have never been so tumultuous as in this century, in music as in all the arts.

All the figures below are currently very much in circulation. Some of them, such as Puccini and Rachmaninov, are well entrenched in the standard repertoire. Some, such as Cage, Messiaen, and Boulez, are seminal Modernists who have wielded great influence while rarely interesting the general public. Some of the composers mentioned will surely decline in importance over the years. A few, such as Janáček, Ellington, and Tippett, I suspect will loom larger in histories fifty years from now than they do at present.

The music of **Gabriel Fauré** (1845–1924) has always been appreciated most in his native France, where the refined melodic lines and subtle harmonies of his songs are especially valued. As a longtime teacher at the Paris Conservatory and its director from 1905 to 1920, Fauré had much influence on the next generation of composers; among his pupils were Ravel and Nadia Boulanger. His harmonic innovations and use of modal scales laid some of the groundwork for the impressionists, for whom he was also a model of classical restraint. Though most of Fauré's output is songs and small piano pieces, his best known work is the gentle, lyrical Requiem of 1887, for chorus and orchestra.

Giacomo Puccini (1858–1924) once said, ''The only music I can make is that of small things.'' Born into a musical family, he early gravitated to opera and before long had proved himself the main successor to Verdi and thus of the long Italian opera tradition, which he also essentially completed. His first dramatic work, *Le Villi* (1884), scored a success; nine years later he made himself world famous with *Manon Lescaut*. By the turn of the century his works rivaled Verdi's in popularity, his string of hits following *Manon Lescaut* including *La Bohème, Tosca,* and *Madama Butterfly*.

Puccini based his work on the Italian tradition of full-blooded melodic writing in the most singable of languages. Picking up the supple orchestral style of late Verdi, he added discreet touches from other styles including the coloristic harmonies of impressionism. As a dramatist, Puccini's interest was mainly in intimate stories, the ''small things'' of which he spoke, rather than in large operatic canvases. In that respect he was the heir of the important if short-lived movement called *verismo,* ''naturalism.'' Typified by Pietro Mascagni's *Cavalleria rusticana* (1890), this approach portrayed the lives of everyday people but still featured the highly charged, melodramatic stories long favored in Italian opera.

The best introduction to Puccini's work is, of course, *La Bohème* (1896), his masterpiece and from its first years one of the most

Puccini the elegant.

beloved of all operas. It is a story of penniless artists, their small joys and small tragedies. One finds no big scenes, no towering climaxes, only a steady stream of lyrical music marked by Puccini's strong dramatic instincts. The arias, some of his finest, entirely serve the story. Poet Rodolfo falls in love with the consumptive Mimi, painter Marcello rediscovers his coquettish Musetta; the lovers quarrel, make up, plan for the future, and then one day Mimi shows up in Rodolfo's garret and dies. Her death makes no difference, and makes all the difference. Few characters in opera reach us as deeply as this little band of bohemians.

The story of the great Czech composer **Leoš Janáček** is one of the most curious in the history of music: laboring for much of his life in relative obscurity as a teacher and conductor, he hit his stride as a composer only in his late forties and wrote most of his finest work in the last dozen of his seventy-four years—mainly inspired by a frustrated passion for a younger woman. Though Janáček was being performed internationally by the time of his death, his music went into a long eclipse before reemerging in the 1970s as one of the finer bodies of work in the century, especially in the realm of opera.

Born in the Moravian village of Hukvaldy in 1854, Janáček studied in Brno, Prague, and briefly in Leipzig and Vienna before settling in provincial Brno as a teacher. For twenty years he wrote one conventional piece after another, until his studies in Moravian folk music and language showed him the way to his own voice, first heard in the opera *Jenufa* of 1894–1903. Premiered to great acclaim in Brno, the opera languished in his hometown until a supporter dragged a local singer to Prague to have her perform some of the music for the director of the National Theater. Finally staged there in 1916, when Janáček was sixty-two, *Jenufa* scored a triumph.

From then on, Janáček composed prolifically. His late work included four more operas, two string quartets, the song cycle *Diary of a Man Who Vanished,* the *Sinfonietta,* and the *Glagolitic Mass.* Two fundamental influences combined to inspire these works. First was Moravian language and folk song, which give Janáček's melody and harmony a distinctive flavor similar to that of his predecessor Dvořák, but more richly modal. Unlike Dvořák, Janáček abandoned traditional forms and genres, finding his own rough-hewn but effective ways of developing his material. He used to walk about writing down Moravian speech patterns in a notebook; these patterns he translated into the rhythm and melodic curves of his music. Thus his work often is a mosaic of short rhythmic-melodic cells, which he called "speech-motives." Though one can trace influences from Debussy, his individual handling of the orchestra is spacious and transparent, full of novel instrumental colors.

The other influence of his maturity was his passion for Kamilla Stoesslova, the wife of an antiques dealer. Though the composer was not all that unhappily married, and though the passion for Kamilla was apparently one-sided and unconsummated, the image of this younger woman dominated his last years and is reflected constantly in his work, from the tormented String Quartet no. 2, called "Love Letters," to the opera *The Cunning Little Vixen*. Not that Janáček spent the end of his life pining; in fact, he seems to have thoroughly enjoyed his late success. He worked full steam and at the peak of his powers until his death in 1928, soon after finishing the opera *From the House of the Dead,* after Dostoevsky.

Janáček's orchestral style is never more handsomely demonstrated than in his five-movement *Sinfonietta* (1926) for orchestra. Based on a series of brass fanfares written earlier, the piece proceeds in his usual discrete sections, each concentrating on a short melodic idea. Here one finds his airy orchestration and much sonorous brass music. His *Glagolitic Mass* (1926), named after its text in the Old Slavonic language called Glagolitic, is a spiritual testament from a thoroughgoing humanist and agnostic; when a critic described it as the work of "a pious old man," the seventy-two-year-old composer dispatched a postcard that read, "Neither pious nor old, *young* man!" The piece is marvelously visceral and youthful sacred music, notable for its orchestral imagination, its hair-raising organ solo, its conclusion full of delirious strings and trumpets. For an introduction to Janáček's operas, I recommend one lesser known at the moment, but in fact one of the most magical stage works since Mozart's *Magic Flute: The Cunning Little Vixen,* who is at once a literal fox, Kamilla Stoesslova, and the eternal Feminine.

Britain's **Frederick Delius** (1862–1934) was born into a business family who in 1882 sent him to Florida to oversee a plantation. There his childhood interest in music was kindled into a determination to become a composer. After studies in Germany, he went to

Norway and met Edvard Grieg, who would be a prime inspiration. Some years of wandering and tentative composing followed before Delius settled in Grez-sur-Loing, near Fontainebleau, and found his style—opulent in harmony (somewhat impressionist influenced), rhapsodic in form, the rhythm usually wandering and slow, the tone often dreamily wistful. Delius's work might best be approached by way of his orchestral rhapsody *Brigg Fair* (1907), and *Sea Drift* (1903), for voices and orchestra, on poems of Walt Whitman. Both display his poetic sensitivity to nature. His admirer, the conductor Thomas Beecham, called Delius "the last great apostle of romance, emotion, and beauty in music."

Carl Nielsen (1865–1931) is the closest Denmark has come to a standard- repertoire composer, though his work has yet to attain the international currency it probably deserves. Nielsen was essentially a Brahmsian Romantic in temperament who more or less had to drag himself reluctantly into the twentieth century. This division reveals itself sometimes as humor, as in the riotous trombone smears of the Flute Concerto, and sometimes as frustration, as in his last symphony, the Sixth, which seems to thumb its nose at Modernism throughout and ends with a flatulent croak on bassoon. A good introduction to Nielsen might be the Fifth Symphony, written in response to World War I; the dramatic first movement is woven around a relentless string tremolo and features a snare drum that seems to be trying to machine-gun the orchestra.

We have previously met the puckish figure of **Erik Satie** (1866–1925), a critical influence on two generations of French composers starting with the impressionists and continuing with neoclassic figures such as Milhaud and Poulenc. Restrained in his ambitions, incomparably funny in words and music, and perhaps a little bit loony in the best way, Satie lived a life of self-imposed poverty, played piano in the cabarets of Montmartre, and wrote enigmatic little pieces with modal melodies and a prophetic harmonic freedom. He helped foment his time's anti-Romantic, anti-German revolt; as he told the young Debussy, "We ought to have our own music—if possible, without sauerkraut." Satie pursued that goal with his modest pieces and satirical outlook, designed to puncture pretensions of all kinds (including Modernist pretensions).

Satie's personality is seen in his famous titles: *Three Pieces in the Form of a Pear* (a response to the accusation that his pieces lacked form), *Desiccated Embryos, Pieces to Make You Run Away, Sketches and Annoyances of a Wooden Man.* He directed his short piano piece *Vexations* to be played precisely 840 times in succession, by a pianist with "solemn motionlessness." This brings up the curious performance directions in his scores: "Like a nightingale with a toothache," "Sheepishly and coldly," "With tenderness and fatality." (Obviously, Satie also prophesied Dada, Surrealism, and other explorations of the absurd and irrational.) Later he turned to larger pieces; *Parade,* his ballet for Diaghilev's Ballets Russes, had sets by Picasso and included parts for steamboat whistle, siren, and typewriter. To get to know Satie, one might pick up a recording of his piano works, making sure they include the ethereal *Gymnopédies* (which Debussy orchestrated) and the *Gnossiennes.*

Sergei Rachmaninov (1873–1943) studied piano and composition in St. Petersburg and Moscow and was encouraged by Tchaikovsky, who would be his model in high-Romantic concerto composition and robust Russian melody. At nineteen, Rachmaninov wrote what would become one of the most famous piano pieces in the world, the portentous Prelude in C-sharp minor; he sold it for a song, however, and never reaped the benefit of its phenomenal sales. Rachmaninov traveled and concertized widely, enjoying international acclaim as composer and virtuoso pianist. He also conducted the orchestra of Moscow's Bolshoi Theater and the Moscow Philharmonic. Later, after some American appearances, he would twice be offered the podium of the Boston Symphony, but both times he turned it down. After the 1917 Revolution, Rachmaninov left Russia; he lived in and out of the United States and finally settled in Los Angeles.

His music represents the twilight of the late-Romantic tradition, extended well into the twentieth century: expansive, rhapsodic, tending to heart-on-sleeve melancholy, and virtuosic in the Liszt and Tchaikovsky tradition. Like Tchaikovsky but even more so, he relies for his main effect on the Big Tune, as heard throughout his Second Piano Concerto. Extravagantly expressive, voluptuous in sound, a tour de force for the soloist, this is the most popular concerto of the twentieth century. (At Juilliard, it is known among

Ralph Vaughan Williams, the grand old man of English music, in 1951.

piano students as "Rocky II.") For many concertgoers, his kind of creamy Romanticism is what "classical music" is all about (thus when Hollywood portrays fictitious composers, they usually write like Rachmaninov). Less well known and in smaller scale is the beautiful, brooding orchestral work *Isle of the Dead,* sometimes cited as a Rachmaninov piece for people who don't like Rachmaninov.

Ralph Vaughan Williams (1872–1958) was largely trained in his native England with some touching up in Berlin and in Paris (with Ravel). He early became a student of British folk song, in the way that nationalists around the world were exploring the folk music of their own regions. Vaughan Williams's first celebrated work, the mellifluous *Fantasia on a Theme of Thomas Tallis* for strings, shows another abiding British connection, based as it is on the work of a Tudor-period composer. The fluid modal counterpoint of Tudor and Elizabethan music would be a steady influence. Another was the stately melodies of British hymnody, which Vaughan Williams absorbed while editing the English Hymnal (and writing some hymns of his own, including the familiar "For All the Saints").

While his music would remain relatively tonal and conservative, Vaughan Williams extended his language into milder modernisms such as Debussyian streams of parallel chords. By the thirties, he had become the grand old man of his country's music, inspiring generations with his conviction that "the composer must not shut himself up and think about art; he must live with his fellows and make his art an expression of the whole life of the community." (We found Britten echoing that sentiment.) Besides the *Tallis Fantasia*, a good introduction to Vaughan Williams's art is *A London Symphony* of 1914, an affectionate portrait of the city.

Unlike his prolific friend Charles Ives, New England composer **Carl Ruggles** (1876–1971) spent his creative life writing a handful of carefully crafted pieces of an individual, chromatic, and steadily dissonant cast. "In all works there should be the quality we call mysticism," he wrote. For Ruggles, dissonance itself was part of his atmosphere, its clashes forming the mystical penumbra around his notes. Stories of his fanatical drive to perfection are legion. Once after listening to Ruggles play over a single chord hundreds of times, composer Henry Cowell suggested that he let it stand the test of time; growled Ruggles, "The hell with time! I'll give this chord the test of time *right now*." As seen in his masterpiece, *Sun-Treader* for orchestra, Ruggles achieves a music of immense concentration and virile strength, with craggy melodic lines. This music seems more quarried than composed.

Toward the other end of the Americas worked another individualist, Brazilian composer **Heitor Villa-Lobos** (1887–1959). As composer, conductor, and folklorist he single-handedly jump-started his country's classical tradition and supplied it with an enormous body of work based on the music and traditions of his country. Typical of Villa-Lobos's approach are the series of pieces he called *Chôros*, a synthesis of Brazilian folk styles, and another series called *Bachianas brasileiras,* in which he united folk elements with Bach and the Western classical tradition. His best-known piece is the first movement of *Bachianas brasileiras* no. 5, for soprano and eight cellos, a beautiful and exotic melody accompanied by guitarlike pizzicatos. It was popularized in the United States some years ago in a recording by folk singer Joan Baez.

One of the founding fathers of twentieth-century avant-garde music, **Edgard Varèse** (1885–1965) followed scientific and mathematical studies with musical training in his native Paris. Through the patronage of such figures as Debussy, Rodin, and Richard Strauss, he seemed on his way to a comfortable career as a modestly progressive composer. But his music veered into a radical path, influenced not only by Schoenberg and Stravinsky but also by the Italian futurists, who proclaimed noise and the urban atmosphere as the music of the day. While never a real futurist, Varèse began to write severe, stripped-down textures that indeed sound like an echo of the modern city soundscape.

Varèse emigrated to the United States in 1915 and spent the bulk of his life here, a good deal of the time struggling against indifference and hostility. In the twenties and early thirties, he wrote a series of pieces heralding many of the ideas and sounds that two decades later would characterize a generation of electronic and tone color composers: *Amériques, Offrandes, Hyperprism, Octandre, Intégrales, Arcana,* and *Ionisation.* His preference for scientific and mathematical titles indicates his main purpose, which was to leave behind traditional ideas of thematic and tonal relationships and explore new and rational ways of organizing sound. In contrast to the twelve-tone school, which largely concerned itself with pitch, Varèse turned his primary attention to rhythm (thus his unprecedented employment of percussion instruments) and to patterns of timbres, volumes, and textures. (Following Varèse's lead, later composers would attempt to bring all these elements—pitch, loudness, rhythm, and timbre—under the control of serial procedures.)

In the mid thirties Varèse entered a kind of limbo from which he did not emerge for nearly twenty years. It was a time of financial hardship, of fruitless experiments with electronic media, of writing music one day and tearing it up the next. Finally in the fifties, his music began to circulate in recordings and was discovered by a new generation of revolutionaries in Europe, including Boulez and Stockhausen. Then support appeared that made possible Varèse's rebirth in late works including *Déserts* and the tape piece *Poème électronique*. The latter was composed for Le Corbusier's Phillips Pavilion at the Brussels Exposition, where it played continuously over 425 loudspeakers. Around that time, after a stranger effusively praised him in a restaurant, Varèse said with bittersweet irony to his wife, "It seems that after all these years of people throwing *merde* at me, I've finally become fertilizer."

For an introduction to the world of Varèse, one might start with *Ionisation* (1931), the West's first purely percussion piece (it uses thirty-five instruments played by thirteen performers) and a kaleidoscopic study in rhythm and sonority. *Intégrales* (1925), for winds, brass, and a large percussion group, is even more striking. In its screaming brass and winds, its tumultuous percussion writing, its relentless intensity, *Intégrales* shows a clear relationship to Stravinsky's *Sacre du printemps*. But where Stravinsky's primitivism is lush and nature oriented, Varèse's is steely and urban. In style this work is one of the prime Modernist prototypes; at the same time, in its ferocious integrity it sounds unlike anything else.

French composer **Darius Milhaud** (1892–1974) also spent much of his later life in America, in his case as a teacher and conductor. But while Milhaud began by associating with a group of cutting-edge Modernists such as Erik Satie and the writer Jean Cocteau, the years turned him and his compatriots into mainstream artists. It was a newspaper critic who grouped Milhaud and five other composers—Francis Poulenc, Georges Auric, Arthur Honegger, Louis Duret, and Germaine Tailleferre—around Cocteau and dubbed them *Les Six*. In one way or another these composers followed the lead of Cocteau, who, it was said, had the gift of turning chic into art. The group was attracted to Stravinsky's neoclassicism and to popular arts including American jazz. All deplored the "phony sublimity" of Romanticism and heeded Satie's proclamation of the era of "the circus and the music hall."

The prolific Milhaud made a lifelong habit of composing in railway coaches, autos, cafés, anywhere at all, cultivating a view of creativity as an everyday thing. Besides showing a lyrical con-

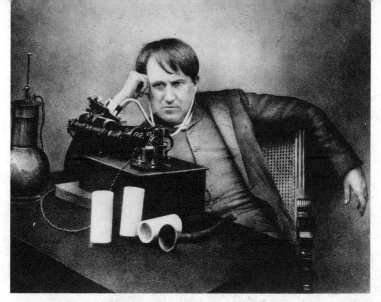

Sound recording revolutionized access to repertoire and to virtuoso performance. It also made possible the editing of sound and electronic music. Above, Thomas Edison with his phonograph. Below, pianist Glenn Gould, having abandoned the concert hall, at home among the knobs and meters of a recording studio.

Les Six: *from the left, Darius Milhaud, Georges Auric, Arthur Honegger, Germaine Tailleferre, Francis Poulenc, Louis Duret. At the piano sits their mentor Jean Cocteau.*

trapuntal style owing something to neoclassicism, his earlier work systematically explored polytonality, an example being the vibrant tonal colors of his 1919 opera *Les Choëphores*. His most familiar work is the 1923 ballet *La Création du monde,* the world's first concert work to use jazz elements (two years before Gershwin's *Rhapsody in Blue*). The scenario, which purported to show Creation in terms of a fanciful Negro cosmology, was premiered as a trendy "Cubist ballet"; the sets and even the costumes imitated Cubist paintings. Milhaud's score has outlasted the ballet. It is far from authentic jazz, but remains a most engaging and colorful piece, with its blues-tinted opening and jazz fugue.

Francis Poulenc (1899–1963), another of *Les Six,* has endured as the quintessential Frenchman of modern composers, the Maurice Chevalier of the bunch. He was once called the "apostle of the Parisian café-concert." Much of his work, vocal or instrumental, is full of urbane lyricism and irony, everything enfolded in his perfumed sweetness. Poulenc is noted for his songs, their tones ranging from the light and satirical to the delicate and touching. Later in life he turned to Catholicism and liturgical music without entirely forsaking his lightness of touch. The familiar *Gloria* of 1959 is a good example of his unique combination of Parisian worldliness and heartfelt piety: it sometimes sounds like a pop song addressed to God.

German composer **Carl Orff** (1895–1982) authored stage works and a much-used system of musical training for children. As a composer he is primarily known for his 1936 dramatic cantata *Carmina Burana* (Songs of Beuren), which was regarded as a showpiece of what music should be in the Third Reich. Based on a medieval collection of songs by wandering students and runaway monks, the work forms a vivacious manifesto of the undergraduate mentality and its perennial agenda. Orff presents these rascally texts in a style of sophisticated primitivism, with a compelling if unsubtle gift for good tunes, striking instrumental colors, and nonstop rhythmic drive.

George Gershwin (1898–1937) is one of the legendary figures of the century, gifted with phenomenal musical imagination and creative energy. An early success as a popular composer, Gershwin remained a true artist who refused to be satisfied with acclaim and riches but insisted on striving toward an unprecedented unity of commercial and classical genres. He died in the course of that effort. Of all those who have tried to achieve such a unity, only he may have had the talent to achieve it.

Gershwin was born in New York to Russian-Jewish parents and studied piano in childhood. Gravitating to the songwriting neighborhood of Tin Pan Alley, he began as a plugger of other people's songs but by 1919 had written his first musical comedy, *La La Lucille*, containing his first hit song, "Swanee." He went on to write hit show after show for the rest of his life, usually with his brother, Ira, as lyricist. Gershwin's list of popular standards is the most impressive of the century, all his songs showing an instinctive melodic genius backed up by equally effective rhythms and harmonies. A very short list includes "Oh Lady Be Good," "Fascinatin' Rhythm," "They Can't Take That Away from Me," and "The Man I Love."

Meanwhile, amidst the glittering showbiz life, the steady output of songs and shows, the money and women, Gershwin never let go of his early interest in the other side of music. That finally resolved into the idea of joining popular and classical music, or as it was put in those days, "making a lady out of jazz." The first of those efforts was *Rhapsody in Blue,* premiered in New York in 1924. Though it was scooped by earlier jazz-inspired concert works of Milhaud and Stravinsky, Gershwin's *Rhapsody* has been by far the most famous. Responding to criticisms that the form of the *Rhapsody* wandered and that he didn't orchestrate it himself, Gershwin got a book on concerto form and tried his hand at one, producing his Concerto in F for Piano and Orchestra in 1925. In that and later works he proved an imaginative handler of the orchestra.

In his pieces for the concert hall Gershwin would remain a blend of naïve and sophisticated, constantly trying to catch up on his technical studies amidst nonstop production in every direction. On one hand, he wrote his concerto more or less from a how-to book; on the other hand, he eagerly absorbed the work of Stravinsky, Berg, Schoenberg, and *Les Six.* The latter were the main models for his half-French, half-jazzy *An American in Paris* of 1928. Legend says he asked both Ravel and Stravinsky for lessons. Ravel declined, saying he did not want to sully Gershwin's instinctive gifts; but Stravinsky, learning what Gershwin's income was, responded by asking Gershwin for lessons. (Stravinsky denied the story.)

While Gershwin's intuitive genius remained his foundation, his technical skill and confidence increased by leaps and bounds. Finally he decided to attempt the first jazz-oriented folk opera. The result, *Porgy and Bess* (1935), is based on a story by Charleston writer DuBose Heyward about poor blacks on Charleston's Catfish Row. From the beginning, music critics picked at the formal and stylistic problems of the opera, black musicians criticized its co-opting of their tradition (Duke Ellington deplored its "lampblack Negro-isms"), and audiences didn't quite know what to make of it. Yet despite everything, *Porgy and Bess* has been revived again and again,

Gershwin, in photos always dapper and poker-faced. What he lacked in formal technique he made up in natural genius and American brashness.

seemingly with greater success every time. Certainly one of the reasons is the ubiquitousness of its "arias"—Broadway-style songs such as "Summertime," "It Ain't Necessarily So," and "I Got Plenty o' Nothin'." Like many Romantic composers, Gershwin had a better gift for melody than he did for large-scale form, but that gift has made his music immortal. When he was cut down at thirty-eight by a brain tumor, his friend and admirer Arnold Schoenberg wrote, "Music to him was the air he breathed, the food which nourished him, the drink that refreshed him. Music was what made him feel, and music was the feeling he expressed. Directness of this kind is given only to great men, and there is no doubt that he was a great composer."

While Gershwin was trying to make a lady out of jazz, **Edward Kennedy "Duke" Ellington** (1899–1974) was shaping jazz into a universal art on its own terms, and doing it so brilliantly as to make him one of the finest composers of the century in any idiom. Ellington began playing piano in his native Washington, D.C., and in 1923 moved to New York, where he organized a ten-piece group that formed the nucleus of the bands he was to lead for the next fifty years. During those years he accumulated a body of work astonishing in quantity (over a thousand pieces), quality, and originality. From the twenties to the early forties, he was the single most important figure in the development of jazz.

Yet that is only part of his achievement. There are comparably seminal figures in early jazz, Louis Armstrong chief among them.

Ellington, turning on the charm
for the "Today Show" with bassist Ernie Shepard.

What takes Ellington beyond the confines of his idiom is that he was a composer in every sense of the word: a man who created forms, melodies, harmonies, colors in a compelling and individual way, and who developed his art throughout his career. As critic Francis Newton wrote, Ellington "solved the unbelievably difficult problem of turning a living, shifting and improvised folk music into *composition* without losing its spontaneity."

One hears the uniqueness of his approach from some of his earliest recordings in 1927 and 1928: in the bluesy "gutbucket" sound of Bubber Miley's wah-wah trumpet in *East St. Louis Toodle-oo*, the tight-muted trumpet and trombone duo that opens *Black and Tan Fantasy*, the novel use of a wordless voice as an instrument in *Creole Love Call*. Classical composers orchestrate for instruments; Ellington orchestrated not only for instruments but for the particular players in his band: the plunger trumpet of Bubber Miley and, later, Cootie Williams, the mellow alto saxophone of Johnny Hodges, the innovative bass playing of Jimmy Blanton, and many others over the years. Ellington put together this kaleidoscopic tonal palette in continually fresh combinations, integrating the improvisations of his players into his works.

Of course, Ellington wrote his share of pop standards, among them *Sophisticated Lady, It Don't Mean a Thing if it Ain't Got That Swing,* and *Don't Get Around Much Anymore.* But he was not really a tunesmith like Gershwin; his concerns were deeper and broader. *Ko-Ko,* one of his string of masterpieces from the early forties, might stand for his mature style—rich in harmony, original in structure and orchestration. It begins quietly with a driving minor tune and builds through a series of solos of increasing nervous energy to a climax of shattering harmonic and rhythmic intensity, with pealing bitonal chords in the brass. At around the same time, the jumpy rhythms and deliberate "wrong notes" of *Cotton Tail* anticipated the coming bebop style of Charlie Parker and Dizzy Gillespie. That style finally took over the trailblazing impetus of jazz, but Ellington and his band remained a vital part of the music world until his death in 1974.

Ellington tried some longer works in his later years, notably the series of Sacred Services and some orchestral pieces. But his prime legacy remains the record sides he did with his band. Besides being one of the glories of African-American music, he is with Schubert and Schumann one of the finest miniaturists in all Western music.

Samuel Barber was obscured by the mid-century triumph of the avant-garde but fares better today, while the avant-garde has declined.

With love and admiration and perhaps only a little hyperbole, composer and jazz scholar Gunther Schuller picked up from the title of Ellington's autobiography *Music is My Mistress* and wrote, "Music was indeed his mistress; it was his total life, and his commitment to it was incorruptible and unalterable. In jazz he was a giant among giants. And in twentieth-century music he may yet one day be recognized as one of the half-dozen greatest masters of our time."

Samuel Barber (1910–1981) spent a long, fruitful career going his own way. As a result, the profession passed him by in some respects while the concertgoing public was making him one of the most popular of American composers. Early trained as a singer, Barber always had a lyrical melodic bent, whether the style is post-Romantic like his early work or more modernistic like his later work. Among his early successes was the sighing, heart-tugging *Adagio for Strings* (1936), recently renewed in popularity by its presence in the film *Platoon*.

His elegant lyricism suffuses the well-known *Knoxville: Summer of 1915* (1947), for soprano and chamber orchestra. Based on an impressionistic evocation of childhood by James Agee, the piece shows Barber's independent mind; in its gentle, nostalgic course it explores folklike material while maintaining a cosmopolitan spirit, suggests neoclassicism while avoiding its hard edges, stays tonal while indulging in considerable chromaticism. Later, in works such as the impressive Piano Concerto of 1962, Barber would court atonality and serialism without losing his individual voice or his forthright expressiveness.

After the death of Sir Benjamin Britten, **Sir Michael Tippett** (1905–) was finally revealed as the powerful figure he had been all along, languishing somewhat in the shadow of his more famous contemporary. Tippett's output is eclectic, as is most British music; in his case it shows a strong influence of Stravinskian neoclassicism and also of African-American music, to which Tippett adds his own gift for counterpoint. His major works include several operas on his own quirky librettos, choral works including the popular *A Child of Our Time* (1944) (with its moving use of black spirituals), and four symphonies of considerable scope and expressive power. A good introduction to Tippett is the *Fantasia Concertante on a Theme of Corelli* (1953), one of the era's freshest essays in string writing, with its

Sir Michael Tippett emerged after Britten's death as the master he had been all along.

roulades of scales and trills that build into grand shimmering textures. His Second Symphony (1958) begins with frenetic strings dancing above marchlike brass figures and goes on to be a masterful symphonic unfolding, startling in a time when the symphonic genre would seem to be in an advanced state of obsolescence.

Elliott Carter (1908–) got into music with the encouragement of his mentor, Charles Ives, and spent a good many years as a composer of mild neoclassic music that had mild success. Then in 1951 Carter suddenly leaped to the front rank of the avant-garde with his String Quartet no. 1. The work features an unprecedented exploration of *metric modulation,* a technique of changing tempos analogous to changing keys in tonal music. Ives had first explored this concept; in his mature works, Carter elaborated on that and related rhythmic ideas of increasingly greater complexity. Meanwhile his sound palette also grew more and more complex. Describing his music as "stubborn sounds," Carter seems to have an almost Puritan disdain for beauty of effect or ease of listening. In his later music he takes to extremes Ives's idea of separate personalities and musical styles expressed simultaneously. In his Third String Quartet, each instrument is virtually a world to itself. One of the more approachable works from Carter's maturity is the *Sonata for Flute, Oboe, Cello, and Harpsichord* of 1952.

John Cage (1912–1992) is another seminal figure in twentieth-century music—part composer, part guru, part myth. One of Schoenberg's American pupils, he early took to his own path. In 1937 Cage made the prophetic declaration that noise was the next frontier, that harmonic density and stylistic exploration in Western music would continue until all possible sounds were available to the composer. At the same time, he predicted the significance of electronic instruments in the music of the future. After writing some pathbreaking percussion pieces, in 1938 Cage invented the "prepared piano," in which screws and other objects are placed on the strings to create what amounts to a percussion ensemble playable from the keyboard. This has been a favorite device of composers ever since.

From his interest in Zen and Hindu philosophy, Cage developed an aesthetic of systematic openness to all sounds and phenomena, of egolessness, non-meaning, non-emotion: the spiritual cipher of

Zen, at the furthest remove from Romantic expressiveness and subjectivity. "My purpose," runs one of Cage's aphorisms, "is to eliminate purpose."

If all sound is equal, Cage reasons, then it follows that silence is also a valid musical experience. Thus his notorious *4' 33"* of 1952. At its premiere, Cage's colleague David Tudor "performed" the work by sitting silently at the piano for four minutes and thirty-three seconds. Of course, the audience inevitably made sounds during that period; those random accidents were, in effect, the music. This piece also illustrates Cage's concept of *chance music* (also called *aleatory,* from *alea,* Latin for "dice"). In chance music some processes are determined and others left indeterminate. Another example is Cage's *Imaginary Landscape No. 4* (1951), in which twelve radios, tuned to different stations, are manipulated according to elaborate instructions, but the actual sound depends on whatever

John Cage,
most charming of
revolutionaries, seems
about to break
into his famous laugh.

happens to be on the air. Cage's approach to electronic media is shown in *Fontana Mix* (1958); though this involves tape, its sound nevertheless changes from performance to performance.

In many ways Cage picked up where Varèse, Schoenberg, and others left off, but everything came out with his own singular spin. His primary ideas—an openness to all sound as musical material, altering traditional instruments and exploring electronic ones, and the explicit incorporation of chance—affected many European and American composers of the postwar generation. Besides his music, Cage wrote a number of essays that explained and elaborated his ideas. Yet his impact has been almost entirely on musicians and avant-garde artists; the concert-going public has largely considered Cage a joker or a pleasant eccentric (he has an artless, childlike charm in person and often in prose). For an introduction to Cage, one should probably start with the sixteen *Sonatas and Interludes* for prepared piano (1946–48), fully notated pieces of surprising attractiveness, an astonishing range of timbres, and considerable rhythmic excitement. In regard to his later music, maybe one would do as well to sit on the front steps and listen to the world go by. Developing that kind of sensitivity to the music of life is a good deal of what Cage has been getting at all along.

Our next composer, **Olivier Messiaen** (1908–92), forms a group with the following two, who were his pupils at the Paris Conservatory. There have been several constants in Messiaen's music over the years: a rhythmic style based on studies of Stravinsky and Eastern music; scales of his own invention; birdsong, of which Messiaen is an avid collector and which he transfers directly into his music (his gigantic piano solo *Catalogue of Birds* is made entirely of notated bird calls); and his devotion to the Catholic Church and its theology, which he interprets with a kind of voluptuous mysticism. It all makes for an idiosyncratic brew of sumptuous post-Debussy harmonies (sometimes a bit overripe), tone clusters, flocks of birds, wild percussion outbursts, and serial rhythmic techniques (the latter having much influence on the next generation). The best introduction to Messiaen's music is the 1941 *Quartet for the End of Time,* written in a Nazi prison camp during World War II for the only available instruments—violin, clarinet, cello, and piano. With its apocalyptic biblical imagery and music by turns lyrically soulful

Olivier Messiaen, a virtuoso on keyboard as well as on paper,
said, "The music I haven't heard yet is the sweetest of all."

dancing, and sulfurously diabolical, the quartet adds up to one of
the classic works of this century.

Of the major postwar avant-gardists, composer/conductor **Pierre
Boulez** (1925–) has long been among the most intellectual and
uncompromising. A zealous believer in the historical necessity of
serialism, he first came to fame for booing Stravinsky's neoclassic
music in concerts and for his 1952 polemic that exalted Webern's
approach to serialism and declared "SCHOENBERG IS DEAD." As
I note in the Webern section, for Boulez's generation serialism
seemed at once a necessary way of structuring atonal music and, I

Detail of a page from Night Music I *by the American George Crumb,*
with novel timbral effects and an improvisatory section.

suspect, a return to rationality after the madness of the Nazi era.

In the 1950s Boulez pursued the idea of total serialization (see Webern essay and Glossary) to its ultimate end in pieces such as *Structures I* (1951–52), which rigorously employs a twelve-tone pitch series, a series of twelve rhythmic values, a series of twelve volume levels, and a series of ten articulations from shortest staccato to legato. Later in the decade, Boulez and his colleagues took up what would seem to be the opposite of total serialism, Cage's idea of indeterminacy. Boulez's later music tends to involve both serial techniques and chance elements. His best-known piece, on surrealist poems by René Char, is *Le Marteau sans maître* (The Hammer Without a Master, 1953–54), for voice and six players. Despite the severe intellectualism of his approach, Boulez has said, "I think that music should be collective magic and hysteria." Perhaps there is something of those qualities in his settings of these enigmatic poems. (*Le Marteau*'s extensive use of mallet instruments, by the way, caused one sarcastic critic to dub it *"L'après-midi d'un vibraphone."*)

The German **Karlheinz Stockhausen** (1928–) studied with Messiaen in Paris alongside Boulez. Stockhausen also began as a thoroughgoing serialist, with a particular interest in electronic music, and helped lead the movement toward indeterminacy in the later fifties. For all his ponderous intellectual framework, Stockhausen has always had a streak of intuitive mysticism that has increasingly manifested itself in works of messianic and apocalyptic import. His epic tape piece *Hymnen* (Anthems, 1969), for example, integrates electronic sound and the national anthems of several countries in a grand unifying vision of humanity, with reference to the composer's personal myth of "the utopian realm of HYMUNION in HARMONDIE ruled by PLURAMON." Despite the moonshine, *Hymnen* remains one of the most impressive works of its time.

Stockhausen calls himself a "tone color composer"; a fundamental purpose of his work has been to explore means of organizing timbres. He regards tone color as the final frontier in music, logically following earlier Western discoveries of ways to structure pitch, rhythm, and volume. One sees his concern with timbre both in his tape music and in instrumental works such as *Gruppen* (Groups) for three orchestras, which also reflects his interest in spatial effects. In recent years Stockhausen has been writing a series of operas, Wagnerian in scale, involving cosmic dramas of humans, angels, and devils. These hermetic works are apt to take some time to digest and comprehend, or even to figure out if they are worth comprehending.

Stockhausen has been one of the most visible of European avant-gardists, partly due to his extensive performing and lecturing, all marked by his intense personality. Much of his popularity originated in the counterculture of the sixties and seventies, whose homespun herbal mysticism he deliberately played to. His tape piece *Gesang der Jünglinge* (Song of the Youths, 1955–56) is the first and still perhaps greatest masterpiece of electronic music, despite the primitive electronic technique of those pre-synthesizer days. Based on the biblical story of three boys magically saved from the burning furnace, the piece mixes evocative electronic effects and boys' voices to create a soundscape at once utterly novel and expressive. *Gesang der Jünglinge* is a good example of what the avant-garde can accomplish at its best: creating work as new and astonishing as something from another world, yet still broadly communicative on this planet. For a look at Stockhausen's more mystical and improvisatory side, one might try *Stimmung* (literally, "tuning" or "mood"), for six singers, in which sustained drones, patterns of vowel sounds, erotic poetry, and the names of gods from around the world are woven into a meditative texture at once sensual and spiritual.

Long allied with Stockhausen and others of the "Darmstadt School" is Hungarian-born **György Ligeti** (1923–). It has been Ligeti's gift to adapt the innovations of others and make them more musical than their inventors did. An example of his art is the *Lux aeterna* for voices and orchestra, one of three Ligeti pieces used in Stanley Kubrick's film *2001;* there this uncanny, spacious, many-stranded music aptly conveys the supernatural powers of the monolith. His comic operas *Adventures* and *New Adventures* represent another side of Ligeti. Both have a considerable variety of characters and situations even though there is no actual plot or word in either piece. Everything comes from a preposterous vocabulary of preverbal shouts, groans, giggles, snorts, expostulations, and the like. When these pieces are performed and staged well, they manage to sound almost classical in their goofy integrity.

Given the steady progression of the musical avant-garde toward arcane personal and technical concerns and away from the general public, a reaction was inevitable sooner or later. The cutting edge of that reaction appeared in the 1960s, in the form of pieces whose material fled as far as possible from the atonal, dissonant, pulseless, and inexorably difficult language of the mid-century avant-garde. This new style had simple ideas strung repetitively along a steady pulse, the material usually modal but clearly tonal, everything designed for easy comprehensibility and mesmerizing absorption. The style came to be called *minimalism*. Its roots lay in the heavy beat of rock 'n' roll, plus elements of non-Western music (especially India, Bali, and Africa) and a whiff of the euphoric sixties culture.

The 1964 *In C* by **Terry Riley** (1935–) can be done by any number of players of any instruments. As it babbles cheerfully onandonandon, either you can sit and get stoned on the sound or you can go out and back for pizza and hardly miss a thing, so slowly do its textures change. The music of **Philip Glass** (1937–) is generally based on simple rippling lines repeated over and over, with slow metamorphoses. In the process the ideas, which are not necessarily interesting to begin with, do not become any more interesting. The result is indubitably hypnotic. *Time* magazine has called Glass the world's greatest living composer, and he has legions of admirers, many drawn from the ranks of rock fans. (Others feel that his fans' idea of a good time is a stupor, and they could get higher cheaper at the local bar.) Glass's massive opera *Einstein on the Beach* (1976) has been heard all over the world, including at the Metropolitan Opera House in New York.

The music of **Steve Reich** (1936–) may be the richest in means and texture of the first generation of minimalists, his pieces some of the first to express something beyond relentlessness. His *Music for Eighteen Musicians* (1975) has the steady pulse and hypnotic effect of the style, but also a novel blending of voices and wind and percussion instruments, sudden shifts of texture, and lively rhythms reminiscent of Latin music. It also manages to sustain a hauntingly melancholy atmosphere.

Regardless of the ultimate value of these works, by staking a claim on the opposite side of the musical spectrum from the serial avant-garde, minimalists opened up a fertile middle ground for composers of the next generation. As the eminent Japanese composer Toru Takemitsu said to me in the mid seventies: "We are free now." He meant that composers at last were free of dogmas of tonality or atonality, mathematics or raw expression, Darmstadt or Los Angeles. We are free to choose from the immense body of musical ideas from all history and all cultures, plus the discoveries of our own hearts and minds. Everywhere, many composers of the last twenty years have embraced expressiveness again, taken up tonality in old and new guises, begun to forge new connections to mainstream audiences with styles drawn from many sources, Western and otherwise. For a good deal of this promising development, we have minimalism to thank.

For a fascinating development of recent years, I would like to touch on the new music emerging from the Soviet Union. After decades of repression, composers there can use without fear a full range of innovative techniques. At times the results can be superficial, with a feeling that the composers are rummaging through the Modernist toy box. But at its best the new Soviet music has a vital seriousness lacking in much of the Western avant-garde: for Russians, atonality and tone clusters and string glissandos can be not merely intellectual games and explorations of new ideas, but shouts of freedom, cries of sorrow for the past, and expressions of concern for the future. Among the most compelling voices to emerge from Russia in recent years is that of **Alfred Schnittke** (1934–), whose Viola Concerto is a sprawling, sometimes beautiful, and sometimes terrifying portrait of his country's soul. The *Offertorium* for violin and orchestra by **Sofia Gubaidulina** (1931–) is a more delicate and controlled modernistic canvas, but a broadly expressive one.

In connection to Gubaidulina, I will close my survey of Western music by welcoming the first major generation of women composers. Or, rather, the first generation to be fully recognized and encouraged. The *International Encyclopedia of Women Composers* lists thousands of creators, all of them active in some degree, most of them with some kind of public in their time. What happened to the music of these women? It does not seem possible that none deserve more notice from history. Along with the other new freedoms and respect gained by women in the middle of this century, the incredible neglect of composers has begun to turn around. The way was paved by the century's older generation of distinguished composers, among them **Louise Talma** in America, **Germaine Tailleferre** and **Betsy Jolas** in France, and the Scottish-born **Thea Musgrave**. Nearly half the present generation of younger composers are women. Still, only in 1983 did a woman finally receive the Pulitzer Prize in music, **Ellen Taaffe Zwilich,** for her Symphony no. 1.

Music by women of the past and present is only beginning to receive the kind of attention that will enable history to place their work in the perspective of the tradition that for so long ignored them. As a result, little common wisdom yet exists about their position in the tradition. Certainly that situation will soon be remedied. In the coming years and centuries, women's voices will be increasingly revealed to the world, in works that may offer ideas and answers men have never suspected. At this point, anyway, there is no reason not to hope for some fresh light on a very old art.

Aand thus all history books trail off into the uncertainties of the present and the future. The portrait I have painted of Modernism has at times been perplexing and even foreboding. Some of the prevailing artistic movements of this century—Dada, theater of the absurd, Surrealism, and various nihilistic currents—have used the means of art to attack art itself, sometimes in furious determination to bring down the edifices of the past. By way of illustration, in a Darmstadt concert of the 1970s, composer and video artist Nam June Paik dissected a piano with butcher knives. In a concert in Holland that included a work of my own, a pianist and tenor performed a piece in which they attempted to sing a lied but soon lapsed into simulated laughter, madness, and violence.

Clearly, there is more to such extreme manifestations of Modernism than unfettered iconoclasm. They are also a reflection of the uncertainties and spiritual malaise of a century of violence and death, and/or of rage at continuing Western social evils. The Romantics had their own malaise, but they were sustained by the humanistic dream of progress, that all things were moving toward something better and more perfect. But science, once seen as the ultimate salvation of humanity, has now produced unprecedented means of mass extermination. As conductor and early music scholar Raymond Leppard has written, the explosion at Hiroshima in 1945 shattered once and for all the myth of progress.

Similarly, it is hard to make a case that Western music has progressed in spiritual and intellectual value since, say, J. S. Bach, whatever the technical advances since his time or the hundreds of masterpieces. Moreover, technical boundaries that for centuries composers saw ahead of them have now vanished: years ago, music reached the final possibilities of harmonic density and dissonance to the point of noise, and explored the furthest extremes both of chaos and of order (which turned out oddly to resemble each other). American serialist Charles Wuorinen lamented, "It's hard to make a revolution when, two revolutions ago, they already said anything goes." More recently, the collapse of serialism as an international language threw composers once again on their own devices, forcing each of us to create our own language from the ground up, using the rubble left from the collapse of past languages. In the last decade or so, Modernism has come to seem a historical style, a thing of the past. We have not yet had time to decide what to make of the Modernist era, or what to do next.

I am not counseling despair. I repeat what I noted at the beginning of this section on the twentieth century: all in all, this has been a very good century for music. While some of the composers we have examined are unlikely ever to interest many listeners, all have found a public, and some will be listened to a hundred years from now. Meanwhile, they and their colleagues have opened up vast new territories of sounds, forms, and concepts. Exploring and settling that frontier, humanizing it, will be the task of future generations. At least, I hope and trust that following generations will accept that challenge rather than attempt to retreat into the past. Whether we like it or not, history goes in only one direction.

We should remember that there remain a tremendous vitality and resourcefulness in the arts, and a ready audience for anything that works. Whatever is going on in classical music, it is anything but dead: Bach lives, and Mozart, and Stravinsky, and very many others. And thousands of women and men around the world are creating new work. Through all the century's turbulence, the dead ends, the challenges of anti-art and popular culture, Western classical music remains one of the finest and noblest traditions on earth.

AFTERWORD

MUSIC: AN APPROACH
TO DEFINING
THE INDEFINABLE

Ludwig van Beethoven, an authority on the subject, once confessed, "I don't know what music is." This was no admission of ignorance or despair. Rather, it recognized the essential mystery of an art that seems to encompass everything and resemble nothing. A sense of awe before that mystery often marks musicians.

One way to get closer to what music does is to define what it can't do. Except when words are involved, music has no subject, no denotation. When we speak of the "language" of music we speak metaphorically, because it isn't a true language: however music moves us, it is not because of *meaning* in the usual sense of the word. By itself, music can't say *hat rat cat* and it can't exactly say *glad sad mad,* either—though each tradition attaches emotions to certain modes and gestures, as I'll come to below. There remains, of course, the indisputable fact that music can evoke feelings. So can a sunset. Yet music does not really contain feelings any more than a sunset does; both are simply things in the air, physical phenomena. Where do the feelings come from?

They come from ourselves. Though a composer's feelings fuel his inspiration, his music does not in the end contain his emotions; instead, the music catalyzes the listener's thoughts and emotions. In other words, the meaning of music or a sunset is not in the things themselves but in the beholder. For some a sunset is lovely and pleasant, for others a melancholy reminder of beauty's evanescence. Most people will feel both ways at one time or another. Like nature, music is a fascinating blank slate that invites us to write on it what we feel and what we are at that moment. Our response, guided by culture and tradition but finally created in each of our hearts, *is* the meaning of music. Thus Wallace Stevens's definition: "Music is feeling, then, not sound."

You may argue that this attitude makes music passive. Because something eludes us, however, does not mean it is powerless. My analogy with nature was deliberate: for all our faiths and theories, in the end we don't really know what, if anything, nature is all about. Likewise music. But aren't major keys bright and happy, minor keys dark and sad? Isn't dissonance frightening? Isn't jazz sexy? In all cases: yes and no. True, we tend to hear major as happy, but it wasn't always so. Bach could write sad music in major, vibrant music in minor. Bartók could make dissonance sound joyous. Our Western major/minor association was cemented in the nineteenth century, notably by Schubert, who regularly made minor keys a signpost to indicate sadness. Jazz used to seem disconcertingly erotic to many; but as happened previously with the waltz, time and still sexier music have bleached much of the sensuality out of it.

While music does not *contain* emotions, it *suggests* them, partly because it can mimic the forms and dynamics and rhythms of emotions. By imitating the bodily sensation of languor, a slow tempo can seem melancholy or sensuous or meditative; by evoking fast movement, a quick tempo can be interpreted as exhilarating or dizzying. Tonal relationships add further dimensions to the effect. Each age and culture will represent "sad" or "exhilarating" with its own tonal signposts. Even so, not every listener in that culture will respond the same way. A piece of music may sound painful to one listener and erotic to another, in part because the physical rhythms of pain and sex are sometimes the same: a buildup to catharsis. Mozart, for one, can seem to linger exquisitely on the border between opposing emotions. Experience plays a central role, too; we must learn how to listen to our culture's music.

So each age and culture erects its own musical signposts, melodic, harmonic, and rhythmic devices to represent emotion, however inexact that representation in practice. These traditional expressive associations are what give music a good deal of its value and meaning for a people. Experienced listeners have an intuitive sense of the signposts: the Greeks had theories of expressive values associated with several kinds of scales; the Western Baroque period had its Doctrine of the Affections; Indian music has its list of emotional flavors called *rasa*s. From culture to culture, however, one finds little agreement about these associations. Plato's moral objections to some of the Greek modes, for example, strike us as quaint; we Westerners don't follow the emotional import of Indian *rasa*s unless we're trained to; and polemics about the moral threat of rock 'n' roll rhythms seem fatuous to most.

In the largest view, across ages and cultures, emotional cues in music trail off into uncertainty. Westerners don't respond to Balinese music as the Balinese do, but we can enjoy it even if we hear it with Western ears. In the end, music strikes deeper than any single group's understanding of it. The only constant, I say again, is each person's individual response, colored by that person's cultural context.

This capacity to catalyze individual feeling makes music the most personal, the most intimate of the arts. The purity of musical expressiveness and form, its ability to evoke emotion without the limitations of story or words, its adaptability to the personality and needs of each listener, is what moved nineteenth-century essayist Walter Pater to declare, "Music is the art to which all other arts aspire."

(You will notice that in this book, for all these convictions about music, I have often used emotional descriptions. A possible excuse is that my personal responses are a representation of the *kind* of responses music evokes in all of us, rather than an attempt to tell you what to feel in a given piece. Anyway, what was it Emerson said about a foolish consistency being the mark of small minds? I hope never to be accused of consistency, foolish or otherwise.)

For all its emotional indefiniteness, we respond no less emotionally to music. An Indian saying runs, "The purpose of music is to produce extraordinary states of consciousness." Clearly, we need to experience those states. I've never heard of a human society without music. In most, music has been regarded as potent magic, from the hunting and warring songs of tribal cultures to the sacred hymns of the Greeks, the trance songs of Native Americans, the religious music of Christendom. Amidst the secular tumult of modern Western society the sense of the sacred in music and in daily life has waned, but just under the surface the magic remains: Mozart's *Don Giovanni* may seem like a simple sex comedy, but within that deceptively fluffy story move primal mysteries, echoes of Dionysus and Milton's Lucifer.

What about the immemorial association of music with dance, movement, the body? The likeliest beginning for music was in connection with dance, which was pursued for magical purposes— to enhance the hunt, to summon the gods, to embody rituals. In all living things, a response to vibration is the most basic of the senses. Many creatures live without light, but none lacks sensitivity to sound. Even to a one-celled animal, sound means things: food, danger, respite. To higher animals, sound means more and higher things.

It would seem then, that the meaningfulness of sound begins at the physiological level of our cells and ascends from there through all degrees of the unconscious and conscious mind. If I'm right about that, it is no wonder that music strikes us on so many levels, from the physical to the spiritual, that music seems to adumbrate whatever we wish to make of it, to resonate with whatever we feel, whatever we *are* for well and ill. When humanity is exalted, music is exalted; when humanity is debased, music is debased. It is entertaining, it is oppressive, it is frightening, inspiring, trivial, exhilarating, sensual, it moves us to awe. It accompanies our orgies and our prayers, our battles and our rituals, our sins and our salvations. At its most profound and best, music is the ideal stimulus for humanity's eternal meditation on the mystery of its own being.

In the end, though, perhaps the greatest importance of music, like that of all the arts, is more immediate and practical: art brings people together. There is a community of people who love Bach, a community of people who love Euripides, and Michelangelo and Shakespeare and Jane Austen and Indian music and African-American music. These connections can transcend every barrier of time and space, language and culture and history. Most people in the modern world belong to many such communities: they are not exclusive; they interlock and overlap. Bach wrote for Christian services, but his music is broader and deeper than that tradition; it touches the wellsprings from which all religions draw, the universal verities of the body and heart and soul.

Those verities we all know: the internal rhythms of our bodies, the daily and seasonal rhythms, pain, joy, despair, hope, pity, love, exaltation. What we perceive in a great artist is less opinions or ideas than one person's feeling response to life. That vision may be obscure or may not agree with our own, but we are gripped by the artist's passion and integrity, his or her act of embodying a compelling vision of the world in moving and lasting forms. It is a heightened version of what we all do, all the time—absorbing the world, responding to it in actions and communications and representations.

Thus the usual way to the universal is through the personal, through the individual voice. When we hear work that moves us, even if we don't know why it does, there is a sense of direct communication, person to person, a sense of, "Yes, that's what it's like to be alive." For a moment that voice speaks for us all as the prophets spoke to God in our behalf. Artists speak to *us* in our behalf. And when an artist moves us, we gather around that voice. Related to the word *community* are the words *communion* and *communication*. The communion of art is a community gathered—in museums, concert halls, homes, on street corners, anywhere the bond is made— around a voice, an image, a story.

A poem, said Robert Frost, "begins in delight and ends in wisdom. The figure is the same as for love." Delight, wisdom, and love are everywhere. Beneath the barriers of culture and religion and ideology, the human heart is universal. Music and the other arts are the most potent demonstration that, in the heart, we are all one community.

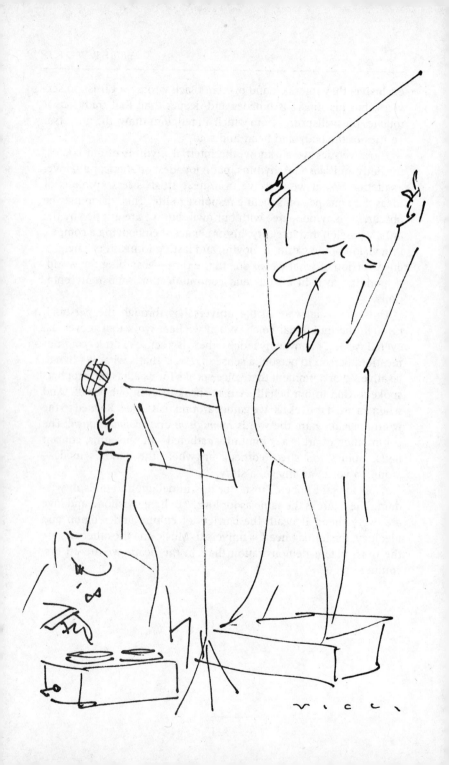

A CLASSICAL LIBRARY

What follows is a chronological listing of composers and works cited in this book. They are given more or less in the order of their citing in the essays, since that order is a suggested means of getting to know each composer.

With one or two exceptions, I haven't included recordings here, for two primary reasons. First, because this list includes most of the standard classical repertoire, there are currently available anywhere from five to twenty recordings of most of the pieces; much of the time it would be too lengthy to list several for each piece. Second, any such list is out of date after a year or so, as new recordings appear and older ones go out of issue.

I suggest that you shop for recordings with reference to one of the standard guides, such as *The New Penguin Guide to Compact Discs,* the *Record Shelf Guide,* or one of the monthly music magazines, such as *Gramophone* or *Stereo Review.* Many stores and most libraries keep these on file. Their ratings will give useful advice, and disagreements from one guide to another will remind you that listening to music, like composing and playing it, is an art and not a science, and thus subject to the glorious unpredictability of our species. In general, using guides is a better method than going for familiar stars: Few famous performers or groups are always at the top of their form, some lesser-known performers have made outstanding recordings, and some quite famous names have never made an outstanding recording.

WESTERN MUSIC

THROUGH THE MIDDLE AGES

GREGORIAN CHANT
Easter chants: *Alleluia* and *Victimae Paschali laudes*
Veni sancti spiritus

ANONYMOUS
Liturgical drama: *The Play of Daniel*

ADAM DE LA HALLE
Secular songs including *Jeu de Robin et Marion*

PÉROTIN
Sederunt Principes

GUILLAUME DE LA MACHAUT
La Messe de Notre Dame
Secular songs

RECORDED COLLECTIONS OF MEDIEVAL MUSIC
(The Gothic Voices: *The Garden of Zephirus: Courtly Songs of the Early Fifteenth Century* and *The Castle of Fair Welcome: Courtly Songs of the Later Fifteenth Century,* both on Hyperion.)

THE RENAISSANCE

GUILLAUME DUFAY
Mass, *L'homme armé,* motets including *Nuper rosarum flores*
Secular songs

JOSQUIN DESPREZ
Secular songs, including "Mille regretz," "El Grillo," etc.
Motets, including *Veni sancte spiritus* and *Absalon, fili mi*
Masses: *L'homme armé* and *Pange lingua*

ORLANDO DI LASSO
Madrigals and secular songs including "Matona mia cara," "Bonjour, mon coeur," and "Ich weiss mir ein Meidlein"

GIOVANNI DA PALESTRINA
Pope Marcellus Mass

RECORDED MADRIGAL COLLECTIONS
(Collegium Vocale Köln, *Madrigals,* 2 CDs, on Odyssey.)

WILLIAM BYRD
Masses and motet *Ave verum corpus*

THE BAROQUE

GIOVANNI GABRIELI
Collections of *Canzone per sonare* for brass and/or winds
Polychoral motets

CLAUDIO MONTEVERDI
Madrigals, including *Se Vittorie si belle* and *Zefiro torna*
Opera: *L'Incoronazione di Poppea (The Coronation of Poppea)*
Vespers of 1610 (a.k.a. *Vespers of the Blessed Virgin*)

HEINRICH SCHÜTZ
Sacred Symphonies, including *Saul, was verfolgst du mich?*
Musikalische Exequien (German Requiem)
Christmas Oratorio

GIACOMO CARISSIMI
Oratorio: *Jephte*

JEAN-BAPTISTE LULLY
Opera excerpts

ARCANGELO CORELLI
Concerti grossi op. 6

HENRY PURCELL
Ode for St. Cecilia's Day
Dido and Aeneas

FRANÇOIS COUPERIN
Harpsichord suites

JEAN-PHILIPPE RAMEAU
Pièces de clavecin en concerts
Opera excerpts

ANTONIO VIVALDI
The Four Seasons
Assorted concertos, including *L'Amoroso* and the collection
L'Estro armonico

JOHANN SEBASTIAN BACH
Collections of shorter pieces including "Sheep May Safely
Graze," "Jesu, Joy of Man's Desiring," etc.
Instrumental works
Brandenburg Concertos.
Harpsichord concertos, including no. 1 in D minor, no. 4 in A
major, and no. 5 in F minor
French and English Suites for harpsichord

Goldberg Variations (Aria with Thirty Variations)

The Well-Tempered Clavier

Unaccompanied Violin Sonatas and Partitas, especially the Partita no. 2 in D minor

Unaccompanied Cello Suites, especially no. 1 in G major and no. 2 in D minor

Organ music, including the Passacaglia and Fugue in C minor, Fantasia and Fugue in G minor, and Toccata and Fugue in D minor

Choral works

Cantatas: *Christ lag in Todesbanden, Ein' feste Burg ist unser Gott, Wachet auf, ruft uns die Stimme*

Magnificat in D

St. Matthew Passion

B minor Mass

DOMENICO SCARLATTI

Harpsichord sonatas including the E major K. 380, F major K. 525, G major K. 549, and D major K. 96

GEORGE FRIDERIC HANDEL

Water Music

Royal Fireworks Music

Concerti Grossi op. 6, especially no. 3 in E minor and no. 7 in B-flat major

Organ Concerto in F major, "The Cuckoo and the Nightingale"

Harpsichord Suite no. 5 in E major, "The Harmonious Black-smith"

Coronation Anthems

Oratorios: *Acis and Galatea, L'Allegro, il Pensieroso ed il Moderato, Messiah, Israel in Egypt, Saul*

THE CLASSICAL PERIOD

JOHANN CHRISTIAN BACH

Concerto for Harpsichord (or piano) and Strings in E-flat major op. 7 no. 5

CARL PHILIPP EMANUEL BACH

Keyboard sonatas

CHRISTOPH WILLIBALD GLUCK
  Operas: *Orfeo ed Euridice, Iphigénie en Tauride*

FRANZ JOSEPH HAYDN
  String quartets
    Sun Quartets, especially op. 20 no. 4.
    Russian (or *Gli scherzi*) Quartets op. 33, especially no. 2, "The Joke"
    Erdödy Quartets op. 76, especially no. 2 in D minor, "Quinten," and no. 5 in D major, "Largo"
  Concertos
    Trumpet Concerto in E-flat major
    Cello Concerto in D major op. 101
  Symphonies
    Early: Symphonies nos. 6, 7, 8 *(Morning, Noon, Evening)*.
    Middle: Symphonies no. 45 *(Farewell)*, no. 48 *(Maria Theresa)*, no. 49 *(La Passione)*
    Late: *London* (or *Salomon*) Symphonies—no. 94 *(Surprise)*, no. 100 *(Military)*, no. 101 *(Clock)*, no. 104 *(London)*
  Choral works
    Mass in Time of War (Paukenmesse)
    The Creation

WOLFGANG AMADEUS MOZART
  Shorter works including *Eine Kleine Nachtmusik* and *Ave Verum Corpus*
  Sinfonia Concertante in E-flat for violin, viola, and orchestra
  Piano concertos
    Concerto in C major K. 467
    Concerto in D minor K. 466
  String quartets
    Quartet in D minor K. 421
    Quartet in C major K. 465 *(Dissonant)*
  String quintets
    Quintet in C major K. 515
    Quintet in G minor K. 516
  Chamber music for winds
    Quintet in A K. 581 for clarinet and string quartet
    Serenade in B-flat K. 361 for winds

Symphonies
  Haffner, K. 385
  Prague, K. 504
  No. 39 in E-flat
  No. 40 in G minor
  No. 41 in C major *(Jupiter)*
Operas
  The Marriage of Figaro
  Don Giovanni
  The Magic Flute

LUDWIG VAN BEETHOVEN
Symphonies
  Nos. 3 *(Eroica),* 4, 5, 6 *(Pastoral),* 7, 9 *(Choral)*
Piano Concerto no. 4 in G major
String quartets
  Rasoumovsky Quartets op. 59, especially the F major *(Cello)* E minor, and C major *(Hero)*
  Late quartets: especially op. 132 in A minor, then opp. 127, 130, 131, and 135
Piano sonatas
  Early to middle: *Moonlight, Pathétique, Waldstein, Appassionata.*
  Late: opp. 109, 110, 111
Opera: *Fidelio*
Piano Trio in B-flat *(Archduke)*
Missa Solemnis

THE ROMANTIC PERIOD

GIOACCHINO ROSSINI
  Collection of opera overtures, including *William Tell, An Italian in Algiers,* and *The Barber of Seville*
  Opera: *The Barber of Seville*

CARL MARIA VON WEBER
  Overtures to *Der Freischütz, Oberon,* and *Euryanthe*

FRANZ SCHUBERT
Symphonies
  No. 8 in B minor *(Unfinished),* no. 5 in B-flat major, no. 9 in C major *(The Great)*

Chamber music
  Trout Quintet
  String Quartet in D minor *(Death and the Maiden)*
  String Quintet in C major
Piano works
  Eight Impromptus, six *Moments Musicaux, Wanderer* Fantasy
  Three Piano Sonatas opus posthumous: C minor, A major,
    B-flat major
Lieder
  Individual songs including "Erlkönig," "Gretchen am Spinn-
    rade," "Heidenröslein," "Nachtstück," "Der Döppelganger"
  Song cycles: *Die schöne Müllerin, Winterreise*

FELIX MENDELSSOHN
  Octet in E-flat major for strings
  Overture and incidental music for *A Midsummer Night's Dream*
  Fingal's Cave (The Hebrides) Overture
  Symphonies no. 4 *(Italian)* and no. 3 *(Scotch)*
  Violin Concerto in E minor

HECTOR BERLIOZ
  Symphonie fantastique
  Overtures: *Roman Carnival* and *Benvenuto Cellini*
  Harold in Italy
  Les Nuits d'été
  Requiem

ROBERT SCHUMANN
  Carnaval for piano
  Song cycles: *Leiderkreis* and *Dichterliebe*
  Quintet in E-flat major for Piano and Strings
  Piano Concerto in A minor
  Symphony no. 4 in D minor
  Cello Concerto in A minor

FRÉDÉRIC CHOPIN
  Preludes
  Impromptus
  Waltzes
  Nocturnes
  Ballades

FRANZ LISZT
Piano Sonata in B minor
Piano Concerto no. 1 in E-flat major
Les Préludes
Mephisto Waltz no. 1 (piano and/or orchestral version)
Hungarian Rhapsodies, especially no. 2
Faust Symphony
Late piano works including *Nuages gris*

RICHARD WAGNER
Orchestral excerpts, including the Prelude to *Lohengrin, Ride of the Valkyries, Siegfried's Rhine Journey* and *Funeral March, Forest Murmurs* (from *Siegfried*), *Dance of the Apprentices and Entry of the Masters* (from *Die Meistersinger*)
Complete operas
Tristan und Isolde
The Ring of the Nibelung

GIUSEPPE VERDI
Operas: *Rigoletto, La Traviata, Aïda, Otello, Falstaff*
Requiem

JOHANNES BRAHMS
Chamber music
String Sextet no. 2 in G major, Piano Quintet in F minor, Clarinet Trio, Quintet in B minor for Clarinet and Strings
German Requiem
Piano Concerto no. 2 in B-flat
Symphonies
No. 1 in C minor, no. 3 in F major, no. 2 in D major, no. 4 in E minor

ANTONÍN DVOŘÁK
Slavonic Dances
Symphonies: No. 9 in E minor *(From the New World)*, no. 8 in G major, no. 7 in D major
Cello Concerto in B minor
Chamber music: Piano Trio op. 90 *(Dumky)*, String Quartet in F major op. 96 *(American)*

MODEST MUSORGSKY
A Night on Bald Mountain
Pictures at an Exhibition (piano version and Ravel's orchestration)
Song cycles: *Songs and Dances of Death* and *Sunless*
Opera: *Boris Godunov*

PETER ILYICH TCHAIKOVSKY
1812 Overture
March slave
Suite from *The Nutcracker*
Romeo and Juliet
Piano Concerto no. 1
Symphonies: nos. 4, 5, and 6 *(Pathétique)*

RICHARD STRAUSS
Tone poems: *Don Juan, Till Eulenspiegel's Merry Pranks, Death and Transfiguration, Thus Spake Zarathustra, Don Quixote, Ein Heldenleben*
Operas: *Der Rosenkavalier, Elektra*
Four Last Songs

GUSTAV MAHLER
Des Knaben Wunderhorn
Symphonies no. 4 in G major, no. 2 in C minor *(Resurrection)*
Das Lied von der Erde
Symphonies no. 5 in C-sharp minor, no. 7 in E minor
Rückert Lieder

GEORGES BIZET
Opera: *Carmen*

CESAR FRANCK
Violin Sonata in A
Symphony in D minor

ANTON BRUCKNER
Symphonies nos. 4, 7, and 8

CAMILLE SAINT-SAËNS
Carnival of the Animals
Symphony no. 3 *(Organ)*

EDVARD GRIEG
 Peer Gynt Suite
 Piano Concerto in A minor

NICOLAI RIMSKY-KORSAKOV
 Capriccio Espagnol
 Scheherazade

ALEXANDER SCRIABIN
 Piano Sonatas 8, 9, and 10
 The Poem of Ecstasy

EDWARD ELGAR
 Pomp and Circumstance March no. 1
 Enigma Variations
 Dream of Gerontius

THE TWENTIETH CENTURY

CLAUDE DEBUSSY
 Piano works: *Suite bergamasque, Children's Corner,* Preludes
  Book 1
 Prélude à l'après-midi d'un faune
 Nocturnes
 La Mer
 Iberia
 Opera: *Pelléas et Mélisande*

JEAN SIBELIUS
 Finlandia
 The Swan of Tuonela
 Symphonies nos. 2, 4, 5, and 7

MAURICE RAVEL
 Bolero
 Pavane pour une infante défunte (piano and/or orchestral version)
 Rapsodie espagnole
 String Quartet
 Ma Mère L'Oye
 Daphnis et Chloé
 La Valse

Orchestration of Musorgsky's *Pictures at an Exhibition*

CHARLES IVES
Symphony no. 2
Songs including "Feldeinsamkeit," "Charlie Rutlage," "Watchman," "Shall We Gather at the River," "General William Booth Enters into Heaven "
Holidays Symphony
Three Places in New England
Symphony no. 4

ARNOLD SCHOENBERG
Verklärte Nacht
Five Pieces for Orchestra
Pierrot Lunaire
Piano Concerto
Violin Concerto
A Survivor from Warsaw
Opera: *Moses und Aron*

IGOR STRAVINSKY
Early ballets: *The Firebird, Petrushka, Le Sacre du printemps*
Les Noces
L'Histoire du soldat
Octet for Wind Instruments
Concerto for Piano and Wind Instruments
Symphony of Psalms
Symphony in Three Movements
Agon
Opera: *The Rake's Progress*
Violin Concerto
Oedipus Rex

BÉLA BARTÓK
Concerto for Orchestra
Divertimento for String Orchestra
String Quartets, especially no. 4, then nos. 3 and 5
Piano Concertos nos. 2 and 3
Violin Concerto no. 2
Sonata for Two Pianos and Percussion
Music for Strings, Percussion, and Celesta

A CLASSICAL LIBRARY

ALBAN BERG
Orchestral excerpts from *Wozzeck* and *Lulu*
Opera: *Wozzeck*
Lyric Suite

ANTON WEBERN
Passacaglia op. 1
Five Movements for String Quartet (or String Orchestra version)
Six Pieces for Orchestra
Symphony
Six Bagatelles for String Quartet

PAUL HINDEMITH
Kleine Kammermusik
Symphonic Metamorphosis of Themes by Carl Maria von Weber
Symphony *Mathis der Maler*

SERGEI PROKOFIEV
Peter and the Wolf
Lieutenant Kije Suite
Classical Symphony
Suite no. 2 from *Romeo and Juliet*
Piano Concerto no. 3
Symphony no. 5

AARON COPLAND
El Salón México
Ballets: *Billy the Kid* and *Rodeo*
Appalachian Spring (full orchestra and/or original ballet version)
Piano Variations
Symphony no. 3 (containing "Fanfare for the Common Man")

DMITRI SHOSTAKOVICH
Symphonies nos. 5, 10, and 13
Piano Trio no. 2 in E minor
String Quartets nos. 8 and 11

BENJAMIN BRITTEN
A Ceremony of Carols
Variations on a Theme of Frank Bridge

Operas: *Peter Grimes, The Turn of the Screw, Billy Budd*
War Requiem

GIACOMO PUCCINI
Opera: *La Bohème*

GABRIEL FAURÉ
Requiem

LEOŠ JANÁČEK
Sinfonietta
Glagolitic Mass
Opera: *The Cunning Little Vixen*

FREDERICK DELIUS
Brigg Fair
Sea Drift

CARL NIELSEN
Symphony no. 5

ERIK SATIE
Piano pieces including *Gymnopédies* and *Gnossiennes*

SERGEI RACHMANINOV
Piano Concerto no. 2
Isle of the Dead

RALPH VAUGHAN WILLIAMS
Fantasia on a Theme of Thomas Tallis
A London Symphony

CARL RUGGLES
Sun-Treader

HEITOR VILLA-LOBOS
Bachianas brasileiras, especially no. 5

EDGARD VARÈSE
Ionisation
Intégrales

DARIUS MILHAUD
La Création du monde
Opera: *Les Choëphores* (or excerpts)

FRANCIS POULENC
Gloria

CARL ORFF
Carmina Burana

GEORGE GERSHWIN
Rhapsody in Blue
An American in Paris
Opera: *Porgy and Bess* (or excerpts)

DUKE ELLINGTON
Collection of band sides through the years, including *East St. Louis Toodle-oo, Black and Tan Fantasy, Mood Indigo, Creole Rhapsody, It Don't Mean a Thing if It Ain't Got That Swing, Reminiscin' in Tempo,* and so on through the great tunes of the early '40s including *Ko-Ko, Concerto for Cootie,* and *Cotton Tail*

JAZZ HISTORY
The Smithsonian Collection of Classic Jazz (a fine recorded compendium, with accompanying historical essay)

SAMUEL BARBER
Adagio for Strings
Knoxville: Summer of 1915
Piano Concerto

MICHAEL TIPPETT
Fantasia Concertante on a Theme of Corelli
Symphony no. 2

ELLIOTT CARTER
Sonata for Flute, Oboe, Cello, and Harpsichord

JOHN CAGE
Sonatas and Interludes for Prepared Piano

OLIVIER MESSIAEN
Quartet for the End of Time

PIERRE BOULEZ
Le Marteau sans maître

KARLHEINZ STOCKHAUSEN
Gesang der Jünglinge
Hymnen
Stimmung

GYÖRGY LIGETI
Lux aeterna
Adventures

TERRY RILEY
In C

PHILIP GLASS
Einstein on the Beach

ALFRED SCHNITTKE
Viola Concerto

SOFIA GUBAIDULINA
Offertorium

ELLEN TAAFE ZWILICH
Symphony no. 1

GLOSSARY

Capitalized terms within definitions have their own entry in the glossary.

A CAPPELLA. Choral performance without instrumental accompaniment.

ABSOLUTE MUSIC. Music having no program or other extramusical associations. Examples include most symphonies and string quartets to which composers have not affixed stories, poems, etc. The opposite of PROGRAM MUSIC.

ACCENT. An emphasis on a note.

ADAGIO, ANDANTE. Standard Italian musical indications for slower tempos; used internationally.

ALBERTI BASS. Steadily moving accompaniment figure outlining a chord. Often played by the left hand in piano music of the Classical period.

ALEATORIC MUSIC. See CHANCE MUSIC.

ALLEGRO. Standard Italian musical indication for fast tempo; used internationally.

ARIA. An accompanied solo song, usually in an opera or oratorio but sometimes freestanding.

ARPEGGIO. The notes of a chord played successively rather than simultaneously.

ATONALITY. Music lacking tonality; that is, without a sense of key or tonal center. (See Tonality and Atonality, p. 268.)

The Annunciation, with angelic musicians,
from a Book of Hours of 1465.

BAR. See MEASURE.

BASS. 1) The lowest part in a composition. 2) The lowest male singing voice. 3) The double bass of the violin family.

BEL CANTO. Italian for "beautiful singing." A style of singing emphasizing beauty and evenness of tone and an effect of effortlessness.

BINARY FORM. A two-section musical form, with each part repeating. The first section usually modulates from the home key to a related key; the second part modulates back to the home key. Most binary pieces use variants of one basic melodic theme; others have two themes. Binary form is an ancestor of SONATA FORM. (See Sonata Form, p. 160.)

BITONALITY, POLYTONALITY. The superimposition of two keys (bitonality) or more (polytonality), as in Stravinsky's frequent stacking up of harmonies and lines from C major and F-sharp major in *Petrushka*.

BRASS INSTRUMENTS. Instruments made of metal—usually brass—having a cupped mouthpiece into which the lips buzz: trumpet, horn, trombone, tuba, bugle, etc.

CADENCE. A melodic or harmonic figure marking the end of a musical phrase, period, or piece. Cadences are said to be "open" or "closed" depending on their degree of finality, as defined by the traditions of tonal music. A cadence marks off musical units similarly to the way commas and periods mark off verbal units.

CADENZA. An unaccompanied passage, often virtuosic, played by the soloist near the end of many concerto movements. Usually improvised in the Classical period, later tending to be written out.

CAMERATA. A group of Florentine musicians and aristocratic dilettantes that played a central role in the invention of opera around the end of the sixteenth century. (See beginning of Baroque section, p. 36, and essay Seventeenth- and Eighteenth-Century Opera, p. 58.)

CANON. A contrapuntal procedure in which a melody line in one voice is exactly imitated by other, overlapping voices. (See Fugue and Canon, p. 72.)

CANTATA. An unstaged composition for vocal soloist(s), instruments, and sometimes chorus, progressing in an operalike way with arias, duets, recitatives, choruses, and the like. It resembles an ORATORIO, but tends to be of medium length.

CANTUS FIRMUS. A preexisting melodic line used as the basis of a polyphonic composition. (See Western Music Through the Middle Ages, p. 4.)

CASTRATO. A male singer castrated in youth to preserve his soprano or alto voice. Common mainly in Italy between the sixteenth and the beginning of the nineteenth centuries, where castrati were used in church choirs and in opera. Some of the opera singers became international stars.

CHAMBER MUSIC. Music for smaller ensembles, usually instrumental, designed for performance in smaller rooms as opposed to auditoriums. Examples are string quartet and trio sonata.

CHANSON. French word for "song." Most commonly used for French secular songs of the medieval and Renaissance periods, including monophonic troubadour songs and also polyphonic works by Machaut, Dufay, Josquin, and many others.

CHANCE MUSIC. Music involving unpredictable or changeable elements. A common technique in the twentieth-century avant-garde, examples including Stockhausen's *Momente* (with its "moments" that can be done in any order), Cage's *Imaginary Landscape no. 4* for twelve radios (which depends on whatever happens to be on the air), and pieces by Lutoslawski and others involving controlled improvisation. Also called *aleatoric* (from Latin *alea*, "dice") and *indeterminate*.

CHORD. Three or more notes sounded together to form a HARMONY.

CHROMATIC SCALE. A twelve-note SCALE using only semitones (also called half steps), the smallest intervals standard in Western music. In contrast is the common seven-tone MAJOR or MINOR scale making up a KEY. Music making much use of semitonal patterns, rather than the usual seven notes of a key, is described as *chromatic*. Examples of "chromatic music" include both late-nineteenth-century music such as Wagner's, and twentieth-century music both TONAL and ATONAL by composers such as Bartók and Schoenberg.

CHURCH MODES. See MODES.

CLAVIER. Literally, "keyboard." General Baroque term for all stringed keyboard instruments—harpsichord, clavichord, piano, etc. (though in some writings organ is also called clavier). In the nineteenth century, it became the usual German word for piano.

CODA. A concluding section of an instrumental piece.

CONCERTO. In the Baroque, usually a CONCERTO GROSSO. In the late Baroque, Classical period, and later, usually a multimovement work for soloist and orchestra—most commonly a piano or violin soloist, though all instruments have had concertos written for them. There are also double and triple concertos and the like.

CONCERTO GROSSO. A Baroque instrumental genre involving the alternation of a larger group, called the *tutti* or *ripieno,* and a smaller group called the *concertino.* (See Baroque section, p. 36.)

CONSONANT. Intervals or chords sounding relatively smooth and stable together are called consonant. The opposite of DISSONANT. (See Consonance and Dissonance, p. 28.)

CONTINUO. The basic "rhythm section" of Baroque music, usually consisting of a keyboard instrument plus a bass instrument, both playing the bass line of the piece, the keyboard also improvising an accompaniment from the harmonies of the piece. Also called *basso continuo.* (See Baroque section, p. 36.)

COUNTERPOINT. See POLYPHONY.

CRESCENDO. Standard Italian musical indication to grow louder; used internationally. Opposite of DIMINUENDO.

CYCLIC SYMPHONY. A symphony in which one or more themes occur in two or more movements. Examples include Schumann's *Rhenish* Symphony and Berlioz's *Symphonie Fantastique* (in which he calls the recurring theme the "idée fixe"). More broadly, works in which identical or similar thematic material occurs in more than one movement are said to have "cyclic form"; an example is the Renaissance cyclic Mass, in which each movement is based on the same CANTUS FIRMUS.

DA CAPO. Italian for "from the beginning." Most often seen in the *da capo aria,* a vocal genre in ABA form, common in the Ba-

GLOSSARY

roque, in which the words da capo appear at the end of the B section to indicate a repeat of the A section.

DIMINUENDO. Standard Italian musical indication to grow softer; used internationally. Opposite of CRESCENDO.

DISSONANT. Intervals and chords sounding relatively rough and unstable together are called dissonant. In traditional tonal practice, dissonant intervals and chords are required to resolve to consonant ones. (See Consonance and Dissonance, p. 28.)

DIVERTIMENTO. General term for various sorts of secular entertainment pieces of the second half of the eighteenth century. A familiar example is Mozart's string divertimento called *Eine Kleine Nachtmusik*. The term appears occasionally into the twentieth century, for example Bartók's Divertimento for Strings.

DOCTRINE OF THE AFFECTIONS. A Baroque expressive aesthetic, common in the seventeenth and early eighteenth centuries, holding that music's main purpose is to arouse the "affections"—i.e., emotions such as love, fear, anger, joy, and so on. Some theorists proposed specific tonal, rhythmic, and other musical/rhetorical devices to suggest specific emotions; these ideas probably influenced Bach, Handel, and many other composers. Another corollary was that each piece, or movement of a piece, should concentrate on a single affect, that is, one emotion.

DODECAPHONY. The twelve-tone technique. See TWELVE TONE.

DOMINANT. 1) The fifth degree above the TONIC and second most important note in a major or minor scale. 2) The harmony built on that tone. A MODULATION to the key based on the fifth degree is called a modulation to the dominant. That key is closely related to the home key because it has only one different note— one less flat or one more sharp. (See Tonality and Atonality, p. 268.)

DRONE. A sustained note that persists through a section of music or a whole work.

FANTASY, FANTASIA. Traditional term for pieces in no standard form, often highly expressive, usually designed to have a quasi-improvisatory effect. The Baroque produced many keyboard fantasias such as Bach's *Chromatic Fantasy and Fugue;* Classical examples include Mozart's Fantasia in C minor. Because of its freedom and expressive associations, it became a favorite term for free-form Romantic character pieces by Chopin and others.

FLAT. A musical symbol (♭) that lowers the pitch of a written note by a semitone.

FORTE, FORTISSIMO. Standard Italian musical indications for "loud" and "loudest." Used internationally; always abbreviated as *f* or *ff*.

FRENCH OVERTURE. A Baroque instrumental genre involving a stately opening in "dotted" rhythms (pah-*dum,* pah-*dum,* pah-*dum*) and then a quick fugal section. An example is the overture to Handel's *Messiah.*

FUGATO. A fuguelike section appearing in a longer, nonfugal work, such as in a Classical symphonic movement.

FUGUE. A contrapuntal procedure in which a short theme, called the *subject,* is treated in imitation. (See Fugue and Canon, p. 72.)

GALANT STYLE. A style in mid-eighteenth-century Rococo music involving a certain delicacy, grace, and simplicity of effect within a homophonic texture. The galant style can be precious and superficial, but at its best it is a vital element in the expressive palette of composers including Haydn and Mozart.

GEBRAUCHSMUSIK. Literally, "useful music" in German. A term originated by Paul Hindemith to indicate music of practical use in situations ranging from private amateur performance to film and theater, as opposed to an attitude of "art for art's sake."

GENRE. As per the dictionary: "genus; kind; sort; style." Musical pieces that belong to the same genre call for the same combination of forces (vocal, instrumental, electronic), are similar in scope, and usually share certain formal characteristics. Thus in this book the symphony, string quartet, and other sorts of pieces are called *genres:* they can vary widely but still have some underlying historical tradition as a type of piece.

GESAMTKUNSTWERK. "Total work of art." Term used by Wagner to indicate the unity of arts in his music dramas. (See essay on Wagner, p. 258.)

GLISSANDO. A musical effect of sliding up or down in pitch without a break. On a violin, for example, it is done by sliding the finger along the string while drawing the bow steadily.

GRACE NOTES. A type of ORNAMENT in which a rapid note or notes precede a main note in a melody.

GREGORIAN CHANT. See PLAINCHANT.

GROUND BASS. A bass line repeated over and over as the basis of a piece, which is composed above the line. See OSTINATO.

HARMONY. 1) The art of chord construction and progression. 2) A particular chord. Harmony is one of the three basic elements of music, the other two being melody and rhythm; and it is the only one of the three unique to Western music. (See Tonality and Atonality, p. 268.)

HOMOPHONY. Music consisting of a melody and harmonic accompaniment. (See Monophony to Polyphony to Homophony, p. 88.)

IMITATION. Broad term for any contrapuntal procedure in which one voice imitates the melodic line of another. Can be rather free, as when one voice begins with an echo of another and continues on its own, or strict, as in fugue and canon. (See Fugue and Canon, p. 72.)

INDETERMINACY. See CHANCE MUSIC.

INTERVAL. 1) A musical measure of distance between notes. 2) The notes themselves, taken together. Intervals are named according to their types: semitone (or half step), whole step, minor third, major third, and so on. They are also classified on a scale from strongly consonant to strongly dissonant. (See Consonance and Dissonance, p. 28.)

INVERSION. Turning a line upside down, making the same melodic shape as the original in mirrored form.

ITALIAN OVERTURE. A type of overture developed for Italian Baroque opera, consisting of three short movements in the pattern fast-slow-fast. Called *sinfonia* during the Baroque, it was an important predecessor of the Classical symphony.

KEY. A collection of seven notes in MAJOR or MINOR mode, gravitating around a main note called the TONIC or *key note*. A key is expressed in terms of a major or minor SCALE and indicated on the page by the *key signature,* a pattern of flats or sharps. There are twenty-four basic keys in Western tonal music, twelve major and twelve minor; pieces are described in terms of their key, as in, "Symphony in B-flat major." (See TONALITY and essay on Tonality and Atonality, p. 268.)

LEGATO. Standard Italian musical indication to play smoothly, with no spaces between the notes; used internationally. Opposite of STACCATO.

LEITMOTIF. In Wagnerian music dramas and works influenced by them, a musical tag representing a character, idea, plot element, or the like. Examples from the many in Wagner's *Ring* include "Siegfried's Horn Call," "The Ring," "The Magic Fire." Wagner uses leitmotifs as if they were symphonic themes as well as reflections of the story.

LIBRETTO. The text of an opera, oratorio, etc.

LIED (PL. LIEDER). German word for "song," generally used in English for Romantic art song.

MADRIGAL. Term used for a wide variety of light secular pieces, usually for three to five voices, popular in the Renaissance and into the Baroque. The genre originated in Italy in the fourteenth century but evolved in many directions. Most familiar of the genre are English madrigals of the Elizabethan period (see Renaissance section, p. 20) and those of Monteverdi.

MAJOR. The "brighter," "happier" of the two common modes in Western tonal music (the other mode being MINOR). A major key is expressed by a major SCALE, a particular pattern of whole and half steps.

MASS. 1) The primary liturgical service of the Roman Catholic Church, involving sections called the Ordinary (always the same—Kyrie, Gloria, Credo, Sanctus, Agnus Dei) and the Proper (which changes from service to service). 2) A musical setting of the Mass, usually the sections of the Ordinary. Examples range from PLAINCHANT Masses, through polyphonic ones by Josquin and others, through the Masses of the Baroque by Bach and others (including the shorter Lutheran Mass), and settings by Mozart and composers into the present.

MEASURE. See METER.

MELODY. A coherent succession of tones arranged into a musical line. One of the three basic elements of music, the other two being rhythm and (in the West) harmony. (See Melody, p. 8.)

METER. Metered music, which is most music in most cultures, is organized by a continuing pattern of pulses, or *beats*. The meter is the continuing pattern of the beats. A single group of beats within the metric pattern is called a *measure*, or *bar* (from the two *bar lines* marking off each measure on the page). Measures in Western music generally have from two to six beats. The written *time signature* identifies the meter, telling the performer how many beats per measure and which kind of note receives a beat; the time signature 2/4, for example, indicates that there are two beats per measure, and that a quarter note gets one beat. The first beat of each measure is called the *downbeat*. There are also strong and weak beats in the metric patterns: in the common meter 4/4, the first beat is the strongest, third second strongest, and beats two and four weak. (Though beats are not usually stressed as strong or weak in playing, they are still perceived as such.) Some genres of music have characteristic meters, among them the two-beat of many marches and the three-beat of the waltz and the minuet.

MINOR. The "darker," "sadder" of the two common modes in Western tonal music (the other mode being MAJOR). A minor key is expressed by a minor SCALE, a particular pattern of whole and half steps.

MINUET. An elegant three-beat dance that emerged in the sixteenth century from folk sources and stayed popular into the nineteenth century. Meanwhile in the eighteenth century the minuet—a nonfunctional abstraction of it—became part of the symphony and other Classical concert genres such as the string quartet. (See Sonata Form, p. 160.)

MODERATO. Standard Italian musical indication for moderate tempo; used internationally.

MODES/MODAL. Generally speaking, any SCALE, that is, an arrangement of whole and half steps in a standard pattern, most often of seven notes. In practice, the term "mode" usually indicates scale types other than the common MAJOR and MINOR scales of Western tonality, especially the ancient church modes called Dorian (on the piano, D to D on the "white notes"), Phrygian (based on E), Lydian (on F), and Mixolydian (on G). These modes have milder tonal pulls than major and minor scales.

Music using the church modes—much of it pre-Baroque and modern—is called "modal."

MODULATION. The process and/or result of changing from one key to another: one modulates to another key; one has then made a modulation.

MONODY. In general, synonymous with MONOPHONY, that is, music based on a single unaccompanied melodic line. More specifically (and in this book), "monody" is used to indicate the homophonic style of Italian solo song in the first half of the seventeenth century, what Monteverdi called *seconda prattica*. (See introduction to Baroque section, p. 36, and Monteverdi section, p. 41.)

MONOPHONY. Music consisting of a single melodic line without harmonic accompaniment, although, as in Indian music, there may be accompaniments in percussion, drone instruments, etc.

MOTET. A polyphonic musical genre first developed in the Middle Ages, when a motet was a short sacred piece usually for three or four voices, with a Gregorian CANTUS FIRMUS and other lines composed around it, each line having its own text. The motet was a common genre through the Renaissance, though its form evolved steadily.

MOTIVE. Also called *motif*. The shortest building block of a melodic line beyond the single note: a pattern of usually two to six notes having a clear identity, which can be assembled and transformed to create themes. An example of a motive is the four-note figure that opens Beethoven's Fifth (its motivic importance in the piece is as much in the rhythm as in the pitches). (See Melody, p. 8.)

MUSIC DRAMA. Wagner's term for his operas, in which music, poetry, and the visual arts are unified in the service of the drama.

NATURAL. A musical symbol (♮) that cancels a sharp or flat.

NEOCLASSICISM. An artistic movement of the twentieth century, led in music by figures such as Stravinsky and *Les Six* in France, that called for an end to Romantic lushness and extravagance and a return to something like the simplicity, clarity, and objectivity that marked the music of the eighteenth-century Classical period. (See essay on Stravinsky, p. 405.)

NOTATION. Systems of writing down music by means of graphic symbols.

NOTE. See OCTAVE.

OBBLIGATO. A term for a subordinate part that is prominently featured, such as a section of a piano concerto with violin obbligato.

OCTAVE. A musical INTERVAL in which the higher PITCH vibrates at double the frequency of the lower. Thus if "middle A" has 440 vibrations per second, "A" an octave above has 880, "A" an octave below 220, and so on. This explains the acoustic phenomenon in which an octave is perceived as a "higher" and "lower" pitch, yet both pitches are also somehow the same. The octave effect also explains why we need only seven names for all the notes, from A to G; all pitches are octave equivalents of these seven notes and their flat and sharp forms (making twelve notes in all). A given "note" has the same name and function in every octave; when men and women sing a tune together, they usually sing its notes in octaves. To summarize: a *note* remains the same in every octave while its *pitch* (that is, frequency of vibration) changes from octave to octave. To jump up an octave on the same note is to double the frequency. In the classification of intervals, the octave is second only to the UNISON in CONSONANCE.

OPERA SERIA. Generally, serious opera; specifically, Italian serious opera of the eighteenth century, usually based on historical or mythological subjects and dominated by the da capo aria. Examples are Handel's *Julius Caesar* and Mozart's *Idomeneo*.

OPERA BUFFA. Generally, comic opera; specifically, Italian comic opera of the eighteenth century, or later works in that tradition. Usually opera buffa used contemporary plots and characters rather than the mythological and historical types of OPERA SERIA. An example of *buffa* is Mozart's *Marriage of Figaro*. Related types are the German SINGSPIEL (Mozart's *Magic Flute*) and the French opéra comique.

ORATORIO. A large work for chorus, soloists, and orchestra, unstaged but proceeding in operalike fashion with choruses, arias, recitatives, etc., and using a text sacred or otherwise elevated in character. An example is Handel's *Messiah*.

ORCHESTRATION. The disposition of music among instruments; the art of arranging combinations of instruments to colorful, expressive, and lucid effect. To put it another way: it is the art and science of coloring the notes of a work by means of its instrumental garb. Orchestration includes the study of the sounds, techniques, and capabilities of each instrument. While the instrumental forces playing various pieces were ad hoc through the Renaissance, in the Baroque composers began to specify particular instrumental combinations for their works and to write them out more or less in modern SCORE form. Through the nineteenth century, composers turned more and more of their attention to the coloristic aspect of music, meanwhile enlarging the orchestra—and adding new colors—with new instruments such as trombones, piccolo, English horn, and so on. In the work of twentieth-century composers such as Mahler and Stravinsky, the orchestral color is nearly as important to the musical substance as the notes, rhythms, and harmonies.

ORNAMENTS. Quick notes that "ornament" the main notes of a line. A regular feature of Baroque and Classical music, in which ornaments are often improvised by the player. Types of ornaments include trills, turns, and GRACE NOTES. A trill, for example, is the familiar scintillation of Baroque and Classical music involving a rapid alternation of a note with the one above.

OSTINATO. A short repeated pattern, most often in the bass, around which a section or whole piece of music is composed. An example is a GROUND BASS piece such as the *Crucifixus* from Bach's B minor Mass.

PASSION. An oratorio on the subject of the death of Christ, based on one of the four Gospels, for example Bach's *St. Matthew Passion*.

PERCUSSION INSTRUMENTS. Musical instruments usually involving something that hits, shakes, or scrapes something. Examples include drums, vibraphone, gongs, maracas, castanets, and sleighbells—and also the piano, in which felt hammers strike the strings.

PERIOD. A term for the next largest musical section after the PHRASE, often marked by a relatively strong CADENCE. In many TONAL pieces, two phrases (called antecedent and consequent) make up most of the periods. Shorter periods in turn combine into longer ones, and groups of periods into *sections*. If the phrase is comparable to the clause in language, the period is analogous to the sentence. Thus the hierarchy of musical articulations runs: subphrase, phrase (two to four measures), period, larger period, section, movement, whole piece.

PHRASE. A musical/melodic syntactical unit roughly equivalent to the amount one can sing in a breath, and roughly analogous to a clause in prose. Always marked off by some sort of melodic or harmonic CADENCE and/or breathlike pause. (See Melody, p. 8.)

PIANO, PIANISSIMO. Standard Italian musical indications for "soft" and "very soft"; used internationally.

PITCH. The perceived highness or lowness of a tone as determined by its vibrational frequency. For example, orchestras tune to the pitch "middle A," which is around 440 vibrations per second. See OCTAVE for the difference between *pitch* and *note*.

PIZZICATO. "Plucked"—a technique for playing stringed instruments, such as the violin, that are normally bowed.

POINTILLISM. A musical texture common in the Webern and post-Webern styles, in which instruments tend to play only one to three notes at a time, and the longer melodic lines are made from these constantly changing instrumental colors. Named after the painting technique of Georges Seurat, who used dots of color to build up textures.

PLAINCHANT. A generic term for the monophonic liturgical music of the Catholic church. The best-known plainchant repertoire is called Gregorian chant. Also called *plainsong*. (See Western Music Through the Middle Ages, p. 4.)

POLYCHORD. A chord made up of two or more superimposed common chords, either from one key or more than one. Examples are the superimposed TONIC and DOMINANT triads in Copland's *Appalachian Spring* and the combined C major and F-sharp major triads of Stravinsky's *Petrushka*.

POLYPHONY. The combination of two or more simultaneous melodic lines. Roughly synonymous with *counterpoint*. (See Monophony to Polyphony to Homophony, p. 88.)

POLYRHYTHM. A technique in twentieth-century and various ethnic musics in which rhythms not in sync with one another (as the West traditionally defines sync) are played together. In African drumming and related African-American and Latin styles, polyrhythm may involve the superimposition of different meters, say, one part outlining 4/4, another 5/8, another 9/8, and so on. In this case the durations of the measure in each part are different, as are the number and duration of the beats. In another technique, superimposed values imply different pulses within the same measure; for example, one part plays four beats in the same time as another plays five and another seven, but everybody has the same downbeat. The latter is a major feature of the rhythmic style of composers including Charles Ives and Elliott Carter. Sometimes called *cross rhythm*.

POLYTONALITY. See BITONALITY.

PROGRAM MUSIC. Works correlated by the composer with a story, a series of scenes, or other extramusical ideas. Familiar examples include Vivaldi's *The Four Seasons,* Beethoven's *Pastoral* Symphony, Berlioz's *Symphonie Fantastique,* and Richard Strauss's *Don Juan.* The opposite of ABSOLUTE MUSIC.

PURE MUSIC. See ABSOLUTE MUSIC.

QUARTER TONES. Musical intervals half the size of the smallest standard interval in Western music, the semitone (or half step); i.e., a note between, say, B and B♭. Quarter tones are common in non-Western traditions such as Indian music; they have been explored in the twentieth century by Western composers including Alois Haba and Charles Ives.

RECITATIVE. A free, proselike accompanied signing style that mimics the normal inflections and rhythms of speech. Invented for and traditionally used in opera, oratorio, and similar genres, both to take care of plot elements and to string together the more melodic sections such as arias and choruses. (See introduction to Baroque section, p. 36.)

REGISTER. Term for a given range of a voice or instrument. One says, for example, "This song stays in the middle register of the soprano voice."

RHYTHM. A general term for the durational patterns of music—the sequence of relatively long and short notes moving through time. We can speak of the rhythmic style of a piece or of a specific rhythmic figure such as the one that begins Beethoven's Fifth Symphony. Rhythm is one of the three basic elements of music, the other two being melody and (in the West) harmony.

RONDO. A formal model diagrammable as ABACADA, and so on. (See Sonata Form, p. 160.)

ROW. See TWELVE-TONE MUSIC.

RUBATO. An indication of a free treatment of the notated rhythm in performance; for example, in a piano piece the right hand may expressively vary the written rhythmic values while the left-hand accompaniment stays steady. (See essay on Chopin.)

SCALE. In the simplest terms, any arrangement of the smaller musical intervals, usually whole and half steps, into a linear pattern in ascending or descending order from one OCTAVE to the next. Examples are the MAJOR and MINOR SCALES of Western TONAL music, the archaic church MODES, and the pentatonic (five-tone) scale of much folk and ethnic music worldwide. A scale lays out schematically the notes in a KEY. Most Western scales have seven tones; for example, a major scale, regardless of what pitch it starts on, is defined by a particular pattern of seven whole and half steps from the tonic (key note) to the tonic in the next octave: whole, whole, half, whole, whole, whole, half. While scales as such are mainly theoretical or didactic constructs, much music uses scalelike patterns constantly; this is why practicing scales has long been a skill-building technique for performers. Beyond their interval patterns, major and minor scales contain complex relationships and tensions gravitating around their tonic. In Western tradition, especially from the nineteenth century on, music based on major scales/keys tends to be interpreted as "bright," "happy," and the like, that based on minor scales/keys as "dark," "sad," and the like. (See Tonality and Atonality, p. 268.)

SCHERZO. Most commonly, one of the middle movements of a symphony, string quartet, or related form: a piece in fast three-beat meter, usually vivacious in character. Haydn first created the scherzo by considerably speeding up the MINUET and trio, but the idea is mainly associated with Beethoven and later symphonists (who also delved into demonic or macabre scherzos). (See Sonata Form, p. 160.)

SCORE. Notation of a piece laid out for all the parts, with all measures and rhythms aligned vertically, as in an orchestral score. When a composer orchestrates a work, he or she is said to "score" it, i.e., turn the sketches into a score. "Score" is also used as a synonym for "piece" or "work," as in, "It was his finest score."

SERIALISM. An extension of Schoenbergian twelve-tone technique in which elements other than pitch—rhythm, volume, and so on—are ordered in rows (see TWELVE-TONE MUSIC) or rowlike arrangements. In serial pieces, all such orderings are referred to as *series;* thus one can have a pitch series, an interval series, a rhythmic series, a series of intensities, and so on. Each of these may be manipulated in various ways including inversion, retrograde, and the like. (See essay on Schoenberg, p. 388.)

SHARP. A musical symbol (♯) that raises a written note by a semitone.

SINFONIA. See ITALIAN OVERTURE.

SINGSPIEL. A German musical/dramatic genre of the eighteenth and early nineteenth centuries, usually comic in tone and with relatively humble characters, that involved arias and choruses as in opera but had spoken dialogue in place of sung RECITATIVE. (Singspiel somewhat resembled, in other words, the American musical comedy.) The most famous singspiels are both by Mozart: *The Abduction from the Seraglio* and *The Magic Flute.*

SONATA. A multimovement work for one or more solo instruments, as in "piano sonata" or "sonata for cello and piano." The term changed meanings in the course of music history, but the term most often refers to the genre as it developed in the Classical period and later, involving movements in sonata form and related forms. (See Sonata Form, p. 160.)

SONATA FORM. A formal model for individual movements developed in the Classical period and typically used in instrumental genres such as symphony, sonata, and string quartet. (See Sonata Form, p. 160.)

SONORITY. A term for the general quality of sound in a work or part of a work: one might speak of the "rich sonority" of a cello or a "characteristic sonority" of a piece. It is similar to the term *timbre*, which means "tone color"; but timbre is most often applied to the coloristic aspect of a specific instrumentation or sound: "a brassy timbre," "a percussive timbre" a "grating" or "smooth" timbre. Modern composers such as Varèse and Stockhausen made timbre into a structural feature of their music.

SPATIAL MUSIC. Music having effects of shifting in space or moving through it; examples are the antiphonal brass music of Gabrieli, Stockhausen's *Gruppen* for three orchestras, and electronic pieces with sounds moving among two or more speakers.

SPRECHSTIMME. Literally, "speech-voice" in German. A vocal technique between speaking and singing, invented by Schoenberg for his *Pierrot Lunaire* and much used since. (Distinct from operatic RECITATIVE, which is done more or less in the normal singing voice.) (See essay on Schoenberg, p. 388.)

STACCATO. Standard Italian musical indication for notes played very short; used internationally. The opposite of LEGATO.

STRING QUARTET. 1) The standard chamber music ensemble of two violins, viola, and cello. 2) A piece written for string quartet, usually a multimovement work analogous to a symphony or sonata. The most widely cultivated chamber music genre.

STRINGED INSTRUMENTS. Instruments having strings that are bowed, struck, or plucked; examples include violin, viola da gamba, and guitar.

SUITE. A multimovement musical form common in the Baroque, usually made up of a sequence of dances or dancelike pieces. (See end of Baroque essay.) In the nineteenth and twentieth centuries, the term often meant a series of excerpts derived from a longer work such as a ballet, for example, Tchaikovsky's *Nutcracker* Suite and Stravinsky's *Firebird* Suite.

STROPHIC FORM. Music organized as a series of repeated sections, often setting a strophic poem; that is, a poem in which each stanza has the same number of lines, same meter, and so on. In a strophic song each stanza of the poem is sung to the same tune.

SYMPHONY. From the Classical period on, the term indicates a sonata for orchestra—a multimovement genre involving sonata form and related forms. (The term *symphony* meant other things in the Baroque.) Beginning as the archetypal "abstract" instrumental genre, during the nineteenth century the symphony was broadened to include programmatic elements (see SYMPHONIC POEM) and voices (e.g., Beethoven's Ninth). Some twentieth-century symphonies, such as Sibelius's Seventh, are in one movement. And in general, by this century the term had come to be applicable to almost any large orchestral work in any form. (See SONATA and essay on Sonata Form, p. 160.)

SYMPHONIC POEM. A type of program music for orchestra, illustrating a literary text or extramusical idea to which listeners are expected to refer. The term was coined by Liszt; an example is his *Les Préludes*. Generally equivalent to a *tone poem*.

SYNCOPATION. A rhythmic technique of emphasizing normally "weak" parts of the meter, such as the middle of a beat, at the expense of a normally "strong" point. While syncopation occurs as a special effect in all Western styles, African-American styles such as ragtime and jazz make it a steady and characteristic feature.

TEMPO. The speed of the basic pulse in music; one speaks of a "fast tempo," "moderate tempo," and so on, traditionally indicated by Italian terms such as ALLEGRO, MODERATO, and ANDANTE, or by the more specific metronome markings such as quarter note = 80 (beats per minute).

TERNARY FORM. The musical form ABA, the middle section being different from the outer section in material and usually in a different KEY as well. An example is the *da capo aria*.

TEXTURE. 1) The quasi-tactile quality of music; the nature of the fabric of sound. One speaks of a "thick texture" or a "thin texture" or a "voluptuous texture." 2) More technically, one can speak of a "contrapuntal texture" or "homophonic texture."

THEME. 1) Any melody used as a basis for a piece or part of a piece, as in, "the opening theme of Mozart's G minor Symphony." 2) The self-contained initial section that forms the basis of a

THEME AND VARIATIONS. (See essays Sonata Form, p. 160, and Melody, p. 8.)

THEME AND VARIATIONS. A musical form based on a series of variations of the opening section, called the *theme*. The whole piece forms the pattern A A1 A2 A3, and so on. (See Sonata Form, p. 160.)

THROUGH-COMPOSED FORM. A piece without strophic patterns, recapitulations, or other repeating sections, such as the Schubert songs that use new music for each stanza of the text.

TIMBRE. See SONORITY.

TIME SIGNATURE. The indication of the METER in musical notation (such as 4/4, 3/4, etc.). It is placed at the beginning of the piece, or notated wherever the meter changes.

TONALITY. In Western music, organization with reference to a primary tone or harmony. Roughly synonymous with KEY. (See Tonality and Atonality, p. 268.)

TONE CLUSTERS. Dissonant harmonies made up entirely of pitches very close together, for example, a stretch of adjacent keys on piano struck with flat hand or with the arm. A common twentieth-century harmonic effect first popularized by composers such as Charles Ives, Henry Cowell, and Béla Bartók.

TONE POEM. See SYMPHONIC POEM.

TONIC. The main tone in a SCALE and KEY, the CHORD built on that tone, and also the home key in a larger work. (See Tonality and Atonality, p. 268.)

TRANSPOSITION. Playing music at a different pitch than its original presentation. In TONAL music, that involves changing the KEY; in CHROMATIC or ATONAL music, it involves changing the pitch of the material by a constant interval. Singers sometimes ask pianists to transpose an accompaniment to a higher or lower pitch so the song will lie better in their particular vocal range. A composer often transposes recurring material during the course of a piece—for example, the second theme group in the recap of a sonata-form piece. Systematic transposition of the row is a basic technique of TWELVE-TONE MUSIC.

TRIAD. A three-note CHORD made of two superimposed INTERVALS of a third, and the basic harmonic unit of Western tonal music.

There are four types of triads: major, minor, diminished, and augmented.

TRILL. See ORNAMENT.

TRIO SONATA. A multimovement piece generally for four players in three parts: two treble instruments and a CONTINUO usually made up of harpsichord and a bass instrument such as cello. The most important chamber music genre of the Baroque.

TWELVE-TONE MUSIC. A compositional method invented by Arnold Schoenberg in which all pitch material in a work—both harmonic and melodic—is based on a chosen series of the twelve notes of the chromatic scale (as opposed to the seven notes of the TONAL scale). This pattern, called the *twelve-tone row*, may be subjected to various manipulations including transposition, inversion, retrograde, and retrograde inversion. (See essays on Schoenberg, p. 388; Webern, p. 442; and Berg, p. 435.)

UNISON. Two or more notes identical in pitch; thus voices singing a melody together are said to be "in unison" (unless they are in OCTAVES).

VIBRATO. A slight, rapid, controlled shaking of pitch used by singers and instrumentalists to give intensity and vitality to the sound. Singers do it by vocal manipulation, instrumentalists by various means: violinists and guitarists rock the left hand, brass and woodwind players rhythmically flex the lips or vary breath pressure. While vibrato has long been used in the West, until the later nineteenth century it tended to be a special effect rather than the inevitable and relentless presence it is today (except in early music performance, where it tends to be used sparingly if at all).

VOICE. 1) The singing or speaking voice. 2) In polyphonic music, each part is called a "voice" whether it is played or sung, by one person or many; thus one speaks of a "three-voiced fugue" for harpsichord. (A useful term because the word "part" can be confused with the successive sections of a composition.)

WOODWIND INSTRUMENTS. Wind instruments originally or presently made of wood, including the single-reed clarinet and saxophone, double-reed oboe and bassoon, and the reedless flute and recorder.

FURTHER READING

Periods and composers are in chronological order, as in the book.

WESTERN MUSIC
THROUGH THE MIDDLE AGES

GENERAL—M. Bukofzer. *Studies in Medieval and Renaissance Music.* Norton, 1950.
MACHAUT—G. Reaney. *Guillaume de Machaut.* Oxford University Press, 1971.

THE RENAISSANCE

JOSQUIN—E. Lowinsky and B. Blackburn, eds. *Josquin des Prez, Proceedings of the International Josquin Festival-Conference.* Oxford University Press, 1976.
MADRIGALISTS—J. Kerman. *The Elizabethan Madrigal.* American Musicological Society, 1962.
LASSO (or LASSUS)—J. Roche. *Lassus.* Oxford University Press, 1982.
GABRIELI—D. Arnold. *Giovanni Gabrieli and the Music of the Venetian High Renaissance.* Oxford University Press, 1979.

THE BAROQUE

GENERAL—F. Blume. *Renaissance and Baroque Music.* Norton, 1967.
MONTEVERDI—D. Arnold. *Monteverdi.* J. M. Dent, 1975.
OPERA—D. J. Grout. *A Short History of Opera,* 2nd ed. Columbia University Press, 1965.
VIVALDI—M. Talbot. *Vivaldi.* J. M. Dent, 1978.
BACH—K. Geiringer. *Johann Sebastian Bach.* Oxford University Press, 1966.
SCARLATTI—R. Kirkpatrick. *Domenico Scarlatti.* Princeton University Press, 1983.

HANDEL—H. C. Robbins Landon. *Handel and His World*. Weidenfeld & Nicolson, 1984.

THE CLASSICAL PERIOD

GENERAL—F. Blume. *Classic and Romantic Music*. Norton, 1970.

HAYDN—K. Geiringer. *Haydn, A Creative Life in Music*, 3rd ed. University of California Press, 1982.

MOZART—W. Hildesheimer. *Mozart*. Vintage, 1983.

  V. Braunbehrens. *Mozart in Vienna*. Grove Weidenfeld, 1986.

BEETHOVEN—E. Forbes, ed. *Thayer's Life of Beethoven*, 2 vols. Princeton University Press, 1969.

  D. Arnold and N. Fortune, eds. *The Beethoven Companion*. Faber & Faber, 1971.

THE ROMANTIC PERIOD

GENERAL—F. Blume. *Classic and Romantic Music*. Norton, 1970.

SCHUBERT—G. Marek. *Schubert*. Viking, 1985.

  E. Blom, trans. *The Schubert Reader*. Norton, 1947.

MENDELSSOHN—W. Blunt. *On Wings of Song: A Biography of Felix Mendelssohn*. Scribner's, 1974.

BERLIOZ—J. Barzun. *Berlioz and His Century*. Little, Brown, 1969.

  H. Berlioz. *Memoirs*.

SCHUMANN—J. Chissell. *Schumann*, rev. ed. J. M. Dent, 1977.

CHOPIN—A. Hedley, rev. M. Brown. *Chopin*. J. M. Dent, 1974.

LISZT—A. Walker. *Franz Liszt: The Man and His Music*. Barrie & Jenkins, 1970.

WAGNER—C. von Westernhagen. *Wagner: A Biography*, 2 vols. Cambridge University Press, 1978.

  P. Burbridge and R. Sutton, eds. *The Wagner Companion*. Cambridge University Press, 1979.

VERDI—F. Walker. *The Man Verdi*. Knopf, 1962.

BRAHMS—K. Geiringer. *Brahms, His Life and Work*, rev. ed.

DVOŘÁK—J. Clapham. *Antonín Dvořák*, rev. ed. Norton, 1979.

MUSORGSKY—M. Calvocoressi. *Musorgsky*, rev. G. Abraham. J. M. Dent, 1974.

TCHAIKOVSKY—E. Garden. *Tchaikovsky*. J. M. Dent, 1973.

STRAUSS—E. Krause. *Richard Strauss, The Man and His Work*. Collett's, 1964.

MAHLER—H. LaGrange. *Mahler*. Doubleday.

THE TWENTIETH CENTURY

GENERAL—W. Austin. *Music in the Twentieth Century from Debussy through Stravinsky*. Norton, 1966.

E. Schwartz and B. Childs, eds. *Contemporary Composers on Contemporary Music*. Holt, Rinehart & Winston, 1967.

DEBUSSY—E. Lockspeiser. *Debussy: His Life and Music*. Casell, 1965–66.

SIBELIUS—R. Layton. *Sibelius*. J. M. Dent, 1965.

JANÁČEK—J. Vogel. *Leoš Janáček: His Life and Works*, rev. ed. Norton, 1981.

IVES—H. and S. Cowell. *Charles Ives and His Music*. Oxford University Press, repr. 1974.

V. Perlis. *Charles Ives Remembered*. Norton, 1974.

RAVEL—A. Orenstein. *Ravel, Man and Musician*. Columbia University Press, 1975.

SCHOENBERG—J. Smith. *Schoenberg and His Circle*. Schirmer, 1986.

STRAVINSKY—V. Stravinsky and R. Craft. *Stravinsky in Pictures and Documents*. Simon and Schuster, 1978.

M. Druskin. *Igor Stravinsky: His Life, Works, and Views*. Cambridge University Press, 1983.

BARTÓK—H. Stevens. *The Life and Music of Béla Bartók*, 2nd ed. Oxford University Press, 1964.

BERG—W. Reich. *Alban Berg*. Harcourt, Brace & World, 1965.

WEBERN—H. Moldenhauer. *Anton von Webern*. Knopf, 1979.

HINDEMITH—P. Hindemith. *A Composer's World*. Associated, 1954.

GERSHWIN—E. Jablonsky. *Gershwin*. Doubleday, 1987.

PROKOFIEV—H. Robinson. *Prokofiev, A Biography*. Viking, 1987.

COPLAND—V. Perlis. *Copland: 1900–1942*. St. Martin's Press, 1984.

SHOSTAKOVICH—S. Volkov, ed. *Testimony: The Memoirs of Dmitry Shostakovich*. Harper & Row, 1979.

BRITTEN—E. White. *Benjamin Britten, His Life and Operas*, 2nd ed. University of California Press, 1983.

INDEX

E

F

M

W

ACKNOWLEDGMENTS
AND PICTURE CREDITS

Grateful acknowledgment is made to:

Harcourt Brace Jovanovich, Inc., and Faber and Faber Limited for permission to reprint an excerpt from "Little Gidding" in *Four Quartets* by T.S. Eliot. Copyright 1943 by T.S. Eliot and renewed 1971 by Esmé Valerie Eliot.

Belmont Music Publishers, Pacific Palisades, CA 90272, for permission to reprint the first four measures of Schoenberg's Minuet from the *Suite for Piano Op. 25.*

CPP/Belwin, Inc., for permission to reprint *Night Music I* by George Crumb. Copyright © 1967 by Mills Music, Inc. International copyright secured, all rights reserved.

ii The Bettmann Archive; vi The Metropolitan Museum of Art, Rogers Fund, 1947 (47.100.1); viii Library, University of Heidelberg; x photo by Mathias Oppersdorff; xii The Metropolitan Museum of Art, Catharine Lorillard Wolfe Collection, Wolfe Fund, 1963 (63.85); xiv, xvi, xviii The Metropolitan Museum of Art, Gift of Lincoln Kirstein, 1959 (JP 3276); xviii Print Collection, Miriam and Ira D. Wallach Division of Art, Prints and Photographs, The New York Public Library, Astor, Lenox and Tilden Foundations; 2-3 photo by Romulo A. Yanes; 6-7 Bibliothèque Nationale; 9 The Metropolitan Museum of Art, Fletcher Fund, 1956 (56.171.38); 16, 18-19 The Granger Collection; 26 Bayerische Staatsbibliothek; 29 AKG, Berlin; 34-35 The Pierpont Morgan Library, Gift of Mrs. Donald M. Oenslager (1982.75.642); 39 The Metropolitan Museum of Art, Harris Brisbane Dick Fund, 1945 (45.82.2 (41)); 42 Library of Congress; 56-57 The Granger Collection; 59 archivio fotografico della Soprintendenza per i Beni Artistici e Storici, Galleria Sabauda, Turin; 64, 66-67 Performing Arts Research Center, New York Public Library at Lincoln Center; 67 signatures courtesy NYNEX; 73 copy photo by Denis Stevens, Accademia Monteverdiana Inc.; 89 Walters Art Gallery, Baltimore; 96 Library of Congress; 102 The Metropolitan Museum of Art, Harris Brisbane Dick Fund, 1932 (32.35 (71)); 106 courtesy Department of Special Collections, Stanford University Libraries; 111 Carnegie Hall Archives; 112-13 The Metropolitan Museum of Art, Harris Brisbane Dick Fund, 1933 (33.56.34); 116 The Granger Collection; 122-3 Library of Congress; 125 Austrian Cultural Institute; **127** The Bettmann Archive; **141** Austrian Information Service, New York; **142** Library of Congress; **143** Austrian National Tourist Office; **148-9** The Granger Collection; **161** Austrian National Tourist Office; **176** Library of Congress; **178** both, Performing Arts Research Center, New York Public Library at Lincoln Center; **179** left, Performing Arts Research Center, New York Public Library at Lincoln Center; right, The Bettmann Archive; **187** Historisches Museum der Stadt Wien; **190-91** New York Public Library; **194-5** Weidenfeld & Nicolson Ltd., London (copyright Philippe Gutzwiller); **198** The Metropolitan Museum of Art, Bequest of Catharine Lorillard Wolfe, 1887. Catharine Lorillard Wolfe Collection (87.15.134); **203** International Museum of Photography at George Eastman House; **204-5** New York Public Library; **208, 210** Austrian Cultural Institute; **223** German Information Center; **229** Library of Congress, Music Division, Loeffler Collection; **237** German Information Center; **241** both: The Bettmann Archive; **247** courtesy Kosciuszko Foundation, New York; **254** Library of Congress; **259** German Information Center; **269** Solomon R. Guggenheim Museum, New York, copy photo by Robert E. Mates © The Solomon R. Guggenheim Foundation (FN 37.262); **279, 280** The Bettmann Archive; **289** courtesy Archivio Mondadori; **290-91** The Mansell Collection Ltd., London; **314-** **15** The Bettmann Archive; **318, 324, 331** Library of Congress; **339** Performing Arts Research Center, New York Public Library at Lincoln Center; **340** The Bettmann Archive; **345** Bettmann/Hulton; **346-7** Indiana University Art Museum, Bloomington; **351** The Museum of Modern Art, New York, Mrs. Simon Guggenheim Fund; **355** Library of Congress; **366** Sony Music; **371** French Embassy Press & Information Division; **379** photo by Frank Gerrantano, courtesy Broadcast Music, Inc.; **388** copy photo by Allan Dean Walker, courtesy Arnold Schoenberg Institute, University of Southern California; **407** Musée Picasso, Paris (copyright Photo R.M.N.-SPADEM); **423** photo by Kata Kálmán; **435** Austrian Cultural Institute; **451** Print Collection, Miriam and Ira D. Wallach Division of Art, Prints and Photographs, The New York Public Library, Astor, Lenox and Tilden Foundations; **467** ASCAP; **474** Library of Congress; **481** Bettmann/Hulton; **488** Library of Congress; **493** Bettmann/Hulton; **497** top, The Bettmann Archive; bottom, photo by Lorne Tulk; **498** French Embassy Press & Information Division; **501** Library of Congress; **502** photo by Raimundo Borea; **504** ASCAP; **505** Bettmann/Hulton; **507** photo by Rex Rystedt; **509** French Embassy Press & Information Division; **522** drawing by Michael Ricci; **538** The Metropolitan Museum of Art, The Cloisters Collection, 1958 (58.71a verso).

ABOUT THE AUTHOR

Composer Jan Swafford began studying music in childhood and received degrees from Harvard and the Yale School of Music. His work has been played throughout the United States and abroad by ensembles including the symphonies of Indianapolis, St. Louis, the Dutch Radio, Vermont, and Chattanooga and by chamber groups including the Pro Arte Chamber Orchestra, Minneapolis Chamber Symphony, Boston Musica Viva, and Scott Chamber Players of Indianapolis. Among his awards are an NEA Composers Grant, a Chamber Music America commission, a Tanglewood Fellowship, two Massachusetts Artists fellowships, and a Mellon Faculty Fellowship at Harvard. His work appears on CRI Records and is published by Peer-Southern.

Otherwise, over the years he has worked as a country schoolteacher, military historian, film composer, college professor, and writer on music. His journalism has appeared in many magazines, including *Gramophone, Symphony, Musical America, New England Monthly,* and *Yankee.* He lives in Cambridge, Massachusetts, where he is composing, and writing a biography of Charles Ives.